The New Poverty Studies

© 2000 Harvey Finkle KWRU R2K March for Economic Rights.

The New Poverty Studies

*The Ethnography of Power, Politics,
and Impoverished People in
the United States*

EDITED BY

Judith Goode and Jeff Maskovsky

New York University Press

NEW YORK AND LONDON

NEW YORK UNIVERSITY PRESS
New York and London

Library of Congress Cataloging-in-Publication Data
New poverty studies : the ethnography of power, politics, and
impoverished people in the United States / edited by Judith Goode and
Jeff Maskovsky.
p.   cm.
Includes bibliographical references and index.
ISBN 0-8147-3115-5 (cloth : alk. paper)
ISBN 0-8147-3116-3 (pbk. : alk. paper)
1. Poverty—United States. 2. Poor—United States. 3. Power (Social
sciences)—United States. 4. United States—Race relations. 5. United
States—Social conditions.   I. Goode, Judith, 1939– II. Maskovsky, Jeff.
HC110.P6 N396 2001
305.5'69'0973—dc21   2001003670

New York University Press books are printed on acid-free paper,
and their binding materials are chosen for strength and durability.

Manufactured in the United States of America
10 9 8 7 6 5 4 3 2 1

Contents

Preface

As the United States enters the third millennium, it is somewhat disheartening to recognize that the poor, the homeless, and the hungry have dropped off the political agenda. As previous historical periods have demonstrated, however, resistance and social change regenerate at unexpected times, and populations that have been the most silenced and oppressed find voices through new forms of organization and new channels of communication.

With its emphasis on ethnography and its insistence on a detailed analysis of the lives of the poor in political and historical context, this anthology draws on the best of the burgeoning field of U.S. anthropology. The book's contribution is also enhanced by its broad and ecumenical approach to disciplinary boundaries, evident both in the research presented in each chapter and in the different disciplinary approaches represented by the authors. Instead of marginalizing the poor, as do terms such as *underclass*, the research presented here confronts the political circumstances, social institutions, and hegemonic ideas that structure the conditions of life for people in the United States. As the book locates the poor within this framework, it also illuminates possibilities for collective action and agency among the poor as well as across traditional boundaries of poverty, ethnicity, and class.

Since 1980, in a variety of ways, the poor have been losing ground. This is amply demonstrated in many of the chapters of this book. Leith Mullings documents the increasing difficulties faced by mothers rearing children in New York City, as public institutional supports such as schools and health care lose funding and city, state, and federal services. Peter Kwong documents the lives of new Chinese immigrants who labor under ties of patronage, which serve to cut them off from the benefits and safeguards that the U.S. worker historically has fought for. Brett Williams discusses the ways in which U.S. lending practices that discriminate against people of color exacerbate the problems of the poor in Washington, D.C. Patricia Zavella demonstrates the different ways in which the Chicano/a population in California is shut out from the American Dream.

There have always been poor people under capitalism. One of the "new" aspects of the poverty today, as Judith Goode and Jeff Maskovsky emphasize in the introduction, is the "regime of disappearance." Under the neoliberal agenda, the poor are portrayed as individually to blame for their lack of funds, and there seems little in the media or the public eye to contradict this perspective. When homeless shelters are closed and homeless people are bussed out of Manhattan, it appears as if the problem of homelessness has been solved. When, on a national scale, public assistance is abolished, and new paperwork and hurdles are put in the way of poor people seeking sustenance, the decrease in the number of people asking for help is taken as evidence of improving conditions.

From two different perspectives, Frances Fox Piven and Carol Stack document the costs of the 1996 Personal Responsibility and Work Opportunity Reconciliation Act. Piven systematically demonstrates the broad picture of increasing work for lower pay, while Stack portrays the personal cost to young women trapped in low-paying, dead-end work with few channels, funds, or assistance to find their way forward. Several chapters in this book document the failures in "training" programs that claim to prepare poor, unemployed people for the workforce but, in fact, place them firmly at the bottom of the ladder, with little hope for any but the lowest-paid jobs, if those. The chapters by Susan Brin Hyatt, Donna M. Goldstein, Catherine Kingfisher, and Vincent Lyon-Callo, which focus on social policies around volunteerism, job training, welfare, and homelessness respectively, are particularly instructive in demonstrating how neoliberal market-based strategies designed to pull poor people out of poverty in fact punish these people in the name of their own empowerment.

This volume does not stop with the documentation of the new poverty, however. In contrast, we see examples of programs that actually have worked, such as Sandra Morgen and Jill Weigt's description of the Comprehensive Employment and Training Act of the 1970s, which placed people in jobs that offered agency and a future. In addition, the chapters by Judith Goode, Nina Glick Schiller and Georges Fouron, and Eve S. Weinbaum examine, with due realism, the potential for political agency among poor people and the shifting grounds upon which political battles are fought. Matthew Ruben's concluding chapter and the afterword by Jeff Maskovsky address the politics of poverty research and policy.

This is a hopeful and important book in that, while it documents the current situation of poor people in the United States, it furnishes the analytical groundwork both for future challenging research on the impact of the dismantlement of the services of the welfare state and for a constructive critique that is built on the agency and voices of the poor themselves.

IDA SUSSER

Professor, Department of Anthropology
Hunter College/Graduate Center
City University of New York

Acknowledgments

This anthology was conceived as an academic response to an immediate and mounting crisis requiring scholarly intervention and popular explanation: the maintenance, intensification, and expansion of inequality and impoverishment in the United States and worldwide. In particular, it strives to serve the urgent political purpose of challenging common sense about poverty, since mainstream popular and political wisdom continues to blame the poor for their own impoverishment rather than explaining poverty as the inevitable consequence of corporate profit-making strategies and state action.

This book was also conceived as a rebuttal to social-scientific literature that continues, despite the persistent efforts of many scholars over the years, to theorize about poverty in the United States and elsewhere in terms that treat the poor as pathological, passive, or in need of moral uplift, and that thereby provide scholarly ammunition for popular and political efforts to justify and excuse the persistence of poverty. The articles collected here advance new arguments about U.S. poverty that account for poverty and inequality vis-à-vis new political economic and ideological developments. In particular, this volume is organized to spotlight the threat posed for the poor by political, economic, and ideological campaigns to promote market-based solutions to the problems of impoverishment and inequality. Although many scholars have been discouraged from making these connections, this book strives to show how the modes of power, politics, economics, and governance that have emerged in the last thirty years—modes designed to encourage the "marketization" of nearly every aspect of social and cultural life in the United States—work against the poor by creating new forms of impoverishment and, importantly, new challenges to poor people's collective efforts to overcome the political, economic, and ideological crises they face.

The New Poverty Studies could not have materialized without the efforts and insights of its contributors and many others. The initial impetus for the project came out of two successive sessions at annual meetings of the American Anthropological Association. The first, in San Francisco in 1996, was titled "The Anthropology of Poverty and Poor People's Political Agency: A Critical Perspective." The second was "Update on the War on the Poor: Anthropological Views on How Public Policy Affects the Urban Poor in the United States," presented in Washington, D.C., in 1997. These sessions, which involved many of the contributors to this anthology, were designed to repoliticize poverty studies in anthropology and in other disciplines. We thank the Society for the Anthropology of North America, which supported both sessions. We also acknowledge the helpful contributions of all those who participated in these sessions, as well as of those contributors who joined us along the way as the book took shape.

We must especially acknowledge the contribution of Matt Ruben, who worked closely with us throughout the duration of the project, intervening productively in our editors' dialogue. Matt's theoretical and political insights helped us organize the volume. We are also indebted to our colleague Susan Hyatt for her valuable and consistent contributions and support. Others who read parts of the manuscript and provided critically important advice were Catherine Kingfisher, Micaela di Leonardo, Sarah Hill, and Ida Susser. We also acknowledge the contributions of many of the anthropology graduate students at Temple University, whose discussions of these very issues in seminars dealing with social policy made us incorporate new perspectives. We also thank Joel Tannenbaum for helping us to complete the index.

At NYU Press, Eric Zinner, Cecilia Feilla, Daisy Hernandez, Emily Park, and Despina Papazoglou Gimbel were enormously helpful. Many thanks to Alfonso for rescuing our manuscript at a crucial moment of its production.

The New Poverty Studies

Introduction

Judith Goode and Jeff Maskovsky

Not long after the world celebrated the turn of the millennium, the *New York Times* dedicated the better part of its Sunday magazine to an extensive article and photo essay on a new phenomenon: the invisible poor. Authored by respected liberal pundit James Fallows, "The Invisible Poor" ruminates over the curious absence of the U.S. poor from popular and political commentary in the turn-of-the-millennium period of economic prosperity and growth. During previous economic booms, Fallows observes, poverty had been a burning question on the public agenda. But now it seems to have fallen off the popular and political radar screen. Fallows asks:

> The last time the United States self-consciously thought of itself as rich, in the early 1960's, discussions of how the wealth should be shared were under way even before real prosperity arrived. Welfare programs, with all their subsequent mixed effects, were expanded.... Before that, America's last significant wave of individual fortune-building, the original Gilded Age, a century ago, touched off decades worth of struggles over the distribution and domestication of that wealth: union battles, antitrust laws, muckraking exposes, the rapid growth of public education, laws establishing minimum wages and maximum hours and even the income tax. Before, whenever we had wealth, we started discussing poverty. Why not now? Why is the current politics of wealth and poverty seemingly about wealth alone? (Fallows 2000: 68, 70)

The answer to this vexing question, Fallows concludes, lies in the structure of the new high-tech economy. Drawing examples from what he calls the "computer-financial complex," Fallows describes a new economic order in which there is an increasingly wide "social and imaginative separation between prosperous America and those still left out" (Fallows 2000: 72). He describes a world in which tech professionals work long hours and take business calls on their cell phones on their way to

1

and from work. The firms in which they work are diverse, but not along class lines. The only example of contact between tech professionals and low-end workers that Fallows describes, in fact, involves himself and an immigrant Russian woman who cleans his office. But she begins works at 9 P.M., long after most of the tech professionals have gone home, and Fallows admits that he knows almost nothing about her. For Fallows, this woman, like many others who are forced to work at the low end of the economy, or worse, who cannot find work at all, is located beyond the microcosmic cultural and political imaginary of the tech firm. Thus, "The Invisible Poor" sets out to make the poor visible, because it presumes that they no longer come into contact with the rich.[1]

Underlying Fallows's argument is the basic but unexamined assumption that the prominence of poverty in the public eye is purely a function of the whims and lifestyles of the rich. The goal of making poverty visible, for Fallows and, for that matter, for most liberals since the beginning of the New Deal, and even before, is to legitimate a charitable response to the problem of poverty.[2] In the current conjuncture, this means providing the poor with market incentives through which they may improve themselves. Previously, in the immediate postwar period, this meant securing services and resources for the poor through the welfare state. In either case, depending on the prevailing political ideology of the time, the question is posed as: What can we, as Americans, do for the poor?

Posing this question in this way has the effect of turning the poor into an object of obsessive contemplation while putting poor people's agency under erasure. For the poor are, of course, not invisible as Fallows claims. Indeed, neither the rise of gated middle-class communities nor the advent of policies designed to remove homeless people forcibly from public space has managed to erase poverty from the cultural, political, and geographic landscape. Thus, the problem lies not in poor people's invisibility but in the terms on which they are permitted to be visible in public discourse. Ironically, Fallows's essay and the photos that accompany it illustrate this point perfectly; for while the photo essay captures, both in pictures and in short anecdotes, the struggles and indignities that the poor must endure, the representations of poor people in the essay form a narrative designed to appeal not to the poor themselves or to their current political allies but to the *New York Times*'s putatively liberal readership, a readership that has largely endorsed political rhetoric and policy shifts that blame the poor for their own impoverishment. Moreover, in seeking sympathy for the plight of the poor, Fallows makes no attempt to challenge the assumption that the fate of the poor lies ultimately in the magnanimous hands of the rich. In this manner the poor continue to be marginalized. They are not permitted full political, economic, or moral citizenship. Alternatively pitied and reviled, they are peculiarly *in* U.S. society but not *of* it.

Accordingly, the rubric of visibility and invisibility functions to screen out alternative understandings of impoverishment. Although perhaps kinder and gentler than the Reagan-era rhetoric of vilification, in making the poor visible Fallows's argument glosses over the roots of poverty. In its compassion, it marks a small shift in the mythology of blame through which poverty in the United States has been justified and excused. But it hardly provides a basis for understanding the new poverty that has emerged in connection with recent political and economic developments.

This book offers an antidote to recent popular and political discussions of poverty such as that of Fallows. Rather than imagining the poor as invisible, passive, pathological, or in need of charity or moral reform, it treats poverty as a political, economic, and ideological effect of capitalist processes and state activity. The essays in this collection are united by their treatment of poverty as a function of power, as an essential and utterly predictable effect of the ideological and political-economic processes of late capitalism. As a result, the essays collected here focus not on diagnosing and describing the isolated behaviors of poor people, but on the "making of poverty" (Susser 1996: 416) and poor people's responses to it. As such, this collection places not only poor people's lives but their *agency* at the center of analysis. By treating the poor as a heterogeneous population, defined in historical and geographical specificity and both within and across various axes of difference, the articles collected here highlight poor people's individual and collective responses to economic restructuring and changes in state policies. This is not to say that this book's intent is to romanticize the poor. On the contrary, it provides ethnographically informed analyses of the contradictory conditions in which the poor find themselves and the often contradictory ways in which they respond to those conditions.

Defining the New Poverty

Mainstream pundits, politicians, and policy experts wax rhapsodic about the economic and moral virtues of a "New Economy" driven by the global flow of finance, information, and technology. If they talk about poverty at all, it is to bemoan the fact that the poor have been "left out." Yet the conditions of U.S poverty have changed in important ways. These changes form the backdrop for the essays collected here; the need to analyze these changes prompted the compilation of this volume. From the point of view of an increasingly large number of poor people, in the United States and worldwide, it is clear that the model of social order that is required to ensure the continued growth and competitiveness of the New Economy is actually a model of social disorder.[3] For, contrary to the rhetoric of mainstream pundits, politicians, and policy experts, the last three decades of the twentieth century have seen the intensification of the very ideological and political-economic contradictions that guarantee the maintenance and expansion of poverty in the United States and abroad. Before turning to a discussion of the limits of mainstream poverty studies and to the specific content of this volume, it is necessary to sketch out, in broad terms, the political, economic, and ideological context of the new poverty. In a general sense, the new poverty can be explained in terms of three interconnected processes—*economic polarization, political demobilization,* and *market triumphalism*—each of which has contributed to the growing social and political disorder affecting the poor.

At the economic level, the gap between rich and poor has widened to an unprecedented distance, both in the United States and worldwide, over the last three decades. Faced with an economic downturn that reached crisis proportions in the late 1960s and early 1970s, U.S. capital imposed strategies designed to lower labor costs and create a more "flexible" workforce (Aglietta 1979; Brenner 1998; Harvey 1989; Davis 1986; Mandel 1975). Having abrogated the "Fordist" contract with labor, the leaders of industry downsized firms and relocated manufacturing activities to low-wage, non-union regions of the South, Southwest, and overseas. Concomitantly, the high-skill service and financial sector was built to manage, coordinate, and speed up production processes that have become nationally and globally dispersed to an unprecedented degree as production has been relocated across the globe (N. Smith 1997). Increased corporate reliance on subcontracting and contract, temporary, and part-time work has also contributed to the decline in the number, quality, wages, and security of low-skill and semi-skilled jobs.[4] Together, these changes have polarized the U.S. workforce, creating a cadre of highly educated and well-paid professionals and managers at the top and a growing population of undereducated, de-skilled workers who receive low pay, no benefits, no job security, and no union protection at the bottom. Corporate leaders, increasingly under the sway of Wall Street financial firms, also began a political and ideological assault on unions, on civil rights, on environmental and other regulations, and on the Keynesian policies that had previously sought to regulate the economy with public investment. Of course, the class warfare practiced by corporations, especially in the 1980s, did not happen in a political vacuum. The U.S. state has, since the 1970s, reoriented its policies explicitly to service big capital at the expense of the workforce and the larger citizenry.

Shifts in domestic policy, especially tax policies and policies related to social spending, exacerbated the tendencies toward polarization brought on by economic restructuring. Driven by a renaissance in coordinated political activity and lobbying by the corporate sector (Edsall 1984), welfare, public health care, public education, and a host of other important social services associated with the New Deal and the War on Poverty were rolled back, privatized, or definitively dismantled through bipartisan legislative action beginning in the early 1970s. Both Democrats and Republicans have gained political legitimacy for rollbacks and privatization in the name of "cost-effectiveness," "competition," and "efficiency," buzzwords designed to legitimate a model of economic restructuring that favors private-sector solutions over the public sector, now vilified as wasteful "big government." Initially, right-wing politicians led the charge in the 1970s for the withdrawal of funds from anti-poverty programs. Famously, they based their arguments on the claim that welfare-state dependency, not poverty, was the evil destroying people's lives. Later, fiscally conservative Democrats joined the attack on dependency in the late 1980s. They allied themselves with Republicans in promoting state and national experiments with workfare programs, such as the federal Family Support Act of 1988. This and other programs imposed the expectation that low-income people should work for the meager benefits that they receive from the state. In other words, benefits were no longer seen as an entitlement of citizenship but as an exchange for labor.[5] The most recent attack on the safety net was the passage of the Personal Responsibility and Work Opportunity Reconciliation Act (PRWORA) in 1996, which sought to "end welfare as we know it." Ignoring the realities of local and regional labor markets, race and gender discrimination in these markets, and the prevalence of low-end wage rates that were so low that families could not hope to subsist on them, this legislation undermined the welfare safety net by mandating rapid attachment to the workforce and putting a lifetime limit on the length of time a household could receive cash assistance (Mink 1998). It is important, of course, to acknowledge that the process of welfare state retrenchment has been highly uneven, with some publicly funded programs expanded and others downsized or eliminated during the same period; yet it is equally important to emphasize that the net effect has been a reduction in what has been putatively called "the social wage" for poor and working people in the United States.[6]

Economic polarization and the dismantling of welfare programs inevitably created a host of social problems that the state has elected to solve in part by incarcerating a historically unprecedented number of poor people. Indeed, the prison industry has experienced tremendous growth at the same time that welfare and other social service programs have been slashed. There are now over 2 million people in U.S. prisons, on probation, or otherwise engaged with the criminal justice system, a disproportionate number of whom are people of color (Buck 1992; Lusane 1994; Parenti 1999). The prison industry has become the major institutional mode of social control in the context of increasing economic inequality. The most important example of this is the criminalization of the poor through the drug war's unequal and racist sentencing guidelines, which disproportionately affect people of color who reside in urban neighborhoods (Buck 1992; Lusane 1991; 1994; Bertram et al. 1996). This and other police-state strategies indicate that the state's new role is to regulate the poor through surveillance and incarceration, not through supportive services. It is now clear that the state, rather than receding in importance or power in the current period, has, from the perspective of the poor, transformed itself from a welfare state to a law-and-order state (Davis 1990; Rouse 1995).

While in recent years pundits and politicians have continually cited government statistics showing low unemployment, decreasing poverty rates, and reductions in welfare case rolls as evidence for the benefits of economic growth for the poor, these figures obscure the economic polarization that has occurred since the 1970s. Low unemployment rates, for example, mask a number of trends that have had a significant and detrimental impact on the poor. These include the end of the family wage system; the consequent increase in household dependency on more than one income; the expansion of women's participation in the paid labor force; the transfer of political and economic power from rural and urban to suburban space; the reconfiguration of power relations transnationally and within and between regions, locales, and neighborhoods; the persistence of disproportionate poverty affecting people of color; and the loss of assets and the crushing debt burden borne by a growing number of working-class households.[7]

Along with these economic developments has arisen a political demobilization that has taken away the political voice of the poor. As the social compact uniting capital, labor, and the state dissolved, the poor suffered politically. No less important was the demobilization of the mass civil rights and anti-poverty politics of the 1960s and 1970s (Davis 1986; Reed 1999). The 1970s saw the rise of what Mike Davis (1986) calls "the Have Revolution," the consolidation and mobilization of a political constituency comprised primarily of middle-class white suburbanites with some white working-class support, particularly at key moments during the Reagan years. Faced with increased economic insecurity, the protagonists of the Have Revolution responded to recession, high oil prices, inflation, and political upheaval with property tax revolts, draconian anti-crime and pro–death penalty measures, and revanchist politics designed to protect what were essentially the suburban entitlements they had acquired in the immediate post–World War II period.

Harsh and racist representations of the poor were intimately connected to the ideologies undergirding the Have Revolution. Popular and political rhetoric sensationalized the pathologies of the poor, fueling a near-fundamentalist moral panic among the middle class as they themselves also faced economic insecurity. Liberal-left rhetoric that once "excused" the poor as victims was neutralized by right-wing attacks that vilified the poor as a moral threat to the middle class. Obsessive references to fecund welfare queens and, later, to the specter of dangerous black men[8] shaped the political culture of the Reagan era and beyond, and the rhetoric of vilification reinforced the racist and sexist ideologies on which the Have Revolution was built. These representations also reinforced a sexualized view of the poor as pathologically "oversexed." This presumption not only treated the poor as an affront and danger to the middle class; it also provided the justification for explaining the persistence of poverty as rooted in poor people's "lack of monogamy" and "hypersexuality."[9] In a relatively short period of time the poor found themselves without a political voice or political defenders.

If there is one ideological claim that has fueled these attacks on the poor and has served to legitimate the political and economic developments described above, it is the belief in the free market as the most efficient means for achieving economic growth and guaranteeing social welfare (Sanchez-Otero 1993; Bourdieu 1998). The equation of unregulated markets, technological innovation, flexible labor, and corporate downsizing is now seen as political and popular common sense. Accordingly, public policies have been reframed away from universal access and toward market-based models in which the goal is the acculturation of the poor to the rules of the market. Now, policy debates center on the moral and political imperative to eliminate dependency and the forms of social insurance that encourage it, rather than on programs that are intended to eliminate inequality. Importantly, distinctions between the deserving poor and undeserving poor that are over a century old have been reshaped in accordance with the ideology of market triumphalism (cf. Katz 1989; 1993). The deserving poor are now those who embrace the spirit of entrepreneurship, voluntarism, consumerism, and self-help, while the undeserving are those who remain "dependent" on the state.

Market triumphalism has coalesced as the ideological cornerstone of recent shifts in mainstream liberalism in the 1980s and 1990s. Indeed, the political ideology of the New Democrats and the Democratic Leadership Council (a group Bill Clinton helped form and once chaired) can be characterized as *neoliberal*, defined as the re-embrace of classic liberalism's faith in the economic, social, and moral attributes of unhindered competition and unregulated markets in the current context of welfare state retrenchment. Yet the neoliberal view does not seek to wish away the role of the state altogether. In fact, one of the most misunderstood and often ignored differences between neoconservatism and neoliberalism is that while the former simplistically (and ironically) rails against government from within the halls of Congress, the latter embraces ideologies of "good government" and "efficient government," acknowledging in code the state's role in promoting the "free" market. Accordingly, George W. Bush's "compassionate conservatism" is best understood as a hard-right variant of the neoliberal project (in contradistinction to other brands of right-wing conservatism such as that of Gingrich and, arguably, Reagan).[10]

The new poverty has thus been shaped by three main factors: polarization at the economic level, demobilization at the political level, and market triumphalism at the ideological level. A large wealth gap, attenuated political activity, and pro-market ideology certainly are not new phenomena in the United States. It is their emergence in the current moment, their level of coordination and mutual reinforcement, that represents a situation of historical significance. The large-scale return of older forms of informal economic activity such as sweatshop labor, piecework, and exploitative labor arrangements under contract farming is in itself striking and quite alarming. Yet these grave developments are merely one aspect of the larger project of dismantling the liberal welfare state, a project virtually without historical precedent. The use of state-sponsored coercion to enforce an economic order is not new; the transition from a welfare state to a law-and-order state in the United States, however, most certainly is new, if not wholly unprecedented—and the conditions of poverty this transition produces are therefore also new and in urgent need of study.

The end of the modern welfare state—not a nonwelfare moment but a *post*welfare moment—has opened the way for a new mode of state regulation and social control that affects the everyday lives of the poor. Influenced heavily by neoliberal privatization policy abroad, domestic neoliberalism has seen the state open the way for private firms to take over the public health and welfare systems. The new primacy of profit over service provision poses dangers for the well-being of the poor, as it does for every other group affected by privatization. More than that, however, it also endangers poor communities *politically*. Privatization removes the poor from a direct relationship with the state, a relationship that historically has been essential to the expression of collective agency for poor communities. Poor people's movements, as Frances Fox Piven and Richard Cloward (1977) demonstrated, have struggled to gain much-needed resources and powers by targeting state-based institutions.

In this context, the neoliberal celebration of the removal of the state from poor people's everyday lives may be seen for what it is: an ideological power play. While privatization has a disempowering effect on the poor, the neoliberal valorization of the market claims the opposite. Everyone, including the poor, is assumed to be possessed of empowerment thanks to the liberating structure of the market itself. Once government gets out of the way of "opportunity," the logic goes, progress will take care of itself. Accordingly, no specific measures need be taken to address the problems of poverty and inequality, since these will eventually be solved by the natural working of the "free" market. Theoretically speaking, this a project of subjectification, of creating "subjects of value," as Paul Smith (1997: 222) has written, well suited to the demands and needs of late capitalism.

The neoliberal valorization of the market thus has a particularly pernicious effect on the creation of alternative political responses involving the poor. For instance, residents in poor and immiserated neighborhoods are increasingly encouraged to purge their ranks of the undeserving poor in order to make their neighborhoods more attractive to private investors. This "localist" agenda is now sold to neighborhood groups by well-meaning state functionaries as the only option for neighborhood improvement and development, with the consequence that tensions and antagonisms *within* and *between* poor communities are intensified. These changes, taken together, have once again made poor people invisible, though this invisibility is not defined or understood in the same terms in which liberal pundits such as Fallows (discussed above) understand it. Rather, it can be attributed to the rise of what we call here a *regime of disappearance:* a mode of governance, economy, and politics in which the poor are not so much vilified as they are marginalized or erased by the institutional and ideological aspects of work, social welfare, and politics that are dominant under neoliberalism.

Toward the New Poverty Studies

Social scientists have long had an uncomfortably close relationship to the dominant ideologies through which U.S. poverty has been justified and excused. In fact, it would not be unfair to say that a good deal of poverty research—particularly that which has had the greatest impact on popular and political representations of U.S. poverty—has contributed, inadvertently or otherwise, to the demonization of the poor. With respect to ethnography, there is no better example than the anthropologist Oscar Lewis, whose work was particularly influential in the policy debates of the 1960s. Lewis is best known for his widely disseminated "culture of poverty" thesis, which made the connection between behavior and the persistence of poverty. He argued that a significant faction of the poor were enmeshed in an intergenerational quagmire of dysfunctional values and behaviors. Interestingly, Lewis did explain poverty as the outgrowth of capitalist development and state policy; yet he tended to view poverty in the United States—a leading industrialized nation—primarily as a result of the persistence of a culture of poverty, while the primary cause of poverty in developing nations was, according to his analysis, the outgrowth of uneven capitalist development. Accordingly, he argued for a "social work" solution to U.S. poverty, which was aimed at changing poor people's values and behavior (Lewis 1966: 404).[11]

This argument resonated with and reinforced the dominant policy positions that corresponded with the prevailing liberal mode of governance in the postwar period. Lewis's influence can be seen, for instance, in Daniel Patrick Moynihan's 1965 report to President Lyndon B. Johnson, *The Negro Family: The Case for National Action*, which relied heavily on the "culture of poverty" thesis to describe black "ghetto" poverty and familial "dysfunction" (Moynihan 1965). Importantly, pundits and politicians such as Moynihan deployed the "culture of poverty" argument, as well as other psychologistic arguments, in order to legitimate the expansion of paternalistic welfare-state interventions designed to "improve" poor people (Katz 1989; 1993; di Leonardo 1998).[12]

In the social sciences, Lewis's work stimulated lively debate. Rebutting his culturalist explanations for social "disorganization," anthropologists and others offered ethnographic portrayals that emphasized the effects of large-scale political and economic developments on the creation and reproduction of poverty (Leacock 1971; Valentine 1968; Katz 1989; Stack 1974; Eames and Goode 1973; Liebow 1967; Valentine 1978; Marks 1991). This endeavor produced much of the classic work on poverty across social-scientific disciplines. These works showed that assumptions about the social and personal incompetence of the poor were in and of themselves ideologically driven. Impoverished people did not have weak egos. Consumption patterns that seemed irrational were shown to be survival strategies (Stack 1974; Eames and Goode 1973). Poor people's behaviors in the labor market were not self-destructive but actually rational choices vis-à-vis dangerous and dirty dead-end jobs (Liebow 1967; Valentine 1978). Family networks and household composition among the poor were not "broken" or "dysfunctional" but rather functional and unnecessarily pathologized simply because they differed from those idealized by policymakers and by the white middle-class.

Although this early ethnographic work was largely successful in rebutting some of the more pernicious assumptions about social disorganization that were implicit in Lewis's "culture of poverty" thesis, it nonetheless treated poverty in very static terms. Significantly, it did not challenge an extremely problematic tenet of Lewis's original formulation: that the culture of poverty produced an incapacity to organize collectively and created an avoidance of mainstream political, economic, and social institutions (outside the criminal justice system, of course).[13] Indeed, rebuttals to Lewis continued to treat poor communities as encapsulated worlds, bounded and isolated from history and wider political-economic developments (Hyatt 1995; Williams 1992). In particular, they focused almost obsessively on impoverished urban black neighborhoods and, as Susan B. Hyatt (1995) has observed, gave almost exclusive attention to either male-dominated "street corner societies" (Hannerz 1969; Liebow 1967) or the domestic sphere of household and family, involving impoverished African American women and children (Aschenbrenner 1975; Stack 1974). The intention here was to demonstrate that in poor communities, informal networks, hardly indicative of the "breakdown" of black family life, are a significant form of social organization and often constitute the most critical bulwark to ameliorate the depredations and crises of poverty. The challenge to the "critics of the Black family" offered by this work, however, conflated minority racial status with poverty and therefore failed to highlight the distinct contribution to immiseration of political-economic developments, including class formation and its effects on black communities, institutionalized oppressive racial formulations, constructions of white privilege, and shifting gender dynamics both inside and outside the household. It all but ignored rural and suburban poverty and failed to treat race, gender, and class as interconnected yet independent processes.[14] Instead, by offering what were intended to be "humanizing"—and therefore apolitical—representations of the poor, early "ghetto" ethnographies inadvertently functioned to reinforce the idea that the family, not public or political institutions or the workplace, was the primary institutional location for intervention into poor life. This construction of poverty, by treating the black poor as deviant objects of public policy that are in need of social intervention from above, accords with the dominant tenets of liberal welfare-state governance (di Leonardo 1998; Hyatt 1995). Thus, although it may have offered a compelling antidote to the Moynihan report, this formulation was nonetheless locked within the dominant ideological framework of the postwar period. As such, it failed to give proper attention to political economy; to the interconnected class, race, and gender dynamics through which poverty is historically constituted; and to poor people's political action (Gregory 1992; Williams 1992).

In the 1980s and 1990s, the ideological drama around the "culture of poverty" thesis replayed itself as the "underclass" debate. Like earlier debates, this one centered on the behaviors of black inner-city residents, though the debate no longer was organized around the question of poor people's social "disorganization" but rather focused on their social "isolation" and "dislocation." First, neoconservative pundits and policymakers on the right used broad-brush statistical correlations to bolster moralistic arguments that poor people's "dependency" and "moral weakness" were caused by welfare programs themselves (Murray 1984; Mead 1992). Supporters of this argument, backed by right-wing think tanks (Stefancic and Delgado 1997), launched a campaign to retrench the welfare state and to delegitimate the Keynesian model of social order (a campaign that correlated, not coincidentally, with neoliberal economic imperatives to boost profitability by privatizing and downsizing state-funded services).

In rebuttal, left-liberal scholars countered the moralistic formulations of the right with demographic analyses demonstrating the "structural" roots of impoverishment. William Julius Wilson (1987; 1996) and Douglas Massey and Nancy Denton (1993), among others, showed that state policies such as affirmative action and market forces had created segregation (apartheid) for the inner-city poor. This, they argued, produced isolation from middle-class role models, resulting in increasingly "pathological" behavior among those left behind (Wilson), and further increased the spatial concentration of unemployment and substandard housing, crime, drug use, and other social ills as a consequence (Massey and Denton 1993). Although supporters of this perspective argue for massive "structural" solutions to poverty, they do not dispute the assumptions about individual pathology that are the cornerstone of the right's attack on the poor. Indeed, Wilson in particular has not only insisted, over the course of his long and influential career, that unwed motherhood, participation in the informal economy, drug use, and crime are measures of bad, ghetto-specific behaviors; he has also admonished the left for neglecting to admit the failings of inner-city residents, arguing that the left's silence on these matters has fueled the rightward shift in social welfare policy (Wilson 1987).

There are numerous critiques of this side of the underclass debate (di Leonardo 1998; Katz 1993; Reed 1999; Williams 1992; Gregory 1992). For instance, Micaela di Leonardo (1998: 117–20) shows how Wilson, by concentrating on the plight of inner-city males, their unemployment, and their paternal responsibility through marriage, incorporates gender into his analysis, but in anti-feminist form. Indeed, in his formulation, women are assumed to be dependent on men, and their education and access to work and child care are ignored. Moreover, Wilson employs what di Leonardo aptly calls "passive-verb political economy" (di Leonardo 1998: 119). He ignores the agency of institutional actors, and by defining racism exclusively in terms of hostile encounters between individuals, he downplays its significance.

Steven Gregory (1992) also disputes Wilson's assertion that race is of declining significance. He shows that class formation *within* black communities has contributed to the reshaping of political interests, power relations, and ideologies affecting inner-city residents. In this context, the deployment of racialized political identities remains significant. These identities may be transformed, but they are hardly irrelevant. Along similar lines, Thomas F. Jackson criticizes Wilson for ignoring the role of black political thought and activism and for an analysis that understates the effects of racist government policies on inner cities (Jackson 1993). Indeed, tax policies, housing policies, and other racially biased policies have had a significant impact on the creation of inner-city black poverty. With respect to labor markets, several economists have demonstrated that race continues to be a barrier for access to low-end jobs (e.g., Cherry 1988).

These critiques remind us of the limits of both sides of the underclass debate. As with the culture of poverty before it, the argument over the "cultural" versus the "structural" roots of poverty actually furthered the image of the pathological poor who are denied political agency, the capacity for activism, and even the rights of citizenship. Indeed, paralleling popular and political treatments of the poor, in emphasizing social isolation, both right and liberal-left positions treat the poor as noncitizens, as a group whose identities—often interpolated through interconnected ideologies of class, race, gender, sexuality, and nationhood—place them outside the U.S. nation (see Gregory 1995; Ruben, chapter 15, below).

Recent ethnographic depictions of the poor have also reinforced this aspect of the underclass argument. For instance, studies of violent street life such as Elijah Anderson's (1999) analysis of "the code of the streets" in Philadelphia became sensationalized as they were popularized. Works such as this are intended to offer a more sympathetic, or at least comprehensible, portrayal of the behaviors of the poor. They are also intended to provide a view of poor people's oppositional consciousness. Yet, by reifing cultural codes and emphasizing individual consciousness (reminiscent, in fact, of early Chicago-school "subculture" and "deviancy" studies), these works construct the beliefs, values, and actions of the poor as products of a locally produced, contagious, deviant culture that ensnares its hapless victims. For example, Anderson's work accentuates invidious moral distinctions between those characterized as either "decent" or "street," without providing sufficient explanation for the wider political and ideological implications of such distinctions. Indeed, he outlines a social typology based on what are presumed to be "emic" moral valuations of individual inner-city residents. This ethnographic strategy makes only the vaguest of gestures toward addressing the effects of dominant ideological, institutional, and political practices through which the poor are divided, and it totally ignores the history of collective action and grassroots activity in the neighborhood in which the research was conducted. Work such as Anderson's is the ethnographic correlate to Wilson's underclass argument. It is complicit with the consistent erasure in poverty studies of politics and collective agency as an aspect of poor people's everyday lives.

Politics and collective agency are also erased or elided by approaches that focus exclusively on the analysis of the discursive construction of poverty. There is no doubt that attention to the ways in which "the poor" are categorized—how sets of discourses and their associated strategies constitute "the poor" as a knowable group—has helped expose how poor people's agency is constrained or compromised by the use of the designation "the poor"; that is, the use of this category has a pathologizing, diagnostic effect, in the Foucauldian sense, as numerous social scientists have demonstrated (see, e.g., Cruikshank 1994). The analytic prioritization of the discursive field, however, can sometimes generate scholarship at a level of abstraction that disregards important aspects of "on-the-ground," historically constituted power relations on the one hand and poor people's agency on the other. Indeed, some take the problem of the discursive construction of the poor to mean that it is inadvisable to talk about poverty at all. This gesture not only ignores poor people's appropriations of various stigmatized and problematic identities as an aspect of their political agency (Piven and Cloward 1971; Naples 1998; Zucchino 1997; for an important discussion of a similar point vis-à-vis "development" in the third world, see Edelman 1999: 7–21). It is also part of a long history of anti-intellectualism in the academy and elsewhere that rejects certain categorizations as "inauthentic" in order to avoid what scholars or other pundits may perceive to be a slight against those who are struggling to survive the indignities of impoverishment. Yet the desire to appear as politically acceptable to constituencies who view the category of "the poor" as "politically incorrect" may short-circuit a materialist analysis of the dynamics of poverty. In fact, academics and others are making *political*, not just scholarly, choices when they elevate the goal of identifying improper naming above the goal of exploring avenues of political agency among that heterogeneous group that is still productively referred to as the poor. Moreover, in the present conjuncture, projects such as these collude with the regime of disappearance that seeks to erase poverty from popular and political consciousness.

This and many of the other arguments we make here have been made before; indeed, they have been repeated often (see Piven and Cloward 1977, for an important and early refutation of the "culture of poverty" argument). Yet we make them again for two reasons. First, they have been all but ignored by a disturbing majority of left-liberal scholars, pundits, and politicians. Second, it is now undeniably clear, particularly in the wake of welfare "reform," that the left-liberal rebuttal to the underclass argument has been largely unsuccessful in delegitimating reactionary moralistic explanations for U.S. poverty or in creating broad support for the "structural" solutions that are posited as the only legitimate policy alternatives. Indeed, the assumption that the poor are lacking in mainstream morality continues to undergird popular and political pity and revulsion toward those who suffer the indignities of impoverishment.

This book charts new directions for cutting-edge research on poverty, policy, and politics in the United States. The essays collected here highlight the ways in which economic restructuring and changes in state policies create new pockets of poverty, transform social relations among the poor, and create new boundaries and tensions between the poor and other groups, within and across various axes of difference. They also attend to the ways in which changes in political and social identities over the last three decades of the twentieth century have affected the social construction of poverty, and they illuminate how poor people have responded to exploitation, domination, and the patterns of inequality that have been imposed on them from above. All this requires a perspective that emphasizes important aspects of poor people's agency that have been underemphasized in much academic literature and that are studiously ignored in mainstream public policy debates. By using new theoretical approaches that situate different groups' experiences of poverty in dialectical relation to global, national, state, and local political-economic change and to the interconnected ideologies of race, class, gender, sexuality, and nationhood, the new poverty studies treat poverty not as a static "moral" *condition* but as a dynamic historically and geographically contingent *process*.[15]

The political economic and ideological production of poverty is unevenly distributed. Certain regions of the country are affected more than others; global competition has affected some industries more than others; part-time, insecure work and other detrimental labor practices affect some populations more than others. Patterns of inequality vary across space and time. This alone requires that we be careful not to define U.S. poverty, or poverty elsewhere, as a singular phenomenon or, as some are now inclined to do, as a uniform outgrowth of "globalization." One purpose of this anthology is to displace such sloganeering with more concrete, empirically informed discussions of economic polarization, political demobilization, and market trimphalism. In particular, this requires us to think beyond simplistic global/local binaries, to understand how economic processes occur on a number of scales—both local and global but also national and regional—and how agents of the state, rather than simply withdrawing from economic regulation, reorient their activity to facilitate the mobility of capital. Similarly, from the perspective of poverty studies, the global/local split effectively ghettoizes the poor, reproducing the dominant ideological assault against the poor by assuming that their social and political agency will always be "local." This is a characterization, generally made by corporate leaders and their allies but not by the poor themselves, that denies the multiple scales and identifications referenced and articulated through the complexity of political identities adopted by the poor (cf. Gregory 1998b).

Accordingly, the wide range of ethnographic treatments in this book is deliberate. Contributors discuss a variety of regions, communities, and political constituencies which are constituted across multiples scales and multiple axes of difference. Included are case studies focusing on residents in "global" cities such as New York and Washington, D.C.; on large regional cities such as Philadelphia and Oakland; and on smaller cities in the Midwest and elsewhere. We also focus on rural areas in California, Colorado, and Tennessee. Populations include immigrants from China, Mexico, and Haiti as well as native-born African Americans, Latinos, and whites. Yet our volume does not attempt to represent the full demographic heterogeneity of U.S. poverty. Moreover, while these diverse representations are designed to disrupt the popular and political obsession with the black inner-city poor, several of our contributors *do* focus specifically on those groups that have been popularly identified with poverty and obsessed over in mainstream poverty studies. The essays selected here, however, are collected for the purpose of advancing the argument that poverty is a direct outgrowth of uneven capitalist development; that the meanings, practices, and identities of those who are impoverished vary across geography, history, and multiple axes of difference; and that poor people engage in a number of collective and individual strategies that are designed not only to survive the conditions of poverty but to change them. This collection aims to overcome the current *regime of disappearance* by redirecting poverty studies toward a repoliticization of poverty and inequality in academia and elsewhere.

The essays in part 1, "New Dimensions of Inequality," explore the historical and geographical specificity of the new poverty. Against those approaches that treat poverty as a static moral condition or that define it exclusively in terms of negation—in relation to some unspoken norm from which people are dislocated, disorganized, and displaced—these essays focus on the complexity of power relations through which poverty is produced, maintained, and reconfigured. All of the essays address poor people's reactions to large-scale economic restructuring and shifts in state policies, showing these reactions to be contradictory: sometimes they secure or mask the practices of exploitation, domination, and subordination, and at other times they challenge and contest them.

Leith Mullings argues against approaches that blame black women for their own impoverishment and that treat female-headed households as inherently pathological. She argues instead that economic and social policies, undergirded by pernicious ideologies of race, class, and gender and imposed on a global, national, and local scale, encourage the creation of female-headed households in poor black neighborhoods even as they vilify those who live in them. She provides a brief social history of Harlem, demonstrating the ways in which economic and social polarization have affected the neighborhood, with particularly negative consequences for low-income black women. She also charts several examples of what she calls "transformative work," collective action on the part of poor black women to expand their options, to ensure the continuity of their families and communities, and to resist or oppose dominant patterns of inequality.

Peter Kwong's chapter exemplifies the transnational context in which both capital accumulation and the restructuring of labor markets are now occurring. Challenging the widely held notion that family ties and ethnic solidarity function to lift immigrants out of poverty, he explores the impact of the transnational smuggling industry on Fuzhounese illegal immigrants in New York. Sent overseas by their families on the Chinese mainland, whose visions of U.S. prosperity and whose community ties to "snakeheads" in the smuggling trade keep them uninformed about life in the United States, illegal Fuzhounese immigrants arrive in debt and face harsh poverty and extreme exploitation. In such circumstances, ethnic solidarity and family ties are actually used by sweatshop owners and snakeheads to coerce undocumented migrants into superexploitative situations.

Brett Williams focuses on one of the most important aspects of the new poverty: debt. Drawing on ethnographic data from Washington, D.C., she shows how impoverished neighborhoods are the new debt frontier. Highlighting "big capital" investments by mainstream banks, other financial institutions, and decision makers in poor communities through check-cashing stores, pawnshops, and high-interest credit card sales, she traces this new form of debt production. She explores how racist and predatory lending practices deny poor Washingtonians access to low-interest loans, forcing them to rely on highly exploitative credit card loans as well as other forms of high-interest borrowing. The result is that poor residents are blocked from succeeding at the very entrepreneurial endeavors they are expected to embrace as a pathway out of impoverishment.

Patricia Zavella discusses the rise of the new nativism in California and its impact on poor women. She shows how economic restructuring on a global scale has made white citizens more vulnerable at the same time that it has spurred on the Latinization of California. The state has become a site of racial tension and social conflict fueled by populist-inspired political measures that do not address the root causes of these transformations. Zavella discusses several case studies in which individuals struggle within and across the boundaries of racial difference to make personal and political connections.

The essays in part 2, "The Fallacy of 'Reform,'" expose recent efforts by federal, state, and local government to roll back health and welfare services, efforts legitimated in the name of "reform." Here, the rhetoric of reform, framed historically in the United States in terms of progress, social improvement, and individual mobility, in the present period masks the material causes of poverty and justifies a range of new policy initiatives that subordinate poor and working people's quality of life concerns to the interests of private enterprise.

Frances Fox Piven argues that one of the most significant effects of the 1996 PRWORA legislation is increased vulnerability among workers in low-end labor markets. After exploring the stagnation of labor markets from the 1970s through the 1990s, she demonstrates the historical role that welfare has played in maintaining a floor under wage rates. She then shows how new welfare policies, particularly the imposition of time limits, benefits cuts, increased use of sanctions, and "workfare," have forced large numbers of welfare recipients into the low-wage labor market. This has increased competition among low-end workers. She argues that sanctions and time limits not only make welfare recipients more materially vulnerable; they also perform the ideological function of stigmatizing those who find themselves at the bottom of the U.S. economic ladder.

Sandra Morgen and Jill Weigt demonstrate how rhetorical attacks made in the name of reform vilified programs such as the Comprehensive Employment and Training Act (CETA) that had been relatively effective in bringing poor people out of poverty. They demonstrate that, in contrast to the current limited "rapid attachment" design of welfare-to-work programs, CETA was a real welfare-to-work program that succeeded in placing women in meaningful work where they learned real, transferable skills. Yet the benefits of this program—as well as its limits—are masked by right-wing political rhetoric that, in a perverse appropriation of civil rights–era concerns with race and class equality, attacks the program for failing to serve the constituencies it was meant to serve.

Carol Stack offers an ethnographic description of life at the bottom of the low-end labor market. She shows the limits of fast-food jobs, currently touted as exemplary for welfare-to-work transitions, especially for young workers. While the young workers look at their work as teaching them valuable and transferable skills, such as teamwork and negotiating skills, their bosses and others do not value what they have learned, and neither teen workers nor employers see a next step on a career ladder. Workers cycle back and forth between fast-food and similar minimum-wage work, unable to find a way into work that will ultimately provide a living wage. By focusing closely on the life experience of one young female worker, Stack shows how such work, when juggled with school and a social life, undermines opportunities for youth to learn leadership skills and creates unexpected contradictions in how youth come to value work, school, and recreation.

The essays in part 3, "Poverty and Neoliberal Governance," demonstrate the extent to which poverty is treated through neoliberal governance as an opportunity for the poor to exercise self-help, volunteerism, and entrepreneurship. This disabling discourse masks the political-economic developments through which poverty is created and maintained, at the same time that it fosters among the poor new, invidious distinctions between the deserving "entrepreneurial" and "volunteering" poor, on the one hand, and the undeserving "dependent" poor, on the other.

Susan Hyatt shows how the discourse of volunteerism, a central part of the neoliberal valorization of unbridled individual agency, is based on racist, classist, and sexist representations that ignore or exclude the cooperative activities of the poor, particularly those of black women. She also shows how the discourse of volunteerism deflects attention from the withdrawal of social services from middle-class constituencies, since it is based on retrograde attacks on "big government."

Donna Goldstein explores one of the most pernicious forms of economic policy development to target the poor: microenterprise. Goldstein shows the impact of such programs—which parallel the failed development strategies that have been imposed, with little success, on the poor in developing countries—in rural and urban Colorado. Programs that teach entrepreneurship often fail to address the wide range of economic and social issues that affect their participants. Instead, they teach participants the abstract "value" of entrepreneurship. As such, these programs create a new subjectivity among the poor, one that promotes the embrace of entrepreneurial subjectivity as the definition of programmatic success.

Catherine Kingfisher spotlights tensions between welfare recipients and welfare workers. In the context of a gendered welfare system, in which women are devalued as both workers and recipients, bureaucratic control over welfare workers limits their ability to meet the needs of poor women seeking welfare services. Workers respond by invoking neoliberal blame ideologies, through which they separate those who are worthy of assistance from those who are not. Poor women, cast in the role of recipients, in turn construct views of the workers as arbitrary and unfair. This erases any sense of common life experience and similar class position between workers and recipients.

Vincent Lyon-Callo uses data from his ethnographic work in a homeless shelter in Northampton, Massachusetts, to explore the relationship of politics to survival for homeless men. He charts how individualized, accomodationist survival strategies become "common sense" for homeless men, one of the most pernicious effects of which is the disabling of collective action on the part of shelter residents. Lyon-Callo shows that homeless men are far from passive in their acceptance of their circumstances and often engage in individual acts of resistance, encoded in which are their own critiques of inequality and homelessness. Many homeless men, however, also accept neoliberal explanations for homelessness, some interpreting their lack of housing as a consequence of their individual shortcomings. In neoliberal fashion, many attempt to engage in self-reform through job training and self-help therapy.

The essays in part 4, "Poverty, Difference, and Activism," examine the dynamics of political action involving the poor. They demonstrate how, in the current conjuncture, the complex articulation of race, class, and national identity works in contradictory fashion to foster collective political action as well as to inhibit it. Importantly, these chapters refute the claim that poor people's political subjectivity is hopelessly or exclusively backward, reactive, and "local" by demonstrating that poor people's protests against inequality, exploitation, and oppression are advanced through the elaboration of political identities that reference multiple scales and multiple axes of difference.

Nina Glick Schiller and Georges Fouron highlight how transnational migration produces polysemous constructions of nationalism for the poor. They show how the imposition of structural adjustment on Haiti, and the resulting debt burden, has impoverished that country. In response to these circumstances, many poor Haitians emigrate to the United States in search of jobs and opportunity. In the process, they become transmigrants who are embedded in both states and who operate in social, political, and economic fields within and between them. The authors argue that long-distance nationalism has emerged from this transmigration process. In some instances, long-distance nationalism hides the relationship of impoverishment, in both Haiti and the United States, to global capitalism's structures of power. In other instances, it reinforces linkages between poor Haitians and global struggles against racism, exploitation, and oppression.

Judith Goode discusses the way in which state institutions deploy contradictory discourses of multiculturalism in order to control anticipated unrest in economically wounded, racially mixed neighborhoods, where many neighbors are engaged collectively in incipient political struggles to improve local conditions. These official state discourses do not fit local realities and are often rejected and replaced by residents. In some cases, this resistance leads to a reinforcement of racial identities and distinctions between the native born and immigrants, which reinscribes difference and separation in the neighborhood. In this way, the common class-based political subjectivity that is developing between cross-racial neighbors is disrupted.

Eve Weinbaum looks at a strike in rural Tennessee. Confronted with an economic crisis of severe magnitude, brought on by the threatened closing of a plant on which town residents depend for jobs, workers engage in grassroots militancy. In the process, they challenge the economic imperatives of globalization. Weinbaum provides an analysis of how these rural workers and their local mobilized in collaboration with other unions, their national leadership, and other labor leaders in a fight against capital mobility. She demonstrates that although they did not achieve their ultimate goal of keeping the plant open, they won on several fronts. They educated the townspeople about the global economy, political practice, and trade and tax policy and were successful in closing a corporate tax loophole at the federal level. Throughout this campaign they maintained an internationalist, antiracist political subjectivity, and the national political labor coalition they built maintained itself for action on other issues.

In part 5, "Conclusions: Theories, Politics, and Policy," Matthew Ruben explores the politics of contemporary research on urban poverty. He draws connections between suburbanization, neoliberalism, and urban poverty research, arguing that ideologies that support suburbanization also form the ideological basis for much mainstream research on urban poverty. Indeed, postwar policies that fueled suburbanization have since become institutionalized through "trickle-down" finance capital strategies, with uneven development, economic polarization, and a stratified geographical and symbolic landscape as a consequence. Ruben shows how the narratives that justify suburbanization have also colonized aspects of academic discourse about the city, which is increasingly aligned with the rhetoric of corporate elites rather than with the oppressed. He offers the class-based rhetoric of a multiracial welfare rights organization in Philadelphia as a corrective to academic research that sensationalizes the urban poor and ignores political economy.

In an afterword to the volume, Jeff Maskovsky challenges poverty scholars to think beyond the dominant policy agenda to envision research projects that can help overcome the political demobilization of the poor.

Taken together, the essays collected here write against the prevailing wisdom in order to show that poor people are inextricably connected to—not isolated from—economic restructuring and state-based institutional power arrangements. This collection therefore provides not only a more dynamic understanding of poverty and immiseration but one that, by insisting on the importance of poor people's agency, poses challenges to dominant moralistic assumptions about the poor and to the prevailing model of social *disorder* through which poverty and inequality have been justified and excused in recent decades.

NOTES

1. With distance, Fallows explains to us, also comes abstraction. Accordingly, Fallows draws a parallel between the U.S. poor and the poor in the developing world: "This is not the embattled distance of the 'Bonfire of the Vanities' period, with its gated communities and atmosphere of urban armed camps. It is more like simple invisibility, because of increasing geographic, occupational and social barriers that block one group from the other's view. Prosperous America does not seem hostile to the poor, and often responds generously when reminded. But our poor are like people in Madagascar. We feel bad for them, but they live someplace else" (Fallows 2000: 72, 78).

2. Fallows dismisses the possibility of crafting public policies that can address, with any immediacy, the growing economic disparity between rich and poor. He writes, "What is happening is a partly logical, policy-driven reaction. Poverty really is lower than it has been in decades, especially among minority groups. The most attractive solution to it—a growing economy—is being applied. The people who have been totally left out of this boom often have medical, mental or other problems for which no one has an immediate solution. 'The economy h.s sucked in anyone who has any preparation, any ability to cope with modern life,' says Franklin D. Raines, the former director of the Office of Management and Budget who is now head of Fannie Mae. When he and other people who specialize in the issue talk about solutions, they talk analytically and long-term: education, development of work skills, shifts in the labor market, adjustments in welfare reform" (Fallows 2000:

72). In this formulation, the poor will need decades of education, support, and acculturation before their integration into the new economy will be possible. The implication here is that a more philanthropic response from the "tech wealthy" is the only way to help ameliorate the privations that the poor will be forced to endure in the meantime.

3. John Gledhill (1994: 151–78) makes this point in a discussion of violence, global politics, and capitalist development in the post–Cold War era.

4. There has, of course, been an international correlate to these developments. A series of U.S.-led agreements on trade and finance since the 1970s have forced the "liberalization" of the economies of developing nations. As is being popularized through the protest efforts of the anti-corporate movement that began in Seattle in November 1999, the U.S.-led hegemony of the Bretton Woods institutions (which outlived the agreement itself) created a world economy in which the majority of nations were forced to become export-driven economies. In the name of "structural adjustment," this was a surefire recipe for economic polarization and widespread poverty. These are the economic imperatives behind what is now commonly referred to as "globalization."

5. For a more in-depth discussion of these policy developments, see Morgen and Weight, chapter 6 in this book.

6. On the effects of welfare state rollbacks on poor and working people's wages, see Shaikh and Tonak 1987.

7. Doug Henwood (2000: 4, 7) provides an analysis of U.S. household incomes and poverty rates by race and gender. This analysis shows that in 1998 the United States had the highest gap in income between rich and poor since the Census Bureau started publishing annual figures in 1947. Moreover, while incomes for rich households have increased dramatically in recent years, this is not the case for middle-class and poor households. His analysis also shows that the poverty rate has remained essentially flat over the last twenty years, despite recent economic growth. With respect to income disparities between racial groups, he writes: "Racial/ethnic gaps are a mixed bag. Though the black/white differential has been closing raggedly since the late 1980s, that's not true of the last couple of years (though it should be pointed out that this is because white incomes were up more strongly than black, not because of a decline in black incomes). So-called 'Hispanic' households—the skeptical phrasing and punctuation is an expression of doubt that this category has much analytical power, given the vast difference between the groups gathered under this single label—have been doing better in recent years. But that bounce barely compensates for the widening of the income gap from the early 1980s into the early 1990s, which is mainly the result of the arrival of poorer immigrants" (Henwood 2000: 4). People of color, he adds, have greater unequal distribution of income than whites. Beyond these statistics, economic restructuring and shifts in state policy have had a differential impact on various populations, communities, neighborhoods, and political constituencies. Karen Brodkin has set forth an important

overview of the social organization of capitalism in the United States in terms of race, class, gender, sexuality, and nation (Brodkin 1999; 2000; Sacks 1989). For a review of the literature focusing on recent political economic shifts and their effects on the poor, see Susser 1996.

8. In an extension of Reagan-era characterizations of women on welfare as lazy and dishonest "welfare queens," George H. W. Bush unleashed attack ads against Democratic presidential candidate Michael Dukakis that sensationalized the violent crimes perpetrated by ex-con Willie Horton, whom Dukakis had freed on parole during his governorship of Massachusetts.

9. On the racial and sexual construction of poverty, see di Leonardo 1997; Williams 1992; Hyatt 1995. Importantly, sexualized representations of the poor were often based on heteronormative assumptions that masked the impact of economic and social policies on a growing number of poor sexual minorities (see Maskovsky 2000).

10. Despite his more conservative social agenda, the vision of government promoted by George W. Bush in the first months of his presidency does not constitute a major shift from the neoliberal vision under Clinton. Indeed, evidence that the Bush presidency is, in fact, a hard-right brand of neoliberalism can be seen in the following quote, which Bush made in support of his proposed $1.6 trillion tax cut: "Government should be active, but limited, engaged, but not overbearing" (quoted in Toner 2001: 4-1).

11. Micaela di Leonardo makes the important point that Lewis's "social work" solutions, unlike those of later poverty scholars such as William Julius Wilson, were intended, at least to a certain extent, to overcome what Lewis saw as the inability of the poor to organize themselves politically. She identifies the implicit, if muted, appreciation for the need for political mobilization involving the poor that is to be found in Lewis's work, which she contrasts favorably with the assumptions about political agency undergirding the arguments of Wilson (di Leonardo 1998: 119).

12. Michael Harrington's *The Other America* is the book that "rediscovered" American poverty amid postwar affluence (Harrington 1962). It was somewhat less influenced by the "culture of poverty" argument than was the Moynihan report. It is interesting to note that Harrington's *Other America* was about Appalachia, and that the urban poor did not become a focus of policy until after Lyndon B. Johnson became president, and after the Civil Rights Act of 1964 and the Watts riots in 1965 put a national focus on urban blacks.

13. It is important to note that work by Anthony Leeds (1971) and others refuted this view but did so by looking at the dynamics of political organization in squatter settlements in Latin America. In anthropology in particular, however, this point was not made in the earliest rebuttals to Lewis that focused on U.S. poverty.

14. More recently, important ethnographic work has paid attention to these areas of oversight. Janet Fitchen (1991), Mary K. Anglin (1992; 1998), and Rhoda H. Halperin (1990) have examined rural poverty, while Douglas Foley and Kirby Moss

(2000) discuss suburban poverty. Pem Davidson Buck (1996) and John Hartigan (1997a; 1997b; 1997c; 1999) have specifically examined the intersection of race and class in the production of poverty, with particular attention to ideologies of whiteness. Buck explores the historical construction of white privilege in Appalachia and how this affects the dynamics of white and black poverty. Hartigan (1999) analyzes the ways in which ideologies of whiteness intersect with class ideologies in the everyday lives and institutional practices of white poor people living in heavily black Detroit.

15. This approach builds on recent work that places the agency of poor and working-class neighborhood residents at the center of analysis and, in so doing, does not sensationalize or pathologize poor people's responses to political and economic changes; see Bookman and Morgen 1988; Gregory 1993; 1994; 1998a; Jones 1977; Maxwell 1988; Mullings 1987; 1996; Sharff 1998; Williams 1988; Zavella 1987; 1988; 1994; Lamphere et al. 1993; Piven and Cloward 1971; Kingfisher 1996; Lipsky 1980; Jones et al. 1993; Sacks 1987; 1988; Susser 1982; 1996; Susser and Kreniske 1987. See also Sugrue 1996; Katz 1993.

REFERENCES

Aglietta, Michel
1979   *A Theory of Capitalist Regulation: The U.S. Experience.* Translated by David Fernbach. London: NLB.

Anderson, Elijah
1991   *Streetwise: Race, Class, and Change in an Urban Community.* Chicago: University of Chicago Press.
1999   *Code of the Street: Decency, Violence and the Moral Life of the Inner City.* New York: W. W. Norton.

Anglin, Mary K.
1992   "Question of Loyalty: National and Regional Identity in Narratives of Appalachia." *Anthropological Quarterly* 65(3):105–16.
1998   "Looking Beyond the Factory: Regional Culture and Practices of Dissent." In *More than Class: Studying Power in U.S. Workplaces.* Edited by Ann E. Kingsolver. Albany: State University of New York Press, 53–72.

Aschenbrenner, Joyce
1975   *Lifelines: Black Families in Chicago.* New York: Holt, Rinehart and Winston.

Bartelt, David
1993   "Housing the Underclass." *The "Underclass" Debate: Views from History.* Edited by Michael Katz. Princeton, NJ: Princeton University Press, 118–60.

Bertram, Eva, Morris J. Blachman, Kenneth Sharpe, and Peter Andreas
1996   *Drug War Politics: The Price of Denial.* Berkeley: University of California Press.

Bookman, Ann, and S. Morgen, eds.
1988   *Women and the Politics of Empowerment.* Philadelphia: Temple University Press.

Bourdieu, Pierre
1998   *Acts of Resistance: Against the Tyranny of the Market.* New York: The New Press.

Bourgois, Philippe
1995   *In Search of Respect: Selling Crack in El Barrio.* New York: Cambridge University Press.

Brenner, Robert
1998   "The Economics of Global Turbulence." In *New Left Review* 229:1–265.

Brodkin, Karen
1999   "Race, Class and Gender: The Metaorganization of American Capitalism." *Transforming Anthropology* 7(2):46–57.
2000   "Global Capitalism: What's Race Got to Do with It?" *American Ethnologist* 27(2):237–56.

Buck, Pem Davidson
1992   "With Our Heads in the Sand: The Racist Right, Concentration Camps, and the Incarceration of People of Color." *Transforming Anthropology* 3:13–18.
1994   "'Arbeit macht frei': Racism and Bound, Concentrated Labor in U.S. Prisons." *Urban Anthropology* 23(4):331–72.
1996   "Sacrificing Human Rights on the Altar of 'Morality': White Desperation, Far Right Explanation, and Punitive Social Welfare Reform." *Urban Anthropology* 25(2)195–210.

Castells, Manuel
1983   *The City and the Grassroots.* Berkeley: University of California Press.

Cherry, Robert
1987   "Theories of Unemployment." In *The Imperiled Economy.* Book 1. New York: The Union for Radical Political Economy, 7–18.
1988   "Black Youth Employment Problems." In *The Imperiled Economy.* Book 2. New York: The Union for Radical Political Economy, 121–32.

Cruikshank, Barbara
1993   "Revolutions Within: Self-Government and Self-Esteem." *Economy and Society* 22(3):327–44.
1994   "The Will to Empower." *Socialist Review* 23(4):30–56.

Davis, Mike
1986   *Prisoners of the American Dream*. New York: Verso.
1990   *City of Quartz*. New York: Verso.

di Leonardo, Micaela
1997   "White Lies, Black Myths." In *The Gender/Sexuality Reader*. Edited by R.
         Lancaster and M. di Leonardo. New York: Routledge, 53–70.
1998   *Exotics at Home: Anthropologies, Others, American Modernity*. Chicago: Uni-
         versity of Chicago Press.

Eames E., and J. G. Goode
1973   *Urban Poverty in Cross Cultural Context*. New York: Free Press.

Edelman, Marc
1999   *Peasants against Globalization: Rural Social Movements in Costa Rica*. Stan-
         ford, CA: Stanford University Press.

Edsall, Thomas Byrne
1984   *The New Politics of Inequality*. New York: W. W. Norton.

Fallows, James
2000   "The Invisible Poor." *New York Times Magazine*, March 19, 68–78, 95,
         111–12.

Fitchen, Janet
1991   *Endangered Spaces, Enduring Places: Change, Identity and Survival in Rural
         America*. Boulder, CO: Westview Press.

Foley, Douglas, and Kirby Moss
2000   "Studying U.S. Cultural Diversity: Some Non-Essentializing Perspectives."
         In *Cultural Diversity in the United States: A Critical Reader*. Edited by Ida
         Susser and Thomas C. Patterson. London: Blackwell, 343–64.

Gledhill, John
1994   *Power and Its Disguises*. Boulder, CO: Pluto Press.

Gregory, Steven
1992   "The Changing Significance of Race and Class in an African American
         Community." *American Ethnologist* 19:255–74.
1993   "Race, Rubbish and Resistance: Empowering Difference in Community
         Politics." *Cultural Anthropology* 8(1):24–48.
1994   "Race, Identity, and Political Activism: The Shifting Contours of the African
         American Public Sphere." *Public Culture* 7:147–64.
1995   "Commentary." From "Race and Racism: A Symposium." *Social Text*
         42(Spring):16–21.
1998a   *Black Corona: Race and the Politics of Place in an Urban Community*. Prince-
         ton, NJ: Princeton University Press.
1998b   "Globalization and the 'Place' of Politics in Contemporary Theory: A Com-
         mentary." In *City and Society* 10:47–64,

Gregory, Steven, and Roger Sanjek, eds.
1994   *Race.* New Brunswick, NJ: Rutgers University Press.

Halperin, Rhoda H.
1990   *The Livelihood of Kin: Making Ends Meet "the Kentucky Way."* Austin: University of Texas Press.

Hannerz, Ulf
1969   *Soulside.* New York: Columbia University Press.

Harrington, Michael
1962   *The Other America: Poverty in the United States.* New York: Macmillan Publishing.

Hartigan, John
1997a   "Establishing the Fact of Whiteness." *American Anthropologist* 99(3)495–505.
1997b   "Name Calling: Objectifying 'Poor Whites' and 'White Trash' in Detroit." In *White Trash: Race and Class in America.* Edited by Matt Wray and Annalee Newitz. New York: Routledge, 41–56.
1997c   "When White Americans Are a Minority." In *Cultural Diversity in the United States.* Edited by Larry L. Naylor. Westport, CT: Bergin and Garvey, 103–15.
1999   *Racial Situations: Class Predicaments of Whiteness in Detroit.* Princeton, NJ: Princeton University Press.

Harvey, David
1985   *Urbanization of Capital.* Baltimore: Johns Hopkins University Press.
1989   *The Condition of Postmodernity: An Enquiry into the Origins of Cultural Change.* Oxford: Blackwell.

Henwood, Doug
2000   "Boom for Whom?" *Left Business Observer,* no. 93 (February). URL: <http://www.panix.com/~dhenwood/IncPov98.html> September 1, 2000.

Hyatt, Susan B.
1995   "Poverty and Difference: Ethnographic Representations of 'Race' and the Crisis of 'the Social.'" In *Gender and Race through Education and Political Activism: The Legacy of Sylvia Forman.* Edited by D. Shenk. Arlington, VA: American Anthropological Association/Association for Feminist Anthropology, 185–206.

Jackson, Thomas
1993   "The State, the Movement, and the Urban Poor: The War on Poverty and Political Mobilization in the 1960s." In *The "Underclass" Debate: Views from History.* Edited by Michael Katz. Princeton, NJ: Princeton University Press, 403–39.

Jones, Delmos
1977   "Incipient Organizations and Organizational Failure in an Urban Ghetto." *Urban Anthropology* 1(1):55-67.

Jones, Delmos J., Joan Turner, and Joan Montbach
1993   "Declining Social Services and the Threat to Social Reproduction: An
        Urban Dilemma." *City and Society* 6(2):99–114.

Katz, Michael
1989   *The Undeserving Poor: From the War on Poverty to the War on Welfare.* New
        York: Pantheon Books.
1993   "Introduction." In *The "Underclass" Debate: Views from History.* Edited by
        Michael Katz. Princeton, NJ: Princeton University Press, 3–26.

Kingfisher, Catherine
1996   *Women in the Welfare Trap.* Philadelphia: University of Pennsylvania Press.

Lamphere, Louise, Patricia Zavella, and Felipe Gonzales, with Peter B. Evans
1993   *Sunbelt Working Mothers: Reconciling Family and Factory.* Ithaca, NY: Cor-
        nell University Press.

Leacock, Eleanor
1971   "Introduction." In *The Culture of Poverty: A Critique.* Edited by Eleanor Lea-
        cock. New York: Simon and Schuster, 1–23.

Leeds, Anthony
1971   "The Concept of the 'Culture of Poverty': Conceptual, Logical and Empiri-
        cal Problems with Perspectives from Brazil and Peru." In *Culture of Poverty:
        A Critique.* Edited by Eleanor Leacock. New York: Simon and Schuster,
        226–84.
1994   "Locality Power in Relation to Supralocal Power Institutions." In *Cities,
        Classes and the Social Order.* Edited by Roger Sanjek. Ithaca, NY: Cornell
        University Press, 209–32.

Lewis, Oscar
1966   "The Culture of Poverty." *Scientific American* 215(4):19–25.

Liebow, Elliot
1967   *Tally's Corner: A Study of Negro Streetcorner Men.* Boston: Little, Brown.

Lipsky, Michael
1980   *Street-Level Bureaucracy.* New York: Russell Sage Foundation.

Logan, John R., and H. Molotch
1987   *Urban Fortunes: The Political Economy of Place.* Berkeley: University of Cal-
        ifornia Press.

Lusane, Claude
1991   *Pipe Dream Blues: Racism and the War on Drugs.* Boston: South End Press.
1994   "In Perpetual Motion: The Continuing Significance of Race and America's
        Drug Crisis." *University of Chicago Law Review* (January): 96.

Mandel, Ernest
1975   *Late Capitalism.* London: NLB.

Marks, Carol
1991   "The Urban Underclass." *Annual Review of Sociology* 17:445–66.

Maskovsky, Jeff
2000   "Sexual Minorities and the New Urban Poverty." In *Cultural Diversity in the United States.* Edited by I. Susser and T. Patterson. London: Blackwell, 322–42.

Massey, Douglas S., and Nancy A. Denton
1993   *American Apartheid: Segregation and the Making of the Underclass.* Cambridge, MA: Harvard University Press.

Maxwell, Andrew
1988   "The Anthropology of Poverty in Black Communities: A Critique and Systems Alternative." *Urban Anthropology* 17(2–3):171–91.

Mead, Lawrence M.
1992   "Should Congress Respond? If Waivers Are Granted, Congress Must Monitor Results." *Public Welfare* 50(2)(Spring): 14-4.

Mink, Gwendolyn
1998   *Welfare's End.* Ithaca, NY: Cornell University Press.

Moynihan, Daniel P.
1965   *The Negro Family: The Case for National Action.* Washington, D.C.: U.S. Department of Labor.

Mullings, Leith
1996   *On Our Own Terms: Race, Class, and Gender in the Lives of African-American Women.* New York: Routledge.

Mullings, Leith, ed.
1987   *Cities in the United States.* New York: Columbia University Press.

Murray, Charles
1984   *Losing Ground: American Social Policy, 1950–1980.* New York: Basic Books.

Naples, Nancy A.
1997   "The 'New Consensus on the Gendered Social Contract': The 1987–1988 U.S. Congressional Hearings on Welfare Reform." *Signs: The Journal of Women in Culture and Society* 22(4):907–45.
1998   *Grassroots Warriors: Activist Mothering, Community Work, and the War on Poverty.* New York and London: Routledge.

Parenti, Christian
1999   *Lockdown America: Police and Prisons in the Age of Crisis.* London: Verso.

Piven, Frances Fox, and Richard Cloward
1971   *Regulating the Poor: The Functions of Public Welfare.* New York: Pantheon Books.

Piven, Frances Fox, and Richard Cloward
1977   *Poor People's Movements: Why They Succeed, How They Fail.* New York: Vintage Books.
1997   *The Breaking of the American Social Compact.* New York: New Press.

Reed, Adolf
1999   *Stirrings in the Jug: Black Politics in the Post-Segregation Era.* Minneapolis: University of Minnesota Press.

Rouse, Roger
1995   "Thinking through Transnationalism: Notes on the Cultural Politics of Class Relations in the Contemporary United States." *Public Culture* 7(2): 353–402.

Sacks, Karen
1987   "Gender and Grassroots Leadership." In *Women and the Politics of Empowerment.* Edited by A. Bookman and S. Morgen. Philadelphia: Temple University Press, 77–96.
1988   *Caring by the Hour.* Urbana: University of Illinois Press.
1989   "Towards a Unified Theory of Class, Race and Gender." *American Ethnologist* 16:534–50.

Sanchez-Otero, German
1993   "Neoliberalism and Its Discontents." *NACLA Report on the Americas* 26(4): 18–21.

Sharff, Jagna W.
1998   *King Kong on 4th Street: Families and the Violence of Poverty on the Lower East Side.* Boulder, CO: Westview Press.

Shaikh, Anwar, and Ertugrul Ahmet Tonak
1987   "The Welfare State and the Myth of the Social Wage." In *The Imperiled Economy,* book 1: *Macroeconomics from a Left Perspective.* Edited by Robert Cherry et al. New York: The Union of Radical Political Economics.

Smith, Neil
1996   *The New Urban Frontier: Gentrification and the Revanchist City.* New York: Routledge.
1997   "The Satanic Geographies of Globalization: Uneven Development in the 1990s." *Public Culture* 10(1):169–89.

Smith, Paul
1997   *Millennial Dreams: Contemporary Culture and Capital.* London: Verso.

Smith, Steven R., ed.
1993   *Nonprofits for Hire.* Cambridge, MA: Harvard University Press.

Stack, Carol
1974   *All Our Kin.* New York: Harper and Row.

Stefancic, Jean, and Richard Delgado
1997 *No Mercy: How Conservative Think Tanks and Foundations Changed America's Social Agenda.* Philadelphia: Temple University Press.

Sugrue, Thomas J.
1996 *The Origins of the Urban Crisis: Race and Inequality in Postwar Detroit.* Princeton, NJ: Princeton University Press.

Susser, Ida
1982 *Norman Street: Poverty and Politics in an Urban Neighborhood.* New York: Oxford University Press.
1988 "Working Class Women, Social Protest, and Changing Ideologies." In *Women and the Politics of Empowerment.* Edited by A. Bookman and S. Morgen. Philadelphia: Temple University Press, 257–71.
1996 "The Construction of Poverty and Homelessness in U.S. Cities." *Annual Review of Anthropology* 25:411–35.

Susser, Ida, and John Kreniske
1987 "The Welfare Trap." In *Cities in the United States.* Edited by Leith Mullings. New York: Columbia University Press, 51–68.

Toner, Robin
2001 "Cutting a Rightward Path." *New York Times*, March 4, 4-1, 4.

Valentine, Betty Lou
1978 *Hustling and Other Hard Work: Life Styles in the Ghetto.* New York: Free Press.

Valentine, Charles
1968 *Culture and Poverty: Critique and Counter-Proposals.* Chicago: University of Chicago Press.

Williams, Brett
1988 *Upscaling Downtown: Stalled Gentrification in Washington, D.C.* Ithaca, NY: Cornell University Press.
1992 "Poverty among African Americans in the Urban United States." *Human Organization* 51:164–74.
1994 "Babies and Banks: The 'Reproductive Underclass' and the Raced, Gendered Masking of Debt." In *Race.* Edited by S. Gregory and R. Sanjek. New Brunswick, NJ: Rutgers University Press, 348–65.

Wilson, William J.
1987 *The Truly Disadvantaged: The Inner City, the Underclass, and Public Policy.* Chicago: University of Chicago Press.
1996 *When Work Disappears: The World of the New Urban Poor.* New York: Alfred A. Knopf.

Zavella, Patricia
1987 *Women's Work and Chicano Families: Cannery Workers in the Santa Clara Valley.* Ithaca, NY: Cornell University Press.

Zavella, Patricia
1988   "The Politics of Race and Gender: Organizing Chicana Cannery Workers in
        Northern California." In *Women and the Politics of Empowerment*. Edited by
        A. Bookman and S. Morgen. Philadelphia: Temple University Press, 202–26.
1994   "Reflections on Diversity among Chicanos." In *Race*. Edited by S. Gregory
        and R. Sanjek. New Brunswick, NJ: Rutgers University Press, 199–212.

Zucchino, David
1997   *Myth of the Welfare Queen: A Pulitzer Prize-Winning Journalist's Portrait of
        Women on the Line*. New York: Scribner's.

Zukin, Sharon
1991   *Landscapes of Power: From Detroit to Disneyland*. Berkeley: University of
        California Press.

Part I

New Dimensions of Inequality

Chapter 1

Households Headed by Women
The Politics of Class, Race, and Gender

Leith Mullings

As income and wealth inequality grows, the public debate increasingly connects poverty with households headed by women. This household form, which, in 1990, comprised over 20 percent of all families in the United States with children under eighteen (U.S. Bureau of the Census 1990a),[1] is frequently cited as the cause of poverty. With the precipitous rise of households headed by women—from 10.7 percent in 1970 to 21 percent in 1990 (U.S. Bureau of the Census 1973: Table 54; 1990a)—the insidious demonization of "welfare mothers" grows. Locating economic failure in the reproductive behavior and household forms of the individual diverts attention simultaneously from the processes through which global and local socioeconomic relations produce poverty and from the reproductive responses to it. These processes form the context for stratified reproduction, whereby "some categories of people are empowered to nurture and reproduce, while others are disempowered" (Ginsburg and Rapp 1995: 3).

For African Americans, the conflict over fertility has always been linked to the political economy—as their efforts to control the conditions of their reproduction clashed with the interests of the dominant class. During slavery, slaveowners encouraged fertility among enslaved women to increase the labor force. In the contemporary economy, as African Americans resist confinement to the low-wage jobs of their parents and grandparents (Collins 1991), they are increasingly considered a "redundant population," an underclass that must be contained. Reproduction is now regulated less directly and less personally than it was during slavery, as the structure of the

Reprinted with revisions by permission from *Conceiving the New World Order: The Global Politics of Reproduction*. Edited by Faye D. Ginsburg and Rayna Rapp. Berkeley and Los Angeles: University of California Press, 1995.

households of women seeking welfare benefits or admission to homeless shelters comes under increasing bureaucratic manipulation and regulation, and as women who head households are stigmatized.

Today, with labor and capital moving around the globe, race, class, and gender, as well as nationality, define boundaries to be held, reclaimed, or challenged. In the global context of population policies, disease, and disasters of all kinds, local populations seek to envision continuity through children and act to ensure that continuity. Using low-income women in Harlem, New York City, as an example, this chapter: (1) describes the global and local socioeconomic relations; (2) explores the ways in which ideologies and social policies reinforce stratified reproduction; and (3) discusses "transformative work," through which people seek to sustain themselves, their families, and their communities.

Global, National, and Local Intersections

That women increasingly raise children themselves is an international phenomenon, characteristic of both industrialized and developing nations. Various factors bear on the rise of these households in different parts of the world. A precipitous increase in the proportion of such households may be associated with war, as in Iraq; genocidal policies, as in Guatemala; neocolonial apartheid and separation, as in South Africa; labor migration, as landless peasants search for work in much of the world; or increasing unemployment, as in parts of the industrialized world. The international labor diaspora places huge burdens on women: in most areas, households headed by women are associated with high rates of poverty, as children become a cost particular to them.

Household structure in both developing and industrialized countries is shaped by global as well as local processes, as policies implemented at national or international levels increasingly mold reproductive experiences. The flight of industry from U.S. cities to areas with cheaper and less-organized labor and the rapid movement of "hot money" around the world in search of speculative opportunities have local consequences: unemployment, destruction of social services, and infrastructural deterioration plague postindustrial cities in the United States.

In the United States, global processes interact with historical patterns of racism and discrimination, sharpening racial and gender disparities. Minority populations in inner cities are most severely affected by the increasing social and economic polarization. Since the 1980s the African American middle class has expanded. But at the same time a growing number of workers have been expelled from the labor force, and unemployment and underemployment among African American and Latino men have reached staggering proportions (Stafford 1991; Wilson 1987).

Because the growth of households headed by women is linked to unemployment and low earnings (see Ross and Sawhill 1975; Wilson 1987), it is not surprising that 50 percent of all African American and 24.2 percent of all Latino compared with 15.8 percent of all Euro-American households with children under eighteen are headed by women (U.S. Bureau of the Census 1990a). While the rise of feminism, growing labor-force participation (which increases women's economic independence), and changing attitudes toward marriage may be factors in rising female headship among Euro-American women (England and Farkas 1986), for African Americans, male unemployment seems to be a major reason for female-headed households (Wilson 1987). The disappearance of "marriageable" African American men—through disproportionate unemployment, consequent participation in an informal underground economy of which crime is only one aspect, and ensuing high levels of incarceration and "excess" death—means that African American women of all classes are less likely to marry or to remarry. But the consequences are greatest for low-income women, who must deal with poverty. In 1990 almost half (42 percent) of all households with children under eighteen headed by women, including 34 percent of Euro-American and 53 percent of African American and 55 percent of Latino households, fell below the poverty threshold (U.S. Bureau of the Census 1990b). Increasingly concentrated in the inner cities, these households become the subject of considerable critical scrutiny in the context of global discourses linking economic development with population control.

Local Communities: Women, Work, and Family in Central Harlem

Central Harlem, a predominantly African American community in northern Manhattan, presents an example of the havoc wreaked in local communities already disadvantaged by centuries of discrimination. But it is also a complex and variegated community, in which people struggle against increasingly difficult conditions. At the turn of the century people of African descent from other parts of New York City, the South, and the Caribbean began to migrate to Harlem. Though it was shaped by segregation and discrimination, Harlem has been a vibrant social, political, and cultural center for African Americans of all classes. In the 1920s it was the hub of a cultural renaissance. Social movements ranging from Marcus Garvey's Back to Africa organization to the election of Ben Davis as the first Communist city councilman have found fertile ground in Harlem.

Many of Central Harlem's residents are currently experiencing severe difficulties, as the effects of global restructuring and the economic policies and cutbacks of the 1970s and 1980s interact with long-standing patterns of racism to produce rapidly deteriorating conditions.[2] Harlemites' limited access to well-paying jobs is reflected in the low median income, which was $13,252 in 1989 compared with $29,823 for New York City, and in levels of unemployment more than double those of New York City (New York City Department of City Planning 1992a; 1992c). Almost half (42.2 percent) of Harlem youth between sixteen and nineteen were unemployed in 1989 (New York City Department of City Planning 1992d), and almost 40 percent of the residents of Central Harlem fell below the poverty line (New York City Department of City Planning 1992e).

As conditions for poor people in the inner cities of the industrial world increasingly resemble those of people without resources in the developing world, it is not surprising that a study found that for men in Central Harlem "the rate of survival beyond the age of 40 is lower . . . than in Bangladesh" (McCord and Freeman 1990: 174).

Less well publicized is the situation for women. "For women, overall survival to the age of 65 is somewhat better in Harlem [than in Bangladesh], but only because the death rate among girls under five is very high in Bangladesh" (McCord and Freeman 1990: 174). Women find themselves in an increasingly difficult position. In Central Harlem, 69 percent of all families with children under eighteen are headed by women (New York City Department of City Planning 1992b). While some women have been immobilized by the crisis conditions, others succeed in raising their children without a stable income from men and are able to maintain their households despite adverse circumstances.

Most African American women have been compelled—by slave holders or necessity—to work outside the home. With the devastating unemployment of African American men, labor-force participation of African American women has become roughly equal to that of men: in 1990 women constituted 52.4 percent of the African American work force, though women made up only 45.3 percent of the Euro-American work force (U.S. Bureau of the Census 1992).

Though differences between African American and Euro-American women in work-force participation are no longer dramatic, their history is. Euro-American women's aggregate participation in the work force has only recently approached that of African American women, who, as mothers, have always worked outside their homes in large numbers (see Mullings 1986b). The obstacles that confront all working mothers are intensified for African American women, who find themselves in the ambiguous position of being primary wage earners in a society where the official ideology designates men as the principal breadwinners. In Central Harlem, 52 percent of women in the labor force have children under eighteen and 43 percent of them have children under six (New York City Department of City Planning 1993). These difficulties are compounded for women with low-income jobs. By the 1980s, as a result of the struggle for civil rights and an expanding service economy, African American women had moved into a variety of professions and occupations. But a large proportion of African American women continue to be concentrated in low-wage jobs, with little job security, few benefits, and difficult working conditions. The poorest women are excluded from the job market altogether. In Central Harlem in 1990, more than half (54.7 percent) of women eligible to work were not in the labor force (New York City Department of City Planning 1990b), with 28.9 percent of the population receiving Aid to Families with Dependent Children (New York City Department of City Planning 1991). Women may work entirely in the informal sector or may augment their income from welfare or low-wage work with such informal-sector jobs as childcare and other domestic work, renting out living spaces, or selling various products. Some develop strategies that combine attending school to improve their job chances with one or more low-wage jobs. Nevertheless, 54.3 percent of all households headed by women that include children under eighteen have incomes below the poverty line (New York City Department of City Planning 1993). In short, many women work a triple shift—work outside the home, additional informal-sector work, and housework—which must be extended to fill the gap left by declining social services.

In addition to responsibility for supporting the household—often with marginal incomes—women must maintain the family in conditions exacerbated by the economic policies of the 1980s. As the federal government decreased its contribution to New York City's budget from 19.8 percent in 1978 to 10.9 percent in 1990 (New York City Office of the Budget 1991), women have had to cope with the problems caused by cutbacks not only in social services but in education, housing, childcare services, and health care.

For example, many African American mothers feel that they can no longer rely on schools. Education has historically been of great importance to African Americans' struggle for equality. They have struggled for equal access to education, and since emancipation, mothers' wages have often been applied to allowing children to continue in school (see Pleck 1979). This strategy has had some successes. Since the 1970s, African Americans have significantly narrowed the gap between themselves and Euro-Americans in number of school years completed, although this improvement has not resulted in narrowing the income gap.

But the gains in education won during the civil rights era of the 1960s and 1970s have eroded since then: racial inequality in access to education has increased (Kozol 1991). Children in New York City schools, for example, receive less funding per capita than children in suburban schools (Kozol 1991), and in Central Harlem, children and schools receive less funding in almost every category than in other districts in New York City (Breslin and Stier 1987). The "survival rate" in these large, underfunded, understaffed schools is low: the two high schools to which the majority of students from junior high schools in Central Harlem are directed have a four-year graduation rate of approximately 27 percent (Mullings and Susser 1992), which does not include those who drop out between the eighth and ninth grades. There is, nonetheless, a belief in the efficacy of education. Parent and community organizations have been successful in instituting after-school programs and in persuading the Board of Education to establish a high school to serve Central Harlem.

In addition to their concerns about education, women must raise their children in neighborhoods where poverty, neglect, drugs, and crime are threatening the social fabric. Since the 1970s, nearly ten thousand units of housing have been abandoned in Central Harlem (Harlem Urban Development Corporation 1990; Mullings and Susser 1992), and at the same time there has been a major reduction in federal funds for new housing units. Consequently, between 1970 and 1990, the number of available housing units dropped by 27.1 percent (New York City Department of City Planning 1990a). The resulting overcrowding, homelessness, and destruction of neighborhoods have had a ripple effect: as families move away, networks that have historically sustained the community and that might control deviant behavior are destroyed, and deterioration and crime increase (see Wallace, Fullilove, and Wallace 1992).

Drugs are a case in point. With the inability (or unwillingness) of the federal government to stop the importation of illegal drugs into the United States, and with police effectiveness significantly curtailed by corruption, strategically located low-income neighborhoods become marketplaces for the sale of drugs to surrounding suburbs. Youth are drawn into the sale and distribution of drugs as meaningful economic or educational opportunities decline. The director of a substance-abuse program in Central Harlem pointed out to me: "The young people today don't have an anti-work ethic. . . . Those kids are out doing the crack thing, that's work. . . . They have a sophisticated understanding of management, organization, distribution, marketing, and competition. But it's all geared to the wrong thing." (Compare Williams 1989.)

The depth of worry about children growing up in these conditions is difficult to convey. The epidemic of violence (the cost of which is borne by these neighborhoods), fueled by the ready availability of firearms, threatens everyone, but people worry most about the youth. Older relatives sometimes give teenage boys guns for protection, and violence spirals. In 1989, Central Harlem had a total of 3,175 violent crimes, ranking seventeenth among seventy-five community districts in New York City in number of violent crimes per person (New York City Office of Management Analysis and Planning 1989).

People are adamant about trying to keep children safe. Women spend an extraordinary amount of time escorting children, limiting their movement, and trying by any means to keep them away from the violence of the streets. There are building-by-building and block-by-block struggles (often unsuccessful) to expel drug dealers. At the same time, proceeds from the sale of illegal drugs may be the only income for some families. As I interviewed residents of Central Harlem, people repeatedly expressed acute concern about losing the children—to the drug culture, to early death as a result of substance abuse, to the often random violence associated with illegal drugs in poor neighborhoods. Today, the leap of faith to envision continuity through children must be as great as during the days of slavery.

In these circumstances, it might be argued that women are making "adaptive" reproductive decisions in a situation where the population is endangered by excessive morbidity and mortality. As with unemployment rates, infant mortality rates among African Americans are over twice the national average. In Central Harlem, the infant mortality rate in 1988 was approximately three times the national rate; between 1985 and 1988, children up to the age of four were dying at three times the expected rate for the

United States (Health and Hospitals Corporation 1991). Indeed, in all age groups except for those between the ages of five and fourteen and those over sixty-five, residents of Central Harlem die at higher rates than among the broader U.S. population (Mullings and Susser 1992; Health and Hospitals Corporation 1991).

It is not surprising that among pregnant young women I interviewed in Central Harlem, death of family members was not an unusual occurrence. For example, one unmarried nineteen-year-old stated that her mother had urged her to bring this pregnancy to term, though she had terminated a previous pregnancy by abortion. In the course of discussion, it became clear that in the last two years several family members had died unexpectedly: her brother had been killed by a stray bullet; a cousin had died of AIDS; and another cousin had died of respiratory distress in a hospital.

Though women through their childbearing behavior may, in a sense, replace people lost to early death (compare Sharff 1987), it is important not to underestimate the cost of all these burdens to women themselves. Between 1985 and 1988, the annual excess death rate (see Mullings and Susser 1992 for an explanation of this index) of women in Central Harlem was ten times that of New York City, with heart disease being the leading cause (Mullings and Susser 1992), no doubt reflecting the stresses to which these women are subject. One might conclude that while excess death among men reflects direct confrontation with the social system, women die of indirect effects.

As conditions in these communities decline, the potential for violence directed at the larger society escalates. While AIDS and illegal drugs function as forms of population control, the public discussion of fertility escalates. As women attempt to raise children in crisis conditions, they find themselves the focus of representations that in effect obscure and even blame them for those conditions.

Ideology and Public Policy

Elements of strongly held ideologies concerning race, class, and gender are reflected in the public discussion of women who head households. Ideologies of race portray them as promiscuous women and inadequate mothers; ideologies of class blame them for their poverty; and ideologies of patriarchy label nontraditional family forms "pathological." The convergence of these beliefs and their reproduction at so many locations render the representation of women who head households particularly deleterious.

Race, Motherhood, and Sexuality

Stratified reproduction is reinforced and reproduced by gender constructions that have emphasized motherhood for Euro-American women (Davin 1978; Laslett and Brenner 1989) but sexuality for African American women. Both sides of this fractured imagery have implications for reproduction, as motherhood, womanhood, and race are symbolically intertwined and contested.

For elite Euro-American women, motherhood has been a major defining element of gender identity. Women as mothers—who are involved in both biological and cultural reproduction—become master symbols of family, race, and civility and are central to the authorized definition of the national community (compare Stoler 1989). When boundaries are threatened, rhetoric about fertility and population control escalates, and native Euro-American women, preferably those of the dominant class, are exhorted to have children. Deviation from traditional roles is presumed to promote race suicide, and women who do not or cannot conform are censured as contributing to the decline of civilization. For example, abolitionists were labeled "shameless amazons" and "unsexed females" (Scott 1970: 20); suffragists were accused of contributing to race suicide by concerning themselves with matters outside the home (Rosen 1982: 45).

In the face of rising discontent with the widening division of wealth and challenges to cultural hegemony, and as international migrations again modify the face of the United States, the oratory of the recent Republican conventions bore a striking resemblance to Nazi rhetoric, which demanded motherhood for the "mothers of the master race" versus compulsory sterilization for others and "race hygienic sterilization . . . [as] a prelude to mass murder" (Bock 1983: 408). Along with a call to arms for "a cultural war . . . for the soul of America,"[3] "family values" became a ringing slogan at the 1992 Republican Convention. But not just any family: the model was the (Euro-American) nuclear family with the father working and the mother at home, characteristic of less than one-sixth of U.S. families. Not surprisingly, traditional gender roles, anti-abortion laws, attacks on households headed by women, and defense of the traditional educational curriculum were linked to the preservation of the nation.

The dominant class's construction of gender has throughout history portrayed African American women as inadequate mothers and promiscuous women. Not only were enslaved women vulnerable to sexual exploitation, but slavery required fertility without motherhood:[4] children could be and were sold away from them. In Sojourner Truth's famous 1851 speech to the Akron Convention for Women's Suffrage ("Ain't I a Woman?"), so often quoted as an emblem of multiracial solidarity, she poignantly described motherhood under slavery: "I have bourn thirteen children, and seen them most all sold off to slavery, and when I cried out with my mother's grief, none but Jesus heard me! Ain't I a Woman?"

When slavery ended, segregation and discrimination dictated that African American women work outside the home, but their opportunities were initially limited to domestic work. Representations of African American women as sexually provocative, which had rationalized the vulnerability of slaves to the sexual advances of Euro-American men, continued to excuse advances toward African American domestic workers.

Images of African Americans as bad mothers, as ineffective mothers, as matriarchs (see Collins 1991; Mullings 1994; and Morton 1991, for a discussion of these notions in popular culture and scholarly literature), also conceal and justify the difficult conditions in which they work and raise children. But, oddly enough, these same women, who are said to run amok in their own communities, are thought to be entirely competent at parenting the children of the elite—as mammies during slavery, as domestic workers during segregation, or as childcare workers today. Thus, the popular images of low-income African American women who head households emphasize not mothering but sexuality. They are not portrayed as mothers with limited resources struggling to care for children. Their public image as nurturers depends entirely on the care they "offer" to the children of Euro-American families. At the same time, the problem of endangered African American manhood is laid at the door of the "weak" mothers who cannot "discipline" them.

Class and Patriarchy

Ideologies of class come into play in depicting these women and their children as the crystallization of the urban underclass. Several works (see, for example, Lemann 1986; Murray 1984; Jenks 1991) attribute the contemporary poverty in minority communities to the growth of households headed by women. This literature has been reviewed and critiqued elsewhere (for example, Mullings 1989; Williams 1992; Reed 1992), but these views persist despite work demonstrating the relationship between unemployment and the rise of female-headed families.[5] By blaming these women for their own poverty and, indeed, for the economic ills of the entire nation, attention is diverted from the injustice of the racial and gendered labor market and from the "savage inequalities" increasingly characterizing U.S. society.

Notions of normative gender roles continue to pervade those works that attempt to analyze the structural conditions that give rise to these households (for example, Wilson 1987). Despite the lack of significant evidence that single-headedness is, in itself, harmful, these households are invariably described as inherently pathological (for discussion of these concepts in the social-policy literature, see Schorr and Moen 1979; Schlesinger 1986). One might conclude that the intensity of affect and scrutiny to which these households are subject at some level reflects "a fear of women without men" (compare Tiffany and Adams 1985 on the "matriarch fixation"); households headed by women are seen as "the other" of the patriarchal family (Sands and Nuccio 1989), just as the underclass is "the other" to the middle class.

Limiting Options through Policies and Representation

Powerful ideas of class, race, and gender are central to social policies, which, by imposing constraints on the experience of reproduction according to race and class, replicate and reinforce structural inequality. Public policies regarding childcare, women's work, and compensation, rationalized by notions about appropriate gender roles, promote the male-headed nuclear family by reinforcing the dependence of women (see Mullings 1989). For the working class, and increasingly for middle-stratum women who must work, these policies make their lives difficult.

For poor women, however, state policies that structure access to social benefits often reinforce and encourage matrifocality. As the lack of employment and educational opportunities constrains women's access to men's income and they are forced to rely on the state, social policies function to further encourage matrifocality. Benefits such as income support (Stack 1974) or Medicaid (Davis and Rowland 1983) are virtually unavailable to men or to households that include men (Stack 1974). Ida Susser's (1989) ethnographic study of homeless shelters in New York graphically documents the role of the state in structuring the composition of households through its regulation of who may sleep where and with whom and whether parents may stay with children. As low-income housing becomes unavailable and the homeless population grows, the shelter system routinely separates men from their children and the mothers of their children. In some facilities, boys over the age of nine are not permitted to stay in the shelters with their mothers. Families are defined as women and young children, and men are considered irrelevant and dangerous.

These public policies combine with popular perceptions to further limit already limited options. Images of the promiscuous welfare mother deflect attention from the role of the society in producing African American mothers and children who are dependent on the state. Michael Harrington suggested that the image of "a welfare mother with a large family, pregnant once again [the poor as promiscuous and lazy], . . . [has] done more to set back the struggle against poverty than have all efforts of reactionary politicians" (1984: 179). These representations are then used to rationalize policies ranging from forcing Norplant birth-control implants on welfare recipients to cutting welfare benefits of parents whose children exceed a designated limit (Reed 1992: 36). The limitations on educational and occupational opportunities, which create the conditions in which young women are more likely to have children, are then reinforced.

Some feminists (for example, Hartmann 1987) suggest that households headed by women may be a positive development, contributing to women's autonomy and control. We do need to "denaturalize" (Rapp 1987) the family: to understand the nuclear family as a historically particular form, characteristic of a minority of humankind for a relatively small proportion of time. We do need to point out that male or female "headship" in and of itself does not determine the consequences widely attributed to it, but that the social context of the family (whatever its form), especially access to material and social resources, seems to be crucial.

Nevertheless, feminist analyses emphasizing increased independence tend to underplay the costs to women, children, and the community and to verge on adopting the conservative view that these women are making an unrestricted lifestyle choice. While this is a complex issue, I think it reasonable to assume that for a majority of African American women who head households, their situation is both imposed and chosen (compare Lebsock 1984). To the extent that they choose, they do so within a range of options severely limited by hierarchies of race, class, and gender. The task, then, is to transform the structure that limits options for both men and women.

Women, Reproduction, and Resistance: Transformative Work

As described above, women work outside the home and in the home rearing children in difficult circumstances. But they also engage in what we might call transformative work. I use *transformative work* in two senses: efforts to sustain continuity under transformed circumstances and efforts to transform circumstances in order to maintain continuity. These efforts have spanned the domains of work, household, and community.

A History of Struggle

In their efforts to sustain continuity under transformed circumstances, women in Harlem have a long tradition to draw on. In slavery, some women resisted increasing the property of slavers through their fertility by using various contraceptive and abortion techniques that Southern medical journals referred to as "medicine," "violent exercise," and "external and internal manipulation" (Gutman 1976: 81). Others imagined their continuity through children even within the "peculiar" institution of slavery. To bear children, who became the property of the slaveowner, must have given an especially poignant meaning to "alienation"; nevertheless they bore and raised children, creating families in which woman-centered networks figured prominently (Gutman 1976; Mintz and Price 1976; Mullings 1986a; 1986b).

Within the constraints of segregation, African American men and women attempted to maintain some control over the conditions in which they bore children. Though planters (Gutman 1976) and poverty forced many married women to work, they often chose to work as laundresses rather than as live-in domestics, increasing the time they could spend with their families and limiting, as best they could, their vulnerability to sexual exploitation.

In their effort to maintain continuity and support survival through the conditions of slavery, segregation, and deindustrialization, African American women have often utilized women-centered networks. These "blood mothers and other mothers" (Collins 1991) embedded in larger networks have a long history in the African American community as an alternative family form (see Omolade 1987). They have sustained and supported survival, caring for children and adults when immediate relatives were unable to do so. In Harlem, these networks continue, often supported by community-based organizations.

Efforts to sustain the family have always been inseparable from efforts to assist the community. African American women have a long history of community work (see Gilkes 1988). Inevitably, the attempt to sustain the community requires measures to transform the larger society. Most African American women and men have been actively involved in individual and collective efforts that foster resistance and empowerment. As a result, African American women were able to make impressive gains in educational attainment and inroads into occupations previously dominated by Euro-American women (Almquist 1989: 419) and have more recently had a significant impact on the political process.

Conditions and Constraints

African American women and, particularly, poor women in communities such as Harlem now face one of the greatest challenges since slavery. In the face of deteriorating conditions, many women in Harlem continue to engage in efforts directed at both sustaining continuity and transforming conditions. Kin and nonkin networks continue to be important in raising children, but the extent to which these networks are threatened by the crisis conditions (DeHavenon 1988) is indicated by the record number of children in foster care. These networks and other institutions are particularly weakened by the spread of illegal drug use among African American women.

Though the decline of working-class movements has undercut a major area of potential advance, women in Central Harlem, many of whom head households, are the backbone of militant unions, such as Local 1199 of the Hospital Workers Union, and they continue to try to change the workplace. They are active in community efforts to build associations and tenant organizations, to improve housing and schools, and to eliminate drugs from buildings and neighborhoods. Community-based activities such as the church-led movement to protest extensive billboard advertisement of cigarettes and alcohol and two environmental movements focusing attention on pollution in low-income neighborhoods have been highly publicized. These local struggles have sometimes been the building blocks of larger, citywide political actions, such as the election of the first African American mayor of New York City and the formation of the New Majority Coalition, a multiracial organization that was active in voter registration, supporting progressive candidates for election to the city council, and organizing for a civilian review board.

With the failures of liberal integration (Marable 1992), however, and the destruction of the left movement (Horne 1993), the political context for collective movements for empowerment and basic social reform was severely restricted in the 1990s. The repressive environment, which had a negative impact on efforts for collective empowerment, lent itself to the resurgence of ethnically based political and cultural movements. This development was evident to the casual observer in the rise of various Afrocentrisms; the adoption of neo-African hairstyles, jewelry, and clothing; the iconization of Malcolm X and the growing influence of the Nation of Islam; as well as in expressions of concern about loss of history, culture, and community. Explanations such as "we need to return to our values" and "we need to build our own cultural and moral base for our children" were typically given by people I interviewed in Central Harlem. On the one hand, this concern with culture represented an attempt to contest hegemonic constructs of race and culture, to repossess history, and to create new definitions of community (Mullings 1997: 189). On the other hand, fundamentalist nationalist movements are frequently patriarchal and authoritarian. In these cases, the status of women, who are often seen as culture bearers, becomes highly problematic (Mullings 1994).

In doing transformative work, then, women seek to construct a space in which they can ensure continuity for themselves, their children, and their communities. We need to increase our understanding of the conditions in which these efforts are successful and the circumstances in which they develop into larger social movements. But what is unique, perhaps, about the experience of African American women is the dramatic way in which their experience has linked the domains of household, community, and the larger society. For women of color, working-class women, and, increasingly, middle-stratum women, protection of their children, which mobilizes their activism, requires the protection and transformation of their households, communities, and the larger society. For this reason, efforts to sustain and maintain continuity inevitably involve significant social transformations.

If we are to understand and address the causes of poverty, not only must we reject the wrongheaded assumptions that all we need is an assault on households headed by women and problematic individual reproductive decisions. We also need to recognize and build on the ways in which the desire to protect children and to ensure continuity mobilizes activism and moves toward transformation.

NOTES

1. Nearly one-third (28.7 percent) of all households were headed by women (U.S. Bureau of the Census 1990a).

2. Health, employment, housing, education, and social services in Central Harlem are described in greater detail in Mullings and Susser (1992).

3. From Patrick Buchanan's speech to the Republican National Convention, August 1992.

4. In some cases, interest in adding to property seemed to mandate easing the burdens of pregnant women (Fox-Genovese 1988), and demonstrated high fertility might bring privileges to a woman and perhaps decrease the likelihood of sale and separation from her kin (Gutman 1976: 75–77). Yet we have numerous accounts of pregnant and nursing women being subjected to grueling working conditions. Jones points to the brutal whipping of pregnant and nursing mothers, "so that blood and milk flew mingled from their breasts," and to the special trenches found throughout the South, designed for administering a beating to a pregnant slave while minimizing harm to the fetus: "They were made to lie face down in a specially dug depression in the ground" (1985: 20). The conditions under which African American women conceived, bore, and raised children varied according to historical period, geographical area, plantation size, and the disposition of the planter. But in no case was the slave family legal.

5. Wilson demonstrates that, despite popular beliefs, the rate of childbearing among African American women decreased 40 percent between 1960 and 1983. But because there are fewer employed men to marry, there are higher statistical rates of out-of-wedlock births for African American teenagers (Wilson 1987: 194). Other analyses point to the lack of evidence that family structure causes poverty—indeed, for people of color, the two-parent family is no guarantee against poverty. (See Baca Zinn 1989 for a review of such studies.) More recently, a Census Bureau study concluded that poverty is a major factor contributing to the dissolution of families in the United States (Hernandez 1992).

REFERENCES

Almquist, Elizabeth M. 1989. The Experience of Minority Women in the United States: Intersections of Race, Gender and Class. In *Women: A Feminist Perspective*, 4th ed., edited by Jo Freeman. Mountain View, Calif.: Mayfield.

Baca Zinn, Maxine. 1989. Family, Race and Poverty in the Eighties. *Signs* 14: 856–74.

Bock, Gisela. 1983. Racism and Sexism in Nazi Germany: Motherhood, Compulsory Sterilization and the State. *Signs* 8: 400–421.

Breslin, Susan, and Eleanor Stier. 1987. *Promoting Poverty: The Shift of Resources Away from Low Income New York City School Districts*. New York: Community Service Society of New York.

Collins, Patricia Hill. 1991. *Black Feminist Thought: Knowledge, Consciousness, and the Politics of Empowerment*. Boston: Unwin Hyman.

Davin, Anna. 1978. Imperialism and Motherhood. *History Workshop* 5:9–65.

Davis, Karen, and Diane Rowland. 1983. Uninsured and Underserved: Inequities in Health Care in the United States. In *The Sociology of Health and Illness: Critical Perspectives*, edited by Peter Conrad and Rochelle Kern. New York: St. Martin's Press.

DeHavenon, Anna Lou. 1988. Where Did All the Men Go? An Etic Model for the Cross-Cultural Study of the Causes of Matrifocality. Paper presented at symposium, Female Headed/Female Supported Households, Twelfth International Congress of Anthropological and Ethnological Sciences, July 21–31, Zagreb, Yugoslavia.

England, Paula, and George Farkas. 1986. *Households, Employment and Gender: A Social, Economic and Demographic View*. New York: Holt, Rinehart & Winston.

Fox-Genovese, Elizabeth. 1988: *Within the Plantation Household: Black and White Women of the Old South*. Chapel Hill: University of North Carolina Press.

Gilkes, Cheryl. 1988. Building in Many Places: Multiple Commitments and Ideologies in Black Women's Community Work. In *Women and the Politics of Empowerment*, edited by Ann Bookman and Sandra Morgan. Cambridge, Mass.: Harvard University Press.

Ginsburg, Faye, and Rayna Rapp, eds. 1995. *Conceiving the New World Order: The Global Politics of Reproduction*. Berkeley and Los Angeles: University of California Press.

Gutman, Herbert G. 1976. *The Black Family in Slavery and Freedom, 1750–1925*. New York: Pantheon.

Hacker, Andrew. 1992. *Two Nations: Black and White, Separate, Hostile, Unequal*. New York: Scribner's.

Harlem Urban Development Corporation. 1990. *Bradhurst Revitalization Planning Document*. New York.

Harrington, Michael. 1984. *The New American Poverty*. New York: Holt, Rinehart & Winston.

Hartmann, Heidi I. 1987. Changes in Women's Economic and Family Roles in Post–World War II United States. In *Women, Households, and the Economy*, edited by Lourdes Beneria and Catherine R. Stimpson. New Brunswick, N.J.: Rutgers University Press.

Health and Hospitals Corporation, Office of Strategic Planning. 1991. *A Summary Examination of Excess Mortality in Central Harlem and New York City*. New York.

Hernandez, Donald J. 1992. *When Households Continue, Discontinue and Form: Studies on Household and Family Formation*. Current Population Reports. Series P23-179. Washington, D.C.: U.S. Bureau of the Census.

Horne, Gerald. 1993. Myth and the Making of Malcolm X. *American Historical Review* 98: 440–50.

Jenks, Christopher. 1991. Is the American Underclass Growing? In *The Urban Underclass*, edited by Christopher Jenks and D. Peterson. Washington, D.C.: Brookings Institution.

Jones, Jacqueline. 1985. *Labor of Love, Labor of Sorrow: Black Women, Work and the Family from Slavery to the Present*. New York: Basic Books.

Kozol, Jonathan. 1991. *Savage Inequalities: Children in America's Schools*. New York: Crown.

Laslett, Barbara, and Johanna Brenner. 1989. Gender and Social Reproduction: Historical Perspectives. *Annual Review of Sociology* 15: 381–404.

Lebsock, Suzanne. 1984. *The Free Women of Petersburg: Status and Culture in a Southern Town, 1784–1860*. New York and London: Norton.

Lemann, Nicholas. 1986. The Origins of the Underclass. Parts 1 and 2. *Atlantic Monthly* (June): 31–35; (July): 54–68.

McCord, Colin, and Harold P. Freeman. 1990. Excess Mortality in Harlem. *New England Journal of Medicine* 322(3): 173–77.

Marable, Manning. 1992. Race, Identity and Political Culture. In *Black Popular Culture*, edited by Gina Dent. Seattle: Bay Press.

Mintz, Sidney W., and Richard Price. 1976. *An Anthropological Approach to the Afro-American Past: A Caribbean Perspective*. Philadelphia: Institute for the Study of Human Issues.

Morton, Patricia. 1991. *Disfigured Images: The Historical Assault on Afro-American Women*. New York: Praeger.

Mullings, Leith. 1986a. Anthropological Perspectives on the Afro-American Family. *American Journal of Social Psychiatry* 6(1): 11–16.

———. 1986b. Uneven Development: Class, Race and Gender in the Urban United States before 1900. In *Women's Work: Development and the Division of Labor*, edited by Eleanor Leacock and Helen Safa. New York: Bergin.

———. 1989. Gender and the Application of Anthropological Knowledge to Public Policy in the United States. In *Gender and Anthropology*, edited by S. Morgen. Washington, D.C.: American Anthropological Association.

———. 1994. Symbols, Ideology, and Women of Color. In *Women of Color in America*, edited by Bonnie Dill and Maxine Baca Zinn. Philadelphia: Temple University Press.

———. 1997. *On Our Own Terms: Race, Class and Gender in the Lives of African American Women*. New York: Routledge.

Mullings, Leith, and Ida Susser. 1992. *Harlem Research and Development: An Analysis of Unequal Opportunity in Central Harlem and Recommendations for an Opportunity Zone*. New York: Office of the Borough President of Manhattan.

Murray, Charles. 1984. *Losing Ground*. New York: Basic Books.

New York City Department of City Planning. 1990a. *Community District 10*. New York.

————. 1990b. *Persons 16 Years and Over by Labor Force Status and Sex, New York City, Boroughs and Community Districts.* DCP 1990 #317. New York.

————. 1991. *Community District Needs FY 1993.* DCP 1990 #91-14. New York.

————. 1992a. *Civilian Labor Force 16 Years and Over by Employment Status and Sex, New York City, Boroughs and Community Districts.* DCP 1990 #315. New York.

————. 1992b. *Demographic Profiles: A Portrait of New York City's Community Districts from the 1980 and 1990 Censuses of Population and Housing.* New York.

————. 1992c. *Household Income in 1989, New York City, Boroughs and Community Districts.* DCP 1990 #309. New York.

————. 1992d. *Persons 16–19 Years, Enrollment, Education and Labor Force/Employment, New York City, Boroughs and Community Districts.* DCP 1990 #321. New York.

————. 1992e. *Selected Poverty Tabulations in 1989, New York City, Boroughs and Community Districts.* DCP 1990 #310. New York.

————. 1993. *Socioeconomic Profiles: A Portrait of New York City's Community Districts from the 1980 and 1990 Censuses of Population and Housing.* New York.

New York City Office of the Budget. 1991. *1990 Annual Average Labor Force Data Disaggregated by Community District.* Brooklyn: New York State Department of Labor.

New York City Office of Management Analysis and Planning, Crime Analysis Unit. 1989. *Statistical Report: Complaints and Arrests.* New York.

Omolade, Barbara. 1987. The Unbroken Circle: A Historical and Contemporary Study of Black Single Mothers and Their Families. *Wisconsin Women's Law Journal* 3:239–74.

Pleck, Elizabeth. 1979. A Mother's Wages. In *A Heritage of Her Own,* edited by N. Cott and Elizabeth Pleck. New York: Simon & Schuster.

Rapp, Rayna. 1987. Toward a Nuclear-Freeze? The Gender Politics of Euro-American Kinship Analysis. In *Gender and Kinship: Essays toward a Unified Analysis,* edited by Jane Collier and Sylvia Yanagisako. Stanford, Calif.: Stanford University Press.

Reed, Adolph. 1992. The Underclass as Myth and Symbol: The Poverty of Discourse about Poverty. *Radical America* 24(1): 21–40.

Rosen, Ruth. 1982. *The Lost Sisterhood: Prostitution in America, 1900–1918.* Baltimore: Johns Hopkins University Press.

Ross, Heather L., and Isabel V. Sawhill. 1975. *Time of Transition: The Growth of Families Headed by Women.* Washington, D.C.: Urban Institute.

Sands, Roberta, and Kathleen Nuccio. 1989. Mother-Headed Single Parent Families: A Feminist Perspective. *Affilia* 4(3): 25–41.

Schlesinger, Benjamin. 1986. Single-Parent Families: A Bookshelf: 1978–1985. *Family Relations* 35(1): 199–204.

Schorr, Alvin L., and Phyllis Moen. 1979. The Single Parent and Public Policy. *Social Policy* 9(5): 15–21.

Scott, Ann Firor. 1970. *The Southern Lady*. Chicago: University of Chicago Press.

Sharff, Jagna. 1987. The Underground Economy of a Poor Neighborhood. In *Cities of the United States: Studies in Urban Anthropology*, edited by Leith Mullings. New York: Columbia University Press.

Stack, Carol. 1974. *All Our Kin: Strategies for Survival in a Black Community*. New York: Harper & Row.

Stafford, Walter. 1991. *Black and Latino Men in New York City*. New York: Association of Protestant Welfare Agencies.

Stoler, Ann. 1989. Making Empire Respectable: The Politics of Race and Sexual Morality in 20th Century Colonial Cultures. *American Ethnologist* 16(4): 634–60.

Susser, Ida. 1989. The Structuring of Homeless Families: New York City 1980–1990. Paper presented at the American Anthropological Association annual meetings, November, Washington, D.C.

Tiffany, Sharon, and Kathleen Adams. 1985. *The Wild Woman: An Inquiry into the Anthropology of an Idea*. Cambridge, Mass.: Schenkman.

U.S. Bureau of the Census. 1973. *1970 Census of Population and Housing, Characteristics of Population, U.S. Summary*. Washington, D.C.

———. 1990a. *1990 Census of Population and Housing, Summary Tape File 1C*. Washington, D.C.

———. 1990b. *1990 Census of Population and Housing, Summary Tape File 3C. Poverty Status in 1989 by Family Type and Presence and Age of Children*. Washington, D.C.

———. 1992. *Detailed Occupation and Other Characteristics from the EEO File for the United States. 1990 Census of Population and Housing, Supplementary Report*. Washington, D.C.

Wallace, Rodrick, M. Fullilove, and D. Wallace. 1992. Family Systems and Deurbanization: Implications for Substance Abuse. In *Substance Abuse: A Comprehensive Textbook*, edited by Joyce Lowinson. Baltimore: Williams & Wilkins.

Williams, Brett. 1992. Poverty among African Americans in the Urban United States. *Human Organization* 51(2): 164–74.

Williams, Terry. 1989. *The Cocaine Kids*. New York: Columbia University Press.

Wilson, William J. 1987. *The Truly Disadvantaged*. Chicago: University of Chicago Press.

Chapter 2

Poverty despite Family Ties

Peter Kwong

Popular wisdom has it that new immigrants armed with strong family ties and kinship support are less likely than other U.S. workers to be unemployed and therefore less likely to live in poverty. Fuzhounese immigrants certainly exhibit some of the strongest kinship ties among all Chinese. This essay intends to show that Fuzhounese immigrants, many of whom are illegals and are therefore burdened with huge smuggling debts and suffer exploitation from their co-ethnic employers, cannot escape the curse of poverty in a society where labor enforcement is weak and organized labor is in decline.

Current social science literature is full of articles lauding the value of family as a powerful institution that can deflect individuals from sliding into poverty. Following this line of thinking, new immigrants, who generally have stronger family ties (due primarily to the selection process stipulated by U.S. immigration laws)[1] than the U.S. native born, are much less likely to be impoverished. The efficacy of family in helping immigrants to upward mobility is well documented. It is also well established that immigrant families are able to build safety nets through pooled resources, in order to prevent individual members from falling into degradation. In this essay I show that there are limits to the influence families can exert over the fate of individual members. Drawing on ethnographic data from a study of Fuzhounese immigrants, the group that constitutes the majority of illegals from mainland China, I argue that these limits are not necessarily the result of the weaknesses in the immigrant family structure; rather, they are due to the hostile larger political and economic environment in which a growing number of illegal migrants find themselves struggling to survive. In particular, illegals and their families are increasingly unable to overcome the marginal, impoverished status they automatically assume once they have arrived in the United States.

This chapter is a revised and modified segment of my new book *Forbidden Workers: Illegal Chinese Immigrants and American Labor*, published by the New Press in January 1998, which focuses on illegal immigrants from mainland China since the 1980s. Most are from the rural outskirts of the city of Fuzhou in the southern province of Fujian. In comparison to other groups of U.S.-bound illegal immigrants, the Fuzhounese are small in number.[2] The circumstances of their entry into the United States, however, and its consequences for their everyday survival after they have migrated, make their situation particularly gruesome. They are victims of a large-scale and sophisticated international human smuggling network. After arrival in the United States, they are forced to work for years under what amounts to indentured servitude to pay off large "transportation" debts. They face constant threats of torture, rape, and kidnapping. Their experiences index the kinds of brutal exploitation of illegals by employers who violate American labor laws.

I have studied Chinese American communities for more than two decades. Since 1991, I have conducted hundreds of personal interviews with Chinese undocumented workers in their living quarters, at their workplaces, in coffee shops, in prisons, and on waiting lines of employment agencies in all parts of New York City, from the relatively circumscribed precincts of south Manhattan's traditional Chinatown to the ballooning Chinese neighborhoods of Queens and Brooklyn. These contacts have brought to my attention circumstances affecting Chinese workers far beyond the New York metropolitan area, from Connecticut suburbs to newly opened restaurants in North Carolina and even into southern California and elsewhere around the country.

My access to these illegal immigrants has been anything but automatic. It takes years of painful cultivation to gain the trust of someone whose daily work is carried out in constant fear of detection by immigration officials, and whose private life is shadowed by the threat of torture from fellow Chinese debt enforcers. In-depth interviews have been very difficult, especially with regard to sensitive issues concerning their smugglers and employers. The problem is compounded by their lack of free time from their long working hours to talk with me. I have to intrude on them late at night, when they are usually exhausted, or on their days off, when they are usually busy with personal chores among their families and relatives.

Aside from these critical personal interviews, my knowledge of illegals is informed by regular contacts with federal and local police officers, immigration officials, social workers, immigration lawyers, and Chinatown reporters. Moreover, after the infamous appearance of the smuggling ship *Golden Venture* as an unannounced seaside attraction for Rockaway Beach tourists in 1993, I traveled to China to investigate the origins of Fuzhounese illegal emigration. There I had the opportunity to interview human smuggling operators called snakeheads, local party officials, and average citizens, including those who had made great sacrifices to send a relative on the dangerous journey to the United States. The data I collected have given me a fairly complete picture of Fuzhounese smuggling networks and the system of family-centered chain migration.

The Political Economy of Southern China

The illegal immigrants from mainland China come mostly from the cities of Fuzhou and Wenzhou, or rather, from the rural outskirts of these cities. These areas are two of the fastest-growing economic regions in China, where development is fueled by foreign investments. The village outskirts of Fuzhou and Wenzhou have always been highly productive as food suppliers for city dwellers. The residents of villages on the outskirts of these two cities commanded favorable positions even during the days of the People's Commune under Mao Zedong. Deng Xiaoping initiated his economic reform first in rural China, allowing rural producers to break up collectives and sell their products in free markets. Many rural producers accumulated wealth quickly by selling produce based on market values. They then invested the earnings into handicraft and small-scale manufacturing industries, such as making shoes and clothing. Thus, Deng's reforms initially brought remarkable gains in rural productivity. Between 1978 (the beginning of the reform) and 1984, the gross output in the countryside grew at an impressive annual rate of 9 percent. In a very short time, rural producers became wealthy in contrast to urban residents who worked for state enterprises on fixed salaries.

By the middle of 1980s, the Chinese government permitted foreign firms to set up factories in special industrial zones. This policy was intended to build cash reserves from these enterprises as a means to modernize state industries. Immediately, multinational firms such as Nike and K-Mart set up production plants to take advantage of China's cheap labor pool. Much of China's most dynamic expansion has occurred in export-oriented sectors, the development of which was financed mainly by foreign investors and often managed by subcontractors from Taiwan and Hong Kong. Most growth is concentrated in the southern coastal areas, in places like Fuzhou and Wenzhou.

With new high-wage jobs available in southern coastal cities, expectations among various sectors of China's rural population heightened. Migrants from rural and interior regions, where there had not been such development, rushed to China's southern coastal cities looking for jobs. China's internal migration is also encouraged by factory owners, including foreign owners, who prefer out-of-province workers because they are "less demanding and work harder." Some factories recruit only young out-of-province girls, who live and work in barracks under sweatshop conditions. Still, workers compete for these jobs because the wages are higher than what they can make at home. In many foreign investment zones, the out-of-province population surpasses the local population.

This rural-to-urban, north-south migration has brought inflation, overcrowded housing, open sewage, street congestion, depressed wages, high unemployment, petty crime, and general social disorder to the cities. Unaccompanied young girls and boys sleep in the open air and sell their labor and bodies in city markets to anyone willing to pay. Some of them become street urchins, barefoot and dressed in rags, scabby-headed, with flies gathering in the corners of their eyes. Their presence recalls the human deprivation of pre-1949 China under semi-colonialism.[3]

Foreign investment has also destroyed newly established domestic industries. Village enterprises simply cannot compete with newer, urban ventures equipped with modern machinery and backed by foreign capital. As one small rural entrepreneur, who is also a relative of an illegal who came to the United States on the *Golden Venture*, described in an interview, "As more people got into making shoes and clothing like ours, the profit margins declined and the markets dried up." This individual, who had prospered earlier in shoe manufacturing, explained: "We are left to fend for ourselves in a highly risky business. . . . Without government connections, we cannot get into the more lucrative export markets. Where can we sell our products?"

Since 1985, rural output has slowed considerably, in contrast to growth in the urban areas. Some analysts suggest that once rural producers abandoned grain production for the more profitable cash-crop and rural industries, they soon fell victim to the cyclical process that begins with heated market competition, is followed by raw materials shortages and price inflation, and ends with overproduction and glut.

Certainly, those rural producers who had the opportunity to taste the fruits of free enterprise are resentful of these new developments, and increasingly they blame the corrupt political system for their troubles. Indeed, Chinese Communist Party officials are using their positions to monopolize the most lucrative enterprises for themselves. It is now a common complaint that party officials allocate public funds to invest in their private business ventures. During China's Eighth National People's Congress, Fifth Plenary Session, held in Beijing in March 1997, delegates castigated the government for its inability to halt the massive exodus of $100 billion (U.S.) stolen government funds since 1979. An estimated $17.8 billion left in 1995 alone. The culprits are top managers of national enterprises and sons and daughters of high-ranking officials—known in China as princelings—who use their privileged positions to channel state funds to private savings accounts outside the country.

In response to these developments, Chinese workers and peasants have mobilized. In the first nine months of 1996, for instance, there were 1,520 reported incidents of mass demonstrations by threatened and laid-off workers in 120 cities. They marched under unofficial, unsanctioned banners reading "Unemployed Workers Alliance," "Anti-Capitalist Restoration Association," or simply "Chinese Labor Association." In the countryside there is also a great deal of unrest, due to the imposition of heavy and arbitrary taxes by local officials. When the peasants cannot pay, officials resort to confiscation of property and imprisonment. These harsh measures have led to violent revolts in half a dozen provinces, including Fujian. The worst reported incident happened in one county of Hunan Province, where the peasants, angered by a variety of unreasonable taxes, demonstrated in front of the county government building. More than ten thousand gathered and sacked the government offices. Eventually, thousands of police and militia were called in from other regions to quell the uprising.

The Chinese leadership is now facing an immediate crisis of survival. Members of the Communist Party have, in effect, arranged for themselves and their children to be first in line to benefit from China's transition to capitalism. Yet the environment of corruption is so suffocating that many Chinese who are less prosperous than party elites feel they have no future in China. Meanwhile, the party hopes to solve its problems by joining the

World Trade Organization (WTO). WTO membership would enable China to gain trade and tariff benefits, but it would also open China's lucrative insurance, banking, and communication markets to foreign ownership. In a way, the Chinese leaders are counting on Western powers to pull the country out of economic crisis in order to stay in power. Thus, the current Chinese Communist leadership is no less comprador in nature than the Nationalist Party leadership that was overthrown fifty years ago.

In this context, the pressure to emigrate has been building. China has a rural workforce of approximately 440 million. At the current rate of agricultural production, only 200 million rural producers are needed. Although newly sprouted village and township enterprises alleviated this unemployment temporarily by employing 126 million rural producers, this still leaves China with millions of unemployed. China's rural and urban unemployment has reached 130 million people, many of whom are roaming around the country in search of work.

China's economic growth, impressive as it has been, is not likely to absorb the surplus labor force created by recent economic developments, so the Chinese leadership has increasingly looked to the West for help. But to get help, it has been forced to agree to "privatization programs" designed to liquidate all unprofitable state enterprises. The result of this policy shift has been an added 5 million unemployed persons per year, just as the economic slowdown occurred in Asia.

The government is now encouraging emigration. China's labor department has intensified its effort to export workers to wealthy nations. The government is making money out of these transactions. The desperation of the government's effort can be seen from the way in which it tries to please its clients. A local Chinese court in Sichuan Province recently sentenced an individual to a two-year prison term for his leadership role in organizing a strike in Kuwait, where he had worked. The strike by Chinese laborers was against Kuwaiti construction companies that forced them to work over thirteen hours a day—a clear violation of their contract, which stated a maximum of nine hours a day.

Indebted Immigrants

The Fuzhounese who are the subjects of this chapter have responded to the political and economic developments described above by migrating to the United States. They participate in a "chain" migration network based on kinship. Migration operates like a family project and runs like a relay team. The family first pools all its resources and social connections to send one young, capable, and dependable male abroad. In the beginning, he has to work for others in the United States to pay off his debts. The ideal narrative from here on goes like this: Once his debts are paid, he begins to save to bring other family members over. He familiarizes himself with his new environment and selects a business that is likely to succeed as a "family enterprise"—a take-out restaurant, for instance. The migration relay then begins. The next in line to be sent overseas may be his wife, or more likely it is another male sibling who will maximize the family's capacity to earn wages. A wife is considered a prime candidate for migration as soon as the family wants to have a child born in the United States. This will secure the family's future legal footing. Once this early core group, the "seed population," is established, other family members are brought over one by one: wives and sisters to help out as cashiers, grandparents to look after the children, and so on. The children will be put to work as soon as they are old enough to act as translators and delivery boys. They form the second generation of the family's "corporate venture." The migration engine does not stop there. Wives often try to link their original families—their siblings and parents—into the migration chain. The siblings can then start a new cycle of family migration, thus extending the network to people with different surnames. Ideally, this strategy may eventually encompass an entire community of neighbors and fellow villagers, each connected to the other through family ties and kinship loyalty.

The present migration chain often fails to meet this ideal, however. It is increasingly under the control of a sophisticated smuggling network, which charges smuggling fees that are either paid up front by relatives or, more commonly, advanced by the smugglers (snakeheads) and then paid off by the illegals after their arrival in the United States, through many years of hard labor in this country. The current price for getting to the United States from Fuzhou is between $35,000 to $40,000. Individuals who intend to come have to raise $1,000 in advance (a hefty sum, considering that the average yearly per capita income in China stands at $400). The rest of the sum is expected to be paid by relatives within seven days of the illegal's arrival in the United States. Typically, the newly arrived illegal immigrant then pays off the relatives within three years, at 3 percent interest. Paying off $30,000 in three years means paying approximately $10,000 a year, or $800 a month —uncomfortably close to the monthly income of the average undocumented worker.

But kin, already burdened with debts of others who came earlier, find it increasingly difficult to pay their debts to the snakeheads. As a result, new arrivals are forced to borrow from the snakeheads at 30 percent interest. Often, illegals earn only enough to pay the interest portion of the loan. Unable to pay off the principal, the illegals become entangled in a complicated arrangement with smugglers that extends considerably the amount they owe and the length of the loan. When this happens, the relationship between smugglers and illegals is transformed into an indentured servitude relationship. What the Fuzhounese migrants are caught up in, then, is no longer a cooperative, kinship-based migration chain but rather a profit-making enterprise that traffics in living human beings and then makes money off of them through long-term usury obligations.

Snakeheads have targeted Fuzhounese migrants for two reasons. First, many Fuzhounese can afford to pay the snakeheads. A seed population of Fuzhounese was established in New York in the early 1970s, by seamen who had jumped ship. This seed population was expanded with the 1986 amnesty program and President George Bush's 1989 executive order, which provided legal status for Chinese already in this country. The resulting relatively large, legal resident community of Fuzhounese had accumulated enough savings to pay smugglers for shipping their relatives over. Second, the snakeheads have practically immunized migrants and their families from being critical of the human smuggling process. In particular, immigrant family members have a very different understanding of the smugglers and work and living conditions in the United States than might be expected of an exploited population. After years of indoctrination, many would-be migrants and their families in China have come to believe that the United States is a land of opportunity, where anyone can work for two years to pay off their smuggling debts and then, in a couple more years, buy a business. Thus, those who are waiting to emigrate see smugglers as the providers of an essential service. When informed of the safe arrival of a family member in New York, the family in China often invites the snakehead for a big community banquet, sets off firecrackers, and puts up big, red wall posters in front of the family home to celebrate. If there is a debt-payment dispute, the family in China tends to side with the smugglers. When I confronted the relatives of illegals in China with accounts of torture, kidnapping, rape, and other abuses perpetrated by the snakeheads, they usually responded that the snakeheads have every right to punish those who are lazy and unwilling to pay off their debts. Those unable to do so are considered *mei-zu-shi*, useless and lacking in ambition. Even those family members not expecting to come to the United States want to make sure the migration project succeeds, so that their future in China will be assured by overseas remittances.

Of course, illegals who are forced to live like indentured servants and who have experienced the cruelties of the smuggling operations often have a different view from that of their relatives who remain on the Chinese mainland. Yet they are not in a position to challenge the snakeheads. Fighting back may jeopardize the chance of other family members to make the trip, and their relatives in China are vulnerable to violence and extortion perpetrated by snakeheads. Local authorities in China are not likely to intervene. More than anything, however, the immigrants keep quiet in order to maintain their "face" and family honor. One illegal immigrant, who told me he was beaten and abused during the sea voyage to the United States in 1994, explains, "I try not to think about it, treat it as if nothing has even happened. Most of all I work as hard as I can, and don't bother with whatever happens to others. I hear nothing and I know nothing." The smugglers thus exploit the strong kinship ties of illegals to keep them in line, and since smugglers need new clients to generate more profits, the smugglers' interests coincide with those of elite Fuzhounese immigrants, who use newly arrived, indentured illegals as cheap labor. The smugglers also need access to kinship networks to gain information on possible new recruits and the help of kin in advising them on the dependability of particular clients. They further need the kinship connection to gain the trust of their clients. In a way, the snakeheads, the illegals, the illegals' family members in China, and elite members of the Fuzhounese community in the United States are all locked in a deadly embrace.

Violence, Crime, and Migrant Indebtedness

There are limits, however, to how far migrants can be exploited. Smuggling operations are increasingly limited by the U.S. Fuzhounese immigrant community's finances. As more Fuzhounese come, the debts are accumulating and will eventually reach a point where the indigenous community will no longer be able to service the debts. Paul Smith of Pacific Forum estimates that between 1991 and 1994, twenty-five thousand Fuzhounese illegals were entering the United States yearly.[4] This suggests that at least one hundred thousand illegal Fuzhounese, not counting the thousands who came before and after that period, paid $30,000 each, a grand total of $3 billion. No new immigrant community can withstand this amount of debt.

By 1992, the influx of Fuzhounese illegals had reached a saturation point, and many illegals had run away or gone into hiding in order to avoid the burdens of overwhelming debt. To counter this trend, the snakeheads tried to squeeze more out of the illegals and their relatives by force. Kidnapping and torturing of illegals was the inevitable consequence. In the meantime, again exploiting the family structure and kin ties, the snakeheads kidnapped and tortured illegals in order to encourage relatives to make payments. They also enlisted the support of debtors' families in China to exact pressure on clients, and they forced illegals themselves to collect funds from their own relatives.[5]

Violence and criminal activity have escalated as snakeheads invent new coercive measures to force payment from impoverished illegals. For instance, a Fuzhounese gang nicknamed "Meihua" (Peach Blossom; also King of Spades in Chinese) specializes in kidnapping garment ladies returning home from work in the evening. They are known for their terrifying tactics in extracting ransom money from victims' relatives. Their methods have included enslavement, torture, sodomy, and rape. Guo Liqin, a thirty-eight-year-old illegal immigrant woman who worked in a Queens garment factory, was snatched off the street in August 1995 by three members of the gang and locked in a basement cellar of a Brooklyn house. She is the wife of an undocumented dishwasher and the mother of two children, and she had borrowed $29,000 from her friends and relatives to come to the United States in 1994. Her family in China received threatening phone calls demanding $38,000. The family panicked. They still owed $30,000 for sending Guo's daughters to the United States and did not see how they could borrow more. After three days, the family scraped together only $5,000.[6] Enraged, the kidnappers chopped off one of Guo's fingers, raped her in front of the gang's two other victims, then wrapped a plastic bag around her head and tried to strangle her with a telephone wire. When that failed to kill her, they smashed her skull with a television set. Before the kidnappers left the apartment, they picked out a king of spades from a poker deck and placed it on the coffee table as a signature. Along with it they left a written warning: "Only death for anyone who refuses to pay ransom."[7]

Snakeheads have adopted more violent, criminal strategies as debt payments from illegals dry up. Rather than coercing just the illegal immigrants and their relatives, unemployed snakeheads have turned up pressure on the entire Fuzhounese community for "easy money." Chinatown newspapers have received regular reports of kidnappings of the sons and daughters of established, well-to-do residents who have nothing to do with migrants' debts.[8] The victims are often released for several thousand dollars. In the winter of 1996, for instance, a restaurant owner in Wallingford, Connecticut, a suburb of Hartford, reported the kidnapping of his son Wei Yang. The FBI was alerted, and the whole suburban community was soon up in arms, in fear and bewilderment. A week later the owner got his son back, without the help of the FBI, by paying $88,000.[9] The restaurateur was evidently familiar with the customs of the smuggling trade—many of his employees, who live in his house near the restaurant, are from Fuzhou. In fact, according to one newspaper report, that was not the first time Wei Yang had been kidnapped. He was a victim a few years earlier.[10]

The impact on the Fuzhounese community is clear: Paying off debts and staying away from kidnappers are every newcomer's main concerns. The debt-paying period is getting longer, the interest charged by the snakeheads higher. Some migrants try to avoid these problems by moving to other states, but they often fail to escape because enforcers find them. A municipal judge in Seattle sent a Fuzhounese youth, who had been kidnaped by enforcers, to a local youth home for protection, but he soon disappeared. He returned with a gang six months later to the same facility in Seattle and kidnapped another Fuzhounese youth there. After his arrest he pleaded not guilty, claiming that he had been threatened by his snakeheads, to whom he still owed money.

We Are All Nothing but Slaves

The flood of desperate, undocumented aliens willing to work under any circumstances has benefited Chinese employers, who have depressed wages and established poor labor conditions, creating slavelike conditions for many workers. Wages in Chinatown's garment industry, for instance, already low by U.S. standards before the arrival of Fuzhounese migrants, have declined significantly. Testifying in 1995 at a Senate hearing for anti-sweatshop legislation, Mrs. Tang, once a schoolteacher in Guangdong Province who had emigrated ten years before to Brooklyn, recalled that in the early 1980s she worked eight hours a day and earned $40–$50 a day. By 1995, with competition from Fuzhounese migrants, she slaved twelve hours a day to make a paltry $30. For her, it is almost as if she has had to work twice as long to make the same amount of money.[11] Those who have worked in the industry for some time and are physically no longer able to keep up the pace are assigned to lesser jobs, such as cutting threads, and make even less money. Immigrants from Fuzhou, who are usually younger and choose to work at nonunion shops in order to get more take-home pay, earn about $40 a day.

Competition from illegals is forcing documented Chinese workers to settle for less if they want to maintain steady employment. Not surprisingly, illegals have the best chance to get and keep a job. The employers like them for being young, committed, willing to work long hours, and for their docility and uncomplaining nature. Longtime residents must either follow their example or lose their jobs. Employers lay off workers as soon as their work orders are completed. In the slower months, from November to the end of the year, seamstresses make less than $200 a month. For immigrants paying off enormous debts, this sum is absurdly, desperately low. Paid per piece of garment sewn, many line up outside the factory long before the doors open to be the first ones to begin work. At night, they refuse to quit even after ten, just to be able to get a few more pieces done for a few more dollars. Some of the seamstresses on sewing machines are known not to drink anything during the day lest they interrupt their work, calculated on a piece rate, by going to the bathroom. One Cantonese garment worker testified to a congressional committee that Fuzhounese illegals work until two in the morning, sleep in the factory, and start again right after sunrise. Sometimes, if they are not able to complete a given order, they ask their children to come in to help.[12] Now even Fuzhounese men work on the sewing machines, competing with the traditionally all-women labor force.

Employers increasingly force workers, both documented and undocumented, to accept many obviously illegal labor practices. Home work, thought to have disappeared in the United States fifty years ago, is a common phenomenon in New York City's Chinatown, as is child labor, which has pushed down the already low wage scale in the garment industry. Employers are using every trick in the book to squeeze extra profits, including laying off workers to collect unemployment compensation while still asking them to work for less cash, or forcing them to work on contract-mandated legal holidays at no pay whatsoever. Some workers are forced to rely on public assistance. Their employers help them "cook" their W-2 forms so that their incomes appear to be below the poverty level, which would make them eligible for food stamps and Medicaid. In another common scam, by now familiar to the New York City Fire Department, gangs set up dungeons, decorated to look like living spaces, in Chinatown basements (with the cooperation of the local landlords). They then recruit dozens of Fuzhounese tenants to move in. A day later, the gang starts a fire and alerts the fire department. When the fire department arrives and discovers the inhuman living conditions, it declares the residence in violation of fire regulations and evicts the tenants. Under New York City laws, those evicted under such unforeseen circumstances—even illegal immigrants—can get city public housing. In fact, they automatically jump to the head of the waiting list when they become homeless. Undocumented workers who receive public assistance like this are actually allowing the employers to pay them even less. The state has, in effect, been manipulated into subsidizing the sweatshop industry.[13] Seamstresses from Hong Kong—reputedly the most unregulated free-enterprise zone in the world—insist the working conditions in their homeland are better than those they witness in the United States. In Hong Kong, for instance, all work stops at six in the evening, when building complexes shut down. Employers who intend to open the factories after hours have to obtain approval from the labor authorities. In Brooklyn, by contrast, garment factories where mainly Fuzhounese migrants are employed stay open until 4 A.M.

The most egregious practice at both union and nonunion Chinese garment factories in New York—and something far from common in Hong Kong—is withholding workers' legitimate wages. This problem has reached epidemic proportions. Previously, the normal withholding period was three weeks; now anything under five weeks is considered good. The duration of wage withholding has become the single standard on which garment workers choose a factory to work for. Street wisdom suggests quitting after six weeks of nonpayment. Of course, some workers never get paid at all. After employment starts, the employer can claim cash-flow problems or manufacturers' nonpayment to postpone payments to workers. After a few weeks of unpaid wages, the workers are faced with the difficult decision of whether to continue to work, in order to be eligible to collect back pay, or to quit and cut their losses. Workers at Hua Great Procetech in Brooklyn, many of whom are Fuzhounese migrants, were forced by their Chinese employer, Jian Wen Liang, to toil routinely in a windowless factory for eighteen hours a day, seven days a week. Sometimes they worked as many as thirty hours straight. In the spring of 1998, when eight of them objected to being forced to work as long as 137 hours a week, they were fired instantly, without months of back pay, which was calculated to be as much as $130,000.[14]

As poor working conditions and low wages are adopted across segments of the economy that rely on undocumented workers, distinctions between legal and illegal immigrant workers have been erased. Yet Chinese workers of legal status blame the illegals rather than the employers for this situation.

Complaints in the restaurant business echo complaints among garment workers. "Dish-washing jobs used to pay $800 a month," a waiter told me. "Then the Amigos [Mexicans] came, willing to work for $750. Now we have the Fuzhounese, who take it for $500." In discussion about workplace conditions in Chinatown that I have heard, Fuzhounese illegals, the *wu-sun-fun* (people with no status), are increasingly targets of scorn. It is not surprising that legal immigrants from China have grown to resent undocumented interlopers.

The Lack of Legal Protection: A Business Class Tactic

Taking legal action against employers almost never succeeds. Although the illegal status of many workers discourages them from filing complaints, the New York State Labor Department has nonetheless received hundreds of complaints filed against Chinese employers for back wages. So far, however, there have been only two convictions. The first occurred in 1993, but the workers have yet to collect any back payment. More recently, in September 1996, workers won back wages totaling $59,000 for work done between August 1992 and November 1993. These are exceptions to the rule. More typically, employers simply take advantage of legal loopholes and opt for bankruptcy proceedings whenever they face pressure for back wages. Workers arrive one morning to find the factory gates closed without a forwarding address or any other information. The same owners soon reopen nearby, under a new corporate title with an altered partnership, refusing legal responsibility for the defunct factory.

State labor agencies are ineffective at overcoming these loopholes to help workers. The New York State Apparel Industry Task Force, regarded as the watchdog of the industry, has just five inspectors to monitor more than four thousand clothing factories. Once they cite a factory for a violation, the task force rarely reinspects it to ensure compliance. Besides, the majority of the cases cited for violations involve failure of registration for firms doing business in the apparel industry. This is the absolute minimum level of compliance. The task force has not devoted much effort to dealing with registered firms that violate labor laws right and left. It usually complains of "workload problems" to justify its inefficiency.

Unionized shops do not offer much help in prosecuting the violations, either. Even the International Ladies' Garment Workers' Union (now UNITE), which has organized nearly 90 percent of the shops in New York's

Chinatown, has proved a surprisingly ineffective foe of unscrupulous sweatshop operators.[15] In 1995, of all the thousands of sweatshop violations, only eleven cases were referred to attorney general's office for criminal prosecution; eight cases were disposed of, and no one employer received a criminal sentence that included jail time. Moreover, despite serious violations, the state has given employers a way to avoid monetary penalties by allowing them to send their management to "educational seminars" to learn about labor laws. A cynical state-level staff worker doubts there is much Chinese employers don't already know about abusing the system: "Their accountants work to a science. They know exactly how many weeks to withhold wages, avoiding taxes, before they close the operation and reopen under another corporate title to get the maximum out of the system. They need no educational seminars."[16] These occurrences accord with wider legal trends that favor employers over workers.

The lack of labor protection for immigrants must be seen as a structural aspect of capital's current labor strategy. Historically, immigrants have been recruited as workers for two reasons: First, during times of economic expansion, when both skilled and unskilled laborers are in great demand, employers turn to immigrant labor, both documented and undocumented. Second, immigrant labor is brought in to increase the labor pool in order to reduce wage levels, by undermining the bargaining power of existing domestic labor organizations. Today's immigration is no different: Professionals are recruited from abroad to service the technical, financial, and high-tech fields, which continue to expand and less-skilled immigrants are recruited to serve the needs of the decentralized, restructured U.S. economy, which has all but eliminated union protections for unskilled labor. In addition to moving production overseas, to locations where labor is cheaper and less organized, U.S. firms subcontract with smaller domestic production sites, whose operations remain more flexible because they employ unregulated labor. The cited rationale for this restructuring is cost cutting, but its much more important objective is a readjustment in the balance of power between labor and capital. The destruction of the powerful labor movement, which emerged in decades past and was able to make significant gains in collective bargaining, higher wages, health and retirement benefits, unemployment compensation, and other social welfare safety nets, is the chief objective of this new business order in the United States.

The best way to achieve this objective is by hiring the least-organized and most-vulnerable workers. New immigrants or, preferably, undocumented aliens who have no protection at all fit this category. The U.S. labor market is increasingly polarized, with highly paid native-born unionized and professional workers at the top and native-born historically disadvantaged minorities, who work in lower-wage competitive industries, unorganized new immigrants, and completely unprotected illegal aliens at the bottom. Among this last group, the Fuzhounese are among the most disadvantaged, primarily because of their indebtedness to smugglers. This leaves the Fuzhounese with the unpleasant distinction of being one of the lowest rungs on the ladder of labor, a status that business owners can use against the rest of the U.S. labor force.[17]

In addition, the possibility of hiring illegal Chinese workers at low wages can undermine the wages of other workers. In 1994, the owners of Silver Palace Restaurant—one of Chinatown's largest restaurants, which was unionized in 1980—locked out all their union workers, claiming that their wages were too high. The locked-out union workers picketed the restaurant for more than seven months. "If the owners win this one," the leader of the picketing workers emphasized, "employers all over Chinatown could impose any kind of conditions they want on the working people, no matter whether they are legal or undocumented. We are then nothing but slaves." The issue is no longer just the treatment of illegals. In Chinatown, where employers use illegals to depress wages for all legal workers, they have transformed the problem into a class struggle between labor and management.

Debts Will Be the Death of Us

After several years of working like machines, twelve hours a day and seven days a week, some Fuzhounese illegals begin to develop physical ailments. Restaurant workers complain of pinched nerves, back and shoulder pains, swollen feet, stomach cramps, and insomnia. Kitchen help can be temporarily blinded by the sudden rush of steam to the eyes from pots or dishwashers. Seamstresses complain of sore arms, headaches, dizzy spells, and heart palpitations. Bronchial asthma is common, caused by exposure to the chemicals used in treating fabrics. The worst problems develop from working with polyester, whose shredded fibers, if inhaled over a long period of time in the dry, unswept conditions of most workplaces, can cause nosebleed and asthma. Some workers who handle the material develop loose skin and swollen fingers. The most dangerous job, however, is sewing on buttons. On old machines, a worker has to move the fabric around fast enough to allow the needle to go through all the button holes, but if she is tired and unable to concentrate after long hours, the needle can easily injure her fingers. Other times, snapped-off needle fragments inflict wounds in the eyes of seamstresses.

Yet what Chinese workers fear most—next to having their wages withheld—is getting sick. This is especially true of illegal workers, for whom not being able to work is tantamount to death. If they get sick, they take herbal medicines, and only if that doesn't work will they consult an unlicensed doctor. It's hard not to notice the inordinate number of pharmacies and Chinese herbal doctors on East Broadway in Chinatown.

Doctor Ling is a graduate of Guangdong Chinese Medical School who works frequently with this population, charging $10 per visit. After a diagnosis, established by feeling the pulse and looking into the patient's mouth and eyes, he prescribes an herbal medicine that costs around $15 for one week's dose. Dr. Ling confirms that his patients are mostly Fuzhounese with work-related illnesses. Some of his patients suffer from excessive hard work. He says that their bodies sometimes *zuo-huai-le,* that is, they break down like machines. The symptoms are dizziness, heart palpitations, generalized body aches, and finally numbness of the hands and inability to move them. Dr. Ling's advice is to rest. But none of his Fuzhounese patients listen, blaming him for his lack of medical acumen. They simply must continue to work.

Western doctors at several city hospital emergency rooms have also reported that Fuzhounese illegals come in complaining that their bodies have turned limp, that they have lost all energy, and that they can no longer exert any force. Without legal status, insurance, or money, the only place illegal aliens can get professional medical care is in these emergency rooms. When the doctors at one emergency room tell them the same thing Dr. Ling has— that they need rest—the patients move on to another hospital, hoping to find a miracle cure.

The specialists I talked with said symptoms such as chronic headaches, intense stomach cramps, fainting spells, menstrual irregularity, and loss of energy cannot be proven to be directly related to work. Although the Workers' Compensation Board and the unions have generally accepted only claims related to repetitive stress injuries and work-related asthmatic problems, Dr. George Friedman-Jimenez, a nationally recognized expert on occupational and environmental medicine, suggests that the symptoms I describe are nevertheless likely to be real. Their causes, however, are normally too complex to be attributed directly to a person's present job. Some of these illnesses may be related to previously existing health problems, exacerbated by working such long hours under primitive, nineteenth-century-like conditions. The fact is that, so far, there has not been any research done in the United States to determine the negative physical effects of working seventy to eighty hours a week for a long period of time. Although problems such as repetitive stress syndrome can be avoided by taking regular breaks and by working shorter hours, back and shoulder aches can be reduced or eliminated by a change in the chair design, and readjustment of one's seating position could minimize problems, none of these options, particularly working shorter hours, is available to the vast majority of Fuzhounese illegals.

The consequences of physical collapse can be devastating. Mr. Lan, who left his wife and children behind in Fuzhou, came here illegally five years ago and worked hard to pay off his huge smuggling debt. Under heavy pressure and emotional stress, his health declined. His wife, realizing his predicament, came illegally to help him out. But this doubled his debt, and his health deteriorated to the point that he could no longer work. His family was then forced to depend solely on his wife's income as a seamstress in order to survive. The debts remained. One day, when his wife was out working, Mr. Lan hanged himself.[18]

Dysfunctional Families

The effects of hard work and indebtedness can also affect kin and family ties. A husband and wife who both work twelve to fourteen hours a day can hardly see each other. Having children is next to impossible, even though many illegals want to have children in the United States in order to protect themselves from deportation by being parents of American-born citizens.[19] Those parents who do have children are often forced, because of grueling work schedules, to send them back to China to be raised by other relatives. The subversion of conventional family functions comes with heavy social costs. When children raised in China, particularly in Fuzhou, return to America, they are strangers to their parents. Moreover, they often have difficulties catching up in the U.S. school system, since bilingual teachers are not available for them.[20]

Migrant parents face other obstacles to childrearing as well. Parents are often forced to raise their children outside traditional extended-family environments. This places increased pressure on both parents and children, as children struggle to adjust to life in the United States. The situation is so bad that parenting has become an increasingly important concern in New York City's Chinatown. I went to a parents' workshop, organized by a group of concerned social workers where Western-trained, bilingual experts tried to convince Fuzhounese parents to adopt a "liberal way" in dealing with their children: be patient, reason with them, listen to their problems, give them praise whenever possible instead of scolding them, and, above all, never use physical punishment. Yet this model, rather than addressing the economic basis of familial "dysfunction," simply blames parents by figuring them as unrealistic upholders of "backward" tradition.

These problems are complicated by the need to have the children work to contribute to their parent's debt payments. It is common to have children as young as ten working full time in restaurants and garment factories alongside their parents. Some youngsters report to work seven days a week: on weekends they work eleven hours a day, and during the week they start right after classes, working from 3 in the afternoon until 10 at night. Alexandra Jacobs, a former teacher at Seward Park High School, located on the outskirts of Chinatown, recalls that many of her students worked in factories and came to school exhausted, without having done their homework, only to fall asleep in class. It is usually difficult for a teacher who becomes aware of this problem to reach parents, either because the parents have difficulty understanding English or because they are out working all the time. Nor do the parents realize that their children need to devote extra time and effort to learning English and adapting to American society.[21]

As a result of these pressures, school dropout rates among the Fuzhounese migrant children are high. Many of the frustrated dropouts are easily recruited into gangs. They become enforcers and drug runners. Without the help of an extended family, without free time, without English, and without education of their own, the immigrant Fuzhounese illegals are incapable of fulfilling the responsibilities of being good parents. In fact, many of the Fuzhounese families are dysfunctional—a bitter irony, since strong family ties are what brought the Fuzhounese to the United States to begin with.

In some situations, the pressure of debts turns relative against relative. For instance, when Mr. Ling, a part-owner of a take-out restaurant in Brooklyn who had come to the United States eleven years earlier, sponsored his nephew's emigration from China, the understanding was that the nephew would help out in the restaurant in exchange for room and board. Mr. Ling would, in return, pay the $30,000 smuggling fee. After working for his uncle for a year and half, however, the young man left to work for someone else. Mr. Ling was stuck with the debt. In response, Ling had a gangster threaten the impetuous young man, to force him to come back. The nephew gave a different story. He claimed his uncle ordered him around, demanding all kinds of chores, as if he were a slave. The last straw was his uncle forcing him to ride a bicycle in one of the worst Brooklyn neighborhoods to deliver take-out orders. The nephew was beaten, robbed, and had his bike stolen. Each time something like this happened, the uncle showed no sympathy, scolding him instead for the property loss and threatening him, saying, "At this rate, you will be working for me forever."

Conclusion

Family conflicts of this nature have become all too common within the Fuzhounese immigrant community. Ironically, it is precisely the tightness of traditional Fuzhounese families that originally gave strength to their migration network, and it is to a certain extent this celebrated "virtue" that has placed migrants in such serious jeopardy. The strong family sentiments and family ties of Fuzhounese immigrants are manipulated by smugglers, who are in pursuit of profit, not collective ethnic advancement. Through the smugglers' use of family and ethnic ties, immigrants, particularly illegals, are tied down and forced to labor under grievous sweatshop conditions. In short, the magnitude of their debts, the exploitation by their employers, the lack of labor law enforcement, and the weakened American labor movement have all combined to destabilize the family structure of Fuzhounese immigrants in the United States, throwing many into poverty and desperation.

NOTES

1. Since 1965, U.S. immigration laws have allocated over 70 percent of the yearly quota to close relatives of U.S. citizens and permanent residents.

2. It is estimated that approximately two hundred thousand Fuzhounese are illegal immigrants in the United States. A conservative estimate of the number of illegal immigrants currently in the United States is 5 million, and over 60 percent of them are Mexicans and Central Americans (Eric Schmitt, "Total of Illegal Immigrants Reached 5 Million in 1996," *New York Times*, February 8, 1997, p. 9).

3. See, e.g., Kathy Le Mons Walker, *Chinese Modernity and the Peasant Path: Semicolonialism in the Northern Yangzi Delta*, Stanford, CA: Stanford University Press, 1999.

4. Paul Smith, "The Strategic Implications of Chinese Emigration," *Survival* 36, 2 (Summer 1994): 60–77.

5. Since 1992, hundreds of kidnapping cases perpetrated by Fuzhounese have been reported. This rash of activity has kept the New York police busy. The police department has sped up the recruitment and training of Fuzhounese-speaking officers. But some of the kidnapping cases are fraudulent. FBI agents who work on this beat have complained that it is difficult to tell if a kidnapping is for real. In one case, the bureau had worked long and hard to convince kidnappers to bring their victim to meet his uncle, who was delivering the ransom money at the drop site. Much to their surprise, when the FBI rushed in to arrest the kidnappers during the exchange, the victim tried to escape, refusing to embrace his uncle. As it turned out, the "victim," long unhappy with the uncle's familial authority, had staged his own kidnapping to extort money from the family. These wayward indebted illegals are recruited to be enforcers. At times they simply go off on their own to prey on others as a way of paying off their own debts. They have been known to seize clients who have already paid and to torture them in safe houses in order to force their relatives to pay again. The cost of a ransom ranges from $1,000 to as high as $80,000, depending on the ability of the victim to pay. The head of the New York City FBI office, James Fox, believes that these crimes are usually the work of ad hoc freelancers on the fringe of the criminal community. These marginal groups are also responsible for stealing other snakeheads' clients at Kennedy Airport, by snatching arriving illegals before they are picked up by their own enforcers. They then demand money from the illegals' relatives.

6. "The Worsening Fuzhounese Gang Violence," *World Journal*, March 1, 1995, p. B2.

7. Seth Faison, "Brutal End to an Immigrant's Voyage of Hope," *New York Times*, October 3, 1995, p. A1.

8. *World Journal*, March 27, 1997, p. B4.

9. The number eight is a lucky amount in Chinese folklore, for the character for eight is pronounced "bar," which rhymes with the character "far," meaning prosperity.

10. Dan Morrison and Graham Rayman, "Boy Had Been Kidnapped Before," *Newsday*, December 5, 1996, p. A7.

11. *World Journal*, September 26, 1996, p. B4.

12. Lin Baoqing, *World Journal*, August 26, 1996, p. B1.

13. Ying Chan, "Dungeon Landlord Blames Mob Scam," *New York Daily News*, October 12, 1995, p. 1.

14. Caroline Gonzalez, *New York Daily News*, May 5, 1998, p. 5.

15. "Made in the U.S.A.: The Clothing Is Brand Name, and Millions of Americans Wear It Every Day. Who Knew It Was Made in Sweatshops?" *U.S. News and World Report*, November 22, 1993, p. 55.

16. Interview and information from State Senator Franz Leichter's office.

17. Casualization of labor is therefore not because of the shortage of labor-law enforcers but because of the strength of business-class political power, which has been extremely successful in recent decades in undermining labor laws and the effectiveness of enforcement agencies. In other words, employers can count on the impotence of the law departments to assist them to break laws and make profits.

18. *World Journal*, August 27, 1996, p. B1.

19. One major hospital in Lower Manhattan established a Chinatown prenatal care clinic in 1994. Most of their patients turned out to be Fuzhounese who, even though undocumented, could legally receive full services. One of the counselors at the clinic was disturbed to find that most Fuzhounese women expressed little enthusiasm for having children. What they really wanted were the birth certificates to verify that their children were American-born. In the meantime, they took full advantage of the clinic's free services: free prenatal counseling, free checkups, free hospital delivery, and free supply of baby nutritional supplements.

20. What distressed the clinic counselor the most was that, invariably, the parents sent their babies back to China as soon as they were old enough for air travel, for fear that caring for the babies would slow down the couple's earning power. Moreover, they knew their families in China, particularly the grandparents, would take good care of their children—after all, they are the family's ticket for legal immigration to America. A well-known travel agent in Chinatown estimates that there are one thousand such births each year, based on the tickets sold to the parents. She also helps them find trustworthy individuals who are going back to China to carry the babies—at the cost of $1,000 a head. The children normally rejoin their parents in the United States when they are old enough to attend school.

21. Immigrant children normally have problems with English and cultural adjustment. In the past, Cantonese immigrants had to confront such problems, too. In the early 1970s, after the first wave of Cantonese immigrants from Hong Kong arrived, there were no Cantonese-speaking teachers and counselors in the public school system. The few Chinese with educational qualifications generally spoke Mandarin. It took another decade for the schools to recruit and train a pool of Cantonese-speaking staff. By the 1990s, however, most of the new immigrants turned out to be Fuzhounese speakers. In the whole public school system in New York in 1997, there are only a handful of Fuzhounese-speaking teachers. Their services are in demand elsewhere as well.

Chapter 3

What's Debt Got to Do with It?

Brett Williams

Will Jenkins is a gifted designer, crafting exquisite compositions from living plants as well as the black and white silk flowers he arranged during our interview one Saturday morning. Born in 1945, he grew up on a small hog and vegetable farm on North Carolina's coastal plain. His parents, sisters, and he worked as sharecroppers, rising before dawn each morning to strip and process tobacco from before he was "even tall enough to reach the leaves hanging from the ceiling." They earned $200 a year. He built up a healthy resentment of white landowners but felt that these early lessons in working hard have helped him work hard all his life.

In the summer, kin and friends who had moved north sometimes returned, "driving nice cars and wearing suits," and Jenkins finally decided that "there must be something better than this." In 1961, along with his brother, cousins, and many other rural African Americans, he traveled to Washington, D.C., to look for work in the expanding service sector. After staying briefly with his uncle, he lived in a series of apartments and worked at an array of restaurant jobs before encountering an established florist who took him on as an assistant, nurturing and disciplining the gifts that Jenkins had cultivated as a farmer and then gardener deft at wrestling stalwart greens, ruddy tomatoes, and lush grapes from the city soil.

Married twice, Jenkins has steered his two older children through a string of troubles. His son now drives part time for Federal Express and does home repairs on the side. Jenkins's third child is a university honors student (already carrying student loans), and his wife, Mary, with whom he shares a small suburban house, works for the government. After the deaths of his uncles and, more recently, his father, Jenkins has become even more central to a dispersed group of kin: his mother and brother (now back in North Carolina), his sisters in New York and Texas, and many cousins, mostly scattered around the Washington area. Jenkins has worked full time, sometimes every day, and with few vacations, for the past thirty-four years. He once worked straight through the busy season with a dangerously swollen right leg, arguing: "I been hopping all this long, I can hop till after Mother's Day." His troubles today stem from one piece of bad luck and the nefarious workings of credit and debt.

In 1991, Jenkins's employer died, leaving the business to his wife. Feeling pinched, and lacking the loyalty her husband had felt toward Jenkins, she slashed his salary from $15 to $7 an hour. Although his daughter had worked at after-school jobs (on an ice-cream truck, in McDonald's, and in a beauty parlor) since she was fourteen, and although Mary had a good job that included health insurance, he found that he could not support his new suburban mortgage on this salary. Also, he was then forty-six. The salary seemed unjust and humiliating, and he decided to live out a longtime dream of starting his own business. Customers, friends, and family held his work in high regard; with his reputation, talent, and discipline for unrelenting work, his chances seemed good.

Jenkins's only problem was that he lacked the capital to open a shop. His mother lent him $10,000, all of her savings. He applied to several banks (including the one next door to his shop) and then to the government for a small business loan for minorities. He believed that his work history, residential stability, and plans to open a business in an underserved neighborhood would favorably dispose lenders toward his plans. He met repeated rejections, however, as he sought to borrow $50,000. As he remembers, he had to demonstrate that the flower shop would make $10,000 a month. He replied, "I don't know if I can make $10,000 a year." Then the loan officer replied, "You're better off trying to find you a nine-to-five job," a scenario Jenkins saw as increasingly unlikely, given the high unemployment rate and predominantly low-wage service-sector jobs available in Washington. "I'd rather be nine to five any day, and have a little time to myself. It's been three years and I haven't had a paycheck yet. No vacation. I told the guy I had to open the shop because I didn't have a job.

"Of course I had no problem getting a credit card, because that's money for the bank." In October 1991, Jenkins opened his shop in a working-class African American neighborhood in suburban Maryland. He did so using credit cards newly acquired and collected through the years. He charged a delivery van for $2,500 (which has cost him many repairs and headaches since), his counters, a refrigerator, all of his supplies, and he describes running back and forth to the cash-advance machine on a Sunday to accumulate money for the deposit and first month's rent.

Jenkins faced many of the difficulties inherent in small business, especially the brutal competition exacerbated by the entry of grocery store chains into mass-marketing flowers: "You would be surprised at the florists in D.C. and Maryland, hundreds and hundreds, and the Chambers Funeral Home chain. The little florists can't compete with Giant and Safeway ... they buy a whole tractor-trailer truckload and we have to buy it by the box. They say they're trying to make it convenient for the customers, the one-stop shop." The flower business, like agriculture, is a seasonal enterprise. Most profits come during the Valentine's Day–Easter–Mother's Day ritual cycle, with the rest of the year lean and heavily reliant on funerals and weddings. For example, Jenkins could count on doing $6,000 around Mother's Day (over a week), but in the summer, sales might only reach $200.

He was vulnerable also to personal setbacks, spending six months in the hospital for blood clots in his legs induced in part by constant standing. He missed the crucial Valentine's Day crowd, relying on his wife, children, brother, and cousins to carry the shop. He says, "They did a hell of a job," but they had to work without an accomplished designer.

Jenkins' most serious problems, however, lay in the debt he carried from starting the shop and, like a double-edged sword, the credit he had to offer customers to stay in business. "The shop pays for itself, but I can't make the bills." Interest on his initial charges totaled $1,000 a month. When he became seriously delinquent, he visited a credit counseling service, which helped him consolidate his debts into one $900-a-month payment. This was difficult to make in addition to his house note, the $3,000-a-month rent he had to pay for his shop, and hefty gas and electric bills of at least $500 a month from cooling and heating the large open space and refrigerating the flowers. At that point, determined to sever himself from consumer credit, he cut up all his cards and mailed them back. Still, he got cards in the mail, which he dutifully filed away: "I don't see why they go right on sending me more."

As a small merchant, Jenkins was trapped by the seller's end of consumer credit as well. In many ways his shop harked back to an earlier mom-and-pop era. A local high school girl helped him out by copying items from a catalog onto index cards. His younger daughter worked there on school vacations and during summers; his son helped with deliveries; his older daughter, raising two children and receiving welfare, helped out several days a week, as did his first cousin. On the Saturday morning when I was there last, a woman and her niece came in to buy wedding runners. She had heard about Jenkins because her father, who was getting married, lived in the same neighborhood as Jenkins' brother-in-law: "I was so happy to hear there was a florist in this area." Several men popped in to chat and lingered to socialize. Despite the small-town feel, though, a florist must also do business with strangers.

Jenkins had to offer credit to be competitive, yet he could not afford the expensive technology that authorizes credit at the point of purchase and thus lowers the risk of offering credit to customers he does not know. Many of his customers used credit cards, often by telephone, and especially on holidays. He sought authorization from Visa and MasterCard by telephone but found that the companies do not always honor such authorizations. He showed me one example, when a customer charged a silk corn plant for $125 and a centerpiece for $65. He called it in: "They don't ask for no names, just our authorization number and the card number and expiration date. They don't say they're not going to be responsible 'til you send the money and it's not right." Jenkins learned by telephoning the woman who had received the flowers that the customer was not the cardholder but was rather in prison out in Rockville. When the Massachusetts cardholder signed a statement testifying that he had not made the purchase, the bank next door refused to pay the charge. (He hand-carried his charge slips to deposit there, and they transferred the money into his account but deducted it when it was not authorized.) In another example, a woman called in a charge of $99 for roses. The transaction was authorized by phone even though the Iowa cardholder was over the limit, but Visa again refused to pay after the cardholder signed a statement denying the order. "They don't have to steal the card . . . they can be working at a place and see the number and just call it in."

Call-in problems were not the only difficulties Jenkins faced. Sometimes people simply signed the wrong name. And when he got busy, he made mistakes. One time he forgot to call in the charge until after the customer had left and was refused authorization. "This was my fault. He came and used a card. At the time I didn't call to authorize it, and they rejected it." He always tries to trace the buyers through the people who receive the flowers, but "you can't charge them, they're not responsible."

Even more important than fraud, however, were the multiple niggling fees, which escalated despite the "relationship banking" (a phrase used by bankers to describe holistic, comprehensive customer services) that he enjoyed with his next-door bank. For example, his bounced-check fees rose from $2 to $5 in two years, and, more importantly yet inexplicably, so did his merchant's discount fees. When he opened the shop in October 1991, the rate was 3.45 percent. In January 1992, his statement simply announced that the fee was going up to 3.53 percent. In March it went up to 3.55 percent, and now it is 4 percent. "They said it was because Visa and MasterCard [which always charge the same fee] had raised their processing fees."

How did Jenkins survive and remain hopeful? In addition to working the long hours and drawing on the family resources that some Americans stereotypically associate with immigrants, he developed at least one under-the-table strategy to save money. When customers paid in cash, he sometimes filed the money in a drawer without ringing it up so that he could avoid the 5 percent sales tax. This stash helped him pay his credit card bills: for example, on one lucrative Mother's Day he earned the whole $900 payment for that month. Jenkins also loved his work and felt that his store, anchored its small shopping center, classed up the street and acted as a force for the good in the community.

By 1997, Jenkins had spent more time in the hospital, lost both legs, and begun a draining course of dialysis. His brother came up from North Carolina to help Jenkins's son close up the shop and auction off the equipment. Will Jenkins has a strong, clear sense of the little injustices that have dogged his path and of how more equitable access to credit might have boosted his chances. But from where he sits, he cannot possibly piece it all together. This is partly because he blames himself at the same time that he feels ambivalent toward the companies.

Jenkins's ambivalence and confusion reflect vast political and economic processes that reach far beyond his shop. He has a strong sense of social justice and a keen consciousness of politics. He worries about Republican strategies to reduce social programs: "If they think crime is high right now, just wait, because people are not going to let their children perish." While he has struggled with racism all his life, he has made many exceptions for white people he knows and trusts. Yet he feels hopeless about social change, for the demonstrations and social movements of the 1950s and 1960s do not appear to him to work anymore. Furthermore, like many Americans, he finds it difficult to link the clear posturing of the state to the murky workings of credit and debt.

Will Jenkins's shop and its neighborhood pay dramatic witness to these larger forces at work, as race intersects place and debt drains resources and sucks capital away from more productive uses. Banks denied him money because they preferred high-interest loans to more constructive and equitable investments. Their policies thus have propelled the polarization definitive of our time, denied Jenkins a shot at his dream, and left him remorseful, angry, but confused. In the second half of this chapter, I look more closely at the institutions and residents of his neighborhood in order to contextualize his experiences and piece together the forces that have left a hard-working and talented man mired in debilitating illness and debt. Banking institutions rejected his applications for affordable credit, and he has been obliged to rely on usurious credit cards as the only credit available, as well as customary strategies used by the poor to mobilize kin. As these informal support systems become strained, new mechanisms for producing debt grow ever more voracious. In Will Jenkins's neighborhood, corporate finance capital is heavily implicated in fringe banking. Their storefronts are misleading, signaling to poor customers that they belong while masking the major role of corporate finance, public trading, heavy investment, and heady profits.

A Crossroads of Race and Place

In the 1990s, banks entered the poverty debt market in earnest. This $5 billion-a-year trade in financial services for the bankless makes Visa and MasterCard seem, in the words of investigative journalist Mike Hudson, like "kindly nonprofits."[1] Their shift to high-interest, debt-generating businesses marks a disturbing decline in productive investment in central cities. We will see that the widely alleged and imagined isolation and cultural pathologies of central cities mask the destructive strategies of the nation's largest banks and corporations, busily generating debt and deterioration there.

First, imagine a community without any banks. Washington, D.C., reflects national trends. Downtown Washington and its affluent upper northwest section teem with banks, now offering extended hours and special dividends. But on South Capitol Street, in a poor neighborhood, customers stand twenty deep in line at a tiny branch, and only two banks serve one entire ward lying east of the Anacostia River. Fewer than nineteen banks operate in south-central Los Angeles, which has as many residents as all of Washington; 90 percent of the banks in the poorest Brooklyn neighborhoods and 20 percent of those in the Bronx have closed since 1978.[2]

Imagine now the African and Latin American neighborhood where Will Jenkins tried to set up shop. This community is littered with rent-to-own centers, finance companies, tax brokers offering "refund anticipation loans," check-cashing outlets, and pawnshops. You can find such fringe-bank strips in practically every American city. Hudson describes Roanoke, Virginia's "Hall of Shame" on Williamson Road. Less regulated than Washington, the debt industry of Virginia is particularly inventive, featuring Credit Tire and Audio, Mr. Car Man, Town and Country Pawn, Prime Time Rentals, Avco Financial Services, Beneficial Finance, the Kar Korral, USA Rents, the Automobile Exchange, and Bankers Optical. Adam Levy describes the intersection of Memorial and Columbia Drives in Atlanta, Georgia, as a "haven for the shadow bankers," and I promise that most readers can find them in poor and working-class neighborhoods near where they live.

"They Will Gladly Take a Check"

Across the street from Will Jenkins's shop lies an America's Cash Express check-cashing outlet, one of three in his neighborhood. It is a plain, grim storefront, staffed by one woman behind ceiling-high Plexiglas, offering pagers for $80, laser tear gas for $10, and myriad one-stop financial services. Customers can apply for a telephone calling card or a secured credit card for a $25 processing fee and a $300 deposit (to be charged against) in First Deposit National Bank in New Hampshire. The annual fee is $35 and the annual percentage rate is 19.8 percent. You can wire a moneygram to pay a bill (for 10 percent of the total and a 10 percent discount on Greyhound) or "wire money in minutes worldwide" through an American Express moneygram. (In some places American Express charges as much as 24 percent of the amount wired.)

You can file a tax return and receive a refund anticipation loan ("After all . . . it's *your* money!" beams the promotional material). If you want ACE to prepare your return, that costs about $30. You can pay gas, water, telephone, and electric bills; play the lottery ("We've got your ticket!"); and purchase money orders with the cash you receive when you cash your payroll, government, insurance, or tax refund check. Some call these outlets "welfare banks" because of their heavy traffic in public assistance checks, and sometimes the government sends checks and food stamps directly there.

Customers must first become "members" for an initial $1 fee and cool their heels while the staffer undertakes a thorough investigation by telephone. She then verifies the check by telephoning the party that issued it, as well as the bank that backed it, identifying herself as a representative of Signet Bank. For the most routine checks, the outlet charges 2 percent of the total, but this varies quite a bit depending on the amount and type of the check and whether or not you have ID. It can cost as much as 6 percent to cash a payroll check and 12 percent to cash a personal one. The most outrageous, expensive, and quasi-legal transactions are called "payday loans," advances secured by a postdated personal check. These loans can charge interest from 20 to 35 percent of the amount advanced; a typical transaction would offer the customer $200 for a $260 check. Customers at ACE often feel humiliated and helpless, because the staffer snatches the check behind the Plexiglas before explaining what will happen. When asked how much it will cost, she gestures at the price list behind her, which is almost indecipherable.

Despite the shame, expense, and tedium of the process, many residents of this neighborhood conduct all their bankless business at places like America's Cash Express. Citizens in poor urban neighborhoods find it increasingly difficult to get to a bank. Even if there is a local bank, residents often cannot afford its minimum balance requirements, fees for checks, or high bounced-check penalties. They may not have enough money in their account at the end of the month to cash a paycheck to pay their bills. They may need immediate cash to deliver to the phone company in person. Some residents do not have the major credit card that is to serve as a second major ID; some cannot manage a bank's restricted hours. Some cannot open checking or savings accounts because of even minor problems with their credit or immigration histories. Some find banks discriminatory and insensitive. Check-cashing outlets have blossomed in this harsh climate, with thousands operating nationally—several hundred in Washington, and sixty-nine of these outlets for America's Cash Express alone. In 1993 these outlets cashed 150 million checks and charged $700 million in fees, for a total value of $45 billion.

Using check-cashing outlets further impoverishes and disenfranchises residents, leaving them with no records or proof of payment, no ongoing relationship to build up a credit history, and in greater personal danger from carrying cash (itself in jeopardy from fire, theft, or loss). From where they stand, residents may find it hard to connect the storefronts to the larger financial system or to the injustices they endure. Levy describes the views of Atlanta snack-food salesman Ronald Hayes, who makes a weekly visit to cash his $400 paycheck and buy a money order to pay a bill per week. The total cost to Hayes is $15 a week. "That's cheaper than belonging to a bank," claims Hayes, mistakenly embracing the outlets' misuse of the concept of "membership" in civic life. He fails to recognize that he is probably paying ten times more than a bank would charge. Even if some poor residents recognize the cost, others bow to hand-to-mouth demands for immediacy, safety, or convenience. One homeless man, coping successfully with the dangers of carrying cash, purchases a money order made out to himself each month, cashes it repeatedly at a 2 percent rate, and then buys another money order to carry the balance. He carries his money more safely, but at a huge cost. Hudson interviewed two men in Manassas, Virginia, who paid $270 to cash a $4,500 insurance check because they didn't have time to wait for the check to clear. At the Eagle Outlet, where they cashed their check, owner Victor Daigle claimed that his customers "would rather pay a little bit more to us and have their convenience. They go to McDonald's because they want their hamburger right now. . . . They can come to us and get their money right now."

The primitive hands-on processing and tawdry exterior of the outlets both exude welcome to poor customers and mask ACE's close ties to and substantial financing from large corporations and big banks, as well as the fact that it is part of a large corporate chain. America's Cash Express is a national, publicly traded chain with hundreds of outlets and financial backing from American Express. The chain is growing so rapidly that it maintains a hotline to notify potential customers of new locations.

As banks have fallen to mergers and acquisitions, restructuring has led them to close less-profitable branches and to flee low-income neighborhoods, where the primary business opportunities lie in relatively low-profit retail banking. But the banks come right back in another guise, soaking the poor clients they abandoned through patriotic-sounding storefronts such as America's Cash Express. Protected by expensive lawyers, utterly unregulated, these outlets reap profits from the devastation of the 1980s and, ultimately, make it worse. (Only eleven states regulate check cashing. Douglas Merrill, director of the Georgia Check Cashers Association, argues, in yet another McDonald's analogy, that "this is America. We don't order McDonald's to set the price of hamburgers.") They displace failing small stores and even locally owned fringe banks. Throughout the 1990s, national chains continued to displace the smaller regional chains, leading to frightening centralization in these predatory financial services for the poor.[3]

"That's Why They're My Customers"

Another, more venerable fringe bank is the pawnshop, a familiar sight in cities for many years. Elliot Liebow spotted one straightaway on

Tally's Corner in 1963. These have proliferated in Washington, D.C., and throughout the nation, doubling during the 1980s to number 10,091 in 1994 and certainly many more today. They have changed in other ways as well, to become centralized and chain-operated, backed by upscale marketing, ruthless acquisitions, and persistent pressure on local governments to raise usury rates. Like check-cashing outlets, they displace small businesses, family-owned pawnshops, and local chains, offering young residents of urban neighborhoods downscale, minimum-wage, no-benefits financial services jobs.

For example, Cash America, founded in 1983, operates hundreds of shops. One of five chains to be publicly traded, it boasts NYSE: PWN (for "pawn") as its symbol, turns lush profits for investors, and has tried to upgrade the pawnshop image as it eyes markets all over the world. If you multiply its monthly rate by twelve, its average annual percentage rate (APR) hovers at around 200 percent, not unusual in an industry that often charges 240 percent, and it recorded $5 million in net income from lending activities in the last quarter of 2000, up 17 percent from the year before. In Washington, D.C., Famous Pawn has been enormously successful by gobbling up mom-and-pop stores including pawn shops in poor neighborhoods.

Famous Pawn began with one storefront in the small shopping center where Will Jenkins struggled to sell flowers. During his time there, the pawnshop expanded to such an extent that by the time he had to close his business it occupied the spaces of four stores, with his presumably next to go. Staffers stand behind floor-to-ceiling Plexiglas to greet customers. The store is stuffed with former collateral for these expensive secured loans: from gold chains, wedding bands, and watches to baseball cards, leather jackets, computers, VCRs, television sets, compact discs, cameras, pianos, guitars, saxophones, power tools, and lawnmowers. To the pawnbroker, the stories behind these treasures are probably unimportant. From Chicago, Steve Mills writes:

> But the musical instruments, electronics equipment, and jewelry do carry with them stories of bad luck and heartbreak, misfortune and need—musicians waiting for the next gig, shoppers deep in debt, lovers who no longer look fondly on their gifts.[4]

Customers pawn these items for 10 percent interest each month, a relatively low rate set by Maryland and the District. A borrower would receive $100 for a pawned item and redeem it in thirty days for $110. One customer complains: "They don't give you nothin' for it. But when they sell it, that's when they mark it up." If a customer is unable to redeem it after thirty days, the shop will keep it on hold for as long as he or she can pay each month's interest. Often, pawnshops' profits lie in nurturing these long-term relationships with borrowers, who come in to pay their "dues" on the first of each month but eventually give up and let their treasures go. Their misfortune allows Famous Pawn to bulge out of its space, overflowing with pawns, featuring a long line of borrowers every day, and swallowing its neighboring establishments. Secondary buyers cruise through periodically, buying up items in bulk and boosting profits in the retail side of the business, long less profitable than the interest-collecting side.

Most neighborhood residents pawn rather than buy, although pawnshops offer the only shopping opportunities here. One man worries about the trend: "They're like McDonald's, springing up all over. Whenever a store closes down, a pawnshop takes its place." He believes that some, but not nearly all, of the goods are stolen, because pawnshops provide a rare source of cash in this capital-starved neighborhood. "I won't even buy a VCR," he explains, "because it's just an invitation to steal." Although the shop staff are supposed to record a borrower's address from a driver's license, this man feels that kids often steal the goods and ask a friendly adult to pawn them.

But other people's experiences belie this understanding. For example, Walsh's son Kenny had by age forty pawned all of his tools and his wife's jewelry to get cash. People slink and slouch into pawnshops so that they can buy food, pay bills and rent, fix the car, replace bald tires, visit a clinic, or fund Christmas and birthdays. Some pawn to stretch out cash until payday. One man pawns his bicycle regularly each month for ten days and redeems it when he is paid. Some resort to pawnshops in emergencies, like the Chicago postman who pawned his color television and Genesis video game player for $75 because he had lost $450 on a riverboat casino.

Borrowers, like buyers, are increasingly diverse as formerly middle-class people suffer layoffs, bankruptcies, foreclosures, medical debt, widowhood, and divorce. Levy met expensively dressed Tony Lawrence at EZ Pawn in Atlanta, toting a Yamaha stereo receiver and a Fisher amplifier. "I have a bank account and credit cards," Lawrence explained. "But I'm maxed out on those." A pawnbroker in Florida told Levy that he had recently lent $2,000 to a small-business owner in exchange for his gold Rolex watch so that the businessman could meet his payroll!

But the vast majority of borrowers are poor, with incomes between $9,000 and $17,000 a year, according to fringe-bank researcher John Caskey. They are young, in and out of work, and disproportionately of color. Cash

America's *Annual Report* describes them this way: "The cash-only individual makes up the backbone of America. He's [*sic*] the hard-working next door neighbor, the guy at the corner service station, or the lady who works as a checker at the local supermarket." Caskey quotes Jack Daugherty of Cash America to somewhat different effect: "I could take my customers and put them on a bus and drive them down to a bank and the bank would laugh at them. That's why they're my customers."[5]

"And You Don't Need Credit to Get It"

Late at night, if you turn on the television, you will find a barrage of slickly produced commercials. A middle-aged white woman asks, "If somebody goes to work every day and they have bad credit or no credit, there's really no reason why [they] shouldn't be able to have nice things. With Rent-A-Center you can." And a Latina in her early twenties claims, "For what it cost me at the laundromat, I got a washer/dryer at Rent-A-Center . . . an' you don't need credit to get it!"

By redefining what they are doing as "renting," rent-to-own stores have emerged to evade usury laws that limit the interest paid by people who buy appliances and furniture on credit. Profits in this $3.7 billion-a-year business stem from astounding markups, as customers often pay five times what they would for retail. By the mid-1990s rent-to-own stores had tripled in number, so that by 1994 there were some seventy-five hundred rent-to-own outlets nationwide. Like check-cashing outlets and pawnshops, they increasingly come in corporate chain sizes.

The Rent-A-Center chain boasts twelve hundred stores, a large share of this market. But another patriotic chain, RentAmerica, dominates the Washington, D.C., area. Mostly located in two poorer suburbs (including Jenkins's) and southeast D.C., RentAmerica is a temple to consumption. To walk in is to discover a lush cornucopia of household consumer goods: florid bedroom furniture; leather couches; brightly colored, blaring television sets; giant, gleaming refrigerators; and shimmering gold jewelry. The store offers impoverished customers a shot at the postwar American dream.

But the American-flag sign that soars from the parking lot, the giddy interior, the slick brochures, and the "convenience" (or urgency?) of instant purchases and free delivery belie RentAmerica's harsh and greedy terms. A glossy flyer hawks televisions ranging from $9.99 (GOOD) through $15.99 (BETTER) to $24.99 (BEST) a week; refrigerators; home entertainment centers; bedroom and living room suites; boomboxes; gold jewelry; and VCRs at $9.99 (BETTER!) or $11.99 (BEST!) a week. The superlatives are printed perhaps one hundred times larger than the microscopic terms at the bottom of the ad. The terms explain that the baby-bear TV requires seventy-eight weekly payments of $9.99, or $779.22 (plus tax); the twenty-seven-inch TV costs seventy-eight weekly payments of $15.99, or $1,247.22 (plus tax); and the thirty-two-inch TV will not be yours until you have paid in full: 104 weekly payments of $24.99, or $2,598.96 (plus tax). Retail prices are much lower. RentAmerica has the good sense *not* to mention either the alleged or actual prices for gold jewelry, refrigerators, freezers, the "bedroom suite," or the "living-room group." The brochure recommends: "Ask for Details!"

To qualify, applicants must fill in boxes supplying "Government Financial Assistance Information" and provide the names and addresses of six references, two of whom must be relatives. No wonder that consumer groups across the country have targeted rent-to-own stores for shoddy sales practices, shady tack-on fees, abrupt, humiliating collections, and all manner of harassment and psychological torture.

To understand their excesses, it might be helpful to contrast rent-to-own terms and interest rates to the consumer credit available to residents of wealthier neighborhoods, who can receive a 10 percent discount on a purchase up to $300 at Woodward and Lothrop, for example, just by applying for a store card—though if they do not pay on time and in full, they owe 21 percent interest. Or at CompUSA, a computer store in the Maryland/Virginia suburbs, approved customers can charge a computer and pay no interest for six months; they pay accumulated interest, however, if they do not pay in full at that time. Seeing RentAmerica helps put these admittedly harsh, austere, and misleading terms into perspective.[6]

A Festival of Debt

These days, banks hawking secured credit cards set up booths right beside vendors selling African folk art and Asian jewelry or grilling pupusas and steaming tamales at multicultural street festivals. Secured cards are thus far the latest and most profitable banking foray into a new market, one composed of people who are too poor or whose credit histories are too shaky to qualify for ordinary credit cards. Marketed by mail and 900 telephone numbers to people with poor credit; through radio and television spots, newspapers, magazines; and in stores, fringe banks, and carryouts through-out working-class neighborhoods, their invasion of festivals celebrating di-versity and community is particularly galling.

A secured card works like this: You open a savings account with a bank for a relatively small amount (usually several hundred dollars) and receive a bank card with a credit line equal to between 50 and 100 percent of your savings account balance. Usually you pay a processing fee of up to $65 with your application, relinquish access to your funds as long as your credit card account is open, and agree to allow the bank to apply your savings to your credit card balance "in case of default." You make monthly payments on your credit card account and send in additional savings deposits whenever you want to increase your credit line. If your balance is paid in full, you may close your credit card account and receive your savings back, but only after forty-five days so that all charges can clear. Promotional materials proclaim: "Get all the benefits of Visa: build your credit record; make motel or car rental reservations; shop by mail or phone; access cash at any hour!" Build-ing credit appears to be a prime incentive. For example, BANKFIRST in South Dakota has founded what it calls the American Fair Credit Associa-tion, so that its "members" can restore their creditworthiness through se-cured cards. Promotional materials say nothing about high annual fees ranging from $20 to $75, low or even no interest paid on your savings ac-count, or the credit card interest rates that run as high as 22 percent. "Basi-cally, you're lending someone back their own money and charging them a lot of money for it," Chicago financial services consultant John M. Stein told reporter Suzanne Wooley.[7]

Secured cards are controversial even within the industry, for several rea-sons. Some find it distasteful to work from lists of people with bad credit. Others believe that "trading of derogatory information is permissible if it results in a useful offer." The Federal Trade Commission has wondered if it is even legal. Some bankers worry about contaminating their image through sleazy television commercials and 900 numbers, which might result in short-term profits from telephone charges and application fees but damage a bank "seeking long-term profitability by the development of their card portfolios."

Other analysts, however, argue that "banks can make rich profits from poor credits"; "for banks able to manage the process, battered consumer balance sheets may turn out to be a gold mine." On an outstanding balance of $1,000, a bank offering a card with an 18 percent rate and paying 5 per-cent on a cardholder's deposit can make a 5 to 7 percent after-tax return.

The bank's risks are quite small because the loan is collateralized, and if se-cured-card holders do manage to build a credit history, they might remain loyal to the bank that got them started.

Although it was pioneered by Key Federal Savings and Loan in 1982, the major credit card issuers generally ignored this market niche until the late 1980s. Today, however, this is the most profitable segment of the credit card portfolio, due to high interest rates, lack of defaults, and requisite annual fees. Not surprisingly, Citibank is the industry leader in these accounts, which it recruits largely from its own "turndown list."

Poor neighborhoods teem with other high-profit debt-generating schemes, such as credit repair sharks, or clinics, including those Hudson calls "foreclosure doctors"; income tax "refund anticipation loans"; many fake, uninsured, unchartered "credit unions"; renters' credit, offered by apartment locators; and lots of opportunities to sell or rent cars and car ac-cessories and then take them back. In less-regulated states, customers can find stores like Roanoke's Credit Tire and Audio (for tires and car stereo sys-tems), rent-to-own cars, and transmission jobs on credit. Washington's Metro buses carry cards for riders wishing to apply for E-Z Auto Loans, es-pecially designed for people with bad credit. Many cities offer car-title pawns, where the title to the car serves as collateral for a high-interest loan with an APR of up to 1,000 percent. "Second-Chance" Auto Financing op-erations require expensive warranties, insurance, and 50 percent interest. Hudson notes that these are often "churning operations," because busi-nesses sell a car, collect the down payment and a few installments, then re-possess and resell it.

Poor neighborhoods in Washington, D.C., are plagued by finance com-panies peddling loans, to consolidate debt or to make home repairs, to peo-ple who are financially desperate or credit starved. These firms target mi-nority, fixed- or low-income, low-wage, and Social Security–dependent households who often hold substantial equity in their homes as their sole resource. Not surprisingly, the finance companies charge high interest: from 36 to 50 percent. They tack on worthless, expensive "credit insurance." They offer shoddy work and pursue ruthless, haranguing collection policies. Sometimes they refinance these loans several times, piling on fees along the way: prepayment penalty fees, more credit insurance, and loan origination fees. They front for some of the country's largest financial institutions: Na-tionsBank (after it acquired ChryslerFirst), Ford Financial Services (whose Associated Services division may keep it afloat), Chemical Bank, ITT, Fleet Financial Services, BankAmerica (through its Security Pacific division),

General Motors, General Electric, Westinghouse, and Citicorp. These large lenders front money through lines of credit to finance companies, then buy up and bundle the loans and sell them on Wall Street via secondary securities markets. The customer may be left with shoddy repair work, a huge debt, the threat of foreclosure, and nobody to hold responsible.

"Our Dream Was to Buy a Home"

In 1993, Lowell Spencer reported to Congressman Joseph Kennedy's Subcommittee on Consumer Credit and Insurance of the House Banking Committee:

> I am originally from Jamaica and I came to this country in 1973. I have worked for the Brooklyn Hospital for over 15 years. Our dream was to buy a home. We had tried several times but never accomplished our goal. . . . Approximately two months ago, I applied for a mortgage with Chemical Bank. The branch manager told me that my application was quite favorable and that I should get some good news in about four days. My credit was not perfect but it was not bad. I always paid my bills, I had a steady job and my wife also works for the Brooklyn Hospital with good incomes. Since we had been approved for a mortgage a year ago I felt confidant [sic]. Four days passed and I called the branch manager. He told me "confidentially" that the mortgage application was denied. I was shocked and disappointed because I thought that after twenty years in this country my dream of buying a home was in my grasp . . . my application was denied because I didn't have enough money for closing costs, which was not true!

In the last few years, leading newspapers have thoroughly reported discriminatory practices by mainstream banks in offering what Americans widely regard as "good debt." For example, the 1991 Boston Federal Reserve Board study on mortgage and home equity loans documents much higher rejection rates for African and Latin Americans at all income levels, paralleling known discrimination by secondary lenders nationally and in Washington, D.C.

In the District of Columbia, black applicants were rejected at double the rate of whites in 1991, with one-third of all black applicants rejected for mortgages and even well-to-do black applicants turned down 23.2 percent of the time. Despite the publication of these results, it happened again in 1992, when things appeared to have grown worse; and in 1993, black and Hispanic applicants were still twice as likely to be rejected, with loans to white neighborhoods approved at twice the rate as loans to black neighborhoods.

Several banking policies undergird this discrimination: the antiquated postwar evaluation system that certifies a narrow slice of Americans who are white, middle-class, and use banks; the abandonment of branches in unprofitable neighborhoods; the failure of banks to develop good working relationships with black realtors; a reluctance to fund mortgages deemed too low to be profitable; and an unwillingness to lend money for semi-detached houses or to finance mortgages in neighborhoods where more than half the units are rented.

The banks' most favorable records in black neighborhoods involved consumer loans, especially credit cards. "Our business is in consumer loans—that's how we serve minorities," Citizens Bank president Jeffrey Springer told the *Washington Post*. Chevy Chase Bank's attorney told *Washingtonian* magazine:

> In the credit-card business, customers have lots of options, and a lot of people, both black and white, would simply choose not to do business with an institution branded as racist.[8]

The Reverend Charles Green, president of Roanoke's chapter of the National Association for the Advancement of Colored People (NAACP), told Mike Hudson, "I don't guess that a week goes by that I don't get something in the mail from somebody who wants to give me a second-mortgage loan on my home—just because of my address." In offering mortgages and home equity loans, once again, alternative institutions replace mainstream banks. Mortgage companies, and their staff working entirely on commission, fax and pepper minority neighborhoods with lending opportunities, trolling for high-interest loans with fees and points that may double the effective rate, with useless credit insurance, and with obscure and dangerous features such as balloon payments. Offering small mortgage loans averaging $40,000, United Mortgage Company charged 11.8 percent interest and fees of 7 percent in 1993, far above prevailing rates.

In Washington, the industry leader Monument Mortgage advertises in the *District Merchandiser*, flaunting a photograph of its African American "senior loan officer." It offers potential applicants a checklist that includes "No Savings," "Bankruptcy," "Looming Foreclosure," "Too Much High Interest Debt," and "Kid in College." Monument also offers same-day appraisals, one-week approvals, "Bad Credit O.K." "We specialize in bad credit . . . our multiple sources of funds permits more creative and flexible loans."

Indeed. Since the 1980s, lenders have been allowed to increase their cash flow by selling "mortgage-backed securities," or bonds collateralized by income from bundles of mortgages. This loophole allows lots of shady lending and profits for Wall Street. "This is one cheap growth stock," an analyst at Oppenheimer and Company told *New York Times* reporter Michael Quint. It is also pernicious, reverse redlining. Mortgage companies can hide behind laws that protect investors who buy mortgage loans after they are made; also, because they do not collect deposits from the community, the companies are not bound by the Community Reinvestment Act.

These national mortgage trends have sinister implications. The house is the main source of equity for those working-class people fortunate enough to have squeezed into the racially subsidized housing market of the 1950s and 1960s, often through expensive, trying, and perilous blockbusting in the wake of white flight. After the ravages of the 1980s, the house may have become one's only wealth to pass on to the next generation, itself increasingly unable to buy houses. When banks fail to lend in minority neighborhoods, they contribute to deterioration and reinforce the downward economic spiral in several ways. Houses may sit on the market longer, reducing neighborhood demand, offering easy prey to speculators. Mortgage companies have no ready source of cash and must depend on investors and, thus, high volume. They rope in marginal buyers at such extravagant rates that, as owners, they cannot maintain their payments. When these loans are insured by the government, the companies simply foreclose, an action that can leave neighborhoods with many abandoned properties and thus further eroding housing stock. In 1992, eight hundred Federal Housing Administration–insured properties were foreclosed in Washington, D.C. In addition, denying black property owners home equity loans helps set the stage for neighborhood abandonment and disinvestment, warehousing of emptied but livable quarters, urban renewal, gentrification, displacement, doubling up, and homelessness. Loan denials become a potent strategy to separate citizens from their property.[9]

For years, American ethnographies have disclosed broad social networks of reciprocity and exchange, credit and debt, sharing and pooling, through which people cope with poverty.[10] Today, two circumstances have changed. Everyday credit and debt, through which people entail friends and allies and manage crisis, operates in the context of debt in its other traditional and more oppressive sense, as it tethers people to costly obligations and onerous penalties while they lack the means to pay it off. Also, popular media and political speeches blast the non-poor with a vision of the poor that vaunts their supposedly greedy, violent, self-destructive, nihilistic nature. I am interested in how residents of poor neighborhoods and others survive, maneuvering in a deteriorating labor market, assaulted by the state, building on long-term but increasingly battered networks of pooling and swapping among friends and kin, resorting to the underground economy and fringe banking when they must. How have the new debt-generating institutions affected life in poor communities?

In this "reverse-redlining" world, residents have access to different kinds of credit. Some, like Jenkins's cousin, a long-term homeowner, receive high-interest credit cards. James Allen, a Washington native, has been on his own since his parents died when he was young. He has worked in data processing and banking; he briefly started his own overnight office-building cleaning service, which failed; he tried to run a dry-cleaning business, which also failed; and he currently works as shift manager for TrakAuto. During periods of unemployment he built up credit card debt, available to him because he bought a house thirty years ago, which is paid for, and because he and his wife have long employment histories. Nonetheless, at sixty-two, he still carries some burdens from the needs of his adult children, and he feels humiliated by his tight economic circumstances and the failure of TrakAuto to recognize and compensate him for his work experience or to pay him overtime. He makes $7 an hour, with no benefits, and this salary is reduced when he works extra hours, which he often does.

Another resident, Luis Perez, grew up with his mother in a small apartment. Ms. Perez is a domestic who works about twelve hours a day, covering as many houses as she can. Often on his own as a teenager, Luis Perez hung out at a local restaurant, where he developed a close relationship with a cook and worked sometimes as a busboy. When he graduated from high school, he began working two jobs, installing cable television during the day and ushering at a movie theater at night. He was never able to amass enough equity to buy a car or a house and rented a small apartment instead. Because he had trouble paying his bills, he decided to pursue his dream of becoming a wrestler. After expensive training in Florida, a promoter promised that he could wrestle professionally in the Caribbean. He applied for his first credit card at the age of twenty-five. (The proportion of families earning under $10,000 who had credit card debt rose from 11.1 percent in 1983, during the worst of the recession, to 23.7 percent in 1992. For those earning between $10,000 and $25,000 annually, credit card debt rose from 26.8 percent among all households in 1983 to 43.2 percent in 1993. So this young man is clearly part of a pattern.) Perez received a secured card at 24 percent interest from Key Federal Bank, but when the wrestling promises proved fraudulent, he quickly became too indebted to pay his minimum. He now dodges his creditors as best he can while working double shifts as a waiter to try to accumulate enough money to pay his rent and his debts. The bank's dunning letters to him began:

Dear Luis,

Allow me to introduce myself. My name is Joan and my job at Key Federal is to contact cardholders, such as yourself, who may be experiencing difficulty in meeting their monthly payment obligations. . . . I have found that once an avenue of communication has been established, most problems are easily resolved. . . . I sincerely believe that together we can work this problem out and put your account back on the right track.

They now sound more like this:

(No greeting) *Your account is now delinquent in the amount of $40.00.* Until your account is current and below your established credit line, we must insist you do not use your card. We must also inform you that failure to make at least the minimum monthly payment will leave us no other alternative but to turn your account over to our Collection Agents, and, if required, our Collection Attorneys. Please be advised your account is also being reported as delinquent to a local credit bureau.

Key Federal Savings Bank

Others, like Irma Workman, who has worked as a domestic servant in Washington, D.C., for the past thirty years, operate on a cash-only basis. She asks that employers pay her in cash, and she in turn pays her bills in person, often traveling straight from work downtown to pay at the last minute to avoid disconnection of services. When she has extra money, she starts a layaway account. A member of a large, once cooperating but now dispersed and battered family, she has had to cast off two problematic male members, a nephew and a cousin she tried to support until their legal problems became too disruptive and expensive. Other families are forced to practice this kind of triage as well. Between 1969 and 1979, the prevalence of extended households among the poor increased, but their pooled ability to raise household income was halved. In the 1980s, their antipoverty effectiveness suffered a precipitous decline. Long distinguished by both flexibility and strength, the extended social networks of the inner city now practice what Kim Hopper terms an "economy of makeshifts," weighing traditional hospitality to kin against the interests of household stability. James Allen's son will enter a community college in the fall of 1995, deferring his dream for something more. Will Jenkins has had to ignore the needs of his chemically dependent daughter, focusing household resources on the younger daughter, who does well in school.

Some resort to the drug business, sometimes with the hope of helping their families, sometimes with the desire to raise enough money to start a small business, thus cashing in on the social capital of the underground economy amid the lack of mainstream labor force opportunities. They must overrely on the informal economy, lining up early in the morning, hugging their power tools, at "shape-up" pickup locations; taking sporadic part-time and seasonal employment at construction sites, sporting events, and cultural festivals; selling drugs, guns, or their bodies; freelancing in plumbing, painting, landscaping, carpentry, babysitting, gypsy cabs, car maintenance, and masonry; setting up informal street markets for buying and selling clothes, videotapes, VCRs, antiques, and beepers. They "package" income from relatives, the market, and the state, thus meeting daily subsistence requirements most of the time. But crises occur often: illness, rent hikes, heating failure, eviction. Expected expenses mount, such as new shoes or winter coats for children, as do unexpected expenses such as school trips, illnesses, complications in pregnancy, and telephone or utility disconnections.

While the poor have developed many creative strategies to provide the essentials of life, such as doubling up, working under the table, managing collective living, and negotiating ongoing exchanges with friends and kin, they are increasingly vulnerable in the current economic climate. When intergenerational network flows, employment, and government assistance fail them, when relatives can no longer provide small loans between checks or the exchange of food stamps for cash, poor people develop strategies to work the fringe banking system: pawning televisions and VCRs when between checks, redeeming them when they can; cashing their checks at America's Cash Express; paying their bills with money orders and moneygrams they purchase ar ACE; using the poor person's telephone, the pager; and "renting" their grossly overpriced furniture and appliances for as long as they can.[11]

The storefronts may look grim and tawdry, but they squat on a financial quagmire. Famous Pawn now occupies Will Jenkins's flower shop, testifying to Jenkins's inability to find affordable credit for his business. The same developers who refused to maintain or build low-cost urban housing have gone bust on overpriced condominiums, unnecessary office space, and underutilized shopping centers in the suburbs. The same lenders who disinvested in cities, jobs, workers, and infrastructure squandered their money on junk bonds and takeovers. Now they're back, extending credit to fringe banks for loans of last resort and thus passing on high-cost debt to the poor.

NOTES

1. Mike Hudson, "Going for the Broke," *Washington Post*, 10 January 1993, C1, C4–6. See also Hudson's edited collection *Merchants of Misery* (Monroe, ME: Common Courage Press, 1996), which gathers together many important articles on the business of poverty. I quote Hudson many times in this chapter because he was the first to spot the emergence of these debt-generating operations. He has shared and publicized his findings widely, won several awards, and, perhaps most important, encouraged others to do similar research and then shared *that* research, because he is more concerned that the story get out than with simply advancing his own career. He emerges as a hero in this tragic story.

2. Hudson, "Going for the Broke," C1, C4–6; Mike Hudson, "The Poverty Industry," *Southern Exposure* 21, 3 (Fall 1993): 16–27; Mike Hudson, "Robbin' the Hood," *Mother Jones*, July/August 1994, 25–29; Adam Levy, "Shadow Banks," *Bloomberg*, October 1994, 7–11; "They Will Gladly Take a Check," *New York Times*, 1 December 1992, D1, D2.

3. See John Caskey, *Fringe Banking: Check-Cashing Outlets, Pawnshops, and the Poor* (New York: Russell Sage Foundation, 1994); Hudson, "Going for the Broke," C1, C4–6; Levy, "Shadow Banks," 7–11.

4. Steve Mills, "The Pawnbroker," *Chicago Tribune*, 11 June 1995, 1, 5.

5. See Cash America, Inc., Letter to Shareholders. URL <www.streetlink.com> (April 15, 2001); Hudson, "Poverty Industry," 16–27; N. R. Kleinfield, "Running the Little Man's Bank," *New York Times*, 13 August 1989, 37 (also quoted in Caskey); Levy, "Shadow Banks," 8–11.

6. Alix Freedman, "Peddling Dreams: A Marketing Giant Uses Its Sales Prowess to Profit on Poverty," *Wall Street Journal*, 22 September 1993; Mike Hudson, "Profiting from the Disadvantaged," *IRE Journal* (January–February 1995): 8–11; Mike Hudson, "Renter Beware," *Washington Monthly*, October 1993, 12–15.

7. Linda Punch, "A New Effort to Scrub Up Secured Cards," *Credit Card Management* 4, 4 (July 1991): 74–77; Ray Schultz, "Hungry Marketers Chew on the Credit Starved," *Business and Society Review* 78 (Summer 1991): 33–38; U.S. Information Bureau, *Credit Card Guide* (1991 ed.); Suzanne Wooley, "Plastic—For a Pretty Penny," *Business Week*, 18 May 1992, 118.

8. Spencer's testimony appears in *Credit Availability in the Inner City* (Washington, D.C.: Government Printing Office, 1993), pp. 85–87; Joel Glenn Brenner and Liz Spayd, "Mortgage Loan Bias Persists, Fed Finds," *Washington Post*, 28 October 1992, A1, A4; "A Pattern of Bias in Mortgage Loans," *Washington Post*, 6 June 1993, A1, A24; "Bankers Describe Roots of Bias," *Washington Post*, 8 June 1993, A1, A10;

Jim Campen, "Lending Insights," *Dollars and Sense*, January–February 1994, 16–20; Joe Catalono, "Testing Bias at a Bank," *Newsday*, 22 January 1992, 63; Kirsten Downey and Paul Taylor, "The Fading American Dream," *Washington Post*, 10 November 1991, A1, A30; Jonathan Glater, "Justice Said to Find Bias in Lenders," *Washington Post*, 25 October 1994, C5; "Fed Reports Disparity in Area Lending," *Washington Post*, 29 October 1994, E1, E6; Mike Hudson, "Bankers, Critics at Odds," *Roanoke Times and World News*, 11 December 1994, A1, A6ff.; H. Jane Lehman, "Fed Finds Wider Low-Income Gap," *Washington Post*, 2 November 1991, F1, F9; "Loan Goals Fall Short in Central Cities," *Washington Post*, 23 April 1994, E1, E15; "Affordable Housing Reforms Asked of S&Ls," *Washington Post*, 30 April 1994, F1, F9; "HUD Looks at Future of Ownership," *Washington Post*, 27 August 1994, E1, E11; Ann Mariano, "Blacks See Bias as Obstacle to Buying," *Washington Post*, 18 June 1994, F1; Alicia Munnell, Lynn Browne, James McKaney, and Geoffrey Tootell, *Mortgage Lending in Boston*, Federal Reserve Bank of Boston, Working Paper no. 92-7 (1992); Peter Passell, "Redlining under Attack," *New York Times*, 30 August 1994, D1, D3; Jacqueline Salmon, "Affordable Housing Eludes Poor Families," *Washington Post*, 19 October 1991; Carolyn Sedgwick, "Debt in America: The Secondary Mortgage Finance System" (unpublished paper, Department of Anthropology, American University, Spring 1995); Liz Spayd and Joel Glenn Brenner, "Learning to Spot the Signs of Bias," *Washington Post*, 8 June 1993, A10; David A. Vise, "The Financial Giant That's in Our Midst," *Washington Post*, 15 January 1995, A1, A20, A21.

9. Albert Crenshaw, "Abusive Mortgages under Fire," *Washington Post*, 23 March 1994, F1, F10; Peter Marcuse, "Gentrification, Abandonment, and Displacement: Connections, Causes, and Policy Responses in New York City," *Journal of Urban and Contemporary Law* 28 (1986): 107, 195–240; Kathleen Keest, "Some of the Poor Pay Even More: Is There a 'Discrimination Tax' in the Marketplace?" *Clearinghouse Review*, special issue (1993): 365–69; Jerry Knight, "Lenders Agree to Anti-Bias Pledge," *Washington Post*, 13 September 1994, D1, D8; Michael Quint, "Profits from Higher-Rate Loans to Low-Income Home Buyers," *New York Times*, 9 November 1994, D10; Liz Spayd and Joel Glenn Brenner, "Mortgage Companies Fill Gap—For a Price, *Washington Post*, 6 June 1993, A25; Paul Tosto, "Regulating Finance Companies," *Business South Carolina*, 16 January 1995, G1, G5; Brett Williams, "Babies and Banks: The 'Reproductive Underclass' and the Raced, Gendered Masking of Debt," in *Race*, ed. Steven Gregory and Roger Sanjek (New Brunswick: Rutgers University Press, 1994).

10. Brett Williams, *Upscaling Downtown* (Ithaca, NY: Cornell University Press, 1988). See also St. Clair Drake and Horace Cayton, *Black Metropolis* (New York: Harcourt, Brace and Co., 1945); Elliot Liebow, *Tally's Corner* (Boston: Little Brown, 1967), and *Tell Them Who I Am* (New York: Free Press, 1993); Carol Stack, *All Our Kin* (New York: Harper and Row, 1974); Betty Lou Valentine, *Hustlin' and Other Hard Work* (New York: Free Press, 1978); "Migrants on the Prairie," in June Macklin and Stanley West, eds., *The Chicano Experience* (Boulder: Westview Press, 1979);

Chapter 4

The Tables Are Turned
Immigration, Poverty, and Social Conflict in California Communities

Patricia Zavella

In popular culture, California is the "golden state." Premised on its founding as a state soon after the gold rush, and with the convergence of plentiful sunshine, fertile land, and the importation of water, California has abundant natural resources upon which to build agribusiness, tourism, and eventually manufacturing which attracted those seeking the good life. From the point of view of booster historians, the golden state is replete with stories of early white migrants of European origins, who quickly became the majority, as having found paradise. And in myth and reality, California became the place that invents the future, then markets it to the rest of the world.[1] Sunny California is where new products, new life styles, and new communities were formed, a place where everyone—from dust bowl Oakies to Cambodian peasants to Mixtecos from Oaxaca—could come and find work and a home of their own. California once epitomized the American dream. Currently, however, we hear more about how California living is harsh, no longer the state of golden opportunities, a place where the "rush" is out of the state.

In *Racial Fault Lines*, Tomás Almaguer shows how California history can been seen as a series of racial divides where white supremacy was constructed through racializing discourses and practices, a "fundamental pattern [that] took shape during the last half of the nineteenth century."[2] The new nativism we see in California—expressed through the attempt to pass the English-Only proposition, and more recently in the passage of

Reprinted by permission from *Immigrants Out! The New Nativism and Anti-Immigrant Impulse in the United States,* edited by Juan F. Perea. New York: New York University Press, 1997.

103

Proposition 187 and the introduction of the California Civil Rights Initiative—reflects a sense of loss of white control over the affairs of the state. Indeed, Proposition 187 was an explicit attempt to "save our state" from inundation by immigrants, who—in this wave—are predominantly of color. This sense of California as "paradise lost" by white citizens is one of the cultural undertones of the current racial tensions we are experiencing in the state today, especially regarding Latinos. The sense of "loss" is ironic, for from the point of view of people of color, California history has been filled with repression and struggle, with the displacement of Native Americans and then Spanish Mexican *Californians* from their land and culture, and the importation of a series of different racial groups—Chinese, Japanese, Filipinos, and more recently, Asians and Latinos from a variety of countries—who were recruited to labor in the fields, factories, and shops.

Once settling in California, Mexican immigrants are stigmatized on the basis of race and gender.[3] Racialization is a process by which social, economic, and political forces determine the content and importance of racial categories, and by which they are in turn shaped by racial meanings.[4] What is new about the fin de siècle nativism is that white supremacy has been undermined by global economic restructuring, which has created tremendous wealth while increasing the vulnerability of white citizens and has spurred the Latinization of California—the massive migration and settlement of Latino workers, increasingly with families who utilize schools and social services. Fueled by populist-inspired political measures that do not address the root causes of these transformations, California has become a site of racial tension and social conflict.

The contemporary sense of loss that originated in the California economy, beginning in the 1980s, began a process of restructuring that had profound implications for the state and local communities. In particular, the changing Santa Cruz County economy has relied heavily on immigrant labor, and may serve as a case study of the reactions and tensions felt by different demographic and social groups. Two low-income families—Mexican farm workers and a white female single parent—are profiled here, illustrating how these tensions are experienced by human actors.

Recent Changes in the California Economy

One set of changes in the economy is the result of restructuring of particular industries, such as electronics, food processing, and garments, seeking ways to remain competitive in an increasingly global market place where labor costs in the third world, or in the U.S. sunbelt, make California too expensive by comparison. The more dramatic phenomenon is the movement of firms out of the state, especially the labor and/or pollution-intensive activities. A recent study of business migration from California over the past decade estimates job loss at between 168,000 to 224,000, with Mexico receiving over one fourth of those cases.[5] The reasons are fairly well known— high overhead costs in California, especially dealing with industrial waste, water shortages, workers compensation, inflated rents, increasing insurance rates, or rising litigation costs. But the overwhelming factor is the cheaper labor, especially in nearby Mexico. These plant closures brought devastating economic and social dislocations for California communities.

When you couple these job losses with the thousands of jobs lost through military base closures in the 1980s, the picture becomes truly grim.[6] Between 1988 and 1993, twenty-two major bases in fourteen counties have been designated for closure or realignment in California, which affected over 29,000 civilian staff and almost 81,400 military staff.[7]

Another form of job migration has been the loss of expansion in jobs. In electronics especially, the frenzy of introducing new products that will organize our lives and provide instantaneous access to global telecommunications masks uneven internal industrial development. What is less readily apparent are the firms with large market shares and research and development budgets that are expanding employment in areas such as the Silicon Valley or southern California as well as establishing new factories in less expensive areas of the United States. The "Silicon Gulches" or "Silicon Deserts" of the sunbelt offer tax incentives, city sponsored industrial parks, lower housing costs, and especially cheaper labor that make for a more attractive site for new factories.[8] The other source of expansion has been to the Third World, especially to the U.S.-Mexico border region.[9] Like electronics, garments and food processing have experienced their own "out sourcing" to the Third World and the sunbelt, and to the extent that they remain in California, increasingly rely on immigrant labor forces.[10]

Less visible are the changes occurring in California agriculture, the "backbone" of the state economy. It is well known that California farms have become efficient producers of capital on the strength of immigrant Mexican labor.[11] California agriculture is a fifteen billion dollar industry that provides the "salad bowl and fruit plate of America." In the late 1980s, the state produced 98 percent of the nation's broccoli, 63 percent of celery, 75 percent of cauliflower, 98 percent of processed tomatoes, and

74 percent of lettuce.[12] The overwhelming majority of California's one million farm workers are migrants from Mexico. Unknown to many Californians, Mexican rural communities have become specialized reproducers of agricultural migrant workers who, with small land holdings, must rely on U.S.-earned wage remittances to ensure basic survival at home. Palerm and Urquiola argue that these two phenomena constitute a "binational system of agricultural production and reproduction," and this relationship is so intertwined that neither link can be correctly understood without reference to the other.[13]

The Bracero Program of 1941–64—an Executive Agreement between Mexico and the United States—initially was designed to make up for World War II–led labor shortages (including the internment of the Japanese), but eventually became Public Law 78 on the basis of growers' pressure for contract workers. In the peak year of 1956, 445,000 Mexican workers were recruited through this program and Braceros (contract workers) averaged 11 percent of all farm labor and 30.2 percent of all hired labor in the state.[14] In important agricultural counties, Braceros formed much larger percentages of the seasonal farm worker population.[15]

During this period in Mexico, hundreds of Mexican men flocked to Bracero recruitment centers. Eventually, peasant small land holders became the core group of Braceros because landless peasants often relocated permanently either to the U.S.-Mexico border region, or settled permanently in the United States. In the central Mexican state of Guanajuato, up to 85 percent of the adult male population in one community had participated in the program. With high local unemployment and favorable wage differentials because of a devalued peso, Braceros received up to ten times the prevailing local wage.

Of more long term consequence, the Bracero program provided migrants with a knowledge base and with personal relationships with employers: these individuals then began to migrate to California on their own, without documentation. With the aid of employers who provided housing or employment letters, many of these early migrants established immigrant communities which would provide the infrastructure of support for other migrants to find jobs, housing, and adjust to life in the United States.

Beginning in the early 1980s, U.S. agriculture experienced a crisis as export markets dissolved, farm prices dropped, and land values eroded, creating severe economic strains on farmers. California farmers survived by shifting to specialized high-value fruit and vegetables and marketing to high income markets such as in Japan. These were labor intensive crops, however, and required the expansion of farm worker jobs. This in turn spurred increased migration from Mexico. Fruit crops have distinct peak harvest periods and tend to create seasonal employment, while vegetable crops tend to create permanent or semi-permanent jobs because production occurs almost the whole year. (With subsidized water and cheap labor, one of the largest farm worker jobs is irrigators, workers who move the irrigation pipes around the fields.)

During the 1980s, Mexico experienced its own economic crisis, precipitated by the decline in oil prices, which resulted in difficulties repaying foreign loans, the devaluation of the peso and increased value of the dollar, defunding of state rural agricultural programs, as well as the stock market crash of 1987. Mexican citizens experienced this crisis in terms of the erosion of real wages, high unemployment in many industrial and service jobs, increased underemployment, and spiraling inflation.[16] Meanwhile, the wage differential between Mexico and the United States had skyrocketed. The only alternative for many was to migrate to the United States, risking apprehension by the Border Patrol. The remittances sent back to home communities in Mexico not only amounted to a significant cash inflow, but enabled remaining household members to survive and to lessen the number of migrating workers. The human capital characteristics of migrants began to change, with more workers with higher education and skill levels and/or urban labor market experience. Beginning in the 1980s, more women began migrating as well, accompanied by male kin or utilizing their own social networks. They too sought work in California fields, or found jobs in food processing, in the service sector, or in urban low-waged jobs.

The availability of long-term jobs has enabled many migrants to establish a second home in California, in which they remain for longer periods of time, and they are increasingly settling permanently. These processes have fueled the *Latinization* of rural California, where immigrant farm workers have become the majority population and have changed the character of rural life in these communities.[17] Moreover, increasingly Mexican migrants are originating in indigenous communities in Mexico, with Mixtecs and Zapotecs forming the newest wave of migrants who often experience increased discrimination and exploitation not only by whites but by Chicanos and mestizo Mexicanos.[18] Rural Latino communities have become places of concentrated and persistent poverty, dual societies in which a few Anglos are the landowners, professionals, and white-collar workers. In these communities, social relations—including networks, church affiliations, political differences, and ethnic expressions—often resemble those in Mexico from which the migrants came.

The presence of Latinos in urban areas is somewhat different, in part because they do not form a majority of the population in large cities, but certainly with their barrios and vibrant social and cultural life, migrants are a strong presence as well. Latinos in urban and suburban areas also experience disproportionately high poverty rates, visible even in the third generation after settling in the United States.[19]

Integral to the system of binational production and reproduction is the construction of binational kin relations among Mexicanos. While Mexicans have a long history of utilizing kinship and social networks for support in coping with migration, recently there have emerged "binational households" that maintain homes on both sides of the border and practice income sharing, resource pooling, and mutual assistance.[20] According to one study, 90 percent of Mexican migrants in California sent money to family members, maintained businesses, constructed homes in Mexico, or attracted relatives and friends to California as permanent settlers or seasonal migrants.[21] Household members can move easily between the two countries, not only to find employment but to attend weddings or other social gatherings, a process facilitated by members becoming U.S. citizens or permanent residents. Given the transnational nature of Mexicans' work and family lives, scholars increasingly are abandoning the term "immigrants" for "transnational migrants."[22]

The system of binational agricultural production and reproduction has become further integrated recently through the post-NAFTA economic crisis in Mexico, which sparked another migrant flow[23] and increased American corporate investment in agriculture in Mexico, which has led to some California job loss.[24]

One of the consequences of the economic changes of the 1980s and 1990s was that the U.S. wealthy got richer while the middle and working classes saw real wages decline and became vulnerable, unable to survive health catastrophes or struggling to pay rising college fees for their children or the purchase of new homes in rising housing markets. This widening class divide is exacerbated by a transference of wealth along racial lines, as family incomes and net worth increased for whites overall, while they fell among blacks and Latinos.[25]

The poor, meanwhile, fell further behind. One study found that 12.5 percent, or 3.6 million, Californians lived in poverty in 1989: "By 1992, California was experiencing the worst economic downturn since the Great Depression: 4.9 million Californians (15.9 percent) lived in poverty, including one out of every four children."[26] It has been estimated that 2.7 million Californians use emergency food services, and nearly half of low-income California families spend at least 70 percent of their income on housing.[27] Using 1993 population and income data, Linda Neuhauser and her colleagues conservatively estimate that "8,400,000 Californians are 'food-insecure'— that is, they may have uncertain access to adequate food through normal channels and are at risk of some degree of hunger."[28] People of color have disproportionately high poverty rates. In one study where the poverty rate was 12.2 percent for whites, it was 33.1 percent for African Americans, 30.6 percent for Hispanics, and 15.3 percent for Asians.[29] And the statistic that too often gets overlooked: most poor people are white.

Some scholars are arguing that these changes are not the product of cycles of expansion and recession but reflect more serious structural changes in the California economy. Regional Planner Stephen Cohen and his colleagues predicted in 1993 that "a moderate national recovery will not translate into a comparable California recovery,"[30] and indeed their predictions have been realized. Despite the recent announcement that the number of Americans living in poverty dropped by 1.2 million in 1995, the first decline since 1989, California remained the exception. California's 1994 poverty rate of 17.9 percent was essentially unchanged from the previous year, and California was one of the few states where median household incomes actually fell—by 2.1 percent—between 1992 and 1994.[31] With some of the highest housing markets and costs of living in the country, the dream of home ownership is becoming increasingly remote for Californians. The social expectation that hard work would pay off in tangible benefits or economic mobility is no longer applicable to thousands of people.

The California economy might be the basis of social cleavages, but immigration and politics played a role as well. Nationally, Latinos experienced unprecedented demographic growth, at nearly ten times the rate of non-Hispanic whites and more than five times that of blacks between 1980 and 1990.[32] In California, we experienced a great deal of that growth in population, with the majority of in-migrants coming from Mexico and Latin America. Data on immigration are notoriously unreliable because of census undercounts, especially of the undocumented who make it their business to go unnoticed. Despite this, the census bureau estimates that about half of the national total of undocumented immigrants came to California.[33]

Despite the structural reasons for their immiseration and migration, the media and conservative political pundits worry whether the "brown hordes" of Mexican and Central American immigrants, with their high fertility rates, will soon deplete American jobs and social services, and bemoan the "culture of poverty" among the poor.[34]

The most sensitive issue regarding this new wave of immigrants is their possible use of social services. The only public services that undocumented immigrants can receive, however, are emergency medical care, prenatal care, and K–12 education.[35] "Except for refugees, immigrants who arrived in the past decade [1980s] receive public assistance at significantly *lower* rates than native-born Americans."[36] Compared to blacks and whites, Latinos receive the lowest amount of cash derived from income-transfer programs such as Social Security, welfare, and unemployment and other social programs.[37] Moreover, "when refugees are excluded, immigrant use of public benefits actually *decreased* during the 1980s."[38] The major cost of immigrants settling in California is in the education of their children. These costs, however, are offset by the taxes paid by settled migrant workers, which rise with length of time in the United States. "The average household incomes of both legal immigrants and refugees who entered before 1980 are higher than natives. Overall, annual taxes paid by immigrants to all levels of governments more than offset the costs of services received, generating a net annual surplus of $25 billion to $30 billion."[39]

Despite evidence to the contrary, the concern with abuse of social services was evident in the passage of the 1986 Immigration Reform and Control Act (IRCA). Ostensibly designed to impede illegal immigration, legislators (with grower pressure) allowed for a period of transition, recognizing the importance of migrants to California agriculture. Thus, the Special Agricultural Worker Program provided a window of opportunity for farm workers who qualified to apply for legal permanent residence and eventually U.S. citizenship. The Replenishment Agricultural Worker Program (RAW) allows new immigrant workers to enter the United States between 1990 and 1993, and after working three consecutive seasons, they too would qualify for permanent resident status. The H-2A program allows seasonal workers to be brought in to work temporarily when farmers cannot meet their labor needs. It has been estimated that about one million California Special Agricultural Workers applied for "amnesty" so they could receive permanent residence.[40] Ironically, based upon the hopes of qualifying for the RAW program or possible family reunification legislation passed by Congress, it appears that even more Mexican migrants have moved to California.

The 1994 vote on Proposition 187, where almost 5 million Californians voted in favor, demonstrates a statewide attempt to control the border. Latinos who work, pay taxes, and contribute to society certainly felt as if they had been disfranchised in this election. It has been estimated that there are 4.5 million non–U.S. citizen Latinos—legal and undocumented—who if they had voted might have significantly altered the outcome of a ballot measure directly affecting them.[41]

Racial and class divides are clearly evident in California today. Middle and working class whites find themselves becoming a minority population, surrounded by immigrants who seem to thrive with their growing numbers, and unable to make the American dream a reality for themselves. In Santa Cruz County, we see these fault lines in microcosm.

Santa Cruz County

With spectacular coastline, accessible beaches with strong surf, and abutting pine-forested mountains, Santa Cruz County has long been an important vacation and retirement area. Tourist infrastructure—beginning with the construction of private rail roads (built with Chinese labor), grand hotels, the now over one-hundred-year-old Boardwalk, and a plethora of beach side cottages—was designed for bourgeois pleasures, and luring tourists continues to be a major source of revenue for the county today.[42] Agriculture was the other half of the foundation of the Santa Cruz County economy beginning in the nineteenth century, concentrated in south county. Like their counterparts elsewhere in the state, recruiters sought out Chinese, Japanese, and Filipino workers, who then settled in the area.[43] By the mid–twentieth century, the area experienced a gradual settlement of whites of European heritage who became the majority population. As in other parts of the state, local developers continue to advertise Santa Cruz County as a paradise, a place to shop, have fun, retire, or raise a family.[44]

Mexicans were relatively late arrivals to the area. Donato's study of Mexicans in the Pajaro Valley's schools in south county indicates that in 1930 there were only seven Mexican-descent students enrolled at Watsonville High, followed by eighteen in 1940, fourteen in 1945, and ninety-four in 1950.[45] Unlike large metropolitan areas like Oakland or Los Angeles, without World War II–led industrial development, Santa Cruz County never attracted large numbers of blacks. Donato shows that it wasn't until the late 1950s that Mexican American students became a noticeable group in the Pajaro Valley in south county. When the University arrived in the mid-1960s, Santa Cruz County was a sleepy retirement and agricultural community, with conservatives at the helm, whites in the majority.[46] The pressing political issues centered around zoning and congestion in neighborhoods near the beaches, and there was a decidedly pro-growth sentiment in the political arena.

Beginning in the late 1960s, Santa Cruz County began experiencing a number of dramatic changes. Chicanos and Mexican and Central American immigrants began settling in the area—the latter displaced by immiseration and political turmoil in their home countries; all attracted to jobs in agribusiness and the service sector, and facilitated by social networks and small immigrant communities, such as the Beach Flats, that enabled people to find housing and jobs. In 1973, Spanish-surname students constituted 34 percent of the total enrollment of the local high school, although Mexican American teachers were only 7 percent of the staff. By 1984, Latinos made up 57 percent of total enrollment.[47] Meanwhile there was noticeable "white flight" as Anglos moved to the suburbs, escaping the Latinization occurring in south county.[48] In some south county classrooms today, its hard to find any Anglo students, and the Latino children are predominantly Spanish speakers—that is, children of immigrants. Like other California counties, Santa Cruz found itself suddenly "Latinized"—containing enclaves, where about 30 percent of their residents are Latino. Watsonville in south county is easily a "majority enclave," a city where two thirds of the residents are Latinos—especially during peak harvest season.[49]

The presence of Latinos can be seen in a number of ways. Local outdoor markets, for example, resemble those in Latin America, with products sold bilingually and varied costumes or accents indicating migrants from far to the south. Even Safeway was spurred into a multicultural response, offering tortillas and other foods for the burgeoning Latino population in a large section of local stores. Unique to Santa Cruz, official census tallies find that 75 percent of the total county population is white, and Hispanics are officially 20 percent. This figure significantly undercounts Latinos, however, especially undocumented immigrants. Local activists argue that south county is 60 percent Latino. In contrast to other counties, the census finds that in Santa Cruz County, blacks are only 1 percent of the population, Asian or Pacific Islanders are over 3.4 percent, and American Indians are less than 1 percent.[50] Besides the visibility of many Latino residents, there are numerous Latino-run businesses, a bilingual newspaper, Latino cultural and arts organizations, and increased political clout by Latino activists.[51]

The transformations in populations can be seen in the local labor market. The county economy diversified over time so that agriculture now provides only about a fifth of total employment. The service sector—fueled by Silicon Valley spillover in software development (primarily in small firms) and retail trade—is highly dependent on tourism and these areas provide another fifth each. The public sector and schools (including the University of California) provide 16 percent of all employment, while manufacturing—some generated by electronics production—provides 13 percent of total employment.[52] The better paying jobs—software engineers, professors—are overwhelmingly male and white; while retail clerks, clerical workers, electronics production workers, or fast food workers are usually female and often of color.[53]

In this diversified economy, unemployment consistently remains high—especially in Watsonville, where it has hovered around 22 percent—even as the state is moving out of the recession.[54] As would be expected with low-paying jobs and seasonal industries, official poverty rates are high. Among adults in 1990, 20 percent of Hispanics, 19 percent of blacks and American Indians, and 9 percent of whites and 9 percent of Asians were living in poverty. Seventy-three percent of those who live in poverty in this county are white (these rates are actually lower for Asians and higher for whites in the state as a whole).[55]

As in the robust informal economy, each sector of the economy has race and gender segregation. "Surf City" (the City of Santa Cruz, the county seat) still attracts major sports tournaments and regional day-trippers.[56] Tourist spots are likely to employ Mexican immigrants at the bottom of the job ladder as busboys and gardeners for men, and maids and domestics for women, while waiters and managers in the fancy hotels or restaurants are usually white men or women. There is anecdotal evidence that in some night spots, stereotypical looking "beach bunnies" or "surfers" (those who are blond and blue-eyed) are hired first.

In south county, agribusiness continues to be a major employer, despite contraction in food processing that provoked a strike by Watsonville cannery workers in 1985.[57] Farm workers are over 90 percent Latino, more often male than female;[58] while food processing's race and gender matrix replicates what I found in the late 1970s in the Santa Clara Valley—predominantly Mexican women.[59] Those who found jobs in agriculture became ensconced in the increasingly longer work season, so that Latinos now include long-term settlers and temporary migrants.[60] With the decline of the United Farm Workers union, agricultural wages for some jobs have fallen to below minimum wage, based on piece rates. In 1993 a strawberry picker earned $3.70 an hour plus 60–65 cents per box.

Housing has been a problem in this county. Political initiatives, including the 1978 statewide Proposition 13 and local ordinances that created a countywide green belt and restricted apartment construction (Measure O, passed in 1979), and repeated rejection of rent control created a situation where rental housing is very limited and expensive. This was exacerbated after the 1989 Loma Prieta earthquake, which destroyed a significant number of housing units, especially in south county. (One-room, unfurnished studio apartments start at $500 and go up; the cost of buying a home is one of the highest in the country, and is beyond the reach of most low-income residents.) Coupled with lax enforcement of building codes, especially in south county, there has been a proliferation of illegal housing units. It is not uncommon to find multiple family households, or very large households of men living in cramped conditions, especially during the harvest season. Farm worker housing is in such demand that attempts to tear down the old, partially renovated Murphy's worker camp were delayed because it would displace two hundred people with nowhere to go.[61] In addition to the lack of housing is the persistence of residential segregation, with several Latino barrios located throughout the county. The Beach Flats, located next to the Boardwalk, is the most visible and is considered a political embarrassment since incoming tourists can see the lack of recreational facilities, overcrowded conditions, and Latino men hanging out on the streets.[62]

Besides the local ordinances and Proposition 13, other political events were important. Grassroots neighborhood organizing, a coalition of liberal-left organizations, and help from the student vote culminated in the "take over" of City Council beginning in the 1981 election. The liberals elected a male socialist, feminist mayor. Since then, local politics has become highly polarized and rancorous.[63] The "progressives" have successfully pushed for increased funding for social services at the expense of business interests, and according to a current City Council member, Santa Cruz has better social service funding than almost any county or city in the United States. In the mid-1980s, when the homeless became a visible national problem, a study conducted on the local homeless made the following observation: that about one third were "the new poor"—that is, white males with relatively high educational levels—another third were displaced mental health patients, and another third were "voluntary street people." The voluntary homeless apparently preferred living on the streets, and found

Santa Cruz a congenial place because of the temperate weather (it doesn't snow), forests to camp in, liberal climate offering shelters and soup kitchens, and "quality of street life"—that is, friendly fellow travelers.[64] By 1993, it was estimated that there were over 3,000 homeless people living in Santa Cruz County, with 450 of them being children and youth.[65] The increase in homeless white men can be seen today in a local highly visible labor shape up that used to include mainly Latinos but on some days includes predominantly white men.

Beginning in the 1970s, Santa Cruz County also became a site of gay and lesbian visibility, as local gay and lesbian activists joined the City Council electoral campaigns, and pushed for queer-sensitive social services. There is a gay-lesbian-bisexual community center oriented toward youth, a magazine *(Lavender Reader)* which profiles gay and lesbian couples, local businesses and political events, a pride parade (carefully organized so as not to conflict with the one in San Francisco), bars, a large entertainment venue (the annual fund raiser, a Gay Evening in May, in local parlance, GEM, is held in the Civic Auditorium), and there was an openly gay City Council member. There is talk of a local lesbian baby boom, with births through artificial insemination, and lesbian mothers can find support through local workshops aimed at their special problems. Gay and lesbian leaders have raised community consciousness about "alternative families," and when Queer Nation organized a "kiss-in" demonstration at the mall, they made the point "We're here, we're queer, and we're not going shopping." Santa Cruz has been dubbed a lesbian utopia. Santa Cruz County, then, has become a center of diversity, where race, gender, sexuality, and class refract to create various visible "communities"; this particular mix is somewhat unusual for suburban California.

The political discourse about the poor is highly charged and polarized. Along with predictable hand wringing over these demographic, social, and political changes, conservatives allege that Santa Cruz is becoming a liberal bastion. They reacted by contesting several liberal-led symbolic fights—whether Santa Cruz should be declared a sanctuary for Central Americans in the mid-1980s, the 1994 infamous "lookism" ordinance that was implicitly about gay and lesbian rights. And the discourse often includes stereotypes about the poor and uses underclass terminology—such as allegations that drug dealers are taking over Beach Flats or that immigrants come here to use social services. Epithets—such as "voluntary homeless," "street bums," or "grunge factor"—are used to blame the homeless for their plight.[66] Coded terms like "the new poor" or "alternative poor"—that is, white people—contain the implicit notion that these people are different from "traditional poor"—that is, people of color.

Besieged by immigrants and the homeless, struggling to fund social services because of recessionary pressures and Proposition 13, increasingly looking to federal support for social agencies, Santa Cruz County's dilemmas are classic Californian. And as in other counties, political pressure recently pushed the City Council to the right. After numerous skirmishes where local business people protested the deleterious effects of street people and local activists protested that the camping ban (in effect since the late 1960s) and inadequate shelters force people onto the streets, the City Council took action. With the Council's blessing, health officials started enforcing ordinances that restrict a local organization, "Food not Bombs," from feeding the poor on the streets. The City Council passed constitutionally questionable ordinances regulating panhandling and forbidding sitting on side walks. (One suggestion was that panhandlers should apply for permits, although that did not pass.) Like San Francisco and Los Angeles, the City of Santa Cruz is now at the vanguard of regulating the behavior of the homeless, with other communities rushing to copy these local ordinances.

In this complex and shifting local political economy, where the political discourse about poverty has become contested terrain, I have been conducting life histories among the multiracial poor—mainly during 1992–1993 prior to the passage of Proposition 187. I am trying to find the "hidden poor," that is, those who are not homeless and therefore highly visible (there are good national and local studies) or not necessarily fitting criteria for being officially poor, that is, the "working poor." I have explicitly sought out "low-income people." Informants, then, self-selected based on their own perceptions that they are "low income." Replicating the major racial groups settling in the area, I am seeking out whites and Latinos—mainly Chicanos and Mexican immigrants.[67] I am trying to get a sense of the practice of daily life—that is, how people manage with low incomes—and whether this varies from cultural constructions of what "family" should be.

These subjects reveal the complex ways they try to support themselves, the contingencies of constructing households where social support and sharing of resources ease their difficulties, and what "family" means in the context of troubled circumstances and underclass ideology in popular culture. The overwhelming pattern is the flexibility of their lives, especially in work, intimate relationships, and support networks.

Being poor in this county means that one's relation to the means of production is tenuous at best. Women as well as men struggle and strategize—

often unsuccessfully—to find stable jobs with good pay and benefits in the area, or hang onto them in the face of contracting employment. Among the poor, then, there are strata, ranging from those who struggle to make ends meet, at the bottom of the working class, to those provided material aid from the state (such as AFDC, workers' compensation, or social security), to those with informal economy incomes so low that one wonders how they survive. Some fit traditional expectations of the poor with their low educational levels. The poor in this county also include those with very high educational levels—all sixteen of the white people I've interviewed have some college (usually community college courses taken when they were virtually free); a few have college degrees either from Mexico or the United States. In this county, a college education will not necessarily translate into a good job. A significant percentage of those who are officially poor in this county have a college education. The highly educated Mexican immigrants find themselves especially vulnerable, putting in stints as day laborers before moving up to bilingual semi-professional jobs that are underpaid for their educational requirements or prior experience, and which are often temporary because of soft money funding.

Race is embedded in this social construction of class, including racial difference in experiences (completing an education, finding work in the labor market, or moving to Santa Cruz to begin with). At one extreme are the Mexicanos (particularly the undocumented), with stories of numbing poverty and no job options in Mexico, differential proletarianization and internal migration there, and perhaps domestic violence or male abandonment for women. Immigrants provide classic stories of extraordinary borrowing of resources to make the journey *al norte*, harrowing tales of crossing the border and the final long journey to northern California, avoiding Border Patrol check points and thieves, coping with vehicles breaking down or lying in trunks the whole time. People spend huge amounts on repaying loans back home or becoming documented through unscrupulous lawyers, providing economic and social support to others in similar situations, and living in cramped conditions, often for years at a time. More so than others, Mexicanos are living in the margins, leading, as Leo Chávez says, "shadowed lives."[68] Many travel back and forth between the United States and Mexico, saving the huge sums for bus, air fare, or the use of their own cars from their meager incomes. My informants behave like others in this transnational labor pool, supporting businesses or kin in Mexico, and occasionally are able to unite disrupted "binational" families, often a difficult project economically and socially.

The stigmatization of transnational migrants can be seen in their treatment once arriving to the United States. Despite internal variation—regarding educational levels, for example—most immigrants have completed elementary schooling, while a few have college degrees—and different regions of origin in Mexico (most are mestizos from classic sending areas such as western Mexico, while others are indigenous people from Oaxaca in southern Mexico), once settling in Santa Cruz County, Mexicanos are treated alike, like "Mexicans." Many informants expressed their anger or fear of verbal or occasionally physical assaults; they have experienced what they characterize as discrimination in hiring, or finding housing, or are forced to work extra hours or tasks without extra pay.

Among the Chicanos, the social construction of race and ethnicity is varied and complex, often in reaction to stereotypes about Mexican immigrants. Second and third generation Chicanos sometimes find little in common with Mexican immigrants (evidenced in statements supporting the regulation of immigrants). These informants often have integrated social networks with whites, and, if their parents are immigrants, may contest aspects of "traditional" Mexican culture while experiencing little economic mobility themselves. Dominique Ponce, for example, found a "good" job with the county as a clerical worker with her high school education, youth, and bilingual skills—a job her mother could never have taken. Yet when Dominique became pregnant, had to return home, and started receiving AFDC, she submitted to her family's strict norms regarding parenting and dating. She characterized moving in with her parents as, "It is really hard." And, while Chicanos will occasionally find discrimination in the labor market or in finding housing, they do not have the same experiences of "super exploitation" described by Mexican immigrants.

The whites also had varied ethnic origins and expressions of ethnic identity, from those who claim none or who only serve ethnic dishes at holidays, to those immersed in or contesting ethnic families.[69] White women often expressed a sense that being single parents was difficult and a concern for their ethnic kin. Sullivan Green, for example, saw her Italian American parents (who wanted her to "settle down") as too "old country." Single parent Esther Strange contested her parents' Swiss-Lutheran military strictures that she should marry. (In speaking about ethnicity, white informants often referred to family.)

There are also gender differences, ranging from getting social capital to enter the job market, to contending with sex segregated work, and gendered families. Often discouraged from pursuing education, women struggled to move up the job ladder, coping with sexism and poor working conditions. Some women—Mexican, Chicana, and white—contested traditional expectations that marriage would provide them with economic stability, for their own experiences showed the fragility of men's employment and of marriages. Others, like Shirley Bywater and Minifred Cadena, attempted to fulfill the American dream of an intact nuclear family despite the temporary job forays into other parts of the country by their spouses. These women are single parents in circumstances, but not by self-perceptions. The quotidian struggles of low-income families reveal how families are trying to survive in this local political economy.

The Cabañas Family

Lucio Cabañas was born in Jalisco, Mexico, and finished the sixth grade in school. He is thirty-eight years old, lives in Watsonville, and identified himself as "Hispano." Lucio has lived in Santa Cruz County since 1970. When he was fifteen years old, he migrated to Tijuana; then, with the help of some relatives, he migrated illegally to the United States (he has since become a permanent resident). He moved to Watsonville and worked in the field for several months. [The quotations that follow throughout this chapter are excerpts from interviews with the referenced person—*Ed.*]

> Well, the work ended. In that time we didn't have the right to unemployment benefits, well we worked in the fields. After the season the people would travel back to Mexico, no? Because the work had finished and the little work there was during the winter, well they gave it to the supervisors or persons with more influence. So the majority returned back to Mexico. And being illegal, well we had to suffer on one side [of the border] and then the other, because, well, also we suffered the crossing, not the *coyote* (smuggler), no?

Lucio returned to Mexico and lived in Tijuana with a group of families of fellow workers. He returned to Watsonville and worked in the fields again. He lived in a number of different apartments before meeting his wife, María, and settling down. The Cabañas returned to Mexico to celebrate their church wedding in María's home community.

In 1977, Lucio got a job at the Green Giant food processing factory, where he worked for thirteen years. María worked there as well, and was laid off when he was. During this time Lucio and María had five children, all of whom were born in Watsonville. Lucio was laid off when the factory closed to move operations to Mexico in 1990. He was unemployed for one and a half years, and during this time Lucio took English as a Second Language classes, learned to read and write in English, and received job training in construction. He appreciated learning English and the ability to figure out strategies for how to proceed in finding a job. He found the training in construction, however, of little value (he did not get a job in construction) and he believed that the training was too costly for U.S. taxpayers (of which he was one).

After a long job search, Lucio returned to farm work, picking strawberries. He earns $3.70 an hour plus 60–65 cents per box. He picks between 25 and 26 boxes a day for a total wage of $41.75 a day, or about $200 a week. María also attended ESL classes and received some clerical training. She has worked in various jobs, then experienced carpel tunnel syndrome in her wrist and can no longer work. She has a worker's compensation case pending and worked part time at a school cafeteria. Meanwhile her mother, who had lived with them for years, became ill and María helped her mother travel to Mexico so she could live in her own home.

Through a process of "down skidding," Lucio and María have become part of the working poor. They did not qualify for AFDC for their U.S.-born children since they were homeowners and were making payments on a car. Yet they were in danger of losing their home and had a hard time making ends meet.

Lucio and other members of his village in Mexico decided that they wanted to form an organization to deal with migrant workers' problems at work and with human rights abuses. Their initial goals were oriented toward their home communities:

> We saw the necessity of taking up again the consciousness of those people, especially with those from my village, and we formed a mutual aid committee. Among ourselves we rediscovered the necessities that were lacking in our little village. And what we could do. Then we got together many of the necessities that there were and between—well it was a group of about twenty participants, sixteen or twenty in the committee—that we met periodically and well we did a few projects that lasted a long time.

Eventually, Lucio and María belonged to four other organizations. María was also active in the predominantly Mexicano parent-led demonstrations against the School Board's spending cuts and threats to dismiss teachers. (These demonstrations resulted in the reinstatement of busing of children to school, facilitated when one of the parents discovered some missing funds on a computer printout of the budget.) María explained her participation in these different organizations by saying, "I'm marginalized, but I want there to be justice." Lucio is now working in the United Farm Workers' new organizing campaign. Their oldest daughter is attending a California university, majoring in math, and is doing well in school.

While their political participation may be somewhat unusual, the Cabañas family is very similar to other farm workers in the area regarding their household structure. A recent local survey found that farm worker households are large (6.8 members on average), with 2.6 workers per household. Forty-eight percent are nuclear families, while 41 percent are households formed by extended family groups. Thirty-five percent had full time, year-round employment, while 65 percent had seasonal/temporary farm jobs. The vast majority earned income below the official poverty level (gross averages of $15,203). California farm workers like Lucio and María Cabañas live in overcrowded rural communities characterized by concentrated and persistent poverty, despite their best efforts to improve their lot. While life seems hard to them, it is an improvement over their situations in Mexico, and they came to the United States with expectations that they would struggle to better themselves.

Sullivan Green

Of Italian American heritage and a strict Catholic family with eight children, forty-two-year-old Sullivan Green was a single parent with one child. Her former spouse was an immigrant from Latin America and Sullivan left the marriage because of domestic violence. Sullivan's early labor market experience included working in fast food, as a retail sales clerk, in telephone soliciting, and then in several nurseries, propagating plants, planning landscaping, working as a sales representative, driving a large truck around the northern part of the state, then managing a nursery. Despite her high level of on-the-job training and increased skills, most of these jobs paid close to minimum wage. Meanwhile she took classes part time, working toward a degree in horticulture. Eventually she became certified by the State of California Nurserymen, passing tests in etymology and landscaping. Her best job was working for the City of Santa Cruz, which provided higher hourly wages and medical benefits. She recalled this job with pride. The downtown mall was beautiful with the flowers she planted, and local newspaper articles about her work turned her into a minor celebrity: "We were always in the papers, were admired, and we were respected. And I had full control as an adult, to handling situations and plants and ordering and it was really fabulous. I got to use my education and my learning to its maximum."

The passage of Proposition 13 put her job into jeopardy, and with her "attitude" for asking people not to smash the flower beds, she was told she would be cut back to part-time work. She resigned instead. Her marriage to a man with no English skills, and therefore limited labor market options himself, and birth of her son meant that her part-time jobs in the service sector, as waitress or as sales clerk, were even more important. Feeling threatened, her spouse took charge of her wages, then changed the bank account to his name so she did not have access to it. She went back to school, commuting by bus to San Jose State University, thirty miles away: "I decided to go back to school because of that drive, where you're losing your life." As her marriage deteriorated, she quit school three courses shy of her B.A. She has held her current job as a food sales clerk for many years, and her hourly wage is a respectable $9.80 an hour. But her job provides no medical benefits. Because her asthmatic son is often sick, she frequently misses work, and her annual gross income in 1992 was $10,800. Sullivan believed that she would have been more aggressive about pursuing her education if she had been encouraged: "Education was not expected for women. Matter of fact, it was better to do typing, possibly if you needed to work, go to secretarial school or get married and they would take care of you. This was how I was raised. We were not expected to be bright, we were expected just to be women."

After asking her for a residence and job history, I asked the general question "Have you ever experienced any discrimination or prejudice?" Sullivan responded, "Sure, living here, because I'm white. It's very interesting. The tables are turned." Sullivan qualified for subsidized housing and lives in an apartment complex in which the overwhelming majority of residents are Latinos. Sullivan considers herself to be racially tolerant; "my parents didn't raise me to believe that all white is right. So therefore the best thing that I thought I could pass to my son would be the same thing. But it doesn't work." Particularly galling is that, in contrast to her own hard work, her neighbors do not seem to follow her example: "Of the sixteen places that are here, there's only three women who work and we're all white. All of us are single moms. Everyone else that lives here are not single parents; they have families and they don't work. Sometimes neither of them [the couple] work."

Moreover, Sullivan and her son experienced a series of rebuffs from their neighbors. Her son was teased by the Latino children, with occasional fights or exclusions from parties, and she characterized this as prejudice. She found that her efforts to work with the parents of the offending children produced few results: "I went over that and said, 'Well, we need to work this out. You need to apologize to him; you need to shake hands like this.' But you always have one parent—me—going out there." She felt hurt that her neighbors would not afford her customary courtesies, like informing her when the laundry was free: "All of a sudden, no one seems to understand English, right? Sometimes I get in such a tizzy." Sullivan does not speak Spanish so her attempts to communicate with her neighbors are difficult. And her attempts to get her neighbors to turn down their music received a "patronizing" response: "They say, 'Well, you could write a letter and get signatures; we're not too sure it's going to work.'" She characterized these experiences as "subtle things" that heightened her awareness of racial prejudice: "And I understand now. I'm among it. I get to see now how they have felt in their past, or how they feel now. It makes me think, 'Now I know what it's like, but no one should ever feel like that.'" These social conflicts, despite her best efforts not to be prejudiced herself, and to teach her son not to name call, are evidence that prejudice is "a social thing," something that "I'm going to rise above."

Sullivan feels extreme pressure by her parents to "just find a nice guy and settle down," yet finds the possibilities for meeting men difficult. She is well aware that as a single parent, the expectations of achieving "normal" social rewards are minimal. "I have no idea what my life has in store for me. My goal is, I want to be a homeowner; I would love to own a house. I would love to have a job where I'm respected and appreciated, and I really want medical benefits. That was on my Christmas list. For me, health insurance would be fantastic. To get a mammogram maybe would be a delight." With over $4,400 in debts, including a student loan, her health takes low priority.

Sullivan could qualify for Medi-cal or food stamps but refuses to apply for several reasons: "I'm trying not to be part of the system. I will take other things that come my way [such as subsidized housing and her son's free lunches at school], but I'm trying to pay my way." Furthermore, "I hate them [eligibility workers] interrogating me, asking all these questions. I dislike that they know everything about me anyway. They make you feel bad, like you're cheating them. Make you feel like a victim. I'm not a victim. I'm a very happy woman and I try to take advantage of being positive on all the things that are given to me. I feel more in control. I feel I'm proud of myself. You don't have to feel as though you're down and out." Her independence and control come at quite a price. Recently her son had a critical asthma attack, in which she had to rush him to the emergency room. "They asked me, 'How are you going to pay for this' and my son's in the back room yelling, 'I'm getting a headache,' then I say 'cash.' 'Are you sure?' I just got paid, and I take out my wallet and lay it down—$480. They'll take my son now." Her sense of fury was mitigated by her belief "that was the hardest thing I ever did, but I never weakened for him. It was a very sad thing."

Sullivan scrupulously manages her money, purchasing clothing and household items at the local flea market, and once a year selling items with her son to generate cash. "We go out to dinner afterwards and we usually break even. It's a fun thing to do, and then we give the rest to the Women's Shelter. That's how I raised him. There's always less fortunate than what we are. And sometimes I tell him, I don't have the money right now. We might be broke, but we're not poor." Despite her difficult economic situation and social tensions in her apartment complex, Sullivan does not want to see herself as a "desperate single mother," someone who says "poor me, I do it all myself." She is proud of her self-sufficiency and distances herself from "the poor." Poor people are people like her neighbors, Latinos with large families, sometimes out of work, receiving food stamps or Medi-cal. To identify with the poor would threaten her self-esteem and force her to confront that her situation of being "broke" is not temporary and continues despite her best efforts. Sullivan attempts to establish some modicum of control over her life and a sense of self-respect despite being in circumstances in which "the tables are turned," she as a white person does not have access to the good life. Despite her good intentions, she resents that others appear to have a free ride.

Conclusion

Low-income people in Santa Cruz County experience poverty as multilayered and complex, certainly grounded in the regional political economy which in the early nineties (like the rest of the state) revealed the underside of the California dream. In contrast to underclass theory and popular images about their dysfunctional culture, however, these informants are both active historical agents and vary enormously in lives they construct under extraordinary constraints.

The sense that paradise is lost is a cultural undertone we experience in

California today. Of course this is a one-sided metaphor, for some of "us" believe that the paradise was never accessible. And those of us who feel that they no longer have control over their lives do not realize that this paradise was never under their control to begin with. The myth of the California dream, seemingly played out in real lives, seemed possible as long as the engine of economic growth and unlimited resources drove development. As we now see the mobility of capital, the downsizing of federal resources in base closures and lost military contracts, the inability of cities to house, feed, police, or transport their multiracial populations under scarce resources, the illusionary nature of the California dream is laid bare. Meanwhile, Mexican and white families in California work and struggle toward fulfillment of their own dreams.

NOTES

For their helpful comments on different versions of this chapter, I would like to thank John Borrego, Micaela di Leonardo, Ramón Gutiérrez, Mike Rotkin, and Paule Cruz Takash. Thanks to the UC MEXUS program and the Chicano/Latino Research Center at the University of California, Santa Cruz, both of which provided financial support for this project.

1. Stephen S. Cohen, Clara Eugenia García, and Oscar Loureiro, "From Boom to Bust in the Golden State: The Structural Dimension of California's Prolonged Recession," Working paper 64, The Berkeley Roundtable on the International Economy, University of California, Berkeley, September 1993.

2. Tomás Almaguer, *Racial Fault Lines: The Historical Origins of White Supremacy in California* (Berkeley: University of California Press, 1994), p. 1.

3. This view contrasts with that of immigration theorists who focus on settlement as a process, or who focus on internal variation in the transnational immigrant pool such as gender and legal status. For studies of settlement processes of immigrants, see Douglas Massey, "The Settlement Process among Mexican Migrants to the United States," *American Sociological Review* 51 (1986): 670–85; Leo R. Chávez, *Shadowed Lives: Undocumented Immigrants in American Society* (New York: Harcourt Brace Jovanovich College Publishers, 1991). For a discussion of the importance of gender and legal status, see Pierrette Hondagneu-Sotelo, *Gendered Transitions: Mexican Experiences of Immigration* (Berkeley: University of California Press, 1994).

4. Michael Omi and Howard Winant, *Racial Formation in the United States: From the 1960s to the 1980s* (New York: Routledge and Kegan Paul, 1987), chap. 2.

5. Stephen S. Cohen, Clara Eugenia García, and Oscar Loureiro, "From Boom to Bust in the Golden State: The Structural Dimension of California's Prolonged

Recession," Working paper 64, The Berkeley Roundtable on the International Economy, University of California, Berkeley, September 1993.

6. Base closures have been mitigated by federal assistance, most often before job loss actually began. For a discussion of plant closures during the 1980s in California, see Philip Shapira, "The Crumbling of Smokestack California: A Case Study in Industrial Restructuring and the Reorganization of Work," Working paper 437, Institute of Urban and Regional Development, University of California, Berkeley. For a discussion of plant closures in the food processing industry, see Patricia Zavella, *Women's Work and Chicano Families: Cannery Workers of the Santa Clara Valley* (Ithaca: Cornell University Press, 1987), esp. chap. 6.

7. Cynthia A. Kroll, Josh Kirschenbaum, Mary Corley, Lyn Harlan, et al., "Defense Industry Conversion, Base Closure, and the California Economy: A Review of Research and Planning Activities for Recovery," Institute of Urban and Regional Development, Working paper 632, February 1995, p. 7. The conversion of Fort Ord in Monterey to educational usage, including the opening of California State University, was the result of over fifteen million in federal funds.

8. For a discussion of Silicon Valley spillover to the sunbelt, see Louise Lamphere, Patricia Zavella, and Felipe Gonzáles, with Peter B. Evans, *Sunbelt Working Mothers: Reconciling Family and Factory* (Ithaca: Cornell University Press, 1993).

9. Patricia Fernández-Kelly, *For We Are Sold, I and My People: Women and Industry in Mexico's Frontier* (Albany: State University of New York Press, 1983); Devon G. Peña, *The Terror of the Machine: Technology, Work, Gender and Ecology in the U.S.-Mexico Border* (Austin: University of Texas Press, 1996).

10. Karen Hossfeld, "Hiring Immigrant Women: Silicon Valley's 'Simple Formula,'" in Maxine Baca Zinn and Bonnie Thornton Dill, *Women of Color in U.S. Society* (Philadelphia: Temple University Press, 1994), pp. 65–94; Louise Lamphere, Alex Stepick, and Guillermo Grenier, eds., *Newcomers in the Workplace: Immigrants and the Restructuring of the U.S. Economy* (Philadelphia: Temple University Press, 1994); Maria Patricia Fernández Kelly and Anna M. García, "Economic Restructuring in the United States: Hispanic Women in the Garment and Electronics Industries," *Women and Work: An Annual Review* 3 (1988): 49–65.

11. Carey McWilliams, *Factories in the Field* (Boston: Little, Brown, 1939); Walter Goldschmidt, *As You Sow* (Glencoe, IL: Free Press, 1947); Ernesto Galarza, *Farm Workers and Agri-business in California, 1847–1960* (Notre Dame: University of Notre Dame Press, 1977); Ernesto Galarza, *Merchants of Labor: An Account of the Managed Migration of Mexican Farm Workers in California, 1942–1960* (Santa Barbara: McNally and Loftin, West, 1978).

12. Ann Foley Scheuring, *A Guidebook to California Agriculture* (Berkeley: University of California Press, 1983), cited in Juan Vicente Palerm and José Ignacio Urquiola, "A Binational System of Agricultural Production: The Case of the Mexican Bajio and California," in Daniel G. Aldrich, Jr., and Lorenzo Meyer, eds., *Mexico and the United States: Neighbors in Crisis* (Berkeley: Borgo Press), pp. 311–66, at 314.

13. Palerm and Urquiola, "A Binational System of Agricultural Production," p. 311.

14. Ernesto Galarza, *Merchants of Labor*, p. 79, cited in Palerm and Urquiola, "A Binational System of Agricultural Production," pp. 323–24.

15. There is regional variation in Mexico regarding the length of time that migrants have been coming to work in the United States. In a heavy sending area of Guanajuato, 1930–40 is the time when the Cárdenas administration enforced land reform, which spurred the migration of small peasant farmers to work in the United States, so the period of migration is about sixty years. The migration history of western Mexico (the states of Jalisco, Michoacán, Zacatecas, Colima, Aguascalientes, Nayarit, and Guanajuato) is over one hundred years, initiated by U.S. recruiters who journeyed to Mexico. For a discussion of the history of migration from Guanajuato, see Palerm and Urquiola, "A Binational System of Agricultural Production," p. 313; for a discussion of migration from western Mexico, see Douglas S. Massey, Rafael Alarcón, Jorge Durand, and Humberto González, *Return to Aztlan: The Social Process of International Migration from Western Mexico* (Berkeley: University of California Press, 1987).

16. Alejandro Álvarez Béjar and Gabriel Mendoza Pichardo (translated by John F. Uggen), "Mexico 1988–1991: A Successful Economic Adjust Program?" *Latin American Perspectives* 78:20 (Summer 1993): 32–45.

17. Juan Vicente Palerm, "Farm Labor Needs and Farm Workers in California, 1970–1989," unpublished report for the State Employment Development Department, 1991.

18. Carol Zabin, Michael Kearney, Anna García, David Runsten, and Carole Nagengast, *Mixtec Migrants in California Agriculture: A New Cycle of Poverty* (Davis: California Institute for Rural Studies, 1993).

19. David E. Hayes-Bautista et al., *No Longer a Minority: Latinos and Social Policy in California* (UCLA: Chicano Studies Research Center, 1992); Aída Hurtado et al., *Redefining California: Latino Social Engagement in a Multicultural Society* (UCLA: Chicano Studies Research Center, 1992).

20. Carlos G. Vélez-Ibañez and James B. Greenberg, "Formation and Transformation of Funds of Knowledge among U.S.-Mexican Households," *Anthropology and Education Quarterly* 23, no. 4 (1992): 313–34; Carlos Vélez-Ibañez, "U.S. Mexicans in the Borderlands: Being Poor without the Underclass," in Joan Moore and Raquel Pinderhughes, eds., *In the Barrios: Latinos and the Underclass Debate* (New York: Russell Sage Foundation, 1993), pp. 195–210; and Juan Vicente Palerm, "Farm Labor Needs and Farm Workers in California." Also see Aída Hurtado, "Variations, Combinations, and Evolutions: Latino Families in the United States," in Ruth E. Zambrana and Maxine Baca Zinn, eds., *Latino Families: Developing a Paradigm for Research, Practice, and Policy* (Thousand Oaks, CA: Sage Publications, 1994).

21. Juan Vicente Palerm, "Farm Labor Needs."

22. These scholars stress the construction of "transnational" lives by Latinos, where economic relations, political power, cultural forms, and identities are situated in and contextualized by Latin American and U.S. social formations. See Roger Rouse, "Making Sense of Settlement: Class Transformation, Cultural Struggle, and Transnationalism among Mexican Migrants in the United States," *Annals of the New York Academy of Sciences* 645 (July 1992): 25–52; Carol Zabin et al., *Mixtec Migrants in California Agriculture*.

23. Esther Schrader, "Peso Plunges Mexico into Uncertainty," *San Jose Mercury News,* November 10, 1995, p. 1C.

24. Kirby Moulton and David Runsten, "The Frozen Vegetable Industry of Mexico," Cooperative Extension Working Paper, University of California, Berkeley, 1986.

25. Rebecca Morales and Frank Bonilla, eds., *Latinos in a Changing U.S. Economy* (Newbury Park, CA: Sage Publications, 1993), p. 1.

26. Linda Neuhauser, Doris Disbrow, and Sheldon Margen, "Hunger and Food Insecurity in California," *California Policy Seminar Brief* 7:4 (April 1995): 3.

27. Linda Neuhauser et al., "Hunger and Food Insecurity in California," pp. 3 and 4.

28. Linda Neuhauser et al., "Hunger and Food Insecurity in California," p. 5.

29. R. A. Zaldivar, "Poverty Rate Hits '90's High," *San Jose Mercury News,* September 7, 1994. In a 1992 survey, approximately 22 percent of Latino families were living in poverty, compared to 22 percent of blacks, 18 percent of Asians, and 7 percent of Anglos. See David Hayes-Bautista et al., *No Longer a Minority,* p. 13.

30. Stephen S. Cohen et al., "From Boom to Bust in the Golden State," p. 3.

31. "Number of Poor in U.S. Declines," *San Jose Mercury News,* October 6, 1995, p. 4A.

32. Rebecca Morales and Frank Bonilla, eds., *Latinos in a Changing U.S. Economy,* p. 1.

33. *San Francisco Chronicle,* August 7, 1993, p. 1, cited in Stephen S. Cohen et al., "From Boom to Bust in the Golden State," p. 33.

34. For one example of this hysteria, see Michael Meyer, "Los Angeles 2010: A Latino Subcontinent," *Newsweek,* November 9, 1992, pp. 32–33. For a critique of cultural models which blame the poor for their own immiseration, see Maxine Baca Zinn, "Family, Race, and Poverty in the Eighties," in Barrie Thorne and Marilyn Yalom, eds., *Rethinking the Family: Some Feminist Questions* (Boston: Northeastern University Press, 1992), pp. 71–89; Patricia Zavella, "Living on the Edge: Everyday Lives of Poor Chicano/Mexicano Families," in Avery Gordon and Christopher Newfield, eds., *Mapping Multiculturalism?* (Minneapolis: University of Minnesota Press, 1996).

35. Estevan Flores, "Research on Undocumented Immigrants and Public Policy: A Study of the Texas School Case," *International Migration Review* 18, no. 3 (1984): 505–23.

36. Michael Fix and Jeffrey S. Passel, with María E. Enchautegui and Wendy Zimmermann, *Immigration and Immigrants: Setting the Record Straight* (Washington, DC: Urban Institute, 1994), p. 6, emphasis in the original.

37. Hayes-Bautista et al., No *Longer a Minority,* p. 166; also see Mark Testa and Marilyn Krogh, "Nonmarital Parenthood, Male Joblessness, and AFDC Participation in Inner-City Chicago" (final report prepared for the Assistant Secretary for Planning and Evaluation, November 1990), p. 83.

38. Michael Fix, Jeffrey S. Passel, et al., *Immigration and Immigrants,* p. 6, emphasis in the original.

39. Michael Fix, Jeffrey S. Passel, et al., *Immigration and Immigrants,* p. 6.

40. Palerm and Urquiola, "A Binational System of Agricultural Production," p. 350.

41. Approximately 4.8 million people voted *yes,* while 3.3 million voted *no* on Prop. 187. See Alexander Cockburn, "Beat the Devil," *The Nation,* December 5, 1994.

42. Sandy Lydon, *Chinese Gold: The Chinese in the Monterey Bay Region* (Capitola: Capitola Book Company, 1985); Betty Lewis, *Watsonville: Memories That Linger* (Santa Cruz: Otter B Books, 1986), vols. 1 and 2.

43. There is evidence of a few blacks who settled in the area beginning in the nineteenth century. Betty Lewis discusses "Jim Broadis—Runaway Slave," who arrived in Watsonville about 1850, and she mentions a south county place known as "Nigger Hill." During the nineteenth century, there was a local "colored school" for south county black children. See Betty Lewis, *Watsonville* (vol. 2), chapter 12, and (vol. 1), p. 101.

44. One commentator dubbed the Central Coast California's "middle kingdom." See Dan Walters, *California: Facing the 21st Century,* 2d ed. (Sacramento: California Journal Press, 1992).

45. Ruben Donato, "In Struggle: Mexican Americans in the Pajaro Valley Schools, 1900–1979," Ph.D. Dissertation, Stanford University, 1987. Also see in Maria Eugenia Matute-Bianchi, "Ethnic Identities and Patterns of School Success and Failure among Mexican-Descent and Japanese-American Students in a California High School: An Ethnographic Analysis," *American Journal of Education* 95 (1986): 233–55.

46. Michael E. Rotkin, "Class, Populism, and Progressive Politics: Santa Cruz, California, 1970–1982," Dissertation, University of California, Santa Cruz, History of Consciousness Board, 1991.

47. See Ruben Donato, "In Struggle," pp. 82 and 128. Also see Maria Eugenia Matute-Bianchi, "Ethnic Identities and Patterns of School Success and Failure among Mexican-Descent and Japanese-American Students in a California High School: An Ethnographic Analysis," *American Journal of Education* 95 (1986): 233–55.

48. Ruben Donato, "In Struggle," p. 83.

49. See Juan Vicente Palerm, "Farm Labor Needs and Farm Workers in California"; and Paule Cruz Takash, "A Crisis of Democracy: Community Responses to the Latinization of a California Town Dependent on Immigrant Labor," Dissertation, Anthropology Department, University of California, Berkeley, 1990.

50. U.S. Bureau of Census, *1990 Census of Population and Housing: Population and Housing Characteristics for Census Tracts and Block Numbering Areas, Santa Cruz, CA PMSA* (Washington, DC: U.S. Government Printing Office, 1993), p. 38, Table 8.

51. League of United Latin American Citizens, for example, was one of the plaintiffs in the redistricting suit against the City of Watsonville; activist Celia Organista has a column in the notoriously conservative newspaper, *The Santa Cruz Sentinel.* For a discussion of the lawsuit, see Paule Cruz Takash, "A Crisis of Democracy."

52. Employment Development Department, Annual Planning Information, Santa Cruz Metropolitan Statistical Area, Report, 1990, pp. 8, 11.

53. University of California, Santa Cruz, "Executive Order 11246 Affirmative Action Program for Minorities and Women, September 1, 1994–August 31, 1995," unpublished report.

54. For nonagricultural employment, see Employment Development Department, *Annual Planning Information, Santa Cruz Metropolitan Statistical Area,* 1990, pp. 8, 11; for agricultural employment, see Santa Cruz County Farmworker Housing Committee, County Farm Worker Housing Needs.

55. Children's Network, "The Santa Cruz County Report Card: The State of Our Children, 1992–93," unpublished report, 1993.

56. Community Chautaugua, "Focus Group Report: Tourism," report by the Beach Area Outlook Conference, 1994.

57. See Frank Bardacke, "Watsonville: How the Strikers Won," *Against the Current* (May/June 1987): 15–20. This strike was immortalized in the award winning documentary "Watsonville on Strike," directed by Jon Silver. Also see Brian Frith Smith, "Stereotypes about Mexicanos in the Mass Media: News Coverage from the Watsonville Cannery Workers Strike, 1985–1987," Honors Senior Thesis in Latin American Studies, 1993.

58. Based on a survey of 688 farm workers and 81 farm worker employees, this study aimed to provide information for the development of farm workers' housing in Santa Cruz County by public and private entities, and to help alleviate substandard conditions of existing farm worker housing. Santa Cruz County is eligible for Community Development Block Grants, and housing has been identified as a pressing need. The Santa Cruz Housing Market Area includes the unincorporated Pajaro, just over the Monterey county line, and other small neighborhoods where many farm workers reside. See Santa Cruz County Farmworker Housing Committee, "Santa Cruz County Farm Worker Housing Needs," unpublished report, 1993.

59. See Frank Bardacke, "Watsonville: How the Strikers Won"; and Frank Bar-

dacke, *Good Liberals and Great Blue Herons* (Santa Cruz: Center for Political Ecology, 1994).

60. Santa Cruz County Farmworker Housing Committee, "Santa Cruz County Farm Worker Housing Needs," p. 10.

61. Marianne Biasotti, "Farmworkers Seek to Keep Camp Open," *Santa Cruz Sentinel*, January 26, 1994, p. 1.

62. See Community Chautaugua, "Focus Group Report: Property Owners," report by the Beach Area Outlook Conference, 1994. Once the focus group reports were compiled, the Beach Area Outlook Conference (sponsored by the Seaside Company which owns the Boardwalk) convened various community forums, whose purpose was to discuss how to redevelop the Beach Area. Several wild schemes were suggested, ranging from constructing a children's museum (competing with one in San Jose, half an hour away) to building a conference center. Also see Nicole Dubis, "I Am Not Heard Here," Community Studies senior thesis on women in the Beach Flats.

63. See Rotkin, cited *supra* n. 46.

64. These observations were based on a survey of 103 homeless people, as well as in-depth interviews with 31 participants, and interviews with shelter workers and participant observation. See William Friedland and Robert Marotto, "Streetpeople and Straightpeople in Santa Cruz, California: A Report of the Downtown Study," University of California, Santa Cruz, 1985 (unpublished report).

65. *Santa Cruz Sentinel*, January 14, 1993, cited in Children's Network, "The Santa Cruz County Report Card: The State of Our Children, 1992–93" (unpublished report, 1993), p. 28. Also see Toni Nelson Herrera, "CASAS HOY!" Community Studies senior thesis on women in a Watsonville homeless shelter.

66. Lee Quarnstrom, "It's Time to Get the Bums Off Our Streets," *San Jose Mercury News*, November 20, 1995, p. 1B.

67. I have interviewed 35 individuals thus far: 11 Mexicanos, 10 Chicanos, and 14 whites; all were found through "snowball sampling."

68. Leo R. Chávez, *Shadowed Lives.*

69. For discussions of white ethnicity, see Micaela di Leonardo, *The Varieties of Ethnic Experience: Kinship, Class, and Gender among California Italian-Americans* (Ithaca: Cornell University Press, 1984); and Ruth Frankenberg, *White Women, Race Matters: The Social Construction of Whiteness* (Minneapolis: University of Minnesota Press, 1992).

Part II

The Fallacy of "Reform"

Chapter 5

Welfare Reform and the Economic and Cultural Reconstruction of Low Wage Labor Markets

Frances Fox Piven

In the summer of 1996 when the national program called "welfare" was overhauled, academic theories of the welfare state were in a sense taken by surprise. In the past, most such theories posited the gradual expansion of social programs, and the gradual centralization of responsibility for their administration. Instead, American welfare reform in 1996 meant new tight limits on cash assistance to poor women and children, and the devolution of responsibility to state governments. Many state governments, in turn, are turning program authority over to localities or to private organizations, and the emphasis has shifted from income assistance to a "service and sanctioning strategy for behavior change" (Nathan and Gais 1998:7), eerily duplicating the pre-1935 local arrangements for poor relief. These and other changes which restricted aid were accompanied by what was virtually a national revival movement calling for the restoration of moral compulsion to the lives of the poor. I think these developments begin to make sense when we examine the bearing of changes in welfare policy, including the moral crusade with which these changes are intertwined, on labor markets, especially low wage labor markets. This aspect of welfare policy, which was largely ignored during the national debate over welfare, is hugely important, and it is the main focus of this article.

Reprinted by permission from *City and Society Annual Review* (1998): 21–36.

The Peculiarity of the Contemporary Labor Market

Obviously, the American workforce is very large, and even at its peak, "welfare," which most people took to mean the Aid to Families with Dependent Children (AFDC) program, was rather small, reaching fewer than five million adults, the overwhelming majority of whom were women, and nine million children. Created in 1935, the program required the federal government to underwrite roughly half of the cost to the states of providing assistance to single parents. But the states were free to set grant levels, and they set them very low, far below the poverty line. As a result, the program never accounted for more than one percent of the federal budget.[1] Just how, then, could changes in the one have a big impact on the other? To make the case for the significance of welfare, I have to first attend to the distinctive sources of labor weakness in market relations today.

Consider a much remarked upon anomaly, often pointed to (and celebrated) by market analysts and financial pundits. Unemployment is at its lowest level in twenty-five years. But wages remain more or less stagnant, failing to recoup even in this economic boom from the long term decline in earnings since 1973. Moreover, as the real wages of most workers drifted downward over the past two decades, the real wages of the lowest paid fell faster. Between 1979 and 1989, the earnings of the lowest ten percent fell by sixteen percent. Despite the legislated increase in the minimum wage as the 1996 election approached, the real value of the minimum wage remains thirty percent below its peak in 1968 (Burch 1997; Freeman 1996).

Why the anomaly? The main reason I think is the growing insecurity of many jobs, lower overall unemployment levels notwithstanding. The term usually used to describe the labor market changes which make work insecure is restructuring, and it includes increased reliance by employers on outsourced production on the one hand, and the spread of new forms of less secure employment within the U.S. on the other. The work that once was done by full-time and long term employees who receive benefits and paid holidays and vacations is increasingly done by temporary employees, or by part timers, or by workers dubbed "independent contractors." The result is pervasive uncertainty about the stability of employment. Everyone understands that rising unemployment shifts the balance of power in labor market relations because workers worry that they can more easily be replaced at a time when jobs are harder to find. But so do insecure patterns of job tenure shift the balance of power in the labor market from workers to employers. Workers worried about their jobs don't usually bid for higher wages or benefits or better working conditions, and they don't readily join unions that bid for wage or benefit or working-condition improvements. By the mid 1990s, the proportion of workers belonging to unions had fallen to the level of the mid 1930s, and strikes virtually disappeared from the repertoire of labor in its dealings with management (Brecher 1998).

The telling indicator of this power shift is the seismic change that has occurred in the relative size of pieces of the American economic pie. Profits are at a thirty year high, and are growing at the expense of wages. The richest 10 percent of households accounted for 61.1 percent of the nation's wealth in 1989; by 1994 their share had jumped to 66.8 percent. Similarly, earnings at the very top are growing, indeed CEO earnings are spiraling to historic peaks. Meanwhile, the wages of the lowest paid fell further and further behind and, instead of accumulating wealth, they accumulated debt (Morley and Petras 1998:130; Wolff 1995; Henwood 1996).

Is It Globalization?

The usual explanations for job restructuring and the growing inequalities with which it is associated point to large and anonymous forces, and particularly to the rise of new information technologies and the spread of global markets in finance and trade that the new technologies facilitate. These are awesome, even frightening explanations, because they argue an economy and society in the grip of technological and market forces that are beyond anyone's reach, and certainly beyond the reach of particular workers in particular employment relations. But it is misleading to talk of globalization as a kind of uncaused cause, presumably resulting from the natural and inevitable unfolding of market trends. Accelerated trade and capital movements are made possible by government policies, and by the political forces which shape those policies. The lightning movements of capital around the globe would not be occurring without the deregulation of financial markets accomplished by national governments, and most importantly the U.S. government, or without the protective shield of the World Bank, which was also a creation of governments, and primarily the U.S. government. Similarly, the accelerating international circulation of goods and services is encouraged by the international and regional trade pacts accomplished by governments.

There are other compelling reasons to be skeptical of globalism as the catch-all explanation. While technologies are changing, and capital and trade movements are increasing, these developments affect all industrial countries. Indeed, the United States remains less exposed to international financial movements and trade competition than most other rich countries. Yet the job restructuring and sharply growing inequality attributed to technology and globalization is far more advanced in the U.S. than in other comparable societies. Wages have fallen further here, for example; poverty is deeper and more extensive; unions have been battered far more severely; social programs have been rolled back much more. All this cannot simply be the result of the new "post-Fordist" economy. In fact, I think these trends are compounded of globalization and the policies and politics which promote it, and of the sharp turn against the Keynesian welfare state in domestic policies, also promoted by politics, and particularly by the rise of aggressive American business politics.

Domestic Policy Shifts and Labor Markets

In any case, a series of domestic policy initiatives were important causes of growing insecurity and inequality. The social compact between business and labor forged in the tumult of the 1930s and 1960s began to come undone, as employers mobilized in what Robert Reich, former Secretary of Labor under Clinton, recently called "the relentless drive among American companies to reduce their labor costs . . ." One way was to whittle back union protections and regulatory controls on business. More directly relevant to my argument here, the income protection programs that are widely acknowledged to constitute a floor under wages were gradually rolled back, often through arcane changes in formulas that received little public attention (Piven 1997).

Consider some examples. When unemployment insurance was initiated in the mid 1930s, the intention appears to have been not only to aid the unemployed, but to moderate the impact of high levels of unemployment on the wages and working conditions of those who were employed. Consistently, when unemployment levels rose during the recession of the mid 1970s, the federal government extended unemployment benefits to cover longer periods of unemployment, and unemployment centers were kept open for longer hours, with the result that the percentage of the unemployed receiving benefits rose from fifty percent to seventy-six percent (Meerpol). During the 1980s, little-noticed changes in the formula defining unemployment, together with changes in formula which triggered federal support for longer term benefits, resulted in contracting coverage. With virtually no public discussion, the program shrank, so that on average only one-third of the unemployed were covered during the decade.

A similarly little-noticed process occurred in the social security program. As with unemployment insurance, social security pensions were initiated in the mid 1930s with the intention of removing older people from a labor market that not only treated them badly, but put them in competition with other workers for jobs. In the 1980s, the intent of policy seemed to have been reversed. The age at which people become eligible for pensions is being raised, although so gradually as to attract very little attention and comment. When the change takes full effect, the age of eligibility will have been raised from sixty-five to sixty-seven, and the talk is of age seventy in the future, with the result that many millions of older people will remain in the labor market. Meanwhile, cost-of-living adjustments in benefits are being shaved down, and the rules have been changed to encourage even those receiving benefits to work or search for work by reducing penalties on earnings.

Or consider the new restrictions on social supports for immigrants that were also incorporated in welfare reform, or the Personal Responsibility and Work Opportunity Reconciliation Act of 1996 (PRWORA). Legal immigrants are no longer entitled to Medicaid, food stamps, or cash assistance.[2] If most of the public appeared to go along with these exclusions, it was probably because they didn't think immigrants should enter the country unless they could support themselves. But the idea that benefit cutoffs will deter immigration finds little confirmation in data or experience (Massey 1998). More likely, the exclusions will simply ensure that the immigrants who do come here will remain without any public protections to tide them over periods of unemployment or low wages. This may indeed be just what was intended, since the business think tanks and congressional bloc that fought strenuously against tighter controls on immigration, also fought to slash the benefits for which immigrants would be eligible. During 1996, the year that cutbacks on aid to legal immigrants were made law, almost a million legal immigrants were admitted to the U.S., the largest number since 1914 (Schuck 1998).

The legislation that cut welfare also included cuts in food-stamp benefits, by almost twenty percent, reducing the average benefit per meal from eighty cents to sixty-six cents (Henwood 1996). This cut affects not only welfare recipients, but the elderly and the working poor. In addition, unemployed adults without dependent children are now limited to three months of food stamps in any three-year period of unemployment, thus ensuring that it will be more difficult for these unemployed to weather a stint of unemployment.

Welfare Reform

The most dramatic cutbacks occurred in AFDC, or "welfare," the main program that provides cash assistance to impoverished families. A new five-year lifetime limit on eligibility was imposed. Even higher limits were imposed on cash assistance as opposed to one or another form of workfare. Unless a state opts out of this requirement, women are required to work at "community service" after two months in exchange for whatever benefits they get. In any case, they must work for their benefits after two years, and this provision is backed up by federal "quotas" establishing the proportion of recipients who must be working and the number of hours they must work. The quotas and the hours rise each year, and states that fail to conform risk fiscal penalties (AFL-CIO Public Policy Department 1996). There were also work requirements under the old AFDC law, but they were far less stringent. Moreover, and this is important in assessing the impact of work requirements on labor markets, the old law included elaborate provisions to prevent the use of welfare recipients to displace existing workers. Most of those provisions have been eliminated or weakened (Dietrich, Emsellen and Williams 1998; Diller 1998). Aside from these restrictions on generosity, the new legislation gives the states wide latitude to design their welfare program, now renamed Temporary Assistance to Needy Families (TANF). Many states are using that latitude to reduce benefits, to impose shorter time limits on assistance, or to introduce sanctions which penalize families with benefit cuts for even minor rule transgressions, and for undesirable behaviors, such as the birth of an additional child, or the failure to get children immunized, or the truancy of a child (Center on Hunger and Poverty 1998). As a result, welfare caseloads are falling rapidly.

Taken together, these several policy developments will inevitably have a large impact on the contemporary American labor market. The reason is simple and can be stated as a kind of policy law. Public programs which provide people with income that is not conditional on work create a floor under wages. In 19th century England the law was recognized as the principle of "less eligibility," a principle which meant that no one receiving poor relief should be as well off as the meanest independent laborer. Of course, people take jobs for many reasons beyond material incentives. Nevertheless, if people can survive without wage work in a manner judged reasonable by the standards of their community, many will, at least if the only work available to them entails dreary toil at low wages with little reason for pride. It follows that when these public supports are slashed, or when the stigma or harassment associated with receiving them is increased, more people will be willing to search for work, they will search more intensely, and more will take whatever job they can find.

During the turbulent 1960s, income-support programs expanded in all rich countries. Some social scientists applauded this expansion and the "decommodification" of labor that resulted when workers were shielded from the market by welfare state income protections (Esping-Andersen 1985: 31–36). Others bemoaned the expansion, pointing to the same relationship to draw a very different moral, that the terms of labor had become unresponsive to the market, or "inflexible," because income support programs were too generous. Either way, the "law" holds: Income protection programs come to constitute a floor under the terms of the labor market. The broad comparative evidence is compelling, and it has become more compelling in the last two decades, as income programs have been rolled back. Haveman points out that in countries where income support programs, such as unemployment benefits or assistance for poor families, provide only low benefits, particularly the U.S., the United Kingdom, and Japan, wages for the low-skilled fell sharply during the 1980s, by between ten and twenty-five percent. But in countries with generous programs, the wages of the less skilled did not fall, and measures of income inequality did not rise as they did in the United States, a development often pejoratively labeled "wage inflexibility" (Haveman 1997; Organization for Economic Cooperation and Development 1994; Esping-Andersen 1990). A similar relationship between welfare benefit levels and the wages of poor women eligible for welfare has been shown in the United States. Even under the old AFDC program, it was the states that set benefit levels, which varied widely. Elaine McCrate shows that these state-to-state variations in benefit levels were correlated with variations in the earnings of less-educated women. With each one-hundred-dollar drop in the benefit package, the wages of women with a high-school degree or less fell by three percent (McCrate 1997). Similarly, Michael Hout shows that cuts in the real value of AFDC benefits in the 1980s combined with the erosion of the real value of the legal minimum wage to depress the earnings of less-educated women (Hout 1997; Moffitt 1992).

So one way that welfare cutbacks will affect labor markets is clear. It will lower wages, especially in the already low wage sectors of the labor market.

As hundreds of thousands of women lose welfare benefits, whether because of time limits or sanctions or bureaucratic snafus, they will stream into the labor market to compete with other women (and men) for less-skilled and low-paying jobs. And wages in these sectors of the labor market will fall, by estimates as high as twelve percent (Mishel and Schmitt 1995). They will fall more in states where proportionately more families are on welfare. Chris Tilly estimates a wage reduction of twenty-six percent in New York City or the displacement of 58,000 workers, or some combination of the two (Tilly 1996). A cautionary word, however. The emphasis on the impact of welfare cutoffs on wages does not mean that all or even most of the people cut from the rolls will actually get jobs. Cutoffs depress wages even if their effect is only to enlarge the pool of people searching for work. In fact, the vast majority of people dropped from the rolls in New York State did not find work, at least not legal work, and similar albeit less dramatic findings are reported from other states (Parrott 1998).

Constructing the Culture of Work Enforcement

I said at the outset that the bearing of welfare on labor markets is not only the result of the interplay between the material incentives of wage work and welfare. Welfare programs amid the discourse which surrounds them also help to define the identities of those who participate in the labor market and those who don't. The campaign to reform welfare was itself a powerful intervention in American culture which argued the worthlessness of poor women raising children on the dole. And the new punitive practices ushered in by the legislation—sometimes called "tough love"—reinforce those denigrating meanings. Indeed, at first glance the campaign to reform welfare seemed to be entirely about questions of the personal morality of the women who subsist on the dole. Certainly it was not about labor markets. The problem was, the argument went, that a too generous welfare system was leading women to spurn wage work for lives of idleness and "dependency" (Fraser and Gordon 1994). Also, too generous payments, too laxly administered, were undermining sexual and family morality among the poor. Women, even teenagers, were having sex and bearing out-of-wedlock babies whose fathers easily walked away, all because they knew they could turn to welfare.

These sorts of charges had been aired by Republicans for decades. As early as 1960, Barry Goldwater asserted that welfare "transforms the individual being into a dependent animal creature." Republican political leaders, and especially Richard Nixon and later Ronald Reagan who used the bully pulpit of the presidency to popularize the image of the "welfare queen," kept up the assault, rightly perceiving that the association of the Democrats with welfare was a vulnerability for the Democrats and an opportunity for the Republicans. Kevin Phillips, for example, lists welfare with rising crime, judicial permissiveness, riots, and the death penalty in accounting for "much of the critical GOP momentum in the Nixon and Reagan years" (Phillips 1993:248). Meanwhile, conservative think tanks sponsored the policy intellectuals, the books, articles, conferences, and reports that kept welfare in the news (Williams 1996).[3] Then in the 1990s, and especially during the 1992 presidential campaign, the Democrats joined in. Bill Clinton, eager to show his credentials as a "New Democrat," hit upon "End welfare as we know it" as a campaign slogan and the lid was off; Democrats and Republicans began to compete for the political support that could be gained by tapping the deep antipathies in American culture toward the poor, toward Black and Latina minorities who were widely understood to be the main beneficiaries of welfare, and also tapping the energy and excitement evoked by talk of women and sex and sin.

None of this talk was about labor markets. Rather, everyone focused relentlessly on the ostensibly perverse effects of welfare on the creatures who received it. Yet it had a good deal to do with labor markets, for it created a national drama which heaped insult on women who were poor if they were presumed not to work.[4] The politics of the 1960s had reduced the stigma of being on the dole, and as a consequence, more people in need applied for welfare and the rolls rose; the politics of the 1990s increased stigma, and beginning in 1993, the rolls began to fall rapidly.[5]

All this began before the legislative overhaul of welfare. Encouraged first by the Bush administration and then by the Clinton administration, the states began to experiment with new restrictions, with lower grant levels, or new behavioral conditions on the receipt of aid, or simply the requirement that people work instead of receiving cash assistance. In Wisconsin, for example, the state welfare department announced it would require "immediate, universal work—no exemptions, exceptions or delays" (DeParle 1997). Meanwhile, the use of sanctions for presumed rule infractions increased, especially after the federal welfare overhaul. In March 1998 a federal study showed that in one three-month period the previous year, thirty-eight percent of the recipients who were dropped from welfare nationally were dropped because they were sanctioned. Georgia families who received two sanctions were banned from assistance for life. The *Washington Post* of March 23, 1998 reported that in Alabama, recipients could lose benefits for failing to show up for an appointment.[6] Mississippi succeeded in slashing the number of families receiving assistance by more than half between 1993 and 1997, and the ready use of sanctions for rule infractions appears to have been the main method for reducing the rolls (Brister et al. 1997). At the same time, investigative procedures to determine the eligibility of new applicants, including fingerprinting and drug tests, were elaborated, all justified by the need to root out fraud, but all with the inevitable consequence of reducing the numbers of poor families who complete the application process.

The point I want to make about these new practices is that they are simultaneously material and cultural in their effects. Grants are reduced, or terminated, obviously a very material change. But material practices, especially material practices with such awesome consequences as the loss of a welfare grant, are also cultural because they help to shape the way people think about themselves and their world. Conversely, so are cultural practices also material, because by helping to shape the way people think about themselves and their world, they change the way they respond to material conditions. The years-long campaign against welfare was a kind of theater which changed the way many Americans thought about welfare, and even changed the way recipients thought about welfare, making it less likely that women would apply for aid if they could somehow survive without it. In the same vein, welfare practices which require fingerprinting and intrusive investigations as a condition of aid heighten the stigma of welfare receipt, which leads many women to shun the dole for whatever work they can get. In fact, many women have always chosen to work rather than be exposed to the shame of welfare, even when the wages they earned did not make up for their added costs in day care and transportation, leaving them worse off than welfare recipients (Edin and Lein 1997). Inevitably, as stigmatizing rituals proliferate, the shame of welfare increases, and more women will work.

Workfare

A good number of states and localities are responding to mandatory work requirements by creating "workfare" programs, and these new programs illustrate the way material and cultural sanctions interact to weaken labor markets. Usually this means that women are given job assignments with public or private employers, for whom they work in exchange for their grants. Sometimes the grant itself is "diverted" to the employer, and the recipient is paid a wage, usually the minimum wage. The labor market implications are clear and dramatic. In New York City, for example, where some 34,000 recipients are enrolled in the city's dubiously named Work Experience program, recipients work for city agencies in exchange for their benefits. (After the Labor Department ruled that recipients were entitled to the equivalent of the minimum wage, the number of hours they were required to work was limited in New York City to about twenty hours.) These people clean the parks, the streets, and the subways, doing the work that until recently was done by tens of thousands of unionized city workers whose jobs were lost through attrition (Greenhouse 1998).

Elsewhere, recipients are being assigned to private sector employers. The roster of corporate partners includes some of the biggest companies in the country: Bell Atlantic, Federal Express, United Parcel Services, National Telecommunications, Marriott, and so on, according to a 1997 memo from the Office of the Governor of New Jersey. The incentives to employers are substantial. They can virtually deduct wage costs from their taxes, and they often receive direct subsidies from the welfare budget as well.[7] There is no systematic accounting of just what is happening to people in these private sector workfare arrangements, but local press reports give reason for alarm. In Kentucky, for example, the minimum wage requirement is evaded by defining these work placements as training, in punctuality and personal hygiene. This enables the state to assign recipients for a full forty-hour week, according to the *Lexington Herald-Leader* of October 27, 1997. In Georgia, a welfare program with the acronym PEACH has launched an initiative called WORK FIRST, through which it enlists businesses to hire recipients in return for subsidies and tax credits. The businesses can also receive the recipients' welfare checks. In Mississippi, welfare recipients are sent to work in chicken- and catfish-processing plants. A catfish plant comptroller praised the Mississippi Department of Human Services for refusing welfare to those who quit. These businesses pay only $1 an hour for the first six months, and the state provides the $4.15 required to bring earnings up to the minimum wage, using in part welfare and food stamp money, according to the *New York Times* of November 26, 1997. In Salt Lake City, the head of a temp agency told the press that without workers from welfare, they would have to raise wages, maybe by five percent (Uchitelle 1997).

In Baltimore, $6.00-an-hour janitors in nine public schools were replaced with recipients who cost the schools only $1.50 an hour. The

City-Wide Bus Company there made the same deal, hiring recipients at a cost to the company of $1.50 an hour. Also in Baltimore, Johns Hopkins University put its staff of full-time food service workers on part time, and made up the difference with workfare recipients (Baldwin 1998). And when the Baltimore Omni Inner Harbor hotel became embroiled in a wage dispute with unionized housekeepers, it began using welfare recipients as cleaners. These sorts of arrangements obviously create an extremely vulnerable and cheap workforce, and that is part of my point. But the other part is that coerced and very low wage work degrades people on the dole, and displays that degradation to a wider audience. These practices follow in the tradition of age-old relief rituals which branded paupers with the iron, the stocks, or the workhouse. A similar ritual is contained in contemporary practices. Mickey Kaus understands that well:

> [W]hat's most important is not whether sweeping streets or cleaning buildings helps Betsy Smith, single teenage parent and high school dropout, learn skills that will help her find a private sector job. It is whether the prospect of sweeping streets and cleaning buildings for a welfare grant will deter Betsy Smith from having the illegitimate child that drops her out of school and onto welfare in the first place—or, failing that, whether the sight of Betsy Smith sweeping streets after having her illegitimate child will discourage her younger sisters and neighbors from doing as she did. (Kaus 1986)

Look again at the New York City workfare program. Workfare recipients are a cheap replacement for city workers, an arrangement that threatens to weaken the unionized municipal workforce. They are also being made into a kind of public display of what it means to be on the dole. The workfare recipients wear bright orange vests, and they move through the parks, the streets, and the subways carrying big wire trash cans. They complain of being denied regulation equipment issued to other workers, and sometimes of being denied elementary decencies like bathrooms or lockers. It is not easy for them to complain, since sanctions for rule infractions of one kind or another are used wantonly. Some forty percent of the people who moved through the program have been punished with benefit cuts (Center for Law and Social Policy 1997). Just how arbitrarily sanctions are imposed is suggested by the fact that eighty-five percent of the sanctions that were appealed were reversed at fair hearings. Taken together, and especially taken together with the barrage of public insult that constitutes our public discourse on welfare policy, these practices go far toward making recipients into public pariahs, just as Mickey Kaus recommended.

The overall conclusion seems to me inescapable, and can be stated briefly. At the close of the 20th century, the United States has reinvented the restrictive and degrading methods of poor relief that we had once thought belonged to the 19th century. Then, coercion and a harsh culture combined to cheapen labor, and to make many workers compliant. But not all workers, and not all of the time. Toward the end of the 19th century, an unbridled industrial capitalism had helped to generate an unprecedented era of protest and tumult. Over the course of the century that followed, successive periods of protest gradually forced the development of public programs that at least partially regulated industry, and provided a measure of economic security to ordinary people.

In recent decades, scholars scrutinizing these programs proposed, reasonably enough, that they served important purposes in maintaining the stability of our economy and polity. It was not only and not mainly that public programs protected people from the most disruptive consequences of a ceaselessly changing capitalist economy, but it was also that the existence of such protections helped to maintain social cohesion and political legitimacy in the face of hardship and social dislocation. Three decades of relative domestic peace seem to have made an aggrandizing business community forgetful of these propositions. It may well be that nothing less than a resurgence of protest and tumult from below, on a scale that threatens to make American society ungovernable, will be required merely to preserve and restore the reforms won over the course of the 20th century.

NOTES

1. To be sure, critics often claimed that welfare absorbed as much as twenty percent of the federal budget, but such estimates are misleading since they include funds for other programs that also reach the poor, such as medical insurance, and tax subsidies to low wage workers.

2. Initially immigrants were also barred from the Supplementary Security Income program, which affects primarily the indigent aged. That restriction was subsequently modified. There are also complicated conditions, some of them the result of modifications introduced subsequent to the passage of the welfare reform law of 1996, under which some legal immigrants remain eligible for aid from some programs.

3. For discussions of the broader business mobilization to roll back government spending and taxation, see Piven and Cloward 1993; Edsall 1984: Chapter 3; Ferguson and Rogers 1986; Burch 1997.

4. I say "presumed" because the data in fact suggest that there is a good deal of movement between work and welfare among poor women, and in fact that a substantial proportion of the women work or search for work while they are on the rolls. For a discussion, see Harris 1993 and Spalter-Roth et al. 1994.

5. The Department of Health and Human Services reported that between January 1993 and September 1997, the recipient population declined by 31 percent nationally.

6. To make matters worse, the sanctioning process appears to be riddled with errors. In the aforementioned *Washington Post* article, a former welfare administrator from Utah was reported to have written that half of the sanctions ordered under a pilot program were done in error.

7. The Balanced Budget Act passed in the summer of 1997 provided a tax credit worth 35 percent of the first $10,000 to employers who hired long term welfare recipients. In addition, the Work Opportunity Tax Credit provides a credit of 35 percent of the first $6,000 paid to individuals in targeted groups. See Center for Community Change 1997.

REFERENCES

AFL-CIO Public Policy Department
1996   Labor Confronts Welfare Reform: An AFL-CIO Guide to State Activity. Washington, D.C.

Baldwin, Marc
1998   Welfare and Jobs: Rebuilding the Labor Market from the Bottom Down. WorkingUSA (January/February).

Brecher, Jeremy
1998   American Labor on the Eve of the Millennium. Z Magazine (December).

Brister, Bill M., Jesse D. Beeler, and Sharon Chambry
1997   Implementation Process Study: Mississippi's Temporary Assistance for Needy Families Program. Center for Applied Research, Millsaps College: Jackson, Mississippi (December).

Burch, Philip H.
1997   Reagan, Bush, and Right-Wing Politics: Elites, Think Tanks, Power, and Policy. *In* Part B: The American Right Wing at Court and in Action: Supreme Court Nominations and Major Policy Making. Research in Political Economy. Supplement 1. Pp. 71–120.

Center for Community Change
1997   Spotlight on the Welfare to Work Partnership. Organizing, no. 6 (November).

Center on Hunger and Poverty
1998   Are States Improving the Lives of Poor Families? A Scale Measure of State Welfare Policies. Tufts University: Medford, Massachusetts (February): 1–13.

Center for Law and Social Policy
1997   CLASP Update. Washington, D.C. (November 25).

DeParle, Jason
1997   Getting Opal Caples To Work. New York Times Magazine (August 24): 33–61.

Department of Health and Human Services
1998   http://www.acf.dhhs.gov/news/caseload.htm, February 19.

Dietrich, Sharon, Maurice Emsellem, and Jim Williams
1998   Comments of the National Employment Law Project to the Proposed TANF Regulations. National Employment Law Project, February 18.

Diller, Mathew
1998   Dismantling the Welfare State: Welfare Reform and Beyond. Stanford Law and Policy Review (Winter):19–43.

Edin, Kathryn, and Laura Lein
1997   Making Ends Meet: How Single Mothers Survive Welfare and Low-Wage Work. New York: Russell Sage Foundation.

Edsall, Thomas Byrne
1984   The New Politics of Inequality. New York: W. W. Norton.

Esping-Andersen, Gosta
1985   The Politics against Markets: The Social Democratic Road to Power. Princeton, New Jersey: Princeton University Press.
1990   The Three Worlds of Welfare Capitalism. Princeton, New Jersey: Princeton University Press.

Ferguson, Thomas, and Joel Rogers
1986   Right Turn. New York: Hill and Wang.

Fraser, Nancy, and Linda Gordon
1994   A Genealogy of Dependency: Tracing a Keyword of the Welfare State. *In* Critical Politics: From the Personal to the Global. P. Jones, ed. Melbourne: Arena Publications.

Freeman, Richard B.
1996   Toward an Apartheid Economy? Harvard Business Review (September–October).

Goldwater, Barry
1960   Wanted: A More Conservative GOP. Human Events, 18 (February): Section II.

Greenhouse, Steven
1998   Many Participants in Workfare Take the Place of City Workers. New York Times (April 13):B8.

Harris, Kathleen Mullan
1993   Work and Welfare among Single Mothers in Poverty. American Journal of Sociology, 99(2) (September).

Haveman, Robert
1997   Equity with Employment. Boston Review (Summer):3–8.

Henwood, Doug
1996   Demote the General Welfare. Left Business Observer, no. 74 (October 7).
1997   Measuring Privilege. Left Business Observer, no. 78 (July 17).

Hout, Michael
1997   The Effects of Welfare, the Minimum Wage, and Tax Credits on Low Wage Labor Markets. Politics and Society, 25(4) (December):513–24.

Kaus, Mickey
1986   The Work Ethic State. New Republic (July 6).

Massey, Douglas
1998   March of Folly: U.S. Immigration Policy after Nafta. American Prospect (March/April):22–33.

McCrate, Elaine
1997   Welfare and Women's Earnings. Politics and Society, 25(4) (December): 417–42.

Meerpol, Michael
n.d.   A Comment on the Wood-Magdoff vs. Cloward-Piven Debate. Unpublished manuscript, Western New England College, Springfield, Massachusetts.

Mishel, Lawrence, and John Schmitt
1995   Cutting Wages by Cutting Welfare. Briefing Paper of the Economic Policy Institute, Washington, D.C.

Moffitt, Robert
1992   Incentive Effects of the US Welfare System. Journal of Economic Literature, 30(1) (March).

Morley, Morris, and James Petras
1998   Wealth and Poverty in the National Economy. In Social Policy and the Conservative Agenda. Clarence Y. Lo and Michael Schwartz, eds. Pp. 121–41. Malden, Massachusetts: Blackwell.

Nathan, Richard, and Thomas L. Gais
1998   Ten Early Findings about the Newest New Federalism for Welfare. Paper presented at the Woodrow Wilson International Center for Scholars Con-

ference on "Welfare Reform: A Race to the Bottom?" Washington, D.C., Smithsonian Institution (March 27).

Organization for Economic Cooperation and Development
1994   The OECD Jobs Study: Evidence and Explanations. Paris: OECD.

Parrott, Sharon
1998   Welfare Recipients Who Found Jobs: What Do We Know about Their Employment and Earnings? Washington, D.C., Center on Budget and Policy Priorities. November 16.

Phillips, Kevin
1993   Boiling Point. New York: Random House.

Piven, Frances Fox
1997   The New Reserve Army of Labor. *In* Audacious Democracy: Labor, Intellectuals and the Social Reconstruction of America. Steven Fraser and Joshua B. Freeman, eds. Pp. 106–18. New York: Houghton Mifflin Co., A Mariner Original.

Piven, Frances Fox, and Richard A. Cloward
1993   Regulating the Poor. New York: Pantheon Books.

Reich, Robert
1998   Broken Faith: Why We Need to Renew the Social Compact. The Nation (February 16):11–17.

Schuck, Peter H.
1998   The Open Society. New Republic (April 13):16–18.

Spalter-Roth, Roberta, Beverly Burr, Lois Shaw, and Heidi Hartman
1994   Welfare That Works. Institute for Women's Policy Research, Washington, D.C.

Tilly, Chris
1996   Workfare's Impact on the New York City Labor Market: Lower Wages and Worker Displacement. New York: Russell Sage Foundation.

Uchitelle, Louis
1997   Push to Put Welfare Recipients to Work Pushes Others from Jobs. New York Times (April 1):1.

Williams, Lucy A.
1996   The Right's Attack on Aid to Families with Dependent Children. Public Eye, 10:1–18.

Wolff, Edward N.
1995   How the Pie Is Sliced: America's Growing Concentration of Wealth. American Prospect (Summer):58–64.

Chapter 6

Poor Women, Fair Work, and Welfare-to-Work That Works

Sandra Morgen and Jill Weigt

In 1964, at the launching of the "War on Poverty," 17.4 percent of families in the United States had incomes below the poverty line (U.S. Census Bureau 1997a). Within a decade that percentage had dropped to 9.7 percent of families (U.S. Census Bureau 1997a). But in the last twenty years the number of families in poverty has grown rapidly, and by the late 1990s over 12 percent of families fell below the poverty level, including over one-fifth of all children (U.S. Census Bureau 1997a; U.S. Census Bureau 1997b). That the percentage of those in poverty is once again so high, reversing the gains achieved in the immediate aftermath of concerted social policies to reduce poverty, should be a matter of grave public concern.

Instead, today's political rhetoric is vastly more concerned with ending welfare dependency than with ameliorating poverty. Almost all the social programs that were the battalions in the War on Poverty have been demobilized, defined as dependency-creating programs that the world's most powerful economic power cannot afford financially or socially. The climax of a concerted two-decade attack on liberal social welfare and labor policies was congressional passage of the Personal Responsibility and Work Opportunity Reconciliation Act (PRWORA) in 1996. This legislation ended the more than one-half-century old Aid to Families with Dependent Children (AFDC) program, devolving the authority to develop the new welfare program—Temporary Assistance to Needy Families (TANF)—to the states.

The TANF program is based on the assumption that the cure for poverty is participation in the paid labor force for all able-bodied adults, including single mothers of infants and young and/or disabled children. The intent of the program is to reduce drastically cash assistance caseloads and move welfare recipients rapidly into the labor force. The claim that the cure for poverty is work is based on at least two interrelated assumptions: that participation in the paid labor force brings wages into the home and that it sets an example for children about the value of work, thereby subverting the pattern of intergenerational poverty. Current federal and state welfare policy assumes that the primary obstacle to participation in the labor force by the able-bodied adult poor is an inferior work ethic, or at least an unwillingness on the part of the poor to attach themselves in a long-term way to the labor market (Handler and Hasenfeld 1997).

There is a substantial social science literature that challenges the assumptions behind these new welfare policies (Edin and Lein 1997; Epstein 1997; Fitchen 1995; Handler 1995; Handler and Hasenfeld 1997; Schein 1995; Schram 1995; Spalter-Roth, Burr, Hartmann, and Shaw 1995; Swigonski 1996). Much of this research documents the fact that the majority of welfare recipients have worked and often continue to work in the paid labor force either at the same time that they receive welfare benefits or by cycling between work and welfare. Other studies conclude that the assumptions and analysis behind the attack on AFDC and other social programs stem from a failure to recognize structural causes of poverty, focusing instead on human capital explanations, which have never been shown to account fully for the prevalence or demographics of poverty in the United States (Berrick 1995; Handler and Hasenfeld 1997; Katz 1989; Pearce 1993). Nevertheless, "the new [political] consensus on welfare" that resulted in PRWORA in 1996 is, simply stated, that the AFDC program was ineffective and wasteful; that it contributed to a pernicious cycle of poverty by devaluing work and enabling long-term dependency; and that welfare-to-work programs and time limits on receipt of cash benefits best serve both the nation's and the poor's best interest.

In the wake of a social policy change of the magnitude of PRWORA, researchers are now focusing on understanding welfare-to-work programs, the centerpiece of the new social welfare policies in place today. This essay emerges from our contention that social scientists, advocates for the poor, and the poor themselves should carefully evaluate both the current programs and previous labor and social welfare policies that can shed light on how welfare-to-work policies might reduce poverty, not simply welfare caseloads. We join those who argue that job creation should be a central component of a serious policy effort to reduce poverty (Handler and Hasenfeld 1997). Specifically, in this chapter we re-examine primary and secondary research on the most recent large-scale public-sector work program in the United States, the Comprehensive

Employment and Training Act (CETA), the federal jobs and job training program that served millions of Americans between July 1, 1974, and September 30, 1983.

We argue that public-sector employment such as the CETA Public Service Employment (PSE) program can be an important means of expanding and upgrading work options for those in poverty, including TANF recipients. In support of this argument, we re-examine the historical record documenting the successes and problems of CETA. In addition to using secondary sources to assess the nine-year CETA program, we also draw on research that one of us (Morgen) has conducted on the use of state programs such as CETA by social movements and community-based organizations that aim to combine jobs and training programs with social transformation goals.

Our goal in re-examining CETA is twofold: (1) to use CETA as an example of how relatively successful social welfare and labor policies have been defined as failures by conservatives intent on dismantling the welfare state; and (2) to demonstrate the potential of public service employment programs to provide "fair work" (Rose 1995) for poor women who seek assistance from the state. Nancy Rose defines fair work as "public employment job creation and related education and training programs—that respect the dignity of the individual, have voluntary participation, base payments on labor market wages and often develop innovative projects" (1995:3). The concept of fair work appears consistent with the goal of using a labor-force attachment strategy to reduce poverty, but it is an employment strategy that is aimed at paying people living wages and providing employment supports (benefits, training, etc.) that ease the challenges faced by single parents in combining paid labor and family responsibilities.

CETA Revisited: The Value of Public-Sector Employment Programs

CETA was authorized by Congress in late 1973 and lasted for almost a decade before it was replaced by the passage of the Reagan administration's Jobs Training Partnership Act (JTPA) in 1982. CETA was the core of a labor policy that provided job training and job opportunities to a variety of low-income groups, including unemployed workers, the poor, displaced homemakers, and youth. It was the first major public-sector jobs creation program since the Great Depression, though state investment in jobs and job training programs had flourished for a decade before the CETA authorization.

During the 1960s a number of job programs developed that subsidized training or work for low-income youth and adults, including the 1962 Manpower Development and Training Administration (MDTA) and the 1964 Economic Opportunity Act programs such as the Neighborhood Youth Corps, the Jobs Corps, and the New Careers program. Federal work programs for welfare recipients included the 1962 Community Work and Training Program, the 1964 Work Experience and Training Program, and the 1967 Work Incentive Program. As unemployment skyrocketed and recession deepened in the early 1970s, the government developed the Public Employment Program (PEP) (1971–1973) and, finally, Public Service Employment, which was a major component of CETA. With PEP and PSE, the federal government stepped back into the business of large-scale public-sector jobs creation for the first time since the 1943 demise of the Works Progress Administration (WPA) (Naples 1991; Rose 1995).

CETA represented a moment in U.S. labor and social welfare policy that acknowledged a key role for the federal government in creating job opportunities for individuals and communities affected by structural economic conditions that foster and exacerbate poverty. The pressure to develop the program came from a severe economic crisis that began with a sharp recession in 1969. Despite President Richard Nixon's vehement opposition to public-sector job programs, unemployment rates were so high and congressional pressure for a federal jobs creation program so strong that, finally, PEP was created in 1971. Two years later, CETA combined a vast array of jobs and job training programs and dramatically expanded federal support in these areas. While the public-sector employment program was initially only a small part of CETA programming, another major recession in November 1973 greatly expanded the authorization for public service jobs creation.

CETA was a huge program that accounted for $55 billion in expenditures and employed millions of men and women over its nine-year life (Franklin and Ripley 1984:22). PSE accounted for between one-third and one-half of CETA expenditures from the mid- through the late 1970s, dropping to 22 percent of expenditures in 1982 (after Reagan's election), the last year of the program (Franklin and Ripley 1984:25). At its peak, the PSE program had almost three-quarters of a million participants (Rose 1995:110). CETA's critics went after PSE, however, and succeeded in dramatically reducing and regulating that program when CETA was reauthorized by Congress in late

1978. More significant, CETA was replaced by the Jobs Training Partnership Act in 1982. The JTPA was the first programmatic exemplar of Reagan's "New Federalism," emphasizing human capital explanations for poverty and job training programs developed or monitored by private-sector business councils as the primary anti-poverty strategy of the federal government (Lafer 1995).

The program life of CETA overlaps substantially with a period characterized by the proliferation of community-based and state-sponsored programs, which were seeded by the social movements of the 1960s and early 1970s including the women's movement; the Civil Rights movement; and the identity politics movements of African Americans, Latinos, Native Americans, Asian Americans, and gays and lesbians. A stunning array of organizations emerged that sought to sustain and expand the gains of these movements in areas ranging from employment and health care to education, community development, and the like. While it is impossible to determine exactly how many of these organizations were able to hire staff through either PSE or other titled programs of CETA, approximately one-fourth of PSE participants in 1977 worked for a nonprofit organization, and in 1975, 30 percent of those employed in nonprofits worked for community-based organizations (CBOs) (Hallman 1980). Many of these CBOs were founded because mainstream nonprofit organizations and federal and state programs had neglected or ill served many low-income communities, communities of color, women, and others whose political subjectivities were mobilized by the powerful social movements of the period.

Fifteen years after the dissolution of the program, the political dust surrounding CETA may have cleared enough for a reconsideration of labor policies that include a public service jobs creation component. Indeed, CETA succeeded in a number of important ways. A major research study documented modest wage and employment gains for participants, with women registering greater economic gains than men and women of color posting the greatest economic boost of the studied target groups (Westat 1983, reported in Franklin and Ripley 1984:197). Grace Franklin and Randall Ripley conclude that rhetorical claims to the contrary, CETA had "positive and lasting economic benefits for participants" and a "favorable return on public investment from a societal point of view," though these positive accomplishments failed to "affect the political calculus that decided CETA's fate" (Franklin and Ripley 1984:198).

Additionally, CETA provided opportunities to those most disadvantaged in the job market and who were the least likely to have access to traditional job training programs. Over the lifetime of CETA, PSE increasingly targeted women, people of color, and low-income individuals (Rose 1995). Demetra Smith Nightingale and Carolyn Taylor O'Brien (1984) found PSE to have been "extremely valuable" in the development of community and public service careers for many minority and working-class people. Additionally, low-income individuals experienced a decrease in receipt of government aid after CETA participation (Westat 1983).

CETA played another important role that is rarely acknowledged in assessments of its programmatic value or legacy. Because CETA provided funds for job creation, it enabled a wide variety of community-based organizations to survive and provide needed social and human services within low-income communities or to staff nonprofit organizations that aimed to improve the lives of women, people of color, gays and lesbians, the poor, and other disenfranchised groups. Indeed, as we argue later, this aspect of the program provoked strong opposition from conservative scholars and politicians intent on dismantling the social welfare functions of the state.

This dimension of CETA is not well documented in the literature and particularly in the evaluation studies of CETA, which are usually the primary sources used to defend or attack the program retrospectively. Indeed, whatever data are available on this important aspect of CETA are more likely to be found in research on social movement organizations than in the evaluation studies of the program. CETA succeeded both in providing "fair work" for low-income people and in supporting community-based organizations that were an essential component of a federal anti-poverty strategy directed at empowering low-income communities. Thus, policymakers who want to go beyond reducing welfare caseloads to attack poverty should reassess the value of CETA's dual impact on low-income communities.

In this chapter, we have gathered accessible evidence about the use of CETA by community-based or grassroots organizations in order to emphasize the importance of this aspect of public sector jobs programs. We do not claim that the evidence we have gathered comes close to representing the full story of how the PSE program served as a crucial resource for the range of social movement or community-based organizations. Rather, we hope that highlighting this aspect of CETA will encourage other researchers to help tell more of the story.

Other sources confirm that CETA was a valuable resource for a host of feminist nonprofit organizations and CBOs with different but related goals.[1] CETA funds subsidized community development efforts aimed at promoting ethnic and racial empowerment.[2] The program supported workers in organizations that targeted low-income groups as well as affording other disadvantaged groups "fair work."[3] Through the Friends Outside/Family Aide Project, CETA participants assisted inmates and their families with various types of emotional, social, and financial support. Moreover, an Indiana program utilized CETA workers to staff the Park Department's Therapeutic Division, which provides recreation for mentally, physically, and emotionally disabled individuals. A Maryland Big Sisters/ Little Sisters program hired CETA employees to act as caseworkers who performed training, assessments, and interviews. In Virginia, CETA subsidized the training and employment of audio technicians for a nonprofit radio station serving the visually impaired.

In other cases, CETA bolstered training programs that attempted to generate structural change and helped initiate those which, while not explicitly feminist or progressive, provide examples of meaningful, empowering, community development–oriented work.[4] The Vets of Oregon Carpentry Project, for example, trained Vietnam veterans as union carpenters while renovating condemned homes. Similarly, the West Side Planning Group in Fresno, California, developed a family farm program that allowed participants to gain skills in farm management, equipment maintenance, harvesting, and marketing of produce (National Economic Development Law Project 1976). In addition, Nancy Naples's research on the Economic Opportunity Act's establishment and funding of Community Action Programs (CAPs) demonstrates an important precursor to CETA in the jobs programs of the 1960s, many of which simultaneously provided jobs for low-income people and community-based, grassroots services sorely needed by poor communities (Naples 1991 and 1998).

Our own investigations focus mainly on the women's and women's health movements and demonstrate that a number of women's health clinics and other health advocacy, information, or referral organizations turned to CETA as a means of funding paid staff positions and, especially, as a means of attracting low-income women to these organizations (Morgen 1990; Rose 1995; Matthews 1995; Hyde 1995; Schecter 1982). During the 1970s women's health activism flourished across the United States, bringing together the political visions of feminism, the community health movement, and widespread support for women's reproductive rights. Feminist health activists worked on many fronts to challenge women's lack of control over and participation in their own health care. The movement sought to transform women's health care in a wide variety of ways, including health education, health advocacy, providing alternative health care services, and working to change health care policy at the local, state, and federal levels. The broad-based movement built on the visions and energies released by progressive health reform in the 1960s, including the Civil Rights, community health, and free clinic movements.

In the 1960s, community action programs, funded by the Office of Economic Opportunity, multiplied the poor's access to decent health care, which began to increase in 1965 when the then new Medicaid and Medicare programs were established. But funding for community-based health initiatives decreased after Nixon axed most of the categorical programs and much of the federal funding that had been allocated during the War on Poverty. The women's health groups that took root in the mid-1970s had to look for new sources of support for community, primary, and preventive health care projects.

Some clinics refused on principle to take state moneys, fearing co-optation and avoiding the strong hand of what they called the "patriarchy." They relied on fees from services (sometimes reduced and sliding-scale fees); small-scale, community-based fundraising; and a pool of volunteers who comprised a significant portion of the staff in many of these clinics. But for those clinics that aimed to reach out to poor women, a reliance on fees-for-service and volunteer staff was not viable. On the one hand, poor women could not afford to pay enough for services, even with sliding-scale fees, to come close to the actual cost of those services. On the other hand, relying on volunteer staff, even for the nonphysician providers, was inconsistent with the political goals of many of these clinics. As a rule, these alternative health facilities valued having professional and nonprofessional staff who mirrored the communities being served in terms of their racial, ethnic, and/or class backgrounds.

But few poor or working-class women and few women of color could afford or were likely to choose to volunteer their labor to these organizations. They needed or were seeking paid employment; they did not have the resources to cover child-care costs while volunteering; or they did not have a desire to join a feminist organization, which they saw as being run by women whose needs, they imagined, were far different from their own. CETA became a strategy that some women's organizations used to diversify their staffs by race, class, and ethnicity. As one member of a California women's clinic explained:

> If our policy was to hire amongst the volunteers, we are not gonna get diversity in our paid staff . . . because, realistically, how many working class women

and women of color were gonna volunteer for a long time for this organization. . . . Eventually, after many difficult meetings we decided that the only way to diversify was to open up the health collective and to hire from outside (the volunteer pool) and that meant four new positions and finding CETA qualified women for these positions. (Morgen, forthcoming)

Being able to offer paid employment and job training to low-income women, including women of color, became a vital part of a strategy to develop health services and organizations that could meet the dual goal of providing quality health care and diversifying the staff and membership of these CBOs.

For example, in 1977, the Women's Health Clinic in which Sandra Morgen was doing fieldwork submitted an application to the regional CETA consortium to hire twelve women for a one-year health education and training project. The goals of the project were to provide opportunities for CETA-eligible women to work in the feminist clinic, which was imagined to be a supportive and empowering work environment; to learn job skills and work at a job usually unavailable to women without a college education and professional training; and to expand and diversify the staff of the clinic as a means of expanding and diversifying the client base of the clinic. The application was approved. In fact, the consortium added funding for several more than the applied-for CETA positions. With the successful receipt of this CETA contract, the staff of this clinic nearly tripled, and the proportion of staff who were women of color or whose incomes put them at or below the official poverty level more than tripled. Ultimately, the women hired through CETA had their contracts extended and worked at the clinic for eighteen months. Almost half of them were finally hired in permanent (non-CETA) jobs at the clinic, paid by funds from other grants and contracts the clinic received (Morgen 1990).

The PSE program enabled community-based organizations such as this community-based women's health clinic to hire staff, albeit temporarily, with the full wages and benefits paid through the federal program, to do work for which the agency or program could not otherwise afford to pay. In this example, the project enabled the clinic to design educational workshops and programs based on the health needs defined by the surrounding community, to help local women preserve and maintain their health and that of their households and become better health care consumers, to promote preventative care at existing health care facilities by providing client advocates and direct services, and to improve the responsiveness of services to the actual stated needs of consumers—all this while also employing and training fifteen low-income women over a period of fifteen months and creating longer-term job opportunities for a portion of this group. With the human resources to expand and improve programming and services, these temporary positions helped create the conditions that enabled these organizations to be competitive for other funds to support activities.

A number of other features of CETA made it an attractive source of funding for CBOs such as feminist health clinics and also made the program valuable for the women who were its targeted beneficiaries. First, CETA often involved a job training component designed to enhance the skills of employees at the same time that it provided needed work experience. The women employed at the health clinic received training as well as work experience in the content and techniques of community health education, the administration and organization of medical files, peer health counseling, routine lab work and pregnancy testing, and interviewing, as well as in other, more basic clerical and administrative skills. While, admittedly, there were not a wide variety of opportunities for these women to be hired for similar work outside the feminist clinic in this community, there were some such opportunities for community health workers thanks to state-funded community health initiatives begun in the 1960s and continuing through at least the late 1970s. Certainly there could be more such jobs today if the federal government decided to re-fund the much-needed community health programs.

Second, the legislation that authorized CETA mandated that employers pay CETA employees the "prevailing wages" of workers doing similar jobs in that agency or in the community. This meant that the wages received by the women hired through this CETA project were considerably higher than the wages they were likely to receive in the private-sector jobs they would have been likely to get (low-wage service-sector or manufacturing work). The prevailing-wage provision was particularly attractive to collectives such as the clinic discussed here, which paid all workers equal wages for ideological reasons. CETA funds enabled the Women's Health Clinic to attempt to circumvent hierarchical power structures by paying similar wages to all staff members and, in the words of the clinic's CETA application, "to create a feeling of self-worth and importance in all employees." A feminist clinic in California raised its own, very low base salaries when it contracted with CETA to hire employees, so that CETA workers would not earn more than their regular workers. Critics of CETA argued that paying the prevailing wage attracted workers away from the private (and especially minimum-wage) sector and kept CETA workers from seeking other employment, even though the CETA employment was temporary. Indeed, when CETA was reauthorized in 1978, it allowed employers to pay wages below the prevailing rate. The prevailing-wage provision, however, was one of the ways in which CETA worked not simply as a jobs program but simultaneously as an anti-poverty program.

Third, CETA permitted enough leeway in project design so that community-based organizations could launch or support valuable projects that followed from their missions, and the employed workers were given the opportunity to do socially valuable work that they could see was useful for their communities. For instance, in a staff meeting, Women's Health Clinic employees expressed their enthusiasm about the prospect of applying to CETA to "really do what we do, what we want to do," rather than taking money for drug abuse counseling out of necessity. Compared to many of the other jobs available for less-educated, less well trained workers, these positions often enabled employees to enjoy work and to benefit from the reality (not simply the rhetoric) that work could be meaningful.

Participating in purposeful work had a major impact on the CETA workers in intangible ways, which they voiced in staff meetings, personal interactions, and evaluations. Some remarked that they valued the learning experiences their work with the clinic afforded; one CETA participant at the Women's Health Clinic relayed the basis of her commitment: "I want to stay here because I keep learning." Others felt proud to be part of an organization giving back to their communities; by the time of the 1978 amendments, CETA workers in general were significantly integrated into the communities in which they worked (Mucciaroni 1990). One CETA employee, discussing the possible extension of the clinic's CETA funding said, "This place is unique—not a factory or a five and dime. We are making a valuable contribution." Still others expressed the impact of the experience on their own empowerment, on that of other women, and on their personal development. CETA employees' responses to a training evaluation indicated a myriad of positive emotions associated with the Women's Health Clinic, co-workers, the work to be performed, and the training sessions—satisfaction, accomplishment, trust, support, cooperation, comfort, confidence, and empowerment among other reactions. Such responses included "I learned to be more open minded," "I learned to speak calmly in a group," and "I learned not to be ashamed . . . of my ideas."

Moreover, their jobs with the health clinic created the opportunity for women of color and from poor families to participate actively in a grassroots organization and to influence its development and programs in ways that ultimately made the organization more welcoming for other poor and working-class women and women of color. This inclusion was expressed by a staff member on the first day of the CETA workers' training: "You are part of the Women's Center. You may find as you are involved (that) you are part of the Women's Center and part of it changing. You will actually be building this agency." Among the fifteen women hired through the CETA project at the health clinic, some had been on welfare for more than two years; some had never been on welfare; some came from families best characterized as the working poor; some came from families with long histories of dependence on welfare. These different experiences represent the diversity of those who live in poverty in this country, and having women with these different backgrounds on the staff contributed to their collective ability to envision and provide services and programs that met the various needs in the community.

We have presented examples of women's health movement organizations that used CETA to create decent jobs that often provided both training opportunities and meaningful work, in order to illustrate the larger point that CETA, and particularly the PSE program, may offer a model for a jobs creation strategy that could empower both low-income individuals and communities. Indeed, the evidence taken as a whole suggests that CETA may have been defined as a failure precisely because of one of its most significant successes. CETA often succeeded in providing better job alternatives than many private-sector jobs. In fact, private-sector employers and their Republican allies launched a concerted effort to curb programs such as CETA that afforded low-wage workers options in pay and working conditions (Lafer 1995).

The Attack on CETA and the Evolution of the "New Consensus on Welfare"

CETA became the target of a concerted attack by critics almost from the moment of the program's authorization. Positive effects of CETA were often dismissed or ignored, obscured beneath an image its opponents painted of CETA as a wasteful governmental debacle. In part, CETA's demise rested on the long historical ambivalence of U.S. policymakers to public works programs. Viewed as a means of massive pork-barreling by their opponents and as vehicles to employment and skills development by their supporters, public employment programs have long provided an ideological battle-ground for competing perspectives.

Critics lambasted CETA on several fronts. Allegations of political pa-tronage, substitution of regular governmental employees with non-union-ized, temporary CETA workers ("substitution"), and mismanagement were commonplace. While there is evidence in the program's early years that po-litical connections and power influenced prime sponsorships as well as the distribution of individual positions (Dubin 1987; Baumer and Van Horn 1985), there are also data that show the practice of political patronage de-clined as the initial kinks in the program were worked out (Baumer and Van Horn 1985:75–76). Accusations of substitution brought one of CETA's pri-mary objectives—the creation of new jobs—into question. Estimates of substitution ran as high as 40 percent of all CETA placements (Mirengoff et al. 1980, cited in Dubin 1987). Yet at least one team of scholars suggests that the Department of Labor never produced credible proof that localities reg-ularly substituted existing jobs for CETA positions (Baumer and Van Horn 1985:77). In the face of the massive budget cuts, localities that used CETA-supported workers in what may have looked like substitution were often re-placing workers their budgets could not sustain.

Mismanagement, in the form of insufficient trainee workloads and supervision, "ghost" employees, overpayment, and falsification of rec-ords, became a favorite charge and site of investigation for critics (Dubin 1987). Gordon Lafer (1995), however, contends that several audits of the program uncovered only sporadic examples of impropriety. In fact, he conjectures that incidence of fraud under the JTPA at least matches that found in post-1978 CETA. The supposed perpetrators of the alleged fraud (low-income individuals versus private-sector employers) and their corresponding societal power account for the disproportionate attention allotted to each. Moreover, CETA criteria granted room for innovation, giving rise to projects that some critics labeled as frivolous, such as the Artists-in-Residence program, the use of CETA trainees as New York City zookeepers (Dubin 1987), a nude sculpting workshop, and body drum-ming classes (Bennett 1978).

Another oft-repeated criticism of CETA is that employees tended to be among the more educated and employable of the millions of unemployed CETA-eligible population. William Mirengoff and Lester Rindler and their colleagues report that 75 percent of CETA participants in PSE had some post–high school education, and as many as 16 percent had four or more years (1978: 169). This is no doubt attributable to the fact that a proportion of PSE positions were professional or para-professional jobs that required a higher level of education and skills than many other CETA positions. Moreover, while it is true that this group were among the more "employable" of the unemployed, this pool of unemployed included many young people who were the first in their families to get any college education or to complete college. They were beneficiaries of expanded educational opportunities hard won by the Civil Rights and women's movements (affirmative action, expansion of public higher education, increases in student loans) but who continued to be disadvantaged in a job market that was still often unresponsive to people of color and white (especially working-class) women who wanted better-paying, higher-status jobs in occupations traditionally open mainly to whites or men. Rather than seeing CETA as failing because not all its participants were among the poorest of the poor or the least employable, the program might be seen as successful because it extended job opportunity to a broad mix of participants.

CETA critics, including Charles Murray, whose work so influenced the Reagan administration, could not contest the empirical data that demonstrated that program participants benefited from the training and job experience they got through the program. Instead, critics tend to argue that the results were not as impressive as the expectations of the program. Murray, for example, notes that while clients were able to increase their incomes because of job training, "effects of this magnitude were far from the results that had been anticipated when the program began" (1984:38). While a wide variety of scholars acknowledge that CETA did have imperfections, many now agree that CETA was a victim of an ideological agenda, the prevailing political climate, bad press, and a series of institutional shortcomings not integral to the idea of federal jobs training and creation (Mucciaroni 1990; Dubin 1987; Baumer and Van Horn 1985; Mirengoff et al. 1980; Lafer 1995).

The delegitimation of CETA in the early 1980s served the neoconservative agenda in a number of important ways. First, in defining CETA as a failure, the groundwork was laid for a radically different labor policy in the incarnation of the JTPA. Second, the end of the public-sector jobs program served the historically specific purpose of financially destabilizing a wide variety of CBOs whose missions conflicted with the Right's social agenda. Finally, the rhetorical story of the failure of CETA was an important chapter in the evolving "new consensus on welfare" that resulted in PRWORA in 1996.

The "end of welfare as we know it" has been gradually evolving since the early 1980s with reduced federal moneys for a variety of social programs for the poor, the enactment of the Family Support Act in 1988, and a dizzying array of state waivers that constituted significant changes in welfare long before the 1996 passage of the PRWORA. Indeed, the critique and final elimination of CETA were part of this concerted effort to reduce both state social welfare spending and state programs that "interfered" with private-sector labor supply and wages.

In 1982, Richard Viguerie, a key political strategist for the powerful right-wing coalition that included the Republican Party, published an important and revealing editorial in the *New York Times* headlined "Defund the Left" (1982: A23). Viguerie argued that "since the 1970's, hundreds of millions of dollars—maybe more than $1 billion—in taxpayers' money have been spent each year to support and spread political views that the American people have consistently and overwhelmingly rejected." Viguerie specifically refers to federal grants to a long list of "liberal" organizations, including Planned Parenthood, the National Urban League, the National Council of Churches, the National Welfare Rights Organization, and others. Viguerie concludes: "Defunding the left has become one of the top priorities of many conservatives."

It is important to clarify that "defunding the Left" was not about eliminating federal funds for revolutionary or "extremist" organizations (unless anything left of center is extreme). Rather, defunding the Left meant targeting much federal support for human services, community-based organizations, labor, civil rights, and a host of other simply "liberal" causes. A recently published study of conservative think tanks and foundations by Jean Stefancic and Richard Delgado (1996) points out the cruel irony that the "defund the Left" strategy was a very well funded campaign, spearheaded by conservative foundations, to delegitimate the social welfare programs and roles of the state.

The attacks on CETA were part of this effort to defund the Left, and PSE was particularly vulnerable, since nonprofit community-based organizations had successfully used CETA funds to staff and support struggling organizations that simultaneously employed the unemployed and put them to work on behalf of low-income families, women, communities of color, and others on the "Left." It was well recognized that the Reagan administration was especially bent on dismantling CETA (Dubin 1987) in what Timothy Conlan termed "a comprehensive assault on the intergovernmental dimensions of public sector activism" (1988:224).

Republican efforts and the program's increasing political unpopularity among congressional Democrats and the U.S. population eventually brought the demise of CETA in 1982. Its successor, JTPA, became law October 1, 1983, drastically altering federal employment and training policy. The Reagan administration campaigned for the exclusion of public service employment under JTPA, a move that wrought dire consequences for the CBOs and nonprofits CETA had subsidized (Nightingale and O'Brien 1984; Hyde 1995). Even from the early debates over the formation of CETA, Republicans lobbied for policy arrangements they knew would thwart the CBOs created by the War on Poverty (Baumer and Van Horn 1985). PSE itself was eliminated in 1981; of the 400,000 PSE jobs scrapped that year, one-third were with nonprofit organizations (Nightingale 1985:3). Overall, 270,000 jobs in CBOs were lost with the fall of CETA (Nightingale and O'Brien 1984:21).

Nightingale and O'Brien (1984) conducted an overview of the effects on CBOs of the transition from CETA to JTPA in which one-third of those CBOs studied recounted that the viability of their agencies was threatened by the loss of PSE, in many cases forcing them to cut back on direct client services. The termination of CETA and the implementation of JTPA resulted in a decrease of CBO participation in training and employment services. The expanded use of performance-based contracts under JTPA has hindered smaller CBOs, who are often unable to shoulder the necessary cash flow, rendering them unable to compete with community colleges, for-profit training programs, and technical schools. These smaller, independent organizations experienced closures more frequently. The transition to JTPA resulted in less-dynamic, less risk-taking organizations. Respondents in Nightingale and O'Brien's study observed that training and social services, for youth and the disadvantaged respectively, especially suffered with the implementation of JTPA.

By design, JTPA reflected the conservative administration that implemented it. For instance, the policy regarding services for women is generally less specific under JTPA than that of the 1978 CETA reauthorization; JTPA failed to explicitly target women or displaced homemakers in its guidelines (Steinberg and Haignere 1983:30; Rose 1995). JTPA lacked special incentives to target the most needy of the groups it serves, leading some to predict that only the most employable would benefit. Furthermore, JTPA calls for private-sector participation through Private Industry Councils, which act in partnership with local governments. This partnership arguably provides "private businesses with employees rather than, as under CETA, providing individuals with training" (Nightingale 1985:xi).

While CETA's image was one of a programmatic failure, a closer look, as we have seen, suggests its political and ideological situations contributed to the dubious popular perspective of the program. The Republicans, in their rancor over "public-sector activism," profited from CETA's public image. At the core of this perceived activism were the nonprofits and CBOs, established in the 1960s and 1970s with the goal of serving the disadvantaged and minority communities previously neglected by mainstream organizations. The defeat of CETA and the passage of JTPA were tantamount to the undermining of many such CBOs and nonprofits, which, arguably, was the intent of the conservatives. Furthermore, with the advent of JTPA, services for individuals in need took a back seat to the demands of businesses.

The evidence strongly suggests that CETA's programmatic characteristics did not generate its undoing but that it was the target of an extensive conservative agenda, which systematically subverted the efforts of the community-based and grassroots organizations. Programmatically, CETA and PSE provide concrete examples of how "fair work" can be achieved. The incorporation of these practices into present-day welfare policy could offer employment to welfare recipients at livable wages, with more sustainable paths out of poverty.

Public-Sector Jobs Creation Programs for Today?

As this chapter has suggested, public service job creation, such as that administered under CETA, can significantly ameliorate newly implemented welfare-to-work policies. Such a program could go a long way toward making welfare reform simultaneously an anti-poverty policy. A recent Associated Press story paints a disheartening picture of new federal workfare policies in action (1997). Unionized employees for the city of San Francisco performing the same tasks as their workfare counterparts earn $8.25 to $21.25 per hour more, plus benefits. The article reports, "Workfare employees are often struggling to make ends meet, living on the street, with family members or in subsidized housing, and feeding themselves with the help of food stamps" (Associated Press 1997:B1). Furthermore, the jobs San Francisco's workfare employees are assigned hardly develop skills upon which poverty-alleviating careers can be built; the recipients cited in this article clean buses, fold hospital laundry, and pick up garbage.

In comparison to the workfare example above, "fair work" programs like CETA offer recipients a surer avenue for averting poverty. Fair work pays a livable wage, substantial enough to support a family in a manner that fosters their well-being. In comparison, low-wage jobs such as those common to workfare fail to sustain families adequately (Edin and Lein 1997) and inevitably make climbing out of poverty very difficult. Until its 1978 amendments, CETA paid prevailing market wages. With a model like CETA, employees such as those in San Francisco would make at least $28,000 annually, compared to the $11,500 the California minimum wage offers.

Roberta Spalter-Roth and her colleagues (1992) identified job training as a critical factor in avoiding poverty. They found that participating in some job training not only doubles one's chances of averting poverty but also positions women for better-remunerated white-collar and full-time jobs at a higher rate than those without training. They found that job training increases welfare mothers' odds of seeking or finding employment. Under CETA, participants sometimes received formal long-term vocational training segments as well as on-the-job training they would otherwise have been unlikely to receive.

As the examples we have presented or referred to in this essay demonstrate, CETA participants, through their employment and job training, developed skills in a variety of transferable areas, including health care work, social services, nature conservation, legal advocacy, and road construction. Under new TANF policies in many states, higher education no longer qualifies as an acceptable work-related activity. On-the-job training opportunities such as those documented in the aforementioned examples may be the only real hope that entry-level private-sector employees hold to advance occupationally or even to gain access to job ladders. Though the feasibility of such programs serving most TANF clients is limited, even if a small but significant number benefit so that they escape poverty and find fulfilling work, the effort is important to make.

Spalter-Roth and her colleagues (1992) also determined that previous job experience slightly boosts women's chances of moving out of poverty. The more work experience gained, the greater the effect. A public service employment program like CETA can offer participants skills-building work experience, as evidenced by the examples provided here. Fair work provides useful skills upon which women have a chance of building satisfying, well-remunerated careers. One study performed in Connecticut demonstrated that, upon completion of participation in CETA, approximately 45 percent of the women in PSE and 30 percent of the men received jobs requiring higher skill levels than the jobs they had previously held (Harlan 1989). In an evaluation prepared for the Department of Labor, Westat, Inc. (1983) found that those who participated in CETA for forty-one weeks or more, thereby gaining more experience, boasted higher postprogram rates of employment and larger wage increases than their colleagues who participated less.

In addition to boosting human capital, public service employment combats critical factors that normally pull low-wage workers out of the labor force. Kathryn Edin and Laura Lein (1997) document how the low-wage, dead-end jobs most frequently available to welfare mothers discourage labor force participation. These jobs offer little economic incentive and few gains in social or human capital or in self-esteem. Unpublished data collected by one of the authors of this chapter (Weigt 1997) suggest that a lack of satisfying work, defined as meaningful tasks, benefits, adequate pay, and opportunities for advancement, deters former welfare recipients from job retention. Employees are reluctant to commit time and energy to employers whose actions reveal a lack of commitment to them.

Public service employment, as evidenced by CETA, has the potential to compensate fairly and sufficiently, to offer skills development and job advancement, to provide work that may contribute to participants' communities and engage their minds, and to help employees in building occupational networks that will assist them in furthering their careers. Indeed, it has been proposed that CETA contributed to self-sufficiency, confidence, and self-worth in poor persons (Carballo and Bane 1984). PSE participation under CETA was voluntary, not mandatory as is the current workfare policy. Voluntary job creation programs offer participants more options, in contrast to the limits workfare imposes. Workfare obliges individuals either to remain in potentially low-paying, dead-end positions in order to retain benefits or to forgo public assistance and the meager security it affords and work in another potentially low-wage job, with little opportunity for advancement and without benefits.

In addition to the multiple benefits it provides low-income women, public service employment is a much-needed and important mechanism for expanding both jobs and, in some cases, public services. In its resolve to move welfare recipients into the paid labor force, PRWORA failed to make adequate provision for the well-being of families reliant on TANF in economically depressed regions and during economic downturns. In a recent study by the U.S. Conference of Mayors (1997), 92 percent of thirty-four cities surveyed reported that their local economy could not meet the demand for low-skill jobs to fulfill welfare reform's work participation requirements. Many welfare recipients cannot find jobs because jobs they are qualified for do not exist in adequate numbers to absorb the numbers of welfare recipients mandated to work, a fact better recognized by researchers than by politicians or even some policymakers (Illinois JOB GAP Project 1996; Spalter-Roth, Hartmann, and Andrews 1992; Burtless 1994; Holtzer 1996). Though the statistical indicators may suggest that the U.S. labor market is currently thriving, economic hardship during the policy life of PRWORA is not unlikely. Those reliant on public assistance undoubtedly will suffer grave consequences. Controlling for human capital, number of children, and other factors affecting the potential of working, high rates of unemployment represent strong obstacles to work, and they reduce an individual's likelihood of escaping poverty by nearly one-half (Spalter-Roth et al. 1995). Policies that mandate work in markets with high unemployment without a "safety net" of cash assistance will further boost poverty rates (Spalter-Roth et al. 1995:41).

A "fair work" jobs creation program like PSE under CETA could provide that safety net in times of economic fluctuation and in compromised labor markets. Public service employment has been identified as one long-term solution to overcoming unemployment (Hallman 1980). The public sector is ideally positioned to supplement the jobs offered by the private sector. Nancy Rose (1995) argues that, due to the cutbacks in public services during the Reagan-Bush era, substantial work opportunities exist in the public sector. She estimates that millions could be employed performing tasks that are necessary and useful but that fell victim to budgetary cuts of the 1980s. A public service jobs creation program based on community and public needs would allow participants and program developers a much broader range of options. Municipalities surveyed by the U.S. Conference of Mayors (1997) recently rated their ability to generate community service jobs in the public and nonprofit sectors as above average. Child care, school improvement, health care, clerical/office work, recreation, city departments, food industry, elder care, and public housing were the most frequently cited fields for such jobs—all necessary and useful but often overlooked or poorly remunerated in the private sector. The use of PSE creates a win-win situation; the program can sustainably get people off welfare while revitalizing the shrinking public sector.

Fiscal conservatives, or even moderates in the current political climate, often argue that public service jobs creation programs are unaffordable. Despite strong rhetoric to the contrary, surveys suggest that, were the money available, the American public would support assisting the poor. A recent national poll found 89 percent of Americans believe it is their responsibility to help those less fortunate, and 76 percent believe the government should care for those who cannot care for themselves (Covey 1997).

Although a full-scale argument is beyond the scope of this chapter, some noted economists and other scholars who study social policy strongly question the view that massive social divestment in the interest of lowering the federal deficit is a good idea over the long haul (Ball et al. 1995; Eisner 1993; Eisner 1997; Thayer 1995; Tan 1997). Moreover, while the working and middle classes are overburdened by taxes, the primary cause for this lies not with excessive public spending but with tax revisions granting breaks to the wealthy and to corporations, resulting in a massive redistribution of wealth (Bartlett and Steele 1994). Major tax "reform" over the past three decades by the legislative and executive branches has subjected the working poor and middle class to higher rates of federal income, Social Security, local, and state taxes, while lowering rates and widening loopholes for the wealthy and corporations (Barlett and Steele 1994).

NOTES

1. CBOs with expressly woman-centered agendas, such as the Los Angeles Commission for Assault Against Women, the East Los Angeles Rape Hotline (Matthews 1995), or the Committee to End Sterilization Abuse (Rodríguez-Trias 1997), drew upon CETA to support their bids at collective empowerment.

2. Joan Amico and Stephen Boochever (1979) list a number of organizations that secured CETA funds for community-based empowerment projects. The following cases are drawn from their work, unless otherwise noted. The Hupa Oral History Project in California, for example, allowed tribal members to document Hupa history while elders who remembered key events were still alive. The American Indian Council, also of California, received funds to plan and staff a museum at a burial site, to work with state employment agencies to recruit and place Native Americans, and to perform administrative, cultural, and tutoring tasks in educational organizations (Hallman 1980). Project "Exposure" in New Jersey funded twenty-three CETA participants to design and implement a theater and arts education program highlighting the historical contributions of African Americans. In California, the International Institute of the East Bay's Information and Referral Center benefited from the employment of two CETA workers who worked to meet the legal, social, economic, and educational needs of immigrants to the area. Through CETA, the American Foundation for Negro Affairs

established a program (New Access Routes to Legal Careers) to encourage minorities to pursue legal careers.

3. Examples include the Community Action Project in Maryland and Project NORM (Neighborhood Overhaul for Resident Motivation) in Massachusetts. The Community Action Project funded an employee to identify the needs of the local low-income community, to educate the community on poverty issues, and to lobby for their resolution. Project NORM simultaneously offered residents of a public housing development support services and the opportunity to cultivate job skills. The project coordinated a community college outreach educational center, an advocacy and cultural development program promoting ethnic understanding among the neighbors, an environmental/maintenance program, a neighborhood security program, drop-in day care, and guided nature walks.

4. The Southeast Women's Employment Coalition (SWEC), "a multi-state coalition of women working as leaders to achieve economic equity for southern women," contracted with CETA programs to train women in nontraditional employment such as road construction (Lilly 1989:252–53). These programs encompassed "skills and physical fitness, job orientation, and education efforts related to sexual harassment and racism, trade unions, the structure and administration of the federal aid road building program, EEO law, tool identification, and job safety" (Lilly 1989:253). In another example of empowering, fair work, the CETA Mason City, Iowa Door Opener project worked with women to satisfy the locally unmet demand for soil testing (Haignere and Steinberg 1989:354). After establishing and completing a training program at a nearby university for women, the women initiated a prosperous small enterprise. Jane Jerson and her colleagues document that CETA money assisted in the institution of over one hundred programs to train women in occupations typically dominated by men (1988:194).

REFERENCES

AFL-CIO, Public Employee Department. 1995. *Public Employees: Facts at a Glance.* Washington, D.C.: AFL-CIO.

Amico, Joan, and Stephen Boochever, eds. 1979. *CETA Works.* Washington, D.C.: National Association of Counties.

Associated Press. 1997. "Welfare Workers Demand Equal Pay." *Eugene Register Guard,* June 26, pp. B1, B5.

Ball, Laurence M., Douglass W. Elmendorf, and Gregory N. Mankiw. 1995. *The Deficit Gamble.* Working Paper 341, January. Baltimore: Johns Hopkins University, Department of Economics.

Bartlett, Donald L., and James B. Steele. 1994. *America: Who Really Pays the Taxes?* New York: Simon and Schuster.

Baumer, Donald, and Carl Van Horn. 1985. *The Politics of Unemployment*. Washington, D.C.: CQ Press.

Bennett, Ralph Kinney. 1978. "CETA: $11 Billion Boondoggle." *Reader's Digest*, August, p. 72.

Berrick, Jill Duerr. 1995. *Faces of Poverty: Portraits of Women and Children on Welfare*. New York: Oxford University Press.

Burtless, Gary. 1994. "Employment Prospects of Welfare Recipients." In *The Work Alternative*, edited by Demetra Nightingale and Robert Haveman. Washington, D.C.: Urban Institute Press, pp. 71–106.

Carballo, Manuel, and Mary Jo Bane, eds. 1984. *The State and the Poor in the 1980s*. Boston: Auburn House Publishing Company.

Cloward, Richard, and Frances Fox Piven. 1993. "A Class Analysis of Welfare." *Monthly Review* 44, 9 (February): 25–32.

Conlan, Timothy. 1988. *New Federalism: Intergovernmental Reform from Nixon to Reagan*. Washington, D.C.: Brookings Institution.

Covey, Stephen. 1997. "The Beliefs We Share." *USA Weekend*, July 4–6. Arlington, VA: Gannett Co., Inc.

Dubin, Steven. 1987. *Bureaucratizing the Muse: Public Funds and the Cultural Worker*. Chicago: University of Chicago Press.

Edin, Kathryn, and Laura Lein. 1997. *Making Ends Meet: How Single Mothers Survive Welfare and Low-Wage Work*. New York: Russell Sage Foundation.

Eisner, Robert. 1993. "Sense and Nonsense about Budget Deficits." *Harvard Business Review* 71, 3 (May): 99–113.

———. 1995. "Balancing Our Deficit Thinking." *The Nation* 261, 20, December 11, 1995, pp. 743–45.

———. 1997. *The Great Deficit Scares: The Federal Budget, Trade, and Social Security*. New York: Century Foundation Press.

Epstein, William M. 1997. *Welfare in America: How Social Science Fails the Poor*. Madison: University of Wisconsin Press.

Fitchen, Janet M. 1995. "The Single-Parent Family, Child Poverty, and Welfare Reform." *Human Organization* 54, 4 (Winter): 355–63.

Franklin, Grace, and Randall Ripley. 1984. *CETA: Politics and Policy, 1973–1982*. Knoxville: University of Tennessee Press.

Gordon, Linda, ed. 1990. *Women, the State, and Welfare*. Madison: University of Wisconsin Press.

Haignere, Lois, and Ronnie Steinberg. 1989. "Nontraditional Training for Women: Effective Programs, Structural Barriers, and Political Hurdles." In *Job Training for Women: The Promises and Limits of Public Policies*, edited by Sharon Harlan and Ronnie Steinberg. Philadelphia: Temple University Press, pp. 333–58.

Hallman, Howard W. 1980. *Community-Based Employment Programs*. Baltimore: Johns Hopkins University Press.

Handler, Joel F. 1995. *The Poverty of Welfare Reform*. New Haven: Yale University Press.

Handler, Joel F., and Yeheskel Hasenfeld. 1997. *We the Poor People: Work, Poverty, and Welfare*. New Haven: Yale University Press.

Harlan, Sharon. 1989. "Targeted Groups and Program Experiences: Introduction to Part II." In *Job Training for Women: The Promises and Limits of Public Policies*, edited by Sharon Harlan and Ronnie Steinberg. Philadelphia: Temple University Press, pp. 137–42.

Holtzer, Harry. 1996. *What Employers Want: Job Prospects for Less-Educated Workers*. New York: Russell Sage Foundation.

Hyde, Cheryl. 1995. "Feminist Social Movement Organizations Survive the New Right." In *Feminist Organizations: Harvest of the New Women's Movement*, edited by Myra Marx Ferree and Patricia Yancey Martin. Philadelphia: Temple University Press, pp. 306–22.

Illinois JOB GAP Project. 1996. *Are There Enough Jobs? Welfare Reform and Labor Market Reality*. DeKalb: Northern Illinois University, Office for Social Policy Research.

Jerson, Jane, Elisabeth Hagen, and Cellaigh Reddy, eds. 1988. *Feminization of the Labor Force: Paradoxes and Promises*. New York: Oxford University Press.

Katz, Michael B. 1989. *The Undeserving Poor: From the War on Poverty to the War on Welfare*. New York: Pantheon Books.

Lafer, Gordon. 1995. "Job Training as Political Diversion: The False Promise of JTPA." Unpublished doctoral dissertation, Yale University.

Lilly, Leslie. 1989. "Training Women for Jobs in Rural Economies: A Southern Experience." In *Job Training for Women: The Promises and Limits of Public Policies*, edited by Sharon Harlan and Ronnie Steinberg. Philadelphia: Temple University Press, pp. 247–64.

Matthews, Nancy. 1995. "Feminist Clashes with the State: Tactical Choices by State-Funded Rape Crisis Centers." In *Feminist Organizations: Harvest of the New Women's Movement*, edited by Myra Marx Ferree and Patricia Yancey Martin. Philadelphia: Temple University Press.

Miller, Jill. 1989. "Displaced Homemakers in the Employment and Training System." In *Job Training for Women: The Promises and Limits of Public Policies*, edited by Sharon Harlan and Ronnie Steinberg. Philadelphia: Temple University Press, pp. 143–65.

Mirengoff, William, and Lester Rindler. 1978. CETA: Manpower Programs under Local Control. Washington, D.C.: National Academy of Sciences Press.

Mirengoff, William, Lester Rindler, Harry Greenspan, Scott Seablom, and Lois Black. 1980. *The New CETA: Effect on Public Service Employment Programs: Final Report*. Prepared for the National Research Council. Washington, D.C.: National Academy Press.

Morgen, Sandra. 1990. "Two Faces of the State: Women, Social Control, and Empowerment." In *Uncertain Times: Negotiating Gender in American Culture*, edited by Faye Ginsburg and Anna Tsing. Boston: Beacon Press, pp. 169–82.

―――. 1997. "Class Experience and Conflict in a Feminist Workplace: A Case Study." In *Women and Work: Exploring Race, Ethnicity and Class*, edited by Elizabeth Higginbotham and Mary Romero. Thousand Oaks: Sage Publications, pp. 131–52.

―――. Forthcoming. *Into Our Own Hands: The Women's Health Movement in the U.S., 1969–1990.*

Mucciaroni, Gary. 1990. *The Political Failure of Employment Policy 1945–1982.* Pittsburgh: University of Pittsburgh Press.

Murray, Charles. 1984. *Losing Ground: American Social Policy, 1950–1980.* New York: Basic Books.

Naples, Nancy. 1991. "Contradictions in the Gender Subtext of the War on Poverty: The Community Work and Resistance of Women from Low Income Communities." *Social Problems* 38, 3 (August): 316–33.

―――. 1997. "The 'New Consensus' on the Gendered 'Social Contract': The 1987–1988 U.S. Congressional Hearings on Welfare Reform." *Signs* 22, 4 (Summer): 907–43.

―――. 1998. *Grassroots Warriors: Activist Mothering, Community Work, and the War on Poverty.* New York: Routledge.

National Economic Development Law Project. 1976. *Conference Transcripts: Job Development: CETA and Community Economic Development.* Berkeley, CA, March.

Nightingale, Demetra Smith. 1985. *Federal Employment and Training Policy Changes during the Reagan Administration: State and Local Responses.* Washington, D.C.: Urban Institute Press.

Nightingale, Demetra Smith, and Carolyn Taylor O'Brien. 1984. *Community Based Organizations in the Job Training Partnership System.* Washington, D.C.: Urban Institute.

Office of Management and Budget. 1996. *A Citizen's Guide to the Federal Budget.* Washington, D.C.: Executive Office of the President of the United States.

Pearce, Diana. 1993. "Something Old, Something New: Women's Poverty in the 1990s." In *American Women in the Nineties: Today's Critical Issues*, edited by Sherri Mateo. Boston: Northeastern University Press, pp. 79–97.

Petchesky, Rosalind Pollack. 1984. *Abortion and Woman's Choice: The State, Sexuality, and Reproductive Freedom.* New York: Longman.

Quadagno, Jill S. 1994. *The Color of Welfare: How Racism Undermined the War on Poverty.* New York: Oxford University Press.

Rodríguez-Trias, Helen. 1997. Personal communication, April.

Rose, Nancy E. 1995. *Workfare or Fair Work: Women, Welfare, and Government Work Programs.* New Brunswick, NJ: Rutgers University Press.

Schecter, Susan. 1982. *Women and Male Violence: The Visions and Struggles of the Battered Women's Movement.* Boston: South End Press.

Schein, Virginia E. 1995. *Working from the Margins: Voices of Mothers in Poverty.* Ithaca, NY: ILR Press.

Schram, Sanford. 1995. *Words of Welfare: The Poverty of Social Science and the Social Science of Poverty.* Minneapolis: University of Minnesota Press.

Spalter-Roth, Roberta, Beverly Burr, Heidi Hartmann, and Lois Shaw. 1995. *Welfare That Works: The Working Lives of AFDC Recipients.* Washington, D.C.: Institute for Women's Policy Research.

Spalter-Roth, Roberta, Heidi Hartmann, and Linda Andrews. 1992. *Combining Work and Welfare: An Alternative Anti-Poverty Strategy.* Washington, D.C.: Institute for Women's Policy Research.

Stefancic, Jean, and Richard Delgado. 1996. *No Mercy: How Conservative Think Tanks and Foundations Changed America's Social Agenda.* Philadelphia: Temple University Press.

Steinberg, Ronnie, and Lois Haignere. 1983. *New Directions in Equal Employment Policy: Training Women for Non-Traditional Occupations through CETA.* Albany: State University of New York, Center for Women in Government.

Swigonski, Mary E. 1996. "Women, Poverty, and Welfare Reform: A Challenge to Social Workers." *Affilia Journal of Women and Social Work* 11, 1 (Spring): 95–111.

Tan, Kim-Heng. 1997. "Can Budget Deficits Improve Welfare in Both the Short Run and Long Run?" *Economic Record* 73, 220 (March): 16–21.

Thayer, Frederick C. 1995. "Do Balanced Budgets Cause Depressions?" *Social Policy* 25, 4 (Summer): 49–55.

U.S. Census Bureau. 1997a. Table 2: "Poverty Status of Persons by Family, Race, and Hispanic Origin, 1959–1996, Current Population Survey." Available: http://www.census.gov/hhes/poverty/histpov/hstpov2.html.

U.S. Census Bureau. 1997b. Table 3: "Poverty Status of Persons by Age, Race, and Hispanic Origin, 1959–1996, Current Population Survey." Available: http://www.census.gov/hhes/poverty/histpov/hstpov3.html.

U.S. Conference of Mayors. 1997. "Summary of Survey Findings Commissioned by Task Force on Welfare Reform Implementation." Available: http://www.usmayors.org/USCM/news/press_releases/documents/execsumm.html.

U.S. General Accounting Office. 1973. *Public Employment Programs in Selected Rural and Urban Areas.* Prepared for the Department of Labor; Report to the Subcommittee on Employment, Poverty, and Migratory Labor, Committee on Labor and Public Welfare, United States Senate, by the Comptroller General of the United States.

Viguerie, Richard. 1982. "Defund the Left." Editorial. *New York Times*, August 11, p. A23.

Weigt, Jill. 1997. "Barriers to Job Retention and Advancement: Impressions from a

Qualitative Study of Post-Welfare Families." Unpublished report prepared for Adult and Family Services, Oregon Department of Human Resources.

Wellstone, Paul. 1997. "If Poverty Is the Question . . . Re-Thinking Welfare Reform." *The Nation* 264, 14, April 14, pp. 15–18.

Westat, Inc. 1983. *Experiences in the First Two Post-Program Years with Pre/Post Comparisons, for Terminees Who Entered CETA during July 1976 through September 1977*. CLMS Follow-Up Report No. 10. Prepared for the Office of Research and Evaluation, Employment and Training Administration, U.S. Department of Labor, Washington, D.C.

World Hunger Year. 1995. "The Welfare Quiz." *Poverty and Race* 4, 4 (July/August): 6.

Chapter 7

Coming of Age in Oakland

Carol Stack

We know very little about what it is like for teenagers nowadays to start life at the bottom in America, their motivations for work, how they find jobs, what motivates them to toil for low pay when many of their friends and neighbors are giving up on paid work, the demands on their income, or where their work ethic comes from or might take them.

In this chapter, I use data from a large ethnographic study of fast-food workers in Oakland to examine labor market dynamics for fast-food workers: who gets hired and who doesn't, how scheduling and hourly rates fail to produce living wages for adults, and the resulting limitations of this work for mature adults leaving the welfare system. Then, focusing on the actual experiences and interpretations of one young Latina worker, I show that fast-food work, like other demanding jobs in which employers want part-time workers to be readily available, is a serious obstacle to the demands of schooling for poor teenagers. In contrast, being in school may actually impede a hard-working young person's chances for promotion at the workplace. Mobility ladders within fast-food work demand that workers are available all the time. And management benefits from but pays little notice to the invisible skills and competencies workers learn on the job, skills that could more easily be transferred if more widely recognized.

This research was jointly funded by five national foundations and is also the basis for a comparative study of fast-food workers and job seekers in Oakland and central and northern Harlem.[1] Over the course of three years, the Oakland team surveyed two hundred workers working in four inner-city fast-food restaurants in some of the poorest neighborhoods of Oakland—one-third Asian, one-third Latino, one-third African American.

My graduate students and I interviewed over two hundred youngsters in the fast-food labor force in Oakland.[2] Researchers worked alongside these young workers at Flips—the name we have given the fast-food chain we studied. They worked at the counter and at the drive-through window; they mopped floors, witnessed holdups, and hung out with the fast-food workers and their friends. During the course of the study they went along to school—high schools, community colleges, occupational nurses aide or beauty colleges—spent time with the families of workers, and joined in on the action at dance clubs, video game arcades, and basketball courts, researchers juggling busy schedules alongside these teenagers. We then conducted extensive life histories with a representative sample of sixty workers, and from those, selected ten workers, ages sixteen to twenty-one, for an in-depth ethnographic study.

About a dozen of the sixty sampled workers emerged as diarists—introspective young people who recorded the days of their lives, zeroing in on their own coming of age in Oakland. They wrote entries about parents who don't understand, bosses who get on your nerves, little sisters who can't keep a secret, good days, great parties, bad report cards, honor, dishonor, family poverty, and headaches that don't go away.

Many of the young workers in the study were at a transitional moment in their lives (near the end of high school or considering dropping out), questioning how to navigate and negotiate the world of work, money, time management, and jobs. Some were young single parents, male and female. Many were children contributing income to their welfare-supported and/or low-income families. Two-thirds were immigrants.

This study has many findings. The workers come from every imaginable configuration of family; among them they speak seventeen languages. They eat different foods, listen to different music, wear different clothes, drive different cars. "That's Oakland," observes Santos Esposito, age seventeen, one of the workers. In the meantime, all these young people share a particular kind of work experience. While they do not share a single perspective on this experience, nor a single interpretation of its significance in their lives, their experiences are another index of the new urban poverty. These teens want to work to put money in their pockets—and God knows, all teenagers need money. Poor teenagers' earnings furnish the only funds available for their personal needs; their families can spare very little. Some contribute generously to their families in moments of crisis, but generally our data show these young workers using all or most of their earnings to pay for their own basic needs (school expenses, food, transportation, gas, clothes) and luxuries (more clothes, entertainment, more food, cars, gas, CDs, clubs, etc.). Many of these young people seek employment in fast-food restaurants because these are among the few legitimate places where they can get work. In pursuing these jobs, they may also be dodging or escaping from the underground economy.

Like teens from more affluent communities, these young, low-wage workers struggle to manage the obligations of work, school, family, and friendship and in the process learn valuable skills that *should* help them "make it" in the new "information" economy. Yet success is hard to come by. Despite their best efforts, most of these teens end up back where they started, as workers at the bottom of an increasingly polarized U.S. labor market.

The fast-food jobs that young workers hold after they graduate from high school and move on to community college (as do the majority of workers in our study) pay around minimum wage and do not provide full-time work. Among the two hundred nonmanagerial workers we surveyed, 43 percent of the workers earned less than $100 per week; 27 percent earned between $100 and $150 per week; 21 percent earned up to $200 per week; and 9 percent (managers in training) earned up to $300 per week. A young family could not survive on the income from one or more part-time jobs in a fast-food restaurant alone, and typically, part-time work does not provide health care benefits. Managers control the number of hours crew are able to work and their work schedules. These week-to-week schedules are manipulated in seemingly arbitrary ways that make it difficult for these workers to hold down a second job—and for those in school to count on schedules that do not interfere with their classes.

Despite the working conditions and low wages in fast-food restaurants, it is no longer a surprise that competition for jobs in fast-food establishments is fierce. A companion study of fast-food workers in Harlem took a look at job seekers applying to restaurants with "hiring" signs in the windows—fast-food establishments that were hiring to replace workers in an industry with astounding turnover. In this situation, in 1993, where a limited number of replacement workers would be hired, the ratio of applicants to hires was approximately 14 to 1.[3]

In Oakland, we studied job seekers who applied to a new fast-food restaurant that had not yet opened. With the exception of a few managers who would be moved to this restaurant, all new workers were hired in 1994. There were 209 applicants for forty-six jobs. The ratio of applicants to hires in this context, where the entire labor force would be hired (rather than replacement workers), was 4.5 to 1. In both Harlem and Oakland, these jobs are in demand, and a high proportion of individuals seeking these jobs are teens and young adults. At the new store in Oakland, 43 percent of the job seekers were between sixteen and eighteen years of age, and 34 percent of those hired were under eighteen.

Our study also indicates that African Americans have a harder time gaining employment in fast-food restaurants than do Asians and Latino/as of comparable age. In 1990, the population of Oakland was 42.8 percent African American, 13.9 percent Latino, 14.2 percent Asian, 28.3 percent White, and .5 percent Native American. The fast-food labor force we studied in the heart of Oakland is approximately 34 percent African American, 30 percent Latino, and 29 percent Asian (7 percent other), and recent immigrants speak Cantonese, Vietnamese, Spanish, Tagalog, as well as English and several other languages and dialects. The percentage of foreign-born workers at the Oakland work sites we studied is more than three times higher than the percentage of foreign-born residents in the city.[4]

Blacks in our survey of workers in fast-food jobs in Oakland are rejected at a much higher rate than are Latinos and Asians. Early on in the study, we observed and documented a change in management and a mass firing of African Americans in a store located in a primarily Black neighborhood. This drama, which took place under new owners of the restaurant, encouraged us to pay close attention to the location of the restaurants with respect to the labor force and hiring patterns. These hiring (and firing) patterns hold true in store locations where African Americans make up between 50 and 98 percent of the residents in census tracts surrounding the restaurants. Similar to the Harlem study, managers in Oakland appear to prefer immigrants to African Americans for these minimum-wage jobs.

Managers and owners we interviewed indicated that they want the labor force in their stores to reflect the racial and ethnic makeup of the neighborhoods. In contrast to these stated objectives, our data show that the racial composition of the Oakland workforce does not typically reflect neighborhood composition. Indeed, in the four restaurants we surveyed, African American workers generally lived less than one mile from the restaurant where they were employed, while 71.2 percent of the Latino workers and 50 percent of the Asian workers lived three or more miles from the restaurant where they were employed.

Additionally, our data showed that Latino and Asian workers are generally given the daytime, weekday shifts at the restaurants. This presents a unique configuration of the workplace, including the organization of shifts, work stations, and job assignments by language groupings. This pattern creates troublesome workplace barriers with respect to opportunities for employment. Constructing shifts comprised of same-language co-workers (Spanish-speaking) and Asian shifts (many dialects that co-workers do not understand) creates barriers to African American employment that may account for the race/age structure of these workplaces and for race and ethnic patterns of promotion to management.

As a result of the structure of shifts, African American workers in Oakland were younger than the other workers in these stores. One-quarter of the workers in our survey were young African Americans, aged sixteen to eighteen, typically living with single mothers. These young workers, male and female, typically worked evening and weekend shifts while they were in school. Once they graduated or dropped out of school, with few exceptions, they were effectively excluded from daytime or weekday work. Given that the youngest workers in these stores are primarily African American, that these young workers typically work the night shift, and that when they graduate from high school or drop out they find it difficult to break into daytime work, relatively few African Americans have joined the management track in Oakland. Latino and Asian managers, sometimes with very limited English skills, tend to hire and promote their own. The job-gap problem in this study is not only a shortage of jobs; it also reveals racial, ethnic, and age-based patterns of employment.

I think back to my own girlhood over forty years ago, when I began working on my father's bread truck delivering bread to small markets and cafés, double parking, double clutching, yet effortlessly maneuvering the Los Angeles landscape. From age eleven on through high school, from the first day of summer up to beginning of school in September, I was awakened at 3 A.M. and the sun rose as my father and I loaded bread onto the back of the truck and double-checked our order. We returned in late afternoon. I learned to work long hours and to go to work when I was tired and had sore muscles and better things to do; I learned teamwork as my father finely tuned his bread route to the needs of his customers and the claims of co-workers. As a teenager still working the bread route, I shrewdly stole precious hours from sleep in order to spend time with my friends, a talent that sustained me over the long haul as balancing part-time jobs and schooling and, later, motherhood modified my sense of time and possibility.

The young helpers (mainly sons) who accompanied our fathers every summer made friends along the route in different languages, learned Spanish, used Yiddish, and ate well. By lunchtime we met up with another driver and his kid and ate together at the counter of one of the restaurants we served. Once a year I met up with the other kids on the Fourth of July, when we competed over prizes to be won at the Teamsters Annual Union Picnics. Over the years I met those same kids in hospital waiting rooms when word was out that a driver had a heart attack or his wife was ill. Once a driver whose sons all rode the truck with him asked my father, "Why bring a daughter?" My father, who didn't have sons, told him, "I want her to learn how to work!"

That was my girlhood in a working-class immigrant family in the 1950s in Southern California. I learned much of what I needed to know in life working with my father delivering bread, and I had the opportunity to capitalize on that knowledge in an expanding 1950s economy. The times are very different from the 1950s for hard-working youth near the turn of the century. A half century later in the proverbial global economy, a dreadful gap has arisen between the work ethic of many of these young people and the opportunities open to them; an appalling gap in our understanding of these young people has come about as well.

Does experience in fast-food jobs lead to other, better jobs? Are the skills learned at Flips transferable? In our study we found that experienced, steady young workers in fast-food restaurants were continually searching for better jobs. As we followed these young people over the course of two years, few if any of them landed a job that paid above minimum wage or could be characterized as the next tier in the labor market.[5] They expended energy while moving along a treadmill of equivalent jobs, such as security guard positions and cashiers in gas stations, then went back to the same fast-food restaurant, the same chain down the street, or another chain where, rumor had it, there was a good manager. Sometimes friends flocked together in these pursuits, moving over to a "better" restaurant; some young people had no expectation of a better job. One young person whose parents, older cousins, and siblings all worked in fast-food chains or equivalent jobs, when asked what she thought of her job at Flips, answered out of her own particular observations and experiences: "This is [what] work is, isn't it?" The young people in this study, whose relatives appear to be stuck in the low-wage labor market, are not able to see a better future for themselves.

Very few researchers, including those who study the low-wage labor market, have a vision of what constitutes the next tier of jobs for these workers.

Likewise, the young people in this study find it difficult to make their way from regular fast-food employment into the "core" economy. Fast-food employers do not appear to place value on the skills their employees are acquiring. At best, employers argue that these jobs teach people to use an alarm clock, to get to work on time, and to arrive clean and well groomed. The jobs are likened to boot camp; they are routinely seen as dead-end by employers in various sectors of the economy, including, ironically, fast-food franchise managers themselves.

Yet many of the young people we interviewed considered the skills they were learning in fast-food work as indispensable to their own upward mobility. Indeed, they had much to say about these jobs, beyond the fact that life in the fast-food lane can be demanding, exhausting, and nonstop work. Here is a list of what workers perceived and valued as transferable skills:

- Learning about teamwork
- How to do more than one thing at a time (multitasking)
- Short-term and long-term planning on the job
- Time management
- Planning for and anticipating the ebb and flow of work
- Negotiating with workers from different ethnic groups
- Acquiring allies to help you out during the busiest times

In addition, they also learn to recruit other workers and to make recommendations, which reflects on their judgment; they develop new systems, shortcuts, and improvements; they learn the mechanics of fixing machines, computer skills, and how to deal with customers who are often rude and bad-tempered toward them; they practice the notion that the customer is always right; and last but not least, they learn to work with a diverse group of bosses who control both their schedules and the hours they are able to work. While these skills should increase the attractiveness of experienced fast-food workers to the next tier of employers looking for workers in higher-skilled jobs, they are instead ignored, and fast-food workers are treated as unskilled workers with no real job experience. Low-wage work satisfies a real need for money to cover daily necessities and an appetite for money to provide many of the luxury items that middle-class teenagers have (and work for). But the time commitments required by both work and school weigh on these teenagers and take their toll. Work steals from schooling, and being in school becomes an obstacle to the work ethic so strong among these youth. These seemingly complementary practices can work at cross-purposes, especially as youth confront the fact that they do not have enough time in any given day, a reality that hits many of us much later in our lives.

Much to our surprise, we turned up a fascination with time, indeed maybe a fixation, among many of the young people working at Flips. Jobs, schools, and socializing take up many more hours than young people have and want. Given the time pressures they fuss about, these kids are frequently negotiating with managers at the fast-food restaurants for better work schedules and for more money, that is, raises, promotions, and additional hours at work. All these are hard to come by. The big loser in all of the juggling of incessant social lives, homework, and family responsibilities is sleep. Sleep-deprived, the teenagers show up at school just hours after the early-morning or late-night shift and an even later night shift with their friends.

While these young workers often talk with some resolve about the future and the education and skills they will need, the future often appears vague and paradoxical, and schoolwork here and now, that is, today's homework, is not perceived by many as integral to long-term future goals. Here and now, school is obligatory, an agenda to work around and cram into an already cramped twenty-four hour timetable. Time pressures that these hard-working, hard-socializing youth take on require diligent management, a skill many of these young fast-food workers are acquiring.

Somehow, at some level, the kids at Flips know by the ages of sixteen to eighteen that the use they make of their time today is related to the shape of their future. Many other young people in our study insist rather vehemently that time is important. Sixteen-year-old Lidia Valesco, for example, is one of those vigorous, impatient, and unsinkable human beings on whom youth is not wasted. Yet she struggles to manage an amazingly crowded schedule of work, family obligations, school, and social activities. A detailed look at Lidia's experience shows just how hard it is for teens who gain employment in the low end of the service industry to keep up with all the work, family, and leisure obligations that accompany life as a teen.

Lidia Valesco was sixteen when we first met her working at Flips. She was born in Michoacan, Mexico. At the age of five, she came to California by walking for three days across the desert with her mother and baby brothers; the family was reunited with her father in Oakland and obtained legal resident status a few years later. Her father is a roofer and an alcoholic. Lidia left home at the age of fifteen and moved in with a boyfriend and his mother; she returned home a year later when the boyfriend began drinking heavily and refused to let her attend school. Working with Lidia at Flips are her mother, one of her brothers, and the mother of her ex-boyfriend. At her high school she is involved in student government and numerous extracurricular activities. She has also worked as a model and has organized a dance team that performs in Mexican American nightclubs and at exhibitions throughout the Bay Area. She plans to go to college while waiting for her current boyfriend to finish his tour of overseas duty with the U.S. Navy.

Lydia keeps one eye on her watch as she writes in her diary. For the week of March 13, 1994, alone, twenty-six times she reports on what time it is. Thirteen times she discusses punctuality, or rather the lack of it that she observes in herself and the people around her. Lidia kept her diary throughout the spring and summer of 1994, when she was sixteen, and then again in the winter months of 1995, when she was fully seventeen years old and, as we shall see, ever so much more mature.

From the Diary of Lidia Valesco

Sunday, March 13, 1994

Today was my first day back at work because the computer took me off all the Schedules and wouldn't put me back on anymore until I take in my school work permit. I really did have my work permit, I just didn't feel like taking it in until yesterday, that way I didn't have to go to work.

Today I got up at 4:30 am and got dressed in 2 min. And then left to work with my mom. I decided that the car might not need any gas until after getting off from work that day. While going to work the car stopped and we were then stranded in the middle of the freeway with no money, food or a phone to make a call to someone that might of help us. Well anyways, we got some help at the last point and went to work. When I got home I went to sleep and then Gene called and invited me to go out with him. I asked my mom if I could go and she said no but I went anyways. I got back home at 1 o'clock am. Hopefully I don't have to explain why I'm so late. (To mom right now)

Monday, March 14, 1994

Today I was very tired and it was a very borring day. I got up at 10:30am and cleaned the house before my mom got home. I took like five to six hours cleaning the dam house up.

After I finished I took a shower and got ready to go to Leticia's house, to the meeting. It was at 5:00 o'clock. I got there at 5:00pm and I was the only one from the club there. Of course Leticia was there, you know she's the president of the club and I'm the vice president. All the guys got to Lety's house at 6:00pm. I was so put off that I felt like going home and forgetting about the whole thing. But I couldn't do that so I just waited for everyone to get there. At the end it was a good meeting, because all together we were like 38 people, that's a lot. Well I got home until 10:30pm (my mom got mad, too).

Tuesday, March 15, 1994

Right now I'm just starting to write because I'm waiting for the phone to ring. I'm waiting for Juan to call me back because I called him and asked him if he could pick me up for us to go to the club practice, at Lety's house. Its 5:50pm now and I had to be at her house at 5:00pm. Ain't that a shame. The vice-president being late.

Today at school I didn't go to first period because I was already late and any ways, I didn't feel like going to Mrs. Rees class.

It's 6:00pm and I'm steal waiting for Juan to call me back. Dam, what the fuck is taking him so long.

It seems like if I were catching a cold or the flu.

Wednesday, March 16, 1994

Dear Diary, how are you today? I'm kind of tired right now, but I'll get over it.

Today when I got up and got ready to go to school, I felt kind of sick so I decided to take 2 Tylenol PM gel caplets. (Why PM I don't know). When I was walking to school I felt like just lying down on the sidewalk and going to sleep. It was the worst thing I had ever felt, trying to fight off the sleepyness.

Anyways I got to school but it was deserted. Find almost all of the school went on a field trip to a conference, even my stupid friends went. What in the hell are they going to be doing there if they don't even go to their regular classes. Well after being at school for half of third period and all of fourth period, I decided that I was too tired to be at school.

I don't know whats been happening to me. All of the sudden I don't go to school. I really think that its because of me being vice-president of club Banda La Bufa. I've been trying to go to school, work, and then the club, I think that it is to much for me in a way, but the kind of person I am, I like to be doing something every little second.

When I got home the first thing I did was to go straight to my room and into my bed. I slept from 12:30 to 4:30, enough to knock down those two caplets. After I woke up I took a shower and got ready to go to Leticia's house because we were going to meet there to go to Mexicali Rose with Banda La Bufa. It was a great night, we left at 6:00pm and came back at 3:00am the next day. I danced like never before in my life. Seriously, not that I don't dance a lot any other day, but this day was different. O, I almost forgot, Juan gave me two hikies. (That hoe)

Thursday, March 17, 1994

Today I decided not to go to school and stay home and just kick back. My mom told me to stay with her since she wasn't going to work that day. At 5:00 o'clock I had to go to work both me and my brother Jaime.

Friday, March 18, 1994

I didn't go to 1st period again but now I am in my second period, in Algebra Trig. It's really hard doing all this work. I really think about dropping out this class. I'll write in this journal again when I get home.

Now I didn't write until it is 10:05pm. I got home at 3:19. I got out of school at 3:00pm as always, and it takes me 15 minutes to walk home. Today in the afternoon I really didn't have anything worth wile to do. I went with my dad the disemployment office down at 5th street and E.12th st., then he gave me a ride to work.

I went to work at 4:30 and got out at 8:00pm. When I got home I talked to Juan and went to sleep.

Saturday, March 19, 1994

Today I got up at 5:30am because I had to be at work at 6:00am. I got off work at 11:00am and when I got home I called Juan and asked him if he was going to pick me up to go to Real Rock Club Latino to dance. He said that he would be here at 8:15, that way I wouldn't have to pay if we got there at or before nine o'clock. At 3:00 o'clock my brother Chequi went to sell fruit with Steven and Edie and I went to sleep. I woke up at 8:00 just as my sister Gris came into my room and asked me for a dollar that I had told her I was going to give her if she washed the dishes for me. That way my mom wouldn't say that I had to wash the dishes before leaving the house. My mom, dad, Jamie and Mario left to my aunty Alma Rosa's house.

Well of course Juan was late, as usual. I got back at 4:30am; ain't that a shame. My mom didn't know at what time I came in my house, but if she ever finds out she'll KILL ME!

Sunday, March 20, 1994

Today I went to work as usual at 6:00am. . . .

When we first interviewed Lidia, a couple of months before these diary entries, she was one of the youngest kids working at Flips and was still excited about her new driver's license; she insisted that one of the main reasons she'd gotten a job was "to have an excuse to get to drive my Dad's car on the freeway." In addition to driving, which was a new passion, dancing was—and had been, ever since she was a little girl—Lidia's other passion. But incredibly, just six weeks after writing these tales of dancing until dawn and rehearsing until dark, she had resigned the vice presidency of her dance club and lost interest in the whole dance scene. Partly, she was growing up, trying to set priorities and tame her wild calendar. Partly, too, she had a new boyfriend who didn't dance.

For the moment, however, in the middle of March 1995, Lidia is living the life of the blessed. She can dance all night and show up for work at six the next morning. She can clean the whole house, top to bottom, "to try and suck up to my mother so she'll let me go out Saturday night." She could feel sick in the morning, "the worst feeling I ever had," drag herself to school anyway, nap on the couch in the afternoon, and then shower and dress and go out to dance "like never before in my life."

There are eight reports here concerning people who are late for appointments or commitments or—worst of all—who show so little respect for Lidia's own schedule that they make the vice president herself be late. This is one vice president who does not waste time gladly, nor suffer fools who do. But the vice president is late a lot, actually. Sunday, she runs out of gas on the freeway and is presumably late to work. Monday morning, she's tired and sleeps late; Monday evening, she can't begin her dance-club practice until late because thirty-six of the thirty-eight members fail to show up on time. Tuesday, she herself is late to the club meeting (Juan's fault). Wednesday, she's late to school and very, very late for curfew. Friday, she's late to school again, and she also takes herself to task for failing to complete her diary entry until later than she'd planned. And Saturday, Juan is late again, making Lidia run late for the ladies' discount hour at Real Rock Latino.

She is constantly late, but she hates being late, and much of her diary is devoted to distributing blame for tardiness. Juan comes in for the lion's share of the blame, but the vice president by no means escapes her own opprobrium. Running out of gas was her own fault; she was the one who had decided the car might not need gas until after she got off work. Being late to school is always her own fault: she decided to take Tylenol P.M., or to take it easy at home with her mother, or that she couldn't face her first-period teacher, or to stay out all night the night before. Indeed, in these diary entries, "I decided" is Lidia's favorite sentence structure; she clearly likes to take responsibility for decision making and to report on the consequences of her decisions, even when they are not the sort of consequences she was hoping for.

For Lidia, as for most of us, time management is a particularly problematic arena of decision making. Conventional wisdom would have it that adolescents in general—also poor inner-city kids in particular, and perhaps even poor people in general—do not manage their time responsibly or efficiently: they run late; they fail to plan ahead; they lose track of time; they neglect their commitments. The story of Lidia Valesco as a sixteen- and seventeen-year-old is in part the story of a young woman who is struggling to gain control of her time—her life—floundering but continuing to struggle to manage the hours of her days (not to mention the rest of her life).

While some might be inclined to interpret Lidia's diaries as a testament to her irresponsibility, I believe they show quite the opposite. In particular, they demonstrate her overwhelming concern and conscientiousness about time and an amazing capacity to juggle a variety of obligations and to work tirelessly. Typical stereotypes about teenagers include: they have no sense of time; they leave everything until the last minute; they are always running late; they ignore the consequences of their actions; they do not defer gratification; and no matter how small the chore, they say they'll do it later. They appear to be bored, with nothing to do, and at the same time stressed out, with too many demands on their time. In contrast, Lidia's diaries show that she, like other teenagers living in Oakland, was able to develop time-management skills very similar to the driven professional or corporate managers that are celebrated in U.S. popular culture. Yet, because Lidia is poor and is therefore put under intensive scrutiny by individuals who want to blame her impoverishment on her own behavior, she is held to standards of time management that more affluent individuals are not. On some level Lidia understands this perfectly. That is why she tries to rationalize away instances where she justifies to herself (and to us) the reasons she is late.

Like other kids at Flips, Lidia will tell you that how kids do in school determines their future prospects. School prefigures success and failure and stands in for the future. Lidia and all the others insist rather vehemently that educated people have a chance to make it in America, and uneducated people almost certainly do not. Lidia and most of the others are still enrolled in school, still trying, more or less, to educate themselves and hitch their wagons to that star. But many of them, like Lidia, hardly ever show up for class. Why? If they believe school is so all-fired important, why are they not fully engaged in it?

Readers may have noted that Lidia in her diary mentions only one of her high school courses, a math class she refers to as "Algebra Trig." Advanced Algebra with Trigonometry is traditionally the fourth-year subject in the college-preparatory math sequence, for which students must already have completed two years of algebra and a year of geometry. In relatively wealthy, suburban-type school districts, some accelerated students begin this sequence in the seventh or eighth grade, thus enrolling in Algebra Trig in about the eleventh grade and becoming eligible to take college-level calculus in the twelfth grade. The Hollywood movie *Stand and Deliver* looked at a group of poor Latino students in California who tried to follow this suburban success strategy—but most inner-city kids never even begin the college-prep math curriculum, much less make it all the way through to Algebra Trig with a year to spare for calculus.

Lidia could have stolen the scene in *Stand and Deliver*; she enrolled in Algebra Trig not in the twelfth grade, like traditional serious students, and not in the eleventh grade, like accelerated suburban students, but in the tenth grade. In spite of a year of emotional and social turbulence, somehow she scraped by in math. As we learn more about her story and her attempts to imagine a future for herself, one vital question emerges that readers may find it helpful to keep in mind: When does Lidia do her homework?

Lidia's difficulty getting herself to school in the morning is something that's got her completely stumped. Any adult reading the diary would see the problem instantly: this child needs to get to bed on time. But Lidia is baffled that she keeps missing school, partly because sticking with school is a critical element of her self-image, and especially her self-respect—but partly, too, because she considers herself perfectly capable of rolling out of the bed in the morning and going about her business after just a couple of hours of sleep, even after just one hour of sleep. She can simply will herself to get up *now*, no matter what, presumably by promising herself a nap later on. This is a time-management strategy she has practiced often, and it is one that she seems to believe she should be able to call upon any time she wants; no matter how little sleep she got the night before, or the night before that, when circumstances dictate on any particular morning, she can decide to go without sleep now and do her sleeping later.

Needless to say, this approach works for Lidia for a day or two, but not for day after day after day—and school, of course, is the ultimate in day after day, fourth period after third period, semester after semester, year after year after year. Even Lidia, young and healthy as she is, blessed as she is with high energy and fiery determination, cannot subdue the need for sleep.

Why don't her parents rein her in? On school nights, at the least, shouldn't parents see to it that teenagers keep reasonable hours? Lidia's parents make at least a little effort in this direction—and she does go through the motions of seeking her mother's permission before she goes out at night and dealing with parental anger when she stays out late—but clearly there is no effective curfew in the Valesco household. Several explanations seem likely.

The bottom line is that neither of Lidia's parents can stay up late enough to enforce a curfew. Her mother, Alma, is usually in bed by eight or nine o'-clock at night, nine-thirty at the latest; she works the opening breakfast shift at Flips five mornings a week (alongside Lidia on weekends, and also alongside Lidia's brother and godmother and two of Alma's cousins). Alma has to get up by four in the morning to be ready when her ride honks for her at four-thirty. Lidia's father also goes to bed early; he works pouring concrete for a curbing contractor and has to get up in time to drive an hour or more to construction sites in distant suburbs, where the workday usually starts around seven. When the contractor is between jobs or when the winter rains are persistent—as was the case in March 1994—he gets laid off, but then he goes to sleep even earlier in the evening, according to Lidia. She says she hates it when he's out of work because he sits on the couch drinking all day and usually passes out soon after supper time. So if Lidia's parents tell her not to go out on a school night or to be sure to come home by a certain time, they have to rely on her to enforce her own curfew. Mom and Dad are no longer young enough to burn the candle at both ends.

Lidia can break curfew any time she wants and get away with it, as long as she doesn't make any noise fiddling with the three locks on the front door or creaking down the steps between the pantry and the stair landing near her parents' bedroom door. One night, she told us, she got back to the house at three-thirty in the morning and moved so gingerly, tiptoeing slowly through the living room and kitchen and down the hall past her parents' room, that it was already four o'clock before she reached the back bedroom she shares with her two little sisters.

Clearly, Lidia's respect for her parents' authority is less than total. She does seem to respect their expectations for her in terms of assuming responsibility within the household; she spends many hours each week cleaning the house, and she is proud of paying some of the utility bills with her own earnings. But their rule is not her law, as she tells them repeatedly, loudly, combatively. When she is eighteen, she tells them, she'll be moving out of the house; she'll get a place of her own, and nobody on earth will be able to stop her. Lidia's parents are inclined toward the traditional Mexican view that young women who live out on their own are probably whores. When Lidia talks this way, they cry and curse and issue frantic counter-threats and restrictions. They know she is not talking idly, because once before, a few weeks after her fifteenth birthday, she up and left.

It was after she left home and established and ended a romantic relationship with her godmother's son that Lidia first went to work. The one thing she knew for certain about jobs was that she did not want to work at Flips with her mother. And at first she didn't have to: within a week of her sixteenth birthday, she'd found part-time work in an earring store at the mall. She liked the job but also settled down seriously into her schoolwork;

she'd lost a lot of credits when she was romantically involved and hoped to catch up fast. The store owner begged her to work full time as manager of a new store he planned to open, but Lidia couldn't bring herself to leave school. Also, there were gang incidents at the store, and Lidia eventually told the manager she felt she shouldn't work there any more.

She finally accepted her mother's offer to get her a job at Flips. Her former boyfriend's mother, her godmother, in whose household Lidia had briefly resided, became her boss. Going to work felt uncomfortably like doing chores for her mother, especially when they worked side by side on weekends. But Lidia was a good worker, and every time the managers offered more hours, she agreed. Within a few months she was working evening shifts on school nights and predawn breakfast shifts on weekends, virtually a full-time workload for a youngster who was unwilling to quit school and unwilling to compromise a moment of her social life.

Like many youth working at Flips, Lidia's relatives are among her coworkers; she sometimes works the same hours with her mother or with her older brother. Some of the young people in the study work alongside five to eight older relatives at the same workplace. And these are not the old mom-and-pop stores, where the family owns the store, but fast-food franchises where the store owns the family! The restaurants pay minimum wage, employ only part-time workers, and pay no benefits.

By March 1994, Lidia was desperate for a vacation. The Flips Corporation, of course, does not provide vacation time for hourly crew employees. But when Lidia was told her name would be removed from the work schedule until she updated her school work permit, she saw the threat as an opportunity: "I really did have my work permit, I just didn't feel like taking it in." Lidia gave herself a vacation. For someone who insists on being up and doing something every minute, it was a long vacation: five days. During this vacation she went to school and attended club practices and went out dancing most nights. Instead of going to work, she slept.

When Lidia has sleep to catch up on and no vacation time at her disposal, she has to steal time to sleep. She can't steal it from work, and she won't steal much of it from play, so she—and many of her colleagues at Flips—sometimes winds up stealing school time to use as sleep time. Classes are missed; homework is neglected. "You don't have time to study," one community college student told us. "You don't have time to go over the chapters. You don't have time to go find the research, 'cause after you get off, you're tired. You should sleep."

"I put more effort into my job than school," said one high school student who claims to sleep only four hours a night. "I know it shouldn't be like that, but after I get off work, you know, I'm all tired, and then I'll go to school that way. Here I am, lazy, tired, 'cause I'm working all night at Flips. When I'm there I'm alive, since I'm used to working at night. Then I go to school drowsy."

Sleep is not a recognized policy issue. Politicians who propose youth work programs never talk about adolescent sleep patterns. Researchers investigating the school-to-work transition don't talk about sleep. We certainly never imagined that sleep would be a focus of discussion in our study. But the kids at Flips talk about sleep—and especially, about the lack of sleep. One of the lessons they learn from working concerns making sleep a priority.

Sometimes kids who deprive themselves of sleep are surprised when they can't get away with it. A sudden craving for sleep overtakes them outside on the basketball court or on the bench at the bus stop, or they suddenly realize that if they sit down on their work break, their eyes are likely to shut. Needless to say, they sometimes fall asleep in class or over their school books. Many of them—certainly Lidia—occasionally or often don't wake up when the alarm clock rings.

Monday, March 21, 1994

Today I got up at 8:00am because the alarm clock was disconected and didn't ring off. I guess the lights or electricity went off in the middle of the night, because the alarm clock was working pretty well before I went to sleep.

If you are supposed to be at school at eight and you don't even wake up until eight, then of course you will be late to class—perhaps only a few minutes late, if you can dress in a hurry and get over to the school quickly, but perhaps an hour or even two hours late, if the situation is particularly complicated. Lidia sized up the situation and decided the entire schoolday was already shot:

I didn't go to first second or third period, or fourth. After lunch time, me, Gena, Liz and Cirila came to my house and got my dad's car. I picked the girls up a block away from my house. I didn't want my brother to see that we were cutting. Then we left to go to Marina Park in San Leandro. When we past by 98th St., by McDonalds we saw Cuco and Felix, so we stopped to see waz up. When we left they decided to chase us down there. We ran too where there's this kind of steep hill and tried to hide from them. Then me and Cirila decided to walk to this part where it looks like an island. Cuco then called me and told me if I wanted to jog around the island so I said ya. Liz got kind of mad with me.... After we came back I went home and got ready for Juan to pick me up to go to practice for the Club "Banda La Bufa."

To the politicians, employers, and researchers focused on young people's labor-force participation, sleep is not the crux of the matter. Like Lidia, teenage workers think that sleep is the first thing to give up and the first thing to reclaim during a free moment or as time stolen from school, homework, and so forth. Sleep is an account they feel they can borrow from at will. And when asked about time pressures between school and work, kids will often recast the issue in terms of conflicts between sleep and everything else: sleep and school, sleep and work, sleep and sports, sleep and social life, and sleep and diary keeping.

When we are in positions of responsibility, we are more judgmental than we might be otherwise. Attending school and trying to hold down a job, Lidia has little "free" time; she can claim more hours here and there by putting off sleep and by deciding that avoiding school or work is an option worth considering. Like so many adolescents, Lidia crashes for an hour at dawn, then takes a shower and goes to work, then naps on the couch in the afternoon, then takes a shower and goes out with her friends. After a few days and nights at this full-throttle pace, she tends to collapse and sleep right through the buzz of her alarm clock. She always seems surprised when this happens, as if she expects perpetual motion to speed her through all the days of her life, forevermore—but she's just a kid, after all, who has a lot to learn about time and mortality.

The young people in this study, whose relatives appear to be stuck in the low-wage labor market, are not able to see a better future for themselves. They are working in jobs that are critical to sustaining a teen lifestyle that commands some self-respect—a lifestyle beyond their parents' means. These jobs are also providing a number of transferable skills related to planning, teamwork, and time management that should provide some entrée into higher-wage work. Yet characteristics of the work—the low wages, the unpredictable, week-by-week scheduling, the night shifts, the failure to recognize and reward learned skills—conspire to produce a scarcity of time and sleep deprivation, which are incompatible with full investment in schooling. For Lidia, extracurricular activities such as dance club also serve as a training ground for organizing and leadership, an aspect of life valued for its relevance among middle-class suburban students (and for college admissions). Lidia has imagined a good future for herself, but she lives within many personal and structural constraints.

In these times, it is difficult to have a vision of what constitutes the next tier of jobs for these workers. Yet many of the young people we interviewed had much to say about their jobs beyond the fact that life in the fast-food lane can be demanding, exhausting, nonstop work. They told us of the skills they were learning at these workplaces—skills observed by our research team while they were working alongside fast-food workers.

Forty years after I rode my father's bread truck, I see young people learning to work. The skills they are acquiring have a familiar ring. But I also see these young people go on dizzying job searches for better jobs, often passing through equivalent jobs only to return to the same fast-food restaurant or another down the street. Employers in this industry do not acknowledge the skills these young people are gaining; likewise, potential employers are blind to the skills these young people have acquired. And these hard-working young people themselves, with their work ethic and faith in the importance of education (which they say they will get in the future), are blind to the fact that poor academic skills are major stumbling blocks to better jobs. They graduated from high school, after all. They have that certificate! Painfully, I observe these young people on a treadmill, moving while standing in place. In so many ways these young people are coming of age marooned and in exile in urban America.

NOTES

Every project is a community effort and the scholarly community is no exception, especially at its best. I am grateful to Judith Goode and Jeff Maskovsky, who nudged me to finish this piece while I was in the midst of writing a book on the subject. Judith and Jeff, in a hands-on effort, guided this piece to completion. They are anthropologists who never forget their mission, and thankfully do not let the rest of us off the hook as well.

1. I am grateful for research support from the Russell Sage Foundation as well as from Ford, Rockefeller, W. T. Grant, and the Spencer Foundation. The Harlem study is reported in *No Shame in My Game: The Working Poor in the Inner City* by Katherine S. Newman, New York: Alfred A. Knopf and The Russell Sage Foundation, 1999. The Oakland study, *Tales of Luck and Pluck, with Fries,* co-authored with Ellen Stein, will be published by Russell Sage (2002).

2. The energy and wisdom of a fine research team composed of graduate and undergraduate students from the University of California, Berkeley made this study

possible. The following graduate research assistants participated in the study: Kamau Birago, Project Director, now Assistant Professor of Sociology, Connecticut College; Ann Ferguson, Project Director, now Associate Professor of African American Studies and Sociology, Smith College; Julio Cammarota, now Postdoctoral Research Fellow, Education, UC Santa Cruz; Regina Martinez, Social and Cultural Studies in Education; Christine Palmer, Anthropology; Pam Stello, Social and Cultural Studies in Education; Wendell Thomas, Sociology; Maria Yen, City and Regional Planning; Daniel Jerome and Zappa Montag, Undergraduates, all at UC Berkeley.

3. Stack, Carol. Job Creation, Worker's Rights and the Challenge of W-R. Testimony presented to the Senate Committee on Industrial Relations on Working in California. February 5, 1997.

4. Source: U.S. Census, 1990, City Statistics, California.

5. See Saskia Sassen-Koob and Kwame Anthrony Appiah, *Globalization and Its Discontents: Essays on the New Mobility of People and Money* (New York: Russell Sage Foundation, 1999); and Saskia Sassen-Koob, "Changing Composition and Labor Market Location of Hispanic Immigrants in New York City," in George J. Borjas and Marta Tienda, eds., *Hispanics in the U.S. Economy* (Orlando: Academic Press, 1985).

REFERENCES

Newman, Katherine. "Dead End Jobs—A Way Out." *Brookings Review* (Fall 1995): 24–27.

———. *No Shame in My Game: The Working Poor in the Inner City.* New York: Alfred A. Knopf and The Russell Sage Foundation, 1999.

Sassen-Koob, Saskia. "Changing Composition and Labor Market Location of Hispanic Immigrants in New York City." In George J. Borjas and Marta Tienda, eds., *Hispanics in the U.S. Economy.* Orlando: Academic Press, 1985.

Sassen-Koob, Saskia, and Kwame Anthrony Appiah, eds. *Globalization and Its Discontents: Essays on the New Mobility of People and Money.* New York: Russell Sage Foundation, 1999.

Part III

Poverty and Neoliberal Governance

Chapter 8

From Citizen to Volunteer
Neoliberal Governance and the Erasure of Poverty

Susan Brin Hyatt

The "Spirit of Service" and the Arts of Government

In many of the qualitative studies conducted in impoverished communities, a primary interest that anthropologists and other researchers have had has been to contest the notion that the poor are poor as a consequence of their pathological habits and lifeways. Some of this work was undertaken in direct response to Oscar Lewis, who was firmly convinced that one of the most disabling features of poverty was the predominance of asocial or antisocial behaviors. As he wrote:

> It is the low level of organization that gives the culture of poverty its anomalous quality in our highly organized society. Most primitive peoples have achieved a higher degree of sociocultural organization than contemporary slum dwellers. (Lewis 1966:23)

Since that time, a number of anthropologists and other social scientists in the United States have argued that, contrary to Lewis's view of "the culture of poverty," poor communities actually evidence complex systems of social organization. Some turned their attention to the study of "street-corner men" and disclosed their particular modes of sociality (Anderson 1976; Hannerz 1969; Liebow 1966; Suttles 1968; Whyte 1943), while others looked at the structure of gangs (Keiser 1969) and, more recently, at the ways in which informal underground economies are mobilized through the rather entrepreneurial relationships that traverse even the most impoverished environments (Bourgois 1996; Sullivan 1989). Still other studies have focused on the critical role played by extended kinship and friendship networks among women that serve to sustain their households and

neighborhoods through periodic and cyclical crises of privation (Aschenbrenner 1975; Stack 1974; Susser 1982, 1986, 1988). Although several of
these works have been subject to criticism, particularly for their conflation
of issues of poverty and race (see Goode 1980; Hyatt 1995; Williams 1992;
Mullings 1992; Gregory 1998:5–19), all of them share one important feature
in common: that is, their commitment to contesting a popular view of the
poor as victims of their own individual deficiencies.

Most of the ethnographies cited above were undertaken during the period of the War on Poverty or in its immediate aftermath and were either
tacitly or explicitly in support of state action directed toward ameliorating
the worst effects of economic inequality and racial exclusion. By the mid-
1980s, alongside this body of work, a new trend in social science had become visible, epitomized first by the publication of Charles Murray's 1984
work, *Losing Ground*, and then by Lawrence Mead's 1986 book, *Beyond Entitlement*. These authors began to put forth the now almost axiomatic argument that it was not the inadequacies of the poor that explained the persistence of poverty but that the state itself continued to foster cycles of poverty
and "dependency." According to this line of argument, an overly interventionist state, now glossed as "big government," had provided *too much* aid to
the poor, thereby stripping them of their capacities for self-reliance and rendering them incapable of taking responsibility for their own actions. One
remedy for this supposed plight has been the diminution of public support
for those governmental programs, such as welfare, that had once provided
direct assistance in the form of cash benefits to the poor.

If the urban ethnography of an earlier era mirrored a larger public concern with poverty and reflected an interest in Black communities in particular, motivated at least in part by apprehension over the civil unrest that
wracked the ghettos during the latter part of the 1960s, the social science
produced by Murray and Mead was the work of authors whose thinking was
shaped by the ideology of the free market. With the election of President
Ronald Reagan in 1980, social policy initiatives turned away from the kind
of direct interventions that had characterized the War on Poverty—such as
the Community Action Program and Model Cities Program, both of which
brought governmental resources (however inadequate) directly into the domains of poor communities—and toward measures intended to inculcate
in *all* citizens, including the poor, the values of the marketplace. Social programs, such as they were, now emphasized the need to encourage the poor
to be self-managing and entrepreneurial and to rely on themselves and their
own innate abilities rather than on government assistance.

This move away from public-sector interventions intended to address poverty culminated in 1996 with the passage of the Personal Responsibility and Work Opportunity Reconciliation Act (PRWORA), generally referred to as "welfare reform," which put an end to the program Aid to Families with Dependent Children (AFDC), the primary source of cash assistance to poor women and their children since 1935. What is of interest is that the PRWORA legislation was ultimately signed and championed by a Democratic president, William Clinton, who had pledged on the occasion of his first election in 1992 to "end welfare as we know it." The events and rhetoric that surrounded the passage of the welfare reform legislation and those that have taken place subsequently are emblematic of a broader series of transformations that are reshaping a political landscape within which the "problem of poverty" is growing ever more intractable.

If the primary undertaking of the 1980s was to make the free market the basis for the logic that informed social policy, in the 1990s this philosophy was extended even further, undergirding the incremental dismantling of the structures of the welfare state. The current message is that governmental action should not be directed toward reforming the *material* environment within which poverty is lodged; instead, it is now the *cultural* environment, within which the general public's understanding of poverty and of the proper role of the state is being forged, that is seen as in need of a transformation. One phenomenon that can be regarded as integral to these larger processes of cultural change is the current fanfare promoting the virtues of volunteerism and community service as alternatives to state action.

In this chapter, I argue that the rallying call for volunteers is linked to a far more fundamental and broadly based set of political processes. More specifically, I suggest that the public celebration of the values of "service" and "volunteerism," as they are currently being deployed in public discourse, has succeeded in pathologizing not only or even primarily the poor; rather, it has served to reconfigure the relationship between the entire citizenry and the state.

In April 1997, for example, Philadelphia was suffused with excitement as a clutch of national celebrities, ranging from Oprah Winfrey to Colin Powell, along with presidents past and present, converged on the city for a two-day summit on volunteerism. In a guest editorial that appeared in the *Philadelphia Inquirer* on the day of the summit, President Clinton exhorted the citizenry to rise to the challenge of his call to action: "Together we must foster a spirit of service that lasts a lifetime, not merely a week or a weekend. As I have said so many times, the era of big government may be over, but the era of big national challenges is not. Service is a way to meet today's challenges through our oldest and most cherished values" (Clinton 1997).

In the current climate, debates about the alleged dependency of the poor have become intertwined with a renewed emphasis on the importance of volunteerism as a corollary of responsible citizenship for *all* Americans. This is not a wholly new development. Historically, American poor relief had always been somewhat distinctive (in contrast to that of many European societies) in terms of its heavy reliance on voluntary and charitable organizations that work in concert with government to provide services to the poor (Katz 1996 [1986]:271). With the expansion of the role of government in providing poor relief in the 1930s, one of the concerns raised was that an overly activist government would diminish the important role played by America's charitable organizations in providing for the needy (Katz 1996 [1986]:271).

This allegation has re-emerged with new force in recent years as a number of think tanks, policymakers, politicians, and pundits have identified a crisis in America that they describe as the "decline of civil society." According to one recent report, *A Call to Civil Society* (Council on Civil Society 1998), a diverse range of ills, including an increase in crime, reduced confidence in both government and the electoral process, high rates of divorce, and a general "abdication of responsibility," should all be addressed through the implementation of measures intended to resuscitate a civil society presumably in danger of flagging.

That volunteerism and service are now seen as activities that take place within "civil society" and as alternatives to state action was apparent in President Clinton's remarks when he linked a resurgent "spirit of service" with the "end of big government." Similarly, the popular discourse on civil society promulgates the view that civil society operates outside the purview of state action. The definition put forth by the Institute for American Values (Council on Civil Society 1998:6), for example, states:

> To us, civil society refers specifically to relationships and institutions *that are neither created nor controlled by the state.* The essential social task of civil society—families, neighborhood life, and the web of religious, economic, educational and civic associations—is to foster competence and character in individuals, build social trust, and help children become good people and good citizens. (Emphasis mine.)

Contrary to this claim, I suggest that civil society and the relationships and institutions it fosters do *not* exist in some sort of autonomous, self-regulating sphere; rather, they are intimately coupled with the actions and interests of the state. It is the work of Michel Foucault on what he called "governmentality" (Foucault 1991) that helps explain this connection. In Foucault's usage, *government* refers to a complex of institutions far broader than those strictly political functions that comprise the formal structures of the state; he defined government as "the conduct of conduct" (Gordon 1991:2; Cruikshank 1999:4), by which he meant all those forms of expert intervention characteristic of modernity, including systems of welfare, social services, medicine, and urban planning, that encourage individuals to behave in ways commensurate with the interests of a liberal, well-tempered, regulated society.

Under the regimes of liberal rule that once produced forms of expert interventions such as welfare, "[t]he State was to take responsibility for generating an array of technologies of government that would 'social-ize' both individual citizenship and economic life in the name of collective security . . . the political subject was conceptualized as a citizen, with rights to social obligations and social responsibilities" (Rose 1996a:48–49). In contrast to that image of the citizen, whose social contract with the state once included the expectation that the state would take a major role in providing, among other services and amenities, a "safety net" for the poor, the "volunteer" is a new kind of political subject, one who is deemed better adapted to the particular requirements of the present form of neoliberal governance. These include an unquestioned acceptance of the claim that the free market is the most cost efficient and the fairest way of delivering services to both the poor and the nonpoor, the privatization of formerly public and state-sponsored amenities, and an emphasis on competition and consumerism in all spheres of life.

Nevertheless, neoliberalism is, like the liberalism that historically preceded it, also a "positive" strategy of government in the sense that it has *produced* a series of new technologies designed to reconfigure the relationship between citizens and the state (Barry et al. 1996:11). As Nikolas Rose (1996a:53) has put it, "Neo-liberalism does not abandon the 'will to govern': it maintains the view that failure of government to achieve its objectives is to be overcome by inventing new strategies of government that will succeed." Establishing structures of rule within which volunteerism has come to play a critical role is one such strategy.

Given the widespread acceptance of the dictum that the era of big government is over, it is the volunteer who now stands at the ready as the citizen who has been liberated from the morally debilitating belief that the state should be the primary source of such services as schooling, policing, welfare and maintenance of the physical infrastructure, embracing in its stead the far more invigorating notion that people can and should take on the responsibility for providing many of these amenities themselves. Thus, it is not only being a recipient of public assistance in the form of welfare that has come to signal a pathological dependency on the state; now, even the expression of ideological support for such programs casts one as lacking in the ability to live up to the obligations of good citizenship.

This analysis of the multiple and contradictory meanings attached to the public discourse on volunteerism is not intended to impugn the good work of individual volunteers, many of whom toil tirelessly on behalf of their own communities and often for other constituencies as well. Rather, it is intended to provide a look at why discussions of the volunteer *as a political subject* have now emerged with such renewed vigor. I suggest that part of the appeal of the volunteer lies in his or her image as an "empowered" and self-governing person, who appears to operate independently of formal state structures and who acts as a kind of social entrepreneur, creating *social capital* that does not carry with it a price tag that presumes on the largesse of the public purse.[1] As I will show, the emphasis on the notion of "autonomy" from the state inherent in the image of the volunteer is part of how neoliberal governance exercises its power over those whom it rules, in ways that ultimately may prove to be as complex and intrusive as were those older regimes of the welfare state. As Andrew Barry, Thomas Osborne, and Nikolas Rose (1996:11–12) write:

> [W]hat has been at issue is the fabrication of techniques that can produce a degree of "autonomization" of entities of government from the State: here the State, allying itself with a range of other groups and forces, has sought to set up ... chains of enrollment, "responsibilization," and "empowerment" to sectors and agencies distanced from the centre, yet tied to it through a complex of alignments and translations.

In addition to its role in reconfiguring the relationship between the state and the citizenry at large, the current emphasis on volunteerism as a necessarily and laudable public virtue has served to mask poverty as a site of social and material inequality and *to obscure the role that state action continues to play in reproducing such inequalities*. At one level, the notion that the state is now *withdrawing* from active engagement in the lives of the poor, in the interest of liberating them from the shackles of dependency, could not be further from the truth. Recent legislation through which such measures as welfare reform have been enacted, along with changes to the tax code and the relocation of services from the public sector to private interests, has drastically altered the terrain of everyday life that inner-city residents must negotiate daily. The implementation of "workfare," or welfare-to-work programs, for example, designed to facilitate what is called "rapid attachment" to work among the poor, has required the direct involvement of a host of individuals and agencies, both public and private, many of which receive substantial governmental subsidies for this undertaking. What *has* changed is the way in which neoliberal social policies have defined the role of the state, away from its older stance of providing "a safety net" for the poor and basic services for the citizenry at large and toward the notion that it is now the primary job of the state to "empower" the poor, and other citizens as well, to provide for themselves and for their communities' own needs.

The particular way in which volunteerism is currently being invoked in contemporary political discourse advocates the view that all communities, and poor communities in particular, have sunk into a state of torpor, stripped of their capacities for self-sufficiency by the incursions of "big government." Robert Putnam (1995a:666) for example, claims that there has been a drastic decline in "social capital" over the past twenty to thirty years, which he measures in terms of a documented drop of 25 to 50 percent in the membership rolls "of such diverse organizations as the PTA, the Elks club, the League of Women Voters, the Red Cross, labor unions and even bowling leagues." Here, Putnam (like many other researchers who write on this topic) is looking exclusively at the kinds of corporate, hierarchical, and formal organizations that are far more characteristic of social formations in middle-class or even working-class communities than they are in poor communities, where informal, nonhierarchical, and open-ended social networks tend to play a far more important role (see Naples 1998:193).

If anything, ongoing ethnographic work in marginalized communities continues to demonstrate that "social capital" and civic engagement among the poor remain at an all-time high, *if* they are measured in terms of community residents' participation in the open-ended social networks that have long been a critical component of self-help strategies among the poor. These forms of self-help, aptly described by historian Ellen Ross (1983) as "survival networks," developed historically in response to various forms of state action (or inaction) ranging from the complete neglect of the poor to the particular forms of community intervention that characterized the War on Poverty. It was pre-existing networks of mutuality and self-help among women, for example, that facilitated the establishment of the Community Action Programs, once the backbone of the War on Poverty (Naples 1998).

The call to volunteerism promulgates a false egalitarianism that renders both the poor and the nonpoor commensurate in terms of their access to the material resources necessary to carry out effectively those tasks of self-governance now regarded as the prerequisites for good citizenship in the postwelfare state. In addition, this endeavor is clearly *gendered*, as it is overwhelmingly women who are responding to the "call to volunteerism" and it is also women who have traditionally carried out such work, particularly in poor communities.

In the current period, when poverty is one outcome of such nonlocal processes as economic restructuring, the globalization of labor and of capital, patterns of disinvestment, racial discrimination, regulations for taxation that favor the rich, and, perhaps most clearly, the withdrawal of public-sector resources from poor communities, it stands to reason that at least some of the solutions for alleviating poverty will similarly be measures undertaken at the level of state policy. The discourse of volunteerism, in addition to effacing discussion of such policy initiatives from the public record, is also striking for the way in which it has become a rehabilitative strategy, aimed at liberating the poor from their shackles as hapless victims of big government while simultaneously casting the state in the villainous role of "enemy of the people." This shift from the pathologization of the poor to the vilification of the state is significant, and it is this change that has made possible the complicity of the working and middle classes in the larger project of reducing the role of the public sector in all aspects of contemporary life.

Civil Society and the Poor

Much of the dirge bemoaning the passing of "civil society" rests on the assumption that it is a decline in the vitality of civil society that is actually responsible for an increase in poverty. As the report *A Call to Civil Society* (Council on Civil Society 1998:15) avers: "[T]he weakening of civil society, including its moral foundations, is closely connected to the persistence and spread of economic inequality.... Conversely, a fragile civil society worsens material conditions." Likewise, the final report issued by the National Commission on Civic Renewal (1998:5) puts forth the view:

There is no doubt that the civic condition of communities is affected by their economic condition. The breakdown of families, public safety, and neighborhoods is compounded by economic misery and diminished opportunities. The decline in civic and political engagement is especially pronounced among individuals who are sliding down the economic ladder, or who have never taken the first step up that ladder.[2]

In looking more closely at the nature of social relationships in poor communities, however, it becomes apparent that ethnographic work undertaken by anthropologists has revealed just the opposite: that is, informal structures of reciprocity sustained primarily by women have long *flourished* among the poor. Such relationships of mutuality do not arise autochthonously but have emerged in response to the exigencies posed by state policy. In her now-classic ethnography of life in a poor African American community, for example, Carol Stack (1974:32–33) provided a very vivid portrayal of how such networks and relationships functioned:

> Black families living in The Flats need a steady source of cooperative support to survive. They share with one another because of the urgency of their needs. Alliances between individuals are created around the clock as kin and friends exchange and give and obligate one another. They trade food stamps, rent money, a TV, hats, dice, a car, a nickel here, a cigarette there, food, milk, grits and children. . . . Kin and close friends who fall into similar economic crises know that they may share the food, dwelling, and even the few scarce luxuries of those individuals in their kin network. Despite the relatively high cost of rent and food in urban black communities, the collective power within kin-based exchange networks keeps people from going hungry.

One of Carol Stack's primary contributions to the study of poverty was her argument that such networks of reciprocity among poor women were not *natural* formations but that they were, rather, one of many *adaptive* responses to structural constraints such as Black male unemployment and the restrictions imposed by eligibility requirements of the federal welfare program, Aid to Families with Dependent Children, which made marriage and long-term unions between poor men and women nearly impossible.

In fact, voluntary associations sustained by African American women have had a particularly long historical trajectory due to the complete absence of public-sector resources in their communities, though the primary organizers behind such efforts may have been members of the working or middle class.[3] As historian Ann Firor Scott (1990:5) has noted, "[E]ven before the Thirteenth Amendment, wherever northern occupation brought freedom, black women had begun, with whatever meager resources they could gather, to create, first, welfare organizations, and, then, schools, health centers, orphanages and many other institutions." Steven Gregory (1998: 54), writing about contemporary working-class African American women in Queens, New York, notes:

> Like their sisters elsewhere, black women in Corona organized and directed church-based and other voluntary associations through which they not only provided critical labor, funds, and other forms of institutional support for political and social welfare activities but also pursued their own interests as black women and, in the process, shaped the political culture and agenda of black activism.

Under present-day conditions of urban deprivation, organizing skills among African American women remain critical, and their formation of "survival networks" constitutes a tenuous yet essential buffer zone against the most dire predations of poverty. Evidence of the enduring and acute need for such forms of self-help was very visible in a series of articles on life in one of Philadelphia's worst housing projects that appeared in one of Philadelphia's daily newspapers, the *Philadelphia Inquirer*, just six months before the 1997 Summit on Youth and Volunteerism. Titled "Passyunk Homes: Welfare's Ground Zero," the series presented a grim look at life in what was described as "the poorest, youngest, most female, most welfare-dependent and most isolated place in Philadelphia" (Giordano and Lubrano 1996a). One segment of the series focused on the story of two African American woman tenants of Passyunk Homes, Anna White and Juanita Sutton, who together had formed an organization called Passyunk Homes Against Drugs (Giordano and Lubrano 1996b). In their efforts to rid their beleaguered housing project of illegal drugs, to which three out of each woman's four children had become addicted and which had claimed the life of one of Juanita Sutton's daughters, the women had become a local two-woman hit squad, threatening local dealers, taking reports of dealing from their neighbors, and working closely with undercover police.

The newspaper account of Anna White and Juanita Sutton's campaign goes on to chronicle their other efforts to improve conditions in their crumbling housing project:

> Go for a walking tour of Passyunk and see the resident matriarchs in action. Anna greets familiar faces with warm hellos and Juanita passes demure smiles.
> "This is the construction site for the recreation center," Juanita said.

"This is the day-care center," Anna said proudly, as though she herself placed the desks and covered the walls with drawings.

The chatter is nonstop as the women weave their way through Passyunk, noting needed repairs, planned demolitions, proposed renovations. Smoothly, they move from Passyunk apologists—"Isn't this place nice?"—to inner-city naturalists—"These trees here are the best, I think"—to ear-to-ground politicos who know their people—"I told you we'd look into that." (Giordano and Lubrano 1996b)

Although Juanita Sutton and Anna White are engaging in exactly the kind of activities that the call to civil society is invoking, their efforts have been, for the most part, invisible to the public eye *as evidence of volunteerism*, as they struggle day in and day out to continue their ministrations on behalf of their community:

"We're trying to get an office," Anna said.

They were talking to Passyunk Management about it. An office would give their efforts a higher profile. It would give Juanita a place to put all those files of hers and Anna somewhere to keep and readily dispense her athletic equipment. It would give people a place to get drug treatment referrals, to pick up the holiday food baskets Anna and Juanita give out, and to turn to two women they know will get things done." (Giordano and Lubrano 1996b)

What becomes all too clear in published accounts of life in places like Passyunk Homes is not the absence of civil society but rather *the absence of material resources*. At Passyunk Homes, it is Juanita Sutton and Anna White who are single-handedly providing whatever meager amenities exist; the local Philadelphia Housing Authority (PHA) site manager was quoted as saying, "Ninety percent of the programs that are out here for the kids—baseball, basketball—it's Anna White" (Giordano and Lubrano 1996b). Yet, despite the laudatory public rhetoric in favor of self-help among the poor, the PHA was unable—or unwilling—to muster even the scant wherewithal required to provide these women with the office space they so rightfully desired.

In describing poor women like Anna White and Juanita Sutton, the press affixed to them such descriptors as "resident matriarchs" and "sister soldiers," but never were they referred to as volunteers. Through their representation in the media, they are being held up as examples of the "good" poor, who are striving to help themselves rather than relying on the generosity of the state. Despite this falsely positive angle, the harsh reality is that their endeavors are unlikely to gain them either paid employment within their communities or greater access to public-sector resources. Rather, their image as the good poor serves to perpetuate a long-standing and invidious distinction between the "deserving" and "undeserving" poor and acts to quell dissent among the poor by depoliticizing their quest for essential resources.

A few months after the series of articles focusing on life in Passyunk Homes was published, a guest editorial appeared in the *Philadelphia Inquirer* titled "On the Hot Seat: It's Hot Dog Mom." Its author, one Elizabeth McGinley, used humor to discuss her trials and tribulations as a school volunteer:

> I'm a new Hot Dog Mom at my daughter's school, and here I am—doing lunch for 40 kids. By myself. Jill, the other parent-volunteer, had to run home for her son's asthma medication. . . . No need to tell her that my contributions for school bake sales often come back to me unsold. My 7 year old daughter would tell her that—and would readily elaborate on my other failings as a parent and school volunteer. . . . I also can't do crafts as well as Lauren's grandmom, can't act out stories like Sharita's mom, and can't arrange a class trip to a pretzel factory like Rebecca's dad. (McGinley 1997)

This personal commentary makes clear that under the umbrella of volunteerism, the extraordinary notion that parent-volunteers are now expected to fulfill this range of multiple functions in what is certainly a middle-class and most probably a suburban and largely white school has now been seamlessly naturalized. McGinley concludes her article: "The reason I keep volunteering, despite my apparent ineptness, is that I do have one gift to offer—my time. . . . There's a job to be done and I'm here to do it."

The assertion that restoring civil society is up to all of us has served to normalize the strategic withdrawal of public resources from *all* communities, including those leafy, relatively privileged communities where "hot dog moms" live. The honorable figure of the middle-class volunteer, like McGinley, whose good works are intended to help compensate for the loss of services to poorer communities and who cheerfully wallpapers over the cracks in her own neighborhood and school as well, now exemplifies the "ideal" citizen, whose genuine public-spiritedness is being used to legitimate the dismantling of the formal structures of the welfare state that once served the needs not only of the poor but of all citizens.

In this age of neoliberalism, government is increasingly becoming operationalized through the creation of new kinds of subjects, whose own goals as "free" individuals become aligned with those of the state "so that they themselves contribute, not necessarily consciously, to a government's model of social order" (Shore and Wright 1997:6). Moreover, the line between those "technologies of the self" that encourage subjects to seek self-fulfillment through their participation in activities such as volunteerism and the implementation of more coercive strategies is becoming increasingly blurred (see Shore and Wright 1997). While the middle classes are to be redeemed through their willing participation in *unpaid* labor, all of the poor, even the "deserving" poor, must be transformed through their forced participation in *paid* labor, however low their wages may be. As President Clinton stated in his 1996 State of the Union Address: "We have to help those on welfare move to work as quickly as possible . . . anyone who can work must go to work." The fervor with which this statement was uttered sidesteps entirely the question of whose responsibility it is to provide such jobs. Furthermore, in concert with the proliferation of the belief that the state has no positive role to play in alleviating poverty, a small body of recent policy initiatives is attempting to exploit pre-existing survival networks among poor women by incorporating them into local-level bureaucracies, as part of an undertaking aimed at illustrating the rewards of withdrawing public-sector resources from poor communities. What is of note is how the assumptions underlying the execution of many of these programs actually violate those norms of reciprocity and mutuality that predate these policies and that have long sustained poor communities. For one such example, we can look at recent events surrounding the campaign to remove the management of public housing projects from the purview of local housing authorities by putting it in the hands of the tenants themselves.

Tenant Management in Public Housing: "Healing the Hurt Neighborhood Within"

In 1997, PBS broadcast a three-part documentary titled *The New Urban Renewal: Reclaiming Our Neighborhoods*. A viewers' guide to the series describes part of its mission as follows: "Across America, low-income neighborhoods are being reclaimed not by top-down programs out of Washington but by local people using local initiative to address a variety of local needs" (CERT 1997:2). The content of the series continually echoed that sentiment, celebrating the local over the national. Top-down solutions out of Washington, as the viewers' guide had put it, were automatically assumed to be inefficient, tax-wasting, bureaucratic endeavors, inevitably destined for failure and suspected of harboring a furtive intent to continue fostering an unhealthy "dependency" among the urban poor.

The final episode of the series, "No Place like Home," focuses on tenant management of public housing, "through which," according to the viewers' guide, "tenants wrest control from overburdened or mismanaged bureaucracies to revitalize their physical and human environment" (CERT 1997:2). The program concentrated on portraying the three most well known public housing developments that have been managed by tenants: Bromley-Heath Tenant Management Corporation, located in Boston; Cochran Gardens Tenant Management Corporation, located in St. Louis; and Kenilworth/Parkside Resident Management Corporation, located in Washington, D.C.[4] Within one year of the broadcast of this segment of the series, however, two out of the three projects—Bromley-Heath and Cochran Gardens—along with a number of less well known public housing developments that had also participated in the tenant management experiment, were at least temporarily back in the hands of their local housing authorities, their resident management boards having been accused of a variety of misdeeds ranging from the fraudulent use of credit cards to harboring drug dealers. What had gone wrong with a program that Jack Kemp, as secretary of Housing and Urban Development (HUD) during the Bush administration, had once hailed as "one of the most powerful manifestations of revolutionary ideals since 1776" (DeParle 1992)?

The troubles at Bromley-Heath offer a particularly instructive example of the ways in which new government initiatives aimed at encouraging the poor to be "self-managing" actually contravene pre-existing norms of mutuality in poor communities. Bromley-Heath Public Housing Development was originally built in 1947 and consists of 1,047 housing units (see the Bromley-Heath Home Page).[5] According to the organization's home page on the Web, last revised in March 1996, "The current population is nearly 3,000 residents of which approximately 75% are African-American, 23% are Latino, and 2% are of other ethnicities. Approximately 60% of the households have annual incomes of $10,000 or less, and at least as many households are headed by single female parents." Bromley-Heath is the oldest of the tenant management corporations, having been established in the early 1970s, when the crisis in public housing first gained national prominence (Peterman 1998:48).[6]

As the narrator of the PBS episode "No Place like Home," syndicated columnist Clarence Page, explained: "By the mid-1960s, the quality of life in many large public housing developments had become worse than the slums they were built to replace. One reason behind the decline was the neglect and incompetence of bloated city bureaucracies who managed the developments." In an alternative reading of the evidence, however, the rapid decline of the quality of life in public housing, which became particularly acute in the 1970s, was not so much the outcome of "bloated city bureaucracies" as of a drastic reduction in federal subsidies for such housing, which, along with the imposition of new HUD guidelines mandating that tenants pay 30 percent of their income as rent, drove out those working tenants who could afford to pay comparable market rates for privately rented housing (Dreifus 1992; von Hoffman 1998:14; Stockard 1998:244). As Alexander von Hoffman (1998:14) writes, "In the 1960s, public housing had begun to project an image of disaster. Caught between rising costs and falling rents, city officials began to cut maintenance and security budgets for the deteriorating projects."[7] Such was the lack of support for public housing that in 1973, President Richard Nixon was able to put a halt altogether to federal funding for housing (von Hoffman 1998:14; Stockard 1998:248). These policy changes, coupled with the ravages of deindustrialization, which sharply curtailed the availability of jobs for unskilled workers living in the inner cities, meant that public housing had become the residence of last resort for the poorest of the poor, who were mostly single mothers and their children.

Tenant management boards had begun to form in the early 1970s as a result of demands by the tenants, who had understandably become frustrated with the deterioration in local conditions (Peterman 1998:48). Armed with energy and organizing skills acquired as a result of their participation in the Civil Rights movement, the War on Poverty, and the Welfare Rights movement, tenants mobilized to try to restore livable conditions in their beleaguered communities, initially very much against the wishes of their local housing authorities. As Bertha Gilkey, founder of the Cochran Gardens Tenant Management Corporation, recalled of the early years of the experiment:

> When the last manager got shot, the housing authority said, "That's it. You can have it." ... The housing authority did not give it to us because they loved tenant management. They gave it to us not because they wanted us to succeed. They gave it to us because they wanted us to fail. And we took it. We knew we couldn't do any worse. We knew anything we did had to be an improvement. (Gorov 1989:5)

Despite early resistance to tenant management on the part of local governments, and contrary to reports that indicated tenant management was neither particularly efficient nor cost effective (Peterman 1998:48), by the late 1980s it was championed by President George H. Bush's secretary of HUD, Jack Kemp, as the solution for the long-overdue reform of public housing, which everyone agreed had become virtually unlivable.

At Bromley-Heath in Boston, the director of the tenant management board was Mildred Hailey, a sixty-five-year-old African American woman who had lived in the development since 1954. According to a newspaper article from the *Boston Globe* detailing the rise and fall of the tenant management board, the women "who would become part of the core leadership [in the drive for tenant management], such as Anna Cole . . . and Lucille Maxwell . . . were Hailey's childhood friends" (Robertson 1998a). As the article recounts:

> "We were poor, some of us on welfare," Maxwell said. "We always took care of each other's children, shared food. Someone would bring a pan, the other spaghetti, and the other hamburger. We had learned to take a little of something and make something of it."
>
> That philosophy blossomed into community activism. Their first victories were getting an extermination program and outdoor clothesline into the development, Hailey recalls. (Robertson 1998a)

In other words, the tenant management movement did not *create* those relationships of mutuality that are thought essential for restoring a vibrant "civil society"; rather, tenant management boards emerged out of those *preexisting* networks of kinship and friendship among poor African American women that had been studied and described by Carol Stack as early as 1974. Another tenant manager, who is less well known as a national leader in the tenant management movement, Irene Johnson of LeClair Courts in Chicago,[8] described her preparation for taking over her housing development as follows:

> For years, I had been volunteering my time in church work . . . and I was learning all kinds of things that would be useful in saving our homes—speaking, organizing, talking to people about their problems. (Dreifus 1992)

These women took on such positions of community leadership precisely because they were already deeply embedded in local networks of exchange and reciprocity. It was their qualities as indigenous leaders who had risen up to take control of their own communities, often through their earlier experiences of organizing in the Civil Rights movement and through their participation in the Community Action Programs, that made them invaluable to their respective besieged and underfunded housing authorities. Bertha Gilkey, a tenant leader from Cochran Gardens in St. Louis and the most well known advocate for tenant management, emphasized the importance of her role as an insider when she noted:

> I always go into places where people have given up, where the sociologists say it can't be done. . . . People say it's my charisma. But charisma does not stop people from tearing up buildings. It does not stop them from selling drugs. It's not just charisma. It's the fact that I'm one of them. I've lived with them. I live with them. I've been there. It's not like someone coming in from the outside telling them how to live. I can tell them how they got to buy in, how they got to adopt some standards. Not my standards. Their standards. I can do that." (Gorov 1989:3)

Despite the fact that all these women were key to the implementation of tenant management programs precisely because they were "insiders," one of the most persistent charges that has dogged them is that they are guilty of "nepotism." The primary reason given by the Boston Housing Authority for its recent take-back of Bromley-Heath, for example, was the allegation that, despite strict rules against allowing drug dealers to live in the complex, Mildred Hailey had continued to shelter her own grandsons, who were locally known to be dealing.[9] In addition, according to newspaper accounts in the *Boston Globe*, "Hailey admits that her sister, niece, and two sons once worked for the development. But she points out that when her son's work was insufficient, the board treated him like anyone else, and fired him" (Robertson 1998a).

Mildred Hailey was caught between two conflicting sets of cultural expectations that ultimately could not be reconciled. As far as the housing authorities were concerned, the women who rose to positions of tenant leadership were expected to act as "bureaucrats with human faces," exercising their responsibilities in accordance with middle-class norms of professional authority. Yet, in order for them to retain their authority as insiders, which was the very asset that made them effective as housing managers in the first place, they were also required to accommodate the expectations of their friends and family members, who continued to make up their most critical social worlds. In the end, these two sets of expectations collided head-on.[10]

The tenant management boards were also accused of cultivating "special relationships" with governmental agencies in an effort to avoid enforcing rules and regulations. While the ability to forge personal relationships with large organizations is often considered intrinsic to operating an efficient and humanistic bureaucracy (and it is one of the resources that defines the very essence of *social capital*),[11] and while norms of authority are regularly contravened in middle-class settings, in poor communities these same acts were regarded as tantamount to criminality. As one newspaper article reported, "The Bromley-Heath housing development would have been raided for drugs and wrested from tenant control a long time ago if the tenant board did not have a 'special relationship' with federal housing officials in Washington, according to Boston Housing Authority administrator Sandra Henriquez" (Rakowsky 1998).

Models for how to operate an efficient and effective bureaucracy, however, are highly contested and need to be culturally contextualized. In her work on a nongovernmental housing aid office in England, for example, Jeanette Edwards (1994:199–200) shows how it was the "'common sense' and 'caring approach'" of the workers that, in their mind, distinguished them in a positive way from middle-class "bureaucrats," who operated strictly "according to the rules" and were regarded as unable to empathize sufficiently with the clients they strove to serve (see also Heyman 1995).

The importance of maintaining networks of mutual support was openly celebrated in the Bromley-Heath Tenant Management Board's motto "We are family." In the *Boston Globe* article that recounts the fall of the tenant management board, that metaphor was extended even further, with Hailey referred to by the reporter (in a manner that parallels the representations of Anna White and Juanita Sutton) as "a matriarch" and as "the head of this sprawling household" (Robertson 1998a). In her role as "head of this sprawling household," it is clear that Hailey was simply continuing to conform to the norms of reciprocity and exchange among kin that had long obtained in her community. Her adherence to such commitments would have been particularly critical since, although she received an annual salary of $50,000 in compensation for her responsibilities as director of the tenant management board, most of the members of her community remained mired in poverty. For her to sustain her long-standing social relationships within her community, it would have been essential for her to try to redistribute some of the monetary benefits of tenant management to her longtime friends and allies. As their grandmother first and foremost, and their landlord only secondarily, of course she would continue to offer shelter to her grandsons, regardless of their drug dealing (which most likely remained the most lucrative option open to them in the absence of any significant alternative economic development). To do otherwise would have risked her complete alienation from the very community she was supposed to lead.

Contemporary neoliberal social policies frequently target "the family" and "the community" as desirable spheres of governance, which are imagined as lying outside of the formal structures of the state. As Nikolas Rose (1996b:331) has put it, "Central to the ethos of the novel mentalities and strategies of government that I have termed 'advanced liberal,' is a new relationship between strategies for the government of others and techniques for the government of the self, situated within new relations of mutual obligation: the community." Rose (1996b:335) points out that the notion of "the community" (to which I would add "the family") is being operationalized, "not simply as the territory of government but as a *means* of government"; but without, I suggest, any attention to the range of social meanings and multistranded relationships that such metaphors necessarily invoke.

The values of reciprocity and loyalty, for example, are implicit in the use of each of these terms and are widely applauded; yet it was the social expression of those values that ultimately became the sources of conflict between the tenant management boards and outside agencies. At Bromley-Heath, for instance, the tenant management board used some of their funds to hire officers to patrol the housing project as a private police force. Quite different understandings of what community meant in the context of "community policing," however, proved incompatible:

> She [Hailey] and others on the management board also articulated her understanding of "community policing"—which in many cases meant trying to work with the residents rather than against them. . . . Rather than encouraging drug arrests, Hailey preferred sending crack addicts into rehab, officers said. Rather than filing complaints against residents who drank alcohol in public, she encouraged at least one officer—Chappelle—to cut them a break. (Kornblut 1998)

Although Hailey's actions can be interpreted as evidence of the strength of those bonds of community that made the motto "We are family" particularly apt and as an attempt to support the most troubled members of her collective, city agencies construed her behavior as proof of her inability to govern effectively. According to the report in the *Boston Globe*,

> [H]ousing and city officials contend the 12-member tenant board and Hailey ignored the "one strike" law, mandating immediate eviction for drug dealers and the residents that harbor them. The Bromley-Heath board is also accused of providing preferential treatment to tenants who were family members. (Robertson 1998b)

On the one hand, to the city of Boston, community policing meant compelling community residents to collaborate in the criminalization of those underground economies that remained essential to their communities' survival; it meant using the community as, in Rose's apt phrase, a "point of penetration" (1999:175). On the other hand, to Mildred Hailey and the other members of the tenant management board, community meant retaining one's loyalty to one's established networks, made up of friends and kin. The result of this irreconcilable conflict was the city's decision to take back control of the housing project from the tenant management board.[12]

In the case of Bertha Gilkey in Cochran Gardens, one of the accusations leveled against her was the allegation that she had misused the credit cards issued to the tenant management group in order to pay for personal expenses she had accrued as a result of activities associated with her consulting firm, Urban Women (Tuft and Parish 1998). In response to questioning by a *St. Louis Post-Dispatch* reporter, Gilkey replied, "It is obvious that this is a witch hunt. . . . Had anyone else made a mistake, you wouldn't even be doing a story on this. . . . I work for Cochran night and day without being paid" (Tuft and Parish 1998).

Gilkey's brief quotation is instructive: it may be true that her conduct was not any different from that of most CEOs. Of even greater consequence, however, is the fact that these women who took on tenant management responsibilities, whether paid or not, *did* work "night and day." As residents themselves, the tenant leaders were constantly "on call," visited for advice by neighbors at all hours as they patrolled the corridors of their developments, casting their "matriarchal" eye over their dominions. Speaking to the camera in the PBS series, Bertha Gilkey remarked, while making her rounds through Cochran Gardens, "Being poor does not mean you're not responsible. Being poor does not mean that we're not going to hold you accountable. And, being poor is no excuse for not suffering the consequences of your actions and the actions of your children."

As was the case at Bromley-Heath, however, as hard as Bertha Gilkey may have worked to "maintain standards" at Cochran Gardens and to hold her fellow tenants accountable, the majority of her neighbors also discovered that tenant "empowerment" was no panacea for poverty. In his trenchant analysis of the tenant management experience at Cochran Gardens, Jason DeParle (1992:46) emphasized this last point:

> Despite Gilkey's sideline as a one-woman employment agency, only 27 percent of Cochran's household heads have jobs. Forty percent are receiving wel-

fare and twice that are getting some kind of government benefit. Eighty-five percent of the households are headed by single women.[13]

Advocates for programs such as tenant management have linked it to a conviction that such policies work because they liberate the poor from the shackles of big government, thereby allowing them to rediscover their internal capacities for self-help. Such advocates argue that the effects of self-management will extend far beyond the parameters of tenant management itself, providing a route out of poverty. As Jason DeParle (1992:22) wrote of Jack Kemp's enthusiasm for such projects:

> Kemp argues that tenant management has the power not only to transform housing but also to unleash a revolution in spirit—one that will invigorate poor people to excel in school, seek jobs and start businesses. "Bertha Gilkey is living testimony to the idea that when people have access to power and control over their own lives—and some assets to go with it—that changes attitudes, alters behaviors," Kemp said in an interview. "And it is a better answer than simply maintaining them on the Government's liberal plantation."

This alleged metamorphosis of tenants and other poor people, from subjects once conceptualized as dependent on others into beings who are now apparently autonomous and capable of self-government, is part of a broader movement to "empower" the poor. Barbara Cruikshank (1994) has identified the contradiction that lies at the heart of "technologies of empowerment" as they were implemented during the 1960s War on Poverty. As she has written, "Despite the good intentions of those who seek to empower others, relations of empowerment are, in fact, relations of power in and of themselves" (Cruikshank 1994:30; see also Peterman 1998).

In the 1990s, "empowerment" and "self-help" as strategies for governance moved significantly away from their original provenance on the political left and were embraced by politicians and policymakers on the right, largely because of their utility as *post hoc* rationalizations for the removal of public-sector resources from poor communities. Furthermore, technologies of empowerment, such as tenant management, mask those mechanisms that create and maintain economic inequality, social exclusion, and material deprivation in favor of adopting a therapeutic project aimed at refashioning "poor selves" into subjects who are now willing and able to be responsible for governing themselves (Cruikshank 1994; Rose 1989:213–28).

This ideology of the newly empowered poor echoes continually throughout the PBS series. It was apparent in the documentary in the voice of

Robert Woodson, president of the National Center for Neighborhood Enterprise, when he stated:

> A lot of people who approach low-income folks patronize them and say, well, if their children don't go to school, we need a social worker for truancy. If they don't clean their houses, we need a homemaker to help them to do that. If their children are unruly, we need a social worker to teach them to be effective parents. So, what we really do is erode the self-confidence of people by imposing third party program providers. Tenant management leaders have the highest expectations of their peers, and require them to live up to these expectations. And most people living in public housing and other low-income neighborhoods respond to higher expectations.

In the interest of promoting self-confidence among the poor, "third-party providers," such as social workers, truant officers, and housing managers, are now to be withdrawn from these communities in favor of the unpaid local volunteers, who will take over these functions. Defining the mission of antipoverty programs as building of self-confidence among the poor, rather than as alleviating material deprivation, simply recycles the old assumptions attached to the "culture of poverty" thesis: that is, that poverty is fundamentally an outcome of psychological deficiencies rooted in the individual (see Cruikshank 1996:231), rather than a consequence of structural and systemic hierarchies of inequality.

The theme of motivating the poor themselves to rise to the challenges before them was a prominent message communicated by the PBS documentary, which ends with journalist Clarence Page making the following impassioned statement:

> [T]he results of increased responsibility are showing that low-income residents do have the same dreams that other people have. Given a chance, they can show tireless energies and abilities to achieve those dreams. With that, they show what the new urban renewal is all about—people helping people to help themselves. *And helping the neighborhood that lies dormant within every ghetto waiting to breath free and make itself new again.*

In fact, the "neighborhood within every ghetto" was never dormant at all; it has always had to serve as the primary source of sustenance for people on the edge of survival. As Carol Stack (1974), Ida Susser (1982, 1986, 1988, 1992), Ann Bookman and Sandra Morgen (1988), Nancy Naples (1998), and others have shown, a culture of volunteerism, self-help, mutual assistance, and reciprocity has long been well established in poor communities, and it was these strategies for survival that formed the roots from which the tenant management movement was able to grow—not the reverse. It was the formalization of tenant management programs into local-level bureaucracies that ultimately resulted in undermining the very values of mutuality that are currently so heartily lauded by the proponents in favor of a strengthened "civil society."[14]

The community caretaking work that has long been carried out by poor women like Mildred Hailey and Bertha Gilkey has been aptly named by Naples (1998) "activist mothering." Evidence of activist mothering has been treated by the media and by politicians and policymakers as one way of distinguishing the deserving poor from the rest. Yet, when it was co-opted by the state for the purpose of getting women to participate in local-level bureaucracies and when, as a result of this move, there was friction between communities and government agencies, many of those same acts of activist mothering were reinterpreted by the state as evidence of nepotism and as proof of the inability of poor people to become self-governing. As this analysis of tenant management shows, the state is very much present in determining the nature and degree of the participation of the poor in (and their exclusion from) community-based organizations and local-level politics. As long as the tenant management boards served the interests of the state, by containing the poor through the disciplines imposed by such figures as Bertha Gilkey, they were lauded as evidence of empowerment. As soon as there was discord between the tenant management boards and their housing authorities, however, the government stepped in to take back control of these communities. Despite the laudatory rhetoric trumpeted by those advocates for tenant management programs featured in the PBS documentary, then, the territory of empowerment was hardly a space where the poor were liberated from the supposedly dispiriting effects of big government; rather, it became a site where power differences stood out in even sharper relief, and where the state was now able to execute a new technology of governance over the poor, toward the end of suppressing and depoliticizing their attempts to advocate collectively on behalf of their communities' best interests.

Vilifying the State

Although two recently published reports on civil society associate poverty with a decline in the quality of civic life, they also go to great lengths to stress that it is not only the poor who are responsible for this decay but that its causes are to be attributed to the spread of a generalized apathy among *all* citizens. After linking conditions in poor communities to the absence of civil society, a report by the National Commission on Civic Renewal (1998: 6) goes on to say:

> A free society depends on the standards and behavior of average citizens, and of the most fortunate as well. It is an evasion of responsibility to focus only on the inner city, or to place all the blame on "liberal elites" or "right wing extremists." Much of what has gone wrong in America we have done—and are still doing—to ourselves.
>
> Too many of us have become passive and disengaged. Too many of us lack confidence in our capacity to make basic moral and civic judgments, to join with our neighbors to do the work of community, to make a difference.

Despite the claim in the report that "there is no simple or direct relationship between the reach of government and the vitality of civil society" (1998:10), all the recommendations that follow valorize participation in neighborhood groups, faith-based organizations, family life, and other activities that are generally regarded as outside the formal structures of the state. The report ends with the following call to action:

> Get involved. Join with others who care. Hold your fellow citizens and your leaders accountable. See yourself as active agents, not passive victims. Above all, take responsibility. After all, it is your democracy—not a consumer good, not a spectator sport, but rather the work of many hands—starting with your own. (National Commission on Civic Renewal 1998:20)

No distinction is made here between the struggles required to repair the damage done to poor communities and efforts to be undertaken by the middle classes in defense of their own relatively privileged environments. Although the authors state, "We believe that building democracy means individuals, voluntary associations, private markets, and the public sector working together—not locked in battle" (National Commission on Civic Renewal 1998:8), there are no recommendations proposing such measures as reforming the tax system to better redistribute wealth, curbing the free-floating financial transactions that now constitute the global economy, raising the minimum wage, or increasing state subsidies for public schooling, job training, better housing, or policing. The Council on Civil Society of the Institute for American Values (1998:18) is more open in its outright advocacy for a strong civil society as an alternative to government:

The old model is essentially mechanistic, relying on government regulation or economic incentives. As public policy, the old model tends toward centralized authority and direct intervention. It is largely problem-oriented. . . . The old model is aggressively secular, often influenced by a professional social work or "client" approach, and is typically reluctant to employ moral reasoning or offer moral judgments. The new model . . . favors community-based mentors and citizen leaders over outside professionals and experts, and, as a result, is more able to rely upon moral reasoning and to exercise moral judgment.

While one would most emphatically not want to offer unqualified approval for the actions of all public-sector employees, since the conduct of such agents, most notably social workers and the police, has often had negative repercussions for poor communities—particularly for communities of color—replacing such "professionals and experts" with "citizen leaders" does not hold out much promise for eradicating—or at least lessening—the effects of structural inequality that reverberate along the fault lines of race, ethnicity, gender, sexuality, disability, and economic class. On the contrary, it replaces any efforts at structural reform with a kind of moralistic vigilantism that ensures nothing in the way of genuine access to opportunity, economic growth, or personal achievement for our most disenfranchised and disadvantaged citizens.

It is in the context of welfare-to-work programs that the vilification of the state as the enemy of the poor and as the agent most responsible for suppressing their initiative is rendered most visible. In Philadelphia, for example, the welfare-to-work program Greater Philadelphia Works is administered by the Private Industry Council, which pledged to place seventy-five hundred welfare recipients in jobs during 1999 (Yant 1998)—a modest offer at best, since over three times that number of families would soon lose their welfare benefits and be in desperate need of employment. In conjunction with that undertaking, an advertising agency initiated a public campaign aimed at "marketing" welfare recipients as good potential employees. One such advertisement that appeared in local newspapers bore the headline "How about My Mom?" Below a photo of a child with his mother, the text read: "Need a hard worker? Moms coming off welfare are motivated, responsible employees. They have to be. Hire one today" (see Naymik 1998).

In contrast to the negative image of the "welfare queen," who dominated the media coverage of poverty in the 1980s (see Cruikshank 1999:104–21), the welfare-to-work mother is hard-working and responsible; it was only the (unnecessary) handouts from the state that previously prevented her from realizing her own potential. As the head of the advertising firm responsible for this campaign stated: "You can't hire a better worker than a welfare mother because working means the difference between surviving and living on the streets with kids. How much more serious can it be?" (Naymik 1998).

Removing welfare subsidies is now represented as liberating poor mothers from their addictive thrall to dependency on the dole. In that spirit Rudy Giuliani, mayor of New York, who is overseeing one of the most draconian of the welfare-to-work programs currently in effect, was quoted as saying that "his critics do not understand that 'people on welfare are exactly the same as they are'" (DeParle 1998:89).

Twenty years ago, when the attack on the welfare state first began to gain momentum, the poor were hardly represented as "just like us"—they were almost another species in the public eye, a grasping, manipulative, pathological residue of humanity who were content to live off of unearned charity. Now this older view of the undeserving poor co-exists alongside a newer representation of the poor as potentially good workers who have simply been deprived of the opportunity to participate in society by the intrusions of an overly paternalistic state. The "participation" in the larger society being offered to the poor, however, is in the form of the lowest-wage jobs that lack benefits, stability, or long-term guarantees of continued employment (Piven 1998).

At this historical juncture, the celebration of volunteerism and the call to civil society are reaching beyond the poor to reshape the subjectivities of *all* citizens. Whatever else it may be, the move toward volunteerism as a policy stance is an attempt to get the middle class to pick up some of the slack left by government's virtual abandonment of poor communities. In addition, however, it conveniently masks the fact that the public sector is withdrawing from privileged communities almost as rapidly. Even in relatively affluent neighborhoods, decent school programs are now more likely to be the result of successful bake sales and weekend walk-a-thons than of local tax bond issues, and responsibility for neighborhood security is increasingly being left up to the vigilance of walkie-talkie-bearing block watch patrols rather than the police. By recruiting middle-class volunteers for the virtuous mission of serving the needy, the neglect that threatens to fray the tranquillity of their own middle-class communities is rendered less visible, as everyone is cajoled into undertaking a roster of charitable activities, all in the name of countering the soul-depleting incursions of that enemy known as big government.

Absent from these public debates is any recognition of the fact that, were the political will for such action to be present, a commitment to greater public investment undertaken by the state could ensure the kind of stable communities where volunteerism actually flourishes best.[15] Moreover, as Jason DeParle (1992) points out in his article on tenant management at Cochran Gardens, "Though [Bertha Gilkey] is often cited as proof of how liberalism has failed, she draws abundantly on its legacy of social services and Federal Government grants."[16] He notes that the tenant management movement owes its genesis to the programs of the 1960s, and that Cochran Gardens is still "awash" in the social programs that are the legacy of the War on Poverty. He concludes with the trenchant observation that, despite all evidence to the contrary, "[T]enant management is part of an antipoverty vision that assumes the ghettos can be healed from within."

We might extend DeParle's comments to suggest that the call for volunteers assumes that *all social problems and communal injuries can healed from within.* If the state will no longer attempt to meet any of the needs of the poor, neither will it serve the residents of more affluent communities. And many of these needs will be continue to be met primarily through the heroic efforts of *women*, who make up the vast majority of citizen-volunteers.

Given the current zeal aimed at forcing poor women into the workforce at pay levels even below the minimum wage, forms of voluntary action already present in poor communities, particularly those that have been sustained primarily by African American women, have either been ignored entirely or co-opted by the state and incorporated into local-level bureaucracies. The very forms of self-help that embody the best virtues of civil society and that have long been essential for the survival of the poorest communities are under serious threat, as women like Anna White and Juanita Sutton are coerced out of the boundaries of their own neighborhoods and into dead-end jobs.

If some manifestations of civil society *are* in decline in the current moment, others are flourishing precisely as a consequence of state action. New forms of police-citizen partnerships such as Neighborhood Watch programs, for example, are being fostered by the state and, consequently, are proliferating. Gated cities, into which the most well-off citizens are speedily retreating, are governed by resident boards made up of volunteers who are able to marshal private resources to secure for themselves the quality of municipal services they were unable to enjoy in more diverse metropolitan settings.

Neoliberal governance masks the withdrawal of public resources from *all* communities by making volunteerism an *obligation* of citizenship for the working and middle classes, while simultaneously diminishing the significance of volunteerism in poor communities toward the end of creating an extremely low-paid workforce. Perhaps this undertaking is, in its way, no less onerous (and, ironically, ultimately no less expensive) than were the attempts of "big government" to tackle poverty and inequality. What we can predict, however, is that if this trend continues unchecked, the outcome will certainly not be to effect any meaningful redistribution of resources. Despite the best efforts of poor women such as Anna White and Juanita Sutton, Bertha Gilkey and Mildred Hailey, and even with the well-intentioned assistance of a legion of middle-class volunteers, poverty will remain entrenched in their communities and will more than likely spread to other communities as well, a reminder of the failure of "small" government to act on behalf of its most vulnerable citizens and an indictment of the ever more fanciful promises of the do-it-yourself postwelfare state.

ACKNOWLEDGMENTS

Earlier versions of this chapter were presented under a number of different titles on a number of occasions. It was first presented at the 1997 American Anthropology Association meetings at the session "Update on the War on the Poor: Anthropological Approaches to How Public Policy Affects the Urban Poor in the U.S.," held on November 21 and organized by Jeff Maskovsky. On February 24, 1999, it was presented at the University of New Orleans as part of their series "Anthropology in Public," organized by David Beriss; and on March 11, 1999, at Grinnell College in Douglas Caulkins's Urban Anthropology course. I am grateful to all these colleagues and audiences for their valuable comments. Special thanks go to Judy Goode and to Jeff Maskovsky for their feedback and encouragement and to Sue Wright and Julia Paley, who also read earlier drafts of this chapter and made excellent suggestions. Despite all this assistance, any deficiencies in the final product are a result of my inability to do justice to all of my interlocutors' recommendations.

Gratitude is also due to my mother, Barbara Brin Hyatt, who kept me abreast of the activities at Bromley-Heath through her excellent clipping service. This chapter was completed during the 1999 spring semester with the help of a Richard Carley Hunt postdoctoral grant from the Wenner-Gren Foundation for Anthropological Research.

NOTES

1. The term *social capital* is currently most closely associated with the work of Robert Putnam, who describes it as "features of social life, networks, norms, and trust that enable participants to act together more effectively to pursue shared objectives" (Putnam 1995a:664–65; see also Putnam 1995b). The critique of "civil society" that follows in this chapter is also applicable to much of this work on "social capital."

2. A report on *Community Building in Public Housing* makes a similar argument that links a decline in civic life with the old model of the culture of poverty. As that report states: "The community-building approach grows out of new understandings of the dynamics of urban poverty and personal barriers to independence. The work of William Julius Wilson and other urban researchers suggests that the roots of chronic poverty lie in the deteriorated social structure, a weakening of the grassroots network of churches, schools, businesses, neighborhood centers, and families themselves which nourishes and supports the life of a community" (Naparstek et al. 1997:8).

3. Thanks to Frank Johnson for his comments on this section of the essay.

4. See Peterman (1998) for a history of tenant management projects in U.S. public housing.

5. The Bromley-Heath Web site is located at the following URL: http://gis.mit.edu/cbcf/chtm/bthmhome.html.

6. Peterman (1998:48–50) explains that what was originally referred to as tenant management later was renamed resident management, to symbolize the notion that the residents of such communities were no longer tenants of the local public housing authority. According to Peterman (1998:49), after a big push for resident management under the Bush administration, by 1992 only twenty-seven groups were actually participating actively in the management of their communities, and of these, only two "were carrying out some management functions independently and had a management contract with their housing authority." In this chapter, I have tended to use the term *tenant management.*

7. Stockard (1998:244–45) confirms that at the federal level, HUD remains an overregulated and unwieldy bureaucracy; but at the local level, the cutbacks in resources would seem directly responsible for the deterioration in living conditions in public housing.

8. According to an article in the *Boston Globe* (Robertson 1998b), "The Chicago Housing Authority gained control of LeClair Courts in 1996, firing 26 staff workers after allegations of misappropriation of funds."

9. Such episodes wherein particularly draconian measures were taken to expel drug users from public housing escalated greatly after HUD's passage of the "One Strike and You're Out" initiative in March 1996, which is described as "the toughest admission and eviction policy that HUD has implemented." It allows local housing

authorities to evict "individuals with criminal conviction records or who abuse alcohol, use illegal substances, or engage in drug-related activity" (see www.hud.gov/
progdesc/1strike.html).

10. In her study of women's roles in the War on Poverty, Naples (1998) also
shows how processes of bureaucratization and professionalization served to divide
women within communities and had the effect of depoliticizing locally based
movements for community betterment.

11. I am grateful to Sue Wright for this point.

12. In an article written subsequent to the Boston Housing Authority's take-
back of Bromley-Heath, Robertson (1999) reported that eighteen families who had
members who had been convicted of "drug-related or violent offenses" were finally
being evicted from their apartments by the housing authority and were unlikely to
find decent alternative accommodations.

13. DeParle's reporting contrasts markedly with Gorov's considerably rosier
portrayal of Cochran Gardens, which states: "Cochran's 12 buildings are well-kept,
its lawns tidy and its streets relatively safe. Cochran has 3,600 tenants and nearly 70
percent of the adults are working. The Cochran Tenant Management Corp. has
spun off several small companies that employ 220 people" (Gorov 1989:5).

In an attempt to clarify this discrepancy, I consulted the Web site of the City of
St. Louis. With the help of a city librarian, who informed me that Cochran Gardens
is located the Columbus Square Neighborhood and that the majority of residents in
Columbus Square are Cochran residents, I looked up the Columbus Square Neighborhood Statistics, which includes 1990 census information; see URL: http://st-
louis.missouri.org/neighborhoods/62/stat.html. According to this source, about
half (500) of the 1,155 households located in Columbus Square have annual incomes of less than $15,000; the median household income in the entire neighbor-
hood was $16,003. Perhaps more strikingly, out of a total of 2,047 neighborhood
residents, more than half (1,236) were listed as "poor persons," with 843 of those
categorized as "very poor persons." The percentage of unemployed was 39.1 percent. This information suggests that although many more people living at Cochran
Gardens may well have found local employment due to the tenant management
program, there were still a considerable number of families living in poverty.

14. This idea that poor communities should be able to rebuild themselves from
within is also embedded in the current literature on "community building." As the
report by Naparstek et al. (1997:6) states: "As traditional sources of revenue diminish, public housing managers are re-examining a previously little-used resource: the
energy and efforts of residents of public housing themselves. Community building
is an approach to fighting poverty that operates by building social and human capital. Community building encourages residents to take on leadership and responsibility rather than be passive recipients of services."

15. Frances Fox Piven made this point to me in her capacity as discussant for the

1997 American Anthropological Association session in which I presented an early draft of this essay. I thank her for this insight.

16. Bertha Gilkey's story (and stories of other community activists) demonstrate that whatever the implicit intent of such programs as tenant management, their outcomes are often unpredictable. Similar arguments regarding the co-optation and depoliticization of the poor have been made with respect to the War on Poverty (most notably by Cruikshank 1994, 1999). As Naples (1998:186) writes, however, "As this analysis of women's community work demonstrates, the dynamics of gender and race within the War on Poverty also had unintended consequences for politicization and political participation of residents in low-income communities as well as for the establishment of community organizations through which they could express their political interests."

REFERENCES

Anderson, Elijah. 1976. *A Place on the Corner*. Chicago: University of Chicago Press.
Aschenbrenner, Joyce. 1975. *Lifelines: Black Families in Chicago*. New York: Holt, Rinehart and Winston.
Barry, Andrew, Thomas Osborne, and Nikolas Rose. 1996. "Introduction." In A. Barry, T. Osborne, and N. Rose, eds., *Foucault and Political Reason: Liberalism, Neo-Liberalism and Rationalities*, pp. 1–17. Chicago: University of Chicago Press.
Bookman, Ann, and Sandra Morgen. 1988. *Women and the Politics of Empowerment*. Philadelphia: Temple University Press.
Bourgois, Philippe. 1996. *In Search of Respect: Selling Crack in El Barrio*. Cambridge and New York: Cambridge University Press.
CERT (Corporation for Educational Radio and Television). 1997. Viewer guide to the series *The New Urban Renewal: Reclaiming Our Neighborhoods*. New York: CERT.
Clinton, President William J. 1996. "State of the Union Address." U.S. Capitol, January 24. Available on the *Chicago Tribune* Web site: http://www.chicago.tribune.
———. 1997. "Here's a Chance to Help Children." *Philadelphia Inquirer*, April 27.
Council on Civil Society. 1998. *A Call to Civil Society: Why Democracy Needs Moral Truths*. New York: Institute for American Values.
Cruikshank, Barbara. 1994. "The Will to Empower: Technologies of Citizenship and the War on Poverty." *Socialist Review* 23:29–55.
———. 1996. "Revolutions Within: Self-Government and Self-Esteem." In A. Barry, T. Osborne, and N. Rose, eds., *Foucault and Political Reason: Liberalism, Neo-Liberalism and Rationalities*, pp. 231–51. Chicago: University of Chicago Press.
———. 1999. *The Will to Empower: Democratic Citizens and Other Subjects*. Ithaca: Cornell University Press.

DeParle, Jason. 1992. "Cultivating Their Own Gardens." *New York Times Magazine,* January 5.

———. 1998. "What Welfare-to-Work Really Means." *New York Times Magazine,* December 20.

Dreifus, Claudia. 1992. "We Have a Future Now." *Parade,* June 7.

Edwards, Jeanette. 1994. "Idioms of Bureaucracy and Informality in a Local Housing Aid Office." In S. Wright, ed., *Anthropology of Organizations,* pp. 196–209. London and New York: Routledge.

Foucault, Michel. 1991. "Governmentality." In G. Burchell, C. Gordon, and P. Miller, eds., *The Foucault Effect: Studies in Governmentality,* pp. 87–104. Chicago: University of Chicago Press.

Goode, Judith. 1980. "Poverty and Urban Analysis." In Irwin Smith and Estellie Smith, eds., *Urban Place and Process,* pp. 113–35. New York: Macmillan.

Giordano, Rita, and Alfred Lubrano. 1996a. "A Forgotten Pocket of the City." *Philadelphia Inquirer,* October 27.

———. 1996b. "Two-Woman Force Wages War on Neighborhood Drug Dealers." *Philadelphia Inquirer,* October 30.

Gordon, Colin. 1991. "Government Rationality: An Introduction." In *The Foucault Effect: Studies in Governmentality,* G. Burchell, C. Gordon, and P. Miller, eds., pp. 1–51. Chicago: University of Chicago Press.

Gorov, Lynda. 1989. "Bertha Gilkey: 'Come See What I'm Sayin'—The Tenants Are Turning Public Housing Around." *Occasional Papers* 1(2). Chicago: Community Renewal Press.

Gregory, Steven. 1998. *Black Corona: Race and the Politics of Place in a Black Community.* Princeton: Princeton University Press.

Hannerz, Ulf. 1969. *Soulside: Inquiries into Ghetto Culture and Community.* New York: Columbia University Press.

Heyman, Josiah McC. 1995. "Putting Power in the Anthropology of Bureaucracy." *Current Anthropology* 36(2):261–87.

Hyatt, Susan Brin. 1995. "Poverty and Difference: Ethnographic Representations of 'Race' and the Crisis of 'the Social.'" In Dena Shenk, ed., *Gender and Race through Education and Political Activism: The Legacy of Sylvia Helen Forman,* pp. 185–206. Washington, D.C.: American Anthropological Association/Association for Feminist Anthropology.

———. 1997. "Poverty in a Post-Welfare Landscape: Tenant Management Policies, Self-Governance and the Democratization of Knowledge in Great Britain." In S. Wright and C. Shore, eds., *The Anthropology of Policy,* pp. 217–38. London and New York: Routledge.

Katz, Michael. 1996 [1986]. *In the Shadow of the Poorhouse: A Social History of Welfare in America.* New York: Basic Books.

Keiser, Lincoln. 1969. *The Vice Lords: Warriors of the Streets.* New York: Holt, Rinehart and Winston.

Kornblut, Anne E. 1998. "Bromley-Heath Officers Cite Lack of Support." *Boston Globe*, November 24.

Lewis, Oscar. 1966. "The Culture of Poverty." *Scientific American* 215(4):19–25.

Liebow, Elliot. 1966. *Tally's Corner: A Study of Negro Streetcorner Men.* Boston: Little, Brown and Company.

McGinley, Elizabeth. 1997. "On the Hot Seat: It's Hot Dog Mom." *Philadelphia Inquirer*, November 3.

Mullings, Leith. 1992. "Race, Class and Gender: Representations and Realities." Occasional paper. Center for Research on Women, Memphis State University.

Naparstek, Arthur J., Dennis Dooley, Robin Smith, and The Urban Institute/Aspen Systems Corporation. 1997. *Community Building in Public Housing: Ties That Bind People and Their Communities.* Civic Practices Network. Available at: http://www.cpn.org/sections/tools/manuals/bc_in_public_housing.html.

Naples, Nancy A. 1998. *Grassroots Warriors: Activist Mothering, Community Work, and the War on Poverty.* London and New York: Routledge.

National Commission on Civic Renewal. 1998. *A Nation of Spectators: How Civic Disengagement Weakens America and What We Can Do about It.* College Park, MD: National Commission on Civic Renewal.

Naymik, Mark. 1998. "Tough Sell," (Philadelphia) *City Paper*, December 11–17.

"No Place like Home." 1997. Part 3 of *The New Urban Renewal: Reclaiming Our Neighborhood.* PBS video. New York: Corporation for Educational Radio and Television.

"One Strike and You're Out" Initiative. Available at: www.hud.gov/progdesc/1strike/html.

Peterman, William. 1998. "The Meanings of Resident Empowerment: Why Just About Everybody Thinks It's a Good Idea, and What It Has to Do with Resident Management." In D. Varady, W. F. E. Preiser, and F. Russell, eds., *New Directions in Urban Public Housing*, pp. 47–60. New Brunswick: Rutgers University, Center for Urban Policy Research.

Piven, Frances Fox. 1998. "Welfare Reform and the Economic and Cultural Reconstruction of Low Wage Labor Markets." *City and Society 1998 Annual Review*: 21–36.

Putnam, Robert D. 1995a. "Tuning In, Tuning Out: The Strange Disappearance of Social Capital in America." *PS: Political Science and Politics*, December 1995:664–83.

———. 1995b. "Bowling Alone: America's Declining Social Capital." *Journal of Democracy* 6(1):65–78.

Rakowsky, Judy. 1998. "HUD Called Too Close to Bromley Tenant Group." *Boston Globe*, November 19.

Robertson, Tatsha. 1998a. "A Matriarch Sees 'Family' Splinter." *Boston Globe*, November 9.

———. 1998b. "Public Housing Review Is Urged: Tenant-Run Projects to Be Reevaluated." *Boston Globe*, December 20.

Robertson, Tatsha. 1999. "Hard Line on Eviction Hits Home: Families Pay Price at Bromley-Heath." *Boston Globe*, June 18.

Rose, Nikolas. 1989. *Governing the Soul: The Shaping of the Private Self.* London: Routledge.

———. 1996a. "Governing 'Advanced' Liberal Democracies." In A. Barry, T. Osborne, and N. Rose, eds., *Foucault and Political Reason: Liberalism, Neo-Liberalism and Rationalities,* pp. 37–64. Chicago: University of Chicago Press.

———. 1996b. "The Death of the Social? Re-figuring the Territory of Government." *Economy and Society* 25(3):327–56.

———. 1999. *Powers of Freedom: Reframing Political Thought.* Cambridge: Cambridge University Press.

Ross, Ellen. 1983. "Survival Networks: Women's Neighbourhood Sharing in London before World War I." *History Workshop Journal* 15:4–27.

Scott, Anne Firor. 1990. "Most Invisible of All: Black Women's Voluntary Associations." *Journal of Southern History* 56(1):3–22.

Shore, Cris, and Susan Wright. 1997. "Policy: A New Field of Anthropology." In C. Shore and S. Wright, eds., *Anthropology of Policy,* pp. 3–39. London and New York: Routledge.

Stack, Carol. 1974. *All Our Kin: Strategies for Survival in a Black Community.* New York: Harper and Row.

Stockard, James G. 1998. "Public Housing: The Next Sixty Years?" In D. Varady, W. F. E. Preiser, and F. Russell, eds., *New Directions in Urban Public Housing,* pp. 237–64. New Brunswick: Rutgers University, Center for Urban Policy Research.

Sullivan, Mercer. 1989. *"Getting Paid": Youth Crime and Work in the Inner City.* Ithaca: Cornell University Press.

Susser, Ida. 1982. *Norman Street: Poverty and Politics in an Urban Neighborhood.* New York: Oxford University Press.

———. 1986. "Political Activity among Working-Class Women in a U.S. City." *American Ethnologist* 13(1):108–17.

———. 1988. "Working-Class Women, Social Protest, and Changing Ideologies." In A. Bookman and S. Morgen, eds., *Women and the Politics of Empowerment,* pp. 257–71. Philadelphia: Temple University Press.

———. 1992. "Women as Political Actors in Rural Puerto Rico: Continuity and Change." In *Anthropology and the Global Factory,* M. Blim and F. Rothstein, eds., pp. 206–19. New York: Bergin and Harvey.

Suttles, Gerald. 1968. *The Social Order of the Slum: Ethnicity and Territory in the Inner City.* Chicago: University of Chicago Press.

"The Summit's Five Goals." 1997. *Philadelphia Inquirer*, April 28.

Tuft, Carolyn, and Norm Parish. 1998. "Gilkey Charged Thousands on Agency's Card." *St. Louis Post-Dispatch,* January 11. Available at the Web site: http://archives.stlnet.com/archives/.

von Hoffman, Alexander. 1998. "High Ambitions: The Past and Future of American

Low-Income Housing Policy." In D. Varady, W. F. E. Preiser, and F. Russell, eds., *New Directions in Urban Public Housing*, pp. 3–22. New Brunswick: Rutgers University, Center for Urban Policy Research.

Whyte, William Foote. 1943. *Street Corner Society: The Social Structure of an Italian Slum*. Chicago: University of Chicago Press.

Williams, Brett. 1992. "Poverty among African Americans in the Urban United States." *Human Organization* 51(2):164–74.

Yant, Monica. 1998. "Hire Welfare Recipients, Firms Urged." *Philadelphia Inquirer*, December 3.

Chapter 9

Microenterprise Training Programs, Neoliberal Common Sense, and the Discourses of Self-Esteem

Donna M. Goldstein

Introduction

Microenterprise training programs have received a good deal of both rhetorical and financial support during the Clinton era, the same administration that can be credited with permanently altering the structure of welfare. From this context, the enthusiastic supporters of microenterprise training appear to be members of a developing ideological chorus that want to credit individuals with personal economic success or failure and are eager to provide "the helping hand" to do so. Never mind that economic restructuring has left entire regions abandoned and the gap between the richest and the poorest segments of the population greater than ever. Microenterprise training programs embody both the contradictions of neoliberal economics and an evolving neoliberal discursive style: on the one hand, they are often undercapitalized (as my case studies illustrate) and they are aimed at a narrow segment of the poor. On the other hand, through the dispersion of these programs, the individual is encouraged and incited to believe in his or her own powers to succeed and then blamed in the event of failure. The participants in these training programs speak of the effects of the programs in a language reflecting a pride in a newly empowered self, one that has gained self-esteem and confidence in his or her own capabilities.

Nancy Fraser (1993) refers to this developing welfare policy and its accompanying ethos as a kind of "*neoliberal* common sense." According to Fraser, the neoconservatism of the Reagan and Bush administrations and the neoliberalism of the Clinton administration have converged.

This is evidenced by the latter's call for "targeting" specific populations for child care, child-support collection, and job training rather than fostering programs that would guarantee jobs, growth in annual income, a single-payer health care system, universal public day care, and a national child-support insurance system for all (Fraser 1993:16). Nikolas Rose (1993) coins the term *advanced liberalism* in his description of a welfare state that seeks to foster self-government by the poor. Following Rose's work, Susan Hyatt (1997:219) argues:

> In the current climate of advanced liberalism, poverty is represented not as a social problem but as a new possibility for poor individuals to experience "empowerment" through the actualization of self-management.

There is an interesting collusion, therefore, that we can now witness in the work of anthropologists called in by policy experts to "give voice to" participants and to "do ethnography" that engages our field in a new configuration of power. In privileging the voices of the poor, it is possible to see the ways in which individuals themselves contribute to an advanced liberal ideology that focuses on the self as the locus of economic success or failure. And while the rewards of success are often highlighted within this discourse, especially by politicians and policymakers on both the left and the right, underlying this is an ideology of blame, in which failure is identified as a personal fault rather than a fault of the government or of structural changes in the economy.

Such an emphasis on the individual is nothing new in the American ideological spectrum. With the convergence, however, that Fraser discusses of the political left and right over the issues of welfare reform and economic (self-) responsibility, this emergent discourse has embedded itself at the level of popular culture. It represents a particularly powerful expression of American individualism in which economic success or failure becomes wholly equated with an individual's possession or lack of self-esteem. Implicit in this is an essential faith in the market as the proper and level playing field for economic success.

This chapter broadly explores the discourses of self-esteem that have emerged in both popular and policy discussions of welfare reform. It examines the specific case of one federally supported microenterprise training program administered in the state of Colorado. The program, which took place between 1995 and 1997 and originated out of the Department of Labor's Job Training Partnership Act (JTPA), targeted low-income individuals with the purpose of training them to become self-employed microenterprise entrepreneurs. It is analytically evident that there are many downsides to these programs, including their inability to address the wider economic structure of the region, their lack of marketing and credit strategies, and their focus on the mid-level poor rather than the poorest. But while these criticisms are accurate, my focus here is on the limiting nature of the self-esteem discourse within which such programs are conceptualized and promoted among certain populations. The discourse of self-esteem limits the discursive possibilities of new policy and posits responsibility for economic success or failure within the individual character rather than in the program itself or in the structural realities of the economy. I focus on the ways in which both the participants and the administrators of the program readily offer the concept of self-esteem as explanatory of what makes for successful microenterprise entrepreneurs. More important, the concept of self-esteem also figures highly in their understanding of what is needed to alleviate poverty. These discourses assume that the potential for economic success lies in the individual self rather than in more material and economic conditions affecting the availability of decent jobs with decent wages. The proliferation and naturalization of this assumption serves to reinvent, in a new, "neoliberal" light, the dated portrait of the poor as psychologically debilitated and behaviorally problematic.

My argument is not that these programs are "the best that we can do" but rather that we cannot hope to do better until we begin to deconstruct this highly effective neoliberal discourse. It appears to be all but impossible at the moment to call for large-scale "safety-net" social programs, because the discursive space for such a discussion has largely closed. The reason, at least partially, may exactly be the convergence of the discourse of self-esteem from both the left and the right. This essay argues that we need to examine this discourse critically in order to know what alternatives are possible to utter.

The Discourses of Self-Esteem and Welfare Reform

A recent flurry of empirical studies in the social and political sciences use Michel Foucault's concept of "governmentality"[1] to analyze "the government of human conduct in all contexts, by various authorities and agencies, invoking particular forms of truth, and using definite resources, means and techniques" (Dean 1999:3). One particular branch of the governmentality literature proposed by Barbara Cruikshank (1993) focuses on the ways in

which the self-esteem and empowerment movement shifts the terrain of responsibility away from outside sources and toward the self. She examines a
few of the diverse sources of the movement, such as Gloria Steinem's (1992)
best-selling book *Revolution From Within: A Book of Self-Esteem* and the
organization and goals of the California Task Force on Self-Esteem and Personal and Social Responsibility (1990a; 1990b). Cruikshank views the self-
esteem discourse as one that offers a reorientation to problem solving, offering a science of the self as liberatory of the psychological state of particular peoples, "especially poor urban people of color to whom most of the
'social problems' are attributed." She perceives the discourse of "self-esteem
[as] but one in a long line of technologies of citizenship," or rather, "a technology of citizenship and self-government for evaluating and acting upon
our selves so that the police, the guards and the doctors do not have to"
(Cruikshank 1993:330). A crucial point of her argument is that what is
being heralded by social scientists as important to understanding a particular problem—such as poverty—is the "lack" of self-esteem, and in this
process, there is a shift in the types of political action that can be called for:

> The call for self-government and democracy is extended away from political
> institutions and economic relations by the self-esteem movement; the politi-
> cal goals of participation, empowerment and collective action are extended to
> the terrain of the self. (Cruikshank 1993:331)

Evidence of this phenomenon is readily available in popular press depictions of how workers see themselves in the midst of economic restructuring—rather than calling for union organizing or for the replacement of lost
economic opportunities, workers frame the problem of economic restructuring as a problem of the individual and speak in a language that focuses
on the self.

For example, a *New York Times* front-page article headlined "Downsizing
Comes Back, but the Outcry Is Muted" (December 7, 1998), written by
Louis Uchitelle, is subtitled "Rather Than Protests, Unions Are Offering
Transition Advice" and leads into a bleak description of the effects of the
closing down of a television assembly plant (Thomson Consumer Electronics of Bloomington) in Indiana. The argument of the article is that "the
outcries and conflict that characterized the waves of downsizing in the
1980s and early 1990s are largely gone now." The article provides close-up
interviews with former employees of Thomson who are forced to cope with
a plant closing. (The company gave fourteen months' notice and then relocated to Mexico.) In the text of the article, a former employee is quoted at

length. She was retrained as a truck driver and suffered a loss in her wages, but she assimilated her experience, at least partially, in terms of her own self-esteem:

> I don't mind driving a truck. A lot of people would not do it, but I am trying to get back to where I was at Thomson. It takes away from your self-esteem until you find something as good, or better. You know there has to be something better.

The worker quoted above seems to be saying that until she gets back to where she was (i.e., her original wages), her self-esteem will "naturally" be lacking. It is interesting that she focuses on the impact on her self-esteem while ignoring the actual economic hardship of earning less. The article describes a process whereby workers and unions are discouraged from protest because of the new forms by which protest is absorbed, namely, through retraining programs financed by the federal government that seem to normalize downsizing, the movement of capital, and the restructuring of entire regions.[2]

Microenterprise Training Programs and the Belief in the Self

As mentioned above, microenterprise training programs have received a good deal of support during the Clinton era. Hillary Clinton, especially, has been a powerful advocate of microenterprise training programs in the United States. Tracy Ehlers and Karen Main (1998), in a critical appraisal of microenterprise training programs for women, quote Hillary Clinton's message to the preparatory meeting of the Microcredit Summit:

> Microenterprise is the heart of development because microenterprise programs work—they lift women and families out of poverty. It's called "micro," but its impact on people is macro. We have seen that it takes just a few dollars, often as little as $10, to help a woman gain self employment, to lift her and her family out of poverty. It's not a handout; it's a helping hand. Through my travels in my own country and around the world, I have seen the profound impact that microenterprise initiatives are having on families. . . . I have met women whose lives are being transformed because, for the first time, they have access to credit. (Quoted in Ehlers and Main 1998:425)

Despite a few critical voices such as Ehlers and Main, who see such programs as ultimately defeating and detrimental for poor women because they promise more than they can deliver and then blame the victim for failure, these programs have, in the mainstream, come to be seen in an extremely positive light. Indeed, highly visible advocates such as Hillary Clinton hold out such programs as the Grameen Bank in rural Bangladesh as ideal models for economic development and have done much to fashion these types of programs as the "new economic hope" within the popular imagination.

Microenterprise training programs are an interesting programmatic breed within a broad range of federal poverty alleviation programs. Historically, the idea of microenterprise training as a poverty alleviation initiative began as one among many "development" strategies (i.e., the Grameen Bank) in developing countries where access to credit was perceived to be the major problem of the informal sector. The enthusiastic policy literature that praises these programs envisions microenterprise training as a way of bringing marginal businesses and low-income people into the mainstream by giving them access to business skills, information, and, most important, credit; yet such an idea is not limited to standard "third world development" strategies. New York City mayor Rudy Giuliani, interviewed in a (December 20, 1998) Sunday *New York Times Magazine* article, exemplifies the current mainstreamed belief in entrepreneurship as a solution to the inability to find or get a job and to the problem of poverty more generally:

> If you can't get a job, start a small business. Start a little candy store. Start a little newspaper stand. Start a lemonade stand. (Mayor Giuliani, in DeParle 1998:89)

The idea behind microenterprise programs partially rests on the idea that in situations where actual jobs are scarce, individuals with an entrepreneurial talent will be able to start up their own business and generate their own income. The author of the *New York Times Magazine* article, Jason DeParle, a well-known journalist devoted to writing about poverty and welfare issues and seemingly critical of the mayor's conservative position on welfare reform, exhibits the journalistic discourse that attempts to get close to characters by seeming to know something about their psychological characteristics. In the text of the article, he describes what he understands to be the overwhelming psychological characteristics of individuals living in poverty, stating boldly that "the majority rank as troubled souls: depressed, illiterate, infirm, addicted." DeParle's framing of the issue in terms of psychological factors illustrates how the underlying self-esteem discourse refocuses economic success and failure in terms of individual "character" (and thereby shifts the causality of economic matters away from the market and onto the individual self). More important, it shows how mainstream such a notion has become: that a similar position can be shared by these two oppositional figures, the liberal journalist and the conservative politician. Such descriptions are reminiscent of the behavioral descriptions of the poor made by anthropologist Oscar Lewis and other "culture of poverty" theorists in the 1960s and 1970s, which were then criticized by anthropologists for the next three decades.[3] DeParle's depiction is a perfect example of this kind of psychological caricature. William Julius Wilson (1997) argues that such explanations, whether offered in the texts of liberal journalists or in the words of conservative policy analysts, have come to share a common language because liberal intellectuals, in failing to advance significant poverty alleviation programs after 1965,[4] allowed popular media and conservative versions of the culture-of-poverty thesis to dominate the discourse up through the Reagan years.[5]

A Social Science Example

Janet Fitchen, an anthropologist who thanks Oscar Lewis in the acknowledgments section of her 1981 book *Poverty in Rural America: A Case Study*, identifies self-esteem as a factor embedded in hierarchical levels of causality within a more generalized "Failure Syndrome."

Fitchen finds that low self-esteem is apparent among the rural poor, especially among men, and cites it as

> an ongoing cause of intergenerational rural poverty. . . . Repeated experiences of failure, almost unavoidable for many people, lead to low self-esteem and lack of confidence. This, in turn, leads to limited expectations for oneself that are apt to cause further failures and reinforce the low self-image. The cycle continues, in all spheres of life: on the job, in school, in dealings with community agencies and institutions, in social relationships, and in marriage and family relationships. (Fitchen 1981:196)

Low self-esteem is understood to be a limiting psychological factor, although it is embedded in the hierarchy of primary causes and viewed as derivative. Nevertheless, these psychological causes take on a life of their own and, over time, have become part of the standard discourse used to describe the causes of poverty in America—not only among journalists and conservative analysts, as Wilson suggests, but also within the social sciences and within the general population. In the process of recognizing that psychological factors play a role in the production and reproduction of poverty, these same factors have begun to circulate and constitute their own universe and have become the primary explanation for poverty and economic failure. One of the results of this discursive explosion constituting the lack of self-esteem as a major cause of poverty is that the ability to call for collective action—against a corporation or the government, for example—is absorbed in a discourse that posits the self as the only location of power to manifest change, placing the locus of responsibility for economic failure on the individual rather than on the government or on historical or structural factors. Poverty is thus continually constructed as a personal problem—a product or outcome of a lack of self-esteem—therefore making the need for government intervention unnecessary or even negative.

The Context of Microenterprise Training in Colorado

The microenterprise training program carried out in 1995–1997 in the state of Colorado calls into question the "effectiveness" of what Fraser identifies as neoliberal common sense. This program also provides us with a case study of a poverty alleviation program for low-income populations that immediately preceded welfare reform. Rather than lobbying for structural reforms, administrators, policymakers, and participants internalize the message of self-empowerment espoused by such programs. This message of self-empowerment downplays the often ambiguous economic outcomes of such programs. Participants often find themselves no better off in terms of economic vulnerability (or often worse off in terms of debt burden), yet the participants nevertheless value the "entrepreneurial skills" they learn in these programs, buying whole-heartedly into the discourse of self-interest, self-esteem, and self-blame. And the anthropologist as ethnographer reports these findings as part of the "extra-economic" benefits of the program.

During 1995–1997, the Targeted Ownership Project (TOP) carried out a microenterprise training program at various urban and rural sites in the state of Colorado. This training program originated as a federal grant from the United States Department of Labor's (DOL's) Job Training Partnership Act (JTPA) to the Colorado State Department of Human Services and Colorado Capital Initiatives (CCI).[6] The training grants were offered by the Department of Labor on a competitive basis, and each state interested in experimenting with microenterprise training authored (or co-authored) its own grant proposal. Colorado was one of the states awarded the grant money to test this pilot program.[7] As a result, the state was awarded $300,000 per year during two years to carry out a training program in some of the most impoverished rural areas in Colorado.

When the Department of Labor's JTPA offered similar grants in 1997, the mission of the grants was geared toward dislocated workers and the long-term unemployed. During the years discussed here, 1996 and 1997, the overall mission of the grants was to provide benefits for economically disadvantaged persons and to do this through training and technical assistance (Meyerhoff 1997:105–6).

The idea behind the Colorado microenterprise training project was "to provide small businesses with access to credit and business assistance, based on an assessment of business needs by community representatives" (CBDI Proposal 1995:3).[8] The Colorado Department of Human Services had conducted microenterprise training with JTPA-eligible participants in the city and county of Denver for three years prior to the initiation of this more comprehensive project. According to the original proposal, the project would enable the collaborators to "begin another microenterprise start-up program in the Denver area, expand the program to three outstate areas, provide equity money to start-up businesses, significantly expand services to young, emerging business and bring higher levels of loan dollars to JTPA eligible self-employed participants" (CBDI Proposal 1995:4). The programs were meant to be "training driven" (CBDI Proposal 1995:6) and in the first phase would provide the JTPA-eligible participants with the "knowledge, financial means, and local support to start a small cottage enterprise" (CBDI Proposal 1995:7).

The four sites[9] initially chosen for "targeting" by the project showed median household incomes lower than the state median of $30,140 (U.S. Census Bureau 1990). One of the stated major goals of the project, according to the original proposal, was to foster long-term community development by aiding successful microenterprise development; thus an implicit assumption of those interested in promoting microenterprise development is that community development can be built upon self-employment. Access to training and credit (in loan and grant form) were defined as key elements to the success of the project. The program was meant to provide short-term credit to the self-employed, since self-employment already figured significantly in the overall economic activity of the poorest regions in the state. It was also meant to help those capable of thinking through a plan of self-employment realize those plans and then to provide the technical support necessary for ensuring success.

The intended participants in the TOP training program were those who would qualify as JTPA-eligible, that is, those who fell within JTPA guidelines. According to these guidelines, the following levels of family gross income must pertain for six consecutive months in order for the participant to fall within the low-income category: a family of one person must have a gross income below $3,870 ($645/month); of two people, $5,190 ($865/month); of three people, $7,130 ($1,188/month). This act targeted "economically disadvantaged" individuals and defined low income according to a time frame of the preceding six months. JTPA eligibility is granted if the participant either falls within the above prescribed guidelines or provides proof that an agency such as Aid to Families with Dependent Children (AFDC) has certified the individual as "economically disadvantaged."

As a criterion, JTPA eligibility is nuanced across urban and rural sites, and, from the perspective of poverty policy analysts, attempts to address a different population from that which is strictly "welfare"; it is set up to be inclusive of a broadly defined low-income population but also aims to capture those affected by short-term economic hardship. It therefore encompasses a population that is more diverse than that addressed by other programs working toward poverty alleviation.[10] JTPA eligibility thus does not necessarily address the concerns of the most impoverished populations, such as long-term welfare recipients, although this population certainly qualifies as JTPA-eligible. Thus, in 1995–1997, JTPA eligibility included the AFDC and Food Stamp recipient population, but it also captured slightly higher income groups that might be considered middle-income but could (and often do) become economically vulnerable. In theory, JTPA eligibility is supposed to capture a population that is both much broader than and yet inclusive of the welfare population.

Colorado Capital Initiatives

From the perspective of Colorado Capital Initiatives (CCI), which co-authored the state-level grant with the Department of Human Services in Colorado, the hope was to capture a group who would have some of the resources to succeed at both getting loans and establishing or continuing a small business enterprise. CCI was attempting to harness these federal resources in a manner that would contribute to community development, and part of their philosophy depended on setting up guarantor programs in the communities where the training programs were to take place. These guarantor programs sought the expertise and investment of business leaders in these communities so that loans could be administered to small, developing businesses or new, promising small businesses. The not-for-profit corporation found the JTPA guidelines for low income to be limiting. CCI would have liked to have enabled more economically secure people, those whom they viewed to be above the "economically disadvantaged" category outlined in the federal guidelines, to participate in the training because they believed that this "cream of the crop" of the rural population was more likely to succeed in business than those struggling at more basic levels. Also, they wanted the population seeking loans from the guarantor program to be credible as entrepreneurs among a conservative business community.

At some sites, many of the participants in the training sessions were so low-income that they fell far from the range hoped for by the CCI partners. But many of these participants dropped out of the classes without finishing. The federal grant, however, had guaranteed these people admission to the program despite the objections raised by CCI. The different perspectives concerning who should be eligible for the program wound up causing conflict between CCI and the federal manager. CCI felt the federal program was somewhat insensitive to the local, community-based needs of their guarantors, who controlled the revolving loan funds and who wanted to support only businesses that would actually turn a profit. The following is a quote from a CCI official in 1996:

> The objective that we set is, you know, low-income community revitalization, economic growth within low-income areas and communities. And how over the long term can something like this add to that. Something like this consists of three major elements: training, capital, and markets—access to markets. You gotta know what you're doing, you gotta have the money to do it, and you gotta have somewhere to sell it. All right. JTPA concentrated on training. We did the capital and left the markets pretty much up to the business. (CCI official, taped interview, 1996)

There was thus some developing tension between the CCI partners and the federal JTPA administrator in charge of the grant, who was bound by the federal guidelines to address a specific low-income population. This tension is telling because it acts as a reality check on policy. It draws into question the potential effectiveness of the program for the majority of those it was intended to help. It also foreshadows the problems with securing credit and grant money faced by many of the participants. (Indeed, many relied on personal forms of financing—credit cards, family loans—rather than on moneys from the program.) This haphazardness in terms of funding was at least partially due to these disagreements between the federal regulators and the local CCI guarantors over who was an appropriate "risk" for credit (which was implicitly a disagreement over whom the program was actually for). And yet, despite this, the majority of the participants perceived even the haphazard economic benefits of the program (small grants and potential loans, subsidized professional advice, etc.) in an overwhelmingly positive light. Although CCI and the federal government differed in their vision of who would best be suited to these programs, both subscribed to the idea that self-employment initiatives could lead to community development and could address some aspects of rural poverty. What the tension between CCI and the federal government suggests, ultimately, is that these programs would be somewhat problematic if offered to only the poorest segment of the long-term welfare population. Besides lacking specific training and education, microenterprise entrepreneurs drawn from the poorest segments of the population would suffer from the lack of concrete capital investment from the local business community, who would be called upon—through the granting of a loan—to support their fledgling businesses.

Methods and Data Collection

During two years, I designed a research program and coordinated an ethnographic research team of graduate students from the University of Colorado–Boulder[11] whose main purpose, as requested by JTPA and the Department of Human Services, was to examine the effects of the training programs on participants and in their communities.

The first- and second-year sites encompassed parts of rural and semirural Colorado and parts of the suburban and metropolitan Denver area.[12] The Denver sites were distinct from the other sites[13] in that the Denver classes attracted a much lower income population than the population participating in classes at other sites.

Researchers traveled around the state attending the TOP training classes and interviewing participants in the classroom and in their homes (using a tape recorder). Follow-up interviews were conducted with participants six months after the training classes ended. Questionnaires were administered, and in-depth community and individual cases for close study were chosen.[14] I designed the research with two distinct goals in mind: first, to find out "what worked and what didn't work" in the training programs, thereby fulfilling the request of the JTPA officials and Department of Human Services administrators who employed the team to carry out the research; and second, to carry out a broader ethnographic investigation into the lives of the participants in the program, paying particular attention to their discourses and perceptions regarding the effects the program had on their own lives. I personally interviewed the administrators and trainers involved in the project and wrote the final evaluation reports based on the taped and transcribed interviews, fieldnotes, and summaries of the field researchers.[15]

The Participants and the Training Regime

More than 140 participants went through the microenterprise training program—approximately 70 each year of the two-year training program. Forty participants were interviewed during the first year, and eight individual case studies from the original forty interviewed were followed up. During the second year, fifty-one individuals were interviewed and sixteen case studies were followed up. Interviews for the case studies ranged in length from approximately forty-five minutes to two hours; multiple visits and observations were made in many cases.

Participants in the first year were chosen from all four 1995 TOP sites and during the second year from the additional three new sites. The sites encompassed parts of rural and semi-rural Colorado and parts of the suburban and metropolitan Denver area. The counties included Alamosa, Montezuma, Conejos, Morgan, Denver, Fremont, and Mesa.

Our research found that 75 percent of the first year's participants and 59 percent of the second year's participants carried no health insurance policy at all. It is a defining feature of the population. In terms of caretaking responsibilities, 23 percent of the participants in the first year and 33 percent of the participants in the second year were single mothers with children.

The cases discussed in the following sections are representative of the diversity of the total participant pool and were drawn from the total pool (140 participants) with the aim of analyzing both the "successes" and the "failures." I have chosen to present these cases because of their diversity and because of what they reveal in terms of personal circumstance, the characteristics of the training program, and, most important, the participants' generally favorable impression of the self-motivational aspects of microenterprise training.

It is important to keep in mind that the program offered to participants step-by-step training on how to put together a business plan, as well as tips on how to market their products. In some cases, small grants were made to participants in order to help them get their businesses off the ground. While the program had hoped to offer credit and loans through a regulated local guarantor program, there was less success in this area than had been hoped for. The participants were extremely laudatory about the motivational and therapeutic aspects of the program, characteristics that are "extra-economic." These widely divergent participants share with one another and with some of the administrators of the program an appreciation for the kind of individual growth, especially in the area of self-esteem, that they experienced as a result of the program.

What the program did for the participants in concrete terms was serve as a mobilizing space for them to consider their own self-esteem in the context of work. The training programs acculturated the participants into a "can do" attitude of confidence that enabled them to consider how they themselves may have, in the past, contributed to their inability to be perfectly successful in the world of work. Over the course of the two years during which we tracked the training program, a number of teacher-trainers participated as classroom teachers. Each of the teacher-trainers had his or her own pedagogical style, and there was some variation with regard to which entrepreneurial curriculum packet these instructors used during any one course.[16]

Given the variability among the participants, it is not surprising that there was some diversity among reactions to the curriculum. Despite this, almost all participants expressed satisfaction with their experience in the classroom. Suggestions by participants as to how the curriculum might be improved varied sometimes to the extent of contradiction, but these were for the most part relatively minor, fine-tuning issues when compared to the general experience of the curriculum's efficacy. The classes often started with general, personal topics, such as a self-assessment of the participants' entrepreneurial characteristics. The curriculum then led to more specific areas such as concept development, business structure, market analysis and marketing, finance, budget, pricing, and cash flow. During this time, participants were to be working gradually on their feasibility studies.

After these were handed in, read by the instructor, and returned, money sources and management were covered. The actual business plan was due in the seventh class meeting, after which time participants who were moving ahead with their businesses had access to their trainer-teachers. In some cases, this relationship continued for months after the course's end, to the credit of the teacher-trainers involved, for whom this kind of dedication was not part of the original job description.

The curriculum also included four individual coaching sessions in which participants could be helped with areas they had been finding difficult in class, issues with feasibility and business plans were discussed, and their progress was assessed. For the most part, the teacher-trainers were considered decent teachers, and the trainees found the curriculum somewhat appropriate to their needs.

Some participants actually commented that they could have done without some of the "inspirational stuff" at the course's beginning and said they did not need to hear stories about businesspeople who had "made it." But the majority of the trainees brought up the changes in self-esteem that the course had offered them and felt thankful that, at the end, they had found the self-confidence to apply for and succeed at securing a full-time job, or to actually start a business, or to begin thinking about the prospect. One trainee expressed this sentiment most directly:

> We've gotten more confidence since the course because the course showed us a lot of different avenues. . . . One thing they taught us in the course was that if you try to grow too fast, you'll drown. And I think that's one of the most common ways businesses die. They try to grow too fast and they succumb to the financial burden.

In some cases, it was mentioned that the textbook was too advanced for the participants, that it was very dry and seemed geared toward college-level students and thus was not really an introductory course. Another criticism was that the curriculum was not designed for participants' particular needs; in other words, for small, home-based businesses, starting with little in the way of resources, such as the vending business or independent medical transcription services, the curriculum seemed to be poorly matched. Instead, it focused on manufacturing and larger-scale businesses that had no relation to those in the course. This caused some feelings of discouragement, though these were outweighed by participants' sentiments about the "personal growth" aspects of the course. They were also happy to interact with businesspeople from the community, which enabled them to feel more comfortable with "professionals." Participants said things like "I came to class with a dream, and now that dream has become a reality" and "I had an idea, but the class gave me the confidence to go on."

In one class where the teacher-trainer was noted by the students to be particularly effective, a participant in the program equated the training course to dieting: "You have to structure your life differently, change your lifestyle and [learn] how to structure your day." Students mentioned that the teacher-trainer for this particular class had helped them learn self-discipline: how to show up on time, behave professionally, and complete projects.

Two generalized outcomes can be suggested from the statements made by the trainees who were interviewed after the course:

1. The allure of self-employment promoted in the context of the training course contributed to a general sense of increased self-esteem on the part of the participants.

2. The course provided a space for the self to be regulated and judged in terms of personal productivity, one that served to institute among the participants a particular form of self-governance in neoliberal times. This self-governance structured around issues of personal productivity also helped build self-esteem on the part of the participants.

The Allure of Self-Employment: Four Cases

Pete

Pete, now just forty, was born in the same agricultural community in rural Colorado in which he attended the Targeted Ownership Project's microenterprise training program. Neither of his parents completed high school. He says he was born on the "wrong side of the tracks," and, as his father was an alcoholic and his mother "was gone long ago," he and his brother were brought up by their grandmother. He says that, as children, he and his brother "pretty much ran wild," and though he always found school easy, he never did well because he wasn't interested, and he quit after tenth grade. During high school, Pete worked at the sugar-beet factory and the meat plant. Afterward, he started working in the oil fields and soon had his own business maintaining oil rigs. He liked knowing he was making more than the high school principal and thought that "making $600 a week was better than a high school education. . . . I couldn't see past that." He has never relied on any form of public support other than unemployment insurance.

At the age of twenty he considered joining the U.S. Air Force but was told he would be too old to learn to fly jets by the time he had finished high school and college. In the mid-1980s, after oil prices collapsed, he and his third wife moved to the Midwest. They had two children, of whom he says, "There hasn't been anything topped that." He worked as a contractor and later as a long-haul semi driver, which was both his best-paid and least-favorite job: he "had to break every law that was written to do it," and the alcohol problem he inherited became compounded by drug abuse. He was on the road six days a week trying to pay for a farm the family had purchased, and when his marriage deteriorated as well as his finances, divorce and bankruptcy followed. He returned to Colorado, and for three years or so after that, "there wasn't a day I wasn't drunk or on something." When he woke up in jail one morning, not knowing how he got there, he decided he had to change and committed himself to a drug and alcohol rehabilitation program in Denver. He worked as a welder for a company until it went bankrupt and was collecting unemployment when he saw the TOP microenterprise training program advertised. He had started building a custom motorcycle to sell and signed up, thinking "this is going to be a way that I can borrow some money . . . and I'll be able to start my own business."

He completed a business plan, which was reviewed by the local mentors, made the suggested revisions, and was told it was a good plan, before approaching "every bank in town" for a $5,000 loan. Because of his bankruptcy, and probably also because of his being in arrears on child-support payments, no bank was willing to make the loan. While living in a $400-a-month trailer, against the side of which he built an open-air workshop, he did small welding jobs and finished his first motorcycle. He sold this unique, beautifully crafted machine through a $5 advertisement in a motorcycle club magazine. This enabled him to relieve some of the pressure of his child-support debts, which amounted to more than $30,000. Soon after his first sale, he received a $5,000 down payment for his next order and paid down his suppliers' accounts. Less than six months after the end of the course, he had sold two bikes and received orders for two more. He has made more than $5,000 in profit on each sale.

When Pete was interviewed, he mentioned how it may have been a good thing that he didn't get a loan, because it made him more attentive to his cash flow. While he agreed that a loan or an investor would help grow his business more quickly, he was extremely proud to assert that he would do it himself, incrementally, if necessary. While he had the incentive to start his business before the TOP microenterprise training program came along, he credits the program with giving him the self-esteem needed to come as far as he did:

> I wanted to learn if I was able to do this, am I smart enough. Can I keep it to-gether good enough, you know. What does it take? I didn't know what it took. . . . The program helped my self-esteem. It didn't provide me with the big in-spiration. . . . But the program showed me how to do it, you know.

He hopes to develop his business to the point of building ten to twelve bikes a year, and his greatest motivation, beyond getting out of debt, is to be able to give his children some of the things he never had and also to be able to send them to college. For Pete, the allure of self-employment—the ability to make it on his own—had the effect of boosting his self-esteem:

> If I don't do it making motorcycles, I'll do it some other way. I already know: It ain't going to be working for somebody else. I'm never going to make enough money to do what I've got to do working for somebody else. . . . [I want to] help [my kids] in their life.

Karen

Although Karen grew up in Colorado, she spent most of her adult life out of state. She returned to Colorado in 1990 so that she could be close to her mother, after the death of her mother's husband. When she first returned, Karen was working as a Certified Nursing Assistant. Despite the fact that she had received training to be a medical assistant in another state, she had to accept this lower-paying occupation because, at the time she returned, her educational certification was not accepted in Colorado. Although she could have become certified in Colorado, Karen was reluctant to undertake the studying required for the examination. Then, in 1993 she was injured at her job. Her injury has become chronic, preventing her from returning to work in the medical field. Currently, Karen is living with her life partner in a small mobile home in a rural town.

Karen's reasons for wanting to have her own business stem in part from her disability. Being out of work created a financial and personal crisis, requiring her to seek out a new means of making a living. Because she is unable to sit for long periods of time, she cannot work in a typical job. She needs to take frequent breaks, which would be disruptive if she were on a regimented time schedule. Through the Resource Jobs Center, a local nonprofit organization, Karen learned of opportunities to work in the medical transcription field, which fits with her previous medical training and would allow her to work independently, on her own schedule and in her home.

At the time of the interview, she was still in the process of completing the required medical transcription training, which was being paid for by the Resource Jobs Center. The center was also instrumental in getting her connected to the TOP program.

Karen was also motivated to have her own business because she sees the local economy as detrimental to most people who are trying to get ahead. There are very few jobs that pay above minimum wage, and the jobs that used to exist when she was growing up, such as agricultural labor and trucking, are no longer available. This makes it difficult for anyone without an education to earn a reasonable living. According to Karen, "the only way to make a decent living is to have your own business."

Karen attributed to the TOP course the understanding that she now has the commitment required to run her own business. The course "opened doors for her" in giving her access to those people who could answer her questions and assist her in running her business. Through the TOP program, Karen received a $500 Supportive Services Grant, which allowed her to buy a transcribing machine and a printer, both of which are essential for her business. She will have to raise a bit more money so that she can remodel a part of the interior of her residential trailer and buy a computer, but she believes this will be possible through a family loan. Karen, like Pete, values the course for providing her with the information she needed to run her own business and, because of her particular skills and the region she lives in, is attracted to the possibility of self-employment.

Maria

Maria is a young woman with three children all under the age of six. She was, at the time of her interview, in the process of getting a divorce. Maria's financial problems began when she was married and her husband had trouble finding a job. During her marriage there were financial ups and downs, and the family received assistance in the form of subsidized housing. Their financial problems meant credit problems, including problems maintaining public service accounts. Since separating from her husband, Maria and the children have been receiving $400 a month in AFDC. According to Maria, her husband tended to be financially irresponsible and would not allow her to participate in managing money. While she now has less money than before her separation, she feels she is "making it" for the first time.

When Maria began to think of starting her own business, she had in mind learning a clerical trade, such as medical transcribing. Her trainer, however, saw that the clerical fields in the city where Maria lives were becoming saturated. This, plus the fact that Maria would have had to invest in other training, led the trainer to encourage Maria to do something she would enjoy more. Maria actually did have another idea, but she didn't realize at that time that she could turn it into a business.

Maria has a young daughter with long hair, whom she enjoys dressing so that her hair accessories match her clothes. Hair accessories such as barrettes and bows are expensive, however, and also quite difficult to match. So Maria began making her own and came up with a unique way to make them so that various barrettes could snap onto others, creating numerous possibilities of color and design. Maria enjoyed this kind of experimentation and soon was making barrettes out of cloth and other sewing ornaments for her friends' children, as well as making custom boxes (with designs and the children's names) to store them in.

When she told the trainer about this idea, the trainer suggested that she follow it up, and this is the idea for which she wrote her business plan and that she is actively pursuing. In the long run, Maria would like to expand her business to adult hair accessories, and she has already begun to design some of them.

The difficulty Maria has with her products is learning how to price them, taking into account her time and materials. This is something she believes will come with experience. At the time of the interview, Maria had received a few custom orders, primarily from other TOP students who planned to give them as Christmas gifts, but as yet she had not developed any significant marketing strategies.

Through the Technical Assistance program, Maria had made plans to speak with the manager of a local department store and an attorney. Maria was particularly excited about having a contact with "a large retail store" and hoped that the manager would be able to give her advice on marketing. Some time after the interview, in a follow-up discussion with the trainer, the researcher learned that not only had Maria met with the manager but that the manager was apparently very impressed with Maria and her products and has placed a large order with her. In addition, he has arranged for her to meet with his marketing department to see if possibilities exist for selling the accessories outside her hometown. The connection to the department store is an important one for Maria, one she likely would have had trouble making on her own.

In response to questions about the feasibility of Maria's products, the trainer remarked that although this is a business that will take some time to become lucrative, such a longer time frame is ideal for a person like Maria. Because Maria has never lived on her own or supported herself, the time she spends building this business will give her the confidence and business savvy she needs to move on to the next level. In the meantime, she can continue to receive AFDC and in that way ensure that her children will be provided for through this business-development period. Maria may also try to get another type of business loan, although she is concerned that this might be difficult because she has never had credit and therefore has no credit history on which to build.

The trainer emphasized to Maria that whether or not this business proved to be successful was not the only issue. That Maria will have learned to interact with businesspeople and that she can use her ingenuity to go forward in her life is also important. Maria feels the course has changed her life because "it has made me believe in myself, made me more determined, and helped me make a solid decision" so that she can support herself.

Robert

Robert is in his early forties, married, and a high school graduate. His grandmother's family once owned "half the San Luis Valley," but from his perspective, this is no reason to be "stuck in the past," the way some people in the valley seem to be. He has heard stories of hundreds of acres of land being sold "for a pair of boots," and while some view that as evidence of exploitation, he simply sees it as "dumb business." The fact that his family no longer owns the land is irrelevant. "That kind of thinking is a big turnoff for me. . . . I could be pitying myself for being a poor Hispanic or bite the bullet and work."

His parents, neither of whom finished high school, "never saw things in black and white, never saw race," and he is barely concerned by the possibility that there may be discrimination in the community that might affect his business, saying that "prejudice is going to be with us until God cleans up the face of this earth." Because his wife is "Anglo," he says, he has "seen both sides"—not just prejudice directed at him but also the prejudice directed at her, and at himself for marrying her, by members of the Hispanic community.

While he does not share this viewpoint, he says there is much thinking in the Hispanic community along the lines of "the white man took away our land using legal tricks, so we're not going to respect it . . . so pay up, 'cause we're poor abused Hispanics." He sees this kind of thinking as one reason this area is "stuck in the statistics [as] one of the poorest counties in the country."

He worked two jobs for years to achieve his dream of having his own business. One salary went into living expenses, the other into a savings account for his business. Without ever having taken a business course, Robert opened a business seven years ago and has succeeded. He says he found the TOP course to be "even better than I had hoped." Until the course, he had never even heard of a business plan. The plan he completed during the course has been especially useful in helping him better identify his expenses and in organizing and managing his cash flow. The class also taught him to be more consistent in his billing and collection practices, and as a result of better planning and billing, he has seen his income grow in the eight months since he completed the course.

One of the conclusions Robert draws from his experience in the training course is that the Anglo community is trained from the beginning to excel and to save money. "Hispanics don't get that kind of training—at least didn't two or three decades ago. They are not told, this is how to get a good job." He perceives a kind of conservatism in his community that he believes limits the potential for change. The Hispanic community punishes those who break the mold by calling them a "sell-out to the race." For Robert, the training course served to raise his awareness about the "cultural" impediments to entrepreneurship. In this process, his self-esteem was built through the allure of self-employment and in contrast to his ethnic identity.

The Regulation of the Self through Personal Productivity

Ann

Ann was born and raised in Colorado's San Luis Valley. After military service, her father worked at the post office in town, and her mother worked as a registered nurse at the hospital. After graduating from high school, Ann studied nursing until her funding ran out; she then decided to join the air force in order to finish her education without going into debt. She was stationed in California, and her husband worked in a boat shop there. After the service, they stayed in California for a time, but they had spent "seven years wanting to come back" to the Valley.

> That seems to be the general consensus, people who're born here we can't wait to leave but when we're gone, we spend the rest of our lives trying to get back. And there's just something that pulls us, I don't know what it is, but it's almost, it's just kind of a magical place, I mean you can look around, it's not the most beautiful, it's certainly not the most economically sound place to live, but this is just where I need to be, so . . .

The couple had another important element in their lives, the Latter-day Saints' community in their hometown, to return to. Although they had been making a good living in California, they weren't happy there. When they returned, they rented a house for a year before buying one. At the time, they both worked for a mobile-home manufacturer. Ann had been there about eight months when her employers, after finding out that she was pregnant with another child, told her they didn't want her back after the birth:

> They told me that they didn't think I could raise six children and hold down a job at the same time so they didn't want me to come back after my baby was born. And that's when I realized that I was going to get that anywhere I went.

After much thought, Ann came up with a business idea she felt would be viable and good for the region at the same time: developing a catalog of local artists' wares. She worked on the idea for a year and a half before learning of the microenterprise training program from a woman she had approached for advice at the Small Business Development Center. By this time, Ann had already identified potential artists and worked out contractual agreements with them. Because she had no funds to actually produce a catalog, however, she found herself stalled and considered dropping the idea.

She found the training course to be just what she needed. It forced her to refine her idea and to define more specifically what her market was. Ann felt that the training, whether by design or not, naturally weeds out people who are not really ready to be in business. Yet Ann perceives the microenterprise training program, which is supposed to offer skills and assistance to individuals, in an extremely positive manner:

> I still think it's a great program. I know that it's still in its early days and there might be minor things that need to be changed but this is so important. We've really got to have—I'm a firm believer in trickle-up economics. And this is the only way this is going to happen. I hate depending on the government for

anything. I hate that we depend on them even for the grant money to do this. I wish we could get seed money from the communities. But it's got to be done. We can't wait around for people to solve our problems. And I think they've [the government's] got enough of their own problems.

Ann's case is particularly interesting in that she addresses the connections between an anti-government (anti-welfare), anti-corporate discourse and an emphasis on individual effort and self-esteem. When asked about the kind of industry the valley needed, she was very clear about the options she was not enthusiastic about:

> *Ann:* Maybe I should tell you what I wouldn't do. I wouldn't come in and put in a GM car factory, I wouldn't put in a nuclear power plant. That's not what we need.
>
> *Interviewer:* You wouldn't bring industry in?
>
> *Ann:* No, we need to maintain our lifestyle and this is what, why we're here anyhow, because we don't want stuff like that, so we need cottage industry, we need you know, telecommuting, things like that, um, the jobs that are here, should pay a little bit better because people are making money, but I don't see that the traditional "go to work for somebody else" kind of thing is ever going to work very well here in the valley. We need to create our own solutions.

Her privileging of internal, community-based solutions readily collapses into a reinforcement of the American ideology in which economic success or failure becomes wholly equated with an individual's possession or lack of self-esteem:

> *Ann:* If you can't commit to that course and if you're not serious enough to put in the hours that it takes to do that how can you hope to run your business? I put in fourteen-hour days now as it is. And anybody who puts in anything less isn't going to succeed.

For Ann, the course enabled her to depend on only herself—and not the government—to increase her productivity. In this case, the ethos of self-reliance found in much of the social science literature on rural populations is mobilized in the service of the productive self, one that would rather self-exploit than rely on the government.

John and Kay

John and Kay met in Texas in 1979. She was living with her parents, who had moved there from New York for her father's health, and John had just returned from a tour in Korea with the army. Kay's grandparents had been immigrants from Eastern Europe and Russia, and one of her great-grandfathers had been a rabbi. Growing up, Kay had relatives "with numbers on their arms" who had survived the Holocaust. John's father had left his family in southern Kentucky, "where they lived pretty backward," for Detroit at the age of fourteen, where he got a job driving a bread truck (without a license) and then in the steel mills, where he worked all his life. After John quit high school, which he says was violent and uncomfortable with the pressure of the racial politics of the early 1970s, he worked briefly in the mills but considered it a dead-end job. At the age of nineteen he joined the army, which he left three years later, after meeting Kay. They moved back to Detroit, where he worked in the automobile industry until he was laid off; then, only because he felt he had no other options for employment and because by now he had a child to support, he re-enlisted. In 1988 he was stationed in Denver, where they were able to purchase their first house.

In the meantime they had three children, and Kay, who had worked in the restaurant business since before finishing high school, had taken up locksmithing on a dare from her older brother, a successful locksmith in Salt Lake City. She had completed the correspondence course, acquired a few tools, and still considered it a hobby when friends and neighbors started calling on her for help. Eventually she began to advertise, and when she went out on night calls, John accompanied her and started learning the business himself. They incorporated the business, Freedom Lock and Key, with Kay as president and John an officer in the company. In late spring of 1992, John, who suspected he was about to "receive orders" to be restationed, accepted an early retirement package, knowing that if he waited the remaining three and a half years, he would be separated from his family for much of that time. Also, they were happy in Denver and were excited by the promise of their new business.

As the business could not yet support them, Kay worked at a part-time restaurant job while John staffed the new store they had opened, and both went off on call at different times. If John had a call while Kay was working, one of their daughters would staff the shop, so it was always open during the day.

A little more than six months after John left the army, while she was lifting fifty-pound flour sacks, Kay's left clavicle broke, an injury from which she still suffered three years later and which left her with substantial movement limitations that have been diagnosed as permanent. The couple closed the shop while they waited for her workers' compensation payments, which took two and a half months to start arriving. For a few months, Kay was so limited in her abilities that John had to attend to her. He still took calls but was not yet versed in all aspects of the business, and some of Kay's customers wanted her specifically. The business suffered and their savings dwindled. Less than a year after John left the army, they applied for Food Stamps for the first time since their days as young parents in Detroit.

As Food Stamp recipients, they had a choice between attending a job program or the TOP microenterprise training program. As they had never studied business, they chose to attend the TOP course together. Their first class was "a little Mickey Mouse" and left them with doubts, but they continued and soon found it extremely valuable. A year after completing it, they credit the course with their still being in business and have seen business receipts increase from $400 to $500 a month to over $2,000 for the same month the year after they took the course. John draws $400 a month in salary and lends it back to the business in months when it is in the red.

> *Kay:* I don't say that none of it is because of us. I mean we got the information from the course and we ran with it, but we had the opportunity to get this information and, yes, I attribute that to the course. One hundred percent.
> *Interviewer:* Where do you think you'd be if you hadn't taken this class?
> *John:* Closed.
> *Interviewer:* Sorry?
> *John:* I'm sure the business would have been closed.

The course taught the couple "how to utilize our energies in a productive manner versus just scatterbrained here and there." It also taught them "not to spread themselves too thin financially, as well as how to collect money from customers." They have now also chosen to focus on developing repeat customers rather than relying so much on advertising. At the time of our interview with Kay, a year after the course ended and while Kay was still struggling with the insurance company, which doubts her disability, John was about to hire the business's first employee.

Martha

As a child Martha spoke Navajo, as her parents worked on the reservation near Cortez, where she now lives. Her father worked as a maintenance man at the reservation school and later as a plumber, and her mother as a cook. Martha had twelve siblings, and as the reservation was close enough to town, they attended high school in Cortez. In 1973, Martha married her high school sweetheart on the day after graduation, and they bought a house on the outskirts of town shortly afterward. Her husband had been earning $27,000 a year at the dairy, where he had worked for fifteen years until he had recently developed a back problem. Martha worked, as she puts it, "off and on . . . I've had eight children, so it would've had to have been off and on," for various companies, usually carrying out bookkeeping services and managing offices. Two local companies she worked for, a construction company and a clothing manufacturer, went bankrupt.

In 1993, she decided to try turning her sewing, which she had done all her life, into a home-based business. She spent $8,000 on two sewing machines and leather, using her credit card, and started designing and manufacturing leather jackets, skirts, and coats. She sold some through her sister, who has a store in Arizona, and a few things through outlets in tourist towns in southwestern Colorado. She attended a crafts fair and advertised in a catalog but only managed to cover her costs. Then, when her husband was hurt and their income was cut in half, she took a job at a leather-clothing manufacturer for $9 an hour, a wage considered good pay in the area. She worked for nine months before having to return home to care for her husband, whose condition kept deteriorating.

She saw the TOP training program advertised in the local paper and signed up. She says it did just what she needed, and she appreciated the technical assistance part of the project, which provided subsidized professional help to small existing businesses, thereby enabling her to afford the services of a professional bookkeeper for only 25 percent of the full cost:

> I was thinking about going ahead and setting up my books and becoming a business and getting my tax number but I didn't have enough business to really warrant worrying about taxes. I was barely paying for costs. One time they asked when you stop becoming a hobby and become a business and that's when you have to become more full time and it just hadn't happened. So I didn't go ahead and pursue.

She says she learned how to do a business plan but never actually did one, since she dropped out of the course just before the end because she had a big order to fill:

> I didn't have time for both. And I thought, "Well, I'm not getting a loan." I wanted to know how to get a loan. And they taught me that up to that point. They went through how to build the feasibility plan and I felt like I had

learned how but I didn't have time to do it. I wasn't looking for a loan and I had this deadline. I had several orders I had to get out on time.

Since then, neither the business nor her family's situation has improved. Her husband has been diagnosed with spinal stenosis, a deteriorative disease, and because of their religious beliefs, which view God as a healer and doctors and medicine as unnecessary, the insurance company doesn't believe he is really disabled:

> *Interviewer:* Well is your husband in pain now?
>
> *Martha:* Yeah. And that's part of our problem see? It's because the doctors say if you're in pain, you can't take it without the medicine or else you're not in pain. Well that's not true. If you have a will, you can survive. And your pain tolerance goes up.

The business has not developed because Martha has not had the wherewithal to market her product outside her region, and her clothing is too expensive to have a large market nearby. Her sales, perhaps $200 every couple of months, have not changed much in the past year. She has made a few efforts to find outlets for her products and now has three in the area. She has also had some flyers printed up and has sent those out to shops and taxidermists. If she had less on her mind and fewer demands on her time, she might have been able to deal with this; but she is running the household, which now consists of ten people, including her husband, six of their children, a son-in-law, and her daughter's new child. Because two of her children are just starting high school and she fears the negative developments there, she has in the past year chosen to home-school them. She is also involved with their church. She says it is all a matter of priorities. In the meantime, the family is on Food Stamps for the first time ever, and they are preparing to declare bankruptcy in order to deal with the pressure of their credit card debt. While the past two years have been extremely difficult, she says she views this as a new beginning, and that the family has grown closer as a result.

The cases of John and Kay and of Martha illustrate the kinds of regulation of the self that the course aptly trains. In these two cases, despite the medical problems and the hardships, the trainees are conditioned into valuing themselves as "more productive" and, in this embraced regulation of the self, to feel a greater sense of self-esteem. Although the training course is only one element among many that would encourage this kind of self-discipline, in these two cases, the absurdity of the regime is clear in the context these people find themselves struggling in. What is clear is that the course succeeds in conditioning its participants for self-esteem in two distinct ways: through the allure of self-employment and through the regulation of the productive self.

Microenterprise Training, Economic Vulnerability, and Discourses of the Self

One of the biggest disappointments for the participants was the program's inability to provide them with access to credit for use as start-up (or continuing) capital in their self-employment projects. Even though Pete, for example, had started a viable business and completed the program, no bank in town was willing to make him a loan. John and Kay purchased equipment for their business with money from John's retirement package, and Martha bought the sewing machines for her home business on her credit cards. Some participants felt the program misled them into believing that they would be eligible for a loan by the end of the class, but when it came down to actually applying, they were unable to pass the most basic tests of financial creditworthiness.

In some classes, a limited number of grants were awarded to businesses that looked promising to the trainers. Participants who received the grants were pleased with this form of aid, and many more would have liked to receive one. Grants were seen by some of the policymakers, however, as more controversial than loans obtained by the participants themselves. This is partially explained by the fact that the training programs were conceived by the policymakers as a "helping hand" rather than a "handout." Many of the participants expressed their appreciation that the program fostered relationships and connections to others in their community, including the trainer, mentors, and other professionals. In some cases, as with Karen, it was a nonprofit organization in the community that suggested she take the TOP program. Maria made her connection with a local department store through her participation in the program.

It is perhaps obvious to say that economically disadvantaged or low-income populations seem to suffer more personal trauma than other populations. Many of the participants narrate stories of trauma that are obviously related to their economic problems, such as a traumatic health problem that either causes or intensifies financial distress. The case of John and Kay illustrates this point: they are on their way to getting their small locksmithing business up and running when Kay suffers an accident that leaves her partially disabled and forces them to spend their savings. Although none of the participants directly suggested that the program address health-related issues, we found embedded in their narratives an exceedingly strong relationship between the likelihood of health problems and financial disaster. Indeed, it is often health problems that inspire people to think about self-employment in the first place.

Tracy Ehlers and Karen Main (1998) recently published an article in the journal *Gender and Society* that describes microenterprise training programs for women as programs "built on false promises." Their article strongly condemns microenterprise training programs for encouraging women to turn unprofitable pink-collar enterprises into employment options and, in doing so, causing them to forfeit the benefits of other (supposedly available and more lucrative) forms of work:

> Microenterprise development programs can be more detrimental and problematic than they are purported to be. In contrast to the optimism exuded by these programs, their supporters in Washington, and the popular media, we have found that they encourage women to partake in undercapitalized, small-scale businesses that maintain economic vulnerability and social peripheralization in a gender-biased world. (Ehlers and Main 1998:436)

Circumstances such as the economic precariousness experienced by participants due to the lack of health insurance and unavailability of credit, as well as, in many cases, the additional pressures of running a single-parent household, make the attraction of self-employment offered by microenterprise training programs comprehensible as opposed to "far-fetched."[17] What I want to make clear is the following. It is not only that microenterprise training "produces a host of latent consequences that are ultimately more damaging than productive for women," as Ehlers and Main (1998) suggest. Microenterprise training programs also both re-inscribe and are a symptom of the discursive limits through which we are allowed to think through social welfare programs. The participants in these programs for the most part blame themselves for failure, rather than any limitations of the program—for instance, undercapitalization, structural constraints of the economy—and in that process reinforce the implicit assumption that the market is the proper and level playing field in this individual quest for self-sufficiency.

Given the limited circumstances—the inability for individuals to demand economic restructuring—the choice they make to attempt self-employment is sensible. People often remain in economically unstable regions because they have a deeply felt connection to place that attaches them for reasons beyond economic viability. Without the state providing other structured alternatives, self-employment as opposed to nonemployment in these economically anemic regions looks appealing, especially to the limited few who not only participate in the training program but who also manage to set up somewhat successful small businesses. What Ehlers and Main (1998) refer to as "pink-collar employment" may be self-exploiting in comparison to some ideally structured work situation in a new society, but it is anything but far-fetched in the current context. Microenterprise training programs are, more precisely, an imperfect solution offered within the confines of late capitalist neoliberalism. More to the point, in building self-esteem through the allure of self-employment and the encouragement of an increased regulation of the self through personal productivity, microenterprise training programs contribute to a mode of self-governance in the confines of late capitalism that is generic and likely to be found within other, similarly conceived projects of social welfare.

Conclusions

These circumstances highlight the attraction of self-employment offered by microenterprise training programs, rendering them comprehensible. Yet, despite the attraction and "sense" of such programs to participants, it is clear that economic vulnerability remains constant or even increases for most. While our research recognized the small economic returns or high levels of self-exploitation that may be involved in encouraging self-employment among a low-income population, it also tried to make sense of TOP participants' decisions in the context of the prevailing self-esteem discourse.

What the case studies illustrate is that such persistent economic vulnerability is overshadowed by the self-esteem discourse itself. Indeed, the prevalence of this notion of self-responsibility and self-esteem is clearly emphasized as an important feature of the training program. As the trainer-coordinator herself stated:

I think even though it's an entrepreneurial thing, it's also a self-esteem-enhancing thing and I think that if we can get people employed then they may move into self-employment. But if they don't, they're still becoming self-sufficient.

When we consider the last decade of the twentieth century and how it was that, during a "liberal" regime, one of the most sweeping welfare reforms in history was instituted with barely a protest, it may be worthwhile to consider the discursive arenas that have been adopted from popular culture (and pop psychology) and reproduced as themes that locate the self as the center of all political action. This ideology of the self seems to have been firmly institutionalized in poverty-policy programmatic terms. Low-income populations under advanced liberal regimes are encouraged to become entrepreneurs and, in the end, to accept responsibility for their own economic successes and failures.

By focusing on this particular aspect of the microenterprise training programs, I do not mean to suggest that there were no good outcomes from the programs as they were instituted in the state of Colorado. Embedded in the texts and embedded in the stories of individuals are moments of success and, for some, an opportunity for a more stable economic future. On the whole, however, such programs do little in terms of decreasing the economic precariousness and the vulnerability of the poor. Because of the ambiguous returns of such programs, it is important to ask why they continue to garner such broad and uncritical support. I argue that part of the answer is that the attraction of such programs lies not in their real economic benefits to the poor but rather in their ideological underpinnings, which reinforce the thesis that economic responsibility falls squarely on the individual self rather than on government or on the nature of the economic structure.

Despite the questionable nature of the economic benefits, participants nevertheless continue to value the "entrepreneurial skills" they learn in these programs, buying wholeheartedly into the discourse of self-interest, self-esteem, and self-blame implicit in such entrepreneurial solutions to poverty, whereby even the blame for the "failure" of such programs falls upon the individual. Such a discourse masks the real success or failure of such programs, and the desire to make an entrepreneurial self replaces any focused discussion on economic restructuring, thus reinforcing the neoliberal/neoconservative convergence discussed by Nancy Fraser (1993) and already apparent in the current policy of poverty alleviation programs.

NOTES

The author thanks Judith Goode and Jeff Maskovsky for their encouragement to write this chapter and their insightful comments on earlier drafts. The following people have also provided invaluable editorial feedback in their unique fashion: Richard Camp, Guita Grin Debert, Deborah Houy, Joanna Mishtal, Michael Newburg, and Jim Schechter.

1. According to Mitchell Dean (1999:1), Foucault first talked about governmentality in a 1978 Collège de France lecture that is now available in English translation in Burchell, Gordon, and Miller's (1991) edited volume titled *The Foucault Effect*. Foucault defines governmentality as the following:

> The ensemble formed by the institutions, procedures, analyses and reflections, the calculations and tactics that allow the exercise of this very specific albeit complete form of power, which has as its target population, as its principal form of knowledge political economy, and as its essential technical means apparatuses of security. (Foucault 1991:102)

2. William Julius Wilson, who writes about joblessness and urban poverty among inner-city African Americans, traces the problem of poverty alleviation in the United States to the lack of interest in social citizenship and to an American ideology that frames economic and social outcomes in individual terms:

> The basic belief system concerning the nature and causes of poverty and welfare frames economic and social outcomes mainly in individual terms. This allows conservative intellectuals and policymakers to overemphasize the negative aspects of persistent joblessness and the receipt of welfare by playing on the key individualistic and moralistic themes of this dominant American belief system. Accordingly the tragic nature and social causes of such problems are lost on a public that holds truly disadvantaged groups, such as inner-city blacks, largely responsible for their plight. (Wilson 1997:158–59)

To illustrate this American ethos, Wilson notes that even those who belong to disadvantaged populations wind up endorsing a perspective that places responsibility on the individual:

> A 33-year-old welfare mother of five who lives in a public housing project located in a census tract in which 61 percent of the population is destitute introduced a little pop psychology into her endorsement of these views: "I think that everybody has a chance to get ahead but it's all where your mind's at: where you were raised, your self-esteem—a lot of that has to do with getting ahead. If nobody's taught you that there's opportunities out there—I think everybody's got a fair chance to get ahead if they want to." (Wilson 1997:180)

3. Although Lewis's (1966) thesis that what distinguished a culture of poverty from plain old poverty was that it was "a way of life handed down from generation to generation along family lines" and could be characterized by a series of behav-

ioral and psychological aspects was summarily criticized by the next generation of anthropologists, the consideration of chronic psychological and behavioral components within the conceptualization of poverty alleviation has become mainstreamed in the popular press—even in the liberal press.

4. Wilson (1997) locates the failure of liberal intellectuals to advance any significant poverty alleviation programs after the release of the Moynihan report in 1965 as related to their fear of racial politics. "[L]iberal social scientists tended to avoid describing any behavior that could be construed as unflattering or stigmatizing to racial minorities" and instead allowed the popular media and conservative analysts to dominate the discourse during the Reagan years:

> Building implicitly on the basic premises of the culture-of-poverty thesis, these analysts, thrust to the fore of the policy debate by the political ascendancy of Reaganism, argued that the growth of liberal social policies since the mid-1960s had exacerbated, rather than alleviated, ghetto related cultural tendencies. . . . Liberal intellectuals had retreated from the discussion of social dislocations in inner-city ghettos and therefore had no alternative explanations to advance. This allowed conservative analysts to dominate the public discourse on the subject throughout the first half of the 1980s. (Wilson 1997:174–76)

5. In contrast to Wilson, Cruikshank doesn't see the retreat of liberal social scientists from policy discourse as much as she sees a proliferation of social science discovery of "lacks," in this case, a "lack of self-esteem":

> From the "discovery" of an absence of the thing, social scientists have created a tangible vision of a "state of esteem." Here the social sciences can be seen as productive sciences; the knowledges, measurements, and data they produce are constitutive of relations of governance as well as of the subjectivity of citizens. In devising the methods for measuring, evaluating, and esteeming the self, social science actually devises the self and links it up to a vision of the social good and a program of reform. In short, social scientists have helped to produce a set of social relationships and causal relations where there were none before. (Cruikshank 1993:332)

6. CCI is a Colorado not-for-profit corporation devoted to small business development in the state and particularly to providing access to credit. In the early proposal of TOP, the Colorado Department of Human Services was known as the Colorado Department of Social Services (CDSS) and TOP was known as the Colorado Business Development Initiative (CBDI).

7. In the first year, the states that received support were Colorado, Montana, Maine, Vermont, and Massachusetts, with each state receiving approximately $300,000 for the year. During the second year, Colorado, Connecticut, Michigan, Vermont, and Maine participated, again each receiving approximately $300,000.

8. CBDI is the Colorado Business Development Initiative, which included CDSS and CCI. See note 6, above.

9. The four sites initially chosen include parts of the following counties: Morgan, Denver, Conejos, and Montezuma.

10. The original JTPA eligibility application for entrée to the program asked the potential participant for his or her current employment status and earnings but did not ask for the employment status or earnings of a live-in partner or about other assets, such as real estate income, that a potential participant might have. Nor did it ask detailed information about the participant's longer-term economic history. These guidelines left ample room for people who are more appropriately considered middle-income to legitimately participate, especially if their income in the preceding six months was low.

11. Michael Newburg, Carol Kelley, and Julie Hart.

12. The counties in the study included Alamosa, Montezuma, Conejos, Morgan, Denver, Fremont, and Mesa. During the first year, ten participants were interviewed in Montezuma County, eleven in Conejos County, six in Morgan County, and thirteen in Denver. One of the field sites studied during 1995 (in the area between Alamosa and Conejos counties) was followed up in 1996, and three new sites were added, including Canon City (Fremont County), Grand Junction (Mesa County), and two new sites (Sunnyside and Aurora) in Denver. Fifty-one participants were interviewed during the second year.

13. In Denver, it was considerably more difficult to schedule interviews. On a couple of occasions, people hung up when the researcher called. Many could not be reached at all. While in the rural areas all interviews were done within a few days, in Denver it took several weeks, persistent phone calls, and numerous trips to complete the required number. Compared to the participants in the rural sites, the Denver participants were not as appreciative of the opportunity to discuss the program.

14. Michael Newburg carried out interviews during 1995, and Michael Newburg, Julie Hart, and Carol Kelley carried out interviews in 1996. The team benefited from its collaboration with professor of economics Jeffrey Zax (University of Colorado–Boulder), who carried out a series of macroeconomic studies comparing the population in the training program with the population of self-employed persons in the areas where TOP has been active. I take full reponsibility for the interpretations offered here.

15. See Goldstein, with Zax and Newburg, 1996; and Goldstein, with Zax, Newburg, Hart, and Kelley, 1997.

16. During the first year of the project, a few curricula were used: *The Business of Small Business* (WomenVenture, 1994) and *Fastrac* and the *Entrepreneur's Planning Handbook*. During the second year, a curriculum titled *Nx-level* was adopted.

17. While I am sympathetic to Ehlers and Main's perspective, which suggests that microenterprise training is a sorry substitute for the real structural change that a socialist-feminist perspective could imagine, and while I recognize the very real problems these authors point out with regard to these programs, the point I make

here is that even the haphazard financial help people receive from these programs is viewed in overwhelmingly positive terms by the participants themselves.

REFERENCES

Burchell, Graham, Colin Gordon, and Peter Miller, eds.
1991   *The Foucault Effect: Studies in Governmentality: With Two Lectures by and an Interview with Michel Foucault.* Chicago: University of Chicago Press.

California Task Force to Promote Self-Esteem and Personal and Social Responsibility.
1990a   *Toward a State of Self-Esteem: The Final Report.* California Department of Education.
1990b   Appendixes to *Toward a State of Self-Esteem.* California Department of Education.

Colorado Capital Initiatives
1995   Colorado Business Development Initiative (CBDI) Proposal. Colorado Department of Human Services.

Cruikshank, Barbara
1993   "Revolutions Within: Self-Government and Self-Esteem." *Economy and Society* 22(3):327–44.

Dean, Mitchell
1999   *Governmentality: Power and Rule in Modern Society.* London: Sage.

DeParle, Jason
1998   "What Welfare-to-Work Really Means." *New York Times Magazine,* December 20.

Ehlers, Tracy, and Karen Main
1998   "Women and the False Promise of Microenterprise." *Gender and Society* 12(4):424–40.

Fitchen, Janet M.
1981   *Poverty in Rural America: A Case Study.* Boulder, Colo.: Westview.

Foucault, Michel
1991   "Governmentality." In *The Foucault Effect: Studies in Governmentality: With Two Lectures by and an Interview with Michel Foucault,* ed. Graham Burchell, Colin Gordon, and Peter Miller, pp. 87–104. Chicago: University of Chicago Press.

Fraser, Nancy
1993   "Clintonism, Welfare, and the Antisocial Wage: The Emergence of a Neoliberal Political Imaginary." *Rethinking Marxism* 6(1):9–23.

Goldstein, Donna, with Jeffrey Zax and Michael Newburg
1996   Targeted Ownership Project 1995: A Project of the State of Colorado

Department of Human Services and Colorado Capital Initiatives: Evaluation Report. September.

Goldstein, Donna, with Jeffrey Zax, Michael Newburg, Julie Hart, and Carol Kelley
1997   Targeted Ownership Project 1996: A Project of the State of Colorado Department of Human Services: Evaluation Report. August.

Hyatt, Susan Brin
1997   "Poverty in a 'Post-Welfare' Landscape: Tenant Management Policies, Self-Governance, and the Democratization of Knowledge in Great Britain." In *Anthropology of Policy: Critical Perspectives on Governance and Power*, ed. Chris Shore and Susan Wright, pp. 217–38. London and New York: Routledge.

Lewis, Oscar
1966   "The Culture of Poverty." *Scientific American* 215(4):19–25.

Meyerhoff, Diane
1997   "Federal Funding Opportunities for Microenterprise Programs." *Journal of Developmental Entrepreneurship* 2(2) (Fall/Winter):99–109.

Rose, Nikolas
1993   "Government, Authority and Expertise in Advanced Liberalism." *Economy and Society* 22(3):283–99.

Steinem, Gloria
1992   *Revolution from Within: A Book of Self-Esteem.* New York: Little, Brown and Company.

Uchitelle, Louis
1998   "Downsizing Comes Back, but the Outcry Is Muted: Rather Than Protests, Unions Are Offering Transition Advice," *New York Times*, December 7.

United States Census Bureau
1990   State and County QuickFacts Colorado. (http://quickfacts.census.gov/qfd/maps/colorado_map.html.)

Wilson, William Julius
1997   *When Work Disappears: The World of the New Urban Poor.* New York: Alfred A. Knopf.

Chapter 10

Producing Disunity

The Constraints and Incitements of Welfare Work

Catherine Kingfisher

Introduction

> The infrastructure of the welfare state . . . creates the basis for cross-class al-
> liances among women. . . . The welfare state has generated powerful cross-ties
> between the different groups of women who have stakes in protecting it.
> (Piven 1984:18)

If there is a single distinctive genius to the American political/economic/so-
cial system, it has been its ability to create and sustain deep divisions among
oppressed people (Wineman 1984:159).

It has long been noted that the U.S. welfare state is specifically gendered,
or two-channeled (Fraser 1989; Nelson 1990), and that the female channel,
referred to as "welfare" (as opposed to "social security"), is feminized both
in its secondary status vis-à-vis the male channel and insofar as both recipients and providers tend to be women. The nominal feminization of welfare has been the subject of considerable speculation on the part of scholars
and activists interested in social change. While some (Piven 1984; see also
Ehrenreich and Piven 1984) have argued that this feminization offers possibilities for political alliances, others have claimed, equally persuasively,
that such possibilities are negligible at best (Brown 1995; Whithorn 1984;
Wineman 1984).

This chapter explores these competing claims in relation to a seventeen-
month ethnography of a welfare office and two welfare rights groups that I
conducted from 1989 to 1990 in Michigan (Kingfisher 1996a).[1] The argument I make is that, in these ethnographic contexts, the possibility of alliance was not only unrealized but also unreasonable. The lack of alliance

was, in other words, a *sensible* lack, produced by and in a particular politico-economic environment and bureaucratic organization of "welfare" that served to obscure shared interests and systematically to undermine any existing potentials for alliance. Although I explore the positions of both recipients and providers, my emphasis is on providers, known as Assistance Payments workers ("AP workers," or "workers," as they preferred). While both recipients and workers are relating to the same bureaucracy in the same politico-economic environment, they relate to it in different ways. Moreover, workers wield considerable power relative to recipients and thus have greater influence over the tenor of their relationships.

Two data excerpts illustrating the nature of AP worker–recipient relations set the stage for my discussion. The first is from a conversation that occurred during a morning coffee break at the welfare office. The participants include two workers, Fran Knight (F) and Sally Blake (S); their supervisor, Edna Lewis (E); and myself (C). The topic of discussion was the characteristics of effective Assistance Payments workers. (Note that capital letters indicate emphatic delivery, parentheses bound uncertain or undecipherable words, and double parentheses bound nonverbal vocalizations/activities or transcriber's comments.)

> E: The only thing you have to be is intelligent, fast, organized and, a medium line between empathy and hate.
>
> C: ((laughs)) A medium line between empathy and hate.
>
> F: You gotta add the ARROGANCE too, this job isn't any fun without a little touch of arrogance.
>
> C: ((laughs))
>
> E: You have to know when to be empathetic and when to, get out your whip.
>
> F: I already know THAT, see? I'm, I'm empathetic to all my clients 'til they LIE to me, once they LIE to me I HATE them and I won't give them ANYthing. ((laughs))
>
> E: WHOA. ((laughs))
>
> S: ((sarcastic tone)) Not REVENGE (oh yeah).
>
> F: Yes it IS. ((laughs))
>
> E: ((sarcastic tone)) You're supposed to do a TRAINING process with them ((regular tone)) make them over VERIFY but still give them what they're entitled to.
>
> F: Oh they get it EVENTUALLY.
>
> E: Okay, don't say you won't give it to 'em, just say that they have to JUMP MORE ROPES to get it, that's OKAY.
>
> F: Unfortunately they just have to—they just, they just have to wait a while.

This exchange is "backstage" in Erving Goffman's sense (1959); it challenges the official ("front region") bureaucratic imperative of standardization and equality of treatment, indicating hostility (as opposed to "even-handed-ness") toward a particular group of clients deemed "liars." This construction of liars and the attendant hostility are then translated into a policy of deferment. What this transcript segment makes clear is that (1) worker-recipient relationships may be highly personalized, and (2) workers are actively engaged in the production of policy, policy here referring to what actually happens in the bureaucratic encounter.

This personalized, policy-productive relationship is also illustrated in the following narrative, in which a recipient, Leslie Goldenberg, refers to her relationship with her worker in attempting to explain an unexpected change in her food-stamp benefit. This is how Leslie presented her problem at a welfare rights group meeting:

> I've been living in . . . Hamilton ((apartment complex)) for almost three years—no it's been about two and a half years—and my food stamps were down to fifty-five dollars 'cause my rent's seventy-four, and I get child support most of the time, usually it's fifty dollars, but it—my food stamps would be fifty-five, and it just didn't ever seem right, and then about four or five months ago, she ((Leslie's AP worker)) upped it to eighty-nine, and I was getting fifty-dollar child support checks regularly at this time, then all the SUDDEN for this mo—MONTH, I get a hundred and ONE, I've never received a hundred and one, since I've lived there . . . that's the highest I've ever received, 'cause most a the time I lived there I got fifty-five dollars, a month, and all the sudden out of the clear blue sky, it went up . . . and so I was like, there's something wrong. WE ((Leslie and her AP worker)) don't get along, we don't argue, but . . . when I first met her I told her I wanted to go to school full time, she asked me why, and I told her so I could have her seat, so I could sit where she's sitting, and she just looked at me like I had lost every little bit of sense I HAD ((laughs)), and so, we—from that day on we never got along, 'cause I'm very, I speak my mind, and if I find something OUT that she's wrong about I tell her about it, and then I speak to her supervisor, and SO we don't—but if something needs to be raised, she'll never raise it unless I call her, if something needs to be dropped, it's dropped IMMEDIATELY, so . . . we just, you know, so I don't think there's something right.

Leslie's narrative points to what she interprets as, on the one hand, extreme arbitrariness on the part of her worker (the unexpected increase in her food-stamp allowance) and, on the other hand—and in contradiction to her postulated arbitrariness—the systematic unwillingness on the part of her worker to help Leslie.

Together, the two excerpts indicate that all is not well in worker-recipient relations, at least in this particular ethnographic setting. There is nothing in either excerpt that can be read as sympathy for the other, nothing pointing to a sense that the other was playing fair or had good reasons for her actions, or to an understanding of the other's position—let alone a recognition of similarities in those positions. And yet there were similarities, albeit in a rather structural and abstract sense. These included relatively low levels of educational attainment,[2] similar constraints related to occupational segregation and the domestic division of labor,[3] and economic dependence[4] on and subjugation within the welfare bureaucracy.[5]

Both groups voiced complaints about their economic options and vulnerabilities and about their powerlessness vis-à-vis the welfare system; for the most part, however, they neither recognized nor acknowledged that these conditions were shared by the other group. As I have claimed elsewhere (Kingfisher 1996a), the women's blindness to these similarities contributed to the perpetuation of a hierarchical welfare system that oppressed them both. Nevertheless, this blindness, whether deliberate or inadvertent, represented the reasonable practice of knowledgeable insiders. In what follows, I underscore the reasonable nature of this myopia with reference to a double-layered framework for interpreting worker-recipient relations that includes (1) the current ethos of welfare in the United States, and (2) the constraints and incitements of Assistance Payments work. I point to specific features of these two contexts of occurrence that contributed to the production of disunity and hostility, rather than alliance and solidarity, between workers and recipients.[6]

The Cultural Context of Welfare: Neoliberal Discourses of Poverty and Welfare in the Current U.S. Gender Regime

The current politico-economic environment of welfare, within which worker-recipient relations are situated, is not a friendly one for the poor; indeed, we are in the midst of a war against the poor. This most recent war[7] has taken the form of the particular discursive constitution of the poor and of relief encapsulated in the Family Support Act (1988) and the more recent Personal Responsibility and Work Opportunity Reconciliation Act (1996).

It was this particular tenor of U.S. discourses of poverty and relief, which gained ascendancy during the Reagan-Bush era and has in many respects been extended by the Clinton administration, that provided the parameters of recipients' and workers' practices in this study.

These discourses of poverty and welfare are part and parcel of a larger discourse of neoliberalism, which is constituted by a particular set of assumptions and assertions concerning the nature of human beings and the appropriate configurations of the state and market. These assumptions and assertions lead to specific economic and social prescriptions, the most notable in this context being the establishment of a minimalist state—in other words, welfare reform. The argument I make here is that neoliberalism is a specifically gendered discourse, with highly gendered material implications. It is, moreover, inextricably tied to a hierarchical gender regime characterized by occupational segregation and women's primary responsibility for the domestic sphere.

Where, then, do gender, poverty, and welfare fit in a neoliberal framework? In her discussion of the naturalization of poverty, Ruth Smith (1990) claims that the existence of poverty challenges the basic assumptions of liberal society, among which are individual autonomy and self-sufficiency. Smith's exploration of the liberal bourgeois symbolization of poverty, on the one hand, and of society, on the other, highlights a nonpoor/poor binary in which the nonpoor represent society and civilization, maleness, "good" (that is, controllable) nature, order, autonomy and freedom, intentionality, independence, universality, morality, and rationality, and the poor represent femaleness, "bad" (or uncontrollable) nature, disorder, need and necessity, want, desire, particularity, dependence, immorality, and irrationality. Gender is a key axis of this binary, with the various attributes on the "masculine" side having a positive valence in relation to those on the "feminine" side, which are hierarchically and definitionally secondary.

In their attack on the assumptions and organization of liberal bourgeois society, the feminized poor, by their very existence, serve to define the boundaries of ordered society. By being "naturally" outside civil society and thus representative of disorder, the feminized poor establish the outer limits of that society. In other words, civilization is what it is—and those who inhabit it are who they are—by virtue of *not* being uncivilized, with all that that entails. The center is defined by the margins, and the feminized poor become a pedagogical instrument in our own identity and social formation. They are not benign teachers, however, but rather represent the abject threatening the boundary (Kristeva 1982; Sibley 1995).

One can see in this gendered binary a basis for arguments in favor of a minimalist state, that is, a state whose role is simply to enable free exchange between rational, independent (male) individuals. This shift away from the interventionist state and toward a free-market social structure has entailed attacks on the welfare state that are based, at least in part, on the liberal claims regarding "proper" human being that I have just outlined. It is the very old yet newly refurbished idea of possessive individualism, for example, that underpins recent calls for increased "responsibility" and "independence" on the part of recipients of financial assistance. According to Glenn Drover and Patrick Kerans (1993:7), however, "[t]he association of well-being and personal development with individuality, separation, and autonomy may be, at best, a reading of the behavioural development of men in western society, and at worst, a distortion of reality for everyone." The concept of possessive individualism is thus not generic but specifically masculinist, built on the gendered assumptions of contract theory (Pateman 1988; Yeatman 1994). Insofar as women are less able to conform to its prescriptions, neoliberal discourses of individualism are inimical to their interests, particularly when they have sole responsibility for the care of dependent children. Given the currency of these discourses and their inability to recognize various forms and levels of "dependency" and "independence" (Fraser and Gordon 1994), single mothers often find themselves the targets of new welfare programs focused on reforming the "undeserving" poor by bringing them more in line with the tenets of liberal individualism. This targeting of single mothers points to the gendered subtext of social citizenship (Brodie 1996), which requires attachment to the labor market for recognition. Childrearing is thus neither recognized as "work" nor counted as contributory to society (Fraser and Gordon 1992).

Neoliberalism and neoliberal theories of poverty are, then, gendered. Women in general and poor women in particular fail to fulfill the requirements of full individuality and autonomy, indeed, of citizenship. This "failure" is not constructed as a property of any political or economic system, however—it is not recognized as a feature of a gender regime that *produces* male citizens and incomplete dependent women. Rather, this failure is located in individuals (women) who are always already incomplete and dependent. The result in terms of poverty is that policy goals are directed at altering what are constructed as negative personality characteristics, at the reformation of individuals rather than structures: thus the rhetoric of empowerment, motivation, and "tough love" characteristic of U.S. neoliberal welfare reform. It is in this light that Barbara Cruikshank argues that current discourses of empowerment, self-esteem, and self-help reflect a form of governance, in which "the question of governance becomes a question of self-governance" (1996:232). As federal programs are devolved to states, "welfare dependency" is devolved to individuals and pathologized: "welfare recipients are not fulfilling their responsibilities to society because of their lack of self-esteem, a deficiency demonstrated by their being on welfare in the first place" (Cruikshank 1996:239; see also Fraser and Gordon 1994). Nikolas Rose echoes this argument in his discussion of governance in advanced liberal societies, in which emphasis is placed on the production of individuals who will govern themselves; thus the disadvantaged, the marginalized, "are to be assisted not through the ministrations of solicitous experts proffering support and benefit cheques, but through their engagement in a whole array of programmes for their ethical reconstruction as active citizens" (1996:59–60). These programs are focused on various requirements and restrictions for the receipt of welfare, most notably "workfare." The cutting of benefits, either for noncompliance or simply because it is considered harmful for people to be on welfare for long periods (as stipulated in the 1996 act), is constructed as a positive contribution to poor people's "ethical reconstruction as active citizens."

This, then, is the larger politico-economic gender regime within which the U.S. welfare system—and thus worker-recipient relations—is situated. Its current manifestation is not a war on poverty, as in more expansive times, but a war against the poor. It is distinguished by a neoliberal valorization of the market, (masculinist) possessive individualism, and reductions in the orbit of the state, that is, welfare reform. In this regime, women's secondary status is reflected in and produced by a particular gender division of labor and citizenship status to which both recipients and workers are subject, albeit it in different ways, as I describe below. Moreover, the masculinist constructions of proper human nature characteristic of this regime serve to produce a highly personalized and negative view of (gendered) poverty and assistance. These views, in turn, contribute to the production of particular practices of welfare provision, to which I now turn.

Inside the Bureaucracy: The Bureaucratic Positioning of Workers and Recipients

The institutional context of recipient-worker relations, particularly with regard to their positioning within the welfare bureaucracy, provides the second layer of the interpretive framework I am proposing here. The claim I make at this level is that, in the current politico-economic environment of welfare, the structural positionings of workers and recipients and, in particular, the organization of street-level bureaucratic work have provided incitements to very specific worker (and, in turn, recipient) strategies that serve to instantiate and reinforce a hierarchical relationship of hostility and mistrust.

Perhaps the most important structural feature of recipient-worker relations is that applicants/recipients are supplicants of a system for which workers serve as gatekeepers. What is at stake here for recipients is considerable: food, shelter, and the integrity of their relationships with significant others—including not only partners but, perhaps more important, children. In other words, in their roles as gatekeepers, AP workers—personally, immediately, and almost always irrevocably (given the difficulty of appeals)—have immense power over the most intimate and immediate needs of recipients' lives. In this context, AP workers become as much a potential threat as a potential help: they embody the bureaucracy's contradictory roles as guarantor and violator of rights—rights of privacy and rights of subsistence.

Workers also have something at stake in their relationships with their clients. While food and housing are not immediate issues of concern in their lives, controlling their workloads, being answerable to their supervisors, and handling desperate clients are. If, reflective of the hierarchy between the institution and its (outsider) supplicants, workers have some degree of power over recipients' lives, they have little power over their own lives within the institution. They are, in fact, at the bottom of an internal hierarchy, only one step above clerical workers and below everyone else—their supervisors, social workers, and policymakers, who, in contrast to AP workers, are awarded the label "professional," with the attendant status, control, and remuneration.

Nor, from their perspective, do workers exercise a great deal of control in their personal lives. The gender regime to which I referred earlier figures prominently here: low levels of educational attainment, occupational segregation, and a domestic division of labor in which the women have primary (if not sole) responsibility for the household and care of children and in which their income-generating activities, however necessary, are considered secondary to those of their male partners, conspire to make Assistance Payments work the women's most lucrative option. In all but two cases, the workers in this study sought and accepted their jobs out of financial and logistical necessity, needing to contribute to their families' incomes in ways that did not interfere with their partners' work lives or their own caring roles. As is often the case in "women's" work in, for instance, health care or education, so-called natural propensities for "caring" (in this case, for the poor) did not figure prominently in the practice of AP work. Rather, workers felt "trapped" in jobs they did not enjoy and in which they suffered, acutely, from low status and powerlessness.

Low status and powerlessness were reflected in workers' relation to policy, in their positioning at the boundary of the institution, and in their workloads:

Workers' official relation to policy. One of the greatest tensions experienced by workers was that between their official role in policy *implementation* as opposed to *formation*, on the one hand, and the open or vague nature of much policy, on the other, which forced them to exercise some degree of discretion. There is a rigid division of labor in the welfare bureaucracy between policy formation and implementation, the former being the strict preserve of policymakers, with no input from front-line workers. Workers are not supposed to make policy decisions; rather, policy is intended to be "worker-proof," in order to encourage standardization and to keep control where it belongs: in the hands of the policymakers and managers. By contrast, policy is not always as specific and formulaic as it is supposed to be; consequently, workers are often left having to make particular decisions regarding, for instance, whether a client's case should be considered for "emergency needs" assistance.

Workers' positioning on the boundary of the institution. Unlike policymakers and managers, who are completely "inside" the institution, and recipients, who are clearly "outside," workers are positioned at the border. In particular, their job requires that they mediate between the interests of the institution, on the one hand, and of its clients, on the other (Erickson 1975; Erickson and Shultz 1982). In the current politico-economic environment, the interests of the institution are focused on minimizing costs by removing clients from the welfare rolls whenever possible, while those of clients are focused on maximizing benefits, which often means staying on the welfare rolls in order to survive financially. These interests are frequently mutually exclusive.

Workloads. Assistance Payments workers are increasingly overworked. AP workers with long work histories remembered a time when they could keep up with their caseloads and lamented the loss of that control over time. By 1990, for instance, workload expectations for providers in Michigan were so high that, by the Department of Social Services' own standards, workers would have needed an additional two hours per day to complete all their required tasks (Wertkin 1990). For the workers in the welfare office I worked in, these required tasks translated into responsibility for an average of 170 cases each. In addition, workers were expected to keep up with large volumes of interoffice memos and new policy materials, which arrived on their desks with perverse regularity.

In sum, the workers in this site were located close to the bottom of the hierarchy. They suffered severe time constraints and oversized workloads, and one result of these time constraints and workloads was that they were unable to keep abreast of policy changes. They had no official input into policy, and they had little officially sanctioned control over their interactions with clients, although they were immediately responsible for the outcomes of those interactions. In addition, workers were fairly close to their clients in terms of socioeconomic background and had to deal with many of the same issues as their clients, for instance, balancing their roles as mothers and as participants in the (often low) paid labor force.

The Everyday Practice of Provisioning

The inability of Assistance Payments workers to meet the strenuous and often conflicting demands of their jobs, along with their lack of autonomy, low status, and exclusion from official decision making, mirrors the situation of many street-level bureaucrats (Lipsky 1980; Prottas 1979; Wilenski 1990). Their *de facto* decision-making practices also mirror those of other street-level providers. Given this general situation, theorists and practitioners have recently pointed to the problematic nature of the traditional dichotomy between policy formation and implementation and accordingly have called for a recognition of the production of policy at the point of contact between public service bureaucracies and their clients (Lipsky 1980; Prottas 1979; Wilenski 1990). As Michael Lipsky (1980) argues, the most important actors in the policy game may not be policymakers but providers; it is, in fact, at the level of the provider that recipients of public services initially encounter the bureaucracy and benefit or do not benefit from policy as it is practiced. In other words, the implementation of policy—its practice—is its production.

Assistance Payments workers are thus policy producers. As I indicated above, however, they are *illegitimate* policy producers, in an environment in which they are pulled and tugged from two directions and in which they are expected to cope with extremely large workloads. It is this combination of pressures and illegitimacy—in the context of the larger politico-economic environment I outlined above—that produces the particular nature of the policy production work they do.

As students of street-level bureaucracies have noted, the exigencies of street-level bureaucratic work often compel workers to construct their own, officially unsanctioned approaches to the management of their work, which may include various shortcuts that draw on particular categorizations of clients, the control of information, and the manipulation of bureaucratic procedure (Prottas 1979). In the same way, perhaps, that the structure and organization of the welfare bureaucracy often compel recipients to "cheat" in order to survive, so the conditions I have described here incite providers to develop a set of strategies for "making ends meet." The strategies of the workers in this study were developed in the few "openings" available in what was otherwise a tightly controlled system of authority and hierarchy of work procedures and decision-making processes, the most notable being the categorization of clients and the manipulation of time.

The categorization of clients. As boundary workers, AP workers are assigned the key role of transforming applicants—complicated, diverse human beings—into "clients"—simplified, standardized "cases" that can then be processed by the system and provided with or denied assistance (Lipsky 1980; Prottas 1979). In the overwhelming press of everyday demands, various stereotypes and classifications ease this task by simplifying a complex social world and providing a means for apportioning workload—for deciding which cases to concentrate effort on, which to put off to the side, and which to try to get rid of through referral or denial.

As already noted, in the current climate of welfare in the United States, poor people are often blamed for their own poverty, and debates about welfare reform are overwhelmingly concerned with issues of morality and responsibility. The welfare bureaucracy does not stand apart from these views; on the contrary, in many ways it represents their institutionalization.

Indeed, in their role as gatekeepers to the welfare system, AP workers are boundary workers in a double sense: not only do they have to mediate the often conflicting interests of the institution and its clients, but they also have to police the liberal discursive boundary between order (represented by personal characteristics such as responsibility and self-sufficiency) and disorder (represented by the character traits of dependence, irresponsibility, and moral laxity).

The distinction between the "deserving" and "undeserving" poor, so prominent in the current discourse of welfare reform, was thus a key tool available to the welfare workers in this study. They made good use of this tool. As illustrated in the first data excerpt in this chapter, informal conversations (sometimes including supervisors) were the locus of much of workers' deserving/undeserving classificatory work. In the vast majority of cases, recipients were classed as dishonest, manipulative, lazy, and irresponsible, with the exceptions only serving to prove the rule. Having constructed a client as undeserving, workers then took one of two approaches. In a majority of cases, a client's status as undeserving provided justification for curtailed service, including, for instance, slow response (see below) or failure to notify clients of services for which they qualified but that they were unaware of (as indicated in the second data excerpt, above). Given limited time and resources, in other words, workers saved time by neglecting the mass "undeserving," opting to concentrate on helping those (few) poor deemed "deserving"—those constructed as motivated, willing to work to help themselves, responsible, and striving for independence. In other, rare cases, and in contradistinction to discourses of efficiency, workers' construction of a client as *particularly* undeserving could produce more rather than less work, when they attempted to reform the undeserving—a process that often entailed filling out extra forms, making extra phone calls, and otherwise pursuing their recalcitrant charges. In other words, clients who somehow stood out, because they were either particularly deserving or particularly undeserving, received the most attention. Again, however, the majority of clients who didn't stand out were not neutral but undeserving—not only of benefits but also of workers' (reformative) efforts. Thus workers' categorizations served both their own interests regarding the management of workloads and the institution's interests regarding the minimization of costs.

The manipulation of time. Although it was what workers had the least of, time was what they were most able to manipulate. The most obvious manipulations of time occurred in relation to the processing of paperwork. Officially, providers had forty-five days in which to process applications for financial assistance. Whether or not a recipient was constructed as "deserving" or "undeserving" had an impact on when that client's application would be processed. For the mass undeserving, this could mean at the end of the forty-five days. In other cases—for example, "expedited" food-stamp applications (which were intended to be used in dire cases only)—recipients could wait a full five days before receiving food. In still other instances, clients were made to wait for long periods in the waiting room, or they had to leave repeated telephone messages before receiving a response. The rare deserving client, in contrast, received a quicker response from her or his worker (and was in general awarded more time and effort).

What the organization of street-level bureaucratic work produces, then, is a need to create some mechanism for controlling oversized workloads. In this ethnographic setting, it incited the development of different categories of clients who were deserving of different kinds of treatment by the system (workers). These categories were developed out of the resources at hand: in particular, the neoliberal discourses of gender, poverty, and welfare discussed above. These discourses, along with the specific policies of the welfare department, provided resources that workers drew on in the conduct of their day-to-day lives. Workers took their job seriously. Their goal was not simply to save time by getting rid of the undeserving; they were also fundamentally interested in reforming some of the undeserving—in policing them and punishing them so as to provide motivation for their reformation, for their transformation into the deserving. As Lipsky (1980:151–52) observes:

> Thus workers do for some what they are unable to do for all. The street-level bureaucrat salvages *for a portion of the clientele* a conception of his or her performance relatively consistent with ideal conceptions of the job. Thus as the work is experienced there is no dissonance between the job as it should be done and the job as it is done *for a portion of the clientele*. The worker knows in a private sense that he or she is capable of doing the job well and can better defend against the assaults to the ego which the structure of street-level work normally delivers.

In their policing/boundary work, Assistance Payments workers made good use of the available discourses of poverty, reproducing the deserving/undeserving distinction faithfully. I have argued that such "good use" served both their practical interests and those of the institution. This good use may also, however, be related to workers' structural closeness to, and thus fear of, their abject clients (Leacock 1971). Indeed, with the election of a new state governor and the appointment of a new director of social services, workers were facing the prospect of restructuring—a situation that engendered feelings of acute vulnerability. In such a context, by "properly" serving the "deserving" and punishing (and thereby hopefully transforming) the "undeserving," workers could maintain not only a sense of professionalism in their work (Lipsky 1980) but also a sense of their own position in society. By actively upholding the tenets of deservingness—the work ethic, responsibility, and sexual restraint—they could, perhaps, protect themselves from slippage into abjection.

Conclusions

Power, according to Michel Foucault (1977, 1978), is fundamentally productive: it does not simply constrain and repress but also—or thereby—creates. It creates objects of knowledge; it creates truths; and it produces realms of practice. My argument here is that the constraints of street-level bureaucratic work, in the context of a specific cultural environment, are productive of a particular set of truths and practices regarding the relative worthiness of recipients that, in turn, produces the kinds of recipient-worker relations illustrated by my data excerpts. In keeping with the larger discourses of welfare reform, most recipients were produced as "undeserving" (with some thereby being deemed particularly deserving of punitive attention). In other words, the lack of worker-recipient alliance in this ethnographic site was not an accident but a production.

I conclude by way of another transcript segment, this time from an interview during which a worker, Harriet Eaton (H), tells her client, Lana Tucker (L), that she has referred her case to a social worker because she suspects that Lana is abusing her two children. (Harriet's concern was related to background sounds she had heard in a taped telephone message from Lana.)

> H: Okay, and I, um, you ARE, I DID want you to talk to another gentleman in the office this morning.
> L: Who?
> H: Okay his name is Mike.

L: Who IS he?

H: Okay, he IS with Protective Services.

L: I'm not talking to 'im.

H: Okay, the reason I—the reason I DID it is because of that phone message yesterday.

L: WHAT phone message?

H: Okay, when I played my tape.

L: Oh, 'cause a something you heard in the background.

H: Mm huh, right.

L: Oh I'm not TALKing to him, I will NOT talk to him and you can't make me, I REFUSE to talk to him, I will not talk to him.

H: Okay, WHY would you refuse to talk to him Lana?

L: Because I REFUSE to talk to him, I will not talk to ANY Protective Services worker, I have one child already gone and they will NOT get the twins.

H: Okay, well they would have no REAson to take the twins.

L: I don't wanna TALK to him.

H: Okay, I guess TALKing to him would probably—

L: Talking to him won't do any good, I will NOT talk to Protective Services, I will not.

H: Mm 'kay, he'll assume that there's something to HIDE then probably—

L: Let him assume whatever he WANTS to assume, they have to FIND me first if they wanna to talk to me I will NOT talk to him, all he's going to do is say "what did you—" what DIFFerence does it make what you heard in the background of a conversation?

H: Okay, well I guess he'd wanna KNOW what was happening—

L: WHY is it his business "what is happening"? WHY is it his business "what is happening"? You know TV, you know, some of the kids were watching wrestling, people HAVE VCRs.

H: Mm huh.

L: People LIKE wrestling, people LIKE boxing, people LIKE sports, but NO, everybody assumes 'cause you have kids and they hear somein' about kick and hit that somebody's abusing children, I WISH I could go inside people's minds, and really find out where they're coming from.

H: I GUESS the reason I thought it was because it sounded like your VOICE.

L: It WAS my voice.

H: Saying the "kick 'em," the "hit 'em."

L: Oh, I LIKE boxing, and I like wrestling I have, you know, friends who have VCRs who watch, who tape you know, WWF DOES tape their matches, I get very into it.

H: Well, I just thought I should explain to you WHY I did it, WHY I, made the referral.

Lana, who had come to the welfare office to seek assistance with housing, suddenly found herself confronted with the possibility of losing her twins. She had lost a child to the Department of Social Services seven years previously, when she was sixteen years old; thus the threat is real. Experiences such as this led the recipients in both welfare rights groups I worked with to consider trust or honesty vis-à-vis workers foolhardy at best (Kingfisher 1996a, 1996b). This lack of honesty and trust on the part of recipients fueled workers' distrust of their clients, thereby contributing to the perpetuation of the deserving/undeserving distinction.

In sum, we need to think about what we mean when we refer to the possibility of alliances between workers and recipients. The commonalities in their lives and in their relationships to the welfare bureaucracy were, in this case, insufficient. As Steven Wineman (1984:160) has pointed out: "[a] program which articulates common interests is necessary, but by itself is not enough. Something else is needed: a consciousness which enables oppressed individuals and groups to identify with each other's struggles and to forge common demands and goals that challenge all forms of oppression."

We need to consider worker-recipient interactions and workers' decision making (policy production) within their bureaucratic contexts of occurrence, which themselves must be situated within the larger politico-economic environment. This environment is one that is hostile to women in general and to poor women in particular. Far from interpreting individual interactions or street-level policy decisions as simply capricious and accidental, then, this approach situates their improvisational nature firmly within an institutional and cultural context in which they are, to some degree, systematic, and in which they above all make social sense.

Assumptions about solidarity on the basis of gender often suffer from a long-bankrupt essentialism that, when put into practice, does little more than subsume the interests of marginalized women to those of dominant women. This is particularly the case in contexts such as those described here, in which recognition of shared attributes or circumstances is systematically undermined by particular discourses of gender and poverty and their attendant bureaucratic arrangements. Nor, in this case, was the simple fact of involvement with the welfare bureaucracy sufficient to provide grounds for alliance, insofar as providers and recipients were very differently (indeed, in the current climate, antagonistically) positioned in that bureaucracy. That both were subordinated in somewhat parallel fashion (in terms of control/surveillance) can be argued in relation to different people's relationships with a variety of bureaucratic forms and, *in this particular politico-economic environment*, did little to overcome their positional antagonism. As Wendy Brown (1995:173) asks: Do women's ever-expanding relationships with the welfare state "produce only active *political* subjects, or do they also produce regulated, subordinated, and disciplined *state* subjects? . . . Do female staff and clients of state bureaucracies . . . transform the masculinism of bureaucracy or reiterate it, becoming servants disciplined and produced by it?" The nominal feminization of the welfare bureaucracy, in other words, does not automatically result in its substantive feminization. It depends, I would argue, at least in part, on the ethos of the time.

At some theoretical, etic level, workers and recipients may seem like natural allies. Indeed, they may be so, given the fundamental similarities in their circumstances; that these similarities exist indicates that the possibility of alliance and solidarity exists. But the realization of this possibility is at least partially an artifact of received discourses of gender and poverty, which, I have claimed, provide the parameters of workers' and recipients' interactions. What I have endeavored to demonstrate here is not that alliance is always already impossible but that the received discourses in circulation during the time of this study were inimical to alliance—that, in fact, they worked actively to produce the opposite. In this ethnographic setting, then, in these times, workers and recipients were engaged—unfortunately but reasonably and sensibly—in the practice of enmity rather than alliance.

NOTES

I thank Michael Goldsmith, Judith Goode, and Jeff Maskovsky for their critical comments on earlier drafts of this chapter. Portions of this chapter are from Kingfisher 1996a and 1998.

1. Participants in the study included 125 welfare recipients and workers in a welfare office and in two welfare rights groups. The data reported in this chapter are drawn, for the most part, from three months of intensive participant-observation in the welfare office, which included interactions with the seventeen providers in that office and with thirty-nine of their clients. I also had the opportunity to talk with an additional thirty providers at a three-day training session for new employees. All personal, place, and organizational names are pseudonyms.

Methods for the project consisted of interviews and tape recordings of informal conversations among both workers and recipients and of formal worker-recipient interviews. Transcripts of the tapes were then subjected to analyses of both content and process in order to gain access to the interpretation and construction of individuals' subjectivities and of policy. These methods of data collection and analysis are drawn from microanalysis, or microethnography, which is concerned with the fine-grained analysis of the moment-by-moment production of social reality, including perceptions and classifications as well as various kinds of institutional arrangements. The basic claim of microanalysis is that social facts are socially constructed in the interactions between people, between people and documents, between people and physical forces, and so on. Social reality is thus contingent; in other words, "the objective reality of social facts [is] an ongoing accomplishment of the concerted activities of daily life" (Garfinkel 1967:vii). What goes on between people in interaction is seen as a key location for the social construction and expression of meaning and social structure (Erickson 1975, 1986, 1992; Erickson and Shultz 1982; McDermott and Roth 1978)—and, I would add, for the construction and implementation of policy.

2. Only 18 percent of the workers had college degrees, while 25 percent of twelve key recipients I worked with in the two welfare rights groups had college degrees.

3. The kinds of jobs that recipients had held or were currently holding were strikingly similar to those that workers had held prior to becoming AP workers, namely, low-status, low-paying, low-security jobs in clerical and service work. In addition, like recipients, workers had primary responsibility for the domestic sphere.

4. Workers, like recipients, were economically vulnerable. Through their interactions with clients as well as their own experiences, workers were aware that poverty could be just a divorce away. In addition, two of the seventeen workers in the welfare office had either grown up in welfare families or had relatives who were on welfare.

5. Workers and recipients shared not only positions of relative powerlessness in their associations with the welfare bureaucracy but ways of talking about this powerlessness. For instance, both claimed that the people in power "had it easy" and were ignorant of what workers' and recipients' lives were really like; both questioned their "choice" to participate in the welfare system; and both groups believed that the welfare system undermined their efforts to succeed (either as economically independent agents, in the case of recipients, or as effective workers, in the case of AP workers).

6. Given space limitations, I have not been able to include as much ethnographic detail in this chapter as I would have liked. Readers interested in greater detail may consult Kingfisher 1996a and 1998.

7. As Abramovitz (1988) indicates in her discussions of colonial discourses of able-bodiedness and responsibility, we are in some ways just recycling old arguments.

REFERENCES

Abramovitz, Mimi. 1988. *Regulating the Lives of Women: Social Welfare Policy from Colonial Times to the Present*. Boston: South End Press.

Brodie, Janine. 1996. Restructuring and the New Citizenship. In Isabella Bakker, ed., *Rethinking Restructuring: Gender and Change in Canada*. Toronto: University of Toronto Press.

Brown, Wendy. 1995. *States of Injury: Power and Freedom in Late Modernity*. Princeton: Princeton University Press.

Cruikshank, Barbara. 1996. Revolutions Within: Self-Government and Self-Esteem. In Andrew Barry, Thomas Osborne, and Nikolas Rose, eds., *Foucault and Political Reason: Liberalism, Neo-Liberalism, and Rationalities of Government*. Chicago: University of Chicago Press.

Drover, Glenn, and Patrick Kerans. 1993. New Approaches to Welfare Theory: Foundations. In Glenn Drover and Patrick Kerans, eds., *New Approaches to Welfare Theory*. Hampshire, England: Edward Elgar.

Ehrenreich, Barbara, and Frances Fox Piven. 1984. The Feminization of Poverty: When the "Family-Wage System" Breaks Down. *Dissent* 31(2):162–70.

Erickson, Fred. 1975. Gatekeeping and the Melting Pot: Interaction in Counseling Encounters. *Harvard Educational Review* 45:44–70.

———. 1986. Qualitative Methods in Research on Teaching. In M. Wittrock, ed., *Handbook of Research on Teaching*. 3d ed. New York: Macmillan.

———. 1992. Ethnographic Microanalysis of Interaction. In M. D. Le Compte, W. L. Millroy, and J. Preissle, eds., *The Handbook of Qualitative Research in Education*. San Diego: Academic Press.

Erickson, Fred, and Jeffrey Shultz. 1982. *The Counselor as Gatekeeper: Social Interaction in Interviews*. New York: Academic Press.

Foucault, Michel. 1977. *Discipline and Punish*. New York: Vintage.

———. 1978. *The History of Sexuality*. Volume 1: *An Introduction*. New York: Vintage.

Fraser, Nancy. 1989. *Unruly Practices: Power, Discourse and Gender in Contemporary Social Theory*. Minneapolis: University of Minnesota Press.

Fraser, Nancy, and Linda Gordon. 1992. Contract versus Charity: Why Is There No Social Citizenship in the United States? *Socialist Review* 22:45–67.

———. 1994. A Genealogy of Dependency: Tracing a Keyword in the U.S. Welfare State. *Signs* 19(2):309–36.

Garfinkel, Harold. 1967. *Studies in Ethnomethodology*. New York: Prentice-Hall.

Goffman, Erving. 1959. *The Presentation of Self in Everyday Life*. New York: Doubleday Anchor.

Kingfisher, Catherine Pélissier. 1996a. *Women in the American Welfare Trap*. Philadelphia: University of Pennsylvania Press.

———. 1996b. Women on Welfare: Conversational Sites of Acquiescence and Dissent. *Discourse & Society* 7(4):531–57.

———. 1998. How Providers Make Policy: An Analysis of Everyday Conversation in a Welfare Office. *Journal of Community and Applied Social Psychology* 8(2):119–36. Special issue: *Mental Health Consequences of Economic Insecurity,*

Relative Poverty and Social Exclusion: Community Psychological Perspectives on Recession.

Kristeva, Julia. 1982. *Powers of Horror: An Essay on Abjection*, trans. Leon S. Roudiez. New York: Columbia University Press.

Leacock, Eleanor Burke. 1971. Introduction. In Eleanor Burke Leacock, ed., *The Culture of Poverty: A Critique.* New York: Simon and Schuster.

Lipsky, Michael. 1980. *Street-Level Bureaucracy: Dilemmas of the Individual in Public Services.* New York: Russell Sage Foundation.

McDermott, Ray, and David Roth. 1978. The Social Organization of Behavior: Interactional Approaches. *Annual Review of Anthropology* 7:321–45.

Nelson, Barbara J. 1990. The Origins of the Two-Channel Welfare State: Workmen's Compensation and Mothers' Aid. In Linda Gordon, ed., *Women, the State, and Welfare.* Madison: University of Wisconsin Press.

Pateman, Carole. 1988. *The Sexual Contract.* London: Polity.

Piven, Frances Fox. 1984. Women and the State: Ideology, Power, and the Welfare State. *Socialist Review* 74(14):11–19.

Prottas, Jeffrey M. 1979. *People-Processing: The Street-Level Bureaucrat in Public Service Bureaucracies.* Lexington, MA: Lexington Books.

Rose, Nikolas. 1996. Governing "Advanced" Liberal Democracies. In Andrew Barry, Thomas Osborne, and Nikolas Rose, eds., *Foucault and Political Reason: Liberalism, Neo-Liberalism, and Rationalities of Government.* Chicago: University of Chicago Press.

Sibley, David. 1995. *Geographies of Exclusion: Society and Difference in the West.* London: Routledge.

Smith, Ruth L. 1990. Order and Disorder: The Naturalization of Poverty. *Cultural Critique* 14:209–29.

Wertkin, Robert A. 1990. *Assistance Payments Worker Job Satisfaction: A Study of Michigan Workers.* Lansing: Michigan Department of Social Services.

Whithorn, Ann. 1984. For Better and for Worse: Social Relations among Women in the Welfare State. *Radical America* 18 (4):37–47.

Wilenski, Peter. 1990. Competing Values in Public Administration. In *Public Power and Public Administration.* Sydney: Hale and Iremonger.

Wineman, Steven. 1984. *The Politics of Human Services: A Radical Alternative to the Welfare State.* Boston: South End Press.

Yeatman, Anna. 1994. *Postmodern Revisionings of the Political.* New York and London: Routledge.

Chapter 11

Homelessness, Employment, and Structural Violence

Exploring Constraints on Collective Mobilizations against Systemic Inequality

Vincent Lyon-Callo

Jonathan,[1] now twenty-eight years old, stayed at a homeless shelter in Northampton, Massachusetts, during the autumn and winter of both 1993 and 1994. Struggling to survive while working food-service jobs, he relocated to western Massachusetts hoping to attend the University of Massachusetts. As a bright and articulate young, white man, he was quickly able to secure employment while trying to save money for housing and school. He was a model guest during both of his stays at the shelter, frequently helping insightfully to mediate disputes between guests around the shelter. Despite his wealth of skills and consistent efforts, he was never able to locate housing he could afford in the city.

During his first stay, Jonathan worked both as a cashier in a local supermarket and conducting telephone surveys. In 1994, he found a job washing dishes in an upscale local restaurant. Both times the shelter staff were supportive of his efforts, extended his stays, and suggested all "available options" they could think of to help Jonathan locate income and housing. The wages paid in the service work available were just not enough, however, to secure housing.

Jonathan and I discussed his plans one evening during the autumn of 1994. He had been working for the past two months, washing dishes five nights a week. About a month and a half previously he began to look for an apartment with another shelter resident, Tom, who worked with him in the restaurant. They wanted to avoid living in rooming houses because they felt them to be unsafe and inhumane. Instead, they had been saving their money for an apartment. That night, Jonathan told me he was planning to relocate to South Carolina, with the hope of finding cheaper rents during the winter. As he put it, "Minimum wage is just about the same everywhere. I can get an apartment for half-price there during the off-season." His "solution" to his homelessness in Massachusetts was to leave town, give up on school for the moment, and try to locate housing further south, where he envisioned less costly rents.

Jonathan's experience is far from unique. The number of people living on the streets and in homeless shelters throughout the United States continues to increase despite the widely reported flourishing economy of the late 1990s (Burt 1997; National Coalition for the Homeless 1997; Dowdy 1998; Waxman and Hinderliter 1996). In a situation that is sometimes seen as paradoxical, a growing number of people who find themselves homeless are, like Jonathan, employed in the "booming" economy (Hardin 1996; National Coalition for the Homeless 1997). In Northampton, I found that over one-third of the single, adult homeless people staying in one emergency shelter were employed in the years 1994–1996. In 1995, 116 of 193 people utilizing the shelter received income from either paid employment or social security disability insurance (SSI) payments.[2] Many others were involved in training programs or self-reform to prepare for work. Despite some popularly held beliefs about the laziness or learned dependence of "the homeless," many of the people I worked with were working quite hard and were desperate to locate better jobs and more income. As in Katherine Newman's research on the working poor in New York City, I found that the income from available employment did not enable people to escape poverty or homelessness.[3] For example, less than one-third of the employed workers I worked with moved into permanent housing when they left the shelter. How does it make sense that so many people continue to be homeless despite their active participation in the "strong" national economy?

There are several possible ways of understanding these dynamics. One possibility is to interpret homelessness as the result of shortcomings in some people that make them unable to compete effectively in the market economy. Another possibility would be to examine homelessness in relation to recent material and historical conditions that have contributed to vastly increased social inequality. As wealth has been increasingly concentrated in the hands of a small percentage of the population over the last two decades of the twentieth century, homelessness for many extremely poor people has also become an almost routine feature of life in the United States. In that light, the statistics cited above could be read as the result of increasing structural inequalities in the United States during this historical period of neoliberalism. An argument could be put forth that widespread homelessness is simply the result of changing material conditions of life for many people in terms of income and housing costs. That understanding would resonate with much recent work by scholars who emphasize the impact of recent economic restructuring and altered political and cultural conditions on the lives of residents of the United States.

Increased disparity in the distribution of wealth and income[4] (U.S. Bureau of the Census 1996; Albelda et al. 1996) has resulted from the decline in higher-paying manufacturing jobs in much of the country, a growing temporary labor industry, urban gentrification (Williams 1996), corporate conglomeration, increased globalization of capitalist production, the decreased strength of unions in the United States, altered tax policies,[5] and other, related conditions.[6] This restructuring has led both to the rewards of increased wealth for those enacting policies that contribute to homelessness at home and abroad and to a drastic increase in the incidence of chronic unemployment and underemployment (Hardin 1996) in low-paying, part-time, temporary employment for many people[7] (Economic Policy Institute 1997). Homelessness is further exacerbated by policies and practices that have created an increasing shortage of affordable housing units in the nation[8] (Lazere 1995; Kaufman 1996; Kaufman 1997; O'Flaherty 1996) and by political decisions regarding taxation policy, funding for housing, labor laws, and international trade. Domination through processes of class exploitation, racial injustice, unequal educational opportunities, and gendered inequality are also all fairly easy to document components of homelessness.

Historical and material conditions clearly contribute to producing homelessness in the United States. I would argue, however, that this knowledge alone is inadequate for understanding the phenomenon of widespread homelessness here. We also need to analyze how such economic restructuring is allowed to occur.[9] We need to account for issues of human agency and strive to comprehend the seeming acquiescence or consent to political-economic conditions that result in inequality and homelessness. Without such an analysis, one is left with the impression that oppression acts solely as overt coercion and domination. The subtle, more insidious ways in which what is taken for granted as normal, natural, or uncontestable helps produce and maintain inequality are left unexamined.

Examinations of how it has become "common sense" to condone homelessness might entail questioning how "average" citizens consent to the

structural violence of homelessness, why so few practices by people working within the homeless sheltering industry challenge systemic conditions,
how popular imaginings about homeless people are discursively produced,
and how people who find themselves living on the streets come to understand that situation and respond to that experience. As part of that effort,
this chapter attempts to make sense of why it is so difficult to find organized, collective movements of homeless people working to challenge systemic inequality in the United States at the beginning of the twenty-first
century.

As recent ethnographic work by Talmadge Wright (1997) and David
Wagner (1993) demonstrates, homeless people are not simply passive victims. Some people living on the streets or in shelters do engage in organized
mobilizations, even if these efforts most often focus on organizing for improved living conditions in shelters or on the streets. Other ethnographies
of poverty in the United States, by Alisse Waterston (1993), Jagna Sharff
(1998), Gwendolyn Dordick (1997), and Philippe Bourgois (1996), for example, account for issues of human agency by analyzing drug and alcohol
abuse, mental illness, membership in gangs, and similar coping behaviors
that are commonly portrayed as symptoms of disorders that cause people
to live in poverty. They interpret their ethnographic data to argue that such
practices are actually strategies to cope with historical exploitation and
structural inequality. What these ethnographies fail fully to explain, however, is how it makes sense to particular social actors to "choose" coping
strategies that accommodate homelessness instead of collective work challenging the material and discursive conditions that produce or justify the
social relations that result in many people being homeless despite the vast
wealth in the United States. As Joel Blau argued, it still remains much more
difficult to find collective mobilizations *of homeless people* than to locate
charity and advocacy efforts *for the homeless* (1992:93). Blau suggests that
this results from how homeless people have been politically disabled by
their internalization of dominant images toward them. As he puts it, "The
message is a simple one: someone without a home is an inconsequential
person, and the actions of an inconsequential person cannot have political
consequences" (1992:94).

In a slight contrast to Blau's argument, I argue that to understand seeming popular consent, it is necessary both to critically analyze individual and
collective practices and to investigate how engaging in casual resistance and
compliance comes to make more sense to many homeless people than does
working to foster opposition. Utilizing five years of ethnographic research,

I show in this essay how many of the people living in shelters are not passive and do act to "resist" homelessness. To locate such resistance, however, it is often necessary to look at subversions, self-constructions, individual acts of subterfuge, seeming resignation, and behind-the-scenes complaints, rather than only at large-scale, collective insurrections aimed at overthrow or emancipation (Scott 1990; Kondo 1990).

Individual acts of resistance occurred on a daily basis in the Massachusetts shelter I examined. Often, as I show later in the chapter, these acts take the form of individual efforts that largely accept hegemonic explanations of homelessness as being the result of individual shortcomings or deviancy. Examples include practices such as a homeless person trying for a better job or engaging in self-reform through job training or therapy. Alternative efforts that seemingly reject the notion that the solution to homelessness is to be found in reforming homeless people also took place. Some homeless people I worked with actively avoided participation in what they saw as exploitative labor conditions, moved to another community in the hope of finding more favorable wages and housing, or engaged in racist and sexist blaming of other poor people. Sometimes these efforts were confined to complaints and noncompliance with shelter rules and "helping efforts." Very few homeless people whom I knew passively accepted their conditions, but even fewer engaged in collective mobilizations or acted in opposition to systemic inequities.

While being cognizant of such demonstrations of agency, we must avoid romanticizing the often individualized strategies of coping or accommodation. Analyzing the resistance acts that do take place, however, allows us to analyze more precisely power relations in particular settings and at precise historical moments. To understand the conditions maintaining homelessness, it is imperative to contemplate the subtle, insidious nature of how certain social conditions come to be taken for granted as normal, natural, or uncontestable. We need to understand how particular conditions promote particular actions while constraining the possibility of more collective mobilizations against structural inequities. Rather than simply reading "the homeless" as passive victims of misguided social and economic policies or as suffering from the debilitating effects of "false consciousness,"[10] I suggest that the often paradoxical ways in which people see themselves and society helps explain why particular strategies of coping, defiance, or accommodation are employed while other possibilities are marginalized as "unrealistic" or "impractical."

As Lila Abu-Lughod writes, "Where there is resistance, there is power"

(1990:42). Thus, it is imperative to analyze the effects of such power relations if we hope to understand the maintenance of homelessness despite the
vast wealth in the United States. To do that, I explore how particular material and discursive conditions set conceptual parameters constraining the
possibility of collective mobilizations by homeless people against recently
increasing systemic inequalities. What factors, material and discursive,
function to constrain these social actors' collective resistance against social
inequality and homelessness?

Exploring Homelessness within a Thriving Economy

In an effort to analyze the dynamics described above, I conducted ethnographic research at a homeless shelter in Northampton, Massachusetts, between 1993 and 1997. In this research, I spent between forty and sixty hours
each week at the shelter or in public meetings, taking note of the concrete,
everyday practices that various agents enacted in response to homelessness.
While actively participating in shelter routines, shelter meetings, staff hir-
ings and trainings, public forums, and community planning efforts, I observed and engaged with staff members, people who were homeless, policymakers, and local advocates. In particular, I engaged in dialogue with homeless people as they applied for jobs, tried to be "reformed" by social service
workers, and attempted to resolve homelessness through a wide range of actions. Taking part in shelter meetings, discussions, and loosely structured
interviews, I also engaged in debates, dialogues, and discussions with people regarding both our perceptions and our practices. In these discussions,
I urged those I had close relationships with to critically evaluate the effects
of our routine practices and to explore the possibilities of expanding the
range of permissible responses. Through these dialogical relationships, I
gained enhanced access to information regarding both the subtle, sometimes hidden strategies and tactics that people I worked with utilized and
the ideological and material constraints on collective resistance to systemic
inequality.

Conducting such ethnographic research within a homeless shelter in
the city of Northampton provided an ideal setting for analyzing seeming acquiescence to social inequality. Northampton is a small city of approximately thirty thousand people, located along the Connecticut River
in the more rural, western section of Massachusetts. Having undergone
much gentrification in the 1980s and 1990s, the city has managed to

avoid the phenomenon of empty storefronts that plague nearby communities and is widely portrayed as a model of how to thrive despite recent deindustrialization. For example, a 1996 *Boston Globe Magazine* article applauded Northampton as an unusual story of success in the postindustrial, mall-driven economy of 1990s New England (Roche 1996), and the acclaimed 1999 book focused on Northampton, *Hometown*, by Pulitzer Prize–winning author Tracy Kidder, invokes an image of Northampton as the type of successful small city other communities and citizens can only emulate (Kidder 1999).

With four elite colleges and the University of Massachusetts located close by, Northampton attracts many visitors. Urban gentrification has produced a busy Main Street full of art galleries, coffee shops, and upscale restaurants, which ends at the gates of Smith College. Avoiding the trend toward malls and national chains, the downtown area features locally owned movie theaters, bookstores, and a range of shopping options. A thriving arts and music community draws even more consumers to the city. Despite appearances, however, there is another side to the Northampton area: that of increasing poverty and homelessness.

The work experiences of Jonathan reflect an overall economic shift in the region. The entire region has witnessed major political-economic restructuring in recent years. For example, 20 percent of workers in the county were employed in manufacturing in 1980. By 1990, this figure had dropped to 15 percent. By 1991, 51.12 percent of jobs countywide were located in either wholesale and retail trade or services (Market Street Research 1994:60). A 15 percent decrease in manufacturing jobs and a 12 percent increase in service-sector jobs occurred countywide during the 1980s as manufacturing plants were replaced by restaurants, coffee shops, galleries, and large retail chains (Market Street Research 1994:14). This trend continued during the 1990s.

On October 10, 1996, Kellog Brush announced that they would be closing down their manufacturing plant in Easthampton and laying off 220 workers. Kellog Brush had been manufacturing goods in western Massachusetts since 1924. This layoff came on the heels of business decisions by National Felt to lay off one hundred workers in 1994; by Stanley Home Products to lay off sixty employees while eliminating manufacturing operations in western Massachusetts, where they had been manufacturing goods since 1947; and by the Lesnow Manufacturing Company to close its factory in 1995, ending employment for 230 workers. Nine months later, during July 1997, another six hundred jobs (many of them in manufacturing) were lost in the western Massachusetts region due to businesses closing or moving. As a result of these tactical business decisions, 42 percent of all jobs in Northampton in 1998 were located in the service sectors, according to the Northampton Chamber of Commerce. Similarly, 45 percent of new jobs projected to be developed in the region over the next ten years are expected to pay wages below the federal poverty level for a family of two (Turner 1998).

Changes in employment and wages alone, however, do not adequately explain the political-economic conditions in the region. One needs to consider also housing availability and cost. In 1990, the median gross monthly rent for an apartment in Hampshire County was $526 per month (Market Street Research 1994:53). In April 1996, I surveyed the cost of apartments listed for rent in the community and found that the average rent of listed apartments was $665 (or $410 per bedroom). A 1996 study conducted by the University of Massachusetts Off Campus Housing Office found similar rents, with the average one-bedroom apartment costing $650 per month without heat (Watson 1996:16). Coupled with the high rents is an occupancy rate for apartments that routinely exceeds 95 percent.

Given that the income available to many working people in Northampton is inadequate to pay "market rate" rents, the only affordable housing option for many is to move into a rooming house or subsidized housing. Even these options are out of the range of many people. As of May 1996, there were 259 single-room occupancy (SRO) units in the city. This represents only slightly more than one-half the number of units in the city twenty years ago. The loss of SRO housing in Northampton is reflective of an overall trend throughout the nation. "Urban renewal" efforts contributed to eighteen thousand SRO units being lost between 1973 and 1984 in Chicago, more than half the SRO units in Los Angeles being demolished between 1970 and 1985, and Boston losing 94 percent of its rooming houses by the mid-1980s (Burt 1997:34).

A second type of low-income housing once available to poorer members of the society involved government subsidies for apartments. Unfortunately, the waiting list for Housing and Urban Development (HUD) Section 8 housing certificates or subsidized rooms and apartments in the city is virtually closed to anyone not categorized as "disabled" or elderly. Even these people often have to wait several years for a subsidy, and then they need to locate an available apartment and a willing landlord.

For three days during September 1996, the neighboring town of Amherst opened its Section 8 housing subsidy waiting list for applications. These had been the only days that they even took applications during the previous two years. In 1997, the nearby city of Springfield opened its waiting list for three days. More than ten thousand different people placed their names on the waiting lists for Section 8 subsidies in the four-city Springfield HUD region in those days. Workers at the shelter informed current and former guests and helped them fill out many applications, knowing there was very little chance that space for even qualified applicants would become available in the next several years. One housing advocate, Elizabeth, explained this strategy in the following manner: "It's just something to do in case it ever comes through."

Again, the local situation is a reflection of national trends. A 1995 report by the U.S. Conference of Mayors reported that the average wait for Section 8 housing subsidies was thirty-nine months. Applicants had to wait an average of seventeen months from the time they applied until they received assistance (Waxman and Hinderliter 1997). In 1993, 1.4 million households nationally were on waiting lists for housing subsidies for privately owned housing, and 900,000 households were on waiting lists for public housing (Lazere 1995:4). As many housing authorities do not even take new applications, these numbers underestimate the demand for housing assistance.

Despite these dynamics, organized responses by homeless people to homelessness that challenge the availability of affordable housing or the wages paid in local jobs have been difficult to locate in western Massachusetts. This does not mean, however, that homeless people do not understand the impact of recent restructuring or that they have simply been passively acquiescing to those conditions. As I show in the next section, in working closely with homeless people over a several-year period I uncovered myriad ways in which people living at the shelter acted in response to the conditions of their lives and their community.

Responding to Homelessness in Northampton

In Northampton, approximately three hundred people stayed at the shelter where my work was focused during each of the years of this study.[11] In addition, over one-third of the people staying at the shelter during 1994, 1995, and 1996 were employed. Fewer than 20 percent, however, moved into nonsheltered housing after leaving the shelter. Many left town, moved to a different shelter, moved to some type of treatment program, lived in the woods surrounding the city, or doubled up with family and friends. This can partly be explained by the fact that the vast majority of these workers found themselves in low-paying food-service or retail trade jobs. For example, forty-two of the sixty-nine employed people staying at the shelter during 1995 worked in either food or retail trade for near minimum wage with no benefits.

Clearly, Jonathan's case of working for wages inadequate to afford housing is far from unique. Questions remain, however, regarding how homeless people respond to such dynamics and why some strategies make sense and are enacted while others are nearly silenced by being deemed impractical or unreasonable.

I worked with more than six hundred different homeless people in the course of this research. They exercised a variety of strategies in the effort to end their homelessness. Many of these people attempted to work their way out of poverty through paid employment. Others looked for more education or training. Some people tried to work hard at their job, hoping their skills would be appreciated while fearful of being fired if they spoke up. Still others moved from town to town, looking for housing they could afford with available wages. The vast majority of people also engaged in some type of self-reform. Yet these strategies almost always remain individualized, based on largely accepted, dominant notions about homeless people, and rarely challenged systemic inequality.

Through engaging with shelter residents as they negotiated the local political economy and housing market, and through participating in the daily workings of the local sheltering industry over a five-year period of time, it became quite clear to me that the dominant responses involved a great deal of self-government.[12] I uncovered a hypothesis of deviancy dominating within the homeless sheltering industry (Lyon-Callo 1998a). Based on discursively produced, prototypical conceptions of "the homeless" as alcoholics or mentally ill, discourses of self-help and bio-medicalization dominate in the shelters. These discourses and resultant practices combine to reproduce a conceptual framework in which homelessness is understood and responded to, by many homeless people, shelter staff members, shelter administrators, and funders, as being the result of shortcomings or pathologies within each homeless person. In such a setting, it comes to make sense to many homeless residents of the shelter to reform the self.

I found that an assumption that guides the preponderance of shelter "helping" practices is that, through a bio-medicalized search for symptoms, staff and guests can discover why one particular person became homeless. This is hardly surprising, given the dominance of bio-medicalized and individualized explanations for social problems in the United States during recent years. In fact, many of the people I worked with came to the shelter already blaming some type of disorder for their homelessness. For example, when asked what caused their homelessness, over 35 percent of the people who stayed at the shelter between 1994 and 1996 chose "substance abuse." As one woman, Ariel, put it, "I was always blaming myself. Thinking that there must be something wrong with me. Other people have houses. How did I screw up my life to become homeless for so long?" This self-blame is not simply the result of false consciousness but rather the result of being entwined within the dominant discourses operating in the shelter and in the society at large. Homeless people often hold a deep-seated belief in the myth of the American Dream. Many homeless people also remain deeply committed to concepts of individual responsibility and pulling oneself up by one's bootstraps.

Examining shelters' routines, including case management, counseling sessions, staff decisions about how long to allow someone to remain at the shelter, and the response to violations of shelter rules and regulations, I found that shelter helping practices reinforce feelings of self-blame and the need for self-help by training homeless people to look for and treat disorders within themselves as the appropriate way of responding to homelessness. Homeless people are encouraged to look for "the cause" of their homelessness within themselves through self-reflection. They are urged to consider "what did I do to become this way." Each person is understood to have become homeless because he or she has a problem (a biological disorder, an attitude toward life, mental illness, a lack of self-discipline, or an addictive personality, for example) that is within the self.

Through routine practices of detecting and treating pathology, statistical record keeping, maintaining case histories, and self-help efforts, a homeless person becomes a subject who was inclined to be homeless because of something within the self. Routine shelter practices serve to produce "the homeless" and homeless subjects, reinforce social policy based on managing these presumed pathological "others," and hegemonically marginalize alternative resistance possibilities by reconfirming "common sense." Subjectivities are created through the widespread languages of self-empowerment and self-improvement and through diagnosing "disorders" in individuals. The "solution," then, is to treat those disorders through retraining, discipline, confession, punishment, or therapy. Self-governing homeless subjects are often produced.

Having subordinated people believe that they are a danger to themselves without self-reform works quite effectively in producing what appears to be acquiescence. This is precisely where the more insidious forms of self-government come into play. Shelter guests govern themselves (through self-help efforts) and other homeless people (through discussing the benefits of self-help and self-empowerment groups). Suggested remedies for the disorders that lead to homelessness include attending the local skills center and workshops at the shelter, accessing public education, attaining a GED, developing a mentoring program, and attending classes at the local literacy project. Those shelter guests who embrace such responses are often rewarded with extended stays, increased staff attention, and similar privileges, while noncompliance is often diagnosed as a symptom of why those who do not participate remain homeless and used as a reason to make someone leave the shelter. Given these dynamics, it is hardly surprising that there are very few large-scale collective resistance struggles by homeless people against economic or racial inequality and housing policies. Self-blaming and self-governing subjects who are rewarded for looking within their selves for the solution to their individual homelessness can scarcely be expected to spend time organizing collective mobilizations against structural inequalities.[13]

Despite these dynamics, however, not everyone staying at the shelter voiced agreement with the representations of homelessness as the result of inadequacies or pathologies within particular homeless people. People staying at the shelter did articulate concerns regarding costs of housing, wages available at local jobs, and similar concerns about economic restructuring on almost a daily basis. As one young, employed, homeless man argued, "If this was the 1950s I wouldn't be homeless. My father graduated from high school and got a job right away in doing tool and dye work. They gave him good pay and benefits and on-the-job training. There just aren't good jobs like that anymore." Many people shared that sentiment, but they still often engaged in individual attempts to resolve homelessness. To examine more fully how these people did respond to homelessness in the face of such dynamics, let me return to Jonathan.

Jonathan, like many other people I have come to know, utilized individual strategies of hard work and self-responsibility as the pathway toward "success." He always was employed, often worked two jobs at a time, never missed a day of work, and hoped to work his way out of poverty. Yet he continued to be homeless. When his individual strategy of trying to work his way out of homelessness through being a responsible, hard-working person proved unsuccessful, Jonathan displaced the blame from himself by blaming other marginalized groups of people. He came to place much of the blame for his inability to find housing on preferential treatment for students, "minorities," and the "disabled." He stated, "They [the shelter staff, local politicians, and employers] don't want to help anybody in this town unless they're lesbian or Puerto Rican. These people just want to get a check. It takes about two minutes to get a job in this town if you want one. They [minorities] just don't want to work and they get all the help."

Jonathan was far from alone in expressing such sentiments at the shelter. Men and women staying at the shelter quite frequently asserted their whiteness by scapegoating minorities. They voiced their beliefs that "minorities" or "welfare queens" were taking resources and causing them to be homeless. As Susan, a woman in her mid-fifties, told me, "This town isn't a place for someone like me. They only build affordable housing for those 'Spanish' people." Other young white men at the shelter began to openly discuss the need for organizing in militia-like organizations to protect the "rights of real Americans" who were suffering because of government favoring of "minorities." Such sentiments were expressed so frequently at the shelter that some staff members proposed rules banning guests who used such "disrespectful language." These racist responses to poverty by some homeless people are hardly surprising. Despite the extensive historical roots of contemporary state-sanctioned and institutionalized white privilege in the United States (Lipsitz 1995; Sacks 1994; Page 1998), there is also a long history in the nation of poor white citizens embracing racist notions of perceived privileges for nonwhite others as a rationalization of their own less-privileged class position.[14]

While quite disturbing, the blaming of other marginalized or poor people was often combined with other responses. During another discussion, Jonathan mentioned that his bosses at the restaurant where he was working at the time were trying to get Tom (a co-worker who was also living at the shelter) and him to continue working instead of leaving town. "They're trying to get us to stay, but there's nothing they can do. This town hates homeless people. Everywhere else I've been people are more willing to help you. Some places people even help without you asking. Here they just don't want to see you."

I suggested that there was something his bosses could do. "Well, they could pay you enough to live on. How about paying you $7 an hour instead of $5?"

Jonathan did not think that was possible. He replied, "They can't do that. They won't stay in business. They could give me 40 hours every week, but I still won't be able to afford an apartment."

Jonathan could not envision his food-service job paying a decent wage. Like many other homeless and housed people, Jonathan represented as "natural" that such jobs must remain low-paying for the very survival of the business, and that decisions about distribution of the surplus naturally are the province of the employer. The possibility that food-service jobs can become "good" jobs, with high pay and benefits, remains outside the realm of even being imagined. He felt powerless to change the pay in these jobs and instead blamed "minorities" for his homelessness.

Again, Jonathan's feelings of powerlessness to alter conditions of work were widely shared by those people living at the shelter. Many of the people I worked with stated that they were powerless to change the wages paid at local jobs or the local cost of housing. When I brought up such concerns, the most frequent response was "That's the way things are. We don't have any power to change it." This feeling of powerlessness to make any substantive changes in systemic conditions is a frequently articulated explanation for homeless people not participating in "politics" at many levels. As neoliberal, market-oriented policies and practices are taken for granted, structural inequities often seem so all-encompassing and overwhelming that many homeless people believe they can do nothing to alter those conditions. It thus appears to be a more reasonable approach to focus on how to do well individually. As one example of many, Howard, an African American male in his early twenties, came to the shelter when he could no longer afford to remain housed or continue paying to attend the University of Massachusetts. Despite being an academic success throughout high school and his two and one-half years at the university, he had become homeless due to financial aid difficulties. Howard had been staying at the shelter for several months when he complained to me about how he had been working at a local supermarket for over six months and still could not afford to move out of the shelter. Despite a near-perfect work record, he was still stuck with a part-time and inconsistent schedule and minimum wage pay, and he felt powerless to alter those conditions of employment except through possibly demonstrating his reliability and efficiency as an individual employee.

I asked if he had requested more hours. Howard replied that he was told that "you don't get to work full time until you've been employed for a year." What was most frustrating to Howard was seeing the "Help Wanted" sign in the front of the store and seeing management hire people for more part-time jobs but remain unwilling to give him enough hours so that he could afford to become housed. When I asked why he thinks they did not simply offer him full-time hours. Howard replied, "'Cause they don't want to pay for benefits and they want to have you able to be at their call. Like yesterday. I wasn't scheduled, but they called me in to fill for someone else. They know you'll come because you're desperate for hours."

Adding to Howard's frustration was the inability of his union representative from the United Food and Commercial Workers Union to understand his desperation for more hours and greater pay. As Howard explained, "All they [the union stewards] do is tell me that we have a contract. That doesn't help me get money for a place to live." When I asked union leadership at his local about the practice, they argued that they got the best contract possible considering competition from nearby nonunion supermarkets. The "need" for large corporate profits and exorbitant salaries for top management went unchallenged in the union's effort to work cooperatively with management or in any of Howard's practices.

The supermarket where Howard (and Jonathan at one time) worked was part of a chain of 128 supermarkets that employed more than forty-eight thousand people throughout New England in 1995. That year the company reported $73 million in net income on sales of close to $4 billion. The chief executive officer received $1,198,153 in compensation (Spain and Talbott 1996:1351). Yet, despite the profits and high executive salaries, many workers continued to be paid wages inadequate to afford housing. Of course, it was understood as "unreasonable" for homeless people or many of the workers to challenge that tactical business decision.

When I asked what he could do about this, Howard said, "I just go to work and hope that I'll be able to save up enough money to find a place to live before I run out of time here [at the shelter]. You don't want to be thinking about it all the time or else you couldn't go to work. There doesn't seem to be much you can do anyway. . . . You can't make too much of a fuss because none of us who want to work full time are able to risk being fired." Despite the presence of a union, which is an increasingly rare condition in private-sector employment, Howard still could not imagine collective action aimed at challenging structural inequalities. Like many poor or homeless people, Howard (perhaps rightly) came to believe that his most rational move was to individualize his response to his homelessness and his working conditions. Instead of working with fellow employees toward gaining a more equitable distribution of the value of their labor, many workers cope by putting on blinders regarding the exploitative conditions of their work while being virtually forced to compete with fellow part-time workers for hours.

I found that establishing an awareness and mode of action outside set parameters is often seen as too overwhelming for many homeless people. Many people consider this sense of too much awareness as a way of numbing their own professional agency. As one homeless woman, Susan, stated, "Yes, what you say makes sense. Of course the problems are with the economy. I'm not stupid, but thinking about changing the wage structure or getting more housing is just too much. I have no idea of where to even start. I only have so much time here and I have to figure out how to cope with the reality of the situation."

Eventually, Jonathan, Susan, and Howard all left the city, hoping for better luck elsewhere. Jonathan headed south, hoping to find housing in South Carolina. Like 10 percent of those people who stayed at the shelter during 1994–1996, he decided that the only solution to his problem was to leave Northampton and hope for better luck somewhere else. He wanted to improve his income potential and job skills through education but couldn't afford to attend college. He worked hard but became extremely frustrated by his inability to afford decent housing. Feeling that he was powerless to alter the wages paid locally, the cost of housing, or any systemic conditions, he "chose" to leave town and try his luck elsewhere when his time at the shelter ran out.

An alternative response sometimes employed by a few homeless people is that demonstrated by Anthony. A white man in his early forties, Anthony, stayed at the shelter on three different occasions during the five years of my research. Most frequently he traveled throughout the country trying to survive. He offered a rarely articulated perspective on the link between employment, wages, and homelessness. His coping techniques for dealing with homelessness, however, remained an individualized strategy.

Anthony argued that much homelessness was caused by economic restructuring leading to declining real wages for many workers and the effects of unequal opportunities for success in the United States. He argued, "I don't have the opportunities because of how I grew up. All my father's relatives were ethnic Italians who worked in steel mills. All my mother's relatives were very rural Appalachian Mountain folk doing logging or agriculture. I certainly did not have any Mom and Dad down in Connecticut or southern California like you were saying. [I had suggested that one explanation for why he was homeless and I was not was that I had a relatively well-off family.] It's more than just getting the hair cut and putting on the three-piece [suit] and here's the training position working for some stock exchange.

"I have certainly worked all my life. I worked, coming home from junior high school, feeding thirty head of beef cattle. I grew up working constantly on my parent's farm, but that was cool. My father worked at nights at the steel mill. I bought my own school clothes. I do have a work ethic. At times I rebel considering that I have three and a half years of college education and I can't get a decent job. I rebel against the fact that I've never made more than $5.50 an hour, except for when I fought fires for the fire service." Significantly, though, he does not rebel by organizing collectively with other homeless people. Instead, he simply does not work for wages for long periods of time.

Unlike Anthony and a few others, however, the vast majority of homeless people I worked with shared many of the ideological norms and cultural values of dominant U.S. culture. Many who believe most strongly in survival of the fittest, patriotism, white male genetic superiority, and individual responsibility can be found practicing these beliefs at the shelters. Other people use sheltering industry representations of Horatio Alger–type stories, of the rare homeless person who has "succeeded" in pulling him- or herself out of homelessness, as a model to emulate. If a few model shelter guests managed to become "housed," then it must be possible. Therefore, there is no need for anything as drastic as organized, collective mobilization to challenge increasing inequality.

Likewise, it is understood that there is little that can be done about the cost and availability of local housing within the assumed "reality" of the current climate. Efforts at building a social movement to make permanent housing a right for all or even to limit the amount of rent a private landlord can charge are similarly minority efforts. Even when nondominant discursive efforts raise the possibilities of such resistance, they are marginalized by being deemed unrealistic and not worth pursuing. Possible collective resistance against systemic inequality is severely constrained when social agents understand current political-economic relations and class processes as inevitable, natural, or too overwhelming to ever change. Collective mobilization often is also almost mind-numbing to consider and understood as too risky to undertake, thus interfering further with personal agency. There is often little need for explicit coercion. Efforts are focused on how to cure, control, or manage the "disease" of homelessness, which is not at all construed as a problem with any racial, gendered, or class dimensions.

Homelessness persists in part because the material and discursive conditions causing it remain largely uncontested in daily practices.

Many of these social actors do articulate some degree of implicit awareness of the systemic and class nature of homelessness. Yet the possibilities for how they struggle against homelessness are constrained by how local actors understand the impediments to housing homeless people in relation to their own community. In Northampton, it appears that prevailing economic practices are not considered a variable to be contemplated in developing strategies to confront homelessness. Instead, it is taken as a given that decisions about production, appropriation, and distribution of the local surplus will remain in the hands of a few. Resistance to the discursive and systemic dimensions of homelessness will not be organized or amplified. Consequently, it is accepted that food-service employers will pay low wages, offer no benefits, and offer most workers only part-time work, even if this means that homeless people will not be able to afford a place to live in the community. These conditions are tolerated because of the combined impact of prevailing assumptions that there is nothing that can be done to alter structural violence; that market capitalism is natural, or at least inevitable; and that other subordinated people are to blame for homelessness. Added to these are the subject effects of a dominant individualized hypothesis of deviancy and self-government.

Is the Shelter a Possible Site for Collective Mobilization?

Routine, everyday practices by which homeless people, shelter staff, or homeless advocates respond to homelessness rarely include collective mobilization. Rarer still are collective strategies of resistance aimed at responding to homelessness through altering the prevailing conditions of systemic inequality in the United States. In Northampton, I found that interrelated understandings and practices connected with feelings of powerlessness to alter socioeconomic conditions, with individualized self-blame and self-government, and with blaming other oppressed people functioned to marginalize the very possibility of collective action. Although such understandings and practices were dominant, however, they were never total. As Raymond Williams so clearly emphasized, hegemony is always a process and is never all-encompassing (1977).

Particular social and ideological conditions working together produced understandings whereby some responses to homelessness were marginalized as unrealistic while other possibilities became common sense. Yet alternative and counterhegemonic possibilities, while marginalized, nonetheless existed in the shelter. Dominant ways of knowing and being were contested on a daily basis. As noted earlier, the majority of these contestations took the form of alternative approaches or subterfuge, sometimes as coping strategies, rarely as oppositional challenges. Rather than pointing out the inevitability of existing conditions (i.e., the sentiment often expressed at the shelter that "we need to work within the reality of these conditions"), I propose that such dynamics contain the possibilities of potential collective and oppositional mobilization. For such mobilization to emerge, however, the social conditions need to be created where collective understandings and practices become imaginable, are fostered, and are allowed to emerge. Just such a moment was created in one shelter in Northampton, Massachusetts, for a short period of time in 1995 and 1996.

The staff and regular volunteers working at this shelter began to explicitly challenge routine, everyday practices in a variety of ways. As part of my ongoing ethnographic research, I began to engage in increased dialogical exchanges with shelter staff members and with the people living at the shelter about my analysis of the effects of routine shelter practices. I shared the results of archival research and statistical compilations regarding local wages and housing costs, the number of employed people residing at the shelter, the extreme rarity of someone locating housing in the community on the basis of income received through low-paid employment, and how I analyzed shelter helping practices as teaching individualized responses.

None of this information was regularly compiled or publicly available at the shelter prior to my research. Once available, however, this information provided new possibilities for some of the staff to think about their own work at the shelter. This critique resonated well with sentiments that several staff members were concurrently developing. A newly hired staff member frequently articulated a Marxist-feminist critique of what she read as the medicalization of homeless people. Other staff were questioning how to do their work more effectively in the face of an unprecedented local demand for shelter. They were struggling to align their own self-proclaimed progressive, anarchist, socialist, and/or feminist political sentiments with an increasing awareness of how very little their helping practices were doing to decrease homelessness. The disjunction between their stated theoretical understandings and their actual practices in the shelter was articulated, acknowledged, and problematized. The culmination of these convergent practices was an expressed and enacted desire among the vast majority of these shelter workers to contemplate how to approach working in the shelters and with homeless people in new ways. Almost all staff members at this moment embraced a desire to rethink routine understandings and practices.

As those conditions came together, new practices began to emerge, creating discursive space for those staying in the shelter to think and act in new ways. All the shelter staff agreed to dedicate one hour of each weekly staff meeting toward discussing how to work in new ways. Staff debated their roles, their positions in the broader community, the effectiveness of prevailing practices, and the impact of existing hierarchical, distanced relationships with homeless people living in the shelter. Some staff began to discuss these issues with current and former residents of the shelter. Some significant changes in practices resulted from these discussions. One such change was the establishment of a weekly "community organizing" meeting at the shelter.

All staff of the shelter, any current or former guest of the shelter, and invited community members came together at this weekly meeting to discuss how to address homelessness. No set agendas were imposed, and the only rules of the meeting were that there be no physical violence and that anyone could say anything without fear of future reprisals from the staff. The stated intention of the meeting was for staff members and homeless people to begin listening to one another and to begin contemplating how they could work together in collaborative efforts. An institutionally sanctioned practice encouraging collective understandings and actions, rather than individualized strategies, emerged.

Preliminary discussions began to take place at this meeting regarding such practices as the developing and enforcing of shelter rules, funding the shelter without being beholden to state welfare agencies, and determining who would have access to producing the official summary of guest behavior in the daily logs, how intakes would be conducted, what statistical and demographic information would be compiled, and how such data would be conveyed to both the local community and government sources. After a few weeks, several homeless people began to use these meetings to discuss their frustrations with finding employment that paid more than minimum wage or with locating housing they could afford. I, in turn, shared data I had compiled on wages and housing costs in the community, the nation, and around the globe, so that those staying at the shelter could contextualize their struggles within a broader political-economic framework. When people raised racist or sexist arguments to explain their low wages or inability to find housing (and, as people were explicitly told they were free to do or say anything at these meetings except use physical violence, many did just that), staff and other guests began to openly challenge one another to think more critically about both the articulated assumptions and their broader effects. When some people argued that we were powerless to alter systemic conditions, other guests could now engage in dialogue. Often this involved raising historical examples of people who had managed to organize collective mobilization for dramatic changes.

Over time, many staff members and shelter residents began throughout the day, in most of their interactions with each other, to discuss and debate power relations within the shelter, employment issues, and the availability of affordable housing in the city. Dialogue about the connections between systemic inequalities and homelessness were now encouraged rather than being seen as misplaced, a waste of time, or a symptom of the disorder of "denial." After weeks and months of discussion and collaborative learning, more staff, guests, and a few shelter administrators began to attempt to enact new practices. New practices and resistance strategies aimed at possibly altering both the material and discursive dimensions of homelessness began to emerge. The culmination of these converging social conditions was such that collective mobilization became possible for a short moment in this shelter and this community.

Throughout these discussions, I continued to suggest that people could begin to work together collaboratively at the grassroots level to begin thinking and working toward more equality. The discursive parameters of what was thinkable and doable in this situation began to be stretched and altered. Some homeless people and some shelter staff began to consider the commonality of their experiences. Collaborative coalitions began to emerge between local organized labor, activist church members, local youth groups, welfare rights activists, and those working in the homeless sheltering industry. As one example, a living-wage movement was developed and organized from the discussions in the community organizing meetings at the shelter. Other people worked to organize a community center focused on community organizing and a collectively run business venture to provide nonexploitative local employment. Additionally, a coalition focused on issues of affordable housing, an effort to counteract popular imaginings about homeless people through producing a film at the shelter for local cable access television, and increased engagement with the local news media came out of these meetings. Several homeless and formerly homeless people were at the center of organizing these collaborative movements.

Unfortunately, this reflective moment and the related collective efforts lasted less than two years. When these nascent social movements moved into actual practices aimed at challenging inequities, shelter administrators, those funding the shelter, and local politicians became quite upset. It was made explicitly clear that the actions were jeopardizing support and the future economic viability of the shelter.[15] Shelter administrators were told to make their staff behave and return to their "proper" job of reforming homeless deviants. A new staff conduct policy was implemented that mandated a detached and professional relationship between staff and homeless "clients." As staff increasingly felt devalued and unable to work in the way they felt was necessary, many took jobs elsewhere or pursued more education. A new director was hired, who did not support or attend the community organizing meeting. Eventually the meeting was eliminated entirely.

Although short-lived, the practices that emerged out of this set of discursive conditions at this shelter in this community suggest that collective mobilizations of homeless people are possible. Previously accepted restrictions on what is possible and acceptable for both staff and homeless guests may be stretched and challenged. Shelter staff and homeless people can learn to rethink their established and habitual roles, including how they work with one another and the broader community. With these practices, different types of subjectivities might be produced within the homeless sheltering industry. A renewed sense of potential in collectively working together to challenge increasing systemic inequalities might become possible. New knowledge may provide the possibility for producing new kinds of subjects who undertake different resistance strategies aimed at altering structural conditions such as housing costs, housing availability, wages paid, the distribution of wealth and income, and racial inequalities. For such collective mobilizations and resistance to emerge or be sustained, the social conditions where such strategies are thinkable need to be in place. To allow such practices to become thinkable, let alone doable, critical reflections and transformations regarding the discursive and material conditions of homelessness must be established and enacted.

1. The names of all participants in this study have been changed to protect their confidentiality.

2. Sixty-nine (38 percent) of the people staying at the shelter during 1995 worked at least part time.

3. See Katherine Newman, *No Shame in My Game: The Working Poor in the Inner City* (New York: Alfred A. Knopf and The Russell Sage Foundation, 1996).

4. The growth in homelessness has taken place within a two-decade period that is also characterized by an increasingly polarized distribution of wealth. The number of people with incomes at or below the federally defined poverty level increased from 22,973,000 (11.1 percent of total population) in 1973 to 39,265,000 (15.1 percent) in 1993 (Center on Budget and Policy Priorities 1994:11; U.S. Bureau of the Census 1996).

5. Due to the restructured tax code, the percentage of total federal tax revenue from corporate taxes decreased from 23 percent in 1960 to 10 percent in 1995 (Albelda et al. 1996:21).

6. The distribution of aggregate household income in the United States documents this trend toward increased inequality. In 1993, the wealthiest 5 percent of the population received 20 percent of the nation's total income, while the poorest 40 percent received only 12.7 percent. Twenty years earlier, the distribution was 16.6 percent for the top 5 percent and 14.7 percent for the lowest 40 percent of families (Center on Budget and Policy Priorities 1994:57). This trend has continued in recent years. According to U.S. Bureau of the Census data, real median income in 1995 fell to 3.8 percent below that of 1989 (U.S. Bureau of the Census 1996).

7. The Census Bureau reported that the proportion of full-time workers with earnings too low to lift a family of four out of poverty rose from 12.1 percent in 1979 to 16.2 percent in 1993, an increase of one-third (Lazere 1995:18).

8. In 1970, after several years of increased government expenditures on housing as one component of the "war on poverty," the 7.4 million low-cost rental units in the United States represented an abundance of 900,000 more units than the number of low-income renters (6.5 million). In 1973, there were 5.1 million nonsubsidized rental units with costs of $300 per month or less (in 1993 dollars). By 1993, however, the number of low-rent units fell to 6.5 million (only 2.9 million of which were nonsubsidized) while the number of low-income potential renters increased to 11.2 million people. A shortage of 4.7 million units was the result (Lazere 1995:2).

9. The articles in the edited volume *More than Class: Studying Power in U.S. Workplaces* (Kingsolver 1998) spell out related arguments about relationships within the United States under contemporary capitalism.

10. By "false consciousness" I am referring to the notion that ideological or structural conditions obfuscate the truth from people, thus resulting in mystification of their essential interests. Following Michel Foucault (1991), I am suggesting that there is no essential consciousness, but rather all human subjects are always produced through the relations in which they are enmeshed.

11. An additional 100–250 other people were turned away, due to a lack of shelter space, each year during 1995–1997.

12. For related arguments about the growth of self-government as the most

reasonable and practical way of responding to social problems, see the work of Nikolas Rose (1996) and Barbara Cruikshank (1996).

13. For a more detailed argument on the effects of the medicalization of homelessness, see my forthcoming article in *Medical Anthropology Quarterly* (Lyon-Callo, 2000).

14. See, for example, the work of Pem Davidson Buck (1992).

15. For a further discussion of the impact that funding considerations played in constraining resistance, see my article in *Human Organization* (Lyon-Callo 1998b).

REFERENCES

Abu-Lughod, Lila. 1990. "The Romance of Resistance: Tracing Transformations of Power through Bedouin Women." *American Ethnologist* 17(1):41–55.

Albelda, Randy, Nancy Folbre, and the Center for Popular Economics. 1996. *The War on the Poor*. New York: New Press.

Blau, Joel. 1992. *The Visible Poor: Homelessness in the United States*. New York: Oxford University Press.

Bourgois, Philippe. 1996. *In Search of Respect: Selling Crack in El Barrio*. Cambridge: Cambridge University Press.

Buck, Pem Davidson. 1992. "With Our Heads in the Sand: The Racist Right, Concentration Camps, and the Incarceration of People of Color." *Transforming Anthropology* 3:13–18.

Burt, Martha. 1997. "Causes of the Growth of Homelessness during the 1980s." In *Understanding Homelessness: New Policy and Research Perspectives*. Washington, DC: Fannie Mae Foundation.

Center on Budget and Policy Priorities. 1994. *1993 Poverty and Income Trends*. Washington, DC: Center on Budget and Policy Priorities.

Cruikshank, Barbara. 1996. "Revolutions Within: Self-Government and Self-Esteem." In *Foucault and Political Reason: Liberalism, Neo-Liberalism, and Rationalities of Government*. Edited by Andrew Barry, Thomas Osborne, and Nikolas Rose. Chicago: University of Chicago Press.

Dordick, Gwendolyn. 1997. *Something Left to Lose: Personal Relations and Survival among New York's Homeless*. Philadelphia: Temple University Press.

Dowdy, Zachary R. 1998. "Homelessness Rising despite Brisk Economy." *Boston Globe*, 10/12, B1.

Economic Policy Institute. 1997. *Nonstandard Work, Substandard Jobs: Flexible Work Arrangements in the US*. Washington, DC: Economic Policy Institute.

Foucault, Michel. 1991. *Conversations with Duccio Trombadori*. New York: Semiotext(e).

Hardin, Bristow. 1996. "Why the Road Off the Street Is Not Paved with Jobs." In *Homelessness in America*. Phoenix: Orxy Press.

Kaufman, Tracy. 1996. *Out of Reach: Can America Pay the Rent?* Washington, DC: National Low Income Housing Coalition.

———. 1997. *Out of Reach: Rental Housing at What Cost?* Washington, DC: National Low Income Housing Coalition.

Kidder, Tracy. 1999. *Hometown.* New York: Random House.

Kingsolver, Ann. 1998. *More than Class: Studying Power in U.S. Workplaces.* Albany: State University of New York Press.

Kondo, Dorinne. 1990. *Crafting Selves: Power, Gender, and Discourses of Identity in a Japanese Workplace.* Chicago: University of Chicago Press.

Lazere, Edward. 1995. *In Short Supply: The Growing Affordable Housing Gap.* Washington, DC: Center on Budget and Policy Priorities.

Lipsitz, George. 1995. "The Possessive Investment in Whiteness: Racialized Social Democracy and the 'White' Problem in American Studies." *American Quarterly* 47(3):369–87.

Lyon-Callo, Vincent. 1998a. "Hegemony and the Construction of Selves: A Dialogical Ethnography of Homelessness and Resistance." Unpublished Ph.D. dissertation, University of Massachusetts, Amherst.

———. 1998b. "Constraining Responses to Homelessness: An Ethnographic Exploration of the Impact of Funding Concerns on Resistance." *Human Organization* 57(1):1–7.

———. 2000. "Medicalizing Homelessness: The Production of Self-Blame and Self-Governing within Homeless Shelters." *Medical Anthropology Quarterly* 14(3): 328–45.

Market Street Research Inc. 1994. *Health and Human Service Needs of Hampshire County Residents: Need Assessment Report.* Northampton, MA: Market Street Research Inc.

National Coalition for the Homeless. 1997. *Homelessness in America: Unabated and Increasing.* Washington, DC: National Coalition for the Homeless.

O'Flaherty, Brendan. 1996. *Making Room: The Economics of Homelessness.* Cambridge: Cambridge University Press.

Page, Helan. 1998. "Understanding White Cultural Practices." *Anthropology Newsletter* 39(4):58–60.

Roche, B. J. 1996. "Balancing Act: Northampton Is a City That Works." *Boston Globe Magazine,* 8/21, 20–29.

Rose, Nicholas. 1996. "The Death of the Social? Re-figuring the Territories of Government." *Economy and Society* 25(3):327–56.

Sacks, Karen Brodkin. 1994. "How Did Jews Become White Folks?" In *Race.* Edited by Steven Gregory and Roger Sanjek. New Brunswick: Rutgers University Press.

Scott, James. 1990. *Domination and the Arts of Resistance: Hidden Transcripts.* New Haven: Yale University Press.

Sharff, Jagna Wojcicka. 1998. *King Kong on 4th Street: Families and the Violence of Poverty on the Lower East Side.* Boulder: Westview Press.

Spain, Patrick, and James Talbott. 1996. *Hoover's Handbook of American Businesses 1996*. Austin: Reference Press.

Turner, Maureen. 1998. "The Division of Labor: Employment Numbers Look Good on Paper, but They Hide Serious Weak Spots in the Market." *Valley Advocate*, 2/26, 20–22.

U.S. Bureau of the Census. 1996. *Poverty in the United States: 1995*. Washington, DC: U.S. Bureau of the Census.

Wagner, David. 1993. *Checkerboard Square: Culture and Resistance in a Homeless Community*. Boulder: Westview Press.

Waterston, Alisse. 1993. *Street Addicts in the Political Economy*. Philadelphia: Temple University Press.

Watson, Bruce. 1996. "Tight Rental Market Aggravates Annual Housing Scramble." *Daily Hampshire Gazette*, 8/28, 15–16.

Waxman, Laura, and Sharon Hinderliter. 1997. *A Status Report on Hunger and Homelessness in America's Cities: 1996*. Washington, DC: U.S. Conference of Mayors.

Williams, Brett. 1996. "There Goes the Neighborhood: Gentrification, Displacement, and Homelessness in Washington DC." In *There's No Place like Home: Anthropological Perspectives on Housing and Homelessness in the United States*. Edited by Anna Lou Dehavenon. Westport: Bergin and Garvey.

Williams, Raymond. 1977. *Marxism and Literature*. Oxford: Oxford University Press.

Wright, Talmadge. 1997. *Out of Place: Homeless Mobilizations, Subcities, and Contested Landscapes*. Albany: State University of New York Press.

Part IV

Poverty, Difference, and Activism

Chapter 12

"I Am Not a Problem without a Solution"
Poverty and Transnational Migration

Nina Glick Schiller and Georges Fouron

In the summer of 1998, Yvette[1] borrowed $10,000 from the modest pension she has been accumulating while working as a shipping clerk in New York City. She originally borrowed the money so that she and her brother Candio, who had also emigrated from Haiti to the United States, could buy a used car for Michel. Michel, one of their brothers, still lives in the small Haitian rural hamlet in which Yvette and her siblings were born. Before Yvette was able to obtain the money, however, Candio proceeded on his own. From his small salary as a cashier in a supermarket in Matapan, Massachusetts, Candio bought a car and managed to ship it to Michel. The procedure was costly because, in addition to the price of the car, Candio had to negotiate a dense web of bureaucracy, taxes, and bribes. With the vehicle, Michel planned to start a taxi service and earn money. His siblings in the United States hoped that by financing Michel's enterprise they would be relieved of some of the burden of supporting an extended network of kin and old friends in Haiti. But the car soon broke down. The only car that Candio could afford was old, needed repairs, and was no match for the wretched conditions of the roads in Haiti.

A further aspiration underlay Yvette and Candio's decision to buy a car and ship it all the way to Haiti. Those abroad who undertake such projects increase their social standing and prestige among their family and friends in Haiti, even as they make their lives more economically precarious in the United States. By shipping the car by himself, Candio had depleted his meager resources but also reaped the self-respect and the social prestige that come from completing such a project. Accustomed to being the member of her family network who carried the burden of supporting others but also obtained preeminence among her family and friends because of her sacrifice, Yvette did not return the $10,000 to her pension. Instead, Yvette took most of her borrowed capital, traveled to Haiti, and distributed it among relations and friends. Her distribution that year resembled a payroll, and she remarked on that as she tucked the cash in envelopes, each marked with the recipient's name. Her generosity provided crucial funds for persons who had no support and funded a large wedding reception for a relative she barely knew. It also assured Yvette's position as a prosperous member of the Haitian diaspora. When Yvette returned to the United States, she worked long overtime hours to try to pay back the loan, her face gray with exhaustion and her back aching from her labors. "My body," she said, "is like Haiti, sick and tired."

By analyzing why Yvette sees herself as an embodiment of her homeland and why both Yvette and Candio impoverish themselves to provide for those they have left behind, we can gain insights into the relationship between the current global restructuring of capitalism and the worldwide intensification of poverty. Global transformations in the structure of capitalist profit-making are inducing people to migrate but maintain home ties (Sassen 1998). The restructuring of capitalism and the transnational ties migrants maintain also shape the context within which we can build movements against contemporary forms of exploitation and oppression.

Yvette, Candio, and Georges, one of the authors of this article, are all "transmigrants," as are many immigrants in the United States today from Haiti and from a host of countries around the world (Glick Schiller, Basch, and Szanton-Blanc 1992:1). Transmigrants maintain multiple familial, social, economic, and political ties to both their country of origin and their country of settlement and live their lives across national borders. They become incorporated in two nation-states and contribute and participate in the daily life activities and social processes that materialize, maintain, contest, challenge, and revalue structures of power in both locations.[2] In this chapter, we contribute to analyses of the links between poverty and international migration by looking at the transnational migration of Haitians to the United States and its economic and political implications. We explore what poor immigrants like Yvette and Candio gain and lose by their immersion in transnational processes. In particular, we highlight the dynamics through which immigrants embrace forms of long-distance nationalism and, in so doing, contribute to and transform ideologies of nationalism in the restructured global economy. We call the assertion of an essential and eternal connection between dispersed people and a territorially based nation-state that motivates or justifies actions taken on behalf of that ancestral land "long-distance nationalism."[3] As we examine the long-distance nationalism of poor and disempowered Haitians, we identify new vistas from which the legitimacy and increasingly unfettered power of global financial and corporate interests can be challenged.

This essay is based on research that we individually or jointly conducted on Haitian settlement in New York in 1969, 1982, 1985–87, and 1996–98, and on research we conducted in Haiti in 1969, 1990, 1991, 1995, 1996, and 1998. Most of the quotations we use are drawn from a snowball sample of 104 persons we interviewed in Haiti in 1996 in order to explore whether or not persons in Haiti defined those who had emigrated from Haiti as members of the Haitian nation and state. We build on this research to argue that an understanding of transnational migration is essential for those interested in struggling for social and economic justice and equality.

Joining Poverty Studies to Studies of Transnational Migration

Several decades ago, social scientists began to address the ways in which their work contributed to processes of domination. William Ryan (1976), for example, popularized the phrase "blaming the victim" to identify the process by which both social scientists and social service providers explain poverty solely by focusing on the behavior of the poor. In a similar vein, anthropologists such as Eleanor Leacock (1969, 1971) and Charles Valentine (1968) critiqued the ideology that portrayed a maladaptive and dependent culture of the poor as the cause of poverty. The next generation of theorists exposed the concept of the "underclass" as a revisiting of the "culture of poverty" argument (Katz 1989, 1993; Susser 1996).[4] As Wacquant pointed out:

> By focusing narrowly on the presumed behavioral and cultural deficiencies of inner-city residents . . . without paying due notice to the historical structures of racial and class inequality, spatial separation, and governmental (in)action that filter and amplify it, recent discussions on the so-called underclass have hidden the political roots of the predicament of the ghetto and contributed to the further stigmatization and political isolation of its residents. (1994:264–65)

Critiques of the culture of poverty thus contributed to a growing understanding of how the construction of culturalist explanations in state societies itself reflects political and economic relations of domination (Frankenberg 1988; Glick Schiller 1992; Roseberry 1989).[5]

While many anthropologists understood the structural basis of poverty, we nevertheless found ourselves uneasy with the portrayal of the poor as "victims," whether blameworthy or blameless. We stressed the agency of poor people, using ethnographic methods to document the adaptive coping strategies of poor individuals and families that allowed them to survive in a hostile, brutal setting (Stack 1974; Baxter and Hopper 1981). A weakness of this rich and insightful literature was the tendency to define as mutually exclusive three ways in which poor people responded to poverty: adaptation, accommodation, and resistance. Debate raged about the "weapons of the weak" (Scott 1985). Were acts of defiance, from giving an unseen finger to a cop to the arson of an urban uprising, actually political resistance if they were unaccompanied by political critique, class consciousness, and a program for fundamental change (Gutmann 1993)? Or were we only detailing more recent forms of "rituals of rebellion" (Gluckman 1960)? This debate echoed, and sometimes was informed by, historical debates on the left about the significance of spontaneous revolts and daily acts of defiance to oppressive authorities and routines (Lenin 1978 [1902]).

Meanwhile, somewhat removed from debates about accommodation and resistance to poverty, a new scholarship of transnational migration developed. Those of us who sought to forge a new analytical framework for the study of migration tended to see transnational migration as a coping strategy of poor persons from poor countries (Glick Schiller, Basch, and Szanton-Blanc 1992; Guarnizo and Smith 1998; Mahler 1998). We portrayed transnational migration as a "hedge your bets" strategy (Basch, Glick Schiller, and Szanton-Blanc 1994). Persons faced with difficult economic circumstances in both sending and receiving societies coped with economic insecurity by living their lives across international borders and becoming incorporated in two or more states simultaneously (Lessinger 1995; Pessar 1995). Some of this research documents, in disparate locations and transnationally, family strategies of surviving poverty that resemble those described by ethnographers of the poor in the United States (Stack 1974; Sharff 1998; Susser 1982; Rouse 1992; Mountz and Wright 1996; Lewis 1965). In economies of great scarcity, family is one of the few resources an individual can tap in a quest for survival, security, or social or physical mobility.

For example, in Haiti, we have described an economy of *grapiyaj*. Haitians use this term to describe surviving by means of many small transactions. If you survive by *grapiyaj*, you get help from different people, making wide use of all your family ties and connections, pooling tiny pieces of resources together to give you a whole—enough on which to live.[6]

For transmigrants from locations around the world, family is often experienced not as a small residential unit of mother, father, and children but as an extended network of connections that crosses international borders. It is tree with underground roots, not always visible but capable of giving sustenance and support to the various more readily identifiable branches that extend in different directions (LaGuerre 1978, 1982; Smith and Wallerstein 1992).

International Migration: Safety Valve or Long Fuse?

It is easy for ethnographers of transnational family connections to become caught up in the struggles for survival of individual immigrant families and to fail to discuss the long-term structural consequences of the patterns of transnational connections.[7] Yet, for over a century, some scholars and government officials have been aware that migration can serve as a "safety valve" that protects the existing order and its dominant classes (Cinel 1982: 74). Late-nineteenth-century policymakers in both Europe and the United States portrayed chain migration as a means of relieving local population pressure and pressure on scarce resources. They believed that if the poor, discontented, and politically oppressed are able to migrate, the social and political inequalities of the sending society are more likely to remain unchallenged. Or, as an Italian writer observed in 1874, "Whatever we do to encourage emigration is a step in the direction of defusing social tensions and avoiding socialism. Emigration is the only way to keep change in Italy under control" (Leoni Carpi, cited in Cinel 1982:74). By the beginning of the twentieth century, some U.S. advocates of immigration restriction argued that without the safety valve of migration, European governments would have to voluntarily address the "political, religious or economic evils" of their social systems or they "would soon be confronted by revolutions" (Frank J. Warne, cited in Dudley 1990:35–36). The view that migration could defuse potentially explosive situations was also voiced in the 1980s by USAID officials. They saw emigration from Haiti as the short-term solution for the population they planned to displace by fostering agribusiness and export processing (DeWind and Kinley 1988).

Those who have argued that migration serves only as a safety valve have not understood that migration is often a transnational process. Once we treat migrants as actors in two polities simultaneously, other possible political consequences of migration become apparent. Transmigrants transmit and transform ideologies and social, economic, and political aspirations across international borders. While their desire for a better life may initially be channeled into migration from their homeland, experiences in their new land often lead them to participate in transnational activities that can have a profound effect on the family and country they left behind. These effects vary greatly and can produce a politics that reinforces or challenges the structures of inequality of the homeland. For example, currently some Haitian transmigrants in the United States have endorsed a policy of privatization and structural adjustment that benefits U.S.-based corporate and financial capital.[8] In contrast, other Haitian transmigrants who contribute to transnational social movements, such as the international women's movement, challenge current globalization policies that benefit the dominant classes in both the United States and Haiti.

Little research has been done on transnational relationships and their economic and political implications, because of a flawed historiography and ethnography of migration that, since the 1950s, has portrayed immigrants in the United States as displaced persons, permanently uprooted from home and family (Handlin 1973 [1951]).[9] Current transnational research can correct these weaknesses only if we move beyond the stage of celebrating transnational connections and proclaiming the agency of transmigrants. We must begin a systematic examination of the *political* implications of immigrant transnational networks and the long-distance nationalism that contributes to their legitimation. When we examine the historical record of transnational migration from this perspective, we find a complex dynamic of stasis and change. While emigrants may physically have left their homeland, they often have remained connected to it through familial, religious, economic, and political transnational networks (Adamic 1941; Park 1974 [1925], Glick Schiller, Basch, and Szanton-Blanc 1992; Wyman 1993). In various situations, these networks of interconnection have maintained, gradually undermined, or directly challenged the political and economic structure of both the society from which emigrants fled and the society in which they have settled (Moch 1992; Bodnar 1985; Morawska 1987, 1989, 1997).

Toward a Social History of Transnational Political Connection

Historically, as industrial capitalism developed within a system of production that relied on raw materials and labor from diverse regions of the world, increasing numbers of people sought to defend themselves against economic restructuring by migrating both within states and across international borders (Chan 1990; Glick Schiller 1999; Wyman 1993). Some of these migrants left home in order to obtain the money they needed to purchase land in their home regions, which had suddenly become a cash commodity. Migration often was a response to the threat of total impoverishment and an attempt to maintain social respectability or social mobility by obtaining cash to use in the home locality. This was as true of the development of industrial production in Japan and China as it was of Great Britain, France, Germany, and Italy (Cinel 1991; Moch 1992; Chan 1990). By the beginning of the twentieth century, regions of many parts of Europe, as well as Turkey, China, Japan, and Mexico, had become remittance societies (Park 1974 [1925]; Portes and Rumbaut 1990; Wong 1982). John Bodnar, for instance, has argued that the fact that return rates for most European migrants during that period ranged from 25 to 60 percent indicates that people migrated in order to obtain sufficient capital to establish themselves in their home society (1985:53).

The energies, hopes, and aspirations of millions of people were channeled toward improvement for themselves and their families through migration. Despite the fact that transmigrants often encountered exploitation, sickness, loneliness, and despair, some earned enough to send remittances. Emigrants sent home money to improve the family house, to contribute to the social mobility of the family, and to maintain or repair village churches or temples (Chan 1990; Wyman 1993). Return migrants often did not challenge the status quo but sought a secure place within it. From the migrants' perspective, there was change and improvement; yet social divisions remained, and vast inequalities of wealth and power persisted.

At the same time, significant changes were wrought in the wake of the migration that accompanied the development and expansion of industrial capitalism. Migration led to changes in patterns of land owning, investment, and the expansion of capitalism. Individual migrants and migrant organizations, exposed to new ideas and experiencing new identities, became central to movements for change both in the United States and in their homelands. Transmigrants to the United States played central roles in the organization of labor and socialist movements in the United States, as well as contributing to nationalist movements in Europe and Asia (Buhle 1987; Bodnar 1985; Gabaccia and Ottanelli 1997; Glick Schiller 1999; Park 1974 [1925]; Schermerhorn 1949; Tolopko 1991).

But homeland loyalties often divided the U.S. labor force (Fraser 1991). The divisions between black and white labor in the United States developed in a transnational context of "whitening" that we are just beginning to comprehend. Part of this process of becoming white, however, clearly included a stage during which many immigrants in the United States distanced themselves from African Americans by participating in homeland politics (Glick Schiller 1999; Pistalo 2001). First Irish labor and then southern and eastern European labor differentiated themselves from being racialized as nonwhites or "whites of a different color" by highlighting their homeland identities (Ignatiev 1996; Jacobson 1998; Miller 1990; Roediger 1991).

Our growing understanding of the political and economic consequences of past experiences of transnational migration must inform our analysis of the implications of contemporary migration, in which immigrants are once again sustaining remittance economies at home as well as becoming participants in nationalist movements in their homelands. Emigrants to the United States, as well as to other areas that are central to the global economy, continue to live within webs of family obligation. They are enmeshed in a pattern of ceaseless labor that sustains large numbers of people who might otherwise literally starve or be pushed to the very bottom of the society.

U.S.-Haitian Migration: Strategies of Individual Survival and Resistance

The Haitian migration to the United States is part of the vast immigration that has been restructuring the U.S. population since the 1960s. Beginning in the 1960s, the size of the immigrant population began to match the level of migration to the United States at the turn of the century. Between 1960 and 1996, 17,289,266 legal immigrants became part of the U.S. population, together with large numbers of undocumented persons or persons who arrived with visitor visas but overstayed their visas (DeSipio and de la Garza 1998:17–18). Today, it is likely that almost one-fifth of Haiti's 7 million people live outside Haiti, with the largest concentration settled in the United States.[10] The Haitian population in the New York metropolitan area remains the largest and most influential Haitian immigrant settlement in the United States, but South Florida has emerged as a significant site of Haitian settlement.

While the flow of Haitian migration was spurred by the coming to power of the Duvalier dictatorship in 1957, a regime that beat, imprisoned, murdered, or exiled all opposition, Haitian migration is part of broader patterns of contemporary migration. Beginning in the 1970s, the growth of the "global assembly line," export processing zones, and the worldwide distribution of food imports produced by agribusiness spurred the migration of displaced agricultural producers and urban workers (Sassen 1988; UNRISD 1995). In the 1980s and 1990s, impoverishment grew in most countries whose economies were outside capitalist centers. Economic crisis in these states was fueled by massive debt service obligations to international banks, foreign governments, and the World Bank (Danaher 1994; Hancock 1989; Torrie 1983). In exchange for staving off the collapse of these economies, the International Monetary Fund (IMF) imposed structural adjustment programs that restricted investment in health, education, and public services; reduced the employment provided by the state; eliminated the subsidization of food; and made all imported goods more expensive by devaluing local currency. Increasing numbers of people turned to emigration as a way to earn money abroad to provide food, shelter, and education for kin left behind, as well as to improve their own social and economic position in their native land. By the 1990s, small and large economies, including the Dominican Republic, the Philippines, India, and Mexico, had begun to look to remittances as significant sources of foreign exchange.

By the 1990s, Haiti had become a "remittance economy," with a large though untold number of Haitian immigrants sending a steady flow of money, food, clothing, and household goods to Haiti. The U.S. State Department reported that "remittances from abroad now constitute a significant source of financial support for many Haitian households."[11] Migration from Haiti, sustained by U.S. development policies and foreign aid that, in point of fact, "aided migration," had grown rapidly throughout the 1970s and 1980s (DeWind and Kinley 1988).

The wealth sent to Haiti in remittances comes from a population whose per capita income is low and whose income is often insecure. Individual income among Haitian immigrants averaged $11,894 in 1989. In 1990, 21 percent of the families were earning an income below the poverty line, despite the fact that Haitian immigrants as a group have a high level of employment and women are employed almost as frequently as men. In many households, dire poverty is prevented only because there are often several adult wage earners.[12] In New York, Haitians work in industries such as health care, hotels, office cleaning, and transport services. Women in particular work in the home health care industry. Employment in the service sector often means working long hours for low wages and no benefits. In the impoverished neighborhoods where Haitians have clustered, immigrants have begun record stores, travel agencies, restaurants, grocery stores, bakeries, and barber and beauty shops, but most of these businesses struggle to survive and provide few jobs. The reduction of manufacturing jobs since the 1970s in U.S. metropolitan areas, racial discrimination, and the difficulties Haitians face in obtaining legal documentation force many to begin small, informal businesses. Vans operated by male drivers offer regular and inexpensive transportation services in areas with large concentrations of immigrants. Women use their kitchens to cater parties, weddings, and other social events. Their living rooms are also transformed into day-care centers. People earn money by dressmaking, tailoring, repairing automobiles, and working as couriers transporting the remittances of others to Haiti.

Although informal-sector employment is unreported in census figures, official figures portray a stratified population that contains both a professional stratum and a significant working class. In 1990, 34 percent of the population worked in service occupations; 21 percent were factory operatives; 21 percent were clerical or technical workers; 9 percent were professionals; 5 percent were managers; and 3 percent were farm workers (U.S. Bureau of the Census 1990). Forty-one percent of these immigrants had a lower than high school education; 48 percent had at least a high school education; and 11 percent had college degrees or higher. Women are about as likely as men to obtain a high school or college education.[13]

While more research is needed to examine the class backgrounds and current class positioning of Haitian immigrants, and while those who are unemployed or ill are often unable to maintain their home ties, transnational ties to Haiti are found among immigrants of all classes. Our research indicates that many persons who have low-wage service and factory work send remittances home. In a convenience sample of 487 Haitians in New York who sent remittances to Haiti, Josh DeWind found that 91 percent of the persons surveyed sent money at least once a year (DeWind 1987:4). He found no relationship between a person's income or occupation and the amount of money sent. Respondents reported sending an average of $1,528 in the year prior to his survey. Middle-class people in professions such as teaching, nursing, accounting, and computer technical work carry large amounts of debt and remain relatively impoverished because of the constant obligation to support those whom they left behind.

Why Do Immigrants Maintain Transnational Connections?

Why do immigrants such as Yvette and Candio continue, year after year, to carry this transnational burden of a broad network of people that includes kinfolk they barely know as well as non-kin who were neighbors, co-workers, and friends? In other writings on transnational migration, we have examined at some length the political, economic, and social forces that contribute to the transnational strategies of Haitian immigrants of all class backgrounds (Basch, Glick Schiller, and Szanton-Blanc 1994; Fouron and Glick Schiller 1997; Glick Schiller and Fouron 1991, 1998, 1999).

First of all, there is the economic insecurity of daily life in the United States. The U.S. economy, as part of broad processes of economic restructuring and globalization, offers much less than it used to in the way of secure employment for all of us, but those with few skills and imperfect English are at the greatest risk for being thrust entirely out of the formal economy. If Yvette's position as a mail clerk is eliminated in some form of corporate reorganization, she thinks it unlikely she will find another decent job. Since he arrived in 1993, Candio has worked his way up from collecting shopping carts in the parking lot of a supermarket to being a cashier, by proving his reliability and trustworthiness to his employers. But he speaks little English and has few marketable skills and so would not easily be able to find work outside the predominantly Haitian neighborhood in which he lives.

Second, there is the issue of long-term security. For the decade or so after a massive grassroots movement overthrew the Duvalier dictatorship in 1986, Haitian immigrants invested in property and businesses in Haiti, not only to sustain their families there but also as a means of ensuring that they had a safety net outside the reaches of U.S. "welfare reform." In the 1990s, U.S. federal and state policies removed health and educational benefits from U.S. permanent residents and threatened to challenge the rights of naturalized citizens. Yvette and Candio have seen projects such as the car service they planned for their brother not only as a means for making their kin in Haiti more self-supporting but also as providing a more prosperous family. If their family members prosper in Haiti, they will be able to care for Yvette or Candio if illness, disability, unemployment, or old age leads either sibling to return home to Haiti. Many Haitian transmigrants in the United States, including Georges, have been planning to retire to Haiti, where U.S. dollars can provide a comfortable old age. If they become U.S. citizens, they are entitled to live in Haiti and collect the Social Security pension to which they have paid during all their labor in the United States. To avoid a lonely old age in the United States, where elders are seen as burdens by both family and the society, rather than as sources of wisdom and resources, immigrants need to have paved the path of return through a lifetime of sending remittances. By the year 2000, however, many Haitian transmigrants' hopes of seeking refuge in Haiti were being destroyed by the insecurity of Haiti's political situation. It is unclear at this point if continuing insecurity will affect the dynamics discussed in this chapter.

Economic insecurity in the United States is accompanied, for immigrants of color, by the constant context of racial discrimination. As black immigrants, Haitians are never sure they are welcome in the United States. While in Haitian Kreyol the word for all human beings is neg, which means black, in the United States all but whites remain hyphenated Americans. Even when Haitian immigrants become citizens, as Yvette is currently doing, they find they will always be seen as black, and in the United States, black is a location at the bottom of the society, against which all others measure their social position (Baldwin 1971; Delgado 1995). Furthermore, by the 1990s, immigrants faced a new wave of anti-immigrant sentiment and legislation.

The insecurity of life in the United States and the obligations of family are not the only reasons that Yvette and Candio send remittances. There are also the dynamics of social status.[14] Because of their constant obligations to send remittances to Haiti, Yvette may live in her cousin's basement in Queens, and Candio may be just another poor black man in Boston; but in Haiti, both Yvette and Candio are seen by their family and friends as prosperous and privileged. In the United States their earnings make no social mark, and even if they were to hoard them or expend them on consumer goods, the siblings would still be counted among the poor. To the extensive network of people they are supporting in Haiti, however, Yvette and Candio are somebodies. They must, of course, find enough money to enjoy this status. They must not only send remittances to Haiti but also visit occasionally. Visits cannot be sustained without the expenditure of large sums for presents and distributions of cash.

Sometimes emigrants confine their visiting to family funerals because during such times there is less pressure to distribute, while the funeral can be an occasion for a display that gives status both to the immigrant and to those related to him or her. For example, Candio's only trip back to Haiti so far has been for a funeral. Although he earns very little, his supermarket job provides him with access to the best cuts of meat at a low price. On his return to Haiti for the funeral of a sister, he included a suitcase of meat among the six bags packed with gifts and fine clothes. When he arrived at the airport, the airline personnel told him he could take only two suitcases to Haiti. So he brought the meat and the gifts and left all his clothes behind. When Candio arrived in Port-au-Prince, he had to buy new clothes for the funeral.

Transnational Migration and Divisions among the Poor

The broad dissemination of the resources sent from abroad has multiple effects on the political consciousness of poor people in Haiti. Remittances sustain a wide network of people but also divide them from one another and direct their aspirations toward migration rather than collective action. Mimrose's situation provides an example. Mimrose is one of the many people whom Yvette and Candio have been supporting in Haiti. She is their deceased brother's widow and the mother of his five children. Because Yvette has remained unmarried and childless, and Candio has family responsibilities in Boston, Yvette assumed the primary responsibility for these six people. Her support made it possible for Mimrose to lease a three-room house with a cistern and to become a patron of those in the neighborhood with even fewer resources than Mimrose. Impoverished persons in the neighborhood with no support from abroad use the cistern for bathing, share in the drinking water, and recycle her cast-off goods. Yet, even though the remittances that Yvette labors to send support a network of people that stretches beyond her kin, the political effects of this type of redistribution are not to build solidarity among poor Haitians but rather to emphasize social distance. Because they live in a presentable house in what is considered a middle-class neighborhood and are able to redistribute the bounty sent from abroad, Mimrose and her grown children have come to believe they are better and more socially important than their poorer neighbors.

Those like Mimrose who directly receive remittances see themselves as no longer poor. Instead, they identify with the middle class, who disdain the poor. We heard this view from many of the people we interviewed. Thomas, for example, who had not worked in six years and lived on a steady flow of remittances sent by two of his children, explained the ideology of class positioning that is promoted through the remittance economy:

> The class below the middle class have to beg for their food. They have to carry heavy things for people in order to eat or do all types of menial jobs. But if you belong to the middle class there are things that you cannot do because the class above you will notice. This is one of our main problems in Haiti. ... Well that is what is destroying us in Haiti because you will not do a job that the people in classes lower than you would do but at the same time you cannot find job worthy of your class.

Here, poor people with some reliable source of income are divided from those who are more desperate.

At the same time, dependency has its bitternesses, and many who live on remittances like Mimrose and Thomas feel that relatives abroad provide them with only a pittance of the wealth that can be obtained in the United States. Those who receive no remittances from abroad tend toward greater hopelessness, since generally only those with some resources are able to leave Haiti for the United States. Although only a few years before they had built a powerful grassroots movement for fundamental change in Haiti, by 1996 most very poor people felt disempowered.

Despair was constantly present during our interview with Marie, a poor women with grown children who had no education and did not know her age. When we asked her if conditions in Haiti will get better, she told us:

> My children ... are obligated to suffer. If my children could have the opportunity to travel abroad, even if I couldn't benefit from the traveling, they would remember me. I would have a good funeral. But when people were taking boats, my children heard that people died so that they became frightened and they didn't try. I would have loved to see them go because hope keeps you alive. Hope keeps you alive.

At the time, Marie survived by selling water. She described the shelter she had constructed by digging into a hill as "a small house with no door."

Poverty and Political Ideology

These findings do not mean that poor people are incapable of broader political ideologies, identification, and collective action. There is a political consciousness that underlies the distribution of resources along the lines of personal networks both within Haiti and across international borders. It is a view that defines normal human behavior as redistributing resources among those to whom a person is socially connected. Family ties express, re-create, legitimate, and are sanctioned in terms of a morality that has its own dynamic of calculation but that stands outside the profit motive. To know of the suffering of family and not to act is to deny your humanity.

Jerome, a skilled auto mechanic and one of the few people we spoke to in Haiti with a steady employment, explained, "When you are in a position to make money, not big money, you would have to be very hard-hearted, not at all human, not to help a lot of people."

As a Haitian return migrant stated: "In the case of someone who leaves Haiti and doesn't help his family behind, I would send him to a doctor . . . you can say for sure, he is not normal. That person should go get a checkup."

Importantly, we found that for many people in Haiti, including the poor, obligations to family were linked to a visceral identification with the Haitian nation. Yvette could identify her weary body with Haiti as part of a cultural logic that conflates self, family, and nation through an ideology of blood.[15] In other writings we document the ways in which personal identification with the Haitian nation became embedded in quotidian activities of all classes in Haiti, including the poor (Glick Schiller and Fouron 2001). Here, we wish to emphasize that the people to whom we spoke conflated family, blood, and nation so that by fulfilling transnational family obligations, one was simultaneously validating one's connection to and love of Haiti and proving oneself to be a moral human being.

While those in Haiti channel their aspirations for a better future toward migration, and while Haitian immigrants in the United States respond to economic insecurity, racism, anti-immigrant sentiments, and the possibility of social recognition back home through maintaining their home ties, these are not survival strategies disengaged from broader notions of nation and polity. We found no dichotomy between public and private, family and country, in poor people's explanations of their actions. We also found that, though families may be divided by status divisions even while the more prosperous sustain their poorer kin, an ideology of common descent, linking nation as well as family, can motivate political action among the poor.

The conflation of kinship, blood, and nation forms the foundational ideas of many variants of nationalism. Nationalism can be defined as a set of beliefs and practices that link together the people of a nation and its territory. The nation is understood to be people who share common origins and history, as indicated by their shared culture, language, and identity (Calhoun 1997).[16] Claims about common origins translate into a rhetoric of blood ties that underwrites the ability of nationalists simultaneously to evoke the links between a people and national territory and to connect persons dispersed around the world to a geographically situated national territory and government. Long-distance nationalism highlights ideas about common descent and shared racialized identities that have long been a part of concepts of national belonging (Balibar 1991; Miles 1993).[17] For example, as a long-distance nationalist, Georges, although he is a U.S. citizen living in the United States, continues to see Haiti as his homeland; many people in Haiti agree and see him as Haitian, despite the fact that he is not legally a Haitian citizen. They argue that "his blood remains Haitian."

In our interviews, poor men and women moved rapidly and comfortably from discussions of family ties that stretched across national borders to discussions of a transnational Haitian nation. They portrayed Haitian nationality as a matter of descent, not legality. We heard repeatedly: "San, se san natif natal se ayisyen yo ye" (Blood, that's native blood that makes you a true Haitian). The blood ties of the Haitian nation extend transnationally to encompass those of Haitian descent wherever they may be living. For instance, Gregoire, a man whose children sent remittances from the United States, summarized a widespread belief: "There are those who go there and naturalize themselves and become citizens of the country which they are living in but they never forget their country.... [Even if s/he is an American citizen, s/he] is always a Haitian, the blood remains Haitian." This political creed allows those in Haiti to identify with Haitians abroad, and those abroad to identify not only with family left behind but with all of Haiti. Almost all the people we interviewed in Haiti (94 percent) believed that Haitians remained to some degree Haitian despite taking on the nationality of another country. In the view of these people, you can't stop being Haitian.[18] And if you have Haitian blood, you remained deeply attached to Haiti.

Beginning in the 1990s, Haitian political leaders began to reconstitute the Haitian concept of the nation-state by building on the widespread conviction of Haitians that those who have emigrated continue to be Haitian and to love Haiti, regardless of their legal citizenship. They began to speak of Haiti as a transnational nation-state, which stretches across national territorial borders.[19] Jean-Bertrand Aristide, the charismatic priest of liberation theology who turned politician and was elected in 1991 as president with the widespread participation of the Haitian poor, specified that his Lavalas movement should be a cross-class, transnational movement to rebuild Haiti.

The Lavalas movement, which has adopted a good project of government, supposes the participation of all citizens from all social classes. A special place will be reserved for peasants, women, all patriotic movements, and all Haitians in diaspora.

The response of Haitian immigrants in the United States was overwhelmingly positive. According to César Dismay, Aristide's campaign treasurer, two-thirds of the $300,000 spent on his 1990 presidential bid came from the diaspora. A particularly strong base was built in Catholic churches among poor women. When Aristide was elected president, he began to speak of the Haitian diaspora as the "Tenth Department." The territory of the Haitian state is divided into nine geographic divisions called departments. By implication, therefore, the diaspora became part of the Haitian state. The designation of the Tenth Department gave public recognition to the fact that Haitian emigrants have participated in political processes that affect Haiti, through lobbying, demonstrating, and organizing in the United States. While there was no change in the Haitian constitution to allow dual nationality, Aristide set up institutions such as the Ministry of Haitians Living Abroad specifically to mobilize those of Haitian descent to contribute politically and economically to Haiti, and this ministry was continued by his successor.[20]

The experience of witnessing Haitians in the diaspora mobilizing on behalf of Haiti, as well as the daily experience of living within a remittance economy, contributed to the long-distance nationalism we found among impoverished Haitians both in Haiti and in the diaspora. The defining moment for them was the demonstrations staged by Haitian immigrants in New York and Miami on behalf of Aristide when he was ousted from the presidency and sent into exile by a military coup in 1991.

Maurice, age twenty-seven, supported a younger brother and sister while working for only a token salary as a radio broadcaster in Aux Cayes. He had no family abroad and received no support from abroad. Yet he saw possibilities for Haiti because of the diaspora:

> I think that the diaspora aids Haiti. The statistics in the newspaper show each month how much the diaspora sends to Haiti annually. This is a very significant contribution. And the diaspora worked hard [to bring Aristide back]. In Haiti while it was difficult to organize demonstrations and take to the streets, the diaspora did not give up. The diaspora stood firm to bring Aristide back and that helped a lot.

This theme was echoed by nineteen-year-old Franck, who felt comfortable with the rhetoric of the Haitian diaspora as the Tenth Department. In fact, for him this link was an accepted feature of the Haitian state, not a political term of reference:

> The *dixime* [Tenth Department] is a state ("youn eta") that the Haitians occupy and that is where they collaborate together to help Haiti. To work in the interests of Haitian people who live in the United States. To help Haiti and to work for those Haitians who live abroad. To help them defend their own interests.

Franck explained to us that it was from a Haitian radio station, Radio Tropical, originating in New York and owned by members of the Haitian diaspora, that he learned about the ways in which the diaspora was helping Haiti. They can help in many ways, he explained:

> They can pay for people to go to school. They can help the people who are in the streets. All of these things are forms of help that the diaspora can help Haiti. . . . On the cultural and religious plane they can help Haiti. . . . Because they are there to defend the interests of the Haitians, to help them when they are humiliated. They are always there to defend the Haitians, whether they live in the United States or in Haiti. They stood up, they shook up the leadership of the American government to take action to save Haiti.

Importantly, if Haitian immigrants such as Yvette learn from their socialization in Haiti that ties of family are also ties of blood and nation, then these messages are reinforced rather than countermanded by the experiences both they and their children have as they become incorporated into the United States. For instance, they have learned from the U.S. government itself that Haitian blood is different. This was made clear to them when first the U.S. Centers for Disease Control and then the U.S. Food and Drug Administration promoted the idea that Haitians were carriers of AIDS and therefore unacceptable blood donors. These distinctions are also made manifest through immigration policies that differentiate them from other political refugees, such as the Cubans, who have been granted asylum while Haitians have been detained and then returned to Haiti. As one woman who fled the Duvalier regime by small boat and managed to gain permanent residency status recounted, "You may become a U.S. citizen but to the whites you are always Haitian."

Yvette also experiences identification with her nation of origin as part of her daily life in the United States. Her co-workers bring her travel articles about Haiti and newspaper clippings about events in Haiti and what is happening to Haitians in New York. In the English class she attends so that she can become an American citizen, she also finds herself identified as a Haitian. Haitian immigrants who have arrived in the United States find themselves grouped together by a range of U.S. institutions, including Catholic parishes, foundations, social services, and political parties, each of which uses the homeland of an immigrant as the primary identifier of that person (Glick Schiller 1975, 1977; Glick Schiller et al. 1987, 1992 [1987]).

The Varying Means of Identifying with the Haitian Nation

Nation is in many ways a "floating signifier," that is, it means many, often contradictory things to people who organize to obtain sometimes diametrically different views of the future, all waving the national flag. The term *polysemous*, defined as "having a multiplicity of meanings," is also a useful way to understand the power of nationalist ideologies. Nationalism as an ideology can be used by different sectors in a state to organize around fundamentally different agendas. Both the rich and the poor in Haiti speak about the need to rebuild Haiti, but while they use the same words, they envision very different futures.

Poor men and women often use a Haitian nationalist rhetoric to struggle against their daily misery and suffering, as well as to critique oppression and to legitimate struggles against it. By using the language of the nation, the poor legitimate their struggle and build a domain of liberation within the dominant rhetoric. This rhetorical strategy is not an instance of what James Scott (1990) has called a "hidden transcript," a politics of resistance stated clearly and directly only when those who are powerful are absent. Instead, we found that many poor people in Haiti state their agenda openly and publicly, only they do so making use of the multiple meanings of nationalist rhetoric. Moreover, we found that in declaring their identification with the nation, many poor people made claims upon the state. The Haitian poor we interviewed did not envision a nation against the Haitian state but rather a Haitian state that supports the nation, defined in terms of family and blood. Many people told us that the state is "obligated to help the masses."

Josephat, a student supported by remittances from his parents, blamed the state for the failure of the economy to help the poor and for the high price of commodities. He told us:

> Yes, the state knows the problems of the poor even though they don't do anything for them. They always tell you they are trying to solve the people's problems. For example, they say they are fighting to get the price of rice down, but

even though they say that, it never goes down. On the contrary, the price goes up. In Haiti the only thing that goes up and comes down is the flag. Everything else goes up and never goes down. Like the price of gasoline. . . . The people expect the state to address their problems, and to make life a little less costly for them. Only God can tell whether it will come true.

Giselle, a young woman who makes a marginal living as a cashier in a business in Port-au-Prince, told us:

We have the right to demand that the work . . . [They] could create work, paved roads, pave all the streets everywhere, build sewers. The problem is that they don't [do it]. There is too much dirt, we inhale too much dirt when we walk around. I would like jobs for everybody and for Haiti to be luxurious and for all the unemployed people to find jobs so they will not kill people, hold up people, take what they possess. For everyone to be able to live so that all people will have a life. I for one am not living. I do not have a life.

We found that when people who lived by *grapiyaj* struggled to support themselves and their family, they spoke of the need to rebuild Haiti as a nation in which there will be not only personal security but also social and economic justice. Their vision of Haiti was one popularized by the powerful transnational grassroots movement that in the 1980s and 1990s engaged large numbers of people in political struggle. Calling for the uprooting of the old system and for struggle against all forms of oppression, this movement succeeded in ending the Duvalier dictatorship, which had ruled Haiti from 1957 to 1986, and then challenged other attempts to impose military rule. We could still hear echoes of this movement and the goals of social and economic transformation in our interviews in Haiti in 1996. Twenty-year-old Yves, whose mother lived in the United States and sent money to Haiti to support her family, told us that "to see something different in Haiti, people must stop exploiting the masses, the leaders must stop thinking they can exploit the disempowered, everybody must have the opportunity to feed themselves. The leaders must stop thinking that by killing people they can stop the country from changing. If I go to the United States, I will study at the university and as soon as I finish I will come back to work for the Haitian people. . . . My place is in the middle of the Haitian people to struggle with them and help them to overcome their misfortunes."

The movement and its goals also had a strong base among transmigrants in the United States, particularly working-class people. Yvette and thousands of Haitian transmigrants participated in this movement as they went to Catholic mass conducted by priests preaching a theology of liberation, as they listened to passionate discussions of rebuilding Haiti on transnational Haitian radio programs, and as they debated the future of Haiti with family and friends.

This vision draws from disparate sources in Haitian history that, from the 1970s through 1990s, brought memory, ideology, and political practice together in a potent transnational movement of the poor to rebuild Haiti and liberate the nation from poverty, hunger, illiteracy, and misery. The agenda of this movement drew from disparate social experiences and cultural understandings gained by Haitians as they struggled to survive within the transnational social fields forged by their social networks. Their determination to reconstitute Haiti drew upon the daily transnational experiences of collectivity that maintain family life. Their agenda for social justice was also inspired by the liberation theology of the Catholic Church, which was widely disseminated among Haitians in Haiti and in the United States in the 1970s and 1980s.[21]

Members of the diaspora, together with U.S.-based non-governmental organizations that began to work in Haiti in the 1970s, brought into the movement a sense of mass mobilization for popular empowerment learned in the U.S. civil rights and anti-poverty movements. These lessons were also translated into Haitian nationalist rhetoric, linking the memories of the 1804 Haitian revolution to contemporary demands for the empowerment of the poor. Haitians have historically built on their sense of Haiti as a black nation to challenge global racism, declaring the slave uprising that was at the core of the Haitian revolution a legacy of all black people. When, in 1900, Hannibal Price, a Haitian intellectual, stated, "The heroes of [Haitian national] Independence [are] . . . the glory of all Negroes, for it is the noblest, strongest achievement of our common mother, the Black Race," he reiterated beliefs that dated from the Haitian revolution and that can be found among all classes today. This reading of Haitian nationalism has contributed to the political energies with which Haitian immigrants have joined and sometimes led anti-racist struggles in the United States.

This consciousness contributes to the ability of Haitian immigrants to take collective and militant action against racist attacks. Tens of thousands of Haitian immigrants marched across the Brooklyn Bridge and filled the entire space of lower Manhattan to protest their linkage with AIDS in 1989; thousands marched across the Brooklyn Bridge in 1997 to protest police violence against Abner Louima, a Haitian immigrant who was taken to a police station and viciously brutalized (Barstow 1999). The people who took to the streets were empowered by a sense of identity that made their assertion of national pride a contribution to the struggles for equality of all black people.

Identification with the Haitian nation has, in the past, also fostered anti-imperialism. To keep foreign interests from dominating Haiti, from the time of the first Haitian constitution until the U.S. occupation of Haiti in 1915, no foreigners were allowed to own land in Haiti. The U.S. occupation sparked an armed rebellion that had widespread support among the Haitian peasantry and cultural resistance among the intellectuals. Nationalist rhetoric has enabled the Haitian poor, both in the United States and in Haiti, to elaborate an anti-racist, anti-imperialist politics that challenges the dominant political and economic organization of race and class all around the world. As the United Nations and non-governmental organizations began in the 1980s to popularize a discourse about human rights and women's rights, these messages also became part of the ways in which poor people in Haiti and Haitian transmigrants began to interpret the nationalist rhetoric of rebuilding Haiti.

We do not want to romanticize the power of this vision. We are not saying that all poor people agree with one another or share a common set of political goals. In Haiti, as elsewhere, poverty brings with it jealousy of family and neighbors, anger, and desperate acts (Farmer 1994; Richman 1992). Even as people declare their commitment to Haiti, they confront the jealousies and distrust that underlie ongoing family ties and cooperation between neighbors, the vast divisions in experience between rural and urban people and between those in Haiti and those living abroad, the profound divisions of class, and widespread disillusionment with political leaders. We have tried to highlight the tensions and bitterness that exist within transnational family networks, between men and women, between the diaspora and those "they left behind." At the same time, in a profound way, the majority of poor people to whom we talked communicated through their love of Haiti a common set of commitments that constitutes an "agenda" of the disempowered. This agenda focuses on the demand to be treated as human beings.

Long-Distance Nationalism and the Pacification of the Haitian Poor

The identification of the Haitian poor with the Haitian nation, however, can mean that oppressed people speak with the same political rhetoric as their dominant class and, in certain instances and historical moments, can be drawn into political movements that delimit and redirect their efforts to obtain social justice. At the same time, the anti-Duvalier movement, as well as the later appeals by various political leaders, embedded the aspirations of the poor in a language of nation that obscured the connections among poverty in Haiti, the conditions that Haitian immigrants face in the United States, and the global reaches of capitalism. In fact, in certain ways, the widespread acceptance among Haitians both in the diaspora and in Haiti of the legitimacy of long-distance nationalism and the vision of Haiti as a transnational nation-state directs political critique back to the Haitian state and its leadership and away from the global context of capitalism in which this state is situated. Nationalist critiques can make the corruption of particular leaders and the failures of the state to develop the country visible. They also can obscure the degree to which Haitian leaders and the Haitian government are almost totally constrained by the United States and the international financial institutions from taking any actions that would redistribute wealth and resources in Haiti.

We have found voices among the poor in Haiti and in the United States who understand this, but they are in the minority. One young women in Haiti, supported by a relative abroad, mused:

> Haiti is close to the United States—it is like you go up a ladder and they are there and they impose their will on the country. They make it difficult for the country to survive. . . . All Haitians know that it was the Americans who imposed the coup d'état because they spent lots of money for the coup d'état and made it possible for the army to kill people, to brutalize people, to come to your house and steal your money and to rape people. They say Haiti is independent but it is not independent because the United States is running it.

The failure of both the political leaders in Haiti and the diaspora to "save Haiti," however, has been more visible than the underlying configuration of power. This problem has been exacerbated by the fact that, soon after Aristide came to office, his government was overthrown by the Haitian military, with U.S. support, and most of the priests and other political leaders most closely aligned with the poor were murdered. The Haitian military not only murdered, mutilated, and raped members of the grassroots movement but also randomly targeted poor people to repress all efforts at resistance. When the Haitian military was unable, through these means, to establish a climate that would entice foreign investors, the United States brought Aristide to a negotiating table in Paris.

The Aristide government in exile was offered a return to power in exchange for accepting a structural adjustment program put together by a series of global financial institutions.[22] The details, when translated into straightforward language, mean that the taxpayers of ten governments, including Haiti, repaid $81 million in loan payments to banks that represent the richest governments in the world, including a U.S.-financed development bank. In return, these same banks would lend Haiti more money, which would have to be repaid. What is described as "development assistance" can just as easily be understood as a burden of debt that makes any meaningful development of the Haitian economy impossible (U.S. State Department 1998). In this deal, in which the World Bank played an important role, Haiti was to privatize key industries and decrease spending on social programs such as health and education in order to service their existing debt. In return, Haiti would be lent millions of dollars (U.S. State Department).

As in other countries in which structural adjustment policies have been negotiated, global corporate interests ran beneath the neoliberal rhetoric of free trade and privatization as the motor of economic development. The public phone company TELECO, for example, even though antiquated, undercapitalized, and run by corrupt administrators, is immensely profitable, earning more than $20 million in profit a year for the Haitian government and providing one of the few sources of cash that the Haitian government is able to spend without foreign directives (White 1997). When sold to a private corporation, this vital source of funds will be gone. Since the government is not likely to collect taxes from corporations and the rich, tax revenue will not replace any income lost from the transfer of the telephone company to foreign hands. Haitian political leaders who either accepted or embraced the structural adjustment agreements did so without putting aside their nationalist rhetoric. They assured the Haitian poor that the policies they had adopted would set Haiti on the path of economic development, so that their actions were actually saving the Haitian nation.

The Haitian poor immediately began to feel the consequences of the policies. The price of basic food staples was no longer supported and prices rose. While a few token policies were aimed at the poor, such as subsidizing schoolbooks, public services were further neglected, schoolteachers not paid or paid a pittance, and public health unable to provide even basic care in Port-au-Prince or the major towns. And in this situation of ever-increasing poverty, poor people in Haiti have found that the Haitian diaspora, to which they had looked for hope, has been failing them as miserably as the leaders located in Haiti. Aristide's return to power in 1994 brought a host of development projects sponsored by international philanthropic organizations, the United States and other governments, and churches. People from the Haitian diaspora arrived to work in Haiti, stating that they had returned to serve their nation and its people. They were paid high salaries. Nothing changed. While many professionals who filled these positions worked hard to improve conditions without adequate funding, resources, or an infrastructure that could sustain these projects, there have been a host of others who sought only personal opportunity and justified their actions by embracing the ethos of privatization.

Haitian radio personalities and prominent spokespeople, as well as Haitian transmigrants who returned to Haiti as cabinet ministers, government officials, and consultants, promoted efforts to privatize government utilities and services and discounted the responsibilities of the state to serve the people. They downplayed the role the United States played in support of the Haitian military, and they glorified the U.S.-led United Nations occupation of Haiti, which reinforced Haiti's vast economic and social inequities.

In the past few years, much of the national fervor we found in Haiti in the 1990s has subsided. As they have seen themselves betrayed by Aristide and by the politicians who succeeded him, the poor people to whom we have spoken in Haiti have been left with no political analysis to explain the dilemma of Haiti or the failure of all of their leaders. As the leaders who promised to rebuild Haiti after Duvalier have turned to lining their own pockets, and those who might have carried on the struggle have been murdered, there has been little anti-capitalist analysis to expose the neocolonial status of small, poor countries such as Haiti, in which formal political independence is the thinnest sham.

Dispirited and discouraged, increasingly poor people fall back on individual strategies of migration. In 1996 we heard people tell us that "Haiti has no future" and "Haiti is dead," but this was not the dominant theme. After four more years in which political leaders fought for power rather than struggled to build a future for the poor of Haiti, the mood of bitterness and despair grew both in Haiti and among the diaspora. Rose, a woman whose husband had gone to the United States illegally by boat and had managed to obtain permanent resident status and raise the economic position of his family in Haiti, told us, "There is not a problem without a solution." But the solution for Rose, as for so many others, came from the support of family living abroad. She went on to say that those "who are left behind can't do anything by themselves so those abroad have to watch over those in

Haiti. They can't leave them to die so they have to support them. If they don't do it, you just resign yourself." Or as a young man in Haiti who had finished his studies but could not find work told us, "Sometimes . . . the person abroad may send something. And if the thought doesn't cross his mind, there is nothing you can do . . . there are no possibilities."

This sense that nothing can be done in Haiti increases the pressures on transmigrants to meet their endless obligations. Worse yet, demoralization can mean that family members in the diaspora abandon plans to return to Haiti and divest themselves of obligations. But if they do so, they lose not only their long-term investments in both people and property but also their sense of self, family, and nation; because, as one young woman, born in the United States and living on Long Island, told Georges, "Haiti is my pride."

Toward Deepening or Ending Poverty: Nationalism as a Two-Way Street

Nationalism is often used by elites as the ideological fodder for modes of social order that justify increased economic and social polarization. Therefore, the fact that many of Haiti's poor, whether residing in Haiti or in the United States, identify with the Haitian nation and take action in its name can lead the poor to accept and legitimate their own oppression. Efforts by mainstream scholars to distinguish among various forms of nationalism have generally obscured this problem. In the wake of the rise of Hitler and Mussolini in Europe in the 1930s and of post–World War II dictators around the world who built support for their regimes by fanning nationalist emotions, mainstream scholars tried to distinguish between what they saw as the good nationalism of democracies such as England, France, and the United States and the destructive nationalism of dictators (Gellner 1983, 1994; Kohn 1994; Plamenatz 1976). The emergence of a new wave of nationalism after the breakup of the Soviet Union and Yugoslavia, in which genocidal actions are being justified in the name of love of country, revived efforts to make such distinctions (Gellner 1994). Much of this debate has been waged in terms of whether the state that claims to speak for a nation of people is democratic in the sense that it holds free and fair elections for its leaders and legislature.

The left also has had a tradition of categorizing nationalist politics. Nationalisms were judged to be progressive or reactionary, depending on whether they were used to unite populations in struggles against imperialist powers or whether they were used by these powers to rally the populations of imperialist countries to suppress struggles for national liberation (Engels 1974 [1866]).[23] But how do we evaluate nationalism in the current historical conjuncture? Today, most countries are formally independent but poor. They have little if any actual sovereignty in relationship to corporate interests that control more wealth than entire countries; financial institutions such as the IMF and World Bank, which control their flows of capital; and the global military power of the United States, which has made examples of Iraq and Serbia.

We suggest that in the current era of globalization, in which most countries around the world are formally independent but intertwined with the institutions of global capital, ideologies such as nationalism can be understood more fruitfully as "discursive formations" in which shared sets of symbols contain multiple and conflicting meanings and messages.[24]

This chapter has shown that, for Haiti's poor, nationalism is a "two-way street" (Sturgeon 1999).[25] Oppressed people can go in two very different directions, both of which are nationalist. Under the signpost of nationalism, they can find themselves supporting leaders who use the institutions of the state and its laws to increase the wealth of a handful of the population and contribute to the continuing or increasing misery of the majority. But there is another course to be pursued, which contests not just the symptoms of oppression and exploitation but its causes, and the Haitian poor can choose to take this alternative direction. The migration on which Haitian long-distance nationalism is based has the potential either to foster modes of governance, economic survival strategies, and social divisions forged out of structures of domination or to contribute to global movements against these structures.

Many people who migrate believe they have escaped the need to make such choices. They can love Haiti but leave it and find an individual or familial solution to their problems. When the grassroots movement subsides and political leaders seem to be vying for power without offering an agenda for the Haitian poor, increasing numbers of people risk their lives on small boats to search for a better life, fleeing both poverty and political insecurity (Torriero 2000).

Migration can serve as a safety valve, channeling those with energy, imagination, and ambition into the pursuit of individual rather than collective responses to worsening conditions and increased exploitation. The remittances of immigrants sustain whole regions of sending countries. Those left behind may place their aspirations for a better life on migration rather than on fundamental challenges to the class system within which they live. At the same time, employers of immigrants obtain cheap, quiet labor and organize their production system around the fact that they don't have to pay a wage that could support a family in the immigrant receiving country. Moreover, immigrants, when they find new forms of exploitation, discrimination, and injustice in their new land, may channel their anger, disappointment, and aspirations for social recognition into activities in their homeland, including long-distance nationalism, rather than joining in struggles to change the oppressive conditions where they live and work. They can become ever more deeply mired in debts, pouring all available capital into sustaining family at home, without having an opportunity to assess the causes of their entrapment. To the extent that they engage in politics, it may be to reinforce a form of long-distance nationalism that glorifies the homeland rather than challenging the class structure of exploitation in the homeland. Family obligations can become linked to national loyalty, focusing collective anger on the corruption of political leaderships in the homeland in ways that obscure the role of transnational capital.

Recently, analysts of globalization have noted the ways in which transnational financial interests tend to reconfigure rather than demolish state structures (Held 1992; Panitch 1997; Mittleman 1997; Sassen 1996, 1998). Scholars are also beginning to recognize that nationalism can be reconfigured rather than diminished in the wake of globalization and transnational migration (Smith 1998; Guarnizo 1997). Individual and family responses to poverty can provide a foundation for narratives and identities that reinforce the nation-state in ways that legitimate the global inequality. We have begun to explore such connections in this essay through an examination of Haitian conflations of blood, home, and long-distance nationalism.

Occupying a range of class positions, shaped by racialization in the United States, as well as by the politics of gender and sexuality, the transmigrants express their long-distance disparate and conflicting political positions. Some transmigrants embrace the neoliberal agenda for their home country, contributing to widening global disparities in wealth and power within or between nations. The long-distance nationalism they foster serves to keep impoverished populations and their diasporas from understanding the connections between their poverty and global capitalist structures of accumulation. Capitalists' interests are global in their domain of operation, inducting people throughout the world into a shared immiseration. Yet long-distance nationalism may induce people to identify with only a small sector of humanity.

Long-distance nationalism also encourages many of the poor in migrant sending countries to speak and think of national unity as the greatest good, despite the consequences of this unity for the poor. Political leaders and political theorists alike use an imagery of citizenship to hold in check the class and cultural tensions inherent in nation-building projects. Citizenship can be used as a means by which the rich and powerful convince those who suffer from the inequalities of the existing structure to support the system. In Haiti, where the handful of rich live lives of great leisure among the vast majority who wake up and go to bed hungry, nationalism can be a particularly cruel diversion. If followed in one direction, long-distance nationalism can lead Haitian transmigrants to support the broader neoliberal project of restructuring nation-states to serve global financial interests by protecting the holdings and rights of global corporations and facilitating their functioning. Transmigrants who move in this direction serve as contributors to and spokespeople for these neoliberal states. If such states have large emigrant populations, the life possibilities of both those who emigrate and those who remain at home will remain seriously constricted by the burden that emigrants must carry. They face lives of sustaining not only themselves and family in the new land but the people in their homeland. Long-distance nationalist rhetorics of family, blood, and nation will continue to reinforce and justify their carrying of this burden, while government resources are used to facilitate the operations of transnational capital. The contributions of transmigrants and non-governmental organizations will increasingly replace state-sponsored development.

But because long distance nationalism can be a two-way street, it can also provide reinforcement, as it did in the 1980s and 1990s in Haiti, for linking impoverished Haitians with global struggles against racism, exploitation, and oppression. Haitian immigrants, informed by a view of the Haitian revolution as a victory for all black people, have contributed energy and initiatives to struggles against the structures of racial inequality. They have placed struggles against police brutality and against the intensive surveillance and policing of black communities in the United States within challenges to global inequities between nations that have been justified through ideologies of race. They have joined and led unions of hospital workers and hotel workers to demand improved working conditions, with a political consciousness that places struggles in the workplace within global demands for social justice. Haitian long-distance nationalists bring to struggles against all forms of oppression demands for the states to be "responsible," to serve the interests of the poor, and to empower the impoverished majority.

Long-distance nationalists provide a voice within global social movements that directs these movements back toward an engagement with state structures. Their transnational family ties and obligations can embody demands that state structures and powers be reconstituted in ways that challenge the dominance of capital. In the midst of globalization, long-distance nationalism can mobilize people to demand liberation from hunger, poverty, malnutrition, and political oppression. In this sense, it does not stand in opposition to transnational social movements that resist various forms of oppression.

To build struggles for social justice, we need to move beyond analyses of poverty that pose a dichotomy between individual and family adaptative strategies on the one hand and collective strategies of resistance on the other. In contradictory ways, the transnational familial obligations of immigrants restrain or divert political struggle in the short term while laying the groundwork for profound movements for justice and equity. This oppositional long-distance nationalism, which emerges from and reinforces transnational family ties, contains within it a challenge to all forms of exploitation and oppression. "Alternative constituencies of peoples and oppositional analytical capacities" are emerging "within the recesses of national culture" (Bhabha 1990:3).

The message that emerged from Haiti's slave revolts and from its rural, urban, and immigrant poor is a clarion call to live in a world that allows all people to "live like human beings." To be human means having access to the resources to live a decent life. To be human means that people can adequately feed, shelter, and educate themselves and their children; that they can be spared the pain and suffering of curable diseases; and that they have security of person and personal property. That all people should be seen as equal means that they have right to live in a system that makes it possible for all people to obtain all these things from their hard work. But all that is not enough. To live like a human being, we all need honor and respect.

Long-distance nationalism certainly is not the only means, or even the primary means, by which disempowered people are currently organizing to obtain social and economic justice. The demand to be treated as a human being is a demand Georges hears when he teaches reading to African American adults in Harlem, only there the demand is voiced in terms of a black identity. The demand for respect is an important theme among black youth in the United States (Canada 1995). Nina heard it while organizing women on welfare in Cincinnati and Ohio, who spoke in the name of the poor or as women. We only wish to point out that long-distance nationalism is not necessarily contradictory to revolutionary internationalism or the ideologies of indigenous rights, women's rights, human rights, or environmentalism. These ideologies all have proved capable of voicing the aspirations of the "wretched of the earth." "Honor, Respect" is the way in which poor people in the Haitian countryside have traditionally greeted each other. Poor Haitians, whether they live in Haiti or the United States, who express their understanding of what it means to be human by meeting their family obligations and identifying with Haiti, are part of the global struggle.

NOTES

1. To protect the privacy of the people we interviewed we have changed their names. We would like to thank them for sharing their experiences and points of view.

2. Our assumption in this chapter is that nation-state building occurs within the daily life activities of persons of different classes in ways that can legitimate or contest structures of power (Joseph and Nugent 1994:22; Williams 1977:113–14).

3. Here we build on Anderson's use of the term but extend and develop his usage (Anderson 1993, 1994). For a further exposition of this concept, see Glick Schiller and Fouron (2001).

4. The concept of the underclass was popularized both by scholars such as Wilson (1987) and journalists such as Auletta (1983). The literature on poverty and on transnational migration we are reviewing in this article is by U.S.-based scholars. It would be useful to compare the research reviewed here with scholarship from other national locations.

5. In this analysis we built on concepts of hegemony articulated by Gramsci (1971) and Williams (1977).

6. Those who have any type of work are called on to distribute their small earnings among a broad network of people. The support that Haitians in the diaspora give to family in Haiti only continues established patterns within Haiti, where the few with work or any means of support provide sustenance for the many with even less.

7. The opposite side of the same shortsightedness is to interpret evidence of transnational family connections as evidence of a challenge to the constraints or the legitimacy of the nation-state (Kearney 1991).

8. In its cold war efforts to derail leftist struggles in Italy, the United States benefited from its immigrants whose priests organized letter-writing campaigns to influence voting and political organizing in Italy.

9. Although Handlin's prize-winning work, *The Uprooted*, popularized this image of immigrants, Handlin actually also wrote about the conservatism of return migrants. See Handlin (1957).

10. There are no reliable figures on the number of Haitian immigrants and people of Haitian descent in the United States. The 1990 U.S. Census reports 225,000 people born in Haiti who were living in the United States. This total does not include people of Haitian descent who are born in the United States and probably does not count the presence of undocumented immigrants in many households. In 1993 the Immigration and Naturalization Service (INS) estimated that there were 88,000 undocumented Haitians in the United States. Most researchers of Haitian immigration consider that the census and INS figures considerably underrepresent the size of the Haitian population in the United States.

11. U.S. State Department Background Notes: Haiti 3/98: 6/12. Available at www.state.gov/www/background_notes /haiti_0398_ bgn.html.

12. As a result of multiple incomes, the mean household income of Haitians in the United States in 1989 reached $32,161.

13. The class differences among this immigrant population are also reflected in the housing circumstances. In 1990, 30 percent of Haitian households lived in homes they owned, many of them accomplishing this feat by maintaining households in which several adults would contribute income. A large number of Haitian families, however, live in overcrowded, poorly maintained apartments where they pay high rents but are exposed to hazardous conditions that include lead-based paint, falling ceilings, and a lack of heat in winter.

14. For an excellent discussion of social status in transnational social fields, see Goldring (1998).

15. This conflation has been made by Haitian political leaders since the founding moments of the Haitian state, when they declared independence in 1894 after a revolutionary struggle in which free mulattos and enslaved blacks rose up against French colonial rule.

16. We also build on Benedict Anderson (1991); Ernest Gellner (1983); Eric J. Hobsbawm (1990); Eli Kedourie (1960), and David McCrone (1998). These approaches to nationalism all link the concept of nationalism to territory. They differ from uses of the term *nationalism* in formulations such as Black nationalism, Arab nationalism, or Hindu nationalism. Logically, it makes sense to differentiate identities based on common historical origins and shared racialization or religion—the substance of *Black nationalism*—from political ideologies linked to efforts to form, claim, or defend territorially based polities. Political usage, however, is often not logical.

17. Identification with a particular, existent state or the desire to construct a new state distinguish long-distance nationalism from other forms of transborder ideas about membership, such as those based on religion or a notion of shared history and dispersal.

18. Those who used a concept of descent to define Haitians were more likely than those who used other definitions of Haitian to have strong transnational connections with family abroad, but the difference was not statistically significant.

19. Over the years, increasing numbers of Haitians have decided to become U.S. citizens. A growing number of emigrant-sending states, including the Dominican Republic, Colombia, Mexico, Brazil, Greece, Japan, Portugal, and many islands in the Caribbean, have begun to reconstitute themselves as transnational nation-states, changing their laws and their state policies to facilitate the reincorporation of emigrants and their descendants upon their return (Fouron and Glick Schiller 1997; Feldman-Bianco 1992, 1994; Glick Schiller, Basch, and Szanton-Blanc 1992; Guarnizo 1997, 1998; Smith 1997, 1998).

20. In 1994, 40 percent of the Haitians in the United States who held permanent resident visas and who had completed the requisite waiting period have become U.S. citizens. Since the welfare reforms that cut benefits from U.S. permanent residents, ever-increasing numbers of Haitians have applied for U.S. citizenship.

21. The pope's declaration, during a visit to Haiti in 1983, that things *must change* helped ignite the grassroots movement and make the demands for fundamental social and economic change, articulated through a nationalist discourse, central to this transnational movement.

22. Speaking in Paris for the Haiti Consultative Group, an organization of representatives of governments and banks, Mark L. Schneider (1999), an assistant administrator of USAID, announced that "thanks to contributions from the United States Government and the Governments of Japan, Sweden, Mexico, Switzerland, France, Canada, Netherlands, Argentina, and Haiti $81,474,605 in arrears to these three financial institutions were cleared and, in so doing, removing the most serious obstacle to the use of $260 million in frozen funds from these three institutions." In the same speech, Schneider reported that the World Bank was committing $40 million to Haiti, while the Inter-American Development Bank (funded by the U.S. government) was providing another $70 million.

23. A distinction between Eastern and Western nationalism has been made by scholars of nationalism such Kohn (1994), Plamenatz (1976), and Gellner (1983, 1994:112–13). Marx and Engels distinguished *historical nations* of Europe, such as England, France, Italy, Hungry, and Poland, which possessed the right of self-determination, from *nationalities.* They stated that nationalities such as the Welsh were relic "remnants of people long gone" and had no such rights (Engels 1974 [1866]:382–83.

24. As Herzfeld (1992:14) has pointed out, "Any ideology, no matter how consistent its formal expression, may produce radically divergent applications and interpretations." Here Victor Turner's (1985:171) approach to symbols as resources deployed by social actors is also useful. He tells us that symbols are "semantically 'open.' The meaning is not absolutely fixed, nor is it necessarily the same for everyone who agrees that a particular signifier (outward form) has symbolic meaning."

25. We build on Foucault's use of the term *discursive formation* in *The Archeology of Knowledge* (New York: Pantheon, 1969), 3. Calhoun (1997) has applied it to the ideology of nation in *Nationalism*.

REFERENCES

Adamic, Louis
1941   *Two-Way Passage*. New York: Harper and Brothers.

Anderson, Benedict
1991   *Imagined Communities: Reflections on the Origins and Spread of Nationalism*. Rev. ed. London: Verso.
1993   "The New World Disorder." *New Left Review* 193:2–13
1994   "Exodus." *Critical Inquiry* 20:314–27.

Auletta, Ken
1983   *The Underclass*. New York: Vintage.

Baldwin, James
1971   *Nobody Knows My Name*. New York: Dial Press.

Balibar, Etienne
1991   "Racism and Nationalism." In *Race, Nation, and Class: Ambiguous Identities*. Edited by Etienne Balibar and Immanuel Wallerstein. Pp. 37–67. London: Verso.

Barstow, David
1999   "Even after Volpe's Guilty Plea, Jurors Doubted Louima's Word Alone." *New York Times* Vol. 148, Issue 51548 (June 9): B9.

Basch, Linda, Nina Glick Schiller, and Christina Szanton-Blanc
1994   *Nations Unbound: Transnational Projects, Postcolonial Predicaments and Deterritorialized Nation-States*. Amsterdam: Gordon and Breach.

Baxter, Ellen, and Kim Hopper
1981   *Private Lives/Public Spaces*. New York: Community Service Society.

Bhabha, Homi
1990   "Introduction: Narrating the Nation." In *Nation and Narration*. Edited by Homi Bhabha. Pp. 1–7. London: Routledge.

Bodnar, John
1985   *The Transplanted: A History of Immigrants in Urban America*. Bloomington: Indiana University Press.

Buhle, Paul
1987   *Marxism in the United States: Remapping the History of the American Left*. London: Verso.

Calhoun, Craig
1997   *Nationalism*. Minneapolis: University of Minnesota Press.

Canada, Geoffrey
1995   *Fist Stick Knife Gun: A Personal History of Violence in America*. Boston: Beacon Press.

Chan, Sucheng
1990   "European and Asian Immigration into the United States in Comparative Perspective, 1820s to 1920s." In *Immigration Reconsidered: History, Sociology, and Politics*. Edited by Virginia Yans-McLaughlin. Pp. 37–75. New York: Oxford University Press.

Cinel, Dino
1982   *From Italy to San Francisco*. Stanford, CA: Stanford University Press.
1991   *The National Integration of Italian Return Migration, 1870–1929*. Cambridge: Cambridge University Press.

Danaher, Richard, ed.
1994   *Fifty Years Is Enough: The Case against the World Bank and the International Monetary Fund*. Boston: South End Press.

Delgado, Richard
1995   *Critical Race Theory: The Cutting Edge*. Philadelphia: Temple University Press.

DeSipio, Louis, and Rodolfo O. de la Garza
1998   *Making Americans, Remaking America: Immigration and Immigrant Policy*. Boulder, CO: Westview Press.

DeWind, Josh
1987   "The Remittances of Haitian Immigrants in New York City." Unpublished final report prepared for Citibank. In files of authors.

DeWind, Josh, and David H. Kinley III
1988   *Aiding Migration: The Impact of International Development Assistance on Haiti*. Boulder, CO: Westview Press.

Dudley, William, ed.
1990   *Immigration: Opposing Viewpoints*. San Diego: Greenhaven Press.

Engels, Friedrich
1974   [1866] "What Has the Working Class to Do with Poland?" In *Karl Marx: The First International and After*. Edited by David Ferbach. New York: Vintage.

Farmer, Paul
1994   *AIDS and Accusation: Haiti and the Geography of Blame*. Berkeley: University of California Press.

Feldman-Bianco, Bela
1992   "Multiple Layers of Time and Space: The Construction of Class, Race,

Ethnicity, and Nationalism among Portuguese Immigrants." In *Towards a Transnational Perspective on Migration*. Edited by Nina Glick Schiller, Linda Basch, and Cristina Szanton-Blanc. Pp 145–74. New York: New York Academy of Sciences.

1994 "The State, Saudade and the Dialectics of Deterritorialization and Reterritorialization." Paper delivered at Wemner Gren Symposium 117, Mijas, Spain (June).

Fouron, Georges, and Nina Glick Schiller

1997 "Haitian Identities at the Juncture between Diaspora and Homeland." In *Caribbean Circuits*. Edited by Patricia Pessar. Pp. 127–59. Staten Island, NY: Center for Migration Studies.

Frankenberg, Ronald

1988 "Gramsci, Culture, and Medical Anthropology: Kundry and Parsifal? Or Rat's Tail to Sea Serpent." *Medical Anthropology Quarterly* n.s 4:334–37.

Fraser, Stephen

1991 *Labor Will Rule: Sidney Hillman and the Rise of American Labor*. Ithaca, NY: Cornell University Press.

Gabaccia, Donna, and Fraser Ottanelli

1997 "Diaspora or International Proletariat? Italian Labor Migration and the Making of Multi-Ethnic States, 1815–1939." *Diaspora* 6:61–84.

Gellner, Ernest

1983 *Nation and Nationalism*. Oxford: Blackwell.

1994 *Conditions of Liberty: Civil Society and Its Rivals*. London: Hamish Hamilton.

Glick Schiller, Nina

1975 "The Formation of a Haitian Ethnic Group." Columbia University dissertation in Anthropology. Available on University Microfilms, Ann Arbor, Michigan.

1977 "Ethnic Groups Are Made Not Born." In *Ethnic Encounters: Identities and Contexts*. Edited by G. Hicks and P. Leis. North Scituate, MA: Duxbury Press, pp. 23–35.

1992 "What's Wrong with This Picture? The Hegemonic Construction of Culture in AIDS Research in the United States." *Medical Anthropology Quarterly* 6(3):237–54.

1999 "Transmigrants and Nation-States: Something Old and Something New in U.S. Immigrant Experience." In *Handbook of International Migration: The U.S. Experience*. Edited by Charles Hirshman, Josh DeWind, and Philip Kasinitz. New York: Russell Sage Publications, pp. 94–119.

2000 "Who Are These Guys? A Transnational Reading of the U.S. Immigrant Experience." In *Identities on the Move*. Edited by Liliana Goldin. Pp. 15–44. Austin: University of Texas Press.

Glick Schiller, Nina, Linda Basch, and Cristina Szanton-Blanc

1992 "Transnationalism: A New Analytic Framework for Understanding Migration." In *Towards a Transnational Perspective on Migration: Race, Class, Ethnicity and Nationalism Reconsidered.* Edited by N. Glick Schiller, L. Basch, and C. Szanton-Blanc. Pp. 1–24. New York: New York Academy of Sciences.

Glick Schiller, Nina, Josh DeWind, Marie Lucie Brutus, Carolle Charles, Georges Fouron, and Louis Thomas

1987 "Exile, Ethnic, Refugee: Changing Organizational Identities among Haitian Immigrants." *Migration Today* 15(1):7–11.

1992 [1987] "All in the Same Boat? Unity and Diversity among Haitian Immigrants." In *Caribbean Immigrants in New York.* Rev. ed. Edited by C. Sutton and E. Chaney. Pp. 167–84. New York: Center for Migration Studies.

Glick Schiller, Nina, and Georges Fouron

1991 "'Everywhere We Go We Are in Danger': Ti Manno and the Emergence of a Haitian Transnational Identity." *American Ethnologist* 17(2):329–47.

1998 "Transnational Lives and National Identities: The Identity Politics of Haitian Immigrants." In *Transnationalism from Below.* Edited by Michael P. Smith and Luis Guarnizo. New Brunswick, NJ: Transaction Press, pp. 130–61.

1999 "Terrains of Blood and Nation: Haitian Transnational Social Fields." *Ethnic and Racial Studies* 22(2):340–66

2001 *Georges Woke Up Laughing: Long Distance Nationalism and the Search for Home.* Durham, NC: Duke University Press.

Gluckman, Max

1960 "Rituals of Rebellion in South-East Africa." In *Order and Rebellion in Tribal Africa: Collected Essays with an Autobiographical Introduction.* Glencoe: Free Press.

Goldring, Luin

1998 "The Power of Status in Transnational Social Fields." In *Transnationalism from Below.* Edited by Michael Peter Smith and Luis Eduardo Guarnizo. Pp 165–95. New Brunswick, NJ: Transaction Publishers.

Gramsci, Antonio

1971 *Prison Notebooks: Selections.* Translated by Quinton Hoare and Geoffrey Smith. New York: International Publishers.

Guarnizo, Luis Eduardo

1997 "The Emergence of a Transnational Social Formation and the Mirage of Return Migration among Dominican Transmigrants." *Identities: Global Studies in Culture and Power* 4(2):281–322.

1998 "The Rise of Transnation Social Formations: Mexican and Dominican State Responses to Transnational Migration." *Political Power and Social Theory* 12:45–94.

Guarnizo, Luis Eduardo, and Michael Peter Smith
1998   "The Locations of Transnationalism." In *Transnationalism from Below.* Edited by M. P. Smith and Luis Eduardo Guarnizo. Pp. 3–34. New Brunswick, NJ: Rutgers University Press.

Gutmann, Max
1993   "Rituals of Resistance: A Critique of the Theory of Everyday Forms of Resistance." *Latin American Perspectives* 20(2):74–92.

Hancock, Graham
1989   *Lords of Poverty: The Power, Prestige, and Corruption of the International Aid Business.* New York: Atlantic Monthly Press.

Handlin, Oscar
1957   *Race and Nationality in American Life.* New York: Doubleday Anchor.
1973   [1951] *The Uprooted.* 2d ed. Boston: Little, Brown.

Held, David
1992   "Democracy: From City-States to a Cosmopolitan Order? *Political Studies* 40:10–30.

Herzfeld, Michael
1992   *The Social Production of Indifference: Exploring the Symbolic Roots of Western Bureaucracy,* Chicago: University of Chicago Press.

Hobsbawm, Eric J.
1990   *Nations and Nationalism since 1780: Programme, Myth and Reality.* New York: Cambridge University Press.

Ignatiev, Noel
1996   *How the Irish Became White.* New York: Routledge.

Jacobson, Matthew Frye
1998   *Whiteness of a Different Color: European Immigrants and the Alchemy of Race.* Cambridge, MA: Harvard University Press.

Joseph, Gilbert, and David Nugent
1994   "Popular Culture and State Formation in Revolutionary Mexico." In *Everyday Forms of State Formation: Revolution and the Negotiation of Rule in Modern Mexico.* Edited by Gilbert Joseph and David Nugent. Pp. 3–23. Durham, NC: Duke University Press.

Katz, Michael
1989   *The Undeserving Poor: From the War on Poverty to the War on Welfare.* New York: Pantheon.
1993   ed. *The Underclass Debate.* Princeton: Princeton, NJ: University Press.

Kearney, Michael
1991   "Borders and Boundaries of the State and Self at the End of Empire." *Journal of Historical Sociology* 4(1):52–74.

Kedourie, Eli
1960   *Nationalism*. New York: Praeger.

Kohn, Hans
1994   "Western and Eastern Nationalism." In *Nationalism*. Edited by John Hutchinson and Anthony D. Smith. Pp. 162–65. Oxford: Oxford University Press.

Laguerre, Michel S.
1978   "Ticouloute and His Kinfold: The Study of a Haitian Extended Family." In *The Extended Family in Black Societies*. Edited by Dmitri B. Shimkin, Edith Shimkin, and Dennis Frate. Pp. 407–45. The Hague: Mouton.
1982   *Urban Life in the Caribbean: A Study of a Haitian Urban Community*. Cambridge, MA: Schenkman.

Leacock, Eleanor
1969   *Teaching and Learning in New York City Schools*. New York: Basic Books.

Leacock, Eleanor, ed.
1971   *The Culture of Poverty: A Critique*. New York: Simon and Schuster.

Lenin, V.I.
1978   [1902] *What Is to Be Done? Burning Questions of Our Movement*. In *Collected Works* 5:347–529. Moscow: Progress Publishers.

Lessinger, Johanna
1995   *From the Ganges to the Hudson*. New York: Allyn and Bacon.

Lewis, Oscar
1965   *La Vida: A Puerto Rican Family in the Culture of Poverty—San Juan and New York*. New York: Random House.

McCrone, David
1998   *The Sociology of Nationalism*. London: Routledge.

Mahler, Sarah
1998   "Theoretical and Empirical Contributions toward a Research Agenda for Transnationalism." In *Transnationalism from Below*. Edited by M. P. Smith and Luis Eduardo Guarnizo. Pp. 165–95. New Brunswick, NJ: Rutgers University Press.

Miles, Robert
1993   *Racism after Race Relations*. London: Routledge & Kegan Paul.

Miller, Kerby
1990   "Class, Culture, and Immigrant Group Identity in the United States: The Case of Irish-American Ethnicity." In *Immigration Reconsidered*. Edited by Virginia Yans-McLaughlin. Pp. 96–129. New York: Oxford University Press.

Mittleman, James
1997   "How Does Globalization Really Work?" In *Globalization: Critical Reflections*. Edited by James Mittleman. Pp. 1–20. Boulder, CO: Lynne Reinner.

Moch, Leslie Page
1992 *Moving Europeans*. Bloomington: Indiana University Press.

Morawska, Ewa
1987 "Sociological Ambivalence: The Case of Eastern European Peasant-Immigrant Workers in America, 1980s–1930s." *Qualitative Sociology* 10(3): 225–50.
1989 "Labor Migrations of Poles in the Atlantic World Economy, 1880–1914." *Comparative Study of Society and History* 31(2):237–70.
1997 "On New-Old Transmigrations and Transnationalism qua Ethnicization." Paper presented at Social Science Research Council workshop on "Immigrants, Civic Culture, and Modes of Political Incorporation: A Contemporary and Historical Comparison," Santa Fe, New Mexico (May).

Mountz, Allison, and Richard Wright
1996 "Daily Life in the Transnational Migrant Community of San Agustín, Oaxaca, and Poughkeepsie, New York." *Diaspora* 5(3):403–28.

Panitch, Leo
1997 "Rethinking the Role of the State." In *Globalization: Critical Reflections*. Edited by James Mittleman. Pp. 83–113. Boulder, CO: Lynne Reinner.

Park, Robert
1974 [1925] "Immigrant Community and Immigrant Press and Its Control." In *The Collected Papers of Robert Park*. New York: Arno Press.

Pessar, Patricia
1995 *A Visa for a Dream*. New York and Boston: Allyn and Bacon.

Pistalo, Vladimir
2001 "Juggling with Three Identities." Ph.D. dissertation, Department of History, University of New Hampshire, Durham.

Plamenatz, John
1976 "Two Types of Nationalism." In *Nationalism: The Nature and Evolution of an Idea*. Edited by E. Kamenka. Pp. 22–36. London: Edward Arnold.

Portes, Alejandro, and Ruben Rumbaut
1990 *Immigrant America: A Portrait*. Berkeley: University of California Press.

Price, Hannibal.
1900 *De la rehabilitation de la race noire par la République d'Haïti* (Of the rehabilitation of the black race by the Republic of Haiti). Port-au-Prince: Verrollot.

Richman, Karen
1992 "They Will Remember Me in the House: The Pwen of Haitian Transnational Migration." Ph.D. dissertation, Department of Anthropology, University of Virginia, Charlottesville.

Roediger, David R.
1991   *The Wages of Whiteness: Race and the Making of the American Working Class.*
        London: Verso.

Roseberry, William
1989   *Anthropologies and Histories: Essays in Culture, History.* New Brunswick, NJ:
        Rutgers University Press.

Rouse, Roger
1992   "Making Sense of Settlement: Class Transformation, Cultural Struggle, and
        Transnationalism among Mexican Migrants in the United States." In *To-
        wards a Transnational Perspective on Migration: Race, Class, Ethnicity, and
        Nationalism.* Edited by Nina Glick Schiller, Linda Basch, and Christina
        Szanton-Blanc. Pp. 25–52. New York: New York Academy of Sciences.

Ryan, William
1976   *Blaming the Victim.* New York: Vintage Books.

Sassen, Saskia
1988   *The Mobility of Labor and Capital: A Study in International Investment and
        Labor Flow.* New York: Cambridge University Press.
1996   *Losing Control? Sovereignty in an Age of Globalization.* New York: Columbia
        University Press.
1998   *Globalization and Its Discontents: Essays on the New Mobility of People and
        Money.* New York: New Press.

Schermerhorn, R. A.
1949   *These Our People: Minorities in American Culture.* Boston: D.C. Heath
        and Co.

Schneider, Mark
1999   Remarks on behalf of the Haiti Consultative Group. Paris, January 31, 1995.
        Available at: www.info.usaid.gov/press/spe_test/speeches/speech.252. Lo-
        cated April 20.

Scott, James C.
1985   *Weapons of the Weak: Everyday Forms of Resistance.* New Haven, CT: Yale
        University Press.
1990   *Domination and the Arts of Resistance: Hidden Transcripts.* New Haven, CT:
        Yale University Press.

Sharff, Jagna Wojcicka
1998   *King Kong on 4th Street: Families and the Violence of Poverty on the Lower
        East Side.* Boulder, CO: Westview Press.

Smith, Joan, and Immanuel Wallerstein, eds.
1992   *Creating and Transforming Households: The Constraints of the World Econ-
        omy.* New York: Cambridge University Press.

Smith, Robert

1997   "Transnational Migration, Assimilation, and Political Community." In *The City and the World: New York City's Global Future*. Edited by Margaret Crahan and Alberto Vourvoulias Bush. Pp. 110–32. New York: Council on Foreign Relations.

1998   "Transnational Localities: Community, Technology, and the Politics of Membership within the Context of Mexico–U.S. Migration." In *Transnationalism from Below*. Edited by Michael Peter Smith and Luis Guarnizo. Pp. 196–238. New Brunswick, NJ: Rutgers University Press.

Stack, Carol

1974   *All Our Kin: Strategies for Survival in a Black Community*. New York: Harper & Row.

Sturgeon, Noël

1999   "Ecofeminist Appropriations and Transnational Environmentalisms." *Identities: Global Studies in Culture and Power* 6(2–3):255–80. Special issue: *Ethnographic Presence: Environmentalism, Indigenous Rights, and Transnational Cultural Critique*. J. Peter Brosius, guest editor.

Susser, Ida

1982   *Norman Street: Poverty and Politics in an Urban Neighborhood*. New York: Oxford University Press.

1996   "The Construction of Poverty and Homelessness in U.S. Cities." *Annual Review of Anthropology* 25:411–35.

Tolopko, Leon

1991   *Working Ukrainians in the USA*. Book 1: *1890–1924*. New York: Ukrainian-American League.

Torrie, Jill

1983   *Banking on Poverty: The Global Impact of the IMF and World Bank*. Toronto: Between the Lines.

Torriero, E. A.

2000   "Haitians Aground on U.S. Policy." *Sun Sentinel*, January 23:1A, 12A.

Turner, Victor

1985   *On the Edge of the Bush: Anthropolology as Experience*. Tucson: University of Arizona Press.

United Nations Research Institute for Social Development (UNRISD)

1995   *Global Citizens on the Move*. Geneva: United Nations Research Institute for Social Development.

United States Bureau of the Census

1990   *Census of Population: The Foreign-Born Population in the United States*. Washington, DC: Department of Commerce, Bureau of the Census.

United States State Department

1998   "Background Notes: Haiti." March. Page 2 at site www.state.gov/www/background_notes/haiti_0398_bgn.

Valentine, Charles

1968   *Culture and Poverty: Critique and Counter-Proposals.* Chicago: University of Chicago Press.

Wacquant, Loic

1994   "The New Union Color Lines: The State and the Fate of the Ghetto in Postfordist America." In *Social Theory and the Politics of Identity.* Edited by C. Calhoun. Oxford: Blackwell, pp. 234–74.

White, Robert E.

1997   "Haiti: Democrats vs. Democracy." *International Policy Report.* Washington, DC: Center for International Policy. Accessed at http://www.ciponline.org/democrac.htm on January 7, 2000.

Williams, Raymond

1977   *Marxism and Literature.* Oxford: Oxford University Press.

Wilson, William Julius

1987   *The Truly Disadvantaged: The Inner City, the Underclass, and Public Policy.* Chicago: University of Chicago Press.

Wong, Bernard

1982   *Chinatown: Economic Adaptation and Ethnic Identity of the Culture.* New York: Holt, Rinehart and Winston.

Wyman, Mark

1993   *Round-Trip to America: The Immigrants Return to Europe, 1880–1930.* Ithaca, NY: Cornell University Press.

Chapter 13

Let's Get Our Act Together
How Racial Discourses Disrupt Neighborhood Activism

Judith Goode

At an emergency meeting to promote local unity in the aftermath of two interracial youth murders,[1] Ester[2] sat with an angry group of Puerto Rican activists. She had been sent to the meeting by her parish priest, a white male who was an active participant in a local human relations consortium. The assembled group was comprised of leaders from the many human relations organizations in Philadelphia[3] and local residents who had voluntarily given up their evening to develop strategies for responding to the killings, in order to prevent additional violence and improve intergroup relations in this moment of crisis. A few minutes into the meeting, one white resident mentioned racism in relation to the fact that the Puerto Rican youths had yelled, "Let's get whitey," before the murder. In response, Luz, a Puerto Rican activist who had attended the meeting, angrily shouted, "Puerto Ricans are *victims* of oppression. We cannot be racist; only white people can be racist." Ester joined with her fellow Puerto Ricans in the angry shouting that ensued.

Interestingly, Ester did this despite the presence of white community members with whom she had close personal ties. A thirty-eight-year-old single mother born on the island of Puerto Rico, who had emigrated to the mainland when she was eight, Ester had lived in this neighborhood for fifteen years. During this time, she forged strong ties with both whites and Puerto Ricans. The godparent of her children was an Italian American neighbor, and the children of both households moved freely back and forth between them, playing, sharing meals, and sleeping. In her activist parish, Ester maintained a large network of both white and Puerto Rican friends who had lent her money to buy her house. She talked about her affection for and reliance on both her white and her Puerto Rican friends, repeating often, "They are always there for me." Yet, during the emergency meeting, Ester's identity as a Puerto Rican and her loyalty to the multiracial coalition of poor people were split. Ester looked a little embarrassed as she chose sides against her assembled white friends.

Ester's personal ambivalence illustrates the contradictory relationships between the political and social identities through which residents authenticate themselves in impoverished neighborhoods in Philadelphia and in other cities across the United States. As poor whites and people of color increasingly live together in places from which capital investment and public services have been withdrawn, they sometimes forge relationships of trust and interdependence, such as Ester's with her white working-class friends, across racial lines. Yet, though they live in a time and place in which material inequality is rapidly growing, racialized identities and discourses rather than those based on shared poverty continue to dominate in the public sphere.

In national-level political discourse, there are two main ways in which racial inequality is understood. The first is a multiculturalist understanding that ignores class and figures race as a kind of ethnic identity. This model is individualistic, superficial, and unresponsive to the structural economic conditions that shape institutional racism and the racial dynamics of poverty. It does not speak to local economic, racial, or political conditions in poor and working-class communities. The second mode of understanding race and class is more progressive. This model attends to the structural conditions that produce poverty and class stratification. It tends, however, to conflate race and class, implicitly assuming that most blacks and Latinos are poor or working-class while most white people are middle-class. While this assumption has a significant degree of empirical support in the aggregate,[4] it is also limited in the insights it provides into the actual dynamics of multiracial poor and working-class communities.

This essay details the racial dynamics of two poor neighborhoods in Philadelphia. It shows that the policies and political strategies adopted by local government to promote racial harmony follow one (or both) of these oversimplified national-level models and therefore exacerbate the very problems they are trying to alleviate. These strategies deploy racialized identities pervasively, stereotypically, and divisively in public arenas, precluding any analysis of the ways in which race and class intersect in particular local formations. Yet, as John Hartigan (1999:279) demonstrates in his analysis of three Detroit neighborhoods, classed nuances and differences in spatial locations create varying significance for "racialness." He says: "The particular contours of spatial formations, with their distinct racial and class compositions, informs the discursive modes through which the significance of racialness is assessed, manipulated and negotiated." The ways in which these distinct circumstances affect racial relations is relevant to the possibilities for opening or foreclosing options for cross-racial, class-based collective action against the continued production of poverty.

In this essay, I examine the ways in which local decline produced by economic restructuring can harden racial and ethnic boundaries in different situations, at the same time fostering the development of intimate cross-racial ties in order to cope with everyday life. While the white working class generally projects an internalized sense of white privilege and is hostile toward arguments of structural racism and cultural nationalism, grassroots activism can, in some cases, engender the kind of local political spaces in which, as Gregory (1998:213) states, "people through collective actions render power visible and recognize themselves as political subjects." These moments of insight are fragile and difficult to sustain over time.

I will demonstrate that as these neighborhoods become targets of programs to quell racial disturbances, the very state discourses invoked to heal rifts work against the transcendence of racial and ethnic assumptions to actually perpetuate current hegemonic constructions of race and ethnicity and exacerbate boundaries. Thus they interfere with emerging politicized class identities. These messages work in two negative ways. First, disseminated by public officials, professional human relations specialists, clergy, and teachers, whose mission and social experience distance them from neighborhood life, these ideologies mask the larger political and economic power relationships that underlie local conflict. Second, this false view is often resisted by local resident leaders and subverted in ways that reassert racialized identities. Examples below illustrate what happens when powerful institutions, in an attempt to deal with racial tension, resort to dominant ethnic, racial, and multicultural constructions.

This essay uses material drawn from two communities that differ from each other in their political-economic trajectories and in their racial and class compositions. The data in this essay are drawn primarily from the Philadelphia Changing Relations Project.[5] Between 1988 and 1990, a team of fourteen anthropologists engaged in fieldwork in two Philadelphia neighborhoods. For a two-year period, everyday activities on the block, in schools, and on the shopping strip, as well as activist campaigns in community organizations and special events such as neighborhood celebrations and healing events in the wake of disruptive incidents, were observed. Community leaders and members of over fifty households were interviewed. Since 1990, as a member of the boards of several community organizations, I have continued to keep track of continuity and change.

The Setting

Once the largest manufacturing center in the United States, Philadelphia has been more affected than comparable cities by post-1970 economic restructuring.[6] The service economy based on health care and higher education on which the city's well-being rests today is vulnerable to volatile shifts in state funding. Since the 1980s, the major urban development strategy has been to commodify the city as a tourist landscape of consumption for the new corporate professional and managerial classes, a process well described by Matthew Ruben (chapter 15, below).[7] This tourist strategy and the related development policy have encouraged gentrification, which has further dislocated poor people and shrunk the pool of available affordable housing.

As a major player in early and late nineteenth-century industrialization, the city experienced major European immigration waves that provided labor to the expanding economy.[8] Initially racialized and excluded from the mainstream, the descendants of these immigrants were "whitened" after World War II as they entered the new middle-income groups created by organized labor and the expansion of the credentialed professional/managerial and technical class.[9] The city became an important point of new settlement for rural Southern blacks who moved north between 1915 and 1960 into a declining and segregated economy.[10] The downturn in the local economy of today has reduced the role of the city as an immigrant destination. Philadelphia has been a minor destination, in relation to other cities, for the new wave of Latin American, Caribbean, and Asian immigrants. In the context of overall population loss, however, new immigrants make up significant local population groups.[11] These populations are entering a racially divided city that is now 6 percent Hispanic and 3 percent Asian, with the remaining 90 percent divided relatively equally between whites and blacks.

Hit hard by postwar suburbanization and extensive white flight, the population of the city is highly segregated residentially (Goldstein 1986). The eastern part of the city is predominantly white and the western zone predominantly black, a pattern that gradually emerged during the postwar population movements of black in-migration and white flight. The increasingly impoverished neighborhoods in this study are places where this color line was broken in the 1970s, as the once white working-class neighborhoods connected to local industries were destabilized and materially devastated by economic restructuring. Corporate and state decisions produced household downward mobility and economic insecurity through plant closings and the loss of middle-income unionized jobs. New jobs in the service economy became bifurcated as either high-end professional/managerial or low-wage unskilled, part-time, and temporary work. Actions by banks, realtors, and state agencies further increased instability, housing abandonment, and blight through mortgage redlining, public housing and refugee resettlement policies, and realtor practices such as flight-inducing blockbusting. These neighborhoods now accommodate poor whites who cannot afford to relocate, blacks who have moved eastward in the wake of the destruction of their housing stock, and new immigrants.

Olney, in the north, was for a long time a destination for aspiring middle-class whites moving northward from the industrial heartland to the first rung of better housing stock. While it has experienced massive turnover in the past decade, it still houses a stream of newcomer upwardly mobile populations. Today, however, these aspiring middle-class populations consist of African Americans and immigrants from over forty countries. As a group, the downwardly mobile whites who remain are poorer than Asians and Latinos who broke the color line and joined them, which, as we will see, complicates the understanding of race and class. However, households are getting poorer across all populations.[12]

In contrast, Kensington is one of the city's poorest neighborhoods. An industrial mill town since the early 1800s, Kensington's experience with plant closings accelerated in the 1960s. By the 1970s, related actions of financial and government institutions had produced visible urban blight, the destruction of the private real estate market, and increased housing abandonment. Those who could afford to leave moved out of the area. The church congregations and civic associations they had sustained died out. Today, Kensington houses the poorest whites and Latinos in the city.[13] The bulk of Latino institutions are in Kensington. In the 1980s, new residents also included increasing numbers of blacks, Southeast Asian refugees placed by agencies, and some Korean and Palestinian merchants.

The color line had been guarded previously in these two neighborhoods by incidents of harassment and vandalism. In the 1970s, there were many conflict incidents when the first racial minority households moved in. Today there are still some incidents of violence, such as the murders referred to above. There are also pockets of active nativists, organized into formal organizations and informal gangs, who respond to "move-ins." In addition to the incidents perpetrated by the small but active number of visible racist-nativists, downward mobility across racial lines has extended less visible interracial and interethnic tensions (Adams et al. 1991; Goode and Schneider 1994) and produced private discourses of racial resentment. For example, some established residents close ranks and use racial rhetoric to strengthen preexisting social boundaries, in order to defend their sense of seniority and "ownership" of local public spaces. They feel resentment because, in many cases, immigrants/people of color are better off economically. This does not fit the historically formed ideology of naturalized white superiority that allowed poor whites to displace their abjection onto poor minorities (Du Bois 1992; Roediger 1990). The success of racial minorities is resented and explained through a belief that immigrants and native-born blacks receive special benefits from an unfair state.

At the same time, many immigrants maintain strong structures of mutual aid and retain their native language for everyday social interaction. They often participate in cultural identity movements that anticipate and defend against white racist actions. Mobilizing for collective action to bid for power, they develop discourses of cultural nationalism that can deploy essentialist and naturalized ideas about race and ethnicity. This essentialism frequently produces assertions of their own collective moral superiority. Rather than advocating an end to hierarchy and inequality, one woman said, when asked what she had learned in a multicultural workshop, "I learned that one day [my group] may get to be on top." Simultaneously but separately, Puerto Ricans, Koreans, and Afrocentrists talked about their morally superior family structures and communal values and spoke against the selfish, individualistic values of whites.

Nonetheless, there are also dynamics developing in these neighborhoods that push people toward a common identity as neighbors. Philadelphia is a city of row houses. It is important to note that in these two neighborhoods, unlike others in which anthropologists have studied race relations (Rieder 1985; Merry 1986; Gregory 1998; Sanjek 1998), separate populations are not clustered on monoracial blocks or in high-rise housing projects, interacting warily in shared and contested public spaces and institutions. Instead, especially in Olney, the blocks we studied were themselves residentially integrated. It is ironic that these mixed neighborhoods, which are seen by suburbanites as hotbeds of racial conflict, are actually settings for much more everyday interracial collaboration than the segregated settlements and workplaces of the suburbs.

The following discussion focuses on how the common local experiences of everyday life in shared neighborhoods create bonds of intimacy, trust, and interdependence based on exchange as well as empathy for victims of racism. Occasionally, through common political struggles related to local quality-of-life issues, racial boundaries are transcended. Two caveats must be stated at the outset, however. First, friendship and empathy in the absence of political struggle do not automatically create the strong foundation for sustained common political subjectivity necessary to accomplish social change. Second, as Gregory (1998) has so clearly argued, even when there are local struggles, place-bound interests related to property values and quality of life are often limited in their capacity to articulate a broader frame of reference linking local situations to larger political-economic structures in the production of poverty and inequality.

From Intimacy, Empathy, and Trust to Political Struggle

Day-to-day community life in many instances can engender multiracial harmony. As Ester's example demonstrates, however, it is difficult to transform these personal understandings into interventions in public discourse or political action that contradicts the hegemonic discourses about U.S. social categories. In fact, the very actions of state governance, economic policy, and hegemonic discourses of difference often interfere with the conversion of these emerging relations of trust into political identities and actions. As Steven Gregory states, "Hegemony works less on the hearts and minds of the disempowered than on their ability to articulate and exercise a political identity able to realize the social force necessary to change the order of power relations" (1998:246).

Our fieldwork demonstrated that these neighborhoods contained many strong bonds of intimacy, empathy, and trust that crossed such socially constructed boundaries as those between poor whites and people of color or new immigrants and established citizens. For example, intermarried households are common in the communities, and these mixed families feel at home in schools and churches. Sally, a white woman married to a black man, worries about having to move: "Where else can I move in the city where my kids don't get called names? There's nothing they need to feel out of place about here. There are so many other children of intermarriage." Anna, a white woman, describes the warm relationship that developed with the family of her black son-in-law after a rocky start. Linda jokes, "You can't call me prejudiced, all my nieces and nephews [children of her two sisters] are black and Latino."

Meaningful neighborhood exchanges were also common. Elena, a young Nicaraguan, and Ann, a seventy-year-old daughter of eastern European immigrants, spend their days together. Elena drives her older neighbor Ann everywhere in return for English-language lessons on the stoop. Carmen, a woman from Colombia, is arranging for her sister to deliver an almost-new sofa to her neighbor Pat, in return for the "many times she helped me out." Many neighbors are engaged in critical social exchanges such as babysitting. Carol babysits for seven mothers on her block. They include "Spanish [street term for Latino], Turkish, Indian, and from the islands [Haitian] . . . a real United Nations. My mother said, you have everyone but an Oriental. I told her it wouldn't be long. My Korean neighbor is pregnant." Carol often talks about how the common interest in the children's welfare brings the women close together as they share intimate details of their everyday lives. Ester talks about her intimate conversations with white neighbors about problems with ex-spouses: "I've learned their men are just like ours. We're just the same." Mary talks about how her Latino neighbors watch her daughters as they move throughout the neighborhood: "If they get into trouble, I would hear right away. They really watch out for us." In many cases, these relationships do not merely lead to a view that the friend is a rare and exceptional member of her race but provide entrée into intimate and increasingly shared social worlds of extended families and celebratory events.

Through friendship, some whites become sensitized to the ways in which people of color encounter overt racism daily and develop strong empathy for their situation. For example, Anita, an Olney descendant of turn-of-the-century European immigrants, often described her indignation about the way in which one of her husband's workmates in a public transportation job, a black woman and close friend of the family, faced discrimination from customers. We see this process discussed as well in Patricia Zavella (chapter 4, above).

Several conditions foster the move from bonds of intimacy and common subjectivity to active political struggle. First, the context of the neoliberal withdrawal of public services (school overcrowding, loss of security, decreased recreation facilities, and infrastructural maintenance) engenders grievances against state and market practices, producing a potential for community action to wrest improvements in quality of life from the state. Second, many of these households had previously succumbed to pressure for white flight. They describe being "run out" of North Philadelphia a generation ago as a result of realtor-induced panic. They talk about resisting panic flight and digging in their heels to save their institutions through incorporating minority residents as political allies.[14]

Ongoing constructions of common subjectivity among diverse new neighbors create a potential site for mobilizing to confront the state. Most of this organizing is done by women through "activist mothering" (Naples 1998:11–12), defined as "political activism as a central component of mothering," in which women "draw on traditional female identities to justify taking revolutionary action to improve the community and the lives of their families."[15] These activities emerge from friendship cliques, informal block groups, and formal institutions and contribute to a sense of common subjectivity as beleaguered neighbors. In Philadelphia, mobilizations took the form of campaigns for child safety, demands for playgrounds and new recreation programs, protest movements in response to school overcrowding, and actions to get the city to close and seal drug houses. In many instances, these place-based, child-oriented oppositional activities also serve to move these women from personal feelings of empathy and trust to action through politicized identities as poor mothers confronting the state.

Staughton Lynd (2000:21) recently critiqued those who wish to bring about anti-racist ideological change in workers' movements by "preaching door to door." He stated, "Racism too will be transformed by experience and struggle . . . as workers' *actions* change in response to the need for solidarity in which the survival of each depends on the survival of all, *attitudes* will change also." In Philadelphia, too, many local campaigns first engendered by common subjectivity have not only produced new demands on the state but disrupted the old racial order. With increased awareness and anger at the racialized discourses directed against their neighbors, several whites severed relationships with racist relatives, intervened publicly against racial statements, and joined anti-racist movements. For example, in Kensington, we had known Mary for a year when her house burned down. The relatives of Mary and her husband urged the couple to move away from the increasingly Latino neighborhood. One of them, referring to the neighborhood, said, "It's not going down anymore; it already went when Hispanics moved in." Yet Mary and her husband, who were engaged in several community campaigns, told their relatives to leave them alone, decided to stay, and bought another house a block away. Such new, deracialized identities in turn moved the political struggles forward.

Candy provides one example of this shift. Angered by the threats to the safety of her children on the streets, Candy organized a successful block organization with Puerto Rican, Vietnamese, Brazilian, and Palestinian neighbors. The group has met monthly for several years. It demanded that the city close a drug house and provide recreational facilities. As a result of this activity, Candy convinced her husband to stay in the neighborhood and continued to play a significant role in local cross-racial political campaigns (Goode and Schneider 1994; Goode 1998). Loretta tells a similar story. During a crisis in her family, a Latina neighbor became "like a sister" to her. Their children are best friends. She was horrified by how her own extended family talked about the way in which "that Hispanic boy," whom she sees as a fictive nephew, was allowed to come in without knocking and to stay for meals or a sleepover. Her white kin and friends have been exhorting Loretta to leave the neighborhood for years. Yet Loretta, a mother of four, like many other white residents is attached to place. She has actively created bonds with her new neighbors of different backgrounds. She has been active in the home and school association and in her parish for years. She does not drive and finds the local shopping strip to be convenient for everything. Loretta felt she had to cut herself off from her racist relatives. She led parents from different backgrounds to organize and sustain a protest against school district practices of busing children of color out of the mixed neighborhood in order to integrate a more solidly white community.[16] She devoted two years to a campaign to foster new school construction and maximum integration. The campaign ultimately succeeded in attaining limited court-ordered construction.[17] Loretta says, "Look at what we can do if we just stick together and fight for what's best for our kids. It took a lot of work to get us all together, especially the mothers that don't speak good English, but we were all being pushed around by the school district; so we had to do something."

Liberal Pluralism and the Multicultural Consensus

In a city full of public and quasi-public agencies working against racism and violence, the state responds quickly to racial incidents through formal programs. State agents cannot risk making local oppositional activism the foundation for anti-racist campaigns. They are either willfully ignorant or fearful of the many actual and potential cross-racial networks and activities that are developing informally on the ground to demand resources. I argue that instead of building on the potential of these adversarial collectivities, agents of the state respond to actual and potential conflict incidents by sponsoring interventions using a liberal pluralist, multicultural discourse. This diverts attention away from power relations between state and neighborhood and focuses on a myth of structural equality and a discourse of individual blame.

The following cases illustrate how these "healing" events interfere with local political struggles and their promise for transcending racialized political identities.(Instead, activists like Ester are forced to choose a side.) The events also promote a false ideology of equality that hides the actual sources of inequality; at the same time, they allow space for covert messages of separatism and hierarchy to creep in through the reification and naturalization of racial and ethnic difference in the name of pluralism.

As a "nation of immigrants," U.S. nation-building narratives focus on creating unity out of diversity. Prior to World War II, U.S. national unity was promoted through institutional policies of Anglo-conformity and assimilation. At the same time, racializing ideas and practices were used to exclude economically exploited populations, such as former slaves and exploited labor migrants, from understandings of the unified nation.[18] Recent scholarship helps us understand the ways in which race, class, and politics were intertwined in earlier moments of history, such as the nineteenth-century formation of the industrial working class (Roediger 1990; Ignatiev 1995) and the post–World War II period of suburbanization (Sacks 1994; Brodkin 1998). Each significant shift produced new discourses of inclusion and exclusion.

The post–civil rights narratives deployed in some of the following cases reflect new discursive relationships among race, ethnicity, and class. The Civil Rights movement called attention to the history of race-based exclusion and demanded redress. As a result, Office of Management and Budget (OMB) Directive 15 (1977) brought race explicitly and officially into the picture as the state reified five categories of difference largely for the purpose of collecting information to monitor civil rights remedies. Four categories were considered racial (black, white, Asian/Pacific Islander, American Indian) while one, Hispanic, was designated ethnic (based on shared culture and language). Some discursive uses of official racial categories further conflated race and class. They located the source of all social disadvantage in race, further muting the significance of class position, and fostered a view of class homogeneity within racial categories.

This was countered by a liberal discourse of cultural pluralism in the 1970s, which was institutionalized during the celebrations of the bicentennial. This narrative focused on national heritages and interpreted the

United States as a nation of immigrant groups within a context of equality of opportunity, with each group making positive cultural contributions to the "mosaic" or "tapestry" that is the nation. Instead of extolling Anglo-conformity or assimilation, each group was valued for its difference and encouraged to maintain its essential integrity in contributing to a new whole. This new pluralism in asserting the equivalent cultural value of each group effectively denied that hierarchies of worth based on race or class existed. (Williams 1989). In fact, Steinberg (1981) asserts that the revival of the new ethnic pluralism on the part of European origin groups occurred partly to assert the equality of all Americans in order to deny the structural racism revealed through the Civil Rights movement. The shift to an emphasis on culture (ethnic, national-origin heritage) rather than race allowed each ethnic group to claim both valuable cultural contributions of "difference" and an equivalent history of struggle and suffering. The mosaic or tapestry model was institutionalized during the bicentennial celebrations in the 1970s, which funded the organization of groups, museums, and celebrations based on national-origin identities (Goode 1998).

Over time, official OMB racial categories have been appropriated by the cultural pluralism discourse to become semi-official categories of multiculturalism: African American, Asian American, Native American, Hispanic, and European American. In this usage, whites are not placed in opposition to excluded people demanding rights but are included as just another category representing different but equivalent, unranked cultural/behavioral traits.

Since Philadelphia served as the national location for bicentennial celebrations, museums and multicultural festivals proliferated in the 1970s and remain today as part of the rhythm of downtown life. Constituent groups of the U.S. mosaic are represented by ethnic museum exhibits, cultural performance groups, ethnic foods, and folkloric crafts. These festivals can be seen as part of the culture and arts industry that is being developed to turn the city center into a landscape of consumption, attracting the commerce of the overconsuming "haves": suburbanites and urban gentry. For these diversity-seeking populations, such events fill the same desire for authenticity and exotica as does the proliferation of international travel, new restaurant cuisines, and shopping venues such as the retail chain Anthropologie. They allow the new professional and managerial class to become cosmopolitan participants in the new global world scene, liberated from the soulless modernity of bureaucratic work as well as from racism and fear of otherness.

This is the discourse of liberal pluralism and multiculturalism that was invoked to deal with neighborhood conflict in the city as formerly white neighborhoods became racially mixed. Agents of the city government and local institutions, fearing disorder from what they perceived as irrational, unruly masses of white working-class racists, responded to early conflict incidents with a repertoire of therapeutic interventions. Such representatives as human relations specialists, clergy, and teachers, who valued cosmopolitan multicultural consumption in their private lives, thought it to be only common sense that similar events invoking a liberal pluralist mosaic of equivalent cultural differences would resolve conflict in poor multiracial neighborhoods, caused by the ignorant fear of the "Other." Teaching about official categories of racial and ethnic difference and exposing people to exotic cultural performances and aestheticized commodities through "multicultural appreciation" would end this fear.

In two years of fieldwork, we observed dozens of these events in poor neighborhoods. The overwhelming preference for multicultural performances was illustrated by one citywide initiative, the Neighborhood Human Relations Project (NHRP), which distributed several hundred thousand dollars to fund such programming.[19] The administrator of NHRP often stated unlimited faith in such folklore-based programs to solve local problems: "People will eat each other's food and enjoy each other's culture and tensions will melt away. They will know how to understand each other." Soon initiatives titled "Hands across X" and "Building Bridges in Y" dotted the neighborhood landscape. Avoiding race and power, such festivals limited culture to aesthetic domains. They avoided confronting those cultural stereotypes connected to moral conflict zones of family structures and work ethics. Demonstrating the desire for consuming exotic commodities, one workshop sponsor urged the audience to approach multicultural situations "as if you are going into a museum looking for treasures." Another spoke of "the adrenalin rush I get when I hear other languages on the street and see the crafts in store windows."

These remedies totally ignored (1) the material structures of inequality produced by late capitalism; (2) the ideological structures of institutionalized racism, which conflate race and class; and (3) the contradictions between the ideology of white privilege/superiority and the poverty and downward mobility of poor whites. In so doing, they ignored the existence of poverty and continued to produce the anger and displaced abjection that trigger most conflict incidents. In the following analysis of several events, I illustrate the ways in which the simplistic narratives deployed by institutional agents as a means of social control are contested by residents at the same time as they continue to disrupt the developing sense of collective agency in the face of increasing poverty. We can see that, while intending to avoid distinctions in race and power, multicultural celebrations often subtly point out such differences. The attempt to display equivalent cultural components only calls attention to the actual differences in each group's place in the hierarchy, further separating people into categories and not addressing any of the material or ideological roots of racial discrimination and poverty.

An Olney Parish Festival

One activist parish in Olney was the site of many campaigns for neighborhood improvement. As the neighborhood changed, the parish recruited new members along racial/ethnic lines by offering the mass in several languages and by creating separate clubs and musical groups for each newcomer population. While informal activities such as volunteering in the parish school or participating in cleanup and beautification programs created friendships, formal activities channeled people into separate groups. The parish, faced with these self-inflicted divisions, tried to create unity through multicultural appreciation days, which ultimately exacerbated boundaries and produced contradictions and resistance.

Half the parish membership consisted of established residents, descendants of turn-of-the-century European immigrants. The other half was comprised of newcomers to the neighborhood: native-born blacks and immigrants from Puerto Rico, Colombia and Central America, Korea, Laos, Portugal, South Asia, and the Caribbean. Long-term parishioners had expressed some resentment about the special events and masses for new immigrants. They complained that while new parishioners dressed better than long-term parishioners, drove newer cars, and brought expensive video cameras and cell phones to events, they did not donate time as volunteers or contribute to the many necessary parish fundraising drives.

As a tide of NHRP-funded multicultural events flooded Olney in the wake of the Korean sign incident discussed below, the clergy decided that a parish celebration of cultural difference was what was needed to create unity. The unity festival intended to promote the idea that we are all descendants of immigrants who have struggled in the United States. Yet, by treating populations differently, the event further inscribed a line between "whitened" turn-of-the-century immigrants and newcomers who were treated as "subordinated subnationals" (Williams 1989). Ultimately, the priests' attempts to organize the event according to the national narrative of cultural pluralism was contested by both new immigrants and established residents.

The celebration was typical of most local multicultural events. Held in the main public spaces of the parish school, the day's activities included a fair held in the gym and playground, where different ethnic groups offered games of chance similar to those offered at school and community fairs. Immigrant groups sponsored games from their home countries. Individuals and families traveled from booth to booth in the early morning. The main attractions were the communal events that occurred in the large school auditorium/lunchroom. In the morning, women set the eating tables and organized the presentation of food at food tables around the perimeter. The midday meal was followed by a formal sequence of cultural performances on stage.

Two priests had organized the event. National identities characteristic of bicentennial pluralism were ascribed to descendants of European immigrants. In contrast, blacks and new immigrant groups were lumped together in the large pan-ethnic categories of post-1970s multiculturalism. These categories ignored national identities and treated immigrant populations as Asians, Hispanics, and so forth. Ironically, these usages reversed people's self-constructed identities. National labels were used for those for whom they were no longer salient and denied to recent immigrants for whom national origin was central.

In these formerly white working-class neighborhoods, national identity had ceased to be noticeable to descendants of turn-of-the-century immigrants. In the postwar period, the strong circumscription of marriage of descendants of turn-of-the-century immigrants to those of the same national origin gave way to broader intermarriage among all white Catholics.[20] At the same time, the expansion of "whiteness" to these former immigrants in reaction to their war experiences, the creation of a new middle-class suburban whiteness, and reactions to the Civil Rights movement produced a new identity as patriotic white Americans, which generally replaced identities based on national origin. At anti-racist workshops, many individuals refused to provide ethnic labels on their name tags and often joked about their hybrid ancestry as they rejected the old nationality labels that in this context marked them as "other."[21]

The organizers of the Olney parish festival, in emphasizing the national origins of established Americans, were reflecting their experience with bi-centennial national discourses that placed Anglo-European sending nations in the center of our national origin myth. Knowing nothing about the nation-states of other regions that had sent forth the bulk of post-1965 immigrants, the "race"-based OMB pan-ethnic categories were used for new immigrants. They were simple and convenient. Yet treating old and new immigrants differently contradicted the narrative of equivalence and further underscored differences between unmarked whiteness and racially marked others.

The preparation for the festival itself inadvertently reinforced differences between newcomers and established white residents, as no attempt was made to encourage established parishioners to relinquish their "insider" status. At a planning meeting attended by white women regulars accustomed to running parish celebrations, these women were allowed to organize themselves in customary fashion. At the same time, the priest in charge took responsibility for paternalistically organizing those whom he called "the ethnics" (immigrants). He selected brokers he knew from each immigrant group and contacted them by phone, precluding any contact between them and other participants. The priest's constant use of the gloss "the ethnics" for immigrants also marked their separateness, as did the encouragement of the use of native language and exotic costumes and practices. Festival organizers encouraged exoticism in the cultural performances of new immigrants, thus exaggerating difference and separation between them and established residents. We observed advisers criticizing a South Asian Indian and a Puerto Rican group for singing songs in English instead of in their native languages. In both cases, the people had been subjects in English-speaking colonial situations and were indeed reflecting cultural practices from their homelands.

The event ultimately became a series of segregated components. The early morning setup was dominated by established women who were used to controlling the kitchen space in the hall. Two Latina women had begun to participate in these kitchen activities during the year and were developing relations with the old-timers. Though they helped out on the festival day, they were marked as "other" by queries and comments about their cuisine, depicted by whites as "spicy" or "too hot," thereby separating their dishes from the Americanized dishes these women had prepared.

At the event, clergy ran into resistance from European American groups when the women removed the nationality signs and flags (Polish, Irish, German, Italian) placed on the tables by the clergy and put up a hastily constructed American flag. As they had worked together in the rectory kitchen over the years to prepare for food events, the long-term parishioners had developed an integrated "American" menu that incorporated common Anglo, Italian, and central European elements that were now part of our national cuisine. The same foods—different kinds of sausages, deli meats in gravy and sauce, and mayonnaise salads such as cole slaw, potato salad, and macaroni salad—were always prepared collectively the night before in the rectory kitchen and reflected the pattern of avoiding particular ethnic markers. As they prepared the food, women often referred to the similarities between particular national cuisines, commenting on how sausages or cabbage could be found across them all. In contrast, the immigrant groups' food contributions were prepared in people's homes and were highly marked in style and content.

At the same time, new immigrants from Puerto Rico, Colombia, Nicaragua, Guatemala, El Salvador, and Mexico, for whom nationality was critical, tore down the large Hispanic banner the priests had placed on one table and ran home for flags and other items of national pride as they strongly asserted homeland identities. Such national identities remain central for immigrants, who increasingly are living in and imagining futures in transnational social fields. In addition, as Linda Basch and her colleagues (1994) demonstrate, for many Caribbean peoples, strong national identities are deployed to avoid racialization as blacks. In Philadelphia, many non–Puerto Rican Latinos, growing numbers from the Dominican Republic, Colombia, and elsewhere, use national identities to avoid being identified as Puerto Ricans, who are stigmatized as both stateless (colonized) and underclass. We frequently were told by individuals from South and Central America that Puerto Ricans should be ashamed of their commonwealth status (as opposed to national independence), that Puerto Rican women were "too attractive" (overtly sexual), and that Puerto Ricans "just don't know how to behave" (Goode and Schneider 1994:83; Goode 1998).

The event reinforced boundaries in other ways as well. As newcomer groups brought their dishes in, there was some jockeying for the best locations in table space. There had also been some competition over the sequence of performance times. At the festival itself, people clustered at their own game booths and food tables. They also tended to leave after their own group had performed. Moreover, several of the more well-to-do immigrant groups invested significant resources in costumes and props for their performance, thus reinforcing the resentment of less well-off established whites. In spite of this, the event, in marking "the ethnics" as different, served to underscore white ownership of the parish and reinforced bound-aries around each group, both self-ascribed and imposed.

The festival developed by the activist parish was based on the common template of multicultural appreciation: the mosaic notion of equivalent aesthetic cultures promulgated by local elites through the Neighborhood Human Relations Project. The failure of this simplified narrative to encom-pass the complexities and contradictions of group relations in everyday life led to a covert invocation of differences among groups by treating white es-tablished residents differently from immigrants. The latter were placed in pan-ethnic rather than national categories, called "the ethnics" by the orga-nizer, and treated as subordinates needing paternalistic care in the prepara-tion and planning phase. These actions both undermined contact and rein-scribed divisions between unmarked whites and people of color. While sub-tle cues, such as the elaborateness of costumes and stage sets, depicted some newcomer groups as well-to-do, the priests' willful ignoring of the inter-twined class and race issues that underlay parish tensions at the worst exac-erbated those tensions and at least left them intact. For a parish developing collective neighborhood activism, this was an unfortunate outcome.

A Struggling Kensington CDC

Another set of problems, some similar and some different, emerged when an activist Community Development Corporation (CDC) in Kensington organized a cultural pluralist festival under the auspices of the NHRP. In this instance, the festival organizers had the same problem of constructing the descendants of turn-of-the-century European immigrants in terms of national origin. In addition, Latino leaders used their understandings of race and cultural nationalism to create an opposition between whites and racial minorities.

The CDC served a territory with a mixed Puerto Rican, white, and black constituency. The group was attempting to gain rights to local abandoned or tax-delinquent homes in order to rehabilitate and rent them. It was working hard to overcome an earlier local reputation as an organization "for Puerto Ricans only." To change this image, the new executive director, a Puerto Rican professional and activist, had worked to integrate the board, which now represented the mixed makeup of the community. She worked daily with poor whites and African Americans to collectively improve local living conditions. The organization had accepted NHRP money in the way that underfunded nonprofits often accept targeted external resources. They hoped the funds could be used partially to aid their core agenda. In this case, they hoped to fund some local women who worked as volunteers. The money came with an expectation of a multicultural appreciation festival.

Organizers ran into the same problem as in the Olney parish. No household members were willing to identify themselves through the national-origin identities required for the pluralist mosaic. Irish priests in a local mission for the homeless came to the rescue with a food display of colcannon—a potato-and-cabbage dish—and soda bread. The multicultural mosaic model also engendered a major controversy over the language on the flyers. To symbolize unity in diversity, the flyer, written in English, also included the word *welcome* in eleven languages that symbolically represented both turn-of-the-century and current immigrants. In actuality, there were only two languages used in public settings: English and Spanish. The sponsoring community group ran all its meetings in both languages. It was customary for all flyers posted locally to be bilingual. Angered by the absence of expected English-Spanish parity, some Spanish speakers rejected this false symbolic representation of the neighborhood as a multilingual mosaic and wanted the flyers to represent the bilingual social reality. At one event-planning meeting, a local activist diverted the entire meeting to an argument about the flyer: "No Latino will come to this event if you don't have flyers in Spanish as well as English. This is a Spanish-speaking area and people have a right to expect all information to be in their language." The CDC leader explained that it was too late to change the flyers and that they were in keeping with the pluralist message of the event. This resulted in an informal boycott of the event.

The event also caused conflict on the board of the community-based organization because it diverted so much time and energy from the central housing activism of the group. As one woman activist explained, "I can't waste my time on this stuff when we've got all these people desperate for a roof over their heads." Several festival workers withdrew their labor from the festival. At the eleventh hour, much of the grant was used to hire a middle-class African American with festival experience to manage the event. She brought in the upscale museum exhibits, quasi-professional performance groups, vendors, and public relations outlets that had become commonly used in downtown festivals. The event shifted from one that served the local community and dealt with relevant local issues to a standardized display of the American mosaic. The only Asian dance group represented a nation that was not represented among local residents. This reflected the reification and naturalization of the pan-ethnic category of Asianness, which had led to the belief that any Asian could represent all Asians. The Solidarity-oriented display of locally resident Polish refugees was negatively received by several in attendance because it differed from the traditional costumed Polish dance performances used to represent Polish Americans in Philadelphia.

The bulk of those who ultimately attended the event were craft vendors, university students, and professionals from around the city. These were the self-selected diversity seekers and consumers of authentic cultural commodities who were responsible for promoting this type of experience. Many residents stood sullenly on their porches around the square on which the event took place but never ventured over. They complained about the noise and the outsiders who were invading their space. Many were aware of all the contestation about the festival. Moreover, the craft and food booths recruited by the hired multicultural specialist sold expensive items aimed at the upscale diversity seekers. The festival appealed to "downtown" multiculturalists, for whom these festivals provide moments of safe passage into Philadelphia's impoverished communities, transformed for the moment into interesting sites of cultural diversity to be enjoyed and experienced and used to satisfy voyeuristic curiosity.

While the poor whites were relegated to pluralist national-heritage categories, elements of anti-racist, anti-imperialist discourses organized another component of the festival, in which all people of color were constructed as oppressed and whites were implicitly on the other side. In the Spanish space of West Kensington, which is dominated by Puerto Rican institutions, leaders trace their oppression to the imperialist U.S. state that colonized them after the war with Spain in 1898. Racism is talked about not only in terms of skin color but in terms of exclusions based on language (English vs. Spanish), citizenship status (voluntary vs. colonized), and poverty. In all these polarities, whites are seen as opposed to Puerto Ricans and associated with actions of the U.S. state. In narratives of everyday life, distrust of whites and fear of racist actions are carried over in a careful marking of spaces and institutions as white-controlled and threatening or non-white and safe for Latinos (Goode 1998).

This anti-racist, anti-imperialist ideology has been an important part of the mobilization of the Puerto Rican civil rights movement since the Young Lords movement in the 1970s (Whalen 1998). Political solidarity resulted in a successful series of actions, including a voting rights lawsuit to redraw a state senatorial district, campaigns for fairness in the criminal justice system, and hearings before the Human Relations Commission about the underrepresentation of Latinos in public-sector jobs. Yet each victory required cross-racial alliances as the next step. For example, while court-enforced legislative redistricting created the first Puerto Rican–dominated electoral district, the bulk of Latino elected officials depend on alliances with both whites and blacks in the political party structure. These alliances have culminated in greater presence of Latinos in the organization of Mayor John Street, who was elected in 1999.

In high-poverty Kensington, Korean merchants and Palestinian merchants and landlords have played important economic roles while whites, Latinos, and blacks shared poverty. This local reality refuted the simplistic opposition between powerful whites and powerless minorities. Why did the CDC leadership insist on inserting this race-based construction of power into the festival? First and foremost, this was a way of resisting the manner in which the NHRP pluralism theme totally ignored the salience of race in discourses of difference. While sticking to the pluralist mandate in the contested issue of language for the flyers, the leadership added on this segment to counteract the hegemonic ideology of pluralist equality.

Second, this was an attempt to reach out to the economically powerful local Koreans and Palestinians in order to solicit feelings of solidarity with them through depicting shared victimization by U.S. oppression. The organizers invited several Koreans and Palestinians to participate by donating food, goods, and performances. The Koreans and Palestinians, seeing themselves as entrepreneurs whose success separated them politically and economically from neighborhood residents, declined. At the event, these populations were nevertheless represented by films shown during the event that depicted their nations of origin as victims of U.S. imperialism. In attempting to use this pluralist event to communicate a broader political message, the anti-racist framework pushed whites out of collective solidarity with poor Latinos (and blacks) and into the category of those who needed to confront their complicity in U.S. racism and imperialism.[22]

The CDC learned an important lesson from the festival, which engendered a lot of local criticism. Residents complained that the performances and exhibits were not interesting to them. One white church group that had been actively involved with the CDC pulled away. Another group of recent, white Eastern European refugee families felt that their exhibit had been maligned and withdrew from collaborative activities. In the weeks after the event, several meetings were held to critique it. The next year, after much reflection about the festival, a simple neighborhood fair occurred. All references to diversity and narratives of cultural difference were removed. Events to celebrate the neighborhood's strength and projects still occur a decade later.

These celebrations of multiculturalism fail to address the threat of racial incidents in these changing communities. They appeal to human relations specialists, who enjoy the consumption of diversity because they avoid direct confrontations of race and power. In their practice, such events not only fail to achieve their goals but they backfire, reinforcing categories of difference and creating situations in which anti-racist, anti-imperialist rhetoric is deployed in contexts in which the target is not the state or capital but their fellow community members. This case demonstrates that attempts to use U.S. narratives of difference based on liberal pluralism are not merely ineffective, but they disrupt the fragile cross-racial political alliances developing in these neighborhoods. The CDC festival is an example of how a cross-race class mobilization was disrupted. The mosaic model generated the problems with the language on the flyer. Yet in resisting the exclusion of race, the festival at the same time used anti-imperialist discourse to separate white activists from people of color in an attempt to establish commonality with powerful and threatening local immigrant entrepreneurs. This temporarily broke down the fragile alliance between poor whites and people of color.

Producing White Defensiveness

If liberal pluralist events do not work because they ignore race and class, what happens when professionals confront race directly? Here again, liberal state and civil authorities (e.g., human relations specialists, clergy, and teachers) argue for therapeutic psychological interventions aimed at presumed low self-esteem in poor people. Their racist acting out is attributed to these psychological inadequacies. While liberal pluralism sees the flawed individual to be ignorant and the cure to be cross-cultural aesthetic experience, here the flaw is low self-esteem, and the primary cure involves workshop training to teach poor white people to purge their racist ideas. Pluralist events are directed toward all populations, while anti-racism workshops target working-class whites so that "racism" can be excised through a regime of rebuilding egos coupled with teaching self-censorship, conflict resolution skills, and the transfer of other skills for self-governance (Cruikshank 1993). A shared repertoire of generic, "one size fits all" techniques is employed, based on the assumption that once "processed" through a workshop, the individual's behaviors and attitudes will be transformed. Rooting out the racism of poor and working-class whites appeals to state professionals because it displaces the responsibility for racism from institutions of power onto individuals and requires no structural change.

Over the course of the two years of fieldwork, we observed over twenty of these workshops. The goal was to "get inside" individuals clustered in small, artificially constructed groups, by "opening them up" through ice-breaking games and role-play exercises that would instantly improve understanding and empathy. Individuals were asked to make contact either literally (through touching) or figuratively through self-revelatory games. The key was to get people to develop self-esteem. Yet they had to do this in the face of the obvious disdain of workshop presenters. Human relations workers ascribed personal flaws to these white residents who did not dress well and who used dated and tainted group labels such as "Oriental" and "Negro." This implicit class contempt was what had helped produce white working-class racism in the first place, as people displaced their abjection onto people of color.

At one professional's vaunted workshop, which was identically performed in three different localities, the audience was exhorted to "say uh oh to the uh oh," meaning that by carefully censoring one's thoughts, one could eliminate racism. The message was that we are all flawed individuals who can be cured by rooting out our internal evil. The historical and structural processes that nurture the roots of this evil currently and in earlier periods were totally ignored. Experts were also ignorant of the ways in which local events underpinned conflict or created collaboration. They allowed no openings for local knowledge and understandings of these relationships.

Recall the earlier examples of how poor whites who were engaged in close relationships or political struggle with people of color often developed a consciousness of how race works against their neighbors. The following example illustrates the development of such a consciousness in two Olney residents and the ways in which it was stifled in the context of a mobilization against realtor practices. The campaign was being organized by a group of liberal clergy, teachers, and social service workers who saw racism as a disease of poor whites.

In Olney in the late 1980s, the number of realtors operating in the community had increased from four to twenty, as illegal techniques to promote sales played on fears of racial turnover and loss of property values.[23] In an effort to monitor and fight against these illegal tactics, these liberal workers, who were not residents of the neighborhood, were trying to organize the neighborhood. They were unaware, however, of the growing and significant interracial networks of women described above. Furthermore, they viewed all poor white residents as ignorant and unreasonable and all people of color as powerless victims.

Yet in Olney, even more than in high-poverty Kensington, the class relations between whites and non-whites did not fit the national narrative that conflates race and class location. Whites were poorer than many influential people of color, who were significant players in the local economy and political structure. In fact, the residential turnover the group observed was not occurring as a result of white flight, since most of the whites remaining could not afford to leave. It was more a result of moves to the suburbs by upwardly mobile people of color. In addition, many new immigrants were active as realtors and landlords. Their actions were contributing to the turnover.

The issue of differential investment power had underpinned a major conflict over Korean-language signs that had occurred several years before. The shopping strip, a major center of local social life, had been significantly transformed by immigrant investment. This led to restricted access to much of the space on the strip. Residents were being increasingly excluded from important public space as a result of the expansion of a Korean-only sector of retail and wholesale stores, which were locked and opened only for Korean customers.[24] Citywide Korean business organizations, whose political contributions gave them access to city government, had gone directly to city agencies for permission to erect Korean-language street signs, marking this space as Koreatown. Local residents saw this as a new example of their powerlessness in controlling meaningful community space. Local civic groups saw control of local space as their bailiwick and were angry at being bypassed. Clearly, the economic and political clout of an immigrant group that didn't play by local rules was resented.

On the day that the *Philadelphia Inquirer* ran an article headlined "Olney to Become Koreatown," the signs were vandalized. The article highlighted the Korean business leaders intent to make the area a Korean service center for Korean merchants and customers from throughout the Middle Atlantic. The street signs had been requested to orient merchants from out of town. Ignoring the economic and political issues that clearly undergirded these actions, city human rights specialists had responded with multicultural festivals and training in self-esteem and conflict resolution.

At the same time, less-powerful local Korean merchants, whose outlets depended on a mixed customer base, were angry at not being consulted by citywide Korean leaders. Rosemary, active in the local merchant association, had developed close relationships with several of these merchants. While Korean merchants had until now belonged to a separate local organization, Rosemary talked to several Korean store owners whom she saw as facing the same struggles against larger-scale businesses and brought two of them onto the board of the local merchant association. She spoke up for these local merchants at the public meetings in the wake of the crisis, describing them as part of the community. She said later, "I took a lot of heat at that meeting but I couldn't sit there and let them be blamed. These guys are working for the community and they belong here as much as I do." She had spoken to all levels of merchants and often spoke in private about the difference between the powerful actors in the citywide business group, whom she saw as responsible for the incident, and the locally embedded merchants with whom she had a great deal in common.

Linda was another local resident for whom the sign incident was a watershed. Linda was a gregarious, sympathetic person. Her problematic marriage to a man who tried to limit her contact with non-whites did not deter her from her from crossing boundaries every day. Her experience as a local day-care provider for diverse parents on the block, her church work work as a lay home visitor, and her service as a committeeperson for a political party all involved her in home visits with her multiracial neighbors, providing health care referrals, spiritual aid, and constituent service. She counted dozens of minority and immigrant families in her personal network and had an active social life involving constant celebrations of family life-cycle events. Unlike the sponsors of diversity festivals, she understood the actual diversity of immigrant cultural practices. Both Rosemary and Linda daily crossed boundaries between racially defined populations and between established residents and newcomers, in activities that they interpreted as building community in the face of economic and political pressures. They saw the locally embedded Korean merchants and struggling immigrant households as sharing their stake in the local community.

The professionals organizing the anti-realtor movement saw things differently. In discussions about strategy, race and class were conflated. All people of color were stereotyped as struggling and powerless in contrast to white residents: "Immigrants are powerless, they live in a world where decisions of power are made everyday without them." "They come with the clothes on their backs and live on one bag of rice a year." There was no recognition that some immigrants had the resources to manipulate local real estate markets and create political power.

In an interview with one of the local clergy who later took a role in the anti-realtor campaign, I asked what he thought of the local community leadership's view of the sign incident, which condemned the vandalism as inappropriate and uncivil but saw the grievance as justifiable and related to issues of local versus elite power. He responded, "That's true of course, but it is not important. We cannot do anything here if we do not root out the racism in these people first." He did not see that common struggles for the community might ultimately be more useful in ending racism. Nor did he see that failing to listen to the analysis of local white leaders while bringing in programs that pointed the finger at their racism would create resentment.

Rosemary and Linda became active in the anti-destabilization campaign after the non-resident organizers requested an endorsement for the campaign from the major civic umbrella organization. Before this request was made, as they strategized about confronting the civic group, the organizers talked about their expectation that they would either be physically ejected or verbally shouted down by a racist rabble. They were very surprised to find that the local white residents wanted to preserve a mixed population as much as they did. The campaign for ethical real estate practices was unanimously endorsed, and Linda and Rosemary were recruited as volunteers. The two were experts in local life. They had a keen understanding of local power and control. Aware that an immigrant realtor/landlord was acting to encourage people to move from a cluster of blocks in which he had an interest, they wanted to include his actions in the group's agenda for intervention. This ran counter to the campaign leaders' construction of all immigrants as powerless and the view that criticizing any action by people of color revealed the psychological disease of racism. At one meeting, the women presented the issue but were ignored. At the next meeting, their comments were silenced by statements such as "We can't talk about [immigrant realtors], its too close to racism." The two women left the meeting early and never came back. After they left, one of the men said, "They were so good during the Korean sign incident, but tonight you could see their fundamental racism." As all nodded their heads in agreement, it was as if they were relieved to find their diagnosis of racism had been confirmed.

The two women had been publicly critical of the behavior of a racially different immigrant. The leaders saw their role as protecting powerless immigrants from white racists. They reacted accordingly. This had a disastrous consequence. The all-white leadership of the real estate action group continually worried about the racial inclusiveness of their organization. While they talked constantly about their enjoyment of diversity in the neighborhood, they had no close relationships with local people of color. Instead, they sought endorsements from citywide leaders of the appropriate minority categories: a Latino councilman, a Korean business broker, and so forth. These were people who were publicly visible and accessible through their staffs. The symbolic use of their names by the campaign had limited use. In the case of the business broker, who was heavily involved in sales contributing to turnover on the strip, it was even hypocritical.

The campaign needed workers to sustain it. It could have served as a major action that brought people together across racial boundaries to support their common local commitment. Instead, white activists whose developed political subjectivity had crossed racial boundaries were cast as flawed, racist individuals, rather than as women whose interracial social networks were essential to a successful campaign. The best opportunity for recruiting local residents of color to the campaign would have been through Rosemary and Linda, who had intensive and extensive relationships among them. Now they felt driven out of the mobilization. The anti-realtor campaign was an ideal vehicle for a class-based, cross-racial movement to prevent real estate brokers from promoting population turnover, which was a factor that weakened the formation of block organizations and local campaigns for better schools and city services. The organizers, conflating race and class, ignored the relative class positions of the white residents and the people of color from whom they recruited endorsements. This ultimately undermined the emergence of class politics as well as local participation in the campaign.

Conclusion: Toward a New Multiculturalism

We must be wary of the appropriation of multiculturalism by powerful institutions that create discourses denying the significance of poverty and racial inequality in their desire discursively to create a myth of equality through aesthetic cultural equivalence. We must also avoid the pitfalls of overreliance on simplistic oppositions between whites and peoples of color that conflate racial and class dynamics. Similarly, we must avoid the discourses of individual blame that define racism as a personal condition, created by ignorance, fear, and low self-esteem, and that seek to "cure" it through festivals and workshops while ignoring the role of the state and capital in creating the structures that shape both material realities and corresponding social constructions.

Returning to Ester's forced identity choice, which opened this essay, we can see that Ester felt compromised by the discrepancy between the Puerto Rican rhetoric of racism and her own newly politicized subjectivity as part of a multiracial coalition engaged in a local struggle for a better life. There is no question that Ester had experienced acts of racism throughout her life and that structural racism persists in making the overall material conditions of life for poor people of color generally worse than they are for whites. It is understandable that Ester would overcome her ambivalence to side with outspoken Latino activists. The Latina speaker engaged in "getting whites to understand their racism" had a worthy and necessary goal.

Yet, as Lynd's comments about action and experience indicate, this rhetorical tactic at public events parallels those of the organizers Lynd criticizes, who expect to change people "by preaching door to door." It fails to convince these poor whites that they should be scapegoats for all local problems. Instead, we must look toward strengthening the role that common political struggle itself plays in the transformation of people's political identities, in the hope of ultimately strengthening this struggle.

In the cases described above, professional human relations experts who were promoters of local political activism failed to see how their solutions disrupted developing but fragile cross-racial, politicized identities created by local activism. By ignoring the complex power relations of local situations in favor of standard national discourses on race, and by preferring treatments that emphasized the blame and reform of flawed local residents, these experts strengthened racial boundaries and masked the role of class in complicating the nature of local racial relationships.

In all three cases discussed, group tensions were blamed on individual flaws—ignorance and fear of other cultures or racism produced by low self-esteem. Festivals and workshops were used to "cure" individuals while leaving formative conditions intact. The NHRP, which sponsored two multicultural events discussed above, was run by a quasi-state institution funded by local corporations. It encouraged the use of depoliticizing multicultural appreciation festivals, which pushed the locally salient issues of race, class, and power underground. The professionals who initiated the anti-realtor campaign ignored local realities in constructing all whites as privileged and powerful and all people of color as deprived and powerless.

Yet, in each case, the local implementation of such false assumptions led local residents to react to both sanitized portrayals of cultural equivalence and conflations of race and class by reinserting ideas about inequality and hierarchy in ways that either reinforced racial boundaries or ignored local situations of inequality. These reactive processes further reinforced the negative pressures on developing class-based coalitions.

In the parish festival, the priest organizers reinscribed a racialized hierarchy by marking immigrants as exotic and subordinate. Established residents asserted identities as patriotic white Americans in the face of subtle displays of immigrant economic and cultural capital. Latinos asserted national identities and created moral hierarchy within the pan-ethnic Latino social space.

The non-resident clergy, teachers, and human relations workers who began the anti-realtor campaign were doomed to failure because they neglected to examine local relationships of race and class. They diagnosed Rosemary and Linda, newly politicized agents, as racists in need of therapy. In this case, the nuances of class difference in speech and dress contributed to the social construction. Rosemary and Linda exhibited speech patterns and dress codes that marked them as working-class. The gendered nature of the social spaces and institutions in which they operated created further ignorance of their local knowledge, social networks, and actions as anti-racist political actors.

In contrast, the struggling CDC managed to overcome the negative effects of its festival experience. Here the NHRP message was carried through, intact, in the multicultural appreciation component. For this neighborhood, however, ideas about race and power that were central to public discourse could not be silenced. Yet the ways in which they were inserted into the festival, without taking class relations into account, created problems. The powerful immigrant entrepreneurs were symbolically represented through films of oppression in a way that both they and poor whites rejected. In this case, however, the leadership realized the problems the festival had engendered and took steps to restore their activist collaborations and common local cause in future celebrations.

In each case, both the powerful institutions that sought to depoliticize and maintain order and those promoting local political activism produced events that failed to link issues of race to class and power. The possibility of effective poor people's political action requires cross-racial alliance building at every level. To enable this, we must create a new multiculturalism that goes beyond simplistic cultural equivalence or a simple opposition of white and other. Such a turn requires attention to locally nuanced class and power relations.

NOTES

I would like to thank Jeff Maskovsky for his insightful comments on this essay and Susan Hyatt for her contributions to my thinking about poor women's political activism. I am also indebted to my fellow fieldworkers on the Philadelphia Changing Relations Project, especially Jo Anne Schneider, Suzanne Blanc, and Cynthia Ninivaggi.

1. In the summer of 1988, two killings, one month apart, involving groups of white and Puerto Rican teenagers filled the Philadelphia media. In the first case, the perpetrators were Puerto Rican and the victim white. In the second, it was the reverse. A full discussion of the nuances of these incidents can be found in Goode and Schneider (1994:195–206).

2. All personal names have been changed to pseudonyms.

3. Philadelphia has long supported groups promoting tolerance. As the seat of the Society of Friends, the legacy of William Penn's "city of brotherly love" is frequently referred to as a tradition. The city created one of the first human relations commissions (1952), and even before, in 1947, an active Fellowship Commission was formed to promote racial tolerance. During our fieldwork, we encountered dozens of locally generated programs that had emerged from the civil rights era and were tied to the Urban League, Urban Coalition, the Society of Friends, the Cardinal's Commission on Human Relations, and the Jewish Community Relations Council, among others.

4. According to Massey and Denton (1993), the black poverty rate is two to three times the white poverty rate. In the neighborhoods described in this essay, however, the upwardly mobile blacks who have broken the color line tend to have higher levels of income and education than the downwardly mobile whites they have joined. The same is true for immigrant Latino and Asian households who also tend to have higher levels of income and education.

5. The Philadelphia Changing Relations Project was part of the national Changing Relations Project supported by the Ford Foundation. It was comprised of six city projects and used ethnographic data to look at the changing relations between new immigrants and established residents in each of the cities (Bach 1993; Lamphere 1992; and Lamphere et al. 1994).

6. Seventy-five percent of all manufacturing jobs disappeared in the two decades between 1955 and 1975 (Adams et al. 1991), through plant closings or relocation of work to the suburbs, Sun Belt, or out of the country. Summers and Luce (1988) show that more jobs left for the suburbs from Philadelphia than from forty-two comparable U.S. cities. Withdrawal of federal aid also hit this city harder than comparable urban areas. In 1979, 25.5 percent of the budget came from federal aid; by 1988, this had dropped to 7.5 percent (Goode and Schneider 1994:30–31).

7. Yet this entails severe competition for the consumption of history, culture, and the arts with nearby cities such as New York, Washington, D.C., and Baltimore.

8. Philadelphia was an important destination for Irish and German immigrants in the early period of the nineteenth century as well as for southern and eastern Europeans during the turn-of-the-century expansion of industrial capitalism.

9. For a discussion of this process nationally, see Brodkin (1998).

10. Philadelphia has always had a large black population relative to other American cities, housing a significant free black population before and after the Civil War (Du Bois 1992; Ignatiev 1995).

11. Even with overall population loss, between 1980 and 1990, the Latino and Asian populations increased by 40 percent and 145 percent, respectively (Goode and Schneider 1994:49).

12. In the last decade, the local school population shifted from mostly lower-middle-class households to a majority of families who are eligible for anti-poverty programs.

13. As long-term residents left in the 1970s, the city's incipient Puerto Rican settlement began to shift eastward to Kensington, forming a buffer between white Kensington and blacks further west. Today, most of the city's Spanish-speaking peoples are clustered in an intermediate band of space now stretching from the poorest tracts in Kensington northward to Olney.

14. During our fieldwork, there were several formal collective efforts by white residents to welcome and organize new neighbors, including a welcome wagon–type program that used local high school students who were children of immigrants to translate information packets into immigrant languages; a campaign to get all established residents to bring one immigrant neighbor to a meeting; and a door-to-door recruitment campaign for people of color.

15. For the past two decades, there has been a growing literature on women as community builders and political activists, making demands for concessions by the state in this era when the state has withdrawn services from poor communities (Bookman and Morgen 1988; Susser 1982). Many had learned political organizing skills as participants in the Civil Rights and Welfare Rights movements (Piven and Cloward 1979), as well as through the Community Action Program (CAP) of the War on Poverty. Such activism has been studied among poor white women (Susser 1982), African American women (Naples 1998; Stack 1996; Hyatt 1997 and chapter 8, above), and Latino women (Pardo 1998; Naples 1998). Like these women, the women we encountered from different racial categories in Philadelphia were creating alliances to promote their family and community interests.

16. The cash-strapped school district had responded to overcrowded schools in the neighborhood in a way that did not cost money but actually produced income. Instead of rehabilitating buildings to add local space and preserve residentially integrated schools, they bused children (a one-hour trip) to a distant all-white area to integrate those schools and bring in desegregation moneys.

17. Instead of building new buildings, the district converted older local structures into annexes for existing schools.

18. For further discussion of this, see Takaki (1979), Goode (2001), and Merry (2001).

19. The funding for the NHRP projects came from a consortium of developers and corporate leaders who were active in many of the city's public-private partnerships, with strong interests in urban peace. The program was administered by the Urban League.

20. People married before World War II often spoke about pressures to marry within national heritage groups. One woman with Irish ancestry spoke about her husband's German-origin family never accepting her. Murray Dubin (1996) describes the frequent comments about the first "mixed" marriage between an Irish man and a non-Irish woman in another area. For several generations, Italian-origin peoples maintained regional endogamy, emphasizing Sicilian, Calabrese, or Abruzzese origin (Goode et al. 1984). Couples married after the war did not experience these pressures. For white Catholics who belonged to nationality-based parishes, early social life took place in social spaces with common national origins. Archdiocesan high schools, however, were fed by all the nationality parish schools and had a major effect on these early practices of national endogamy.

21. Joking banter about being "one-eighth Irish, one-eighth Italian, and one-eighth Polish, and gosh knows everything else" was frequently heard.

22. Blacks were often seen by Latinos as similar to whites. As far as their contacts with city agencies were concerned, blacks had a lot of power in the political system and held many visible public jobs. They were seen as more successful in taking advantage of affirmative action mechanisms. In the festival, they also were not present as participants but were represented by museum exhibits.

23. The increase in realtors was accompanied by increasing reports of churning activities to increase sales, which violated Human Relations Commission rules: unreasonable solicitation through postcards and phone calls, the use of references to and photos of people of color, steering clients to particular blocks and away from others, and excessive use of sale signage.

24. One community leader reported knocking on the door of a Korean dress store while soliciting advertisements for local publication. She was told, "This store is for Koreans only and besides you cannot afford our clothes." This single comment reinforced her feeling of exclusion from her local space and her sense of class resentment.

REFERENCES

Adams, Carolyn, David Bartelt, David Elesh, Ira Goldstein, Nancy Kleniewski, and William Yancey
1991   *Philadelphia: Neighborhoods, Division, and Conflict in a Postindustrial City.* Philadelphia: Temple University Press.

Bach, Robert
1993   *Changing Relations: Newcomers and Established Residents in U.S. Communities*. New York: Ford Foundation.

Basch, Linda, Nina Glick Schiller, and Cristina Szanton-Blanc
1994   *Nations Unbound*. Langhorne, PA: Gordon and Breach.

Bookman, Ann, and Sandra Morgen, eds.
1988   *Women and the Politics of Empowerment*. Philadelphia: Temple University Press.

Brodkin, Karen
1998   *How Jews Became White Folks and What This Says about Race in America*. New Brunswick: Rutgers University Press.

Chock, Phyllis
1995   Culturalism: Pluralism, Culture and Race in the Harvard Encyclopedia of American Ethnic Groups. In Virginia Dominguez, ed., *(Multi)Culturalisms and the Baggage of "Race." Identities* 1(4):301–24.

Cruikshank, Barbara
1993   Revolutions Within: Self-Government and Self-Esteem. *Economy and Society* 22(3):327–44.

Dubin Murray
1996   *South Philadelphia: Mummer, Memories and the Melrose Diner*. Philadelphia: Temple University Press.

Du Bois, W.E.B.
1992   *The Philadelphia Negro*. Philadelphia: University of Pennsylvania Press.

Goldstein, Ira
1986   The Wrong Side of the Tracts: A Study of Residential Segregation in Philadelphia. Ph.D. dissertation, Temple University.

Goode, Judith
1998   Contingent Construction of Local Identities: Koreans and Puerto Ricans in Philadelphia. *Identities* 5(1):33–64.
2001   Teaching Against Cultural Essentialism. In Ida Susser and Thomas C. Patterson, eds., *Cultural Diversity in the United States*. Malden, MA: Blackwell, 434–56.

Goode, Judith, Karen Curtis, and Janet Theophano
1984   Meal Formats, Meal Cycles, and Menu Negotiation in the Maintenance of an Italian-American Community. In Mary Douglas, ed., *Food and the Social Order*. New York: Russell Sage Foundation, 143–218.

Goode, Judith, and JoAnne Schneider
1994   *Reshaping Ethnic and Racial Relations in Philadelphia: Immigrants in a Divided City*. Philadelphia: Temple University Press.

Gregory, Steven
1998   *Black Corona.* Princeton: Princeton University Press.

Hartigan, John Jr.
1999   *Racial Situations: Class Predicaments of Whiteness in Detroit.* Princeton: Princeton University Press.

Hyatt, Susan Brin
1997   Policy in a Post-Welfare Landscape: Tenant Management Policies, Self-Governance and the Democratization of Knowledge in Great Britain. In Sue Wright and Chris Shore, eds., *The Anthropology of Policy.* London: Routledge.

Ignatiev, Noel
1995   *How the Irish Became White.* New York: Routledge.

Lamphere, Louise, ed.
1992   *Structuring Diversity.* Chicago: University of Chicago Press.

Lamphere, Louise, Alex Stepick, and Guillermo Grenier, eds.
1994   *Newcomers in the Workplace.* Philadelphia: Temple University Press.

Lynd, Staughton
2000   Overcoming Racism. *Monthly Review* 51:16–23.

Massey, Douglas, and Nancy A. Denton
1993   *American Apartheid: Segregation and the Making of the Underclass.* Cambridge: Harvard University Press.

Merry, Sally
1986   *Urban Danger.* Philadelphia: Temple University Press.
2001   Racialized Identities and the Law. In Ida Susser and Thomas Patterson, eds., *Cultural Diversity in the United States.* Malden, MA: Blackwell, 120–39.

Naples, Nancy A.
1998   *Grassroots Warriors: Activist Mothering, Community Work and the War on Poverty.* New York: Routledge.

Pardo, Mary S.
1998   *Mexican American Women Activists: Identity and Resistance in Two Los Angeles Communities.* Philadelphia: Temple University Press.

Piven, Frances Fox, and Richard Cloward
1979   *Poor People's Movements: Why They Succeed and How They Fail.* New York: Vintage Books.

Rieder, Jonathan
1985   *Canarsie: The Jews and Italians of Brooklyn against Liberalism.* Cambridge: Harvard University Press.

Roediger, David
1990   *The Wages of Whiteness: Race and the Making of the American Working Class.* London: Verso.

Sacks, Karen Brodkin
1994   How Did Jews Become White Folks? In S. Gregory and R. Sanjek, eds., *Race*.
New Brunswick: Rutgers University Press.

Sanjek, Roger.
1998   *The Future of Us All*. Ithaca, NY: Cornell University Press.

Stack, Carol
1996   *Call to Home: African Americans Reclaim the Rural South*. New York: Basic
Books.

Steinberg, Stephen
1981   *The Ethnic Myth: Race, Ethnicity and Class in America*. New York: Atheneum.

Summers, Anita, and Thomas Luce
1988   Economic Report on the Philadelphia Metropolitan Area, 1988. Philadelphia: University of Pennsylvania Press.

Susser, Ida
1992   *Norman Street: Poverty and Politics in an Urban Neighborhood*. New York:
Columbia University Press.

Takaki, Ronald
1979   *Iron Cages: Race and Culture in Nineteenth Century America*. New York: Alfred A. Knopf.

Whalen, Carmen
1998   Bridging Homeland and Barrio Politics: The Young Lords in Philadelphia.
In Andrew Torres and Jose Velasquez, eds., *The Puerto Rican Movement:
Voices from the Barrio*. Philadelphia: Temple University Press.

Williams, Brackette
1989   A Class Act: Anthropology and the Race to Nation across Ethnic Terrain.
Annual Review of Anthropology 18:401–44.

Chapter 14

From Plant Closing to Political Movement

Challenging the Logic of Economic Destruction in Tennessee

Eve S. Weinbaum

In the 1980s and 1990s, plant closings all across the United States became the local tragedies of the "global economy." The trend was most pronounced in economically disadvantaged regions of the South, where low-wage and labor-intensive industries had clustered. Towns and their citizens were impoverished and destabilized as companies that had anchored the community fled to distant shores where labor was cheap and land plentiful.

These plant closings, worker dislocations, and the poverty that results are most commonly understood as an inevitable process, integral to the transition from a backward industrial economy to a new, progressive, "postindustrial" age. The workers suffering from job loss and displacement are seen at best as victims caught in an economic sea change and at worst as people who should have prepared themselves for the impending transition, even people who are pitiful for their lack of education and misunderstanding of their own plight.

This essay, based on ethnographic research in Appalachian Tennessee, portrays a very different reality. I investigate the process of economic change in a small Southern community, the type of place considered least likely to be able to challenge "inevitable" economic forces spelling its doom. In Clarksville, the tragedy of the Acme Boot Company plant closing was real. But the Acme workers were not passive victims of the market's invisible hand. They fought capital mobility, and although they did not win, their accomplishments were impressive. They not only educated a community about the global economy, political process, trade policy, and tax code; they also overturned an important corporate loophole and saved American taxpayers millions of dollars. Their story shows that when there are strong unions committed to organizing workers in conjunction with the communities in which they work, many positive consequences are possible. Working people are able to see their plight in a far broader international context, to use national legislative forums to challenge corporate flight, and to create organized campaigns to fight what many have called unstoppable, the global flight of capital and the impoverishment of working-class communities. Given the right organizational assistance, these low-income workers proved they had the ideas and the stamina to take on the largest issues of economic development policy, free-trade politics, and global poverty. They also had the ability to emerge victorious from some, if not all, of these fights, and in so doing, to set the stage for further victories.

For sixty-five years, the Acme Boot Company had been not only the largest employer in Clarksville, Tennessee, but a source of pride and recognition for the community. Then, in 1993, Acme closed, devastating the local economy. By all accounts, it was still an extremely profitable corporation. But like many manufacturers in the apparel and footwear industries, Acme had moved nearly all its production offshore, subcontracting most of it to other manufacturers. The story of Acme Boot's departure from Tennessee is not an account of a company succumbing to tragic but inexorable trends of the global economy. In fact, Acme's conduct in the 1980s and 1990s reveals the opposite. This case study demonstrates how both private and public policies and investment decisions—decisions made by Acme's owners, other corporate executives, and local and national political leaders—transformed economic opportunities, individual lives, and entire communities. And the story of the workers who mobilized against a seemingly inevitable sequence of events exposes the barriers to—but also the possibilities for—democracy and collective action in the context of this political economy.

The Story of Acme Boot

In 1929, the Acme Shoe Company began to manufacture shoes and boots in Clarksville, Tennessee, a small Appalachian city on the Kentucky border. It was founded in Clarksville when its original owners, Jessel and Sidney Cohn, moved the company from Chicago to Tennessee, in an early example of capital mobility. One analyst says the Cohns moved to Clarksville "to take advantage of an exceptional work force."[1] More likely, they were moving south in search of a non-union environment, high unemployment, and a pool of willing and desperate workers in a region with singularly high poverty rates.[2] Acme's beginnings in Tennessee were perhaps an omen: in 1993, Acme would become a "runaway shop" once again. The Cohns turned Acme into a profitable and productive company, and by the late 1930s, they were shipping millions of shoes and boots all over the world. By 1969, five large Acme Boot plants operated throughout the state's rural areas. Throughout the 1970s and 1980s this region of Middle Tennessee produced up to 90 percent of the nation's supply of cowboy boots.[3] Thousands of workers made boots under brand names such as Dingo, Dan Post, Corcoran, and Luchesse. Acme produced the highest-quality casual, dress, military, and cowboy boots, maintaining a loyal clientele in each sector of the boot market and marketing their products worldwide in expensive advertising campaigns featuring celebrities like Joe Namath and O.J. Simpson.[4] Acme was not only the largest manufacturer of western boots in the world but was considered "the Tiffany's of the western boot business."[5]

As recently as 1990, the Clarksville plant alone employed about fifteen hundred people.[6] The company was considered a good citizen and a responsible employer. People in Clarksville remembered how, during the Great Depression, demand had dried up and production was halted. Rather than lay off their employees, however, Acme's owners sent the workers out to cut the grass or paint the building every day, in order to keep them on the payroll as long as possible.[7] To the community, this symbolized the company's commitment to its workers and their families. Other businesses came and went with mixed records, but Acme was seen as a constructive and distinguished participant in the life of Clarksville.

Unlike most factories in rural Tennessee, Acme Boot had been unionized for over three decades. When the Philadelphia and Reading Corporation purchased Acme from the Cohns in 1956, it had cut wages, from about $46 down to $42 a week.[8] In response, the workers began a unionization drive, with support from the United Rubber Workers International Union. After a long organizing campaign, they succeeded in negotiating their first contract in 1962 and became Local 330. With the United Rubber Workers (URW)[9] representing Acme workers throughout the state, the workers were able to achieve steady gains in wages and working conditions, but these gains were the product of much struggle. Throughout the 1960s and 1970s, the union was forced repeatedly to demonstrate its strength. Walkouts and other job actions were common, and the longest strike, in the mid-1970s, lasted eighteen weeks. A leader of the union at that time says, "We stood up for the union then, and that's when we got most of our recognition at that time. They didn't doubt us no more."[10]

By 1980, Acme's employees had won decent working conditions and insurance; they were treated fairly and relatively well paid. Many workers had left family farms or coal mines to work at Acme, migrating to Clarksville from Middle Tennessee and southeastern Kentucky. Jobs at Acme promised better wages, shorter hours, health insurance, the protections of a union contract, and more opportunities for family members in the surrounding community. By all accounts, the workforce in Clarksville was extremely dedicated and loyal. Acme had a very low absentee rate and a low turnover rate—in 1992, the average employee's tenure was twenty-two years.

Plant Closing

In 1985, Northwest Industries, which had assumed ownership of Acme Boot in 1969, was taken over by Farley Industries, a privately held Chicago conglomerate owned by industrialist William Farley, a high-profile takeover specialist who already owned several large companies.[11] Farley bought Northwest Industries, a far-flung conglomerate, for $1.4 billion in what was the largest leveraged buyout to date. The sale, which included only $14 million in equity and the rest in debt financing, was financed by Michael Milken of Drexel Burnham Lambert. A diversified company with interests in automotive components, railroad parts, apparel, and footwear, best known for its Fruit of the Loom brand name, Farley Industries' annual revenue was over $3.5 billion by 1990.[12] Farley himself was known as "Chicago's poster boy for the demise of junk bond–financed leveraged buyouts."[13]

Farley's empire was threatened with several bankruptcies and negotiated several corporate reorganizations throughout the 1990s. Acme was not threatened, for it was always considered to be "financially strong and viable and . . . not involved in the bankruptcy proceedings" that would affect many of Farley's and Northwest's holdings.[14] The parent company, however, was burdened with tremendous debt. Anxious to boost productivity and sales, to elevate profit levels in his strongest subsidiaries, Farley began to consider reorganizing Acme. He notified the workers and their union representatives that the shoe and boot industry in the United States had begun to change dramatically, and that Acme Boot must change along with it.

Industry analysts disagreed with Farley's assessment. Acme boasted productive and technologically advanced factories in a booming industry and was considered a very safe business investment.[15] While some parts of the domestic footwear industry had a gloomy outlook, the western boot sector was booming. There was almost no international competition or imports, and there was a growing market for American cowboy boots.[16] Yet, while most western boot plants in Tennessee were expanding production, Acme's Tennessee plants began to shrink or close.

Although his public statements assured Acme workers that the company would continue the excellent production standards set by previous owners, Farley's actions contradicted his stated goal. Acme Boot opened non-union, lower-wage plants in Texas, Mexico, and South America, and increasingly, the production work was done there, with boots returning to Tennessee only for finishing, repairs, and shipping. Farley decided to follow other companies' example in restructuring and "outsourcing."[17] As Acme Boot Company president Mike Vogel explained later, moving production to lower-cost sites was "part of our strategic marketing plan to put more emphasis on global sourcing and less emphasis on manufacturing."[18] Accordingly, at the same time that workers were being laid off and plants closed in Tennessee, Acme Boot Company was dramatically expanding its national advertising budget, which doubled in 1992 alone.[19] Eventually the company's primary activity would be to buy low-cost boots from makers in Latin America and elsewhere and then to advertise and market them under the Acme labels.[20] Acme workers in Tennessee felt the impact. By 1991, only the Clarksville plant remained, and with the union's assistance, many laid-off Acme workers from other parts of Tennessee had relocated to that town in order to keep their boot-making jobs.

Farley continued to advertise both himself and his company as friendly, committed to communities, and family-oriented. He visited Clarksville and talked with the workers. "He said his daddy belonged to a union—he worked at the post office—and he didn't have nothing against the union."[21] He promised the workers that all the changes he was making were in their best interests. Alan Buckner, a Clarksville native in his early fifties, was an active union member at the time, but since then he has left Acme for a job as a traveling salesman. He remembers, "I go back to what [Farley] told me when he first took over. He patted me on the back, he said, 'We're one happy family—and we're going to grow.' . . . I never forgot it."[22] Still, the workers had their suspicions. Sally Kellam was forty-eight and had worked at Acme Boot for over twenty-five years. Assuming she would stay at Acme until she retired, she had just moved into a relatively expensive house with her new husband. Kellam recalled, to her dismay, "things started to really change when that Farley Industries bought it out. When he came in here, he told us that he wasn't for the union, but he wouldn't work against it. [But] he must have really been against it, because he started making big changes."[23]

The union accepted Farley's demands for cuts, but to no avail. In 1986, in his first round of contract negotiations with the union, Farley demanded serious wage concessions. After a struggle, the union agreed to forgo wage increases for a full four years, until 1990. Their bonuses were eliminated. The production system was re-engineered, and some workers took huge cuts. Long-term workers saw their wages plummet from almost $14 an hour to $5.35.[24] Farley then cut benefits, and the union protested but went along, convinced that the changes would save members' jobs. The workers also conceded to major changes in work rules, resulting in significant speed-ups in the production process.

While workers' positions were eliminated, management's ranks were swelling. A new "Value Engineering" department was responsible for efficiency and management techniques. "We are trying to refocus the way in which we look at containing costs and how we go about reducing costs," said Vice President John Petrovich. "It will be the first time that we have an entire department devoted to taking the costs out of the boot."[25]

Farley persuaded the union to agree to considerable sacrifice by warning that, otherwise, jobs would be lost. "They threatened us, right away: 'Well, we'll just go to Mexico, or El Paso, or wherever—you take what we got to offer, and that's it.' And we did. . . . We could grouse and mumble all we wanted to, but it wouldn't do us any good."[26] The union leadership argued internally about how many concessions to accept. Buckner, Local 330's chief steward in the 1980s, remembers one particularly harsh round of negotiations, conducted while several other Acme plants were still in operation. "We went through negotiations to give concessions to keep the plants open. I tried at that time to get him [the union president] not to do it. I said they're going to close the plants anyways. But cuts and concessions came."[27] As Sally Kellam said, "We did this, you know, to save our jobs. We did everything to save our jobs. We made a lot of concessions."[28] This was not unusual in the downsizing epidemic of the 1980s and 1990s. Even the strongest unions were under extreme pressure to cut their own pay and benefits, and most members did not protest. As *New York Times* surveys showed, a great majority of workers across the country—82 percent of those polled—said they would work more hours, take fewer vacation days, or accept lesser benefits to keep their jobs.[29] Workers voted to go along with the concessions in the hope of helping the factory and saving their jobs and income. Farley seemed to be pleased with the results, and the bottom line showed the impact. By 1990, productivity had increased by a full 35 percent, and profits were higher than ever before.[30]

This good news from corporate headquarters meant no one at Acme was prepared for the bombshell of November 1992. Acme announced plans to close its last manufacturing plant in Clarksville. The workers were shocked. Wilma Mittendorf, a woman in her early fifties who worked as a boot piper and developed crippling repetitive-motion injuries in both wrists, expressed the general consensus: "None of us ever *dreamed* Acme Boot would close."[31] The company would lay off nearly six hundred people within three months, and production work would shift south, mostly to a new plant in Puerto Rico. Some management and supervisory personnel would move to Puerto Rico immediately to begin operations there. The company president tried to reassure the community that, although no manufacturing would remain in Clarksville, they would retain some managerial employees in corporate headquarters there. "Acme will continue to be in Clarksville. . . . Clarksville is home," he said.[32] The fired workers saw it differently.

The decision to close the Clarksville plant had been made in Farley's corporate offices in Chicago's Sears Tower. By 1992, Farley Industries was in serious financial trouble; it had defaulted on $3 billion in junk bonds (from a hostile takeover of West Point-Pepperell textile company), and Drexel Burnham, which had collapsed, was unable to bail out the company. Farley Inc. was liquidated under Chapter 7 bankruptcy, but Farley retained control of both Fruit of the Loom and West Point-Pepperell.[33] Industry analysts were unanimous about Farley Industries' troubles. "Farley is in this fix partly because he used debt to solve his past deals' problems. There are signs that this habit is wearing thin with investors."[34] Farley had huge debts to pay off, and Acme was called into service. Production had tripled in one year in El Paso (with much of the actual assembly work done across the border in Mexico, for much lower wages), and production facilities in Latin America were proving very profitable.[35] There was no longer any compelling reason for Farley to maintain relatively costly plants in Tennessee.

The closing proved to be a terrible hardship for the Clarksville community. Although no one got rich at Acme Boot, and the work was hard and often dangerous, they were some of the best jobs available. When the plant closed, the average employee was forty-seven years old and the average seniority was almost twenty-five years. The loss of work was a blow. Edna

Luttrell was fifty-six years old and had moved to Clarksville with her entire family thirty-four years before, from a farm in rural Stewart County. She had never finished middle school, but she was a hard worker and one of Acme's most senior and most valued employees when she lost her job. "It is horrible. You know, people don't realize what it's like to be in a situation like that, but you can't go out on the street and pick up a job. . . . The only thing you'd probably find was a fast-food restaurant, like McDonald's here. . . . [Even] some of 'em that's got education can't get a job, unless you're working for minimum wage. And you can't make a living off of that."[36] State agencies encouraged job training, but the workers were skeptical that they would find jobs afterward. "Jobs are really scarce around here. Everybody I've talked to so far . . . they can't find jobs."[37] Education did not seem to be the answer, either. "We got people that's been to college; they can't find no job."[38] Poverty rates were high in the area, and many workers had to swallow their pride and apply for public assistance for the first time in their lives.

For many, the situation was even more dire because their entire family had worked at Acme Boot. Edna Luttrell's sister, father, brother, two nephews, and niece earned their livelihoods at Acme. Her elderly parents now depended on her income, and her siblings had families too. After the plant closed down in 1993, with her unemployment running out, Luttrell despaired. "I don't know what we're going to do."[39] Even those who were able to find work suffered. Kellam found a warehouse job that was much more physically demanding than her previous job as a boot sewer. Although it was better than minimum wage, her salary was significantly lower than it had been. "I only make $5.86. And that's not much. But I knew when I lost Acme, I would never make what I was making before. . . . I have to work seven days a week to get what I made at Acme in forty hours. That's hard to accept. . . . Everyone keeps saying, 'Well, it's a job, it's a job.' Yeah, it's a job! But that can be very depressing."[40]

As in every plant closing, workers became scared, discouraged, and mistrustful. They had not anticipated either the material change or the feelings that went with it. "When I got laid off, I got depressed, moody. . . . Then you get bitter. I had a hard time adjusting. I got so depressed that I couldn't even clean my house; I didn't go noplace; I didn't even do nothing. I was just so upset and worried that I wouldn't find a job. It was a real hard time."[41] As in most apparel-related industries, most Acme Boot employees were women. Most workers had worked at Acme for their entire adult lives and had no experience in anything else. Moreover, Clarksville was in the middle of a serious recession, and new jobs would be scarce and low-paid. Even with a strong union, the highest pay bracket at Acme in 1992 was $7.95 an hour—approximately $16,000 a year—for workers who had been on the job more than thirty years. New jobs would pay even less. In a letter many of the workers signed and sent to President Bill Clinton, they wrote:

> Three-fourths of the Acme Boot workers are women, and they only earn $7.95 an hour. The job market in our area is very poor now, and hardly any new jobs offer better than minimum wage. [Moreover, they wrote, they had worked hard for President Clinton's election, at their union's urging, and now they were counting on him to live up to his promises.] In your campaign, you often expressed sympathy for the 100,000 U.S. workers who lose their health insurance each month. Many of the Acme Boot workers are farmers' wives who definitely need their insurance coverage for their families. Most are in their 40s and 50s, and will have great difficulty finding another job.[42]

As in other rural communities, the closing of a large manufacturing plant would reverberate throughout the regional economy.

The Union Fights Back

Local 330 of the URW was in many ways a typical union organization. The leadership was capable and conscientious but never especially militant or visionary. They had a fine relationship with their international body, but as a small local, they did not receive any particular notice. The local rarely reached out to the larger URW for help, preferring to solve its own problems internally. Its president was a full-time Acme worker who handled union business on the side. Like many organizations, the leadership of the union did not reflect the membership. The union president and chief stewards had always been men, although the majority of members were women. When campaigns arose, women did the lion's share of the work—phone-banking, leafletting, letter-writing, gathering signatures on petitions, and remaining loyal rank-and-file members. Yet they were not rewarded for this work within the structure of the union; they were not recognized as leaders and did not think of themselves that way. The leadership group of the union had become relatively small and insular. That would change as the union mounted an aggressive campaign against the plant closing, beginning by educating their own members and ending in a strong coalition with national and international organizations.

When the company announced that the Clarksville plant would close, the union leadership were both surprised and angry. They had been reassured that the Clarksville factory—Acme Boot's first and flagship plant —was doing better than ever. Suddenly they were told that within two months, half the employees would be laid off. The union began a campaign to protest the closing. The effort, beginning immediately after the closing was announced, would last for nearly a year and would change Local 330 forever. Within days of the announcement, the union was holding meetings, brainstorming, and notifying the local press and local officials of Farley's intentions.

Forced by media and politicians to respond to the workers' charges, company officials assured the public that they intended to be a "good corporate citizen" of Clarksville. They argued that the closing was inevitable, a direct consequence of the global economy. Even with all the union's concessions, Acme executives said, the costs of doing business in Tennessee were simply too high in the context of international competition. The closing was an economic necessity. "The last 5 or 6 years have been very tough. What we are trying to do is make this company well so we have jobs for the remaining [managerial] employees."[43] The union leadership began to do some research into Acme's proposed move to Puerto Rico. Acme Boot president Mike Vogel had been quite frank about the anticipated surge in profits: "It's better for us to do it there. It's less costly." He cited the tax advantages, lower costs of wages and benefits, and employee training incentives Acme would receive from the government. Vogel did *not* say that the Clarksville plant was closing because it was doing badly. Indeed, Acme was doing extraordinarily well. The fiscal year 1992 was Acme Boot's second-best profit-making year of all time.[44] Acme's sales of women's boots had been up 50 percent in 1991, and men's sales rose as well. The marketing director exulted, "We're very happy with our business and we're having an excellent year."[45] The decision to close their flagship plant was apparently made for other reasons.

The union found that both the Puerto Rican and the United States government had directly encouraged Acme's decision to move the plant to Puerto Rico, in several ways. Acme Boot had been given a factory building in Toa Alta, Puerto Rico, and invited to take it over immediately, at no cost whatsoever. The structure was owned by the Puerto Rico Industrial Development Company (Pridco), a governmental authority. The Toa Alta plant and its surrounding roads and utilities had been built with U.S. federal government money and had been occupied previously by a pharmaceutical division of Baxter International, which had subsequently moved. In return for the free building, Acme had promised to invest $1 million in its own production equipment and machinery in Puerto Rico and, eventually, to hire six hundred workers.[46] Puerto Rico was overjoyed at the prospect of bringing hundreds of jobs to island residents. Acme's move was touted on the island as a major economic development coup.

The company was also taking advantage of the Possessions Tax Credit, also known as Section 936 of the U.S. Internal Revenue Code. This credit, established under the Tax Reform Act of 1976, allowed Puerto Rico–based subsidiaries of U.S. corporations to send their profits back to their American corporate parents without paying federal income taxes, giving multinational corporations a legal 100 percent tax break.[47] In addition, under Puerto Rico's Industrial Incentives Act of 1948, an American company could escape local Puerto Rican income taxes. Between these two programs, according to the U.S. General Accounting Office, "most U.S. subsidiaries in Puerto Rico have been completely or partially exempt from Puerto Rican taxes as well as from the U.S. income tax."[48] As Vogel said, Farley Industries had a chance to increase its profit margin dramatically: "There are some tax code advantages to doing work in Puerto Rico."[49]

Fighting Section 936—and specifically, opposing its use for "runaway shops" like Acme Boot—became a major focus of Local 330's campaign to prevent the plant closing. The loophole in the IRS code was costing the taxpayers nearly $4 billion annually in taxes—revenue that instead accrued directly as profit to these corporations.[50] In years of recession and budget-cutting, the URW believed it could attract political support for an effort to end unjust "corporate welfare" and tax-code incongruities. During their 1992 election campaign, candidates Bill Clinton and Al Gore both had raised political awareness and outrage against the practice of using tax dollars to subsidize job destruction. The candidates had also vowed to stand up to special interests and crack down on obscure and unfair tax loopholes. The time seemed ripe for action.

The Acme Boot workers became centrally involved in a movement to amend Section 936 of the tax code. With the help of the Oil, Chemical and Atomic Workers Union (OCAW), which had just been through a similar fight against Whitehall Pharmaceuticals, the URW learned more about Section 936. Research and strategy assistance came from the Midwest Center for Labor Research (MCLR), where researchers had identified over fifty mainland communities from which approximately twenty-five thousand jobs had been transferred to Puerto Rican tax-sheltered factories.[51] The companies included pharmaceutical giants such as Merck and SmithKline Beecham; food processors such as Bumble Bee Seafoods,

H. J. Heinz, and RJR/Nabisco; personal care companies such as Colgate Palmolive, Johnson & Johnson, and Avon Products; and other footwear companies, such as Stride Rite Corporation and G. H. Bass. In each case, massive layoffs on the mainland left a community to figure out how to survive without a major source of jobs and revenue. MCLR found over two hundred thousand people known to be employed in Puerto Rican factories that were owned by American corporations.[52] A researcher called this "a case of tax loophole-driven job destruction," supporting the URW's position against Acme's petition.[53]

Union leaders began a campaign to convince the American government to amend Section 936 to block requests such as Acme Boot's. Local 330 and the Clarksville workers were clear about their mission in fighting Section 936. They were not objecting to incentives for jobs in Puerto Rico, but they were objecting to government-sponsored transnational corporate capital flight. The URW and its coalition partners were careful to make this distinction throughout their campaign, for most unions involved represented workers in Puerto Rico as well as on the mainland. As a memo from the Tennessee Industrial Renewal Network (TIRN) to its members put it, "Remember that Puerto Rico is part of the United States. Our objection is not to hurt the U.S. citizens of Puerto Rico. We do object to corporations getting a tax break for moving jobs to Puerto Rico, just as we would—and do— object to corporations getting a tax break for moving jobs from one state to another."[54] It was not unusual for economic development policy to encourage transience and deteriorating work conditions. In this case, the situation was exacerbated because Puerto Rico's status as a territory made it eligible for provisions such as Section 936 that were not open to other states.[55]

The Acme Boot workers and URW staff sent a delegation to Washington. In an intense five days of meetings, they met with the staff of most members of the House Ways and Means Committee, where all tax legislation must originate. They also met with most of the Tennessee congressional delegation, including Senators Harlan Mathews and Jim Sasser.[56] To all of them, the Clarksville workers presented their case for ending corporate "subsidy abuse."

The URW's campaign against Section 936 seemed well timed: it coincided with President Clinton's attempt to cut the federal budget deficit. Because of the pressure the unions had brought to bear and their convincing public call to end an expensive subsidy program for Fortune 500 companies, President Clinton proposed amending Section 936. In his 1993 State of the Union address, Clinton said, "Our plan seeks to attack tax subsidies that actually reward companies more for shutting their operations down here and moving them overseas than for staying here and reinvesting in America."[57] With the support of a Democratic Congress, Clinton included in his budget proposal a plan to change the Section 936 tax exemption into a 65 percent wage credit, so that U.S. corporations in Puerto Rico would receive federal exemptions only on an amount equivalent to 65 percent of their wage bill.[58] This proposal linked tax incentives to the purported justification for Section 936 itself: to create jobs in Puerto Rico. It would also raise $7 billion over the next five years in corporate tax revenues.[59] A U.S. Treasury Department report supported Clinton's proposal, since corporations that created a large number of jobs would "continue to enjoy the tax credit they now receive," while other firms would "lose some of their tax benefits unless they expand their Puerto Rican employment."[60]

The administration's proposal was unacceptable to the large corporations operating plants in Puerto Rico. The unions' burgeoning movement for amending 936 met a strong counterattack as industrial and political leaders quickly mobilized to defend their subsidies. The Puerto Rico-USA Foundation (PRUSA) lobbied on behalf of Fortune 500 corporations, manufacturers, bankers, and stockbrokers controlling more than a trillion dollars in assets, while PRO-S936 (Puerto Ricans Organized for Section 936) represented economic development officials and other business interests. Both began to mobilize Puerto Ricans, in Puerto Rico and in the mainland United States. The business coalitions framed President Clinton's proposal to limit Section 936 tax benefits as an attack on Puerto Rico rather than as a constraint on corporate power. They also stated a clear threat. "Most pharmaceutical manufacturers in Puerto Rico would leave the island over the next several years if Section 936 tax breaks are slashed,"[61] reported the *San Juan Star*.

Workers in Puerto Rico were pitted directly against workers on the mainland, including the Acme Boot workers, who were attempting to save their jobs. Puerto Rican workers were encouraged to see their employers as their allies, protecting their interests and livelihoods against the government and other workers. The conflict was often portrayed as a power struggle between different groups of workers fighting each other to protect their turf and maximize their incomes. But a closer analysis reveals a much more complicated story. The Puerto Rican community and its leadership were deeply divided over Section 936, much along class lines, just as Americans would be divided over the North American Free Trade Agreement (NAFTA) a year later. Organized labor in Puerto Rico, as in the United States, unequivocally supported reforming or repealing Section 936. At a May 1993 board meeting, the Puerto Rico Federation of Labor adopted a resolution to support Clinton's proposal to replace 936 with a wage credit, arguing: "The practice of accepting 'Runaway Plants' in Puerto Rico has undermined the well-being of workers in both Puerto Rico and the United States, putting workers in both countries against each other."[62] Among other things, the Amalgamated Clothing and Textile Workers Union (ACTWU), which represented workers in Puerto Rico, had found out that many Section 936 companies did not provide permanent, full-time jobs but hired temporary and part-time workers through temporary employment agencies. The companies had consistently fought unionization, and they illegally "used lower wages in Puerto Rico as an excuse for . . . concessions from their mainland workers." Almost 70 percent of the workers employed by Section 936 companies were women, who were paid significantly lower wages than their male counterparts.[63] Thus, the labor unions as well as the Puerto Rico Federation of Labor demanded the denial of 936 benefits in cases of runaway shops or when a company had violated labor, health and safety, or environmental laws. Instead, the government should invest in worker training, skills upgrading, infrastructure, and other such improvements, with the democratic involvement of the Puerto Rican people in designing and implementing new policies.[64]

Nevertheless, the corporate lobbying paid off and the PRUSA strategy succeeded. Through an intensive media blitz representing powerful corporate interests, and wielding both veiled and explicit threats, the well-orchestrated campaign had dissuaded congressional leaders from their plans for reform. President Clinton's proposal was withdrawn, and the 1993 budget passed with no changes to Section 936. The URW would not have an impact on the law until the following year.

Clarksville's Struggle Continues

While the political fight about the future of Section 936 was underway, Acme Boot workers were also pursuing more immediate strategies to stop the plant from moving, devising an ambitious and multifaceted campaign. The group's primary focus was on a range of public policies, especially financial incentives, that influenced or facilitated Acme's move. In addition to Section 936, the workers attempted to block the company from taking advantage of the Puerto Rico Industrial Incentives Act, which exempted U.S.

companies from local Puerto Rico taxes on most of their income. Acme Boot had also been offered other subsidies—a free building, infrastructure improvements, and job training funds—in Toa Alta. Local 330 did its homework and found that Acme was actually ineligible for many of the tax incentives it was slated to receive. The union's strategy relied on two legal provisions. First, a 1987 commonwealth law prohibited local officials from waiving local corporate taxes if the company's move to Puerto Rico "would substantially and adversely affect the employees of an enterprise under related ownership operating in any state of the United States." A question on the tax break application asked if the jobs coming to Puerto Rico would cost jobs anywhere in the United States. Acme had answered no. Second, tax exemption laws in Puerto Rico forbade the government from offering tax exemptions to firms opening a plant on the island if they were moving "to avoid contract obligations with labor unions on the U.S. mainland."[65] The URW vowed to save Acme Boot in Clarksville by convincing either the U.S. or the Puerto Rican government to review the case and deny the company's benefits. This was an uphill battle; neither governmental entity had ever refused tax exemptions to any company before. To build its case, the union gathered evidence showing that Acme had shipped equipment directly from Clarksville to Puerto Rico, and that the work planned for Puerto Rico was exactly what had been done in Clarksville.

Union leaders initiated contacts with Puerto Rican officials and met with them in Washington, D.C. The unions urged the officials to enforce their law prohibiting tax benefits to manufacturing companies whose relocation would contribute to job losses in the states. They found some sympathy, especially from Carlos Romero Barceló, Puerto Rico's resident commissioner and delegate to the United States Congress. Clifford Myatt, administrator of Puerto Rico's Economic Development Administration, also promised to recommend that a formal hearing be held on the Acme Boot situation. This would be the first hearing ever held on an exemption application. Myatt assured union leaders that Acme Boot's tax exemption had not been approved yet, and he pledged to weigh Local 330's evidence before granting any credits.[66]

But these reassurances were misleading. The company had already been received with open arms by local politicians desperate for new jobs at almost any price. Local 330 president Mitch Tucker wrote Puerto Rico's Governor Pedro Rosselló to ask that he deny tax benefits to Acme Boot. "We state to you unequivocally that this is a runaway shop. . . . If an exemption has already been granted, you must revoke it. . . . If an application is now pending, it should be denied." Tucker wrote that Acme "plans to perform Clarksville production processes on Clarksville brand name boots with equipment shipped from Clarksville. . . . Any attempt by Acme Footwear, Inc. to represent the facts otherwise, would be fraudulent."[67] Tucker also sent letters to Carlos Romero Barceló and to Vice President Albert Gore. Both expressed sympathy but declined to intervene.

A formal hearing was scheduled for May 26, 1993. Meanwhile, the URW pursued other strategies. Back in November, when the closing was announced but layoffs had not yet begun, the local had contacted TIRN in Knoxville and asked for its assistance in thinking about ways to fight a plant closing. TIRN sent staff and members who had been through plant closings to a meeting in Clarksville, where they brainstormed ideas and discussed with the workers various legal options. With TIRN's help, Local 330 challenged the legality of the shutdown itself, claiming that officials at Acme Boot had violated the federal WARN Act (which requires companies to give employees sixty days advance notice of any potential layoffs or plant closings) by not telling the employees who would be laid off at each stage of the closing. TIRN also contacted the Tennessee American Civil Liberties Union (ACLU) to investigate the possibility of age discrimination lawsuits. Since the average age of the laid-off workers was forty-seven, it seemed possible that Acme's closing was partly motivated by its unwillingness to cover the pensions and health expenses of an older workforce.[68] Moreover, many of the workers—primarily older women, including women of color—would experience further discrimination in their search for new employment.

The workers focused most of their energy on a public campaign, with the goal of increasing public pressure on Acme's parent company. By making their story public, the workers hoped to gain sympathy but also to exercise power. As Greg LeRoy explained, "Acme Boot's customer base is rural and Southern. . . . Word of the plant closing will result in consumer decisions to buy other brands. Already, some dealers have returned shipments, and Clarksville-area outlet stores are vacant of shoppers."[69] If the workers could call into question Acme's reputation and public image—and perhaps threaten the company's bottom line by affecting its sales—then the company would have an interest in negotiating a settlement with the workers. By spreading the word, the workers hoped to persuade the company to continue manufacturing in Clarksville.

In January 1993, the union held a mass rally in Clarksville, focusing on Acme's move to Puerto Rico. Community members as well as workers gathered to hear charges that closing the Clarksville plant was possibly illegal and certainly immoral. Individual workers told their stories. Calling Acme a runaway shop, the URW blamed government policies for Clarksville's expected loss of 480 production jobs in one year. At the rally, Mitch Tucker vowed, "We want to send William Farley a message. We intend to fight this illegal shutdown."[70] The rally also featured Connie Malloy of the OCAW, a laid-off worker and a rank-and-file leader who had helped fight Section 936 in Indiana, and Ricky Mullins, a dislocated worker from the non-union Decaturville Sportswear.[71] Local 330 urged all area unions, community groups, and churches to attend its rallies, demonstrations, and events and to participate in its campaign. "We need all of Clarksville to help us stop this illegal shutdown," said Tucker.[72] TIRN invited its member groups—organizations from all parts of Tennessee—to write to their representatives and to demonstrate in support of the Acme workers.

The media and some public officials began to take notice. Once Local 330 had presented its case publicly, government officials could not condone a blatant violation of the law, but they withheld direct criticism of Acme or outright support for the union. A spokesperson for Vice President–elect Al Gore made a rather weak statement. Acme's proposed move, she said, was "an unfortunate use of the existing tax law, which was intended to create jobs."[73] Similarly, the *San Juan Star* quoted Clifford Myatt: "If it is a clear case (of a runaway), then we will be obliged to make a decision in accordance with the facts." But Myatt also cautioned that there is "a very thin line" between runaways and normal plant closings. "We will have to see the reasons for the closing, whether the company thinks it makes business sense, and if it does not relocate in Puerto Rico, if it intends to relocate somewhere else."[74] None of these criteria was specified in the actual law.

With other groups from Clarksville and beyond, the Acme workers planned event after event. They held demonstrations, press conferences, and marches. With the support of the Clarksville community, they held a three hundred–car motorcade through the small downtown. Workers stood in front of K-Mart and Winn-Dixie every weekend, distributing flyers explaining Section 936 and their plight and encouraging community members to contact all relevant decision makers. On May 4, 1993, the union sponsored a mass public boot-burning, to which hundreds of Clarksville residents brought their Acme-made boots. This dramatic gesture inaugurated a national boycott of Acme, Dingo, and Dan Post boots. A boycott flyer, "The Anatomy of an Acme Boot," designed by award-winning labor cartoonist Mike Konopaki, was distributed by labor unions nationwide.

The URW International Executive Board had declared the boycott, and all AFL-CIO members and supporters were asked to observe it. "URW Local 330 members at Acme Boot in Clarksville, Tennessee have done everything possible to save their jobs," said URW president Kenneth Coss. "In return, they have been stripped of their jobs and their dignity. Acme's actions are an affront to the local community, the state and the nation."[75] The workers' spirits rose when the boycott was announced. They had asked the AFL-CIO to endorse the boycott, and it agreed, making the campaign national and official. Local 330 was optimistic that Farley would act to prevent a sizable drop in sales of Acme's boots. As Coss said, "It is the URW's goal that a boycott, in conjunction with efforts to amend Section 936 . . . will convince the company to reopen the Clarksville facility."[76]

Another crucial component of Local 330's strategy involved attracting media attention. Largely because of the union's connection to a national political struggle—and because of Clinton and Gore's attention to the issue during their campaign—it was unusually successful. Local media coverage, including both written press and TV, was extensive at the outset and continued, at a slower pace, for many months. Both local and national media picked up the story of the struggle around Section 936 and included Acme in their coverage. Dan Rather reported on the situation in Clarksville in a CBS News segment on job loss in the global economy, as did *Prime Time Live* and *This Week with David Brinkley*. The Associated Press picked up Acme's story as the "human interest" side of the political battle being waged in Congress, and Nashville's NBC affiliate produced a special week-long investigative series, including in-depth interviews with Acme workers. On May 29, 1993, the *Walter Cronkite Report* covered the shutdown of the Clarksville plant. Invited by the URW, the TV show had attended the bootburning and other events, including the last day of work at Acme Boot. The *Cronkite Report* aired extensive footage of interviews with dislocated workers and showed the devastating impact of job loss on workers in the already depressed Clarksville economy. It emphasized job flight and the connections between tax policy, job loss, and poverty. The extensive media coverage was very unusual for a plant-closing story. Members of Local 330 were tremendously encouraged by the outpouring of public support that resulted. They received mail and support from individuals and groups around the country.

The boycott, rallies, and media attention encouraged the laid-off workers. With all the activity, Acme workers felt the support of a much wider community, including the national labor movement as well as other groups within Clarksville. All the workers have stories of their friends and neighbors expressing sympathy and even helping out. As Alan Buckner said, "I was talking this morning with a man . . . and he always wears cowboy boots. And I didn't bring the subject up, he did. He said, 'Well, I'll tell you one thing . . . I'll never buy another damn pair of Acme boots.' And see, he had nothing to do with it. He's never worked a day at Acme. He's just a hard-working man and that's his feeling. And I'm glad to hear it."[77] This type of external validation was crucial to the workers as they continued their struggle. In the vast majority of plant closings, this type of support does not materialize—in fact, many laid-off workers report more disdain than sympathy from their neighbors—and workers end up demoralized and isolated. Community support was a direct outcome of the mobilization at Acme Boot.

Victory, Defeat, and Victory

At the height of the campaign, just after the boot-burning and motorcade, the union and the workers learned of a major victory. At least one prong of their strategy had succeeded. Acme suddenly announced that it would not request federal income tax exemptions on profits from the Puerto Rico plant. The company withdrew its application for Section 936 benefits. Its press release announced simply, "Officials at Acme Boot have decided not to seek income tax exemptions offered for the company's operation in Puerto Rico."[78]

Why had Acme given up? A high-ranking Puerto Rican official cited "corporate exhaustion" as the reason for Acme's withdrawal of its application. Myatt said, "I think the union has been so vociferous and unfair in its attack on them that they [Acme] don't want any more bad P.R. Also, they've been inundated with so much paperwork and expenses that they decided to forget it."[79] The workers' struggle had paid off. Rather than endure the barrage of negative media attention, the continuing boycott, and potential harm to its image and sales, Acme decided to forgo a very lucrative opportunity. The union was elated.

But the bad news followed quickly. Acme announced that it was going to move anyway. Vogel explained that, although the company was distancing itself from the 936 controversy, it would still receive local economic development subsidies and was continuing with plans for production in Toa Alta. Although Acme had withdrawn its federal application, its executives refused to concede that the new factory was a "runaway." They would still receive the Puerto Rican tax incentives, as well as job training funds and free infrastructure. Vogel claimed that the Clarksville plant closing and the establishment of a new plant in Puerto Rico were "non-related, coincidental issues."[80] None of the workers believed him.

Acme's decision to give up on benefits under Section 936 was a major victory for the workers' campaign. The U.S. taxpayers had saved some money. But the workers had failed to save their jobs or their community. The Clarksville plant closed on schedule, and the company, without benefit of federal tax breaks, moved the work to Puerto Rico. After months of mobilization, coalition building, public education, media attention, political lobbying, and protest, the Clarksville community nevertheless lost Acme Boot.

Months later, the workers learned that the long battle against Section 936 had ended in a "compromise." The House and Senate had agreed to amend 936 so that, instead of a 100 percent tax break, corporations would enjoy only a 60 percent exemption—without changing the nature of the exemption. The companies had managed to preserve the type of loophole that Clinton and congressional leaders had deplored publicly, the income-based exemption that was already in existence, as opposed to an exemption on the basis of jobs created or wages paid. As the *Wall Street Journal* reported, "Despite the fact that they were the first—and an especially vulnerable—target of the new president's desire to change Washington, the drug companies escaped with much of their coveted tax break intact."[81] In addition, the centerpiece of the URW, UAW, ACTWU, and OCAW campaigns—the provision to prevent runaway plants—was never enacted. Clinton himself had declined to press for the provision, and the Puerto Rican economic development establishment had lobbied heavily against it. Journalists and politicians agreed that the corporations' political campaign had been expensive and ingenious. At the end, four drug companies (Pfizer, Merck, American Home Products, and Bristol-Myers Squibb) paid about half a million dollars to a lobbying firm that included former members of Congress.[82] PRUSA lobbyists had convinced even avowed proponents of tax reform, such as Senators Bill Bradley of New Jersey and Pat Moynihan of New York, to maintain the loophole.[83] PRO-S936 had preserved a major tax break for corporations. And yet, a small group from Clarksville, Tennessee, had succeeded not only in publicizing the case but in cutting the corporate windfall by a full 40 percent.

Although the Acme Boot campaign failed in its specific goal of keeping the Clarksville plant open, it had a major impact in at least four other ways.

First, the workers significantly affected Acme's decisions and corporate behavior, and politicians' actions as well. In an era when the balance of power rests firmly in the hands of the owners of capital, this is not a trivial accomplishment. The workers won some concrete victories. In particular, Acme did not receive the federal tax exemptions it had sought. More important, the union succeeded in changing Section 936. Although the change was not as far-reaching as the workers had hoped, it was significant. The cut in the exemption rate forced corporations to pay approximately \$3.75 billion in additional federal income taxes over five years.[84] This represented a substantial savings for the taxpayers and an important partial correction of a long-standing loophole. Moreover, given the intensity and expense of the pharmaceutical and other industries' campaign to defend Section 936—and most politicians' capitulation in the face of corporate pressure—it was remarkable that Congress implemented any cut in the program. If the labor movement, with the URW in the forefront, had not kept up a grassroots campaign, Section 936 benefits most likely would have remained intact. The union had been surprisingly effective in counteracting an aggressive corporate campaign.

Second, the Acme workers developed a politicized analysis of the closing itself and did not blame one another or find scapegoats for their misfortune. Similar plant closings often have been characterized by divisiveness, scapegoating, and self-reproach, but none of these features was dominant at Acme.[85] Ironically, while unions are usually blamed for antagonizing relations between workers and management, just the opposite can be demonstrated here. The union's nine months of intense mobilization had provided the workers with an appropriate analysis of the situation they faced. Unlike the situation in other plants, no one from Acme Boot blames their immediate supervisors or even their managers. Instead, they blame Acme's owners. In the workers' words: "It wasn't management here. It was Farley Industries, a corporate giant. He just wanted more, more, and more . . . to correct his mistakes."[86] Luttrell believed it was about power and control even more than money. Acme wanted to escape not only the high wages and benefits, she said, but also the rules. With the union, "they had to do things legal, that they wouldn't normally do. . . . They had rules to go by."[87] The workers were effectively educated to understand the national and international political decisions that led to the plant closing. They understood Acme's move as a strategic decision made possible by a series of governmental decisions, under pressure from large transnational corporations.

In the process of their struggle, the workers became more critical of certain ideologies they had always accepted. They began to analyze their workplaces and communities in different terms. This new, politicized outlook remained with them even after they left Acme and moved on. Because of the education they had received during the union campaign, the workers were able to place the events in Clarksville within a much larger context. Rather than blaming immigrants, minorities, or the Puerto Rican people for "stealing" their jobs, as happens in many crisis situations, they found common ground with all these groups, understanding their own place within the global economy. As a result, their political views and behavior changed. Alan Buckner said, "We will not see any changes whatsoever until a new policy has been brought before the president, the Congress and the Senate, to do away with this policy where they do not have to pay their income taxes."[88] The workers understood complex economic issues because of their experiences at Acme.

This analysis was evident in their evaluation of later political debates, in which the Acme workers applied the lessons they had learned. For instance, all the Acme workers interviewed could speak quite knowledgeably about NAFTA and its effects on both American and Mexican workers. Charles Schmidt and his wife, Betty, had both worked at Acme for almost twenty years. Charles worked in the shipping department, packing boots onto trucks. He had never been involved in political issues in his life, but now he had strong feelings. "This is a Republican treaty. It was drawn up by the Bush Administration. . . . All that time, they were strictly anti-labor, strictly."[89] They worried about its repercussions in the future. Kellam says, "Before long, there will be no manufacturing in this country—it's coming to that . . . which has been going on for years. But I didn't even realize how bad it was until this happened to us."[90] Accordingly, when NAFTA came up for a congressional vote in the fall of 1993, many of the Acme workers became involved in the political campaign to defeat or amend the treaty. When the General Agreements on Tariffs and Trade (GATT), "fast track," and other "free trade" proposals came up, the Acme Boot workers got involved in the same context. "They say here will be high-tech jobs, but I don't see many of them. For every five hundred workers at Acme Boot, they may create one hundred if that many, but you can't sacrifice four out of five jobs, regardless of what the pay scale is."[91] When the workers read or heard news reports on issues related to international trade, they paid close attention, because they could relate the stories to their own experience and knowledge. After the closing, Kellam said, "You turn on TV all the time and you hear about a plant closing and part of it going to Mexico . . . you know, I didn't realize it was that bad [until Acme closed]. I just did not realize at all."[92] But the union's campaign had an even deeper impact on the workers' ideas about international issues than their opposition to NAFTA and GATT suggests. The Acme workers fit exactly the demographic profile of Pat Buchanan's supporters in 1995: working-class, mostly white, disillusioned Democrats, culturally conservative, Christian, in the South. Specifically victims of a plant closing, they might have been persuaded to place the blame on immigrants or on the Puerto Rican people for "stealing" their jobs, as Buchanan and other right-wing leaders were advocating. But the Acme workers did not believe this. Not a single worker interviewed blamed Puerto Rican workers. As Mittendorf said, "I might blame the government of Puerto Rico, [but] the poor workers are like us. I mean if they take their job ... there ain't nothing they can do about it. The Puerto Ricans can't do anything. All they could do is refuse to work, and they're not gonna refuse to work if they're starving to death and need jobs."[93] Class consciousness won out against xenophobia.

Third, the workers who got involved in saving their plant learned a lot about politics and means of participating in the system. This knowledge was practical as well as theoretical; the lessons learned could easily be translated into future activity. As one example, even though the union had lost the fight against the plant closing, the Clarksville workers evaluated unions, and collective action in general, much more positively than other groups of workers did. This is remarkable because culturally and ideologically, like most Tennesseans, the workers were not at all predisposed to support unions. Yet, despite their disagreements with URW decisions, the Acme workers unanimously agree that with a union, "they treated you like human beings, they couldn't push you like they normally would, without the union."[94] Buckner summed it up: "It wasn't the old buddy-buddy system, you know, you pat my back and I'll pat yours. Everybody was more treated equal. They had to treat us equal."[95] This general expectation of fair treatment and democratic participation was crystallized during the campaign against Section 936 as well.

In more general ways, the mobilization in Clarksville transformed the participants' political beliefs and their political behavior. In other plant closings, the failure of politicians to stop the closing has left workers embittered and politically apathetic. By contrast, the Acme workers who had participated in union activities were significantly better educated about American politics. Throughout the plant-closing campaign, they had participated in letter-writing campaigns, met with politicians, followed the events around Section 936, and learned about political processes. Kellam said, "We did everything that could be done. We wrote letters to the president, we wrote letters to the congressmen. . . . I stood out in front of Wal-Mart last winter—cold, snowy, handing out literature on that 936 law."[96] And they had succeeded in eliciting a response from their representatives. Congressman Sundquist met with the union's leaders, and Vice President Gore and Senators Sasser and Mathews made some public statements in support of the local's campaign. Even if their political representatives capitulated in the end, their attention and support indicated to the workers that their troubles were important and that they were capable of being heard. All this was essential to the workers' ability to continue mobilizing and acting politically.

The Acme workers' participation also taught them about the limits of the ostensibly democratic political system in the United States. One lesson they learned was that their elected representatives did not take workers' needs and interests very seriously. Sally Kellam expressed a common sentiment: "We [the URW workers] went out here and worked for this man [President Clinton] to get him in office. Now we feel like we've been let down."[97] Charles Schmidt learned, "The power is with these corporations; *they've* got the power."[98] The workers expressed disappointment in local politicians as well as national officials. Luttrell had been shocked that the mayor of Clarksville was unwilling to assist the workers more in their effort to keep the plant open. "What we've had to go through with the mayor, to help us out!"[99] Buckner agreed: "I didn't see any good come out of Acme's people— our mayor and county government—for Local 330 when the plant started closing down."[100] Despite their disillusionment, however, the Acme workers actually maintained their political involvement after the plant closed. As Buckner said, "I still feel like there's a way that this town might benefit the people of Acme Boot. . . . Of course, I'm not a smart man, not an educated man, but I still feel like there's something those politicians might be able to do. See, they floated bond issues when Acme first moved up to that new plant. They done that for [the company]. It looks to me like there ought to be some way they could float some type of bond issue to help the *people* out."[101] Kellam had not been active before the plant shutdown. Now, she says, "I've gotten more involved in a *lot* of things since this plant closing. . . . I had never in my life wrote letters to congressmen and the White House. I never was like this. . . . I feel like we need to stand up because that's important. They need to *know* how the people feel. It could make a change. It could make a difference."[102] Mittendorf is looking for a leader who stands by his word and is committed to "creating more jobs," raising wages, and improving the lot of the working class. Betty Schmidt had a similar standard: "Say John Doe voted for NAFTA—Are you going to vote for somebody that gave our jobs away? . . . I think people get it."[103] The transformation of "apathetic" workers into active citizens who "get it" about American politics is an important victory of the URW campaign.

Although the Acme workers had lost the struggle to save their plant, they had also learned that there were ways they could act to affect their own fate. And they continued to act, even after the campaign to stop the shutdown had ended. Jane Hutchins and Jane Pryor, best friends and co-workers since the early 1970s, walked up and down their streets, ringing every doorbell, to get their neighbors to sign a petition against NAFTA. Mitch Tucker conferred with other union leaders fighting their companies' tax exemptions. Other workers acted in smaller ways, by boycotting Farley Industries and other offensive firms and by choosing goods with union labels. People at Acme found ways to use their new knowledge, to retain a sense of agency in their own lives and in the political economy.

Finally, the impact of the struggle in Clarksville went far beyond the boundaries of Middle Tennessee. Local 330's campaign had ramifications in the wider political world. Its willingness to take on the challenge of fighting some of the most powerful corporations on the planet was an inspiration to other unions and political organizations. To attempt this type of struggle was extremely rare at the time. Local 330's fight was one of the first cases in the country of a union taking an active role in protesting the unregulated mobility of capital. What later became known as corporate welfare, subsidy abuse, or the global assembly line was largely absent from the public debate in 1992. No one had expected OCAW and the URW to fight an obscure and complex tax regulation known as Section 936. The *San Juan Star* noted the bewilderment of corporate executives and government officials at the mobilization that resulted: "When Puerto Rico defended Section 936 tax breaks from proposed cuts in the mid-1980s, U.S. labor unions hardly made a peep. Yet today, labor's voice is shrill in the 936 debate on Capitol Hill."[104] Impelled by the struggles of small local unions in places as unremarkable as Clarksville, Tennessee, organized labor has made these issues a national priority and continued to defend workers against global impoverishment.

The coalition that formed against Section 936 helped lay the groundwork for the national mobilization around NAFTA only a year later, as well as the successful struggle against "fast track" legislation in 1998 and ongoing protests against the World Trade Organization (WTO) thereafter. Like many struggles that take place in the early phases of social movements, the anti-936 movement sowed the seeds for later mobilizations. During Acme's campaign, many unions and other groups either participated in the anti-936 coalition or watched with interest. A process of political education took place across the country. People learned about the importance of the tax code in job creation, about economic development incentives that pit workers and localities against each other, about "runaway shops" and taxpayer-financed job destruction. Workers and organizations began to pay attention to the phenomenon of transnational corporate capital flight. The campaign against Section 936 awakened many political leaders and organizations to the possibilities of abuse under the tax code. But more important, globalization and free trade no longer seemed an arcane and marginal policy topic but instead were very real issues with important ramifications for workers' lives and communities. Inspired by the Acme workers' example, many unions and other organizations went on to protest unfair treatment on their own. Some of this grassroots action came together in the fall of 1999 in the streets of Seattle, where labor groups, environmentalists, students, farmers, international organizations, and others protested the role of the World Trade Organization in furthering the global "race to the bottom." With as many as one hundred thousand people involved, this mobilization made it clear that the landscape of political possibilities was shifting, in small but important ways. Acme Boot workers had been at the forefront of this nascent movement.

Because it failed, the campaign against 936 also taught the labor movement what it was up against. Relatively small unions such as OCAW and URW had fought some of the most wealthy corporations and their powerful political allies, and lost. The power of money in U.S. politics was not news, but the willingness of corporations to spend so heavily on issues like this—and the unwillingness of most political leaders to defend workers and the unemployed—was still unexpected. The unions learned that if they hoped to regulate corporate mobility in the global economy of the 1990s, it would require continued pressure, resources, and grassroots mobilization across state and national boundaries. This lesson provides an important challenge to the labor movement of the twenty-first century.

NOTES

1. John Sisk, letter to Acme Boot workers, June 10, 1993, p. 4.
2. Acme was perhaps a pioneer in a long-lasting pattern of capital mobility in

search of low labor costs. As Bluestone and Harrison said in the 1980s, "Management can move capital by completely shutting down a plant. . . . In a few cases it may even load some of the machinery onto flatcars or moving vans and set up essentially the same operation elsewhere. This last option earned the epithet 'runaway shop' in the 1930s, and again in the 1950s, when industries such as shoes, textiles, and apparel left New England for the lower-wage, non-unionized South." See Barry Bluestone and Bennett Harrison, *The Deindustrialization of America* (New York: Basic Books, 1982), pp. 7–8.

3. Bill Hobbs, "Despite Acme, Boot Makers Like Outlook," *Nashville Business Journal*, June 1, 1992, p. 5.

4. Bonnie Baber, "Give 'Em Ad-itude: A Visual Feast of Footwear's Finest and Funniest Marketing Moments," *Footwear News*, August 14, 1995, p. 16.

5. Jean E. Palmieri, "Badovinus Gave Retirement the Boot," *Daily News Record*, February 20, 1995, p. 56.

6. Hobbs, "Despite Acme, Boot Makers Like Outlook," p. 5. By the time of the plant closing in 1992, the Clarksville factory employed about six hundred people.

7. Jane Hutchins, interview with author, Clarksville, Tennessee, September 3, 1993; Jane Pryor, interview with author, Clarksville, Tennessee, September 3, 1993.

8. Alan Buckner, interview with author, Clarksville, Tennessee, December 14, 1993.

9. The URW's official title was the United Rubber, Cork, Linoleum and Plastic Workers of America, AFL-CIO. In 1995, the URW merged with the United Steelworkers of America.

10. Buckner interview.

11. A "mergers and acquisitions" specialist, Farley had worked for the investment bank Lehman Brothers before going out on his own. In 1984, he had used debt to buy Condec, a defense and electrical equipment company. When Condec fell apart, Drexel Burnham Lambert bailed Farley out with $150 million in junk bonds, but Farley still owed interest of $38 million. Farley's ads for Fruit of the Loom in 1987, featuring himself pumping iron in a T-shirt, denounced the "uncaring attitude" of American management and extolled "feeling good about yourself and your company . . . the only way to win." Farley was for a time considered a potential political candidate, and he entered the presidential campaign in Iowa in the fall of 1987. But his candidacy seemed doomed after he was revealed to have been married and divorced three times and to have an illegitimate daughter. In addition, the media reported in detail on his belief in reincarnation, with previous lives as a high priest in ancient Egypt and as one of Christ's twelve apostles. See Michael O'Neal and Dean Foust, "Bill Farley's $500 Million Needs a Home—Fast," *Business Week*, June 27, 1988, p. 35; Greg LeRoy, "Background and Chronology on William Farley, Farley Inc., and Acme Boot," report for Midwest Center for Labor Research (MCLR) (Chicago, January 4, 1993), p. 1.

12. LeRoy, "Background and Chronology on William Farley," p. 1.

13. Judith Crown, "Meet Bill Farley," *Crain's Chicago Business*, April 5, 1992, p. 1.

14. "Farley Note Holders File Bankruptcy Suit," *Footwear News*, July 29, 1991, p. 67.

15. LeRoy, "Background and Chronology on William Farley."

16. Hobbs, "Despite Acme, Boot Makers Like Outlook," p. 5.

17. Prominent examples include Nike, which produces no shoes in the United States, and Timberland, which closed its last U.S. plants (in Tennessee and North Carolina) in 1995. See Richard J. Barnet and John Cavanagh, *Global Dreams: Imperial Corporations and the New World Order* (New York: Simon and Schuster, 1994).

18. "Acme Boot Co. Declines Tax Exemptions for Puerto Rico Operation," press release (Clarksville, TN: Acme Boot Company, May 6, 1993).

19. Bill Hobbs, "Acme Pumps Up Ad Budget while Mulling Closure," *Nashville Business Journal*, June 8, 1992, p. 5.

20. Farley's business decisions exemplify a national pattern of corporate disinvestment in the 1980s and 1990s. As Bluestone and Harrison explain it, "The essential problem with the U.S. economy can be traced to the way capital—in the forms of financial resources and of real plant and equipment—has been diverted from productive investment in our basic national industries into unproductive speculation, mergers and acquisitions, and foreign investment." See Bluestone and Harrison, *Deindustrialization of America*, p. 6. Farley undertook all three of these with a vengeance.

21. Edna Luttrell, interview with author, Clarksville, Tennessee, December 15, 1993.

22. Buckner interview.

23. Sally Kellam, interview with author, Clarksville, Tennessee, December 15, 1993.

24. Buckner interview; Kellam interview; Luttrell interview.

25. Gary Coffey, "Acme Boot Makes Revisions to Streamline Manufacturing," *Nashville Business Journal*, May 13, 1991, p. 37.

26. Kellam interview.

27. Buckner interview.

28. Kellam interview.

29. Louis Uchitelle and N. R. Kleinfield, "On the Battlefields of Business, Millions of Casualties," *New York Times*, March 3, 1996, pp. A1, A26–29. See also N. R. Kleinfield, "The Company as Family, No More," March 4, 1996, p. A1.

30. "United Rubber Workers Boycott Acme Boot for Runaway Plant," press release (Washington, DC: United Rubber Workers International, April 29, 1993).

31. Wilma Mittendorf, interview with author, Clarksville, Tennessee, December 14, 1993.

32. Douglas Ray, "Acme Plans Boot Plant in Puerto Rico," *The Leaf-Chronicle* (Clarksville, Tennessee), December 27, 1992, p. A1.

33. LeRoy, "Background and Chronology on William Farley," pp. 2–4.

34. O'Neal and Foust, "Bill Farley's $500 Million Needs a Home," p. 35.

35. Stephen Franklin, "Union Wants Puerto Rico to Boot Acme," *Chicago Tribune*, February 1, 1993, p. 1. The El Paso plants employed more than seven hundred employees, a similar number to those fired from the three other Tennessee plants recently closed. The company would not reveal the wages of workers in El Paso or Mexico.

36. Luttrell interview.

37. Kellam interview.

38. Luttrell interview.

39. Luttrell interview.

40. Kellam interview.

41. Kellam interview.

42. Letter to President Bill Clinton, signed by Acme Boot workers, February 10, 1993.

43. Franklin, "Union Wants Puerto Rico to Boot Acme," p. 1.

44. Ray, "Acme Plans Boot Plant in Puerto Rico," p. A1.

45. Western boot executives agreed that the 1990s saw a great surge in the popularity of their product, which they attributed to new interest among women, young people, and urban residents. One reason was the rising popularity of country music. "The boot industry should get up every morning and kiss Garth Brooks' picture," one executive said. See Hobbs, "Acme Pumps Up Ad Budget while Mulling Closure," p. 5.

46. Pablo J. Trinidad, "Acme Boot to Produce Footwear in Toa Alta," *Caribbean Business*, December 10, 1992, p. 1.

47. Special tax provisions for U.S. corporations operating in U.S. possessions have been on the books since the Revenue Act of 1921, primarily to help U.S. firms compete with foreign firms in the Philippines, which was then a U.S. possession. See "Tax Policy: Puerto Rico and the Section 936 Tax Credit," Report GAO/GGD-93-109 (Washington, DC: United States General Accounting Office, June 8, 1993), p. 2.

48. "Tax Policy: Puerto Rico and the Section 936 Tax Credit," p. 2.

49. Ray, "Acme Plans Boot Plant in Puerto Rico," p. A1. It is interesting to note that Vogel later denied having said this. After Acme's use of tax incentives became controversial, Vogel declared, "Neither the tax exemption nor the benefits offered by filing as a 936 corporation were ever determining factors in our decision to open this facility or to close our plant in Clarksville." "Acme Boot Co. Declines Tax Exemptions for Puerto Rico Operation," press release (Clarksville, TN: Acme Boot Company, May 6, 1993).

50. Harry Turner, "Congress Urged to Eliminate 936," *San Juan Star*, May 15, 1992, p. 1.

51. *Job Flight to Puerto Rico: A National Tax Scandal* (Chicago: Midwest Center for Labor Research, 1994).

52. Other studies arrived at different estimates of job loss under Section 936. OCAW had calculated total job loss due to transfers of work to Puerto Rico as high as nearly thirty thousand jobs. The estimates of total jobs created by 936 also vary widely. The Puerto Rican government had estimated that about three hundred thousand jobs depended on U.S. corporations with 936 exemptions. These three hundred thousand jobs accounted for about a third of all jobs on the island in 1993. See Richard W. Leonard, "Statement before the U.S. Senate Committee on Finance concerning President Clinton's Economic Plan and Section 936 of the Internal Revenue Code" (Washington, DC, April 27, 1993); Doreen Hemlock, "Industry Gets Behind 936 March," *San Juan Star*, March 5, 1993, p. 19.

53. *Job Flight to Puerto Rico*.

54. Bob Becker, memo to TIRN members, Knoxville, Tennessee, March 4, 1993, p. 2. Likewise, leadership of both the OCAW and URW were explicit: "We, along with the entire AFL-CIO, support the cause of Puerto Rican workers seeking more jobs and better wages. . . . Puerto Rico, like other states and regions within the U.S., competes for jobs and industries using a variety of incentives. The lack of a national industrial policy allows any state to use its public treasury to subsidize incoming businesses with lower taxes, free improvements, free land. . . . [However,] nowhere in this bidding war for ever-greater tax-financed giveaways to industry does the U.S. Federal Tax Code take sides in the battle among the states for jobs and industry [except in Section 936]." See Robert E. Wages, Kenneth L. Coss, and Greg LeRoy, "Business Viewpoint: Case for Addressing 'Runaways' Issue," *San Juan Star*, February 14, 1993, p. 19.

55. During the campaign, advocates of Puerto Rican statehood frequently noted that if Puerto Rico were to enter the union, its eligibility for Section 936 would be nullified, for precisely the reason that Wages, Coss, and LeRoy identify (in note 54, above).

56. Before the trip, Local 330 had met with a local congressman, Republican Don Sundquist, a member of the Ways and Means Committee. (Sundquist subsequently became governor of Tennessee.) After meeting with the Acme workers, Sundquist made a strong public statement against Section 936. "My attitude is that the tax law has outlived its useful purpose," he said. "The law is no longer needed and I'll vote to end it." See "Congressman Sundquist Denounces 936; Union Leaders Take Case to Congress," press release (Clarksville, TN: United Rubber Workers Local 330, February 2, 1993).

57. President Bill Clinton, State of the Union Address, February 17, 1993. This statement was not directly addressed to Section 936, which rewards American companies for moving to another American territory.

58. Clinton's proposal was a milder version of a bill (S-356) submitted in Congress by Senator David Pryor of Arkansas, who called Section 936 "the most abusive of all tax shelters—maybe of all time." Pryor's bill, which was co-sponsored by Tennessee senators Harlan Mathews and Jim Sasser, would have replaced Section 936

with a 40 percent wage-based credit, applied to salaries up to $20,000 a year. Clinton increased the coverage to 65 percent and increased the maximum salary to $57,600 a year, the amount subject to Social Security withholding. See Jose de Cordoba, "Puerto Rican Businesses Are Terrified of Clinton Plan to End Tax Exemption," *Wall Street Journal*, February 26, 1993, p. B5.

59. In other words, firms would retain tax breaks worth about $13 billion.

60. de Cordoba, "Puerto Rican Businesses Are Terrified," p. B5; and Robert Friedman, "Treasury Report: Capping 936 Will Create More Jobs," *San Juan Star*, February 26, 1993, p. 3.

61. Doreen Hemlock, "Analysts: Drug Firms Will Bolt," *San Juan Star*, February 26, 1993, p. 17.

62. "Proposed Amendments to Section 936: Resolution," press release (San Juan, Puerto Rico: Puerto Rico Federation of Labor, AFL-CIO, May 7, 1993). Interestingly, the federation compromised with Governor Pedro Rosselló not by mitigating its support for Clinton's plan but by endorsing an additional investment tax credit equal to 10 percent of new capital spending by these companies.

63. Jack Sheinkman, "Statement of the Amalgamated Clothing and Textile Workers Union, AFL-CIO, on the Administration's Tax Proposal Regarding Section 936 of the Internal Revenue Code," Washington, DC: Committee on Finance of the U.S. Senate, May 13, 1993, pp. 4–5.

64. Sheinkman, "Statement of the Amalgamated Clothing and Textile Workers Union, AFL-CIO," p. 1.

65. Pablo J. Trinidad, "Acme Boot's Tax Exemption Goes to Hearings," *San Juan Star*, March 11, 1993, p. 13.

66. "Puerto Rico Official Wants Acme Boot Investigation; Union Leaders Press Case to Congress and Clinton," press release (Clarksville, TN: United Rubber Workers Local 330, February 9, 1993).

67. Robert Friedman, "Rosselló Urged to Deny Factory Tax Benefits," *San Juan Star*, January 12, 1993, p. 1.

68. Indeed, Acme had been sued once before on these grounds. Jerry Castleman, a manufacturer's representative, was fired eight months before becoming eligible for a pension. Acme Boot was found guilty of age discrimination, and a U.S. Appeals Court upheld the ruling. See Greg LeRoy, "Background and Chronology on William Farley," p. 4.

69. Greg LeRoy, memo to Judy Pfeifer, January 27, 1993.

70. Terry Batey, "Acme Boot Workers, Union Vow to Fight Closing to Bitter End," *The Tennessean* (Nashville), January 15, 1993, p. 1.

71. In its public campaign and political appeals, the URW repeatedly drew on the parallels between the Clarksville and Decaturville stories. Decaturville Sportswear had moved from Decaturville, Tennessee, to El Salvador with the support of the Agency for International Development. The Decaturville plant closing had been a major campaign issue in 1992. Vice presidential candidate Gore had visited

Decaturville and denounced the pattern it represented. The Clinton administration had invited Ricky Mullins himself to the "Faces of Hope" luncheon at the Clinton inaugural. The URW pointed out the similarity and asked for the administration's support. See Robert Kerr, "Faces of Hope: Soul of America En Route to Inaugural," *The Commercial Appeal* (Memphis, Tennessee), January 15, 1993, p. A1.

72. "Unionists Rally in Tennessee, Demanding Halt to Puerto Rico–Bound Runaway Shop," press release (United Rubber Workers Local 330, Clarksville, Tennessee, January 13, 1993).

73. Robert Friedman, "Acme Boot Company: A Runaway Plant?" *San Juan Star*, January 10, 1993, p. 20.

74. Friedman, "Acme Boot Company: A Runaway Plant?" p. 20.

75. Kenneth L. Coss, quoted in "United Rubber Workers Boycott Acme Boot for Runaway Plant," press release (Washington, DC: United Rubber Workers International, April 29, 1993).

76. "United Rubber Workers Boycott Acme Boot for Runaway Plant."

77. Buckner interview.

78. "Acme Boot Co. Declines Tax Exemptions for Puerto Rico Operation," press release (Clarksville, TN: Acme Boot Company, May 6, 1993).

79. "Acme Boot Withdraws 936 Application," *San Juan Star*, May 7, 1993.

80. Jimmy Settle, "Will Newest Stitch Come in Time for Acme Workers?" *The Leaf-Chronicle* (Clarksville, Tennessee), May 18, 1993, p. A1.

81. Rick Wartzman and Jackie Calmes, "Potent Medicine: How Drug Firms Saved Puerto Rico Tax Break after Clinton Attack," *Wall Street Journal*, December 21, 1993, p. 1.

82. Many millions of dollars were spent on the pro-936 campaign; it is impossible to gauge precisely how much. The Puerto Rican government hired a large Washington lobbying firm on a $50,000-a-month retainer, as well as a prominent public relations firm. New York lawyer Harold Ickes, a friend of the Clintons, was hired by the pharmaceutical firms on a $40,000-a-month retainer. The industry made many campaign contributions during this period, to candidates in Puerto Rico and on the mainland. And many other expensive lobbyists, public relations experts, and consultants were involved in the long campaign. See Wartzman and Calmes, "Potent Medicine," p. A14.

83. Bradley, known as "the Senate's pre-eminent tax reformer," had proposed to eliminate Section 936 completely in his 1986 "Fair Tax" blueprint. Since then, however, he had come to depend on pharmaceutical companies—a top employer in New Jersey and a top funder of Bradley's campaigns. Bradley had received over $100,000 from the pharmaceutical industry in his close 1990 Senate race, more than any other member of Congress, according to the Center for Responsive Politics. Bradley aides could not defend the profit-based 936 incentive on policy grounds but finally explained that they just couldn't "let go of the income credit. It's important to New Jersey." See Wartzman and Calmes, "Potent Medicine," p. A14.

84. Milt Freudenheim, "Drug Makers Are Already Feeling a Cut in Puerto Rico Tax Breaks," *New York Times*, August 17, 1993, p. D4.

85. For a full discussion of this phenomenon, see Eve S. Weinbaum, "Successful Failures: Local Democracy in a Global Economy" (Ph.D. diss., Yale University, May 1997).

86. Buckner interview.

87. Luttrell interview.

88. Buckner interview.

89. Charles Schmidt, interview with author, Clarksville, Tennessee, December 13, 1993.

90. Kellam interview.

91. Buckner interview. Almost the entire Tennessee congressional delegation voted for NAFTA, including many House members who had pledged to oppose the treaty for months before it came up for the vote. Sasser was the only exception.

92. Kellam interview.

93. Mittendorf interview.

94. Luttrell interview.

95. Buckner interview.

96. Kellam interview.

97. Kellam interview.

98. Charles Schmidt interview.

99. Luttrell interview.

100. Buckner interview.

101. Buckner interview.

102. Kellam interview.

103. Betty Schmidt, interview with author, Clarksville, Tennessee, December 13, 1993.

104. Doreen Hemlock, "Labor Flexes Muscle in 936 Debate," *San Juan Star*, May 17, 1993, p. B6.

Part V

Theories, Politics, and Policy

Chapter 15

Suburbanization and Urban Poverty under Neoliberalism

Matthew Ruben

Suburbia and the Neoliberal Development Model

The high-rises of downtown Philadelphia stretch far into the sky, overshadowing the statue of William Penn that stands atop City Hall. For nearly a century an unspoken agreement held that no structure would surpass the brim of Penn's hat. Alas, the temptations of the 1980s real estate frenzy proved irresistible, and one bold developer put up a spire-topped office tower called Liberty Place. Others soon followed. Now there is talk of selling City Hall to developers who will turn the first floor into a shopping mall and rent the rest back to the city. This is the new downtown, a living snapshot of the balance of power in the twenty-first-century city.

The ascendancy of big business in Philadelphia is but one instance of a new urban economy and a new government-facilitated development model that have taken hold in cities across the United States during the past two decades. The manufacturing concerns that dominated the urban landscape until mid-century are by and large gone. Today's city fathers belong to the expanded "FIRE" sector: finance, insurance, and real estate; some high-tech and pharmaceutical; and a smattering of hospital systems and universities thrown in for good measure. The urban economy over which they preside is decidedly postindustrial, based more on selling services and images than on making products.[1] The new development model that sustains this economy relies on trickle-down strategies of privatization, marketization, and consumerism to promote urban economic revitalization. Rather than targeting investment to stabilize neighborhoods and raise living standards, it redevelops the city as a "growth machine" (Logan and Molotch 1987), creating landscapes of cultural consumption for suburbanites and visitors.

Patronized by locally headquartered corporations and accompanied by pockets of residential gentrification, the new model channels municipal resources into high-profile shopping and entertainment centers (including sports stadiums), tourist attractions, and convention facilities, all concentrated in downtown districts.

This local development model is patterned on a national (and global) shift toward neoliberalism during the past twenty-five years. Evident in both elite and popular circles and influential across much of the political spectrum, neoliberalism opposes the New Deal–Keynesian model of direct government intervention in job creation, human service provision and community empowerment. Instead, it advocates a market-based program of deregulation, investment tax credits, downsizing, and outsourcing of public services, and an up-by-the-bootstraps philosophy. Rejecting the libertarianism and hard-line laissez-faire ideology of the right, neoliberalism embraces efficiency and "good government" by shifting public resources away from the promotion of social equality and toward the promotion of targeted economic growth. While it repudiates the right's overtly racialized vilification of the urban poor, neoliberalism retains the age-old distinction between the deserving and undeserving poor (Katz 1989). In the neoliberal view, the undeserving poor no longer consist of the black family and the welfare queen but rather of those who are still "dependent" on state largesse and are not "productive" in the private sector. Those among the poor and unemployed who invest in the ideology and practices of the market re-enter the lowest echelons of the labor market. Those who, for whatever reason, do not become acculturated to the market are written out of the public sphere and subject to malign neglect—or worse.

Because it enacts neoliberal priorities of growth, privatization, and the rollback of government social service provision, the new urban development model may be termed the *neoliberal development model.*

City officials nationwide have hitched their political fortunes to the neoliberal development model, pledging to help create, as former Philadelphia mayor Ed Rendell said in his inaugural address, "a dynamic downtown that can serve as a magnet to conventioneers, tourists, and suburbanites alike" (qtd. in Bissinger 1997: 24). This downtown-as-silver-bullet has become the primary political-economic goal for Philadelphia's political and corporate elite. It also has become a sublime object of ideology, obsessively written about, projected, and imagineered in promotional literature.[2] Take, for example, *The Greater Philadelphia Story* (Greater Philadelphia First 1993), a coffee-table book advertising the "Greater Philadelphia region" to firms, venture capitalists, and high-level professionals who might want to locate or invest in the area. The book contains the testimony of several dozen FIRE sector executives, all recent transplants, as to the educational, recreational, and consumption-related benefits of living in the region. The managing partner at the law and consulting conglomerate Ernst and Young writes:

> From strolling Elfreth's Alley to enjoying a horse and buggy tour through the neighborhood where Ben Franklin and Thomas Jefferson helped shape our nation to exploring some of the world's finest museums, history is so alive and accessible. Although we live here now, we continue to be fascinated tourists in a great city. (9)

The executive's survey of historic sites provides a concise illustration of how the neoliberal development model commodifies urban space. He and his family "enjoy a horse and buggy tour" of a meticulously mani-cured (and meticulously depicted) downtown. They "explore" museums like sojourners in the urban jungle. The body text that accompanies his testimonial represents the city's historic monuments as "America's most historic square mile": "Here, in downtown Philadelphia, just blocks away from department stores and corporate towers, is an endlessly captivating pageant of American History" (9). The artifacts of a long and compli-cated urban history are spatialized and aestheticized, the pleasures and dangers of the city flattened into an attraction—or a "destination," in the now-ubiquitous parlance of corporate boosters in cities across the coun-try. As a destination, Philadelphia's downtown competes with those of other American cities for capital investment, high-skill workers, tourist dollars, and white middle-class residents and commuters. Los Angeles has movie stars; Baltimore has the waterfront; Philadelphia has history. In true commodity fashion, these features become exchangeable, endlessly substitutable for one another. They may be listed on a check-off sheet, counted up and totaled against one another—precisely what *U.S. News and World Report*'s livability index does every year.[3]

It is the argument of this essay that the commodification of urban space is central to our understanding of the neoliberal development model and therefore central to the research agenda of the new poverty studies. The commodification of urban space is predicated on two phenomena that bear directly on the methodologies and politics of scholarship on urban poverty:

1. the erasure of the poor from the public sphere; and
2. the suburbanization of American consciousness.

Poor, homeless, and working-class people are absent from downtown spaces of hyper-investment like the one depicted in *The Greater Philadelphia Story* because they have been displaced by gentrification. Poor people living in other neighborhoods get bypassed by the growth machine, resulting in a major withdrawal of resources (Adams 1988; Harvey 1985; Marcuse 1986). Either way, the poor are absented from both economic and ideological redevelopment, from sites that constitute, in the words of a Philadelphia public relations consultant, "the geographical center of our identity" (Boyd, qtd. in Ruben 1996).

At the same time, the Ernst and Young executive "feels like a tourist," because while he lives in the Greater Philadelphia *region*, he remains a stranger to the *city*. The subject of the postindustrial city is a suburban one. Municipal leaders do not ask urban residents to forgo key public services and countenance obscene levels of corporate welfare in order to make the city a "home" or a "sanctuary" but rather a *destination*. The neoliberal policies and strategies employed to stimulate urban investment are inseparable from—nay, identical to—those employed to attract suburban consumers and tourists. As such, there is no such thing as neutral ground in urban policy, urban scholarship, and urban representational practices. The putatively dislocated, national-level position from which mainstream scholars and policymakers consider the plight of the city is inescapably a suburbanized position that always tends toward the erasure of the poor as active political and civic agents. While the role of suburbanization in urban disinvestment is well known, precious little has been written about the extent to which scholars ourselves are implicated in neoliberal ideologies, discourses, and representations that depoliticize urban policy and relegate the agency of the urban poor to the fringes of discussion.

To illustrate the pitfalls of urban scholarship under neoliberalism and to recuperate a place for the agency of the urban poor, this chapter first outlines the importance of suburbanization in structuring our dominant view of the city and in ushering in neoliberalism as a dominant ideology and policy framework. It then examines the difficulties of producing responsible urban scholarship in the neoliberal moment. Finally, it uses interviews and pop-cultural analysis to propose one way of understanding the urban environment that places poor people's political agency at the center of analysis.

Suburbanization as Nationalization

Suburbanization typically is understood as a pattern of residential development. It may be more thoroughly analyzed, however, as an ongoing project of political and cultural *nationalization* accomplished through socio-spatial transformation. As many scholars have shown, suburbanization represented a major shift in the geography of U.S. metropolises after World War II (Harvey 1985; Jackson 1985; Davis 1986). Although begun in the 1930s, suburban development did not take off on a truly national scale until the 1950s and 1960s, when millions of predominantly white, upwardly mobile urban residents moved to burgeoning communities separate from, but proximate to, cities.[4]

Postwar suburbanization represented a massive channeling of public funds into private investment in order to head off economic crisis. World War II had caused the United States to double its industrial capacity in a historically short period of time, far outstripping demand. The development of thousands of new suburban communities allowed for what David Harvey terms a "spatial fix," that is, "the mobilization of effective demand through the total restructuring of space so as to make the consumption of the products of the auto, oil, rubber, and construction industries a necessity rather than a luxury" (1985: 206). No less than the Marshall Plan and the Bretton Woods monetary agreement revived the postwar markets of Europe and Japan and sought to open markets in less-developed nations during decolonization, suburbanization stemmed a potential economic crisis by creating new markets at home. "For nearly a generation after 1945," Harvey observes, "suburbanization was part of a package of moves . . . to insulate capitalism against the threat of crises of underconsumption. It is hard to imagine that postwar capitalism could have survived . . . without suburbanization and proliferating urban development" (1985: 206–7).

Government mortgage guarantees, the Interstate Highway Act of 1956, and the federal mortgage interest deduction all built on the Serviceman's Readjustment Act of 1944 (the GI Bill) to encourage the development of suburban communities nationwide. More than an economic stimulus package, these interventions used state-sponsored credit, grants, and tax incentives to spur geographic and class mobility for millions of white men and their families. Eight million free college educations and 16 million new suburban homesteads later, these measures had utterly transformed the U.S. landscape. The suburbanization of production and consumption followed soon after. Supermarkets and shopping malls sprang up across the nation. By the 1970s, the suburbs were the main source of employment for the majority of the nation's largest metropolises, and at the dawn of the 1980s, two-thirds of the nation's manufacturing industry was located in suburban industrial parks (cf. Jackson 1985).[5]

These economic spurs to suburbanization had a homogenizing effect on suburban populations. Demographically, suburban migration is well known as "white flight" from urban centers. Yet that familiar phrase ignores the formative role suburbanization played in constructing a homogenous white population to begin with. Suburbanization not only moved people out of cities but also transformed their primary social identifications, consolidating a pan-ethnic, national whiteness. "The suburbs," George Lipsitz writes, "helped turn Euro-Americans into 'whites' who could live near each other and intermarry with relatively little difficulty" (1998: 7). This process of sociocultural unification was abetted by urban renewal in the central cities, which "helped construct a new 'white' identity in the suburbs by helping to destroy ethnically specific European American urban inner-city neighborhoods" (Lipsitz 1998: 7; see also Berman 1982).

Ethnic nationalization was reinforced by a high degree of material homogeneity, both economic and geographic. Postwar suburban development took advantage of economies of scale by using historically unprecedented degrees of automation and standardization, by fighting union regulations (against spray-painting, for example), and by offering no more than a handful of exterior designs and floor plans.[6] This kind of standardization brokered a historic marriage between class mobility and sociocultural nationalization. It allowed unprecedented numbers of people to purchase homes, and at the same time it nationalized suburban architecture and aesthetics. Standardization transformed the *geographical* distinctions of place into *aesthetic* distinctions of fashion. Architectural styles previously associated with particular regions of the country—Cape Cod cottage, split-level, ranch, colonial, and so on—became national fads, implemented one after another as fashions changed from year to year. "By the 1960s," Kenneth Jackson writes, "the casual suburban visitor would have a difficult time deciphering whether she was in the environs of Boston or Dallas" (1985: 240). Thus was accomplished the kind of homogenizing spatialization that would later surface in *The Greater Philadelphia Story* and other documents of neoliberal urban development.

Demographic, environmental, and economic processes of homogenization permeated suburbanization, extending far beyond the kind of social conformity detailed in William Whyte's *The Organization Man* (1957) and other well-known critical works of the time. The role of sameness in suburbia was not *sociological* in the traditional sense of the term. In this respect, Whyte's study, and Herbert Gans's oft-cited rebuttal on suburban diversity in *The Levittowners* (1967), missed the point.[7] Rather, suburbanization constituted a process of *political-economic* homogenization, a process of social *nationalization*. While this process clearly represented a loss of the diversity endemic to the city, its more dominant effect was a kind of liberation. By breaking down ethnic and subnational sociogeographic identifications through architecture, environment, and the relentless imposition of consumption on every aspect of life, suburbanization allowed for the emergence of a putatively deracinated, normative national identity and paved the way for the current electoral dominance of the suburbs. More than any other development, suburbanization created a national American populace that could be more effectively addressed by national politicians, marketed to by national retail chains, and employed (and periodically transferred among the various branch offices) by national firms. It was this same populace whose "revolt of the haves" in the 1970s spurred the rise of neoliberalism. Property-tax rollbacks, opposition to busing and public housing, and a host of other reactionary mobilizations by suburban populations signaled the end of the New Deal coalition and ushered in the neoliberalism of the so-called New Democrats.

Michael Lind (1995) classifies this nationalized population "the white overclass." Unlike the quasi-aristocratic northeastern establishment of the past, he writes, "this relatively new and still evolving political and social oligarchy is not identified with any particular region of the country":

> Nor does the white overclass dominate other sections through local, surrogate establishments, as the Northeastern establishment once did. Rather, overclass Americans are found in the higher suburbs of every major metropolitan area, North and South, coastal and inland. Unlike the sectional elites of the past, members of the white overclass are often not even identified with the regions in which they happen (temporarily) to live. The white overclass, homogeneous and nomadic, is the first truly *national* upper class in American history. (Lind 1995: 143)

Lind's summary highlights the confluence of the dislocatedness of suburbia with the nationalization and homogenization of the "overclass"— among whose ranks may be counted the recent transplants who appear in *The Greater Philadelphia Story*. Antonio Gramsci provides a more apt, less melodramatic modifier for this kind of group: *hegemonic*. Gramsci was adamant that for a class—or "social group," as he often wrote—to exert hegemony, it first had to attain a high degree of sociopolitical homogeneity, and its ideological commitments had to come to appear "universal," which for Gramsci meant *national* (cf. Gramsci 1971: 181–82). Thus did suburbanization help create the class conditions for the rise to hegemony of its inhabitants during the neoliberal era. Suburbanization thus consolidated a three-way equation among location, whiteness, and American-ness.

Urban Development and the Rise of Neoliberalism

The effects of suburbanization on cities were unmistakable and are well known. During the 1950s, suburbs grew forty times as fast as cities (Davis 1986: 191). From 1950 to 1970, the national suburban population more than doubled (from 36 million to 74 million), and 83 percent of total national population growth took place in the suburbs (Jackson 1985). By 1970, more people lived in suburbs than in cities or rural areas, a first for any society in recorded history (Jackson 1985: 283–84). Racist implementation of the GI Bill on top of already segregated housing, lending, and employment markets ensured that suburbia intensified the racial inequality and residential segregation that had always been present in the cities (Marable 1983; Jackson 1985; Massey and Denton 1993). The class effects were equally striking: median household income in cities was only 80 percent of that of the suburbs in 1970 and plummeted to 72 percent by 1983, illustrating the geographic dimension of the nationwide wage depression that began in the early 1970s (cf. Jackson 1985; Harvey 1989).[8] Cities experienced a wholesale reduction in population and resources, as well as a marked increase in the nonwhite population. For African American migrants and their children, suburbanization (along with redlining and deindustrialization) was particularly cruel: just as they became able to get decent-paying industrial jobs, those jobs began to disappear; and just as they found themselves in need of the resources of the welfare state, those resources began to dry up as cities faced shrinking personal and business tax bases—and later, a succession of anti-urban federal administrations.

In addition to its centrality in the process of urban disinvestment, suburbanization also played a determinant role in producing the polarized, pathological view of the city that emerged amid the economic and political changes of the 1950s and 1960s. The construction of the homogenous image of the troubled inner city mirrored precisely the nationalization of the suburbs into a political and cultural bloc. In the nineteenth and early twentieth centuries, a relatively small, blue-blood aristocracy beheld the teeming national diversity concentrated in the cities from the safety of their rural manors. Portions of the burgeoning professional-managerial class periodically moved to outlying areas but soon became urban dwellers again, when their new homesteads were annexed by the central city. Since the mid-1960s, by contrast, it has been a sizable, growing, nationally normative middle class that has beheld an increasingly racialized, impoverished urban environment from their uncomfortably proximate suburban homes. At the same time, annexation has ceased, and virtually no major city has increased its geographic boundaries for more than thirty years (cf. Jackson 1985; Adams et al. 1991).

In this postwar context, the homogenized city and the homogenized suburb are more than mirror images of each other. The nationalized suburban position is *the necessary point of observation and enunciation for urban diagnosis,* providing a vantage point from which the city may be apprehended precisely as a site of national otherness. It may be argued, in fact, that a truly national urban policy was not possible until a national process of suburbanization was largely complete. Indeed, no national-level economic policy targeted specifically at cities was undertaken until the disastrous "urban renewal" of the 1960s, itself carried out in response to the disinvestment wrought by suburbanization. At the same time, the "culture of poverty" and "underclass" debates (U.S. Department of Labor 1965; Lewis 1966; Murray 1984; Wilson 1987; Katz 1993) took the particular shape they did—indeed, took shape at all—because suburban development and subjectivities had taken root and had begun to produce significant shifts in the social and political complexion of the country. The city ceased to become a container for various differences within the national populace and instead became a marker of difference itself, a container of abnormality *from* a national ideal that was being constructed both literally and figuratively in the suburbs. The city was still *in* the nation, but increasingly it was not considered *of* the nation.

It is thus no coincidence that the city rose to the forefront as a most troubling object of policy and scholarship beginning in the mid- to late 1960s, just as the majority white middle class was moving out and becoming suburban rather than urban. Cities were sites of economic disinvestment but also of ideological hyper-investment, playing all manner of roles in relation to the dominant suburban position in public policy and the national imaginary. Much of the literature produced in the intervening years implicitly speaks from the nationalized position of the suburbs, referring to the urban center as "a 'reservation' for the economically disenfranchised labor force in a monopoly capitalist society" (Hill 1984: 228), with groups of poor people "restricted to deteriorating inner cities" (Sugrue 1993: 110). The resulting image, across the political spectrum, typically is that of the "Pariah City" (Hill 1984), in which the central city appears as a victim of both the suburbs and national policy, with precious little distinction made between the two. As Adams (1988) writes, "The dramatic population losses suffered by the aging cities of the northeast and midwest in the period after World War II spawned a whole new lexicon of images to describe the central city, including 'wasteland,' 'doughnut,' and 'bombed-out war zone.' The common theme in this postwar urban imagery is the belief that urban life is gradually receding from our inner cities, as residents and business owners flee from the advancing blight, the deteriorating services, and the social pathologies associated with 'dying' neighborhoods" (2–3). In such formulations, the city appears as a decaying organism: it "ages," it has "suffered," and it is dying as life spatially "recedes" from it.

Much urban scholarship continues to make extensive use of this terminology and remains heavily influenced by the overwhelming images of urban decay, civil disturbance, and fiscal bankruptcy that punctuated the urban environment from the 1950s to the 1980s. The roles and motivations of scholars and policymakers in reacting to—and helping create—these images vary widely across the political spectrum. The right has been concerned to demonstrate how "moral bankruptcy" has produced an urban "underclass" isolated from market forces and the larger society, unwilling to take the responsibility or action necessary to improve urban America (cf. Murray 1984). The left has used the same negative urban imagery to counter the right's arguments by demonstrating the urgent need for government action to save cities and their populations from economic ruin (cf. Wilson 1987). But while the political commitments and policy implications vary greatly, the underlying logic of homogenization has been pervasive across the board. Michael Katz (1993), writing as editor of the definitive anthology on the "underclass" debate, notes: "Most American research on poverty and the underclass always has reinforced images of social pathology because it has focused on bad behavior: long-term welfare dependence, drugs, crime, out-of-wedlock pregnancy, low educational achievement, unwillingness to work." As a result, "[a]reas of concentrated poverty emerge from much of the historical and contemporary underclass literature as monolithic islands of despair and degradation" (21).

It is important to keep in mind the extent to which the liberal-left contribution to such urban scholarship first developed in order to combat the "up by the bootstraps" and "family values" ideologies the right has wielded to oppose the modern U.S. welfare state since the 1930s. Demonstrating the role of racism and government neglect in producing the nightmare of the "inner city" was and remains a crucially important political, ethical, and scholarly task. At the same time, though, it has always been a risky undertaking. Progressive urbanists often have mobilized much of the same behavioral and empirical "evidence" of urban decay as conservatives, banking on the persuasiveness of the structural-economic explanation to win the day for the left.

With the rise of the neoliberal development model, the very foundation on which the left placed its rhetorical and political bets has been altered. The return of private investment to many cities, the partial return of industry (concentrated in the extended FIRE sector), and a marked increase in residential gentrification have made the urban picture more diverse and complex than the persistent organic representations of cities would indicate.[9] Under the neoliberal model, the "Pariah City," left for dead by its national parent, has been replaced by the "Fortress City" (Davis 1990) and the "Revanchist City" (Smith 1996), in which relations of urban neglect and urban inequality make themselves apparent *within* the city itself, beneath the national radar in which cities are seen as simply advancing or declining. To be sure, neoliberal economic development continues a long-standing tradition of uneven development with regard to cities, in which the urban poor have been bypassed by funding and strategies intended to promote growth and prosperity (cf. Smith 1991). But the neoliberal model posits a very different relationship between the urban poor and the city than past models. During the 1960s and 1970s, the obvious solution to urban decline for many centrist, liberal, and liberal-left scholars and activists was increased funding and investment for cities. The spirited advocacy of that solution is no longer a viable political wedge for the left, because funding and investment already have returned to the cities. In a perverse neo-Keynesianism characteristic of neoliberalism, public investment has been used to leverage private investment in ways that benefit corporate interests, large developers, and selected corporatist nonprofit organizations like universities and hospital systems.[10] Thus, new urban development strategies have not significantly improved conditions for the urban poor and in many cases have worsened them. Historically, this situation merely replays the failure of urban renewal and slum clearance. Yet the neoliberal model is

more insidious because it makes no pretense of investing directly in resources and infrastructure for the poor, instead redirecting public moneys
and credit away from social welfare provision and toward large-scale private
development projects. Its proponents thus claim that the model is succeeding, for it appears to be achieving its purpose.

Neoliberal development has been accompanied and abetted by neoliberal ideology. Neoliberal ideologies of governance and welfare reform have
provided cover for the unequal effects of the new development model. Welfare reform, empowerment zones, tax increment financing, and a range of
other supply-side and privatization measures have emphasized acculturat-
ing poor people to the rules of the free market—now that a critical mass of
policymakers, pundits, and capitalists sees cities as places where the market
once again thrives.

Moreover, neoliberal narratives of the city do not accept the gloom-and-
doom imagery of the culture-of-poverty debate. Nor do they make overt
commitments to either the left-structural or right-moral explanations of
urban poverty. They often combine seemingly incompatible aspects of the
two, because causal explanation is not the concern of neoliberal discourse
and policy. The neoliberal goal is simple: to stimulate investment while cutting the costs of social service provision. The causes of urban problems are
considered irrelevant, and any inequalities or discontinuities that might be
created by investment or the redirection of public resources are considered
equally irrelevant.

A cursory look at the documents of the neoliberal policy establishment
illustrates this ideology at work. A 1997 report on "the revival of urban
communities in America" by the Urban Neighborhoods Task Force, a joint
venture of the Center for National Policy and the Local Initiatives Support
Corporation, recognizes that the suburbanization-era image of the decayed
city no longer obtains. It begins with the statement that "American cities
have started to recover from decades of decline" (iv). The report, which
focuses on Philadelphia and five other urban areas, and whose core task
force was co-chaired by Philadelphia mayor Ed Rendell (dubbed "America's
mayor" by the national media), aims to dispel the view of "most of the
American public, most of the media, and many business and government
leaders [that] the state of cities [is] a simple case, and an essentially negative
one at that" (1). The "core message" of the report "is that, while problems
persist, hope and accomplishment are on the rise, even in what were once
among the worst urban places in America" (2).

While the report's main purpose—to promote cities and put them back on the list of national-level funding priorities—is consistent with efforts of progressive scholars since the 1960s to spur the federal government to pour more resources into cities, its analyses and proposed solutions are quite different, taking on a distinctly neoliberal flavor. The report embraces the trickle-down approach that fuels tax increment financing and other business-friendly urban development policies. In trickle-down fashion, it assumes that these supply-side measures taken to return city governments to solvency, revitalize central business districts, and redevelop parts of certain residential areas simply need to be multiplied in order to bring the entire city back. Ignoring the increasing divergence between rich and poor, downplaying the *geographic concentration* of poverty in "comeback" cities, and glossing over the withdrawal of social service funding at all levels of government, the report chalks up the stubbornness of the "persistent problems" to the fact that "[t]his is a success story in the making. . . . The recovery process is not complete," and it punctuates this assertion with a vague moral entreaty that has no relation to the actual processes of public resource allocation and community economic development: "What we do as a nation over the next several years . . . will determine whether the process succeeds or fails" (3). This construction replicates precisely the national-suburban positionality from which both policy and moral judgment proceed under neoliberalism.

In this manner, despite its awareness of recent change and the clear intent of its drafters to encourage urban revitalization, the report holds onto a unitary, totalizing view of the city and its fortunes. Seemingly, there are no internal contradictions in the urban recovery process; there is only unfinished business. In this respect, the report homogenizes the social landscape, exemplifying the neoliberal refusal of questions of social inequality and its embrace of a blanket, supply-side notion of growth instead. The report asserts, for example, that in terms of "rebuilding low income neighborhoods . . . we already know much about what works: local initiatives grounded in self-help; public-private community partnerships; market discipline; and visible results."[11] And the discussion of residential neighborhoods in the section on Philadelphia in particular—Rendell's area of expertise—seems put together with smoke, mirrors and press releases in comparison to the definitive changes cited in the redevelopment of the Center City business and cultural district (33–34).

When applied to urban development, then, neoliberal ideology totally reshapes the context in which urban scholarship operates. When investment picks up and the aggregate statistics that measure urban economies begin to improve, the older arguments—from both left and right—begin to lose their descriptive power and thus their prescriptive efficacy. The previous negative homogenization by both left and right scholars that ignored the potential agency of the poor from the 1960s to the 1980s has been countered and replaced by a positive homogenization by neoliberals in the 1990s and beyond that ignores inequality itself. Progressive cries for more jobs are taken up by neoliberal scholars and politicians, who simultaneously appropriate notions of "personal responsibility" and family stability from the right. Calls for demographic and developmental diversity are selectively appropriated in strategies that commodify diversity in the downtowns while promoting geographic segregation along class lines in the neighborhoods.

Urban Scholarship and Neoliberalism

Compounding the problem of the neoliberal development model is the fact that urban scholars, by and large, have not effectively accounted for the pervasive influence of these new, neoliberal ideologies and measures. Nor have they sufficiently understood the implications of neoliberal development for scholarship and policy targeted at the problem of urban poverty. Persisting, sometimes unconsciously, in the belief that cities still may be represented merely as suckholes of racial otherness and despair, much urban scholarship reproduces the social homogenization of neoliberal policy, even when it seeks to embrace urban diversity. As the following examples illustrate, this scholarship is utterly consonant with the Urban Neighborhoods Task Force's move away from direct government intervention, its focus on the individual, and its embrace of pragmatics over principles.

Editing an edition of *Urban Affairs Annual Reviews*, urban scholars Mark Gottdiener and Chris Pickvance urge a move beyond economically based, structuralist analyses of urban development, politics, and culture. In their introduction to the volume, they argue that "all [current approaches] possess a commonly held understanding that economic changes are the root causes; hence their common concentration on the economic dimension of transformation." While they concede that "the understanding of economic change is central to the study of urban restructuring," they counter that "the sum total of such efforts gives the false impression that people and their respective everyday lives do not exist. Consequently, urban economics becomes the privileged field of inquiry." Their own vision, they write, "is quite different":

We suggest that the drama of change, its operation at the quotidian level and the impact of restructuring on the neighborhood, the household; on class, race, and gender, and, finally on urban institutions such as political leadership, all require examination in their own right. (1991: 4)

Arguing that "[a]ll analyses that privilege the economic dimension stop at the institutional level of society," Gottdiener and Pickvance pledge that the anthology's contributors "will range further in the following pages—down to the street level and into homes[,] stopping just short of gauging the psychic damage resulting from restructuring" (9). Speaking of their own contributions to the anthology, they write:

Our separate chapters place flesh and blood on the more abstract aspects of urban restructuring. The new urban realities that emerge do not lend themselves easily to analysis by existing approaches that aim for sweeping generalizations of change. . . . Perhaps it's time to rethink our ways of comprehending these new urban realities. The closing chapter, "A Walk Around Town," offers just such a transformed perspective. . . . Clearly, . . . we need to pass beyond the abstract categories of class, race, gender; of power and wealth; of institutions and economics, to some greater grasp of what it's like "down there" in our cities, on our streets, and in our homes. (Gottdiener and Pickvance 10)

Gottdiener and Pickvance's introduction thus moves quickly and unequivocally from a discussion of the limits of macroeconomic analysis to a dismissal of class, race, gender, power, and wealth as concepts too abstract to capture the reality of modern urban life. This desire to "pass beyond" virtually every piece of descriptive terminology one might imagine, in order to get to the essence "what it's like 'down there.'" is an unmistakably neoliberal desire to jettison theory and "ideology" in favor of a harsh "reality" that liberals supposedly have resisted acknowledging. According to the authors, scholars need to face up to "the new urban realities" with new, innovative methods because the old ways won't work anymore. This sort of neopragmatism is identical to the message of every neoliberal politician, pundit, and academic when discussing public investment, welfare reform, Social Security privatization, and a host of other social issues in which privatization and marketization have come to dominate the policy agenda.

Even more instructive is Gottdiener's own contribution, in which he demonstrates the "transformed perspective" he and Pickvance prescribe in their introduction. Titled "A Walk Around the Town: Closing Observations with Apologies to F. Engels,"[11] this short chapter closes out the anthology. It consists of a half dozen vignettes that Gottdiener claims as examples of "urban anthropology." The first and longest proceeds as follows:

> It was raining and as we got on the 67th street cross-town bus the crowd squeezed together more than usual. It was also 5:00 and everyone was eager to get home after a hard day's work. Rush hour and rain—not a good combination. The Puerto Rican kid in front of me bounced up the bus steps and then stopped in front of the fare box. He wore Walkman earplugs and apparently had been too busy listening to rap music to prepare his fare. Caught without a token he stood fumbling for the exact change. I pushed past and dropped my token in the box. I heard him yell as I passed by, "You're supposed to say excuse me!" I just ignored him and took a seat.
>
> After paying he came down the aisle and stood in front of me. "You better watch yourself. You're supposed to say excuse me. That's the Right Thing to do." He then sat down at the back of the bus.
>
> I noticed all the other passengers looking away. I was on my own. I thought about ignoring him. I decided not to. I turned toward him and asked "What happened?" He didn't answer. I pressed him on it, "I want to know, what happened?" Just then I noticed him fidgeting in his seat. Was he getting uncomfortable? And then, at once, he looked away. I had him! By looking away, he had backed down. "Fuck you," I said. It was over.
>
> I was lucky. The chances were high that the kid carried a gun or at least a knife. Maybe he didn't and he backed down. It also wasn't his turf. But lately, people have told me, there isn't any neutral territory in the city anymore. The kids roam the city freely and attack when they can. They keep order, too. Adults are so terrorized by random violence, much of it perpetrated by youth gangs, that they live in fear of just such an incident. Everyone defers to them now, even the police. I was lucky. (240–41)

This passage's most striking feature is, of course, the frankness and apparent lack of self-consciousness with which the author reveals his own reactionary impulses and political viewpoint. On the surface, it clearly is not what one would expect given the tone of the anthology's introduction.[12] Yet its fatal intellectual flaw—the absence of a coherent framework within which to understand the narrated events—shows that it is utterly consonant with the introduction, faithfully enacting Gottdiener and Pickvance's entreaty to refuse all those metanarratives and analytical tools they claim are obsolete. The evident exhaustion with theory; the antsiness—not only physically but intellectually—in the face of the rude Latino youth; the inability to escape the ugly "facts of life" that allegedly negate 150 years of progressive social theory: these are all signs of the infection of the social sci-

ences by neoliberalism and key components of neoliberalism's final jetti-
soning of reform liberalism and democratic socialism from the U.S. political spectrum.

At the same time, Gottdiener writes as someone who used to frequent
some of the same New York neighborhoods that today's out-of-control
youth do (242–43). In this manner, his text occupies a distinctly *suburbanized* perspective: periodically or even frequently in the city but evidently no
longer *of* it. He is aware that "there isn't any neutral territory in the city anymore" only because "people have told [him]" this is the case.

This suburbanized point of view pervades urban scholarship that tries to
grapple with the culture of cities: "the city . . . is a place full of sexual anxi-
ety, obsession and verbal assault, litanies of sexual distress. . . . [I]t is a barrage—a veritable eruption—of ordinarily repressed material" (Rainer, qtd.
in Shields 1996: 240). In this example, there is the notion that urban space
is a site of the "ordinarily repressed." One is compelled to ask, What exactly
is ordinary? This is not only a problem of pathologizing the city, albeit in
this case in a way meant to valorize the urban. It is also an indicator that the
intellectual—one with overtly progressive intentions and, in this instance, a
feminist self-positioning—is effortlessly occupying a space of normality
that seems to be in a zero-sum relation with the urban. This space of normality, and the naturalized subject-position that goes with it, is unmistakably a suburban one. Whether the author actually lives in a city or a suburb,
the position from which she writes is identical to Gottdiener's: a dialectical
position of proximity to, and distance from, the urban center. This sort of
proximate revulsion, and its flip-side distant fascination, is the geographic
and ideological foundation of suburbia.

Perhaps the most overlooked manifestation of the suburbanization of
consciousness occurs in the context of the great academic-political issue of
our time: diversity. Theorizing the role of the urban in *Justice and the Politics of Difference* (1990), Iris Marion Young argues:

> City life . . . instantiates difference as the erotic, in the wide sense of an at-
> traction to the other, the pleasure and excitement of being drawn out of one's
> secure routine to encounter the novel, strange and surprising. . . . The erotic
> dimension of the city has always been an aspect of its fearfulness, for it holds
> out the possibility that one will lose one's identity, will fall. But we also take
> pleasure in being open to and interested in people we experience as different.
> We spend a Sunday afternoon walking through Chinatown, or checking out
> this week's eccentric players in the park. We look for restaurants, stores, and
> clubs with something new for us, a new ethnic food, a different atmosphere,

a different crowd of people. We walk through sections of the city that we experience as having unique characters which are not ours, where people from diverse places mingle and then go home. (239)

While truly integrated residential patterns have never been a widespread reality in the United States, it is instructive to compare Young's theorization with, for example, Jane Jacobs's earlier (1961) prescriptions for urban diversity. In Jacobs's work, there is no sense that either the writer or the reader is supposed to be a visitor enjoying "eccentric players," being "drawn out of one's secure routine," or "losing one's identity," as in the paradigmatic theory of the erotic scene. Rather, for Jacobs, the assumption is that one lives in the city, is *of* the city, and that street life and diversity aid in stabilizing the neighborhood environment, increasing safety, and maintaining rich social relations among different kinds of people. One does not lose oneself in a Sunday afternoon of titillating indulgence but rather finds oneself—both psychically and literally—on the street, every day, in the seemingly mundane yet crucial process of commingling that urban life enforces. As Joel Kahn (1995) writes of Young's work:

> [C]ontrary to the impression generated by talk of "diversity," the plethora of urban voices, and so on, what we have here is more accurately seen as a representation from a singular vantage point, a vantage point that appears to exist *outside* the hurly-burly of the diversity of lives that it claims to represent. Rather than being located *within* any single urban voice, what we have here is the bird's eye view of someone privileged to see all that diversity without actually being part of it.

Evincing the same "bird's eye view" that leads Gottdiener and Pickvance to refer to the city as "down there," the passage from Young illustrates the convergence of suburbanization and neoliberalism in the commodification of urban difference. The narratives of tourism, frontierism, and otherness that pervade Young's argument are key markers of a suburbanized point of view, as well as key components of the marketing of cities under neoliberal development. The creation of entertainment-tourist-historic-restaurant-shopping "destinations" and "districts" is predicated on the commodification of diversity and mystery in the city. Even as municipal governments and city fathers fritter away the urbanity of places like Times Square, they depend on the city's "instantiation of difference as the erotic" to draw suburbanites and tourists to the Hard Rock Cafe, the Niketown, the Warner Brothers store, and the downtown Starbucks (it's got a two-story glass facade!), and McDonald's (it's got a mural painted on it!) locations.

The confluence of the suburban and the neoliberal in urban scholarship also makes itself apparent in the humanities, when poststructuralist and postmodernist theorists try to grapple with the urban environment. Rob Shields (1996), writing on "alternative traditions of urban theory," draws on continental philosophy to question the way in which urban scholarship understands the city. In the name of capturing this "tactility of lived encounters," he opposes any representation of the city as an artifact of "socio-economic relations," instead positing "a relationship between the visible and the articulable, between the visual (architecture, urban features) and the tactile (exchange and interaction) existing on the same epistemological plane with neither having analytical or explanatory priority over the other" (242). In this manner, Shields rejects the notion that what one sees in the city can or should be explained through recourse to processes and structures—such as political economy—that are not literally visible.

Shields's language evinces what is by now a familiar resistance, on the part of both non-Marxist and "post-Marxist" scholars, to the analytical primacy of class and its attendant political-economic processes. Notably, it also exemplifies a fetish for the visible and a refusal of large-scale "forces" whose workings and effects must be inferred or theorized. In this instance, then, the rather esoteric poststructuralist idiom actually serves a distinctly anti-intellectual purpose that accords entirely with the pragmatism and anti-structuralism of neoliberal ideology.

Yet Shields's coded argument against materialist analysis is merely a means to an end. Following in the psychoanalytically inflected footsteps of poststructuralist theorists as they jettison "ideology" and "interest" in favor of "desire," Shields writes:

> If desire is the founding impulse of society, how are we to understand the affectual, emotional city (a kind of view from the slum) rather than focusing on the ideally planned rational city (the view from city hall)? The emotional city is perhaps then closer to reality—to the essence of the urban—than the rational urban representation and ordering imposed by state functionaries. (242–43)

The final sentence of the essay drives the point home: "Let us guard a place for the paradox of street life, the irony of contrasting representations and complexity of everyday life" (246).

While Shields's argument stakes its claim on the rejection of a realist epistemology, his approach turns out to have its own notion of the real in mind. The fetish of the slum and the street clearly is a marker for an urban authenticity that provides refuge for the intellectual from the complications of political economy specifically and "rationality" generally. It is the same kind of refuge neoliberals seek from critiques of welfare reform when they disseminate stories of individual women who have "successfully transitioned" from welfare to work. The important thing to realize is that the desire the intellectual sees embodied in the authenticity of the slum is not actually the "emotional city," the "essence of the urban." Rather, the desire at work is the desire of the intellectual himself for a romantic clench with the downtrodden, because methods for theorizing political alliances supposedly are tainted by their vulgar notions of class and economic determination and carry with them the risk that theorization will turn into overgeneralization, that working up a notion of totality will lapse into an oppressive move toward totalization. "Guard[ing] a place for the paradox of street life" turns out to mean guarding the dramatic image of the city from the predations of political-economic analysis. Ironically, as with Gottdiener's mortifying foray into ethnography and Rainer's valorization of the urban-as-irrational, Shields's analysis is mired in the very forms of romanticization, homogenization, overgeneralization, and knee-jerk reactionary politics it is supposed to transcend. The sheer ignorance of how cities work—we are presented with the cartoonish image of "the people" versus "city hall," with nary a capitalist in sight—indicates a disturbing willingness to retreat from the field of battle in the modern city.

It is always rather to the authentic, pathologized, nonsensical, erotic urban dwellers and sites that these intellectuals return, seduced by the neoliberal specter of the undissectable, irrational kernel of "reality." These and many other urban scholars remain locked in the binarism of sameness and difference when writing about the city. From a suburbanized national-level perspective, the city is perceived as a site of racial otherness, poverty, and mystery. At times, as in Gottdiener, this is seen as a dangerous thing, as many conservatives have maintained while lobbying for the end of the welfare state. At other times, as in Rainer, Shields, and Young, this is seen as a good, exotic kind of thing, as the public relations flacks of neoliberal development maintain when they squeeze $100 million tax breaks for already prospering downtown development projects from municipalities that cannot properly feed and shelter the vast majority of their poor residents.

Finally, and perhaps most tellingly, the neoliberal abandonment of political-economic analysis for empowerment and self-help—or the favoring of "culture" over "structure," as many sociologists prefer—is an indicator of the extent to which politics itself has receded into the background of much urban scholarship. In the name of both rhetorical exigency and personal conviction, many scholars and commentators have focused on the national level and portrayed the problems of cities and the communities within them as trickle-down problems of a nation unable or unwilling to share the benefits of economic recovery with cities. This approach has resulted in the curious phenomenon of scholars trying to address policymakers with a moral argument: we should help cities so we can be good Americans. While it trades (in part) on discourses of empowerment and empathy, this sort of entreaty in fact has nothing to do with political organizing or with understanding the feelings, opinions, and agency of the poor. It fails to understand the extent to which the realm of policy has become more and more promiscuous under neoliberalism, taking over areas of public discussion that used to be concerned with "maximum feasible participation" and community empowerment, replacing them with top-down prescriptions, individual empowerment, self-help, and pragmatic, mechanistic debates over tax breaks and market-based incentives. "When [neoliberals] stand in the front of University classrooms," writes one journalist approvingly, "it is to teach economics. Their public pronouncements are simple, measured, and pragmatic, rarely analytical" (Rothenberg 1984: 19–20). This passage, written in the mid-1980s, referred to neoliberal politicians. Today, it might just as well refer to liberal scholars.

Neoliberal Development and the Poor

To meet the political and ideological challenges posed by neoliberalism, urban scholarship must:

- attend to the broad political-economic context of neoliberal development that shapes most U.S. cities in the present moment.
- be self-conscious about the suburbanized identity that constitutes the unacknowledged position from which most representations of the city are produced. Because suburban identities have become nationally normative, it is particularly easy to fall into them when apprehending the city from a position of scholarly objectivity. The perceptual process of approach from a distance is characteristic of both scholarship and suburbanization.
- understand that neoliberal development cleaves apart the interests of "the city" from the interests of poor people who live in cities.

Neoliberal economic development policies create and maintain un-even development, improving cities in the aggregate but ignoring and in many cases worsening the problems of the poor. It is thus imperative to refuse the removal of poor people's agency from the scholarship of cities if we are to address the problem of urban pov-erty responsibly.

Following are provided a few small counterexamples to Gottdiener's "Walking around Town." These examples are by no means any more prop-erly ethnographic than Gottdiener's. They are offered, rather, in the spirit of finding ways to understand how neoliberalism and uneven development play out in regard to poor people and poor neighborhoods, and how urban scholars might begin to address neoliberal development in studies of spe-cific urban locales.

The first example concerns Philadelphia, where the author lives and studies. As part of its improved national image under Mayor Ed Rendell ("America's mayor") in the 1990s, Philadelphia gained a reputation as something of a filmmakers' city, with several major motion pictures being filmed there during the past decade.[13] The emergent local film industry has been coaxed along by the Greater Philadelphia Film Office, which was founded and is funded by Greater Philadelphia First (GPF), the corporate development firm that published *The Greater Philadelphia Story*.

In mid-February 1995, the Philadelphia media provided extensive cover-age of the local filming of *12 Monkeys*, directed by Terry Gilliam and star-ring Bruce Willis, Madeline Stowe, and Brad Pitt. Hailing the filming as a boon for Philadelphia, the *Philadelphia Inquirer* printed a shooting sched-ule, and television news followed up with nightly features. On a day when film crews had traveled to the heart of Center City, the central business dis-trict, to shoot scenes near City Hall, one station broadcast a feature on a family that had been cast as extras. This family, clearly middle-class, con-sisted of a white woman with two children (the husband presumably was at work), who evidently lived far enough from the city limits to drive in for the day, as they were interviewed in front of their late-model sedan. They had intended simply to observe the filming but, quite by surprise, had been en-listed as extras. The reporter had caught up with them on the way home after their exciting day.

This story and the hyping of the production of *12 Monkeys* around town followed fast on the heels of the production of the film *Philadelphia* the year before. In GPF's annual report for 1994, production of *Philadelphia* was featured prominently in two sections: "Economic Development" and "Communicating Regional Strengths." The report stated, "When the film 'Philadelphia' premiered in Paris in March, GPF and the Greater Philadelphia Film Office organized a special screening for executives of the French pharmaceutical industry, investment prospects, and film community representatives" (GPF 1994:7). The French pharmaceutical executives saw the film presumably because a French laboratory had first discovered HIV, and because GPF has had past success in luring French pharmaceuticals to the Philadelphia region. "Film community representatives" were invited to help circulate Philadelphia's reputation and therefore draw more producers and film crews to the city. And "investment prospects" were to be impressed by Philadelphia's importance to the film industry, its international image, and the skill with which GPF had been able to coordinate the special intercontinental screening.

The production of *12 Monkeys* was similarly hyped, with a promotional still featured in GPF's 1995 annual report and the local media running several features on local actors who appeared in various bit parts in the film. As far as GPF and the local news media were concerned, the message was clear: film production in Philadelphia brings in much-needed revenue while providing free advertising for the region, which in turn brings in more revenue, presumably not just in the area of film production.

This message was not so clear in Kensington, the impoverished neighborhood where much of the film was shot. Once a manufacturing center for nondurable products like leather and textiles, Kensington is now one of the poorest areas in all of Pennsylvania, filled with vacant, crumbling buildings that used to house factories and the families of their workers.

Filming centered on the extremely depressed area around the intersection of Kensington Avenue and Somerset Street, which was altered to fit the requirements of the film's script. Film crews draped a two-block length of the El overpass with plastic covers as if it were being painted. A local appliance store was converted into a butcher shop, which (in the film's diegesis) had been taken over by the "Freedom for Animals Association"—the "FAA" sign was nailed on top of a much larger butcher-shop sign adorned with drawings of pigs' heads. Crews had purchased a local merchant's beat-up van, pasted small U.S. flags on it, and spray-painted graffiti over them. Posters advertising fictitious music bands playing at clubs located at fictitious addresses had been pasted on and around the "FAA headquarters." When *12 Monkeys* was released a year later, it became apparent that these modifications, and the placement of dozens of extras on the streets to give the appearance of bustling foot traffic, had helped lend a sinister aura of decadence and decay to the secret headquarters of the Army of the 12 Monkeys, a group of mentally unbalanced urban activists.

Just beyond the range of the cameras stood several crowds of people, primarily white and Puerto Rican residents who lived in the immediate area and African American residents who lived a few blocks due west in North Philadelphia. Most had come out of curiosity, and many had hoped to catch a glimpse of the stars. On-site, numerous exchanges occurred between crew members and spectators as the crowd was continually asked to be quiet, to move away from this or that corner, to get out of the street, and to refrain from flash photography. Spectators reacted to these exchanges in ways that expressed the contradictions, ironies, and social antagonisms of the city's political economy and belied the harmonious representations of the local media. One woman, when told to refrain from flash photography, immediately complied despite the fact that her camera had no flash. As the crowd looked on she said, "Like I have the money for a flash," and then, referring to the crew and actors, added, "They do." I asked a man who lives in North Philadelphia if he thought Philadelphia was getting a lot of attention recently because of film production. He said he did, mentioned the fact that *Rocky* had been filmed in the same area several years before, and added, "There's a lot of money here. . . . [But] they always say we have no money. There are cuts and cuts and cuts, the mayor says we have to have cuts, but all this money's coming in here." The man's understanding of the economy and geography of film production flew in the face of GPF's representation of the same process. In contrast to GPF's neoliberal trickle-down perspective, in which the film would benefit the entire region not only imagewise but as a concrete example of economic development, the man with whom I spoke clearly saw the Kensington neighborhood as a commodity that generated what he felt were massive sums of money coming into the city. He understood the "economic development" process as one of uneven development, whereby money came in "here," in Kensington, traveled to Center City and City Hall, and then disappeared, never to return to the neighborhood.

The same theme became apparent later, when a young woman who had come with her two children, her mother, and a friend stated that although she lives in the area, "I'm afraid to come here. The only reason I'm here is because there's so many police now," referring to police officers who had been specially assigned to assist the production crew in managing automobile traffic and controlling the crowd. "You never see police here. Now they're here and all the drug [trade is] gone." Her mother commented, "This area's gone down in the last twenty years. Why would anyone want to shoot a movie here?" The crew, in conversations with local reporters overheard by many in the crowd, provided the answer. "I overheard the crew talking," said a local woman. "They said Philly is great because it has shiny Center City and also the slums." The stark contrast between Center City and the "slums" allowed Gilliam to get shots of midtown high-rises, City Hall, and Kensington decay, all within a convenient two-mile radius.

But the more important benefit of the proximate spatial contrast accrued in the broader production context: because of neoliberal development, Gilliam and his producers had at their disposal both a ready-made urban nightmare in which to film and a first-rate local film office in the downtown business district to help production run smoothly. The producers brought the stars, director, and other "talent" from Hollywood and London; rented or purchased local labor and equipment; and saved on costs by using worthless lots and devalued buildings for sets, staging, storage, and parking. "We went to Philadelphia looking for rotting America," Gilliam told *Entertainment Weekly*. "It turned out to be the perfect place" (qtd. in Ascher-Walsh 1995: 36). "Throughout their stay," wrote a local reviewer, "[Gilliam] and production designer Jeffrey Beecroft couldn't believe their good fortune: they found the city replete with crumbling buildings and beat sites. They were also greeted with enthusiasm by the mayor. Gilliam recalls, 'We met Sharon Pinkenson [executive director of the Film Office], and [Mayor] Ed Rendell, who's a very keen guy. They understand that when films come to your town, it makes your town famous'" (Fuchs 1996: 16). An article on the film's economic impact on the city noted that "hotels were chief among the beneficiaries." But while the manager of one upscale establishment noted "an increase in room service and dry-cleaning activity," he explained that "film is a small part of our overall business." More important, he stressed, was "the impact on the cachet and positioning of the hotel [which] is invaluable and totally out of proportion to the number of room nights" (qtd. in Rickey 1995: D1).

Indeed, *12 Monkeys* has been used, just like *Philadelphia* before it, to promote the city's corporations and service industry to a regional, national, and international audience of potential investors, tourists, shoppers, and high-skill management employees. For the years 1992 to 1995, GPF's figures indicate that film production jobs accounted for between 25 and 75 percent of the total annual job creation for which it takes credit (GPF 1995: 8). Like the producers of *12 Monkeys*, Greater Philadelphia First takes advantage of the unevenness and inequalities of the neoliberal development model to craft its own representations and imagery. Low-wage, temporary, film-related employment is added to other numbers to work up a particular picture of job creation that suits the facile optimism of the neoliberal policy establishment while masking the growing inequality of a local economy fueled by service jobs. Film stills from the city's most shamefully depressed areas become promotional images in public relations brochures, and low-wage service businesses happily make do with the indirect benefits of "cachet" and "positioning." All this occurs in an effort to draw more financial, service, and so-called knowledge-intensive industries into the suburbs and Center City, strengthening the geographic stratification characteristic of an economy based more and more on the speedy production of a wide range of commodities, including motion pictures.

Thus it would seem that while Kensington can help the Philadelphia region become a filmmakers' center, the Philadelphia region can do little to help Kensington emerge from its depressed state. In fact, in the example cited here, the Philadelphia region *depends* on Kensington being rundown and depressed for the whole operation to function properly. This, in a nutshell, is how neoliberalism plays out in urban space.

Yet it would be a mistake to think that an impoverished neighborhood like Kensington is merely bypassed and ignored by the "growth machine" of neoliberal development. The commodification of urban space and city life is no less powerful in Kensington than in the historic and business districts that were the subjects of this chapter's introduction. The neoliberal development model does not only produce increased profits and expanded markets. It imposes the logic of consumption on the city, just as suburbanization made consumption the *sine qua non* of suburban life and identity. New wants, needs, and standards of success are created that shape the contours of social life. Consumables—urban amenities, motion pictures, recreational activities—are produced and redefined at ever faster speeds and draw almost at random from a dizzying array of historical sources, influences, and antecedents. As in accounts of the "postmodern condition," aesthetic pastiche becomes a primary marketing tool, as linear narrative is replaced by the immediacy of consumer choice and the ideology of consumption comes to permeate more and more aspects of daily life. "The image, the appearance, the spectacle" of the urban environment and the tourist's paradise, Harvey argues, "can all be experienced with an intensity (joy or terror) made possible only by their appreciation as pure and unrelated presents in time" (1989: 285). Cheri Honkala, director of the Kensington Welfare

Rights Union (KWRU), a citywide poor people's organization named for the neighborhood in which it was founded, relates the effects of this sort of accelerated consumerism on teenagers in poor communities:

> [These] kids have no alternatives. . . . [They] have attempted suicide. I['ve] been in so many hospital rooms with mothers with kids trying to kill themselves. . . . None of these kids ha[s] any money for movies. They are constantly under harassment for not being up to style in clothing, there's pressure to develop drug addictions—you name it. They're living a hell. (Ruben 1995)

Honkala's narrative highlights the psychic trauma of living under constant pressure to keep up with rapid changes in fashion that follow no logical progression and with consuming the unending output of cultural products like Hollywood films. In Honkala's account, even drug abuse is subject to the logic of consumption: in the instances to which she refers, it is not drugs per se that produce the teens' suicide attempts but rather drug addiction as one more item in a regime of consumption of products with short "life spans" that fit the fast-turnover logic of modern-day capitalism. As the pace, pervasiveness, and social importance of consumption increase, the relative deprivation of the poor rises along with them. Put simply, there are more and more things that one notices one does not have and cannot get, and the fact of not having becomes increasingly central to one's identity as a social being. The middle-class consumer, who may go to see *12 Monkeys* and marvel at its dramatic imagery, experiences the acceleration of consumption as a "pageant," an intense spectacle of joy. But the impoverished urban teenager, who cannot afford to see the movie and for whom the film's decrepit images constitute documentary photographs of his or her neighborhood, experiences the flip side of spectacular joy: terror and violence.

While Honkala's account of poor teens' experience is quite powerful, it is also quite depressing. If the only choices are media images of teenagers killing each other for a stylish new pair of sneakers or Honkala's image of teenagers killing themselves because they cannot afford a stylish new pair of sneakers, then we are back to the superpredator-versus-passive-victim binary that has structured the underclass and culture-of-poverty debates, and that has allowed scholars like Gottdiener and Shields to spin their yarns (both ominous and celebratory) about "the essence of the urban" and "the ghetto." It would seem that, while neoliberal development facilitates agency for certain Philadelphia business interests and for the producers of *12 Monkeys*, it tends to close off possibilities for agency among the women and children who belong to KWRU. Even Harvey's argument reaches its limit at this point, when it relegates the difference between consumptive joy and spectacular terror to a parenthetical.

The effects of neoliberal development are not merely empirical facts whose phenomenal status must be debated. For the urban poor, uneven development represents both a political threat and a political opportunity. KWRU, in fact, was founded to fight the implementation of neoliberal welfare policies: it was formed to protest statewide welfare cuts that were being proposed just as economic prosperity was returning to Philadelphia. As Honkala says, "The first reason [for KWRU's existence] is to meet basic needs. But the game, or the fight, is to provide people with political education."[14]

Which Way Welfare Rights? a pamphlet authored in part by Honkala, proposes a way to understand struggle and empowerment for poor people:

> No end or objective can be accomplished without means or resources and their proper utilization.... [History places] means at the disposal of political leaders ... in the course of social development. History is the unfolding of the stages of development of society. It is rooted in the constant changes in the economy, changes in the way the necessities of life are produced and distributed. On the basis of these changes, conflicting economic interests of different sections of the population compel them to take up historically evolved forms of struggle and fight it out. (National Welfare Rights Union 1993)

In postmodernist discourse and urban scholarship, in English departments and sociology programs, this sort of narrative is regularly dismissed for being linear, rigid, retrograde, and masculinist. In fact, it is fair to say that a number of subfields, schools of thought, and careers have been founded on a strict and specific opposition to just this sort of teleological discourse. But when it is *situated*, placed in the context of the confusing and disorienting workings of the economic system it critiques, this linear, teleological narrative, written by and largely for poor women, can be understood as one appropriate tool in and for a particular conjuncture characterized not only by its historical location but also by its *geographic* one.

Similarly, a KWRU organizing pamphlet (1993) addresses itself to "the victims of poverty," making an appeal across the racial and ethnic lines that often separate neighborhoods from one another:

> We as poor people, especially women and youth, are often isolated from one another.... We tend to blame each other, i.e.: poor whites will blame poor blacks, poor blacks blame poor Asians and the cycle goes round and round. And we see this tool of division taking place every day in the Kensington area,

even though we all stand in the same soup lines, welfare lines and our children go to school together. (KWRU 1993)

This passage features neither the supply-side optimism of the Urban Neighborhoods Task Force report, the eroticization of difference evident in much urban cultural scholarship, nor the agentless pessimism of much progressive policy literature. Rather, it evokes a vision of urban neighborhoods that are heterogeneous with respect both to the redeveloped city center and to one another. It appeals to "the victims of poverty" across the racial lines that often separate neighborhoods from one another. It speaks to poor people who must increasingly avail themselves of the shrinking services of the welfare state, and it uses that shared experience to break the temporal "cycle" that goes "round and round" by organizing poor people across the urban landscape on the basis of *class*.

In the end, it is class, and its attendant political-economic processes, that has risen to parity with race as the most important factor in understanding and fighting neoliberal development. It is therefore not surprising to see neoliberal discourse and policy promoting individual responsibility, self-help, and "market discipline," as a way of obscuring the fundamental class inequalities created by the modern urban landscape of uneven development. It is rather surprising and disappointing, however, to see urban scholars condemning political-economic analysis and dispensing with "metanarratives" in favor of romantic, impressionistic, individualistic narratives of urban poverty and difference that fail to subvert or resist the processes of uneven development and the policies and cultural practices of neoliberal governance.

The reintegration of class into the language of urban representation can serve as a countervailing force to isolation and division without falling into the trap of homogenizing and erasing the material realities of people's lives. It also makes a fairly obvious point to urban scholars and policymakers. A study that begins by asking, "How can we save the city?" makes ideological assumptions about the nature of urban space, the unity of the polity, and the way the economy works (or doesn't work) to provide the means of survival for urban residents. "How can we save the city?" when asked uncritically and unreflexively in the current climate, inevitably produces a supply-side answer that balances budgets on the backs of the poor, leaves neoliberal development unchallenged, and clears the way for the vilification and marginalization of grassroots poor people's movements that protest new forms of development and state policy. The nature of the neoliberal model requires us to consider prior questions: Who are "we" to save the city? What if we start from the fact that poor people in cities are fighting and will continue to fight, and that their struggle is central to the future of urban areas? Then, as intellectuals who often live in suburbs and gentrified urban enclaves and work in institutions integral to the reproduction of the producer-service economy and the policy establishment, we might more rigorously situate ourselves, our readings, and our global epistemologies in an ethico-political relation to that context. We might set about trying to help poor people be makers of policy, rather than its object, and return poor people's agency to the center of analysis.

NOTES

1. The concept of the postindustrial economy has been misused extensively in both the humanities and the social sciences. The term *postindustrial* is used here only to refer to the local urban context. Hundreds of books and articles on globalization notwithstanding, neither national nor global economies are postindustrial. Over the past thirty years, large corporations based in the leading industrial nations have greatly stepped up the internationalization of production, moving manufacturing facilities across nations and around the world in search of cheap labor, minimal regulation, and low taxes. *Deindustrialization* refers to a very specific phenomenon in which a particular area experiences a significant loss of manufacturing industry as a result of these national and global relocations. More often than not, spaces of deindustrialization are cities, being that cities constituted the locus of most manufacturing infrastructure up until the 1960s. In sum, while the economy of a city like Philadelphia may be referred to as postindustrial (or deindustrialized), it is inaccurate to refer to "the economy"—i.e., the national or global economy—as postindustrial.

2. The phrase "sublime object of ideology" is taken from Zizek's book of the same name (1989). The term *imagineer* is taken from Disney's "living history" attractions at its theme parks (Imagineers 1996).

3. Much work in the humanities and social sciences takes considerable liberty with the term *commodity*. While I am using this term outside the context of the manufacture of a specific tangible good, I nevertheless aim to preserve the strict meaning of the concept of commodification. The subsumption of Philadelphia's space under an agenda of competition with other cities for tourist dollars inevitably submits that space—which is, after all, material and therefore produced and reproduced through various kinds of labor—to the logic of exchange, which Marx (1990) says is the "mystical character" of the commodity (as opposed to the mere produced object) under capitalism (163). Philadelphia's historical space competes as a *prod-*

uct on the basis of its distinctiveness; but the very notion of such a competition implies the potential substitutability, or exchangeability, of this space's distinctiveness for that of any other city's space, according to criteria of recreation, safety, beauty, availability of land or finance capital, and so on.

4. Postwar suburbanization also signaled the end of the image of the United States as a rural nation. While urban outmigration was by far the main source of population for suburban communities, rural outmigration constituted the beginning of the end of the family farm as a major player in agricultural production and allowed more and more suburban communities to be built on farmland that had been sold or auctioned off.

5. It is worth noting in this regard that the vast majority of firms that have left U.S. cities since World War II have relocated in U.S. suburbs, not in other countries as is commonly thought.

6. The Levitts, of Levittown fame, were among the earliest and best-known adopters of mass-production and off-site construction techniques in the home-building industry (Jackson 1985).

7. The legacy of Gans's study is particularly disturbing. While the work itself is of considerable importance, it has been taken all too often as "proof" of the extensive, hidden diversity of suburban communities. This tack has led to an entirely unproductive scholarly debate about whether or not suburban residents should be vilified or blamed for the problems of cities, diverting attention from the political-economic dimension of urban-suburban inequities.

8. Income levels, of course, do not begin to capture the actual dynamics of class difference and class relations. They do, however, serve as a basic indicator of differentials in the geographic concentration of poverty, which is a major focus of this chapter and this anthology.

9. On the rise of the producer-service sector, see Sassen (1994, 1991). On gentrification, see Smith (1996).

10. The role of the large nonprofit firm in neoliberal urban development is too complex to detail in this chapter. Three basic observations may be made in this limited space. First, certain large, highly rationalized nonprofits are seen by municipal authorities as potential "anchors" for economic development, and so cities often provide such organizations with tax breaks and devote resources to stabilizing the surrounding real estate in hopes of stimulating commercial investment or gentrification. Second, many of these nonprofits have for some time been adopting the fiscal policies and service priorities of the for-profit sector, seeking to serve more affluent clients and customers at the expense of social equity, universal access to health and education, and their employees' livelihoods. Finally, economic contradictions often work against efforts by these nonprofits to "corporatize" themselves successfully. The most frequent example is that local and regional hospital systems go bankrupt because they do not get sufficiently reimbursed for the cost of care by local and regional HMOs. Both types of institution often are courted by municipal

authorities, yet the essential competition for resources between them works against the municipal growth agenda.

11. The title refers to Friedrich Engels's own observations of mid-nineteenth-century Manchester in his foundational *The Condition of the Working Class in England* (1999 [1845]). For the definitive analysis of Engels's book and an explanation of its importance to both Marxism and urban studies, see Katznelson (1992).

12. Indeed, many of the anthology's contributions are rigorously theorized, persuasively argued, and quite useful.

13. Prominent recent examples include *Philadelphia* (1994), *12 Monkeys* (1996), *Beloved* (1998), and *The Sixth Sense* (1999).

14. Throughout its seven-year existence, KWRU's ability to provide political education to new members has varied greatly, based on available time and resources, the nature of its struggle at particular moments, and the changing priorities of its leadership.

REFERENCES

Adams, Carolyn Teich. 1988. *The Politics of Capital Investment;:The Case of Philadelphia*. Albany: State University of New York Press.

Adams, Carolyn, David Bartelt, David Elesh, Ira Goldstein, Nancy Kleniewski, and William Yancey. 1991. *Philadelphia: Neighborhoods, Division, and Conflict in a Postindustrial City*. Philadelphia: Temple University Press.

Ascher-Walsh, Rebecca. 1995. "Making Monkeys Shine: It's a Pitiful Life in Brad's New World." *Entertainment Weekly*, October 20, p. 36.

Berman, Marshall. 1982. *All That Is Solid Melts into Air: The Experience of Modernity*. New York: Simon and Schuster.

Bissinger, Buzz. 1997. *A Prayer for the City*. New York: Random House.

Davis, Mike. 1990. *City of Quartz: Excavating the Future in Los Angeles*. London: Verso.

———. 1986. *Prisoners of the American Dream*. London: Verso.

Deleuze, Gilles, and Felix Guattari. 1983. *Anti-Oedipus: Capitalism and Schizophrenia*. Translated by Robert Hurley, Mark Seem, and Helen R. Lane. Minneapolis: University of Minnesota Press.

Engels, Friedrich. 1999 [1845]. *The Condition of the Working Class in England*. Edited with an introduction and notes by David McLellan. New York: Oxford University Press.

Fuchs, Cynthia. 1996. "The Monkeys Man"/"*12 Monkeys*" (linked feature and review). Philadelphia *City Paper*, January 5, pp. 16–18, 50–51.

Gans, Herbert J. 1967. *The Levittowners: Ways of Life and Politics in a Suburban Community*. New York: Pantheon Books.

Gilliam, Terry. 1995. *12 Monkeys*. Los Angeles: Universal Pictures/Atlas Entertainment.

Gottdiener, Mark. 1991. " A Walk around Town; with Apologies to F. Engels." *Urban Life in Transition: Urban Affairs Annual Reviews*, Vol. 39. Edited by Mark Gottdiener and Chris G. Pickvance. Newbury Park, CA: Sage Publications, pp. 240–43.

Gottdiener, Mark, and Chris G. Pickvance. 1991. "Introduction." *Urban Life in Transition: Urban Affairs Annual Reviews*, Vol. 39. Edited by Mark Gottdiener and Chris G. Pickvance. Newbury Park, CA: Sage Publications, pp. 1–11.

Gramsci, Antonio. 1971. *Selections from the Prison Notebooks*. Edited and translated by Quintin Hoare and Geoffrey Nowell Smith. New York: International Publishers.

Greater Philadelphia First (GPF). 1995. *Report of Progress 1995*. Philadelphia: Greater Philadelphia First Corp.

———. 1994. *Report of Progress 1994*. Philadelphia: Greater Philadelphia First Corp.

———. 1993. *The Greater Philadelphia Story*. Philadelphia: Geater Philadelphia First Corp.

Harvey, David. 1989. *The Condition of Postmodernity*. Cambridge, MA: Blackwell.

———. 1985. *The Urbanization of Capital*. Baltimore: Johns Hopkins University Press.

Hill, Richard Child. 1984. "Fiscal Collapse and Political Struggle in Decaying Central Cities in the United States." In *Marxism and the Metropolis: New Perspectives in Urban Political Economy*. Edited by William K. Tabb and Larry Sawers. 2d ed. New York: Oxford University Press, pp. 213–40.

The Imagineers. 1996. *Walt Disney Imagineering: A Behind the Dreams Look at Making the Magic Real*. Foreword by Michael D. Eisner. New York: Hyperion Books.

Jackson, Kenneth T. 1985. *Crabgrass Frontier: The Suburbanization of the Untied States*. New York: Oxford University Press, 1985.

Jacobs, Jane. 1961. *The Death and Life of Great American Cities*. New York: Random House.

Kahn, Joel S. 1995. *Culture, Multiculture, Postculture*. London: Sage Publications.

Katz, Michael B. 1993. "The Urban 'Underclass' as a Metaphor of Social Transformation." In *The "Underclass" Debate: Views from History*. Edited by Michael B. Katz. Princeton: Princeton University Press, pp. 3–23.

———. 1989. *The Undeserving Poor: From the War on Poverty to the War on Welfare*. New York: Pantheon Books.

Katznelson, Ira. 1992. *Marxism and the City*. Oxford: Oxford University Press.

Kensington Welfare Rights Union (KWRU). 1993. *Link Up the Struggle* (pamphlet). Philadelphia: Kensington Welfare Rights Union/United in Strength.

Lewis, Oscar. 1966. "The Culture of Poverty." *Scientific American*, vol. 215, no. 4: 19–25.

Lind, Michael. 1995. *The Next American Nation: The New Nationalism and the Fourth American Revolution*. New York: Free Press.

Lipsitz, George. 1998. *The Possessive Investment in Whiteness: How White People Profit from Identity Politics*. Philadelphia: Temple University Press.

Logan, John R., and Harvey L. Molotch. 1987. *Urban Forturnes: The Political Economy of Place*. Berkeley, CA: University of California Press.

Marable, Manning. 1983. *How Capitalism Underdeveloped Black America: Problems in Race, Political Economy and Society*. Boston: South End Press.

Marcuse, Peter. 1986. "Abandonment, Gentrification, and Displacement: The Linkages in New York." In *Gentrification of the City*. Edited by Neil Smith and Peter Williams. Boston: Allen and Unwin.

Marx, Karl. 1990. *Capital*. Volume 1. New York: Penguin.

Massey, Douglas S., and Nancy A. Denton. 1992. *American Apartheid: Segregation and the Making of the Underclass*. Cambridge, MA: Harvard University Press.

Murray, Charles. 1984. *Losing Ground: American Social Policy, 1950–1980*. New York: Basic Books.

National Welfare Rights Union. 1993. *Which Way Welfare Rights?* (pamphlet). Philadelphia: Annie Smart Leadership Institute and *Voices from the Front*.

Rickey, Carrie. 1995. "*Twelve Monkeys* Takes the Turnpike; Futuristic Film Leaves Town after Pumping Millions into City's Economy." *Philadelphia Inquirer*, March 27, p. D1.

Rothenberg, Randall. 1984. *The Neoliberals: Creating the New American Politics*. New York: Simon and Schuster.

Ruben, Matthew. 1996. Interview with Kelly Boyd, May 25.

———. 1995. Interview with Cheri Honkala, March 10.

Sassen, Saskia. 1994. *Cities in a World Economy*. Thousand Oaks, CA: Pine Forge Press.

———. 1991. *The Global City: New York, London, Tokyo*. Princeton: Princeton University Press.

Shields, Rob. 1996. "A Guide to Urban Representation and What to Do about It: Alternative Traditions of Urban Theory." *Representing the City: Ethnicity, Capital and Culture in the 21st-Century Metropolis*. Edited by Anthony D. King. New York: New York University Press, pp. 227–52.

Smith, Neil. 1996. *The New Urban Frontier: Gentrification and the Revanchist City*. London: Routledge.

———. 1991. *Uneven Development*. London: Blackwell.

Stallone, Sylvester. 1978. *Rocky II*. Los Angeles: Chartoff/Winkler Productions.

Sugrue, Thomas J. 1993. "The Structures of Urban Poverty: The Reorganization of Space and Work in Three Periods of American History." In *The "Underclass" Debate: Views from History*. Edited by Michael B. Katz. Princeton: Princeton University Press, pp. 85-117.

United States Department of Labor. 1965. *The Negro Family: The Case for National Action*. Washington, DC: U.S. Government Printing Office.

Urban Neighborhoods Task Force. 1997. *Life in the City: A Status Report on the Revival of Urban Communities in America*. Co-sponsored by the Center for National Policy and the Local Initiatives Support Corporation. Washington, DC: Center for National Policy.

Whyte, William Hollingsworth. 1957. *The Organization Man*. Garden City, NY: Doubleday.

Wilson, William Julius. 1987. *The Truly Disadvantaged: The Inner City, the Underclass, and Public Policy*. Chicago: University of Chicago Press.

Yates, Pamela, and Peter Kinoy. 1996. *Poverty Outlaw*. New York: Skylight Pictures.

Young, Iris Marion. 1990. *Justice and the Politics of Difference*. Princeton: Princeton University Press.

Zizek, Slavoj. 1989. *The Sublime Object of Ideology*. London: Verso.

Afterword
Beyond the Privatist Consensus

Jeff Maskovsky

The New Rules of the Game

The corporate offensive of the past three decades has been waged on many fronts. A shifting and sometimes unwitting conglomeration of large corporations, right-wing ideologues, centrist politicians, and liberal policy experts have pushed government to scale back or eliminate key regulatory mechanisms, social services, and community funding streams, all to the detriment of poor and working-class Americans. State-facilitated economic restructuring has restored corporate profitability in many sectors of the economy; but it has done so by creating an historically unprecedented degree of economic polarization and inequality. This capitalist offensive has been accompanied—and helped along—by a wholesale shift in the national culture, a move toward the pro-market ideology of neoliberalism. In this climate of what Robert Kuttner (1997) calls "everything for sale," privatization has been figured as the panacea for all of the social ills in the United States.

It should not be surprising, then, that the effects of neoliberal ascendancy in the United States are most starkly apparent in the new war on the poor. The right-wing attack on welfare in the 1980s (itself an outgrowth of the post-1960s backlash in the 1970s) quickly morphed into a kinder, gentler neoliberal project in the 1990s, with intensified salvos against "dependency" and a concomitant attenuation of the racist rhetoric of the Reagan era. The basis of popular compassion and political support for the poor now rests more than ever on their ability to conform to market-based notions of consumerism, responsibility, initiative, and entrepreneurship. In the wake of welfare reform, those whose social value cannot be defined in terms of the market are vilified as "irresponsible dependents," unworthy of state largesse or even charity.

Herein lies the most important characteristic of the new war on the poor. Neoliberal market ideology has reformulated the historical division between the deserving and undeserving poor around the category of *productivity*, rather than race, gender, or morality. This market-based focus allows proponents of welfare reform to identify their project with the national interest. In keeping with the putatively non-ideological ideology of neoliberalism, the new war on the poor avoids division and vilification and instead concentrates on the pragmatics of prosperity. In short, the new war on the poor claims not to be a war at all.

This is the central dynamic to which current research on poverty must respond. With popular and political support for a policy agenda defined almost exclusively in terms of the market model, scholars with alternative perspectives and concerns for social and economic justice confront a popular, political, and scholarly environment in which our viewpoints are marginalized and our findings ignored. This is, of course, entirely consistent with the neoliberal way of dealing with the poor themselves. Overcoming this kind of forced invisibility—what Judith Goode and I refer to in the introduction to this book as a *regime of disappearance*—will require us to rethink the goals and objectives of contemporary poverty research. I argue here that our research must aim beyond specific policy questions and legislative debates and instead aspire to promote fundamental social change. In particular, we should tailor our research agenda so that it contributes to the grassroots efforts of the poor, as well as other mobilization efforts allied with or politically relevant to the poor.

Barriers to Effective Poverty Research

The challenges neoliberalism poses to poverty research are many. The most pervasive, and the most insidious, is depoliticization. Identifying itself with national prosperity, embracing diversity, eschewing "ideology" for pragmatics, neoliberal policy shelves the question of poor people's political agency. This is of course a political move, part of neoliberalism's imposition of market subjectivity across the spectrum of everyday life. Yet, as it relates to poverty research, it plays into certain conceptions about objectivity prevalent in the social sciences. The result is that as the public policy spectrum has narrowed during the past twenty years, so, too, has the social scientific research agenda. In attempt to remain "relevant" to policymakers and legislators, an alarming amount of recent scholarship on poverty has restricted itself to program evaluation. This approach focuses on assessing the efficiency and effectiveness of policies relative to their stated goals, leaving unexamined the merits of the goals themselves. At best, such scholarship provides insights into the relative utility of various mildly reformist programs. At worst, it amounts to a tacit endorsement of a policy agenda that has given up entirely on eliminating poverty and promoting social equality (Piven and Cloward 1997: 243–67). Here I sketch some specific factors that undermine the ability of poverty research to contribute meaningfully to the reversal of current patterns of economic polarization and social inequality.

First, there is increased pressure on poverty researchers to join what I here term the *workist consensus*. The workist consensus holds that participation in the low-end labor market is the primary goal of anti-poverty policy and an unquestionable social good. Under the rubric of self-sufficiency, the workist consensus promotes labor conditions that often are not beneficial to the poor and working classes. Shunning the use of income transfer payments and job creation programs to equalize wages and tighten the labor market, neoliberal anti-poverty policy works to loosen the labor market and polarize income, promoting lower wages as a counterbalance to the frenzy of credit-driven consumption that has sustained national economic growth for the past decade. Poverty researchers are now asked to consider the workist consensus as axiomatic, to conceive of privatist policy interventions that do not disrupt the overarching pattern of labor-market polarization.

A case in point is research on welfare policy. Welfare "reform" has spawned a torrent of research organized around the question of how to best enhance the capacity of poor women to gain access to and success in low-end jobs. Although much of this scholarship has demonstrated the need for income supports such as child care and health care for women and their families who are forced, as a result of Temporary Assistance to Needy Families (TANF), into low-end jobs, it does not challenge the racist, sexist, and classist devaluation of poor women's child-rearing and community work. In fact, this scholarship ignores and implicitly devalues the work poor women do at home and in their communities (Mink 1998; Kahn and Polakow 2000; Hyatt, chapter 8, above). Indeed, by embracing the politically retrograde position that everyone who can work should work, such research offers remedies designed to make poor people more comfortable in low-end labor markets, rather than challenging the structure of the labor markets themselves. The roots of inequality are masked and the poor, particularly poor women, are now more vulnerable, whether they can find paid work or not (Piven, chapter 5, above). Lost in the entire enterprise is any strategy for actually reducing or eliminating poverty.

Similar examples abound in policy arenas beyond welfare. In fact, the implications of privatization for health, education, and welfare services is something many researchers have failed to grasp. As public institutions are scaled back and the role of private entities, corporate or otherwise, expands, many researchers have ignored the question of whether this shift is beneficial in a broad sense to poor communities. Instead, they confine themselves to research focusing on the best ways to improve what is already assumed to be the dominant organization of poor relief, work opportunity, and "empowerment" for the poor. This research, whatever its specific programmatic contributions, reinforces the retrograde idea that self-help is the only legitimate way for the poor to pull themselves out of poverty, and that state action cannot be relied on to provide long-term solutions to immiseration and impoverishment. Arguing for the central political and policy importance of "equal proprietorship of public institutions" for black Americans, Adolph Reed has said:

> From this perspective the predominance of self-help rhetoric marks a capitulationist evasion whose dangers are obscured by its enshrinement of class prejudice and the soothing patter of class self-congratulation in an insipid discourse of "role models" and special middle-class tutelage as an antidote to impoverishment. That the self-help program is a strategic dead end is clear in the spectacle of the tremendous expense of effort poured, in communities all over the country, into Black Family Weekends, marches to Stop the Violence, proclamations of firearms-free or drug-free zones, failed attempts at economic development, gang or youth summits—which mainly produce platitudes and homilies and moments of orchestrated conviviality.
>
> I by no means wish to disparage grassroots activism and community initiative in principle; the problem with self-help ideology is that it reifies community initiative, freighting it with an ideological burden that reduces it to political quietism and a programmatic mission that it is ill equipped to fulfill. (Reed 1999: 127)

This point is particularly applicable in light of the kinds of projects that are now increasingly targeted not only toward black inner-city residents but toward poor people everywhere, projects that poverty researchers are increasingly asked to endorse. Accordingly, research, particularly applied "evaluation" research on the efficacy of volunteer service corps, the voluntary (and sometimes publicly funded) efforts of faith-based organizations, high school and university service learning programs, and development projects based on social and human capital formation, to name several of the current fads, often accepts, to one degree or another, individualized, privatist definitions of personal responsibility and self-help, ignoring the implications of these programs for the capacity of poor community members not only to elaborate demands on the state in the face of growing inequality but even to envision the state as a site of struggle.

The second factor undermining poverty research is that, while the political spectrum of policy has narrowed, the arena of policy implementation remains fragmented. Despite the scaling back of welfare, existing programs and policies designed to meet poor people's needs continue to be arrayed across a complex and multilayered bureaucracy. This corresponds with the promotion of pathologized and medicalized identities for the poor. Indeed, as social programs continue to be dispersed among more specialized bureaucracies, poor people are ascribed different identities—homeless, drug addict, welfare mom, Medicaid recipient, and so forth—each with its own prescription for social change. Not only do these labels obscure the political and economic basis of inequality by reinforcing psychologistic models of individual deviance; they and their associated assumptions also shape the ways in which poor people view themselves and their relation to the state. Some might argue that devolution has somewhat complicated these dynamics, with increased "discretion" and "flexibility" in policy development and implementation now possible at the state level. Federal mandates, however, continue to define the intended goals of social policies such as welfare while giving the states the power to determine how best to meet those goals, and state-level bureaucracy thus continues to reinforce federal-level categorizations of the poor. Given this arrangement, the impact of devolution on the cultural landscape of social policy should not be overstated (Soss et al. n.d.).[1]

The limits of current social policy are by now well known to policymakers and the researchers who work with them. For example, mainstream policy experts occasionally elaborate policy alternatives that contradict the dominant assumptions about social policy's role in shaping labor markets. Yet some proponents of these alternatives are as ambivalent about poor people as they are about current social policies. No small number have refused to demand an expanded role for the poor in shaping policy; and many avoid overt alliance or identification with the political movements that can give voice to poor people's collective demands. Prominent poverty scholar William Julius Wilson, for instance, has elaborated a policy framework designed to create better-paying jobs and reduce growing wage and social inequalities (Wilson 1996). Drawing on comparisons with welfare-state policies in industrialized nations such as Germany, France, and Japan, Wilson argues for the expansion of employment opportunities through a number of measures, including a universal WPA-like jobs program. Interestingly, Wilson realizes that this suggestion is politically unfeasible in the current conjuncture. He writes:

> My aim, therefore, is to galvanize and rally concerned Americans to fight back with the same degree of force and dedication displayed by those who have moved us backward, rather than forward, in combating social inequality. I therefore do not advance proposals that seem acceptable or "realistic" given the current political climate. Rather, I have chosen to talk about what *ought to be done to address the problems of social inequality*, including record levels of joblessness in the inner-city ghetto, that threaten the very fabric of society. (Wilson 1996: 209, emphasis in original)

Unfortunately, Wilson's political relationship to politics is never revealed.[2] In fact, as compelling as his social-democratic policy recommendations are given the current situation, they mask an agenda that is somewhat hostile to grassroots activism and political struggle, an agenda in which he prefers to appeal to the unspecified, politically ambiguous, and ultimately empty category of "concerned Americans" rather than to the poor themselves. Though his recommendations are cloaked in rhetoric about the need to "rally concerned citizens to fight back," Wilson does not suggest strategies for generating the political will for more progressive social policy. His recommendations are therefore easily ignored, and his work, which continues to endorse the idea of ghetto pathology, then becomes ideological fuel for further right-wing attacks on what remains of the welfare state.

Those who dare not offer policy recommendations such as jobs programs have often justified and excused their acquiescence to the current retrograde policy agenda as a practical tactic designed to accord with the "realities" of current politics and policy. One of the greatest limitations of this strategy is its fantasy that policy research can somehow separate itself from the domain of politics. For instance, in her important and influential book *No Shame in My Game*, Katherine S. Newman (1999) outlines a series of narrow policy solutions, such as wage subsidies and tax breaks and educational reform for the "working poor." These solutions are elaborated based on the presumption that more sweeping alternatives, such as the kinds of public works programs that Wilson proposes, are politically unfeasible at the present moment. She writes:

> William Julius Williams has argued . . . that without creating a Marshall Plan for the nation's ghettos, complete with a substantial public job creation program for those who cannot find private employment, we will see little improvement in the lives of inner-city residents. This, coupled with intensive job training and child care support, Wilson suggests, is essential for any meaningful transformation of the dismal conditions of many isolated urban ghettos. He is surely right. Yet political support for federal jobs creation is weak, to say the least. Until the tide changes, it would be worthwhile to consider alternatives. (Newman 1999: 273)

Few liberal or progressive scholars would disagree with Newman's assessment of the struggles and indignities that poor people who are forced to work low-end jobs now face. And few would reject her policy proposals. Yet the suggestion that the role for social scientists is to offer narrow policy alternatives while we passively await a tidal change should be challenged, for it assumes a categorical split between politics and policy, and this division of labor, while presumably designed to preserve the "objective" aspects of liberal policy design, actually functions in the ideological domain to reinforce rightward shifts in the policy arena. Indeed, the very mention of the category of "the working poor" reinforces the retrograde and false policy assumption that there are a good number of poor people who do not work.[3] Of course, it could be argued that there are a variety of good reasons for this type of acquiescence at the present moment. Most compelling is the desire to leave some sort of liberal or progressive imprint on what might otherwise be a policy agenda that would have even more catastrophic consequences for the poor. Yet, although maintaining a progressive foothold such as Newman's in the current policy landscape is surely relevant, it is equally important to recognize that the incrementalist strategy of offering partial and politically compromised adjustments to a bankrupt policy agenda is nonetheless a tacit acceptance of an agenda that has been designed to excuse the persistence of poverty by dividing the poor into the categories of the deserving (those who are worthy of assistance because they work) and the undeserving poor (those who are unworthy because they do not receive wages for the work that they do).

The third major factor affecting poverty research concerns the "empowerment" of the poor themselves. As the social value of the poor is increasingly defined in terms of the market, it remains necessary to challenge pervasive ideologies of individual uplift and mobility that blame the poor for their own impoverishment. Moreover, it is now increasingly necessary to highlight the contradictions that ensue when the "empowerment" of the poor becomes implicated in policy changes to which the poor have historically stood in opposition. Unlike the Keynesian welfare-state models of the past, the forms of neoliberal incorporation to which the poor are now exposed tend to celebrate—and romanticize—poor people's agency. Researchers who strive to "give voice" to the poor now face popular and political pressure to ensure that those voices conform to the dominant tenets of the mainstream policy agenda, including the call for personal responsibility and the disavowal of state "dependency." Indeed, we now hear near continuous testimony from those who have found often-precarious jobs in the low-wage, high-turnover labor force but who talk about turning their lives around and holding their futures in their own hands.

These dynamics are fortified by the actions of liberal foundations and think tanks that support the kind of research discussed here. These institutions tend to concentrate, as Jean Stefancic and Richard Delgado (1997) say, on "good deeds," funding projects that operate within the bounds of political feasibility to accomplish the most incremental of reforms. Unlike their conservative counterparts, which have been far more successful at shaping the policy agenda, liberal foundations have little if any ideological function. In fact, they often work to dismiss and discredit work from an explicitly left position, inadvertently doing the right's bidding. Politically engaged work is often immobilized in the face of attacks, from pundits across the political spectrum, that it is elitist, idealist, and uninterested in the social issues that have garnered mainstream attention, and many who might be inclined to support less draconian policies toward the poor also view dissent from the mainstream as a detriment. Even some on the left have effectively given up the project of envisioning a just society, allowing those from other political perspectives to define the policy agenda. In this context, the central challenge we face is not fashioning policy recommendations in an arena that is, by now, so narrowly constrained by politics; nor is it to envision policy alternatives that are unviable precisely because the political will for their implementation does not exist. Rather, it is to fashion research that challenges the policy consensus itself. This requires us to overcome the current moment of political demobilization on the left.

I want to make clear that what I am arguing here is not the full-scale retreat from policy debates or from applied research. On the contrary, it implies a more thorough engagement in these domains. Policy-oriented re-search can only be successful, however, if it confronts the central contradic-tions that the poor face vis-à-vis capital and the state in the current con-juncture. For instance, state institutions—Housing and Urban Develop-ment, Empowerment Zones, Health Resources and Services Administration, Substance Abuse Mental Health Services Administration—have recently stepped up War on Poverty "maximum feasible participation" models to en-courage community "input" into publicly funded service provision models. Yet this emphasis on community input is occurring at the same time that so-cial services are being withdrawn and privatized. In this context, the demo-cratic limitations of new "participatory" models must be confronted.

In fact, some scholars and activists might now argue that greater com-munity input into service provision models in a context of welfare-state contraction is a cynical strategy to regulate the poor through a model of self-empowerment. This argument accords with the viewpoint that the provi-sion of relief itself has functioned in other historical periods to quell dissent and to regulate the poor (Piven and Cloward 1977). It is my view that poor and working people have consistently demanded better government services and an expanded role in determining how, where, and when those services are provided, and that any attempt to deliver on this promise represents a positive step that is fully commensurate with the goals and objectives of poor people's movements. I also believe, however, that poverty researchers tread on very shaky ground when they participate—through contract work or otherwise—in research designed to help "democratize" service provision in situations where services are being privatized or scaled back. Indeed, the invention of more efficient service provision models, the improvement of communication between providers and recipients, and the development of culturally appropriate services, although all laudable goals in and of them-selves, often do not address the underlying basis of poor people's needs vis a vis the welfare state. In instances where conflicts erupt between state func-tionaries, services providers and the poor themselves, researchers should keep in mind that the line between helpful mediation and participation in a pacification project for the state can become uncomfortably blurred.

The Goal of a New Research Agenda

In recent years, there have been signs that faith in the "free market" is fal-tering. In the wake of the Asian financial crisis of 1997, pundits and politicians began to question whether neoliberal ideologies and practices would continue to fuel economic growth and guarantee social welfare. Moreover, the long-term trend toward political apathy and racial and class demobilization seems now to be reversing itself. From the top, we now hear calls, by George Soros and other financial luminaries, for more market regulation and the possibility of limited job creation (Harris 1999; Robinson and Harris 2000; World Bank 1997). From the bottom, we can now hear calls for economic justice, improved environmental regulations, and greater union democracy, issued in the mass demonstrations in Seattle, Washington, D.C., Philadelphia, and Los Angeles (e.g., Brecher et al. 2000; Hart-Landsberg 2000). These may now only be murmurings—a hiccup in the neoliberal moment. They may also coalesce, however, into a wider political and ideological struggle that unites poor communities, organized labor, left activists, environmentalists, and academics in new and powerful ways. This situation, uncertain though it may be, creates an opportunity to fashion an activist scholarship that challenges the privatist consensus and aligns itself with movements for social and economic justice.

At the same time, a progressive response at the current moment will have to resist the temptation to wax nostalgic for the bygone days of the U.S. welfare state. It is true that the ravages of neoliberalism are most clearly illuminated in terms of privatization and devolution in reference to the Keynesian welfare state. It does not follow, politically or analytically, however, that we should be arguing for a return to that state. Some of the worst aspects of the current neoliberal climate were present (albeit in altered form or different contexts) in the old welfare state, which had racial and gender inequalities structured into it. Moreover, it is possible to trace the neoliberal passion for privatization and marketization to the equation of democracy and Keynesian-style capitalism that characterized official U.S. ideology and foreign policy during the Cold War. Most important, neoliberal policies were born in reaction to the failure of Keynesianism to overcome the corporate crisis in profitability that occurred in the late 1960s and early 1970s. The reinstantiation of welfare-state liberalism, while preferable to neoliberalism, will nonetheless represent a relatively narrow political response to the patterns of inequality and impoverishment that the poor continue to face.

Rather than working toward the replacement of a top-down privatist welfare system with a top-down government welfare system, poverty scholars ought to focus our efforts on the true political empowerment of the poor. The common factor in more than a century of voluntarism, policy, and scholarship related to poverty has been the exclusion of the poor themselves from real political and decision-making power. By studying the mechanisms that continue to keep poor people from the table; that co-opt poor communities through consumerism and other forms of false empowerment; and that use moralism, racism, sexism, homophobia, and other tactics to divide poor and working-class Americans from one another, poverty scholarship can help reorient public discussion back toward the putative goal of poverty policy: to eliminate poverty. By studying and communicating poor people's efforts to organize themselves into coherent, politically effective collectivities, we can work to ensure that poor people are integrally involved in that reorientation. The contributors to this book have taken a step in moving us in this direction. The ethnographically based discussions of poverty and inequality that are collected here serve as a blueprint for the creation of a more politically engaged poverty scholarship, one that stands a reasonable chance of uniting scholars not with the goals and objectives of corporate leaders and their allies, who have waged such an effective war against the poor in recent decades, but with the activist agendas of the poor themselves.

NOTES

1. Thus far, the immediate impact of devolution has not been to significantly alter the policy terrain, which continues to be set at the national level. Rather, devolution represents a shift in degree rather than substance, as states have been granted the flexibility to impose more draconian sanctions against the poor (Soss et al. n.d.).

2. See Di Leonardo (1998) for a more extensive discussion of the politics underlying the work of William Julius Wilson.

3. See Williams (1988) for an important ethnographic portrayal that accounts for both paid and unpaid work in its portrayal of poor people's economic survival strategies in Washington, D.C.

REFERENCES

Brecher, Jeremy, Tim Costello, and Brendan Smith
2000   Globalization from Below. *The Nation* 271, 18 (December 4, 2000): 19–21.
Di Leonardo, Micaela
1998   *Exotics at Home: Anthropologies, Others, American Modernity.* Chicago: University of Chicago Press.

Harris, Jerry
1999   "The Politics of Globalization: Regroupments in the Ruling Class." *cy.Rev.* 6: 3–10.

Hart-Landsberg, Martin
2000   "After Seattle: Strategic Thinking about Movement Building." *Monthly Review* 52, 3 (July/August 2000): 103–26.

Kahn, Peggy, and Valerie Polakow
2000   "Mothering Denied: Commodification and Caregiving under New US Welfare Laws." *Sage Race Relations Abstracts* 25(1): 7–25.

Kuttner, Robert
1997   *Everything for Sale: The Virtues and Limits of Markets.* New York: Alfred A. Knopf.

Mink, Gwendolyn
1998   *Welfare's End.* Ithaca, NY: Cornell University Press.

Newman, Katherine S.
1999   *No Shame in My Game: The Working Poor in the Inner City.* New York: Alfred A. Knopf and the Russell Sage Foundation.

Piven, Frances Fox, and Richard Cloward
1971   *Regulating the Poor: The Functions of Public Welfare.* New York: Pantheon Books.
1977   *Poor People's Movements: Why They Succeed, How They Fail.* New York: Vintage Books.
1997   *The Breaking of the American Social Compact.* New York: New Press.

Reed, Adolf
1999   *Stirrings in the Jug: Black Politics in the Post-Segregation Era.* Minneapolis: University of Minnesota Press.

Robinson, William, and Jerry Harris
2000   "Towards a Global Ruling Class? Globalization and the Transnational Capitalist Class." *Science and Society* 64, 1 (Spring 2000): 11–54.

Soss, Joe, Sanford F. Schram, Thomas P. Vartanian, and Erin O'Brien
n.d.   "Setting the Terms of Relief: Policy Explanations for State Policy Choices in the Devolution Revolution." Unpublished Manuscript.

Stefancic, Jean, and Richard Delgado
1997   *No Mercy: How Conservative Think Tanks and Foundations Changed America's Social Agenda.* Philadelphia: Temple University Press.

Williams, Brett
1988   *Upscaling Downtown: Stalled Gentrification in Washington, D.C.* Ithaca, NY: Cornell University Press.

Wilson, William J.

1996   *When Work Disappears: The World of the New Urban Poor.*

World Bank

1997   *World Development Report 1997: The State in a Changing World.* Washington, DC: World Bank.

Contributors

Georges E. Fouron was born in Haiti. He was educated in Haiti, Trinidad, and the United States. He is an assistant professor and chair at the State University of New York at Stony Brook in the Social Sciences Interdisciplinary Program and in the Africana Studies Department. He has just completed a book with Nina Glick Schiller titled *Georges Woke Up Laughing: Long Distance Nationalism and the Apparent State.* In addition to his research on transnationalism and immigrant identity, he has researched and published in the fields of education, language maintenance, and bilingualism.

Donna M. Goldstein is assistant professor of Anthropology at the University of Colorado–Boulder and writes about poverty issues in Latin America and the United States. She has done fieldwork in Ecuador, Mexico, Brazil, and Hungary and has published articles about AIDS and sexuality in Brazil and on ethnicity and nationalism in Hungary. She is currently completing an ethnography with the working title *Laughter Out of Place: Violence, Sexuality, and Survival in a Brazilian Shantytown.*

Judith Goode is professor of Anthropology and Urban Studies at Temple University. For several decades she has been engaged in research and teaching about the ethnography of race, ethnicity, and class in Philadelphia and the United States. She served as past president of the Society for Urban Anthropology and the Society for the Anthropology of North America and has published five books and many articles.

Susan Brin Hyatt is an assistant professor of Anthropology at Temple University. She has done fieldwork in British public housing and has written on working-class women's engagement in local-level grassroots movements based on that research. Currently, she is working with Judy Goode and Jeff Maskovsky on a project examining poverty and civic participation in three poor neighborhoods in Philadelphia.

Catherine Kingfisher teaches anthropology at the University of Lethbridge in Alberta, Canada. She does research on neoliberalism, welfare-state restructuring, gender, and poverty. Her publications include *Women in the American Welfare Trap* and *Western Welfare in Decline: Women's Poverty in an Age of Globalization* (forthcoming).

Peter Kwong is professor in the Department of Urban Affairs and Planning and director of Asian American Studies Program at Hunter College/CUNY. His research focuses on the intersection of immigration, labor, and racial issues. Kwong is also a labor/community activist, journalist, and producer of video documentaries.

Vincent Lyon-Callo is an assistant professor of Anthropology at Western Michigan University. He also worked as a full-time staff member in New England homeless shelters throughout most of the 1990s. His current research concerns living-wage movements, neoliberalism, and resistance to economic restructuring.

Jeff Maskovsky is an assistant professor in the Department of Anthropology at Montclair State University in New Jersey. His research, writing, and teaching focus on poverty, grassroots activism, and neoliberalism in the United States and worldwide. He is currently engaged in a collaborative study of the effects of state policies on civic participation in three poor neighborhoods in Philadelphia.

Sandra Morgen is director of the Center for the Study of Women in Society at the University of Oregon. She is an anthropologist with a faculty position in the Department of Sociology. For the past three years, she has directed and participated in a study of welfare reform in Oregon. She is the author of *Into Our Own Hands: The Women's Health Movement in the U.S.* (from Rutgers University Press, in press), as well as two edited books: *Women and the Politics of Empowerment* (with Ann Bookman; Temple University Press, 1988) and *Gender and Anthropology: Critical Reviews for Research and Teaching* (American Anthropology, 1989).

Leith Mullings is Presidential Professor of Anthropology at the Graduate Center, City University of New York. Her most recent books include *On Our Own Terms: Race, Class and Gender in the Lives of African American Women* (Routledge, 1997) and *Stress and Resilience: The Social Context of Reproduction in Central Harlem* (with Alaka Wali: Kluwer/Plenum Academic Press, 2001). In 1997 she was awarded the Prize for Distinguished

Achievement in the Critical Study of North America by the Society for the Anthropology of North America.

Frances Fox Piven is co-author, with Richard Cloward, of *Regulating the Poor* (1993), *The New Class War* (1985), and *Poor People's Movements* (1977). Their most recent book is *Why Americans Still Don't Vote* (2000). She teaches political science and sociology at the Graduate Center of the City University of New York.

Matthew Ruben earned his Ph.D. in English and Urban Studies from the University of Pennsylvania. His research and published work focus on contemporary culture and politics in the United States, as well as on the patterns of uneven development affecting cities. He is currently co-editing a volume with Rosemary Hennessy on the culture of neoliberalism.

Nina Glick Schiller is the Class of 1941 Professor at the University of New Hampshire and editor of the journal *Identities: Global Studies in Culture and Power*. She co-authored *Nations Unbound: Transnational Projects, Postcolonial Predicaments, and Deterritorialized Nation-States*; co-edited *Towards a Transnational Perspective on Migration: Race, Class, Ethnicity, and Nationalism Reconsidered*; and has just completed the book *George Woke Up Laughing: Long Distance Nationalism and the Apparent State*, with G. Fouron. In addition to writing on transnational migration and race, ethnicity, and nationalism, she has researched and published in the field of medical anthropology.

Carol Stack, professor of Women's Studies and Education at the University of California, Berkeley, is the author of *All Our Kin: Strategies for Survival in a Black Community* (Harper and Row, 1974) and *Holding On to the Land and the Lord: Essays on Kinship, Ritual, Land Tenure, and Social Policy*, edited with Robert L. Hall (University of Georgia Press, 1982). Her most recent book, *Call to Home: African Americans Reclaim Rural Southern Places* (1996), won the prestigious Victor Turner Prize. She is currently writing a book with Ellen Stein on urban youth working in fast-food restaurants in Oakland: *Tales of Luck and Pluck, with Fries*.

Jill Weigt is a graduate student in the Department of Sociology at the University of Oregon. For the past three years she has been a research assistant at the Center for the Study of Women in Society, participating in a study of welfare reform in Oregon. She is currently completing her dissertation on gender, families, and welfare reform.

Eve S. Weinbaum teaches political science and labor studies at the University of Massachusetts Amherst. Her work focuses on women and union organizing, labor-community coalitions, and social movements among working-class people in the United States and across borders. She has been a union organizer and activist in the northeast and southern United States.

Brett Williams is professor and chair of the Department of Anthropology at American University. She has written about gentrification, displacement, homelessness, poverty, credit and debt, and environmental justice in Washington, D.C., for the last twenty-five years. She has also worked with activist groups and many public programs exploring cultural traditions and social problems in the city.

Patricia Zavella is an anthropologist, professor of Community Studies, and director of the Chicano/Latino Research Center at the University of California, Santa Cruz. Her research interests include the relationship between women's wage labor and family life, sexuality, poverty, and transnational migration of Mexicana/o workers to the United States and of U.S. capital to Mexico. Her most recent publication is *Telling to Live: Latina Feminist Testimonios*, co-authored with members of the Latina Feminist Group (Duke University Press, 2001).

Index